An Inventory of Breeding Seabirds of the Caribbean

UNIVERSITY PRESS OF FLORIDA

Florida A&M University, Tallahassee
Florida Atlantic University, Boca Raton
Florida Gulf Coast University, Ft. Myers
Florida International University, Miami
Florida State University, Tallahassee
New College of Florida, Sarasota
University of Central Florida, Orlando
University of Florida, Gainesville
University of North Florida, Jacksonville
University of South Florida, Tampa
University of West Florida, Pensacola

An Inventory of Breeding Seabirds of the Caribbean

∽

EDITED BY

PATRICIA E. BRADLEY AND ROBERT L. NORTON

FOREWORD BY JOHN CROXALL

GEOGRAPHIC INFORMATION SYSTEMS ANALYSIS BY WILLIAM A. MACKIN

University Press of Florida
Gainesville/Tallahassee/Tampa/Boca Raton
Pensacola/Orlando/Miami/Jacksonville/Ft. Myers/Sarasota

Library of Congress Cataloging-in-Publication Data
An inventory of breeding seabirds of the Caribbean / edited by
Patricia E. Bradley and Robert L. Norton ; foreword by John Croxall ;
geographic information systems analysis by William A. Mackin.
p. cm.
Includes bibliographical references and index.
ISBN 978-0-8130-3329-7 (alk. paper)
1. Sea birds—Caribbean Area. 2. Bird populations—Caribbean
Area. 3. Rare birds—Caribbean Area. I. Bradley, Patricia E.
II. Norton, R. L. (Robert L.)
QL685.7.I58 2009
333.95'828709729—dc22   2008052381

The University Press of Florida is the scholarly publishing agency
for the State University System of Florida, comprising Florida A&M
University, Florida Atlantic University, Florida Gulf Coast University,
Florida International University, Florida State University, New College
of Florida, University of Central Florida, University of Florida, University of North Florida, University of South Florida, and University
of West Florida.

University Press of Florida
15 Northwest 15th Street
Gainesville, FL 32611-2079
http://www.upf.com

This book is dedicated to all who have committed, and given, their lives to securing the future of seabirds in the Caribbean.

Contents

Figures

Tables

Maps

Plates

Foreword

More than 25 years ago, concern about the status of the world's seabirds led BirdLife International to convene a major conference and publish a global review (Croxall et al. 1984) highlighting the many threats seabirds face and the widespread lack of mechanisms and actions to address these.

Since then the overall situation has deteriorated: the global status of seabirds, notably as measured by the IUCN Red List (World Conservation Union 2006), has declined faster than that of any other group of birds. Resources to redress this are still less than 1% of those devoted to landbird conservation, and even where resources exist, awareness and ability to get involved are at least an order of magnitude lower than for terrestrial species and systems. Gradually, however, action plans for the conservation of seabirds and marine habitats are being developed and concerted action is being initiated, largely through the activities of nongovernmental organizations, with increasingly effective advocacy to get national and international management agencies involved.

Such actions are disproportionately under way in developed countries and regions (because the data and resources are usually more readily available), or in relation to critical situations (e.g., the by-catch of albatrosses in long-line fisheries) where iconic species are involved and cost-effective solutions are feasible. Typically, tropical seabirds are the least considered of all: there is a perception that most species are widespread and common and that the marine systems they depend on enjoy adequate protection.

This new book challenges such assumptions. It shows that in the Caribbean, surely a paradigm for tropical systems worldwide, the situation for seabirds and their coastal breeding habitats and adjacent marine systems is already very serious and rapidly becoming critical.

The main chapters, each devoted to one of the nations of the Caribbean, demonstrate the pervasive nature of the population declines of seabirds and the widespread disappearance of their breeding sites; the loss of critical inshore feeding habitat though destruction and pollution; and the increasing threats to offshore habitats and species.

The overview chapters reemphasize this, using data from both national and regional scales to identify many of the key problems, especially lack of adequate protection for breeding and feeding sites and absence of management and enforcement at existing protected areas. Together, the environmental pressure caused by coastal development—involving massive disturbance and destruction of key habitats and including the impact of alien species and direct depredation—and the impending disasters arising from climate change raise serious doubts about the survival of much of the characteristic marine coastal biodiversity of the whole Caribbean realm.

This book not only makes available the key data but also provides guidance on priority sites and advice on the actions and procedures necessary to convert existing knowledge to practical action. All those interested and involved in the wildlife of the Caribbean, and especially its exceptional marine life, should read the concluding chapters. All decision makers, particularly in governments, together with everyone who wants to help redress the current situation should read—and act on—the outline conservation action plan (chapter 30), particularly its call for education, management, protection, and above all active involvement by those who wish the heritage of the Caribbean's unique marine life to survive to the end of this century.

John Croxall, Cambridge

Preface

Although they feed only over or in the ocean, seabirds must come to land to reproduce. Success during this vulnerable terrestrial part of their lives requires the absolute or essential absence of land-based predators, especially mammals. When canoes from the American mainland first landed in the West Indies several thousand years ago, the islands were home to population after population of shearwaters, petrels, tropicbirds, boobies, and terns. Seabirds were common enough that they provided food to the early human settlers, as evidenced in archaeological sites by the prehistoric bones of such species as Audubon's Shearwater, "Black-capped" Petrel, Red-footed Booby, Sooty Tern, Roseate Tern, and Brown Noddy on islands where they are rare if not extirpated today.

The problems that people create for breeding Caribbean seabirds have intensified over the past 500 years of European and African influence. Rats, cats, mongoose, soil erosion, and commercial fishing, among other things, are no bargain for seabirds that are trying to reproduce. With the ever-growing numbers of human residents and the proliferation of tourism-based development, it is probably safe to say that more people now reside in or visit West Indian islands than ever before. A logical consequence of this situation is that the breeding populations of West Indian seabirds that still persist face very real threats to their existence.

Enter Patricia Bradley and Robert Norton, two of the most respected names in West Indian ornithology. In *An Inventory of Breeding Seabirds of the Caribbean*, these two scientists have compiled and edited badly needed, up-to-date information on the 22 species of West Indian seabirds. Never before has there been a book like this one, with a chapter dedicated to the seabirds that nest on nearly every major Caribbean island or island group, focusing on numbers of breeding pairs, current threats, and conservation. The 46 different authors (including Bradley and Norton) are experts on the birds of their particular islands. The four summary chapters tie everything together, supplemented by an outstanding bibliography. *An Inventory of Breeding Seabirds of the Caribbean* will be the launching pad for all future work on Caribbean seabirds.

Lacking confidence in my ability to predict the future, I will not speculate about what the coming decades and centuries will bring to our beloved breeding seabirds of the Caribbean. I will note that it is almost effortless to be pessimistic, but such detachment will do nothing to improve the situation. This volume represents the exact opposite of effortless—it is a hands-on, sleeves-rolled-up approach to understanding the difficult issues in conserving seabirds. We should be inspired by the editors and authors of *An Inventory of Breeding Seabirds of the Caribbean*, who represent a vigorous blend of local and visiting scientists. Because of their hard work and dedication, the future of West Indian seabirds has become brighter. Let us all do our best to maintain the momentum.

David W. Steadman, Gainesville, Florida

Society for the Conservation and Study of Caribbean Birds

The shocking decline in the region's seabirds makes *An Inventory of Breeding Seabirds of the Caribbean*, edited by Patricia Bradley and Robert Norton, a book of great importance. The Society for the Conservation and Study of Caribbean Birds (SCSCB) is fully supportive of the mammoth task undertaken by Patricia and Rob. We hope the book will raise awareness among governments and people throughout the Caribbean about the problems facing seabirds.

Before human colonization, the relatively predator-free islands sustained abundant seabird populations. Today, threats posed by increasing human population, tourism, pollution, invasive species, and overfishing are well known. Now we have to add the likely effects of global warming and rising sea level. Seabirds have disappeared as breeding species from many islands. Some seabirds, notably the petrels, have become globally endangered. Breeding seabirds once numbered in the millions, but now we speak of thousands. Seabirds are in for a hard time, and this book is very timely in suggesting plans of action.

We hope every government and environmental NGO will receive a copy of this book. It supports the need for the collection of further data on seabirds; strengthens the case for Important Bird Areas; assists in the advocacy process for bird conservation; and will help raise funding for seabird conservation.

Seabirds form part of the region's unique heritage. The hope that seabird populations in the Caribbean can be sustained depends on the willingness of all agencies to act now. The relationship between birds and people needs to be raised to a new level, as seabird populations can benefit only if people are willing to act as true guardians of the environment and birds. Local communities can benefit from the income generated from ecotourism, especially the growing number of bird tourists.

For detailed information on the breeding seabirds of 25 island nations, the SCSCB offers thanks to the many contributors who have made this crucial publication possible.

Andrew Dobson, President, SCSCB

The Society for the Conservation and Study of Caribbean Birds is a nonprofit organization dedicated to promoting scientific study and conservation of Caribbean birds and their habitats. SCSCB is the only regional organization dedicated to bird conservation.

1

The Inventory

An Alarm Call for the Caribbean

PATRICIA E. BRADLEY AND ROBERT L. NORTON

An Inventory of Breeding Seabirds of the Caribbean builds on the regional inventories of seabird species presented in *Status and Conservation of West Indian Seabirds*, edited by Schreiber and Lee (2000a), and "The Status and Conservation of Seabirds in the Caribbean" by van Halewyn and Norton (1984). Its completion moves closer to fulfilling a full inventory of Caribbean seabirds, one of the goals of the Seabird Working Group of the Society for the Conservation and Study of Caribbean Birds (SCSCB). SCSCB, formerly the Society of Caribbean Ornithology, is an organization committed to the conservation of wild birds and their habitats in the Greater Caribbean region, and a partner in the hemispheric Waterbird Conservation for the Americas initiative (Kushlan et al. 2002).

We call upon the governments of the region and the international NGOs to work together, as a matter of urgency, to sustain seabirds and their habitats. Together they have the power and expertise to harness the might of the many international conventions (World Heritage Convention, Ramsar Convention, CITES, Bonn Convention, Biodiversity Treaty and Cartagena Convention) that relate to the Caribbean and to justify funding. The central tension in the region must be addressed imaginatively and cooperatively. The benefits of tourism, where an enlarged wage economy has reduced dependency on birds and eggs, are being overwhelmed by its costs. Escalating populations, urbanization, and recreational use of coastal habitats are exerting intense environmental pressures, which, unless halted, will result in ever steeper declines in breeding seabird populations throughout the region.

This volume urges robust conservation actions. It identifies priority species and sites that require regular monitoring and are in need of protection, and sites where new surveys are recommended. The 51 maps produced by the Nature Conservancy and Will Mackin identify the main breeding sites, a herculean effort over

five years that continued until we went to press. Using these new data on status and distribution it will now be possible to build a strategic plan with the goal of sustaining Caribbean seabirds, an important advancement in striving to provide coherence and impetus to waterbird activities under way across the region.

Originally Schreiber and Lee (2000a) intended to include status reports of breeding seabirds as single-genus accounts only. Subsequently SCSCB commissioned island status reports, funded partially by the National Fish and Wildlife Foundation, being convinced that individual island accounts were necessary to complement the regional approach initiated by van Halewyn and Norton (1984). This volume grew out of that initiative. Written by professional and amateur ornithologists, the majority of them resident in the islands, the 25 national accounts provide the most recent inventory of Caribbean breeding seabird populations and breeding sites and also outline specific threats and conservation needs. The new data presented here, collected in situ, would appear to justify the value of island accounts; however, future standardization of data collection is essential. Additional chapters are on regional and global threats, a summary of the status of Caribbean seabirds, a Geographic Information System (GIS) of breeding seabirds, and proposals for conservation actions. The bibliography covers seabirds of the Caribbean region and includes literature cited in each chapter up to 2006 and two 2007 works consulted in drafts before publication. We urge authors working in the region to ensure that they include references to other work and, if they are from outside the Caribbean, ensure that copies of their publications are shared within the islands. The coverage in Schreiber and Lee (2000a) of seabird history, range, research, museum collections, and censusing and monitoring techniques is not repeated here. Maps, figures, tables, and plates are listed in the contents section at the beginning of the book. The

Table 1.1. Synoptic range, status, and estimated minimum populations of breeding seabirds (pairs, individuals, populations) in the Caribbean

Common name	Scientific name	Range.Caribbean
Bermuda Petrel (Cahow)	*Pterodroma cahow*	Bermuda
Black-capped Petrel	*Pterodroma hasitata*	Hispaniola
Jamaica Petrel	*Pterodroma caribbaea*	Jamaica
Audubon's Shearwater	*Puffinus lherminieri*	Caribbean
White-tailed Tropicbird	*Phaethon lepturus catesbyi*	Caribbean
Red-billed Tropicbird	*Phaethon aethereus mesonauta*	Pantropic
Masked Booby	*Sula d. dactylatra*	Caribbean & SW Atlantic
Brown Booby	*Sula l. leucogaster*	Caribbean & tropical Atlantic
Red-footed Booby	*Sula s. sula*	Caribbean & SW Atlantic
Brown Pelican	*Pelecanus o. occidentalis*	Caribbean
Magnificent Frigatebird	*Fregata m. magnificens*	Tropical America
Laughing Gull	*Larus a. atricilla*	Caribbean
Brown Noddy	*Anous s. stolidus*	Pantropic
Black Noddy	*Anous minutus americanus*	Caribbean and S. Atlantic
Sooty Tern	*Oncychoprion f. fuscatus*	Pantropic
Bridled Tern	*Onychoprion anaethetus melanoptera*	Caribbean
Least Tern	*Sternula a. antillarum*	U.S., Caribbean & Venezuela
Gull-billed Tern	*Gelochelidon nilotica aranea*	Eastern U.S. & northern Caribbean
Roseate Tern	*Sterna d. dougallii*	Cosmopolitan
Common Tern	*Sterna h. hirundo*	Cosmopolitan
Royal Tern	*Thalasseus m. maximus*	Caribbean
Sandwich Tern	*Thalasseus sandvicensis acuflavidus*	Eastern U.S., Gulf coasts & Caribbean
Cayenne Tern	*Thalasseus sandvicensis eurygnatha*	S. America & Caribbean

Notes: CARS= Caribbean At-Risk Species; CNIC= Caribbean No-Immediate Concern Species
a. Counts of minimum breeding pairs (Status Chapter: island/species matrices, Tables 5 and 6).
b. Estimate of adult population (individuals) by multiplying number of pairs x2.
c. Estimate of total Caribbean population (adults and immatures) pairs x4.

44 plates are in a central portfolio, illustrating 19 seabirds and some sites, habitats, and conservation management strategies; unfortunately there was not enough space to include the many interesting photographs offered from around the region.

Nomenclature and species sequence follow the American Ornithologists' Union *Check-list* (1998), including the revised classification of the Terns (*Sterninae*) resulting in the resurrection of four genera and a rearrangement of the sequence of names of the 47th Supplement to the Check-list (AOU 2006). There are 22 seabird species: 21 taxa in the Caribbean and one in the Atlantic (table 1.1).

Four species are members of the Procellariiformes: the Jamaica Petrel (*Pterodroma caribbaea*), a West Indian endemic species, is probably extinct and there are no post-1999 data since a search by Leo Douglas (L. Douglas, pers. comm.; Douglas 2000a; Sutton, this vol.); the endemic Bermuda Petrel (*P. cahow*) is extirpated from the West Indies and occurs now only in Bermuda in the Atlantic; and two endemic species, Black-capped Petrel (*Pterodroma hasitata*) and Audubon's Shearwater (*Puffinus lherminieri*). Seven species belong to the Pele-

caniformes: two with endemic subspecies, White-tailed Tropicbird (*Phaethon lepturus catesbyi*) and Brown Pelican (*Pelecanus occidentalis occidentalis*). Twelve are members of the Charadriiformes, the Laridae, two with endemic subspecies, Bridled Tern (*Onychoprion anaethetus melanoptera*) and Cayenne Tern (*Thalasseus sandvicensis eurygnatha*, sometimes regarded as an endemic species, *T. eurygnatha*). English species names are used throughout the text apart from this chapter. (For species codes used in the GIS chapter, see the table in appendix A.)

Map 1, Greater Caribbean region, defines the area covered in this volume. Maps 2–51 accompany the relevant chapters and specifically relate the locations of breeding colonies, with population diversity linked with a code ranking sites in order of regional population and conservation status (chapter 27).

The island accounts are presented geographically from north to south and west. Those from the traditional West Indies region of Bond (1950a, 1985) include the Bahamas, Turks and Caicos Islands, Cuba, Jamaica, Hispaniola and satellites (and Navassa Island, a U.S. territory), Puerto Rico and satellites, the Cayman Islands, U.S. Virgin Islands, British Virgin Islands, Anguilla, French Antilles

Status	Total number of breeding pairs[a]	Adult Individuals[b]	Total Caribbean Population[c]
Endemic sp. Globally endangered	71	142	280
Endemic sp. Globally endangered	<2,000	<4,000	<8,000
Endemic sp. Globally endangered		Extinct?	
Endemic ssp. CARS	2,700	5,400	10,800
Endemic ssp. CARS	4,100	8,200	16,400
CNIC	1,800	3,600	7,200
CARS	750	1,500	3,000
CARS	7,000	14,000	28,000
CNIC	14,600	29,200	58,400
Endemic ssp. CARS	2,400	4,800	9,600
CARS	6,100	12,200	24,400
CNIC	12,300	24,600	49,200
CNIC	42,200	84,400	169,000
CARS	100	200	400
CARS	318,000	636,000	1,272,000
Endemic ssp. CNIC	9,000	18,000	36,000
CARS	4,500	9,000	18,000
CARS	250	500	1,000
CARS	3,600	7,200	14,400
CARS	630	1,260	2,500
CARS	650	1,300	2,600
CARS	1,600	3,200	6,400
CARS	3,900	7,800	15,600

(Guadeloupe group, St. Martin group, and Martinique), the northern Netherlands Antilles (St. Maarten, Saba, and St. Eustatius), St. Christopher and Nevis, Montserrat, Antigua-Barbuda-Redonda, St. Lucia, Barbados, St. Vincent, the Grenadines and Grenada, and the Colombian archipelago of San Andrés, Old Providence, and Santa Catalina. Accounts from the wider Caribbean include the continental islands of the Netherlands Antilles (Aruba, Bonaire, and Curaçao), Trinidad and Tobago, and the islands of Venezuela (map 1). Bermuda is included as the site of the endangered Bermuda Petrel. The rediscovery and recovery of this species is a story of imagination, determination, and long-term commitment and stands as an inspiration and encouragement to all those working with species on the brink of extinction (Madeiros 2004). Accounts from Dominica and the remaining islands in the western Caribbean are missing, sadly, because we could not find authors to write them.

The authors, who are responsible for the content of their chapters, were given a simple format: island description, an inventory of breeding seabird taxa with a table of counts of breeding pairs, methodology, individual species accounts, threats and conservation, and literature cited (combined into a single bibliography). The accounts vary. Most authors attempted to follow the proposed layout, but it was obviously impossible for islands where there were few or no recent observations or long-term data. Some authors, funded by considerable long-term resources backed by governments or institutions, produced comprehensive accounts resulting from regular monitoring of widely distributed seabird populations, for example in Puerto Rico and the U.S. Virgin Islands. Others, although unfunded, were able to conduct regular monitoring of accessible populations confined to small areas, such as in the Cayman Islands. For these, it was possible to report population trends, declines, and site abandonment, and in some cases to correlate these with local threats. For territories such as the Bahamas, with many large islands and thousands of cays and rocky outcrops stretching over 1,000 km, or the Venezuelan islands, completing the inventories will be a daunting task requiring the input of considerable financial resources and the support of trained observers for the foreseeable future. However, their inventories are critical to understanding regional seabird dynamics, as the two nations together most

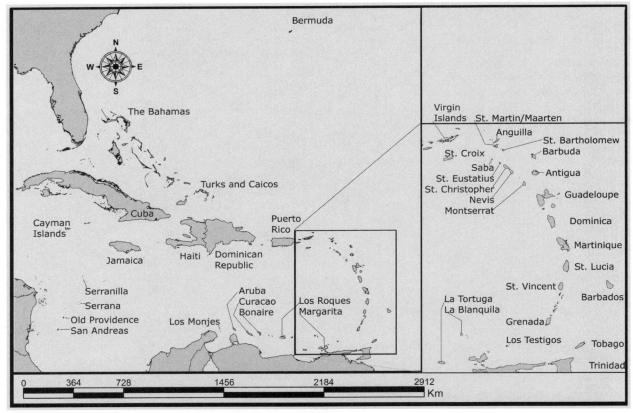

Map 1. Greater Caribbean region including tropical Western Atlantic Ocean.

likely contribute a considerable percentage to the total inventory.

Regional specialists wrote the chapters for island nations where there were no resident observers, for example, Haiti, the Dominican Republic and islands, and St. Vincent, Grenada, and the Grenadines. These data-poor accounts are more descriptive, and the latter chapter was rescued from being solely historical (with much data approaching 100 years old) by timely visits in 2004, funded by the National Fish and Wildlife Foundation. As editors, we have considered it relevant to report a few sightings at sea, close to remote islands or cays, where breeding was considered a probability and where future regional surveys should be directed. Counts from some previously undocumented breeding sites are recorded, including Navassa Island and the Grenadines, and there are new population estimates where previously breeding was known but numbers were not, as in Anguilla, the Venezuelan archipelago Los Roques, and the San Andrés Archipelago of Colombia. Additional data for the British Virgin Islands in 2004 and 2005 are given in appendix B (McGowan et al. 2006a).

Completion of the inventory will likely have to wait due to the scarcity of resources for monitoring and sur-

veys, with the risk that new sites may be destroyed before they can be mapped and can have populations counted, never mind protected. Thus this volume is a partially completed seabird inventory of the Caribbean to 2007 and remains a work in progress. Funding, logistics, political commitment, and training of resident biologists are called for from seabird specialists, governments, and NGOs, who must address together increasing regional and global threats and plan to direct resources toward stabilizing and protecting the priority species and sites discussed here.

This volume and van Halewyn and Norton (1984) provide population estimates for Caribbean taxa and, in three cases, include Atlantic populations in Bermuda. The Sandwich Tern and Cayenne Tern were inventoried separately—one species, two taxa. A comparison of this volume's Caribbean 2007 inventory with that of van Halewyn and Norton (1984) showed that eleven Caribbean populations underwent significant declines in 23 years, a fact backed by known changes in colony size and by colony extirpations. The majority of estimates by Schreiber and Lee (2000a) were for the West Indies, where the populations of ten species in 2007 were greater than those in 2000, largely due to new data.

To raise the profile of Caribbean seabirds and focus attention on the need for conservation actions, two globally endangered species, Bermuda Petrel and Black-capped Petrel, and 14 additional species are proposed as Caribbean At-Risk Species (CARS)(table 1.1). In addition, five species considered less under threat are termed Caribbean No-Immediate Concern Species (CNIC), for which regular monitoring is required but not urgent conservation measures. The region's seabirds are now estimated to number fewer than two million individuals, and colonies with as few as 10 individuals held 1% of the regional population for some species, the criterion for a regional Important Bird Area (IBA) and a valuable method of identifying priority sites. The GIS analysis (chapter 27) estimates that 13% of sites hold more than 5% of the regional population; 73% of sites have moderate populations or are unknown; and 13% rate zero, meaning they are severely declining or are extirpated. The Black-capped Petrel is almost certainly in continuing decline, although there are no new data since Lee (2000a), and monitoring of this endangered species and a conservation strategy are urgent to prevent its extinction.

Despite inhabiting one of 12 global "biodiversity hotspots," Caribbean seabirds continue to come a poor second to the conservation attention, international funding, and nature tourism dollars given to their endemic landbird cousins (Myers et al. 2000). During the preparation of this volume many gaps were recognized in regional population data, including in dynamics at breeding sites and "at sea," and in methods of data collection. These issues are compounded by the paucity of trained regional observers, lack of resources for conservation, and escalating impacts from tourism.

The final chapter focuses on conservation strategies to address the long list of local, regional, and global threats to seabirds. Some threats remain similar to those outlined previously (Halewyn and Norton 1984; Schreiber and Lee 2000b; Schreiber 2000a), only more acute, while others are of greater dimension or are new. Historically in the Caribbean, human predation was the main cause of seabird population declines, followed closely by animal predation. The authors now assess both those threats, although continuing, as having been overtaken by habitat destruction, degradation, and human recreational disturbance. Since we began work as editors on this volume in 2003, the issue of global climate change has shifted from being something only a few scientists recognized to sudden and wide acceptance by decision makers around the world. Sea level rise, sea warming, and increased tropical storm activity are forecast to exert as yet unknown but most likely profound pressures on the region's seabirds, including further loss of breeding habitat and altered foraging areas. Responses to these new threats will challenge the region's biologists to devise ever more innovative conservation management strategies.

Nongovernmental organizations working in conservation must become empowered and lobby their governments and citizens to take responsibility for sustaining seabirds. They should be supported by international NGOs. The SCSCB, with representatives in most island nations, is positioned to take the lead in advocacy and strengthening regional NGOs. Strategies devised to sustain seabirds must include capacity building, research and monitoring, more protected areas, effective management (conservation legislation, management plans for protected areas, and predation control), revenue raising, and protocols for sustainable nature tourism. Strategies must also link into socioeconomic planning including the creation of jobs. Seabird conservation must be raised to a level of political priority in island nations, and the policies and actions that follow should operate in the context of the regional and hemispheric frameworks, such those of Birdlife International, the North American Waterbird Conservation Plan, and the Nature Conservancy.

We urge a prompt response and sustained action to address the issues raised by this volume's dedicated authors. Only a combined effort, with cooperation and determination backed by funding, will arrest the decline in breeding seabirds and ensure that future generations of people and seabirds continue to share the Caribbean Sea. Such joint action has already been achieved in Europe and can be repeated in the Caribbean.

Acknowledgments

Our thanks to the National Fish and Wildlife Foundation for funding toward a seabird report; John Croxall for his support and foreword; Jennifer Wheeler for support over five years; more than 40 authors who contributed chapters and photographs and stayed the course; Phillip Kramer and Michael Palmer of the Nature Conservancy, who, working with Will Mackin, contributed the maps; David Steadman, John Chardine, Herb Raffaele, and the Society for the Study and Conservation of Caribbean Birds. We are grateful to all photographers who generously shared images, especially David Lee, Eladio Fernandez, Juan Papadakis, Rodrigo Lazo, Yves-Jacques Rey-Millet, Roger Craig at the Cayman Islands National Archive, and representatives of the Nature Conservancy and the U.S. Virgin Islands Division of Fish and Wildlife. Our thanks to David Wege, Geraldine Duckworth, Lisa Sorenson, Patricia Sutherland, Helen Huckle, and Tery (Norton) Mattison. At the University Press of Florida, we wish to thank especially John Byram for his faith in the project and his patience and wise guidance over five years, Michele Fiyak-Burkley for getting us to the finishing gate, and Sally Antrobus for sympathetic copy editing.

We especially thank our families, who endured countless hours of temporarily displaced affection, and we offer special thanks to Michael Bradley for proofreading and printing the many evolving drafts.

2

The Bermuda Islands

JEREMY L. MADEIROS

The Bermuda Islands are located in the western North Atlantic Ocean at 32° N and 64° W, some 912 km east-southeast of Cape Hatteras, North Carolina (the nearest point of land) and 1,460 km northeast of the Bahamas archipelago. They have a total habitable land area of 35 km² and are composed of approximately 150 islands of varying size, of which eight of the largest are joined together by bridges or causeways (map 2). The climate is subtropical and frost free, largely due to the warming influence of the Gulf Stream current, which passes around 640 km to the west and northwest of the islands and enables the survival of marine and terrestrial habitats and organisms hundreds of kilometers north of their normal ranges. As a result, the full range of tropical wetlands and marine environments is represented, including inshore ponds, marshes, mangrove swamps, rocky shores and coastal cliffs, sandy beaches, coral reefs, seagrass beds, shallow lagoons, and semi-enclosed harbors, sounds and bays of various sizes.

Bermuda has an interesting geological history, originally formed by two periods of volcanic activity occurring about 100 million and 35 million years ago respectively. This activity formed a steep-sided volcanic seamount rising over 4,000 m from midoceanic depths to the surface and probably initially to a considerable height above the ocean. Over millions of years, all volcanic material above the surface was eroded away by wind, waves, and rain, forming a shallow submerged platform, which was colonized by reef-building organisms such as coral that eventually formed a thick cap of limestone on top of the volcanic rocks. This, in turn, was eroded into sand, which during periods of low sea level was piled by wind into large sand dunes. The layers of sand comprising these dunes were eventually cemented together into Aeolian limestone by the action of rainwater seeping through them. Over millennia of rising and falling sea levels, the islands of Bermuda were built up and eroded

in stages, until today they consist of a mosaic of limestone formations ranging from 1.6 million years to less than 10,000 years in age.

The land surface of the islands consists of rolling hills ("fossil" sand dunes), the highest rising over 79 m above sea level. Rivers, streams, and freshwater lakes are absent because of the porous nature of the limestone, and there are only a few freshwater marshes where a subterranean freshwater lens, formed when rainwater collects in the rock at sea level, reaches the surface. There are, however, a number of saline or brackish ponds and lagoons, many of which are bordered by mangrove swamps. A mild climate, with temperatures ranging from 18°C in February to 27°C in August, and regular rainfall, averaging 1,400 mm annually, produces a thick vegetation cover wherever enough topsoil is found. In common with many isolated oceanic islands, Bermuda was covered by a thick but species-poor forest, with only 146 higher plants being recorded, most of which were endemic. After human settlement, most of this native forest was cleared or burnt off, and the island's vegetation cover is now dominated by over 1,000 species of introduced tropical and subtropical plants.

From subfossil evidence in caves and the descriptions and accounts of shipwrecked mariners and early settlers, it is known that there were large colonies of the endemic Bermuda Petrel, known locally as the "Cahow," possibly numbering over 1 million birds, and the Audubon's Shearwater. The White-tailed Tropicbird, or "Longtail," as it is still known in Bermuda, was also mentioned and remains the island's only common nesting seabird. Early colonists also mentioned the large colonies of "egg-birds" or terns, of which several species probably nested on Bermuda. These probably included the Common Tern (the only present nesting species), Sooty Tern, Roseate Tern, and Least Tern. Mention is also made of boobies, although it is not known what species of sulid

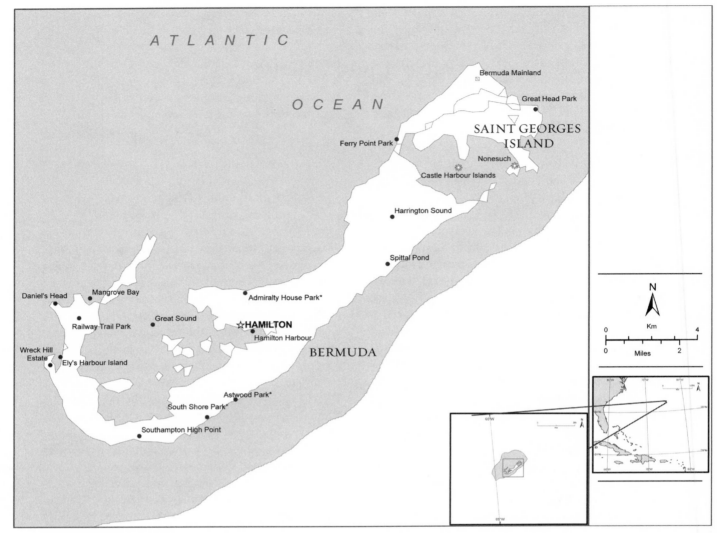

Map 2. The Bermuda Islands.

is meant or whether they were nesting or merely visiting the area.

Some of the most interesting records involve subfossil (not fully fossilized) remains of the Short-tailed Albatross, which include eggs as well as adult and juvenile skeletal remains and so confirm that this was indeed the site of a nesting colony of this species. Just as interesting is the complete bill of a Great Auk, found in the same limestone strata, which date back to 485,000 years before present. More recent subfossil remains include numerous bone deposits of Bermuda Petrel and Audubon's Shearwater in limestone caves and sandy deposits throughout Bermuda.

Portuguese and Spanish mariners first discovered Bermuda in the early 1500s; there is no trace that native

peoples had ever reached the island from the Caribbean area. The Spanish claimed but never settled the islands, believing them to be inhabited by evil spirits because of the tremendous noise made by the large colonies of nocturnal seabirds. They did, however, drop off pigs and possibly other animals, which multiplied rapidly with disastrous effects for ground- and burrow-nesting land- and seabirds. Bermuda also has dangerous reefs. In 1609 the British ship *Sea Venture* ran aground, and all 150 people on board survived and remained on the island for 10 months before continuing their journey to Virginia. This event led to permanent settlement by the British in 1612, with Bermuda remaining a British colony (now Overseas Territory) until the present.

The resident population is well over 65,000 and has

Table 2.1. Species pairs breeding in Bermuda in 2003, 2005, and 2006

Species	2003	2005	2006
Bermuda Petrel	70	71	76
White-tailed Tropicbird	2,000	2,000	2,000
Common Tern	25	8 (no young)	11 (8 young)

become largely suburban in nature—hardly surprising, as Bermuda is one of the most densely populated countries in the world, with over 1,000 people per km². About 14% of the island is covered in concrete. The economy is centered on a financial industry (particularly the international reinsurance industry) and tourism. About 500,000 tourists visit Bermuda annually. Bermuda is divided into nine parishes: Sandys, Southampton, Warwick, Paget, Pembroke, Devonshire, Smith's, Hamilton, and St. George's. The capital city is Hamilton (not to be confused with Hamilton Parish), located in the center of the main island, with the town of St. George, the original capital, remaining an important port at the eastern end of Bermuda.

On September 5, 2003, Bermuda suffered an almost direct hit from Hurricane Fabian, the strongest storm to affect the island since 1899. For more than 10 hours, peak sustained winds were 195 kph, with maximum gusts of 250–270 kph. This hurricane caused loss of life and severe damage to buildings, boats, utilities and roads, especially along the southern coastline. The effect on Bermuda's breeding seabirds was particularly severe as most nested in exposed coastal sites that bore the full force of the 3 m storm surge and 12 m waves along the south coast.

Species Accounts

As of 2006, only three seabird species breed on Bermuda (table 2.1). All are migrants absent at different times of the year: Bermuda Petrel (breeds late October to mid-June; plates 1–3), White-tailed Tropicbird (breeds March to September) and Common Tern (breeds April to September). At least three additional seabird species have been extirpated from Bermuda since the mid-1800s: Audubon's Shearwater (last confirmed nesting about 1980), Roseate Tern (last nesting confirmed in the 1840s), and Least Tern (last attempted to nest sporadically in the 1970s).

Bermuda Petrel

Endemic migrant, which nests only on Bermuda. Listed as critically endangered. Breeds only on four rocky islets totaling less than 0.8 hectares near Castle Harbour at the southeast end of the Bermuda chain. Extreme migrant dates 15 October to 28 June.

Breeding

This rare endemic had the distinction of being rediscovered in 1951 when eight pairs were located after being thought extinct since the 1620s. It was not until after 1960 that intensive further searching uncovered the entire remaining breeding population of 18 nesting pairs. Intensive management has resulted in a slow but accelerating increase in the petrel population, from 18 nesting pairs producing 8 fledged chicks in 1962 to 76 established nesting pairs with 36 chicks successfully fledged in 2006 (table 2.1). In 2008, 85 established nesting pairs successfully fledged 40 chicks. The fledgling departure period extends from 24 May to 15 June.

Due to the direct effects of Hurricane Fabian, three of the four petrel nesting islets were completely overwashed by the waves, destroying nine active nest burrows and damaging most of the remainder. Fortunately, the petrel population was still away at sea at the time of the hurricane, enabling essential repairs to be carried out during the six-week period before the birds returned to begin their nesting season. Ten new concrete nest burrows were built to replace the destroyed sites, but *Pterodroma* petrels exhibit such strong site fidelity that it will most likely be several years before they accept new sites. The effect on breeding success from the loss and disruption of nest sites during the storm was evident during the 2004 breeding season, as occupied nest sites dropped to 65 (from 70 in 2003), and the number of successfully fledged chicks dropped to 29 (from 39 in 2003; table 2.1). By 2006 the species was recovering, with 36 young fledging from 76 occupied nest sites.

Legislative protection

All nesting islets and adjacent larger islands are protected as Nature Reserves (Class A Protected Areas under the Bermuda National Parks Act 1975) under the name of the Castle Harbour Islands Nature Reserve. The species is fully protected under the Protection of Birds Act 1975 and the Bermuda Protected Species Act 2003. The Bermuda Petrel is also classified as endangered under the IUCN Red List and recognized by Birdlife International as a critically endangered species of international significance.

Management

The species has been under management since rediscovery in 1951, by the Department of Agriculture and Fisheries Conservation Division from 1962 to 1993, then under the Bermuda Parks Department from 1993 to 2001. Following reorganization of the Bermuda Ministry of the Environment in 2001, the Cahow Recovery Program is now managed by the Terrestrial Conservation Division (Applied Ecology Section) of the Department of Conservation Services.

Past Management Actions

Following rediscovery of the Bermuda Petrel in 1951, initial emphasis was given to the control of rats (*Rattus norvegicus* and *R. rattus*) on the breeding islands. These were successfully eliminated by the use of anticoagulant rodenticide, a technique used regularly ever since. Efforts were also made to solve a problem with nest site invasion and competition by the White-tailed Tropicbird. In 1954 Richard Thorsell was employed by the Bermuda Government to work on this problem, eventually devising a wood "baffler" plate with a specially sized entry hole that was installed at the nest site entrance, allowing entry by the petrel but preventing access by the larger tropicbird (Thorsell, unpubl.). Thorsell installed baffles of the optimum size in five burrows on two islands before ending his research in 1955.

After being present as a 15-year-old schoolboy at the initial rediscovery of the Bermuda Petrel in 1951, David Wingate became involved in the Cahow Recovery Program in 1957 upon his return from college. In 1966 he took over the program as Bermuda Government conservation officer, a post he held until his retirement in 2000. Wingate first concentrated on repeating Thorsell's work to determine optimum baffler dimensions. He obtained identical results and began to install baffles at all known nest sites, completing this work by late spring of 1961. Ever since then, baffles have routinely been fitted to all new nest burrows as part of the recovery program, and no further petrel chicks have been lost due to tropicbird nest takeovers (Wingate, 1977, 1978).

Deducing that there had to be additional undiscovered nest sites for the species to have survived, Wingate carried out further searching of all islands in the area and by 1961 had found 11 new nesting pairs on three additional islands. The next management action was to develop and build additional artificial nest burrows. This was essential as the nesting islands did not contain sufficient soil cover for the petrels to dig their own nest burrows, and population growth was limited to the small number of natural rock crevices deep enough to be suitable for nesting. Wingate developed concrete nest burrows that could be built on the elevated sections of the islands. An ongoing program of installing new concrete nest burrows has been undertaken ever since, with more than 100 being constructed on the nesting islands by 2006 (plate 31).

These have enabled the petrel breeding population to increase beyond the original carrying capacity of these islands and now are used by almost 75% of all breeding pairs. Wingate also pioneered hand-rearing of abandoned petrel chicks and has guided the ecological restoration of the nearby Nonsuch Island Nature Reserve, which is larger and more elevated than the present nesting islands, as a potential future nesting site for the Bermuda Petrel (Wingate 1985, 1995).

Present Management Actions

Upon the retirement of David Wingate in 2000, Jeremy Madeiros took over management of the Cahow Recovery Program as Bermuda Government conservation officer. Under this program, all active and potential nest sites are monitored regularly through the nesting season. There is also an ongoing program of artificial nest burrow construction to provide additional nest sites for new pair formation on all nesting islands. All nest burrow entrances are fitted with wood baffle plates with specially sized entrance holes to prevent colonization by White-tailed Tropicbirds. All nesting and adjacent islands are monitored for signs of colonization by rats (*Rattus norvegicus* and *R. rattus*), which are eradicated when necessary by use of anticoagulant rodenticide in bait boxes.

A banding (ringing) program for the petrel was initiated in 2002, with 223 birds banded by July 2006 (140 fledglings and 83 adults—the main emphasis has been on fledglings to carry out life studies of known-age birds). In 2006, eight birds banded as fledglings in 2002 returned to the nesting islands, representing 26% of all chicks banded in that year. This gave the first confirmation of the age of Bermuda Petrels when they return to the nesting islands to prospect for nest sites and attract mates. In addition, a study of fledgling growth rates has been carried out since 2002 to confirm variability among individuals in growth and to obtain information on growth to be used in a translocation project. To carry this out, 20 fledglings were weighed every 1–3 days from hatching to departure in 2002, and 18 fledglings were weighed in the same way in 2003 and 2004. Other morphometric measurements were made of adults, chicks,

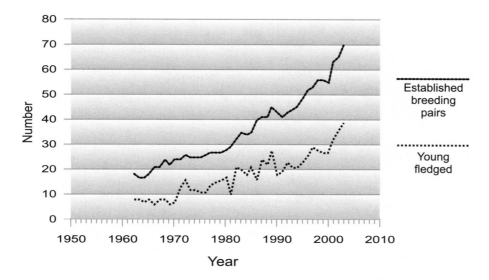

Figure 2.1. Breeding pairs and reproductive success of the Cahow.

and eggs; for example, adult petrels were measured for total head length, bill length, bill depth at gonys, wing chord (flattened), tarsus length, and mass (weight).

Following the hurricane destruction of seven low-lying active nest burrows on one of the nesting islets, a new complex of replacement artificial cement burrows was built at 4.2 m higher elevation because of extreme erosion of the island at the original sites. Because *Pterodroma* petrels exhibit such strong attachment to the original nest sites, sound attraction techniques were used to help attract displaced adult pairs to the replacement burrows. This was carried out by playing a digital recording of petrel courtship calls over a solar-powered, weatherproof sound system via omnidirectional speakers installed next to the new burrow entrances. The equipment was used in the 2004 and 2005 nesting seasons and was successful in attracting pairs of nesting petrels to four of the new burrows by 2006, two of which successfully fledged chicks that year.

Because of the continuing storm damage to and vulnerability of the present nesting islets and their suboptimal nature as nesting habitat, preparatory research was carried out for a translocation project to establish a new Bermuda Petrel nesting colony at Nonsuch Island Living Museum, located 200 m from the nearest nesting islet. Nonsuch Island is managed as a mammal-free restoration of precolonial terrestrial habitats originally found on Bermuda. Between 2001 and 2003, the conservation officer collected data on fledgling growth (weight gain/loss, wing chord development, feeding frequency, and approximate feed size).

In 2003, a translocation site was established on the southern coastal hillside of Nonsuch Island. Fourteen specifically designed plastic nest-boxes and ten cement artificial nesting burrows of the type used for many years on the nesting islets were installed in a forest clearing, under the forest canopy, and along the immediate cliff edge. During May and June 2004, developing chicks were translocated with the nest material from their original nests to the new sites on Nonsuch. A total of 15 chicks were moved and hand-fed every other day on fresh squid and small whole fish until they developed full adult plumage or their wing chords indicated that they were ready for departure. They were then monitored at night while they carried out predeparture exercising and exploration of the area around their burrows. All chicks translocated fledged successfully within normal weight and growth parameters.

In 2005, 21 more chicks were successfully translocated to Nonsuch Island, followed by a further 20 chicks during 2006. A total of 56 petrel chicks have therefore fledged successfully from the new colony site during the first three years of the project. By 2008, a total of 104 chicks were translocated. Also in 2008, the first 4 birds from the 2005 nesting season returned to Nonsuch and prospected for nests, another 6 were overflying at night. So hopes for a new colony on Nonsuch were high.

An education program has been initiated, which includes public and school talks, slide presentations, and articles in the local and international media and magazines, to inform the public better about the petrel and the recovery program. The Bermuda Petrel is the emblem of the Bermuda Parks Department and in 2003 was declared as Bermuda's National Bird.

White-tailed Tropicbird

Spring and summer migrant, nesting in erosional cavities and caves in coastal cliffs and rocky shorelines around Bermuda, and rarely under vegetation on mammal-free islands. The tropicbird has been severely affected on the main island of Bermuda through destruction of nesting habitat by coastal development, predation by introduced mammal predators (rats, cats, dogs), competition for cliff nest sites with introduced feral Rock Dove (*Patagioenas livia*), occasional predation of eggs and young chicks by introduced American Crow (*Corvus brachyrhynchos*), and destruction of nest sites by hurricane waves.

Breeding Pairs

The tropicbird has undergone a significant decline in total numbers of breeding pairs, especially on the main island, although the exact extent of this decline is difficult to determine because of the inaccessibility of many of the cliff nests. Total current population, the largest in the North Atlantic Ocean, is estimated to be approximately 2,000 nesting pairs, significantly less than the estimate of 3,000 to 4,000 nesting pairs in the 1960s to 1970s. The largest remaining populations are on the protected Castle Harbour Islands Nature Reserve (approximately 550–650 pairs) and Southampton High Point–Church Bay area (150–250 pairs). The remainder are scattered on coastal cliffs and rocky coastline around Bermuda, in particular Great Head Park, St. David's Island; Ferry Point Park, St George's Island; Harrington Sound cliffs and islands, Hamilton Parish; Spittal Pond Nature Reserve, Smiths Parish; Admiralty House Park, Pembroke Parish; South Shore Park, Warwick and Southampton parishes; Astwood Park, Warwick Parish; Wreck Hill Estate, Sandys Parish; Ely's Harbour Islands, Sandys Parish; and Railway Trail Park and Daniel's Head on Somerset Island.

The effect of Hurricane Fabian on the White-tailed Tropicbird population was severe, with a minimum of 50% of all natural nest sites in the Castle Harbour Islands being completely destroyed, representing over 300 active nest sites in this area alone. Some of the islands in this reserve lost up to 75% of all active nest sites. The total loss of nest sites along all coastal areas probably approached 1,000. In addition, many of the surviving nest holes were filled with rocks and debris swept in by the high surf, rendering them unusable by the birds. It was fortunate that three-quarters of all tropicbird chicks had already fledged by the date of the hurricane, but mortality among the remaining late-season chicks was high. This is evidenced by the fact that out of 20 tropicbird chicks still being monitored at the time on the Castle Harbour Islands Nature Reserve, only two survived the hurricane. In 2005, an estimated 2,500 pairs bred.

Legislative protection

The tropicbird is fully protected under the Protection of Birds Act 1975 and the Bermuda Protected Species Act 2003 and is listed as a locally threatened species.

Management actions

These include removal of introduced mammal predators from major nesting areas, clearing out of hurricane debris from surviving nest sites, repair of damaged sites, and installation of artificial tropicbird "igloo" nests made of compacted polystyrene strengthened with a fiberglass sealant (plate 32). Igloo nest-boxes for tropicbirds have been developed by the Bermuda Audubon Society, using funds provided by the Bermuda Ministry of the Environment. Almost 100 of these artificial nests have already been installed on the Castle Harbour Islands and other government and Audubon nature reserves, with up to 50% colonization within three years. Work will continue to install additional artificial nests at appropriate sites, and these nests are also offered for sale to the public to be installed at private coastal properties.

A tropicbird breeding survey was undertaken by a master's student in 2007–8 on 335 nest sites in the Castle Harbour Islands Nature Reserve to compare breeding success with that determined by surveys carried out by David Wingate in the 1970s and early 1980s. The conservation officer started a banding (ringing) program in 2002 for fledgling tropicbirds in accessible nest sites, and banding continues as part of the present survey; 260 birds had been banded and measured by August 2006.

Additional breeding surveys have been carried out by the conservation officer and summer intern students at two sites on the main island of Bermuda, Ferry Point Park (68 nest sites) and Spittal Pond Nature Reserve (30 nest sites) during 2001 to 2003. Information gained from these surveys will be used in the production of an Action Plan for the management of the species.

A culling program to reduce the numbers of feral Rock Dove is under way and has already substantially lowered numbers, reducing competition with the tropicbird for cliff nest sites. New, more effective culling methods have been investigated and implemented.

Common Tern

Summer migrant, breeding on small, rocky islands around Bermuda, generally with only one to six pairs per island. Common Terns on Bermuda have never shown a tendency to form larger nesting groups or colonies, although suitable habitat does exist on the Castle Harbour islands. Migrant dates from March to September.

Breeding pairs

A small breeding population on Bermuda has fluctuated between 10 and 25 breeding pairs at least since the early 1960s. This species is more prone to disturbance and predation at nest sites on the small exposed rocky islands. Nesting islands are located in the following areas: Ely's Harbour and Mangrove Bay, Sandys Parish; Great Sound and Hamilton Harbour, Warwick and Paget parishes; Harrington Sound, Hamilton Parish; and Castle Harbour Islands Nature Reserve, St. George's Parish. The population cumulatively produces from 55 to 80 successfully fledged young during the breeding season. These usually band together in a large group in late August and September, often in Harrington Sound, to feed on large concentrations of bait fish.

The Common Tern population on Bermuda appears to have been decimated by Hurricane Fabian, which struck just as the adults were departing the island and as the total population of fledged young had gathered in a large group in the inshore harbors and sounds. Of more than 55 juveniles seen the day before the storm, only two were observed afterward. The full scope of the storm's effect on the adult breeding population was realized during the 2004 nesting season, when only eight pairs of Common Terns returned to nest, compared with the usual recent number of 16 to 25 pairs, with only one chick confirmed as having successfully fledged. In addition, many of the pairs that did nest produced abnormally large "super-clutches" of five to six infertile eggs, indicating that pairs consisting of two females were attempting to nest in the absence of enough males. Monitoring will continue to assess the long-term effect on the Common Tern population. In 2005 none of the eight pairs produced eggs, but in 2006 a total of 11 nesting pairs produced eight fledged chicks, one of the first indications of possible breeding recovery from the effects of the hurricane. Nevertheless, the position of the Common Tern on Bermuda remains extremely tenuous.

Legislative Protection

The Common Tern is fully protected by law under the Protection of Birds Act 1975 and the Bermuda Protected Species Act 2003. It is listed as a critically endangered species on Bermuda. All nesting islands are fully protected by law with no landing except by permit and no approach within 33 m during the nesting season.

Management actions

Nesting islands are monitored during the nesting season and a banding program for chicks has been carried out since the early 1970s. Introduced invasive Casuarina trees (*Casuarina equisetifolia* and *C. cuninghamiana*) have been cleared on some islands where their thick growth had destroyed nesting habitat. A nesting platform was constructed to provide additional nesting habitat on an old concrete railway bridge abutment but had not been used by the birds in 2007.

Conservation

Protected sites on Bermuda

Bermuda is fortunate in already having a fairly comprehensive system of national parks and nature reserves, which, although generally small in area, protect many stretches of pristine coastline and wetland sites. These otherwise would undoubtedly have been lost to development, especially in light of Bermuda's high population density and dependence on tourism. The nature reserves are classed as Class A Protected Areas under the Bermuda National Parks Act 1986 and are managed by the Terrestrial Conservation Division of the Department of Conservation Services (Applied Ecology Section). The national parklands are considered Class B Protected Areas under the same act and are managed by the Bermuda Parks Department. In addition, Bermuda has a number of important NGO-owned nature reserves that protect wetlands, islands, and coastal seabird nesting habitat.

The full list of areas of importance for nesting seabirds is as follows (owners are indicated for those not government-owned): Abbott's Cliff Nature Reserve; Admiralty House Park; Alfred Blackburn Smith Nature Reserve (Bermuda Audubon Society); Astwood Park; Castle Harbour Islands Nature Reserve; Church Bay Park; Cockroach Island Nature Reserve (leased by Bermuda Audubon Society); Coney Island Park; Daniels Head Island; Ferry Point Park; Great Head Park; Lambda Island Nature Reserve (Bermuda Audubon Society); Morgan's Island Nature Reserve (Bermuda National Trust); Pearl Island (Bermuda Audubon Society); Rabbit Island Nature Reserve (leased by Bermuda National Trust); South Shore Park; Spittal Pond Nature Reserve (Bermuda National Trust and Bermuda Goverment); Tern Nesting Islands (Bermuda Government and private nature reserves); Watch Hill Park; and West Whale Bay.

Three additional areas are important for nesting seabirds on Bermuda and require protection: *Cooper's Island* (former NASA Tracking Station), St. George's Parish, is of critical importance for the Bermuda Petrel (Cahow) population, which nests only on islets in close proximity; the area also supports a large number of nesting White-tailed Tropicbirds. The *High Point Property–Talbot Estate* coastline, Southampton Parish, has high coastal cliffs supporting the second-largest concentration of nesting White-tailed Tropicbirds. *Bay Island and Pigeon Rocks*, Hamilton Parish, support nesting White-tailed Tropicbirds and Common Terns. The former NASA Tracking Station on Cooper's Island has been proposed as a nature reserve by the Bermuda Ministry of the Environment, but possible incompatible development proposals for the site could threaten the nearby Nonsuch Island Nature Reserve and Bermuda Petrel nesting islands. In 2008, the Cooper's Island site was officially protected by the Bermuda Government as the Coopers Island Nature Reserve. This has effectively protected this area from most forms of inappropriate development, although there are still some issues with public access of environmentally sensitive areas to be worked out.

Additional funding is required for a public education campaign on the sensitivity of breeding seabirds to human and habitat disturbance.

Although there is sufficient legislation protecting seabirds on Bermuda, enforcement and judicial support have been issues that require improvement.

3

The Bahamas

BRUCE HALLETT

The Bahamas Archipelago lies at the western end of the Middle Atlantic Ocean and consists of two political entities—the independent Commonwealth of the Bahamas and the Turks and Caicos Islands, a self-governing British Crown Colony. This chapter discusses the Bahamas; the Turks and Caicos Islands are addressed in chapter 4.

In 2000, there were an estimated 305,000 people in the Bahamas, of whom 70% (over 200,000) live on New Providence, where the historic capital of Nassau is located. Nassau is the main business center, commercial port, and tourist destination. Another 50,000 people live in and around the town of Freeport on Grand Bahama Island, the other main area for tourists. The rest of the population and tourist destinations are spread throughout the towns and settlements on the other islands (mainly Abaco, Andros, Eleuthera, and Great Exuma), which are known collectively as the Family Islands or the Out Islands.

The low-lying, mostly narrow islands of the Bahamas are spread over an area of 321,000 km² with a land area of only 14,000 km². The islands lie in a northwest-to-southeast direction for over 1,000 km from the northern islands of Grand Bahama and Abaco to the southernmost island of Great Inagua. The western end of Grand Bahama is less than 100 km from West Palm Beach, Florida, and the southern tip of Great Inagua is less than 130 km east of Cuba. While 17 major islands are inhabited, there are literally hundreds of uninhabited smaller islands and cays.

As an aerial view reveals, the northern islands are surrounded by extensive sandy shallows and sand banks, some connected, some separated by deep blue water. Formation of these banks came about in the last ice age (ending roughly 16,000 years ago), when sea level dropped several times, reaching 120 m below present level and creating large areas of land, such as the Great

Bahama Bank and the much smaller Little Bahama Bank. When the sea rose again, it flooded the banks and islands to present levels. Shallow water over the banks averages about 6 m deep.

The geography of the Bahamas is complicated, but Sprunt (1984a) provides a convenient breakdown into five regions in his publication on Bahamian seabirds: Little Bahama Bank, Cay Sal Bank, Great Bahama Bank, the Eastern Islands, and the Southern Islands (maps 3–13). The sequence runs from the northwest portion to the southeast, and any island or cay within the area is discussed from west to east.

Little Bahama Bank

The Little Bahama Bank consists of two major islands, Grand Bahama and Abaco (maps 3, 4). Grand Bahama is very flat and runs mainly west to east, about 128 km long and 11 km wide. The town of Freeport is a popular tourist destination. Peterson Cay National Park, to the south of Grand Bahama, is a known tern breeding site. Abaco has the second largest land mass in the Commonwealth. Shaped like a boomerang, it consists of two large islands—Little Abaco in the north and Great Abaco cover 160 km in length. Off the north and east coasts a string of smaller cays stretches 320 km from Walker's Cay in the north to Cherokee Sound in the south. These islands and cays have been traditional breeding seabird locations, including Pelican Cay Land and Sea Park.

Cay Sal Bank

This remote and isolated bank is roughly 160 km west of Andros and almost equidistant between the southern mainland of Florida and Cuba (map 5). It covers an area of nearly 6,700 km², almost all of which is shallow water averaging 10–15 m deep. The western, northern, and

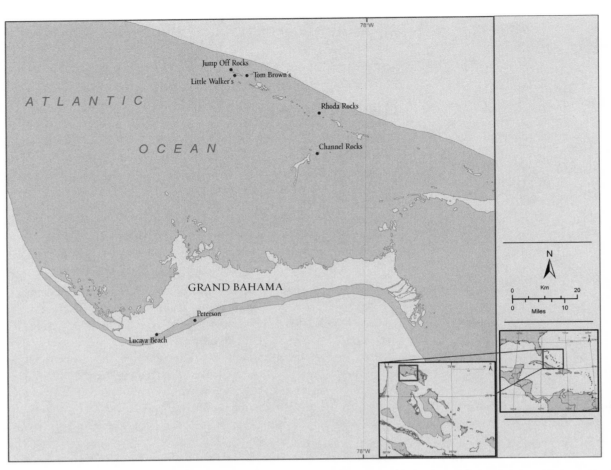

Map 3. Grand Bahama and northern out-islands, Bahamas.

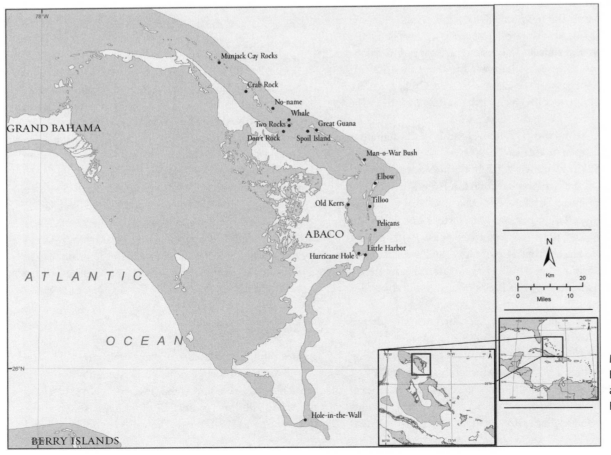

Map 4. Grand Bahama, Abaco, and out-islands, Bahamas.

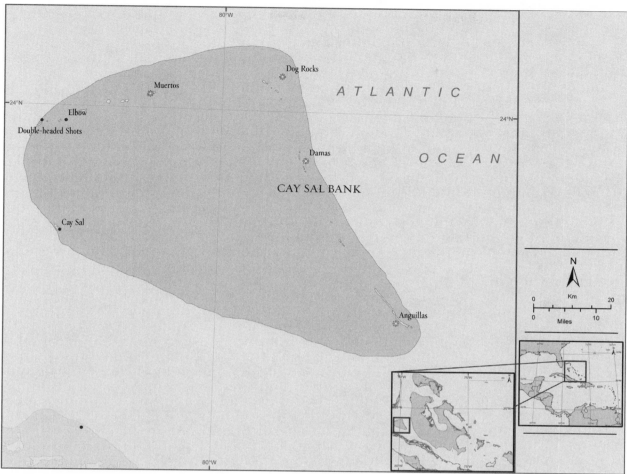

Map 5. Cay Sal Bank, Bahamas.

eastern margins of the bank are lined with an exposed rim of scattered cays and rocks, the most notable for seabirds being the Double-headed Shot Cays (including Elbow Cays), Muertos Rocks, Dog Rocks, Damas Cays, and Cay Sal. Cay Sal Bank is one of the most important locations in the Bahamas for breeding seabirds.

Great Bahama Bank

The Great Bahama Bank (maps 6–12) is the major geographical feature of the Bahamas and covers an area roughly 480 km long and 300 km wide. It stretches from the island chains of Bimini and the Berry Islands in the northwest portion of the bank to the Ragged Islands Range in the southeast. Bimini consists of a north and south island (collectively around 26 km^2) and several small cays and rocks farther south, which have historically been locations for breeding terns. The Berry Islands chain (map 6) claims around 30 islands and cays and runs for about 40 km from north to south, much of it

uninhabited. These islands and cays represent important breeding seabird locations. South of the Berry Islands lies the largest island in the Bahamas, Andros (map 7)—really three large islands (North, Central, and South Andros), which collectively cover 6,000 km^2, some 160 km long and 64 km wide. Andros is thinly populated and has large tracts of unexplored or impenetrable land. A number of cays off the east coast of Andros are important for seabirds—High Cay and Little Green Cay, off North Andros, and Grassy Creek Cays, Washerwoman Cays, and South Cay, southeast off South Andros.

Only 40 km to the west of North Andros is the island of New Providence, home to the capital, Nassau (map 7). The whole island is roughly 34 km across (west to east) and 11 km wide at the widest point. Off the west end of New Providence, Goulding Cay is an established site for nesting terns. East of New Providence starts the northern portion of the island of Eleuthera, 160 km long and 3.2 km wide (map 8). Eleuthera is bordered to the west by the Great Bahama Bank and to the east by the

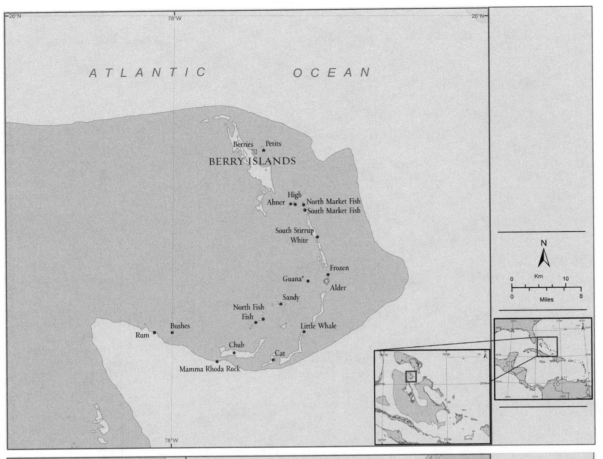

Map 6. Berry Islands, Bahamas.

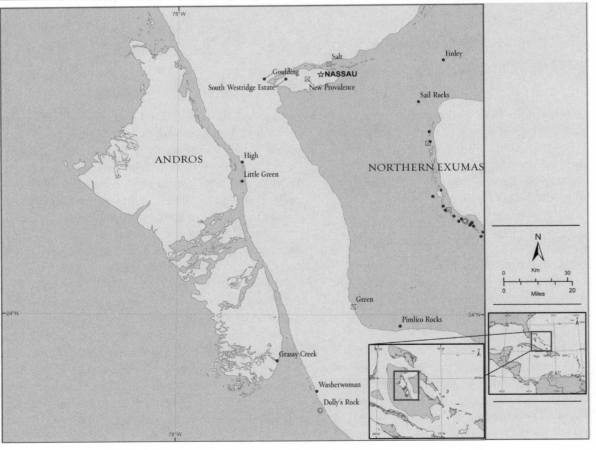

Map 7. Andros, New Providence Island, and Northern Exumas, Bahamas.

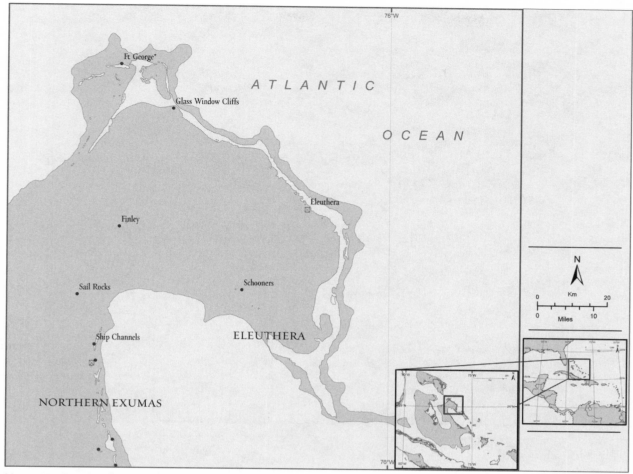

Map 8. Northern Exumas and Eleuthera, Bahamas.

Atlantic Ocean. The Schooner Cays and Finley Cay are traditional seabird breeding sites off the west side of Eleuthera. Between the southern end of Eleuthera and the northern tip of Cat Island sits the Little San Salvador complex (map 9), which includes the main island (Little San Salvador) and three cays off the eastern end: Goat Cay, Long Rocks, and Tee Cay. Known as a historical site for breeding seabirds, Little San Salvador was purchased by the Holland American Cruise Line in 1996, and any current status of breeding seabirds is unknown. Cat Island, shaped like a long and slender boot, is roughly 80 km long, only a few kilometers wide except at the heel (20 km wide) (map 9). Guana Cay off the south end of Cat Island has been a traditional location for breeding seabirds.

Continuing from New Providence, roughly 64 km to the southeast begin the islands of the Exumas (maps 10, 11). This chain of cays stretches for more than 160 km, ending at the two largest inhabited islands of Great and Little Exuma. Many of the cays in the chain are uninhab-

ited. Midway along is the protected 453 km² Exuma Cays Land and Sea Park managed by the Bahamas National Trust. The islands in this group are important historical sites for breeding seabirds, notably the Allan's Cays and Long Cay for Audubon's Shearwaters and Warderick Wells for White-tailed Tropicbird. Furthermore, all the breeding terns of the Bahamas use not only the islands of the Exumas chain but also the rocks and cays off Great and Little Exuma. To the northeast of Great and Little Exuma is Long Island, which stretches for 100 km and averages 1.6–3.2 km wide (map 9), similar in shape and size to Eleuthera and Cat Island. The cays in the harbor off Clarence Town, Long Island, have traditionally been used by breeding terns. The remote Ragged Island Range begins just south of Great and Little Exuma and continues in an arklike fashion for some 160 km from the northern cays (often referred to as the Jumentos Cays) to the settlement of Duncan Town on the largest island in the group, Ragged Island (map 12). Some traditional seabird locations include Water Cay, Jamaica Cays, Seal

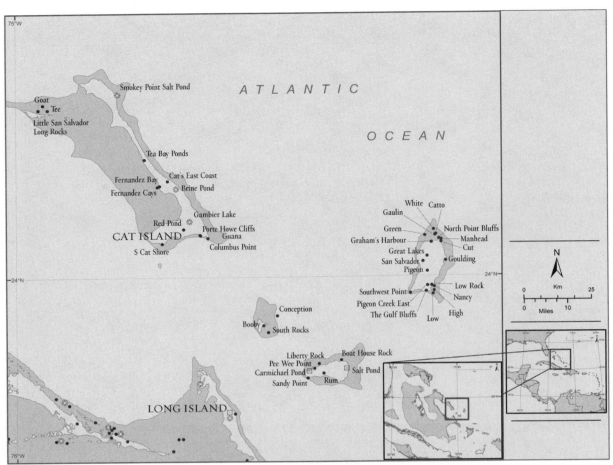

Map 9. Cat Island, Long Island, and San Salvador, Bahamas.

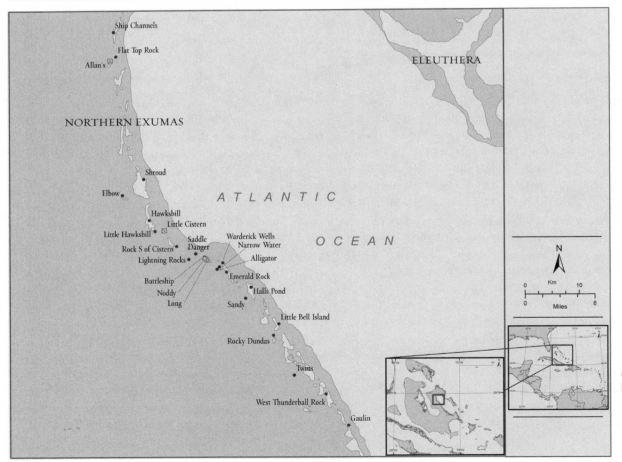

Map 10. Northern Exumas, Bahamas.

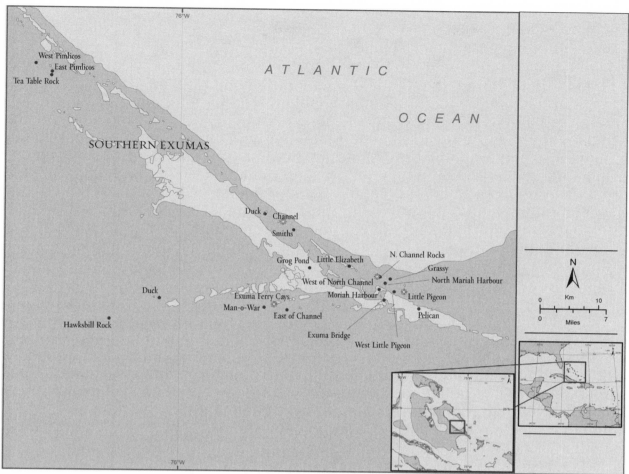

Map 11. Southern Exumas, Bahamas.

Cay, South Channel Cay, and Buena Vista Cay. Both Long Island and the Ragged Islands Range are bordered to the west by the shallower Great Bahama Bank and to the east by deeper ocean water (map 12).

Along the extreme southern and southeastern edge of the Great Bahama Bank are three remote cays, uninhabited and surrounded by vast expanses of ocean. Cay Lobos, with a lighthouse and a beach around the shore, is about an acre in size, roughly 160 km from the tip of South Andros and less than 48 km from the northern islands of Cuba. Cay Santo Domingo sits 48 km due south of Ragged Island. White et al. (1999) estimated the size of Cay Santo Domingo as 180 × 18 m and noted that waves could break over the entire cay, diminishing the potential for breeding seabirds. Cay Verde lies roughly 65 km east of Ragged Island and northeast of Cay Santo Domingo. The cay covers around 4.05 hectares and has high cliffs at the south end, which slope gradually down to the north side (White et al. 1999). Historically, both Cay Lobos and Cay Verde have been considered important locations for breeding seabirds.

The Eastern Islands

The islands of the eastern and southern Bahamas are positioned like isolated pinnacles, surrounded by much smaller banks than the northern and central islands. In turn, deep ocean waters surround each bank. It is believed that this part of the archipelago may have had a more recent origin compared to the sedimentary building process of the northern and central Bahamas.

Approximately 80 km to the northeast of Long Island and the same distance to the southeast of Cat Island is San Salvador, usually known for the first landfall of Christopher Columbus. Covering some 163 km², San Salvador is the easternmost island in the archipelago, surrounded completely by the Atlantic Ocean (map 9). The interior is mostly brackish lakes and mangroves. San Salvador is home to 14 species of breeding seabirds, and the cays of Graham's Harbour (White, Green, Gaulin and Catto cays) on the north side of the island make this probably the most important seabird harbor in the Commonwealth. In the deep water between San Salvador and

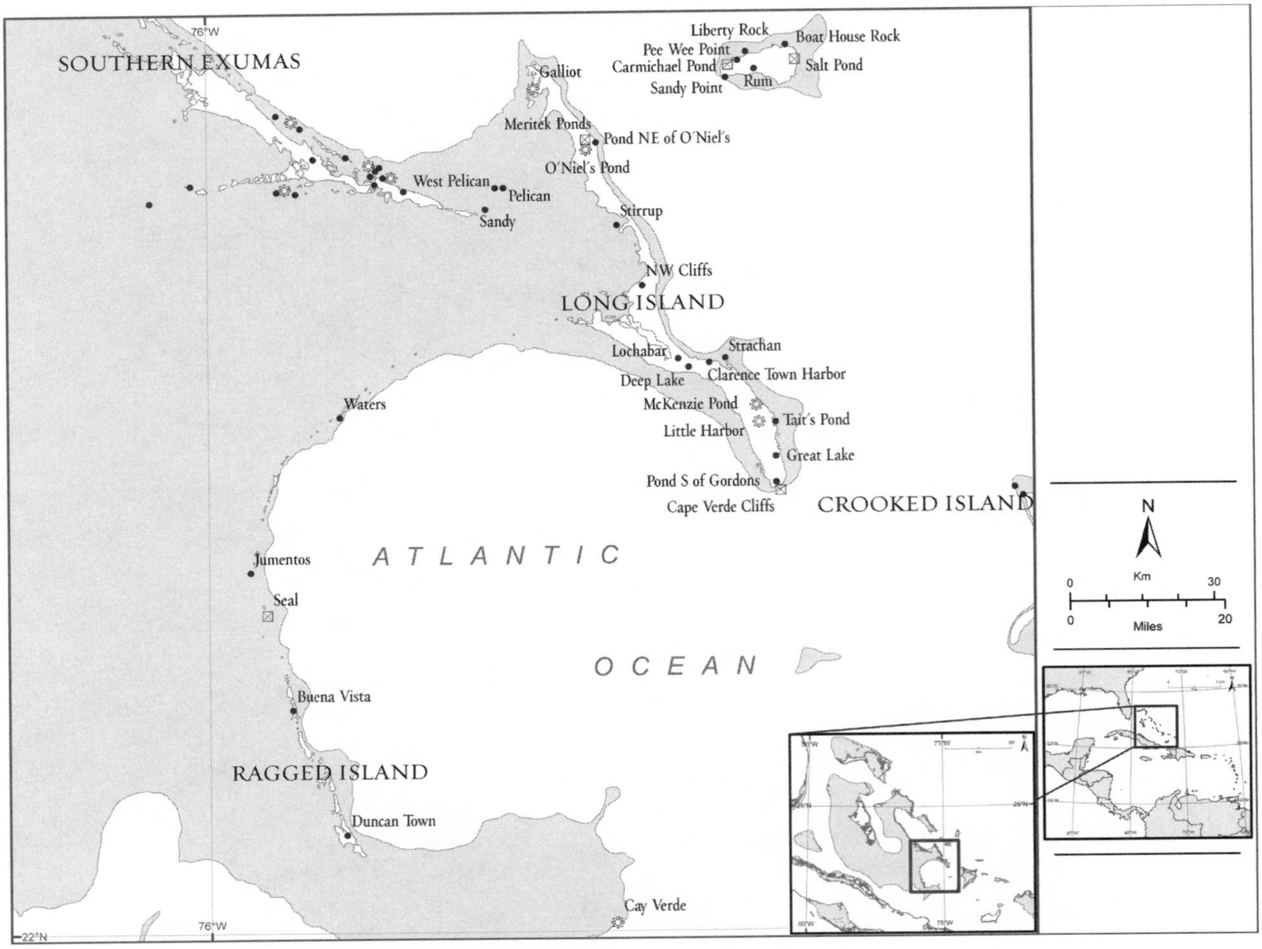

Map 12. Rum Cay, Long Island, and Ragged Island, Bahamas.

Long Island are Conception Island and Rum Cay. Conception Island, an uninhabited dot on the map, 3.2 by 4.8 km and 25 km northeast of Long Island, is protected as the Conception Island Land and Sea Park, managed by the Bahamas National Trust. It has a large interior lagoon on the main island as well as a few cays offshore (West Cay, Booby Cay and South Rocks). Historically a relatively large number of White-tailed Tropicbirds have bred here. Less than 32 km to the southeast of Conception is the larger island of Rum Cay, covering around 130 km², with about 50 people in the only settlement, Port Nelson.

The Southern Islands

Often referred to as the southern Bahamas, this region is hot, dry, sparsely populated, and seldom visited. It consists of the Crooked-Acklins complex, Mayaguana, and the Inaguas. Crooked Island (180 km²), Long Cay to the south, and Acklins Island (310 km²) are close together

(maps 13a, b). Traditional seabird sites are Glen Bluff and Bird Rock, both off the eastern end of Crooked Island; Gold Rock in the north and Salina Point in the south of Acklins Island; and several cays along the southwestern edge of the Crooked-Acklins bank. Included also in this complex are the uninhabited Samana Cay (40 km north of Acklins) and the Plana Cays (24 km east of Acklins). Propeller Cay, off Samana Cay, has historically been a tern breeding site, and West and East Plana Cays are a protected reserve for iguanas and hutias.

Running generally west to east, Mayaguana, east of the Plana Cays, covers some 285 km² but has a human population of only 300. Booby Rock lies off the northwest point of Mayaguana, and Booby Cay sits off the eastern coast, both cays traditionally known for their Brown Booby colonies. Another 105 km to the south of Mayaguana are Little and Great Inagua in the extreme southeastern portion of the Bahamas. Little Inagua, 8 km north and east of its larger namesake, is about 78 km². It is uninhabited and has recently been proclaimed

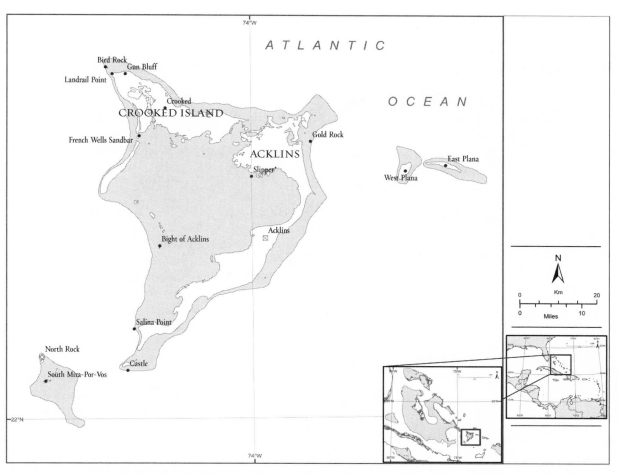

ATLANTIC

OCEAN

Bird Rock
Gun Bluff
Landrail Point
Crooked
CROOKED ISLAND
ACKLINS
Gold Rock
French Wells Sandbar
East Plana
Slipper
West Plana

Bight of Acklins
Acklins

N

Km
0   20
Miles
0   10

Salina Point

North Rock
Castle
South Mira-Por-Vos

22°N

74°W

74°W

Map 13a.
Crooked Island
and the Acklins,
Bahamas.

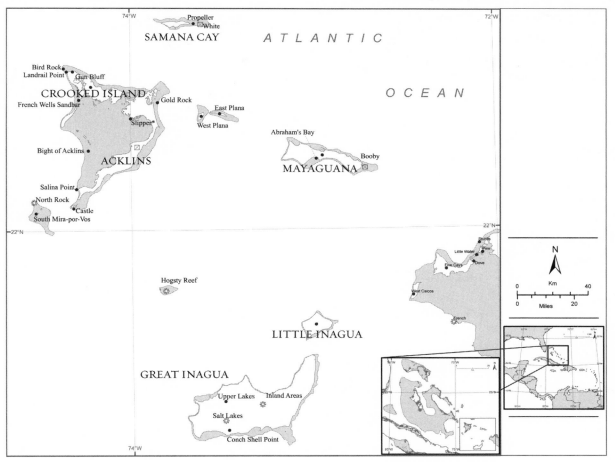

74°W
Propeller
White
SAMANA CAY
ATLANTIC
72°W

Bird Rock
Landrail Point
Gun Bluff
CROOKED ISLAND
OCEAN
Gold Rock
French Wells Sandbar
East Plana
Slipper
West Plana
Bight of Acklins
Abraham's Bay
ACKLINS
Booby
MAYAGUANA

22°N

N

Km
0   40
Miles
0   20

Hogsty Reef

LITTLE INAGUA

GREAT INAGUA

Upper Lakes   Inland Areas
Salt Lakes
Conch Shell Point

74°W

Map 13b.
Samana Cay,
Inagua, and
Mayaguana,
Bahamas.

a national park. Great Inagua is the third largest island in the Bahamas and covers a very flat 64 km across and 32 km wide. Morton Salt Crystal Factory has made its home here for over 100 years and the Inagua National Park, in the center of the island, protects its flamingos. The inland lakes and ponds have historically been important for breeding terns, and Conch Shell Point has been a traditional White-tailed Tropicbird nesting site. It is also the only known breeding location in the Bahamas for the Brown Pelican.

Two remote and uninhabited areas in the deep waters of the southern islands are known as Mira-Por-Vos and Hogsty Reef. Mira-Por-Vos is about 16 km off the southern tip of Acklins Island, a shallow bank that consists of shoals, reefs, exposed rocks (North Rock, Northeast Rock), and one cay (South Cay). Hogsty Reef sits by itself 56 km southwest of Great Inagua and approximately the same distance from the southern tip of Acklins Island. The area is known as a near perfect atoll, a good diving site, and a ship cruncher. At the entrance to the submerged U-shaped reef is the small Northwest Cay and roughly 2.4 km southeast is the smaller Southeast Cay.

Species Accounts

Historical references come almost exclusively from two publications, "The Status and Conservation of Seabirds of the Bahama Islands" (Sprunt 1984a) and the species accounts in *Status and Conservation of West Indian Seabirds* (Schreiber and Lee 2000a). In addition, a number of recent studies provide much of the foundation for this report and population estimates (table 3.1). These include Lee and Clark (1994); reports from White, Carey, and Dean's trip in 1999; Steinkamp, Carey, and Dean on the breeding seabirds of the Berry Islands (*in* Norton et al. 2002a, b), and Hayes's (2003) report from San Salvador. Walsh-McGehee, Lee, and Claridge (1999) reported specifically on the population status of White-tailed Tropicbirds in the Bahamas. White (1998, 2004) provides an overview of seabird occurrences in the Bahamas Archipelago. Table 3.2 provides a geographic distribution from the northwestern terminus to the southern islands. No recent field work was conducted to confirm estimates.

Fifteen species of seabirds breed in the Bahamas (table 3.1). Four species are resident throughout the year:

Table 3.1. Estimate of seabird pairs breeding in the Bahamas, 1994–2004

Species	Estimate of breeding pairs
Audubon's Shearwater	1,800–2,000
White-tailed Tropicbird	305–450
Brown Booby	450–550
Red-footed Booby	2
Brown Pelican	50
Magnificent Frigatebird	148–150
Laughing Gull	1,305–2,000
Brown Noddy	2,475–4,300
Sooty Tern	5,184–7,200
Bridled Tern	1,975–2,200
Least Tern	440–600
Gull-billed Tern	32–100
Roseate Tern	560–800
Royal Tern	110–200
Sandwich Tern	160–335

Table 3.2. Distribution of breeding seabirds within the Bahamas Archipelago

Species	Area 1	Area 2	Area 3	Area 4	Area 5
Audubon's Shearwater		N	EB, N (few)	EB	N
White-tailed Tropicbird	N		N	N	N
Brown Booby			N	N	EB
Red-footed Booby				N (few)	
Brown Pelican					EB, N (few)
Magnificent Frigatebird	N		N	N	
Laughing Gull		N (few)	N	EB	EB
Brown Noddy		EB	N	N	N (few)
Sooty Tern	N	N	N	N	N
Bridled Tern	N	N	N	N	N
Least Tern	N	EB	N	N	N
Gull-billed Tern			N	N	N
Roseate Tern	N	EB	N	N	EB
Royal Tern		N	N	N	N
Sandwich Tern		EB	N		N

Notes: Area 1 = Little Bahama Bank; Area 2 = Cay Sal Bank; Area 3 = Grand Bahama Bank; Area 4 = Eastern Islands; Area 5 = Southern Islands; EB = Estimated breeding; N = Nests found; blank column = breeding not confirmed.

Brown Booby, Red-footed Booby, Brown Pelican, and Magnificent Frigatebird. Eleven are migrants absent for part of each year: Audubon's Shearwater, White-tailed Tropicbird, Laughing Gull, Brown Noddy, Sooty Tern, Bridled Tern, Least Tern, Gull-billed Tern, Roseate Tern, Royal Tern, and Sandwich Tern.

Audubon's Shearwater

Little Bahama Bank

Lee (2000b) indicated Walker's Cay and Tom Brown Cay, Abaco, as possible historic breeding locations.

Cay Sal Bank

Sprunt (1984a) reported breeding on Elbow Cay, part of Double-headed Shot Cays, and reported birds present in 1996 (Sprunt report to SCSCB meeting, 1996). Five to six nests found with birds on eggs or single chicks at North Elbow Cay, 27 April 1999 (Hallett, pers. obs.); approximately 200 carcasses found in piles near the lighthouse on North Elbow Cay, 27 April 1999, presumably consumed by refugees from Cuba (Hallett and White, pers. obs.).

Great Bahama Bank

Breeding reported by Sprunt (1984a) on Washerwoman Cay and Green Cay off South Andros; Lee (2000b) listed these two cays and two others off South Andros as historic breeding locations. About 200–250 birds were seen around Blossom Channel at the Tongue of the Ocean off South Andros on 23 June 1998 by White et al. (*in* Norton 1998).

Exumas: Lee and Clark (1994) estimated a minimum count of 500 nesting pairs on Long Cay in the northern Exumas but thought an estimate of 1,000–2,000 pairs not unrealistic; Mackin (2004, 2005) estimated 1,100 pairs nesting on Long Cay. In addition to Long Cay, Lee and Clark (1994) estimated 200 nesting pairs on Allan's Cay, 2 nests on Noddy Cay, and 1 nest on Malabar Cay and reported that Buden (in ms.) found individuals nesting on Little Cistern, Sandy Cay, Twin Cays and Rocky Dundas; 200 birds sitting and occasionally flying off Staniel Cay, Exumas over deep water on 22 June 1997 (Hallett and White, pers. obs.); Lee and Clark (1994) and Baltz et al. (1998) believed there could have been hundreds of nesting pairs on Allan's Cay and perhaps the same on a similar cay north of Allan's. Macklin noted 100 pairs nesting on Channel Cay, Exumas, 1 June 2002 (*in* Norton et al. 2002b). Lee (2000b) listed Cay Lobos and Cay Verde as historic breeding locations; White et al. (1999)

made no observations of shearwaters on Cay Lobos but noted that on Cay Verde there were many possible nesting holes with tracks leading to them.

Eastern Islands

The Conception Island Complex was noted by Sprunt (1984a) as a breeding area. Lee (2000b) listed San Salvador (15 pairs) as a breeding location; Hayes (2003) estimated 200 pairs on the main island and 9 pairs on the offshore cays of San Salvador.

Southern Islands

Breeding confirmed by Sprunt (1984a) and Lee (2000b), on Propeller Cay off Samana Cay, East Plana Cay, and Mira-Por-Vos.

White-tailed Tropicbird

Little Bahama Bank

Walsh-McGehee et al. (1999) indicated South West Point (known as Hole-in-the-Wall), Abaco, as a confirmed breeding location and confirmed nesting at Hole-in-the-Wall (10 pairs) and Tilloo Cay (7–8 pairs) in 1996 and reported 30–40 birds seen between Lantern Head and Fishes Hill in April 1997 (D. Claridge, pers. obs.); T. White (pers. comm.) noted the species at Little Harbour and Great Guana Cay, Abaco. Walsh-McGehee et al. (1999) estimated breeding population on Abaco at 50 pairs on 21–22 June 2003; 3 pairs observed either flying into holes or returning with food on Whale Cay, Abaco (Bracey 2003).

Cay Sal Bank

No breeding records.

Great Bahama Bank

Walsh-McGehee et al. (1999) noted the Berry Islands as a historic breeding location, and Sprunt (1984a) confirmed breeding on Grassy Creek Cays off South Andros. Connor and Loftin (1985) noted 4 to 6 pairs nesting just north of the Glass Window, Eleuthera. Sprunt (1984a) and Walsh-McGehee et al. (1999) confirmed the Little San Salvador complex as a breeding location and the latter also included the south end of Cat Island; 3 birds observed by Buden (1987a) on 3 July 1986, between Port Howe and Columbus Point, Cat Island.

Exumas: Confirmed breeding reported on Shroud Cay, Warderick Wells, and Little Bell Island in the Exuma Cays Land and Sea Park by Sprunt (1984a) and Walsh-McGehee et al. (1999); from 20 May to 1 June

1991; Lee and Clark (1994) estimated 30–50 nesting pairs (26 actual nests found) on Warderick Wells and one nest on Little Bell Island; Buden (1987a) reported nesting on Shroud Cay, Elbow Cay, Little Hawksbill, and Hall's Pond Cay; birds seen by Lee and Clark (1994) but no breeding records on the following cays: Shroud Cay, Compass Cay, Long Cay, rocks southeast of Marion Cay, Soldier Cay, Stanial Cay, Hog Cay, and Hall's Pond Cay; B. Smith reported more than 20 nests on Man-o-War Cay, southwest of Exuma, on 13 June 1998 (*in* Walsh-McGehee et al. 1999). Walsh-McGehee et al. (1999) estimated a maximum of 170 breeding pairs in the Exumas. However, affecting the overall count of breeding pairs in the Exumas is the disturbing report by Lee et al. (2004) that roughly between 1999 and 2002, two to three free-ranging dogs, owned by the warden of the Exuma Cays Land and Sea Park managed by the Bahamas National Trust, actively hunted the tropicbird colony and killed 80% of the adults, reducing the colony from 70 pairs estimated in 1999 by Lee to 6 pairs in late May 2003 (pers. comm.).

Walsh-McGehee et al. (1999) noted Long Island as a confirmed breeding location; Buden (1992a) noted several tropicbirds flying around cliffs at the north end of Long Island (*in* Walsh-McGehee et al. 1999). Sprunt (1984a) listed Buena Vista Cay in the Ragged Islands Range as a confirmed breeding location, and Walsh-McGehee et al. (1999) noted this cay and two others in the Raggeds as historical breeding locations; Buden (1987b) listed breeding season individuals on Seal and Frog Cay, Ragged Islands, and B. Smith (pers. comm.) reported individuals around Water Cay area on 5 June 1998.

Eastern Islands

Sprunt (1984a) noted the Conception Island Complex as a breeding location and considered the population there (estimated at 75 pairs) to be the largest in the Bahamas; Conception Island, 2 birds seen in a nest hole and approximately 40 birds flying around the area 3 May 1999 (Hallett, pers. obs.). Walsh-McGehee et al. (1999) noted Conception Island, Rum Cay, and San Salvador as confirmed breeding locations; Buden (1990a) found at least 14 nests and estimated 100–150 breeding pairs on Rum Cay between May and July 1989. At Graham's Harbour, San Salvador, 25 breeding pairs were estimated in mid-June 1997 (Walsh-McGehee et al. 1999); estimated 12 birds circling and calling along the cliffs there, 20 June 1999 (Hallett, pers. obs.); Hayes (2003) estimated 100

pairs breeding along the bluffs (north, east and south) of San Salvador.

Southern Islands

Walsh-McGehee et al. (1999) noted one location each on Crooked and Acklins islands as historic breeding locations; 5 to 6 birds flying off the cliffs of Gun Bluff and flying off the cliffs west of Landrail Point, Crooked Island, 4 May 1997 (Hallett and White, pers. obs.); several birds seen flying off the cliffs on the north side of Castle Island (just off southern tip of Acklins), 12 May 1999 (Hallett, pers. obs.). Buden (1987a) confirmed nesting on Samana Cay and West Plana Cay; Walsh-McGehee et al. (1999) indicated the Plana Cays as a historic breeding location; 20 birds circling over ridge where there were many cavities on East Plana Cay on 6 May 1999 (Hallett, pers. obs.). Walsh-McGehee et al. (1999) listed two breeding locations on Mayaguana and Little Inagua; one chick observed in hole and several adults entering holes, roughly 20 birds circling the cliffs at the western end of Little Inagua, 9 May 1999 (Hallett, pers. obs.). Sprunt (1984a) and Walsh-McGehee et al. (1999) confirmed breeding on Great Inagua; White (1998) indicated Conch Shell Point as a nesting site.

Masked Booby

Little Bahama Bank and Cay Sal Bank

No breeding records.

Great Bahama Bank

Schreiber (2000b) indicated Cay Santo Domingo as a historic breeding location, now extirpated or thought to be extirpated (20 pairs, Bryant 1859). White et al. (1999) visited Cay Santo Domingo by boat on 22 June 1998, and found no sign of Masked Booby or of any breeding seabirds.

Eastern Islands

Schreiber (2000b) estimated 6 pairs on White Cay in Graham's Harbour, San Salvador in 1999; however, D. Lee (pers. comm.) indicated that this number and notation were in error and should have been a reference to Hayes's (2003) report of a pair of Masked Boobies courting at White Cay, San Salvador, on 12 June 1998, although he was unable to confirm breeding.

Southern Islands

No breeding records.

Brown Booby

Little Bahama Bank

No breeding records.

Cay Sal Bank

No breeding records but over 20 birds sitting on the Elbow Cays, 27 April 1999 (Hallett and White, pers. obs.).

Great Bahama Bank

White et al. (1999) observed 25 birds sitting on Cay Santo Domingo but believed no nesting could take place because the cay is vulnerable to waves; Schreiber (2000b) noted this location as extirpated. Sprunt (1984a) confirmed breeding on Cay Verde in 1979 with an estimated 550· pairs, and White et al. (1999) estimated 150–200 nests on 22 June 1998.

Eastern Islands

No seabirds observed on Booby Cay off Conception Island on 3 May 1999 (Hallett, pers. obs.). Over 300 birds were seen and roughly 200 probable nest sites counted on White Cay in Graham's Harbour, San Salvador, 24 January 1997 (Hallett, pers. obs.), where Schreiber (2000b) noted 100+ pairs; Hayes (2003) estimated 200 pairs on White Cay and Catto Cay in Graham's Harbour, San Salvador.

Southern Islands

Sprunt (1984a) confirmed breeding in 1979 on North Rock within Mira-Por-Vos and estimated 600 breeding pairs; more than 20 boobies were feeding over deep water about a mile east of Castle Island, Acklins, 12 May 1999 (Hallett, pers. obs.). Booby Rock, off the northwestern end of Mayaguana, estimated to have 70–80 nesting pairs, October 1997 (Schreiber 2000b), and over 50 birds were seen circling there, 7 May 1999 (Hallett, pers. obs.).

Red-footed Booby

Little Bahama Bank

Cay Sal Bank and Great Bahama Bank: no breeding records.

Eastern Islands

One or two pairs have nested on White Cay and/or Catto Cay in Graham's Harbour, San Salvador, at least since 1988: Sprunt photographed a pair on White Cay 16 May 1988 (White et al. 1996); Bainton and Hallett photographed a pair with one downy young on 28 April 1995 (White et al. 1996); 3 adults, 1 immature, and 1 juvenile photographed, 20 June 1999 (Hallett, pers. obs.); Schreiber (2000b) noted 2 nesting pairs on White Cay, San Salvador; Hayes (2003) noted 2 nesting pairs there with data from 1993 to 2003; 3 pairs nesting, 25 February 2005 (Hayes, pers. comm.).

Southern Islands

No breeding records.

Brown Pelican

Little Bahama Bank

Cay Sal Bank, Great Bahama Bank and Eastern Islands: no breeding records.

Southern Islands

M. Robertson noted a pair nesting on Slipper Cay, Acklins Island, in May 2003 (Norton et al. 2003). Sprunt (1984a) estimated between 100 and 200 pairs breeding on Great Inagua, mostly in the inland area locally called the "Upper Lakes"; Collazo et al. (2000) estimated 50–100 pairs. Even though there has been no confirmation of breeding since Sprunt (1984a), the Brown Pelican is still a fairly common bird on Great Inagua and it is assumed that it still breeds there.

Magnificent Frigatebird

Little Bahama Bank

Lindsay et al. (2000) indicated Abaco as a historical breeding location with no reports that the colony had been extirpated; J. Kushlan and Steinkamp reported 40 nests in a colony on Man-O'-War Bush, The Marls (west side), Abaco, 26 June 2002 (Norton et al. 2004).

Cay Sal Bank

No breeding records.

Great Bahama Bank

Lindsay et al. (2000) listed Bimini and New Providence as historic breeding locations that are extirpated or thought to be extirpated, as was Seal Cay in the Ragged Islands Range, from a report by Buden (1987b). Sprunt (1984a) counted 99 nests in 1979 at Cay Verde, and White et al. (1999) counted 75 chicks on 22 June 1998.

Eastern Islands

The following are breeding observations from White Cay in Graham's Harbour, San Salvador: 30+ birds observed over potential nest sites, 4 May 1995; 50 nests counted, 24 January 1997, and 20–25 chicks on 20 June 1999 (Hallett, pers. obs.). Hayes (2003) estimated 33 pairs on White Cay and Catto Cay; and 70 nests on Catto Cay, with around 200 adults in Graham's Harbour, 25 February 2005 (Hayes, pers. comm.).

Southern Islands

Buden (1987a) estimated 10 nesting pairs on Atwood Key off Samana Cay. Lindsay et al. (2000) listed Booby Cay off Mayaguana as a historic breeding location.

Laughing Gull

Little Bahama Bank

No breeding records.

Cay Sal Bank

Sprunt (1984a) indicated no confirmed breeding at this location but reported a few pairs in 1996 (Sprunt report to SCO meeting, 1996).

Great Bahama Bank

Seabird surveys from the Berry Islands in 21–24 May 2002 indicated nests on the following cays: N. Fish Cay (250), Sandy Cay (25), S. Market Fish Cay (25), White Cay (40), and N. Market Fish Cay (20+), and species was present on S. Stirrup Cay, Cat Cay, and Frozen Cay (in Norton et al. 2002a); J. and P. Kushlan counted 400 gull nests at Petit Cays, near Great Harbour Cay, Berry Island, on 12 June 2002 (in Norton et al. 2002b). Sprunt (1984a) counted 300 pairs courting and building nests on the Schooner Cays, Eleuthera, in May 1981.

Exumas: Sprunt (1984a) counted 150 pairs courting and building nests on Sail Rocks in May 1981, reported by Chardine et al. (2000a) as a historic breeding location. However Lee and Clark (1994) mentioned that Sprunt (pers. comm.) noted the largest colonies in the Bahamas are on Ship Channel and Sail Rocks Cays in the northern Exumas, where there were an estimated 1,500 pairs; Lee and Clark (1994) reported from the Land and Sea Park that about 50 birds appeared to be sitting on nests on the Malabar Cays on 25 May 1991, and 5 pairs nesting on Riding Rocks; Bailey Smith (pers. comm., 2003) reported that hundreds of Laughing Gulls nest on Duck Cay off Great Exuma and have done so for many years.

Sprunt (1984a) confirmed breeding on Buena Vista Cay in the Ragged Islands. White et al. (1999) reported 35 pairs nesting on Cay Verde.

Eastern Islands

Hayes (2003) estimated a population of 260 pairs from the Pigeon Cay area on Great Lake, San Salvador.

Southern Islands

Sprunt (1984a) confirmed breeding on the South Cay (also known as Wood Cay) in the Bight of Acklins, which is to the east of Acklins Island along the edge of the Crooked-Acklins bank.

Brown Noddy

Little Bahama Bank

Chardine et al. (2000b) indicated a cay or cay(s) off Abaco as a historic breeding location; Bracey (2003) reported Brown Noddy as a summer resident on cays off Treasure Cay, Abaco, but no nesting activity detected.

Cay Sal Bank

Breeding reported by Sprunt (1984a) on Double-headed Shot Cays, Muertos Cays, Dog Rocks, and Damas Cays; 3,500 pairs estimated in 1996 (Sprunt report to SCO meeting, 1996), indicated by Chardine et al. (2000b) as a historic breeding location.

Great Bahama Bank

Breeding reported by Sprunt (1984a) on Bimini, and Chardine et al. (2000b) indicated the area as a historic breeding location. Estimated nests on Berry Islands: Mamma Rhoda Rock (150), Frozen Cay (400), Alder Cay (50), High Cay (17), 21–24 May 2002; J. and P. Kushlan counted 6 nests at Petit Cays near Great Harbour Cay, Berry Island on 12 June 2002 (in Norton et al. 2002a, b). Breeding reported on cays on east side of Andros Island, High Cay, Grassy Creek Cays, and Washerwoman Cays; Sprunt (1984a) and Chardine et al. (2002b) indicated these areas as historic breeding locations. More than 40 birds observed in and around known breeding site, Goulding Cay off west side of New Providence, 6 May 1995 (White and Hallett, pers. obs.), an established colony for at least 6 years, estimated 150 breeding pairs (Hallett, pers. obs.). Sprunt (1984a) indicated breeding on the Little San Salvador complex (Goat Cay, Tee Cay, Long Rocks), off the northern portion of Cat Island; Chardine et al. (2000b) confirmed a breeding location on the southern part of Cat Island and indicated a historic breeding location for the Little San Salvador complex.

Exumas: Breeding reported by Sprunt (1984a) on Saddle Cay; Lee and Clark (1994) estimated several thousand breeding pairs in the Exuma Cays Land and Sea Park portion of the Exumas in late May 1991, where nesting cays included Sandy Cay (50–75 pairs), Emerald Cay (30–50 pr), Alligator Cay (100 pr), Narrow Water Cay (100 pr, Peggy Hall, pers. comm.), Hawk Fish Rocks (200 pr), Danger Cay (200 pr), Saddle Cay (200 pr), Harbour islands on Staniel Cay (100s of pairs); White counted 200 birds at Thunderball Cay, Exumas, but gave no nest estimates, 22 June 1997 (Norton 1997a); Bailey Smith (pers. comm.) estimated 100 pairs using North Channel Rock off Great Exuma, 2000–2003. Chardine et al. (2000b) noted two locations on Long Island, one as a confirmed breeding location and one as a historical breeding site. Breeding confirmed by Sprunt (1984a) on Water Cays, Ragged Islands, and the remote cay of Cay Verde. Fifty birds sighted off Buena Vista Cay, Ragged Islands, 14 May 1999 (Hallett, pers. obs.). White et al. (1999) counted 300–350 nests on Cay Verde in June 1998.

Eastern Islands

Breeding confirmed off Conception Island (South Rocks, Booby Cay) by Sprunt (1984a), and Chardine et al. (2000b) confirmed breeding; no birds observed, 3 May 1999 (Hallett, pers. obs.). Hayes (2003) estimated 400 pairs with data from Catto Cay, Gaulin Cay, Green Cay, and White Cay in Graham's Harbour, San Salvador, 1993–2003.

Southern Islands

An estimated 75 pairs breeding on Gold Rock off Pinefield Point, Acklins Island, in 1997 (White and Bainton, pers. obs.). Breeding confirmed on Mira-Por-Vos by Sprunt (1984a) and Propeller Cay off Samana Cay; over 150 birds seen off south end of Acklins (near Mira-Por-Vos), 11–12 May 1999 (Hallett, pers. obs.) and over 100 birds to and from Propeller Cay off Samana Cay, 4 May 1999 (Hallett, pers. obs.).

Sooty Tern

Little Bahama Bank

Breeding reported by Sprunt (1984a) off cays north and east of Abaco—Walker Cay Complex, Mamma Rhoda Rocks, Fish Cays, and Pelican Cays; Saliva (2000a) in-dicated Walker Cay Complex as a historic breeding location; R. Pagliaro confirmed 24 nesting terns at Tilloo Cay and Pelican Cays National Park (*in* Norton et al. 2002b). Bracey (2003) reported Sooty Tern as summer resident on cays off Treasure Cay, Abaco, but no nesting activity detected.

Cay Sal Bank

Sprunt (1984a) reported breeding on Double-headed Shot Cays, Muertos Cays, Dog Rocks, and Damas Cays and estimated that this area had the largest numbers of Sooty Terns in the Bahamas; he estimated 20,000 pairs in 1996 (Sprunt report to SCO meeting, 1996).

Great Bahama Bank

Breeding reported by Sprunt (1984a) on Bimini, indicated by Saliva (2000a) as a historic breeding location. Estimated nests on Berry Islands: Mamma Rhode Rock (100), Rum Cay (1,000), Frozen Cay (700), and Alder Cay (100); birds also present on four other cays but no breeding evidence, 21–24 May 2002 (*in* Norton et al. 2002a). Breeding reported on cays east and southeast of South Andros—Little Green Cay, Grassy Creek Cay, Washerwoman Cay, and South Cay (Sprunt 1984a); Saliva (2000a) indicated these areas as historic breeding locations. More than 50 birds observed in and around known breeding site at Goulding Cay off west side of New Providence, 6 May 1995 (White and Hallett, pers. obs.); 80 pairs estimated, June 2004 (Hallett, pers. obs.). Sprunt (1984a) reported breeding on Finley Cay and Schooner Cays off the west side of Eleuthera and on the Little San Salvador complex off northern portion of Cat Island; Saliva (2000a) indicated these areas as historical breeding locations.

Exumas: Breeding reported by Sprunt (1984a) on Saddle Cay; Lee and Clark (1994) estimated a minimum of several thousand breeding pairs, but this was an educated assumption because colonies were still forming and birds were difficult to census by boat; confirmed nesting on following cays: Narrow Water Cay (5–10 pr), Fish Hawk Rocks, Danger Cay, Saddle Cay, Sandy Cay (150–200 pr), Emerald Cay, Lighting Rocks (25 pr), Sooty Cay, Noddy Cay, and Richard's Rocks; Bailey Smith (pers. comm.) estimated 150 pairs on North Channel Rocks and Little Pigeon Cay off Great Exuma, 2000–2003; 30 birds seen off Buena Vista Cay, Ragged Islands, 14 May 1999 (Hallett, pers. obs.). Sprunt (1984a) and Saliva (2000a) both confirmed Cay Verde as a breeding location; White et al. (1999) estimated 30 nests on Cay Verde in June 1998.

Eastern Islands

Breeding confirmed off Conception Island (South Rocks, Booby Cay) by Sprunt (1984a); no birds observed, 3 May 1999 (Hallett, pers. obs.). Hayes (2003) estimated 500 pairs with data from Catto Cay, Gaulin Cay, Green Cay, and White Cay in Grahams Harbour, San Salvador, 1993–2003.

Southern Islands

Sprunt (1984a) reported breeding on Mira-Por-Vos and Propeller Cay off Samana Cay; 20+ birds in and around Propeller Cay, Samana Cay—probably early arrivals, 4 May 1999 (Hallett, pers. obs.).

Bridled Tern

Little Bahama Bank

Erika M. Gates (pers. comm.) reported 100 birds and more than 20 nests on Peterson Cay, Grand Bahama, June 2004. Sprunt (1984a) reported breeding on Rhoda Rocks and Channel Rocks off north and northeast Abaco, and Chardine et al. (2000a) reported these areas as historic breeding locations; Bracey (2003) confirmed breeding on Don't Rock (12 pr), Whale Cay (20 pr), Two Rocks (2 pr), and No Name Cay (no number given) off Treasure Cay, Abaco; also confirmed nesting on Tilloo Cay (1 pr) and Third Pelican Cay (10 pr), Abaco.

Cay Sal Bank

Sprunt (1984a) reported breeding on Double-headed Shot Cays, Muertos Cays, Dog Rocks, and Damas Cays; 400 pairs estimated in 1996 (Sprunt report to SCSCB meeting, 1996); Chardine et al. (2000a) indicated this area as a historic breeding location.

Great Bahama Bank

Sprunt (1984a) confirmed nesting on Bimini, and Schreiber and Lee (2000a) indicated this area as a historic breeding location. Nest estimates on Berry Islands: Mamma Rhoda Rock (25), Rum Cay (200), Frozen Cay (300), Alder Cay (50), White Cay (20) and High Cay (5), birds present on five other cays but no nests observed, 21–24 May 2002; J. and P. Kushlan counted 48 nests at Petit Cays, near Great Harbour Cay, Berry Islands, June 2002 (*in* Norton et al. 2002a, b). Off Andros, Sprunt (1984a) confirmed breeding on Little Green Cay, Grassy Creek Cays, Washerwoman Cays, and South Cay, and Chardine et al. (2000a) noted these cays as historic breeding locations. White (pers. obs.) saw 30+ birds in

and around Goulding Cay off west side of New Providence in 2003; Goulding Cay has been a breeding site for these terns for at least 6 years—estimate 20 breeding pairs (Hallett, pers. obs.). Sprunt (1984a) reported breeding on the Little San Salvador complex off the northern end of Cat Island and Pt. Howe Rock off the southern end of Cat Island, both listed by Chardine et al. (2000a) as historical breeding locations. Hallett and White (pers. obs.) observed around 10 birds around cays in Fernandez Bay, Cat Island, a probable breeding site, 1 May 1995.

Exumas: Lee and Clark (1994) found no evidence of breeding, but Sprunt (pers. comm.) subsequently confirmed nesting on Saddle Cay and rocks west of Little Bell Cay—no estimate but conveyed as breeding in small numbers; Bailey Smith (pers. comm.) estimated 20–25 pairs nesting on cays off Great Exuma during 2000–2003. Sprunt (1984a) confirmed breeding on cays off Clarence Town, Long Island. Sprunt (1984a) and Chardine et al. (2000a) both confirmed Cay Verde as a breeding location, where White et al. (1999) estimated 50 nests on Cay Verde in June 1998.

Eastern Islands

Sprunt (1984a) and Chardine et al. (2000a) both confirmed the Conception Island complex as a breeding location; no birds observed, 3 May 1999 (Hallett, pers. obs.). Hayes (2003) estimated 70 pairs breeding on the following cays of San Salvador: Catto Cay, Gaulin Cay, Green Cay, and White Cay in Graham's Harbour; Manhead Cay; Goulding Cay; and Low Cay and Low Rock in Pigeon Creek.

Southern Islands

Sprunt (1984a) confirmed Mira-Por-Vos and Propeller Cay off Samana Cay as breeding locations. An estimated 50 pairs breeding on Gold Rock off Pinefield Point, Acklins Island, in 1997 (White and Bainton, pers. obs.).

Least Tern

Little Bahama Bank

Six pairs raised 7 chicks on a gravel roof of a condominium at Lucaya Beach, Grand Bahama, noted by Erika M. Gates (*in* Norton et al. 2002b). Twenty birds counted and confirmed nesting at Tilloo Cay and Pelican Cays National Park, Abaco, by R. Pagliaro (*in* Norton et al. 2002b); Spoil Island (off Great Guana Cay), Treasure Cay, Abaco, has supported as many as 10 breeding pairs during June–July 2000–2003 (Bracey 2003).

Cay Sal Bank

Sprunt (1984a) indicated breeding on Cay Sal and confirmed breeding during a 1996 visit (Sprunt report to SCSCB meeting, 1996); Schreiber and Lee (2000a) indicated Cay Sal as an historic breeding area.

Great Bahama Bank

Sprunt (1984a) confirmed breeding on Bimini, and Jackson (2000) noted it as a historic breeding location; 12 birds sighted on a boat trip with short stop into North Bimini, 27 April 1999 (Hallett and White, pers. obs.). Nest estimates on Berry Islands, Chub Cay (2) and birds present on other cays, S. Stirrup Cay, Frozen Cay, S. Market Fish Cay, Abner Cay, but no nests observed, 21–24 May 2002; J. and P. Kushlan counted 6 nests at Petit Cay, near Great Harbour Cay, Berry Island, June 2002 (*in* Norton et al. 2002a,b). Jackson (2000) indicated a historic breeding area on New Providence and two locations on Eleuthera. Dean and White estimated 35 pairs nesting at South Westridge Estates, New Providence, on 15 July 2003 (*in* Norton et al. 2004); White (pers. com.) saw 10 pairs in August 2004.

Exumas: Sprunt (1984a) reported breeding on Little Bell Island in the Exumas chain and Duck Cay off Great Exuma; Jackson (2000) noted both sites as historic breeding locations. Lee and Clark (1994) observed breeding behavior on the following cays in the Exuma Cays Land and Sea Park—Warderick Wells (5–10 pr), Marion Cay (15–20 pr), Little Bell Cay (2 pr), and on a rock just south of Cistern Cay (20 pr); nesting at Grog Pond, Great Exuma and Staniel Cay, estimated total of 5 pairs, 23 June 1997 (T. White, pers. obs.); Bailey Smith (pers. comm.) observed 75–100 birds (estimate 40 pairs nesting) in a traditional colony at Moriah Harbour Cay, Great Exuma, 12–16 June 2000. Jackson (2000) noted two confirmed breeding locations on Cat Island with 8–20 pairs estimated; 7 birds seen on a visit to Cat Island, 5 May 1995 (Hallett and White, pers. obs.). Schreiber and Lee (2000a) reported breeding locations on Long Island with an estimate of 4–10 pairs. Breeding reported by Sprunt (1984a) on Water Cays, Ragged Islands, listed by Jackson (2000) as a historic breeding location; 15 birds were noted at Buena Vista Cay, Ragged Island, on 14 May 1999 (Hallett, pers. obs.). White et al. (1999) estimated 29 nests at Cay Lobos on 23 June 1998.

Eastern Islands

Jackson (2000) confirmed breeding on Rum Cay with an estimate of 40–50 pairs. On San Salvador, at a large beach expanse known as Sandy Point or Southwest Point, 75–100 adult birds and 20+ downy chicks were seen (est. 40–50 pairs) on 18 June 1999 (Hallett, pers. obs.); Hayes (2003) estimated 100 pairs on High Cay and scattered sand bars on inland Great Lake, San Salvador.

Southern Islands

On Crooked Island 50+ birds were observed but no nesting was detected, 3–7 May 1997 (Bainton, Hallett and White, pers. obs.). Sprunt (1984a) confirmed breeding at Salina Point, Salina, Acklins Island, and Jackson (2000) listed an area on the island as a historical breeding location (not known if the same site); in the same general area 50+ birds were seen on Castle Island (off southern tip), Acklins, on 12 May 1999, most of them on a rock bar in an interior pond (Hallett, pers. obs.). Three birds were seen flying over an interior wetland in Abraham's Bay, Mayaguana, on 7 May 1999 (Hallett, pers. obs.). Sprunt (1984a) confirmed breeding on Great and Little Inagua (noting one group of 300 pairs) and Jackson (2000) indicated both islands as confirmed breeding locations with estimates of 250–350 pairs; 25 birds on Great Inagua, 10 May 1999 (Hallett, pers. obs.).

Gull-billed Tern

Little Bahama Bank and Cay Sal Bank

No breeding records.

Great Bahama Bank

Chardine et al. (2000a) indicated the Berry Islands as a historic breeding location. Birds were observed but no numbers indicated or any evidence of breeding at Cat Cay and Guana Cay in the Berry Islands, 21–24 May 2002 (Norton et al. 2002a). Four breeding locations on Cat Island were confirmed by Chardine et al. (2000a); more than 50 birds seen over coppice and inland ponds but no breeding confirmed, 1–3 May 1995 (Hallett and White, pers. obs.). Two breeding pairs noted at South Westridge Estates, New Providence, in August 2004 by T. White (pers. comm.).

Exumas: Lee and Clark (1994) noted individual birds on Warderick Wells, 25 and 29 May 1991, with breeding suspected, despite lack of evidence. Estimated 10–15 pairs nesting on beach and 30–40 birds in flight over area at Moriah Harbour Cay, Great Exuma, 12–16 June 2000 (Hallett, pers. obs.). In 2003, Bailey Smith (pers. comm.) indicated that an estimated 20–25 pairs have nested on that beach or near Moriah Harbour Cay, Great Exuma, for several years. Chardine et al. (2000a) noted 2 confirmed breeding locations on Long Island. Six birds observed over inland areas of Duncan Town and Buena Vista Cay, Ragged Islands, 13–14 May 1999 (Hallett, pers. obs.).

Eastern Islands

Two breeding locations were confirmed by Chardine et al. (2000a) on Rum Cay. Eight birds seen during trip to San Salvador, 26–29 April 1995 (Hallett and White, pers. obs) and Hayes (2003) estimated 5 breeding pairs on scattered sandbars of Great Lakes, San Salvador.

Southern Islands

Five birds in flight during afternoon, one bird carrying small lizard near Abraham's Bay, Mayaguana, 7 May 1999 (Hallett, pers. obs.). Sprunt (1984a) reported 12 pairs breeding on Great Inagua in 1967 and 1972, and Chardine et al. (2000a) indicated Great Inagua as a historic breeding location, where 12 birds were seen over inland waters, 10 May 1999 (Hallett, pers. obs.).

Roseate Tern

Little Bahama Bank

Sprunt (1984a) confirmed breeding on Fish Cays, off northern Abaco; B. and E. Bracey found 80 terns on Whale Cay and 50 terns at Crab Rock on 24 June 2001 (Norton and White 2001); Bracey (2003) recorded breeding off Treasure Cay, Abaco, at Don't Rock (5 pairs), No Name Cay (nesting for three years but no numbers), and rocks off Munjack Cay (12 birds present but breeding only suspected), 2000–2003. Ten birds were counted and confirmed nesting at Tilloo Cay and Pelican Cays National Park, Abaco, by R. Pagliaro 2002 (in Norton et al. 2002b); Kushlan and Steinkamp reported a colony with 29 nests near Old Kerrs, Abaco, on 26 June 2003 (in Norton et al. 2004).

Cay Sal Bank

Neither Sprunt (1984a) nor Saliva (2000b) reported any breeding records from this area; however, in 1996 Sprunt estimated 795 breeding pairs (Sprunt report to SCO meeting, 1996); 30+ birds with breeding caps on rocks off Anguilla Cays with other terns, 25 April 1999—possible breeders or migrants (Hallett and White, pers. obs.).

Great Bahama Bank

Saliva (2000b) confirmed breeding on the Berry Islands; 75 nests were found on a rock off Little Whale Cay and 200 nests on Alder Cay, and birds present but not breed-

ing on Mamma Rhoda Rock, S. Market Fish Cay, White Cay, and Abner Cay, 21–24 May 2002; 15 nests counted by J. and P. Kushlan at Petit Cays near Great Harbour Cay, Berry Islands, 12 June 2002 (in Norton et al. 2002a, b). Colony of terns (est. 10–20 pairs) at Salt Cay off Paradise Island, New Providence, abandoned in 1997 after depredations by rats, according to White (Norton 1998). Sprunt (1984a) and Saliva (2000b) both confirmed the Little San Salvador complex off the northern end of Cat Island as a breeding location.

Exumas: Sprunt (1984a) reported breeding on Hawksbill Rock and Little Bell Island in the Exumas, confirmed by Saliva (2000b). Lee and Clark (1994) reported over 100 individuals but no actual evidence of breeding on Marion Cay, Sandy Cay, Hall's Pond, Bell's Cay, and Little Bell Island, and 2 pairs with eggs were recorded on Lighting Rocks; White estimated 50 pairs nesting on North Channel Rocks off Great Exuma on 19 June 1997 (in Norton 1997a); 15 pairs estimated on an unknown cay to the east of Channel Rocks off Georgetown, Great Exuma, 12–16 June 2000 (Hallett and B. Smith, pers. obs.). Sprunt (1984a) confirmed breeding from Clarence Town, Long Island; B. Smith (pers. comm.) reported 50–100 birds in and around Stirrup Cay, off Indian Hole Point, Long Island, during the summer of 2003—probable breeding but not confirmed. Saliva (2000b) confirmed breeding on Cay Lobos, where 20 nests were estimated, 23 June 1998 (White et al. 1999).

Eastern Islands

Schreiber and Lee (2000a) indicated Rum Cay as a confirmed breeding location. Hayes (2003) estimated 50 pairs on 5 offshore cays off San Salvador—Catto Cay, Gaulin Cay, and Green Cay in Graham's Harbour; High Cay and Low Rock in Pigeon Creek (colonies irregular).

Southern Islands

Up to 15 terns resting on sandbar at French Wells, Crooked Island, 5 May 1997, and over 30 birds feeding off the south end of Castle Island, Acklins, on 12 May 1999, suggesting some colony nearby (Hallett, pers. obs.). Both Sprunt (1984a) and Saliva (2000b) confirmed breeding on Great Inagua.

Royal Tern

Little Bahama Bank

No breeding records.

Cay Sal Bank

Breeding pairs numbered 150 in 1996 (Sprunt report to SCSCB 1996); over 60 birds sighted (20 on rocks off Anguilla Cays) with full dark caps, 24 April–2 May 1999 (Hallett and White, pers. obs.).

Great Bahama Bank

Present in Berry Islands on Mamma Rhoda Rock, Bushes Cay, and Frozen Cay, 21–24 May 2002 (*in* Norton et al. 2002a). Sprunt (1984a) confirmed nesting of 75 pairs on South Cay southeast off the island of South Andros and 9 pairs on Schooner Cays, off southern Eleuthera; Chardine et al. (2000a) confirmed both locations. J. Parnell in 1998 indicated 50 pairs on Cat Island (Schreiber and Lee 2000a).

Exumas: Lee and Clark (1994) found no evidence of nesting on their visit to the Land and Sea Park but individuals (approx. 15) were seen on the following islands: Sandy Cay, Bell Cay, Warderick Wells, and Hawksbill Cay. Buden (1992b) found 27 pairs with eggs off the northeast tip of Hawksbill Cay on 3 June 1991; Bailey Smith (pers. comm.) photographed roughly 10 pairs with chicks on Smith Cays off Great Exuma in June 2000.

Eastern Islands

Sprunt (1984a) confirmed 14 pairs laying on South Rocks off Conception Island on 15 May 1981. J. Parnell reported 5–10 pairs breeding on Rum Cay in 1998 (*in* Chardine et al. 2000a). Observations of 25–30 birds (10–15 pairs) sitting together on low grasses separated by an arm's length were likely birds on nests, seen on top of Catto Cay, Graham's Harbour, San Salvador, 20 June 1999 (Hallett, pers. obs.); Hayes (2003) reported 10 pairs using the following cays irregularly: Catto Cay and White Cay in Graham's Harbour and Low Rock in Pigeon Creek, San Salvador.

Southern Islands

Sprunt (1984a) reported nesting on Great Inagua with 12 pairs in July 1967 and 20 pairs in June 1972, and Parnell reported 12–20 pairs in 1998 (Chardine et al. 2000a). Sightings, with numbers in parentheses, occurred at the following locations: Atwood Harbour, Acklins (3), Plana Cays (10), Mayaguana (2), and Great Inagua (15); this may indicate breeding birds, but no breeding was confirmed, 3–16 May 1999 (Hallett, pers. obs.).

Sandwich Tern

Little Bahama Bank

No breeding records.

Cay Sal Bank

An estimated 136 breeding pairs were noted in 1996 (Sprunt report to SCSCB meeting 1996); 20 birds in breeding plumage with other terns off Anguilla Cays may have been potential breeders or migrants, 25 April 1999 (Hallett and White, pers. obs.)

Great Bahama Bank

Sprunt (1984a) reported 400 pairs breeding on South Cay (also known as Dolly's Rocks) off South Andros in July 1977 and 3 pairs with eggs on Schooner Cays, Eleuthera, in May 1981. Norton (2000) indicated both areas as historical breeding locations.

Exumas: Lee and Clark (1994) noted breeding pairs in and around Exuma Cays Land and Sea Park at Lightning Rocks (4), Sandy Cay (2), Malabar Cay (several), and Pirate Cay (1); and reported Buden (1992b) finding 30 adults with 15 nests off the northeast tip of Hawksbill Cay on 3 June 1991; White counted 15 pairs nesting on North Channel Rocks off Great Exuma on 19 June 1997 (Norton 1997a); B. Smith (pers. obs.) reported 100–150 birds using North Channel Rocks and an unknown cay to the west (both near entrance to Elizabeth Harbour, Georgetown, Great Exuma), 1999–2003, but had no breeding estimates. White et al. (1999) estimated 95 nests on Cay Lobos 23 June 1998.

Eastern Islands

No breeding records.

Southern Islands

Sprunt (1984a) noted breeding on Bird Rock off the northwest point of Crooked Island, and Norton (2000) indicated this area as a historical breeding location; 10 birds resting on sandbar at French Wells, Crooked Island, on 5 May 1997 seen by White and others (*in* Norton 1997a). Sprunt (1984a) noted around 150 pairs were preparing to breed on Hogsty Reef in May 1979, and a subsequent visitor confirmed that nesting took place; 8 birds seen flying near Hogsty Reef but no evidence of breeding—may have been too early, 11 May 1999 (Hallett, pers. obs.) Sprunt (1984a) estimated 150 pairs in 1967 and 125 pairs in 1972 from the interior salt lakes of Great Inagua, listed by Norton (2000) as a historic breeding location.

Threats

As with other birds, seabirds cannot survive without productive nesting areas and sources of food. In addition, they are particularly vulnerable because they concentrate on relatively few breeding sites and have to remain at these sites for long periods to care for (typically) one slow-growing chick per year. Seabird viability can be compatible with human wants and needs, but more often than not, increasing human populations put more pressure on seabird survival requirements, making this relationship incompatible. A large, even sustainable, seabird population over a large area may be able to withstand some loss or depletion no matter what the causes, but it is not known what constitutes a large and sustainable population. Given the current human population estimates, it makes sense to protect what we have or what is left. The main threats to seabirds and their colonies in the Commonwealth of the Bahamas are:

- Loss of breeding habitat from development for homes, condominiums, recreational and resort facilities, and marinas. This includes areas where birds need isolation to rest and preen.
- Human disturbance, whether intentional or not, from boaters, fishermen, walkers and joggers, tourists, etc. Disturbance exposes eggs or young to excessive heat or predation, thus decreasing nesting success, which already is low for seabirds. Too much disturbance may cause the adult birds to abandon the colony completely.
- Taking eggs and birds for food by various groups or individuals such as poachers, illegal fisherman, careless boaters, or refugees. Concentrated breeding sites make seabirds especially vulnerable to these practices.

- Human introduction of non-native animals, whether intentionally or not, near or at seabird nesting locations: goats, donkeys, pigs, cats, dogs, and rats which trample or eat the habitat, cause disturbance, or prey on the eggs, young, or adults.
- Degradation, pollution or overfishing of coastal or ocean environments, affecting the food chain of seabirds.
- Lack of interest, will, skill, or money by individuals, groups, or governments to ensure reasonable protection for seabirds.
- Natural threats include hurricanes, storms or unusually heavy rains, and predation by Barn Owls and Peregrine Falcons on adults and by Laughing Gulls, iguanas, and crabs on eggs or chicks. Impacts of natural threats intensify when human disturbance at some sites effects birds' habitats.

Acknowledgments

First, my thanks and gratitude to all those researchers, surveyors, ornithologists, and birders who have taken the time and effort (blood, sweat and tears no doubt) to gather information about breeding seabirds in the Bahamas. Also, many thanks are extended to Patricia Bradley for her help and guidance on the project and for asking me to take this on in the first place. Tony White, Bailey Smith, Elwood Bracey, and Dave Lee have always been helpful with information and assistance, and this project has been no exception. Word processing was graciously done by my neighbor, Christine Bos, who offered to do it; I cannot thank her enough.

4

The Turks and Caicos Islands

MICHAEL W. PIENKOWSKI

The Turks and Caicos Islands lie on two shallow limestone banks, Turks Bank being 254 km^2 and Caicos Bank 5,334 km^2 (21°–22° N, 71°–72° 30' W). Water depth in much of the area is less than 2 m, but the two banks are separated by about 30 km of deep ocean. The maximum altitude of the islands is about 50 m above sea level. Further shallow banks to the southeast (Mouchoir, Silver, and Navidad), some within the territory of the Turks and Caicos Islands (TCI), are important for whales and probably for feeding seabirds. The Bahamas lie on separate banks to the northeast and share some aspects of the geography (e.g., Sealey 1994). There are about 38,000 ha of intertidal sand banks and mud flats. Of the 500 km^2 (50,000 ha) total "dry land" area of the Turks and Caicos Islands, 26,669 ha, more than half the land area, consists of wetlands.

On the Caicos Bank, the largest islands lie along the northern edge, including inhabited Providenciales and North, Middle, and South Caicos (map 14). Several very small cays, important for breeding seabirds, lie on the southern edge of the Caicos Bank. Turks Bank holds the inhabited islands of Grand Turk and Salt Cay as well as numerous smaller cays, several of which are important for seabirds. The Turks Bank islands generally have very short vegetation. The dry-land areas of the Caicos Bank Islands are covered mainly by dense thorn scrub in various stages of recovery to the natural tall, dry tropical forest. Shore types include cliffs, rocky shores, sand beaches, mangrove marshes, and extensive flats. Sizes of the larger islands can be seen on the map. Sizes of smaller cays on Caicos Bank are French 8 ha, Bush 16 ha, White 2 ha, Little Ambergris 328 ha, and Fish 10 ha; those on Turks Bank are Long 19 ha, Penniston 4 ha, East 45 ha, and Big Sand 52 ha.

In pre-Columbian times the islands were important centers of population (Keegan 1997). Archaeological studies from a site in Grand Turk occupied between AD 705 and 1170 suggest that less than 1% of meat intake was from birds but that the most frequent birds in the sample were boobies. There is a good case (Menzies 2002) that the first explorers to reach the area were Chinese fleets in the 1420s. The next wave, when islands of TCI or nearby in the Bahamas were the first landfall of Columbus, wiped out the indigenous population within a generation. The area remained largely unoccupied following this. Subsequently, the Turks Bank islands plus South Caicos (the "salt islands") were used to supply salt, important as a food preservative, from about 1500. They were settled from Bermuda for this purpose from the 1660s. The salt pans (salinas) remain, after close-down in the twentieth century, as undervalued historic features and places where birds in large numbers can be viewed closely with great ease.

The Caicos Islands, because of their shallow and complex channels, became a main refuge of some of the more famous pirates. From 1787, land in the Caicos Islands was given to "Empire Loyalists" who had lost their lands in the newly created United States, because they wished to remain British. The resulting plantations (initially mainly for cotton) cleared much of the high forest, which appears to have survived until that time in largely pristine state, the pre-Columbian population having apparently used forest and marine products, rather than clearing large areas. Although leaving a substantial archaeological heritage, the main plantation period lasted only a few decades and met a series of natural and economic misfortunes. Most of the plantation owners eventually left the Caicos Islands or moved to the salt islands. Former plantation slaves and their descendants developed a subsistence economy and a great knowledge of the medicinal and nutritional uses of the native vegetation as it was reestablishing toward tropical dry forest. There were some later cotton and sisal plantation initiatives in the late nineteenth and early twentieth centuries.

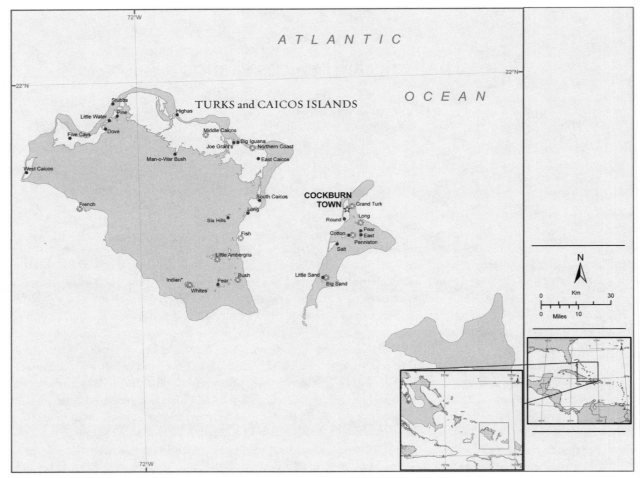

Map 14. The Turks and Caicos Islands.

The marine and wetland habitats of the Caicos Islands were probably largely untouched by human impacts until the last quarter of the twentieth century, when the land grant of much of Providenciales to U.S. development companies led to the establishment of holiday resorts and private homes. Providenciales has been converted from an island of three small villages (probably rather like the present Middle Caicos) to a largely unplanned urban sprawl and commercial center. The human population of the Turks and Caicos Islands is about 20,000, mainly on Providenciales, with significant numbers also on Grand Turk (4,000), South Caicos (2,000) and North Caicos (2,000) and smaller communities on Middle Caicos (300) and Salt Cay (100). There are resort developments on some of these islands as well as on Pine Cay and Parrot Cay, with others under construction or proposed at West Caicos, Water Cay, Joe Grant Cay, East Caicos, and Big Ambergris Cay. Economic activity includes tourism, offshore finance, and fishing. Only a small area is under cultivation.

Methods of Survey

The material in this chapter is based partly on the cited earlier work, especially of D. Buden, P. Bradley, A. White, and R. Ground. The more recent sightings and numeric information have drawn together published and unpublished records by workers listed by Pienkowski (2006). Several projects since 1998 have been designed to cover as much of the area as possible and, where feasible, at different seasons and in different years. For example, systematic surveys through the Middle Caicos woodlands and wetlands, as well as the areas on North Caicos and Grand Turk, have been achieved on several occasions each year in this period. Systematic efforts have been made to fill gaps in coverage, leading to several specially organized visits to Salt Cay, the seabird cays, East Caicos, and other sites. Filling major gaps in the seabird coverage was targeted in 2002 by Pienkowski et al. (2005).

In this survey, small, powered boats were used to visit the cays. All cays were viewed initially from the boat. In the case of some small, rocky cays with few birds, or with the birds essentially viewable on sea cliffs or slopes, numbers were estimated from the boat. In the case of larger cays, those with large bird populations, and those with birds on land not viewable from the sea, landings were made and ground surveys undertaken.

On cays with few or moderate numbers of birds in relatively open ground, direct estimates were generally easily made. Two or three observers counted the same sections independently and reached good agreement. The difficulties in counting large seabird colonies in (usually tropical) areas of ground cover are well known (Bibby et al. 2000). A combination of the methods indicated by Bibby et al. (2000) was used. These included the following:

1. Direct counts of apparently occupied nests (AON) were made of small to medium colonies on open ground, following the definitions for AON used by Bibby et al. (2000).
2. Mapping and quadrant counts were used in larger colonies. Nests were usually under cover of vegetation, producing a severe case of the conflict identified by Bibby et al.: keeping disturbance to less than half an hour but obtaining enough data for useful estimates. In the present case, the distributions of different apparent densities or markedly different habitats were mapped, both in relation to published maps and charts and by using a portable GPS device. Use of the maps and charts was assisted in that the nesting cays were small, and the areas of colonies were large in relation to the cays. Sample counts of nests were then made within the areas of similar density. Because of the low visibility through the vegetation under which birds were generally nesting, quadrants were generally smaller than the examples given by Bibby et al. (2000).
3. Flushing counts were used in some cases, generally alongside one of the other methods. Bullock and Gomersall (1981) and Bibby et al. (2000) report a fairly reliable relationship showing that three flushed terns equate to two breeding pairs. Observations during the current study indicate that this underestimates the number of breeding pairs in the Turks and Caicos colonies, because many terns

did not leave their nests even when humans were a few meters away and many terns were already in the air giving alarm calls. This was thought to be due to the density of the vegetation under which many birds were nesting.

Numbers estimated are generally given to 1 or 2 significant figures, to avoid giving misleading implications of higher precision. Further information is given by Pienkowski et al. (2005). Financial limitations prevented visits to all seabird sites, notably several cays near South Caicos. Priority was given to those remote cays from which data were most lacking, and which are most difficult to visit, as well as less remote cays known to be important. The totals given are consequently underestimates for Turks and Caicos as a whole, although less so for the priority seabird species than for others.

Species Accounts

Thirteen species of seabirds breed in the Turks and Caicos Islands, and regular breeding is suspected in another. Three are resident: Audubon's Shearwater, Brown Booby (suspected breeding), and Magnificent Frigatebird; and eleven are migrants, with at least some of the population absent for part of each year: White-tailed Tropicbird, Laughing Gull, Royal Tern, Gull-billed Tern, Sandwich Tern, Roseate Tern, Common Tern, Least Tern, Bridled Tern, Sooty Tern, and Brown Noddy. Studies on seabirds have so far largely been limited to surveys and censuses. However, once funded, the implementation of the *Plan for Biodiversity Management and Sustainable Development around Turks & Caicos Ramsar Site* (Pienkowski 2002a) and related proposals in the Environment Charter strategy (discussed later) would involve developing the monitoring programs for seabirds and other aspects of biodiversity.

Tables 4.1 and 4.2 summarize the seabird counts and current status records available. These are mainly in the five years up to 2004, with few numeric records earlier (or numeric records that probably do not relate to systematic coverage). Reporting follows the units of the original reports, whether individuals, pairs, or the standard measures of apparently occupied nests (AON) or territories (AOT) (Bibby et al. 2000). In several cases the reports are noted as minima because the nature of the terrain meant that observers knew they were underestimating totals.

The coasts of West Caicos and northern North Caicos were surveyed from the sea in May–June 2002, with few seabirds recorded. The inland marsh and pond areas of

Table 4.1. Minimum estimate of seabird pairs breeding in the Turks and Caicos Islands

Species	Estimate of Pairs
Audubon's Shearwater	Probably at least hundreds of pairs, but no counts
White-tailed Tropicbird	300
Brown Booby	3
Magnificent Frigatebird	100
Laughing Gull	200
Brown Noddy	27,000
Sooty Tern	48,000
Bridled Tern	3,500
Least Tern	700
Gull-billed Tern	100
Roseate Tern	200
Common Tern	100
Royal Tern	10–100
Sandwich Tern	10–100

several Caicos islands, even including parts of Providenciales, are difficult of access, and could hold substantially more of a certain species of seabird than recorded so far.

Audubon's Shearwater

Range and status: Common resident, at sea and on small, remote cays (Buden 1987a); uncommon breeding summer visitor (Bradley 1995). These hole-nesting birds, which visit their nests at night, are generally seen only at sea. There are breeding records for "a small islet off Providenciales," Long Cay and West Six Hill Cay near South Caicos, and East Cay (Buden 1987a), and local reports indicate significant breeding numbers, probably in internationally important numbers, on the small rocky cays off northwestern Middle Caicos and near Drum Point on mainland East Caicos (Walsh-McGehee et al. 1998; Pienkowski 2006; Pienkowski et al. 2005). Information

Table 4.2. Status of seabirds in the Turks and Caicos Islands in the decade up to 2004, plus any earlier total counts

Island or Cay	Audubon's Shearwater	White-tailed Tropicbird	Brown Booby	Magnificent Frigatebird	Laughing Gull	Brown Noddy
PROVIDENCIALES						
Five Cays to Bonefish Point	Breeding 2004	50+ AON in 2002				
MIDDLE CAICOS						
Highas Cay		20 AON in 2002				10 AON in 2002
Other northern cays & headlands	Breeding	80+ prs in 2004				
Marshes					1050 birds in 2002	
Man O' War Bush				100–200 prs 1998, 60 AON 2001, 35 AON in 2002		
EAST CAICOS						
Joe Grant's Cay		10+ prs 2004				
Northern coast of East Caicos	Breeding 2004					
Marshes					150 in 2004	
SOUTH CAICOS						
Long Cay, S. Caicos	Breeding	30+ AON in 2002				
Six Hills Cays	Breeding 2004	Breeding 2004				

gathered during survey work for other species indicates (by sounds at night) significant numbers breeding in May 2004 at East Six Hill Cay and Middle Cay in the Five Cays (B. N. Manco, pers comm.)

Breeding data: Land records relate mainly to May and June, but the sample is small, and a longer breeding period is likely.

White-tailed Tropicbird

Range: Common summer visitor, probably breeding (Buden 1987a), recorded March to October; uncommon breeding summer visitor (Bradley 1995). Recorded at Providenciales, Water Cay, Pine Cay, Stubbs Cay, Middle Caicos, Iguana Cay, South Caicos, Dove Cay, Long Cay (Caicos), Grand Turk, Long Cay (Turks), Pear Cay, East Cay, Salt Cay, Cotton Cay, Big Sand Cay (Buden 1987a), plus Turtle Rock, Five Cays, Highas Cay, and cays off

northern Middle Caicos (Pienkowski et al. 2005). The eastern coasts of East and South Caicos have not yet been adequately checked.

Status: There are few numeric records. Pienkowski et al. (2005) noted that the survey methods they were using in May–June 2002 were not designed for this species and that numbers would be underestimated. This was both because not all cliff areas likely to be used were covered and because the survey method was not designed to detect all birds in nest burrows. The minimum estimates for the most important areas they found were the southwestern shore of Providenciales and nearby islets, especially from Bonefish Point to Five Cays (minimum 48 pairs), Highas Cay (min 20 pairs), Long Cay (Caicos, min 30 pairs), and Big Sand Cay (min 6 pairs), with an additional at least 80 pairs on the cays and headlands of Middle Caicos in 2004 (pers. obs.). There is some indica-

Sooty Tern	Bridled Tern	Least Tern	Gull-billed Tern	Roseate Tern	Common Tern	Royal Tern	Sandwich Tern
	15+ AON in 2002						
	20 AON in 2002						
	Breeding 2004						
		150 birds in 2002	Breeding in large numbers (30 pairs and 50 birds in small parts of area) 2002			270 birds in 2002	200 birds in 2002
		30+ AON in 2004			200 pr birds 2004		
		100 in 2000	40 in 2000			60 in 2000	50 in 2000
Breeding	Breeding						

continued

Table 4.2.—*Continued*

Island or Cay	Audubon's Shearwater	White-tailed Tropicbird	Brown Booby	Magnificent Frigatebird	Laughing Gull	Brown Noddy
CAICOS BANK OUTER CAYS						
Fish Cay						100 AON in 2002
Little Ambergris Cay					Large breeding colony 1999	
Bush & Seal Cays:						
Bush Cay						2750 AON in 2002
Pear Cay						50 AON in 2002
Indian Cay						2800 AON in 2002
White Cay						2800 AON in 2002
French Cay					20 AON in 2002	11000 AON in 2002
TURKS BANK CAYS						
Grand Turk		33 pairs 1987–93			Breeding: no count. 900 birds in 2003	
Gibbs Cay						
Round Cay						100 AON in 2002
Long Cay						6000 AON in 2002
Pear Cay						
East Cay	Breeding				150 AON in 2002	
Penniston Cay			3 birds 2002	25 prs 1966, 30 birds 2002		1300 AON in 2002
Salt Cay		25 pairs 1987–93			Breeding: no count. 900 birds in 2003	
Big Sand Cay		6 AON in 2002				20 AON in 2002
Little Sand Cay					Breeding	
MINIMUM TOTAL AON/AOT	N/A	224	?3	35–235	170	26930
MINIMUM BREEDING SEASON POPULATION (rounded to 2 sig. fig.)	N/A	450	?6	70–470	3300	54000

Sooty Tern	Bridled Tern	Least Tern	Gull-billed Tern	Roseate Tern	Common Tern	Royal Tern	Sandwich Tern
25 AON in 2002	25 AON in 2002			200 AON in 2002			
				300 birds in 2002		30 birds in 2002	200 birds in 2002
1750 AON in 2002	970 AON in 2002						
1200 AON in 2002							
1200 AON in 2002	1 AON in 2002						
130 AON in 2002	1 AON in 2002						
		420+ AON 2004				40 birds in 2003	60 birds in 2003
	1 AON in 2002						
	60 AON in 2002						
		30 AON in 2002					12 birds in 2002
	2000 AON in 2002						
		140+ AON 2004		Breeding 1998		30 birds in 2003	60 birds in 2003
44000 AON in 2002	240 AON in 2002	20 AON in 2002					
				Breeding			
48305	3333	640	?	200	100	?	?
97000	6700	1700	150	700	200	470	580

tion of changes of distribution, as White (1998) advised bird-watchers to visit East Cay to see tropicbirds, but Pienkowski et al. (2005) recorded none there. P. Bradley estimated up to a maximum of 25 pairs at Salt Cay and 33 pairs at Grand Turk, 1987–1993.

Breeding: Nests with eggs or young have been reported mainly in May and June (Buden 1987a; B. N. Manco, pers. comm.).

Brown Booby

Range, status, and breeding: This species has been recorded from Penniston Cay since 1930 (Buden 1987a), and breeding has long been suspected but not proved (Bradley 1995), although Schreiber and Lee (2000a) indicated breeding. Pienkowski et al. (2005) flushed 3 birds during survey work on this cay in June 2002; they were probably nesting, but direct confirmation remains lacking due to inaccessibility of the probable sites. This is the only site in the country regularly used by this species.

Magnificent Frigatebird

Range: Seen in flight throughout islands, with two current breeding localities.

Status and breeding: Uncommon breeding resident (Buden 1987a; Bradley 1995). The Penniston Cay colony has been known since a report of 25 pairs apparently breeding in August 1966 (Buden 1987a), with breeding more recently indicated by Schreiber and Lee (2000a). The larger colony at Man o' War Bush on the south side of Middle Caicos was found (at least by ornithologists) more recently (cf. Bradley 1995), but the opinion of local residents is that numbers there have been stable for many years. Walsh-McGehee et al. (1998) reported 100–200 pairs. Estimates by Pienkowski et al. (2005) in 2000 and 2001 were about 60 AON, and 35 in 2002. However, the apparent decline may simply be seasonal, as the 2000 and 2001 counts were in April, whereas those in 2002 were in June, and the breeding season is apparently spread through much of the year. Of more concern is the absence of active nests at Penniston Cay in June 2002, despite the presence of 30 adults, as well as the presence of remains of at least 6 dead frigatebirds, half of these looking relatively recent (weeks, rather than months) in what was thought to be the traditional nesting area here. Buden (1987a) refers to a report of a breeding colony at North Creek, Grand Turk, in November 1977 that has not been present more recently. An older possible colony is implied by a location on the west coast of South Caicos being labeled as "Little Man o' War Bush" on the Department of Overseas Surveys maps (originally produced about 1960).

Laughing Gull

Range: Seen throughout the islands but few breeding localities confirmed.

Status: Common summer breeding visitor, occasionally seen at other seasons (Buden 1987a; Bradley 1995). Walsh-McGehee et al. (1998) noted the lack of breeding records and that local fishermen said these gulls nested regularly on the Caicos Bank, but the only specific site mentioned was Little Water Cay. Although the birds are seen throughout the cays and islands, locations of breeding colonies have been recorded only by P. Bradley (pers. comm.) on Little Sand Cay, near Big Sand Cay, and by Pienkowski et al. (2005) on East Cay (at 150 apparently occupied nests, internationally important at 2% of the Caribbean population; Wege 2002) and French Cay (20 AON). A larger colony was found in northeastern Little Ambergris Cay in 1999 (pers. obs.), but it has not been possible to check this more recently. Small numbers were recorded breeding among large numbers present in summer on the salinas and beaches at Grand Turk and Salt Cay. It seems likely that there may be other breeding sites.

Breeding data: Nests with eggs or young reported mainly in May to July (Buden 1987a; Pienkowski et al. 2005).

Brown Noddy

Range: Breeds mainly on small, remote cays; at other times at sea. These breeding areas include Six Hill Cays, Bush Cay, White Cay, French Cay, Round Cay, Long Cay, and Penniston Cay (Buden 1987a). To these can be added Highas Cay, Fish Cay, Pear Cay, Indian Cay, and Big Sand Cay (Pienkowski et al. 2005).

Status and breeding: Abundant breeding summer visitor to the colony areas (Buden 1987a; Bradley 1995), with records mainly from May to September, with some at sea outside this period. Nests both on the ground and in low bushes. In June 2002 Pienkowski et al. (2005) estimated 100 AON at Fish Cay, 2,750 AON at Bush Cay, 2,800 AON at each of Indian and White Cays, 11,000 AON at French Cay, 100 at Round Cay, 6,000 AON at Long Cay, 1,300 AON at Penniston Cay, and 20 AON at Big Sand Cay. These represent a significant proportion of the world population and a major component of the population in the Caribbean. The densities of nests tended to vary considerably between cays but rather little within a habitat type on any one cay. Average densities of nests ranged from 0.01 to 0.5 per m^2, with most around 0.1 per m^2, thought to be underestimates because of the difficult nature of the terrain and vegetation.

Dean (1999) reported thousands of Sooty Tern on French Cay and hundreds of Brown Noddy sitting on eggs. This is the reverse of the relative proportions of species surveyed there by Pienkowski et al. (2005). However, Dean's visit was in early March and that of Pienkowski et al. in early June. It is not known, therefore, whether this reflects a difference between years, or sampling of a regular annual pattern at different seasons in different years, or some other difference. The breeding cycle of Sooty Tern at Ascension Island in the mid-Atlantic famously averages a 9.6-monthly, rather than annual, cycle (Ashmole 1963a), and this is thought to be an antipredator adaptation. At St. Helena, 1,300 km south of Ascension, the same species has an annual cycle (Rowlands et al. 1998). Clearly, more information is required on the biology of these species in the Turks and Caicos Islands before a formal monitoring program can be developed.

Sooty Tern

Range: Breeds mainly on small, remote cays; at other times at sea. These breeding areas include Water Cay, Middle Caicos, Iguana Cay, Dove Cay, Six Hill Cays, Bush Cay, White Cay, French Cay, Round Cay, Long Cay, East Cay, and Penniston Cay (Buden 1987a). To these can be added Fish Cay, Indian Cay, and Big Sand Cay (Pienkowski et al. 2005).

Status and breeding: Abundant breeding summer visitor to the colony areas (Buden 1987a; Bradley 1995), with records mainly from May to August. Nests mainly in sand scrapes, often under at least partial cover, where available. In June 2002 Pienkowski et al. (2005) estimated 1,750 AON at Bush Cay, 1,200 AON at each of Indian and White Cays, 130 AON at French Cay and 44,000 AON at Big Sand Cay. These represent a significant proportion of the world population and a major component of the population in the Caribbean. The densities of nests tended to vary considerably between cays but rather little within a habitat type on any one cay. Average densities of nests ranged from 0.01 to 1.25 per m², thought to be underestimates because of the difficult nature of the terrain and vegetation. The Sooty Tern colony on Ascension Island in the mid-Atlantic stood at 194,000 pairs in 1997, at an average density of 2.12 per m² (Rowlands 2001). See Brown Noddy for some information on temporal variability.

Bridled Tern

Range: Breeds on small, remote cays and a few headlands, favoring rocky hollows; at other times at sea. These breeding areas include Six Hill Cays, Bush Cay, French Cay, Round Cay, Long Cay, and Penniston Cay (Buden

1987a). To these can be added Little Sand Cay, north of Cotton Cay (P. Bradley, pers. comm.), as well as Turtle Rock, Five Cays, Three Mary Cays, Highas Cay, other small cays and headlands of Middle Caicos, Fish Cay, White Cay, and Big Sand Cay (Pienkowski et al. 2005 and unpubl.).

Status and breeding: Common breeding summer visitor (*S. a. recognita*) to the colony areas (Buden 1987a; Bradley 1995), with records from May to August. The importance of the Turks and Caicos Islands is suggested in that almost all of Buden's (1987a) records are from here, rather than from the much larger area of the Bahamas. In June 2002 Pienkowski et al. (2005) estimated 20 AON at Highas Cay (with more at the other Middle Caicos northern cays observed in June 2004), 970 AON at Bush Cay, 60 AON at Long Cay, 2,000 AON at Penniston Cay, and 240 AON at Big Sand Cay. These represent a substantial proportion of the world population and probably the largest population in the Caribbean.

Least Tern

Range: In coastal and other wetland areas throughout the islands.

Status and breeding: Common breeding summer visitor, recorded April to October (Buden 1987a). Buden (1987a) reported nesting, in May and June, from Providenciales, North Creek (Salt Cay), and a colony on Fort George Cay, which moved to Pine Cay following beach erosion. Some counts of nests are given, but it is thought that these do not represent systematic counts. In June 2002 Pienkowski et al. (2005) found colonies of at least 30 apparently occupied nests on East Cay and at least 20 (and probably many more) AON on Big Sand Cay. Systematic counts of the salinas on Grand Turk and Salt Cay in June 2004 revealed minima of 420 and 140 AON, respectively. The salinas remain important throughout the seasons for presence of the terns in the islands, and the Creek Mouth area of Salt Cay is an important post-breeding resting (possibly molting) area, with over 400 birds recorded (pers. obs.). The author found a colony of at least 30 AON at Thatch Cay, off northern East Caicos, in June 2004.

Gull-billed Tern

Range: In coastal and marsh areas throughout the islands.

Status: Uncommon to locally common breeding summer visitor (Buden 1987a; Bradley 1995). Breeding is thought to be irregular, using salt pans and marshes on the larger islands, with large numbers attempting to breed in extensive marshes flooded by rains in Middle Caicos in May–June 2002, when only a small area could be surveyed (Pienkowski 2002a, 2006).

Roseate Tern

Range: In coastal areas throughout the islands.

Status: Uncommon breeding summer visitor (Buden 1987a), and uncommon winter visitor (Bradley 1995). White (1998) reported breeding on rocks south of Salt Cay, and P. Bradley (pers. comm.) reports breeding on Little Sand Cay, near Big Sand Cay. In June 2002 Pienkowski et al. (2005) found a breeding colony of about 200 apparently occupied nests on Fish Cay and a roost of about 300 birds on Little Ambergris Cay.

Common Tern

Range: Occasional records throughout the islands (Buden 1987a; Bradley 1995); breeding colony found on East Caicos in June 2004 by the author.

Status and breeding: Previously recorded as transient only, with records March to October (Buden 1987a). Colony of at least 200 birds (about 20% of the Americas summer population), with eggs at Rocky Point, East Caicos, in June 2004. This is one of the most remote locations from human habitation in the TCI, with a difficult sea approach, making the late discovery (and occasional sightings on other islands over the years) less surprising.

Royal Tern

Range: In coastal and other wetland areas throughout the islands.

Status: Common breeding summer visitor and present also in winter (Buden 1987a; Bradley 1995). Buden noted reports by K. Hesse of breeding on sand spit at Little Water Cay in several summers in the 1970s, but this spit has now linked to the next cay, possibly with more disturbance, predation, and invasion of alien plants, and there are no recent records despite conservation observations in the area. Recorded recently in various areas (Pienkowski et al. 2005), with some breeding behavior, particularly at the salinas at Grand Turk and Salt Cay. Ground (2001) reports breeding on remoter cays. Breeding may be fairly irregular, as for some other tern species in these desertic conditions. Little Ambergris Cay was found to be an important resting area for several terns, including 30 Royal Tern (Pienkowski et al. 2005). Comparable numbers have been recorded also at the salinas at Grand Turk and Salt Cay.

Sandwich Tern

Range: In coastal areas throughout the islands.

Status: Uncommon to locally common breeding summer visitor (Buden 1987a), and uncommon winter visitor (Bradley 1995). Pienkowski et al. (2005) recorded the species mainly in nonbreeding situations (although in some cases in pairing displays). Breeding may be fairly irregular. Little Ambergris Cay was found to be an important resting area for several terns, including 200 Sandwich Tern (Pienkowski et al. 2005). Comparable numbers have been recorded also at the salinas at Grand Turk and Salt Cay.

Threats

The greatest current threat to the seabird populations in the Turks and Caicos Islands is the potential loss of habitat. This is the case across much of the archipelago. The rate of built development, largely without any strategic plan, has been rapid on Providenciales for 30 years. In the present century, this has accelerated greatly to what appears to be one of the highest rates in the world in proportion to area. Such rapid built development is spreading to almost all the islands in the country, even impacting statutorily protected areas. These protected areas need governmental commitment to effective long-term protection and management by an appropriate governmental or non-governmental body, such as the Turks and Caicos National Trust.

The impacts on the globally important wildlife (with many endemics and vulnerable species) of many taxa are major and continuing. In respect of seabirds in particular, the main impacts are likely to be via the loss of wetlands and nesting areas throughout the islands, loss of and damage to the old salinas in Grand Turk and Salt Cay, and loss or disturbance of coastal habitats in these and other islands.

The salinas are of international importance to breeding terns (and shorebirds) as well as to large numbers of shorebirds in the nonbreeding season. They also provide exceptional bird-watching opportunities and historic interest for tourists and residents. At present, these salinas are largely unprotected and totally undervalued. Although theoretically protected under the planning regulations, in practice, the salinas are subject both to casual and medium-scale infilling and to major proposals that would remove them in their entirety. Similarly, built developments elsewhere threaten coastal populations. Ironically, pressure for development in Grand

Turk, related to increasing tourism, is destroying the Salinas—actually and potentially one of the major features of interest for tourists.

The major increase in the numbers of tourists in Grand Turk at the time of writing results from the current rapid development of a cruise ship port, leading to very large numbers of short-term visitors, in contrast to the previous pattern of smaller numbers of longer-stay visitors. Vigilance and enforcement will be needed to ensure that the introduction of cruise liners does not lead to oil pollution incidents. However, the larger impacts may result from habitat loss and increased disturbance. Catering for the hugely increasing number of visitors is putting pressure on the seabird cays near Grand Turk. It will be important to try to limit landing visitors to the already damaged Gibbs Cay (see later discussion), with controlled non-landing boat visits to view birds on nearby Round Cay, but no visitation to the highly vulnerable major seabird cays.

The southernmost seabird cays are protected largely by their remoteness or difficulty of access. However, their sensitivity and sanctuary status (meaning that visiting without license is theoretically banned) is not widely realized, and there are many unauthorized landings by yachts and probably by boats carrying illegal immigrants. During the first Haitian crisis in 1989, refugees in boats fleeing Haiti told of relying on eggs on the Sand Cays and French Cays, etc. Such activity probably continues. Lack of wardens prevents effective management.

It is thought that the collecting of seabird eggs and unfledged young may have been common but has probably largely died out. However, it may still be undertaken by illegal immigrants, and concern exists that the southern seabird cays may be particularly exposed to this. This factor or disturbance seems to have had an effect. P. Bradley reports that in the early 1990s, egg collecting was common at Gibbs Cay, which still held thousands of Sooty Tern and Brown Noddy. Hardly any seabirds now breed on this cay, and conservation efforts tend to center on limiting visits (now mainly diving and picnicking) to this cay and avoiding the spread of disturbance to the other nearby seabird cays.

The introduction of cats and rats has had undoubted effects on the endemic iguanas and may well have affected nesting seabirds, as noted earlier as a possibility. Introduced plants, such as *Casuarina* sp., tend to consolidate beaches, thereby reducing nesting habitat for some seabirds as well as turtles.

Conservation

In September 2001, UK signed Environment Charters with UK Overseas Territories. In 2003, with the support of the UK Foreign & Commonwealth Office, the UK Overseas Territories Conservation Forum facilitated an exercise with Turks & Caicos Government and other TCI stakeholders to develop a strategy for action to implement the Environment Charter. In addition to its local use, this was designed to provide a model for other U.K. Overseas Territories (Ground and Pienkowski 2004). Most of the conservation issues indicated would be addressed by full implementation of this strategy for action. However, personnel changes have impeded this. A strong commitment by government and an able and committed coordinating official are needed.

The Ramsar, Bonn, World Heritage, Cartagena, London, and MarPol conventions have been adopted by the Turks and Caicos Islands, which are also moving toward adoption of CITES and the Convention on Biological Diversity. One large Wetland of International Importance has been designated under the Ramsar Convention. Progress is needed on designating some of the other seven qualifying sites identified in a review commissioned by the U.K. government and undertaken in collaboration with the TCI government and other stakeholders (Pienkowski 2005).

Table 4.3 indicates TCI's important seabird breeding sites for species listed in table 4.1 and their status in relation to protection. Designation as a protected site does not in itself achieve conservation, and needs for management are addressed in the following strategy for action.

Several breeding seabird species are well covered by the protected areas. However, other species are barely covered. The following actions (as suggested by the TCI government-appointed Environment Charter Working Group and by international reviews) are recommended for site protection:

1. Town Salina and Pond, and the other Grand Turk salt pans, as well as North and South Wells need Nature Reserve (and Area of Historic Interest) status, for breeding and feeding terns and many other features.
2. The northeastern area of Middle Caicos (including Crossing Place Trail, Blowing and Juniper holes, Fish Ponds, and Highas Cay as well as other small cays and headlands on north side of Middle Caicos) need Nature Reserve status, for breeding Audubon's

Table 4.3. Important seabird breeding sites in the Turks and Caicos Islands and their status in relation to protection

Site	Status
Providenciales	
Five Cays to Bonefish Point	Small part lies within Pigeon Pond and Frenchman's Creek Nature Reserve, but mainly unprotected
Middle Caicos	
Highas Cay and other northern cays and headlands	Unprotected
Marshes	Some protected as part of North, Middle and East Caicos (International Ramsar Site) Nature Reserve; other areas proposed for extension of this.
Man o' War Bush	Protected as part of North, Middle and East Caicos (International Ramsar Site) and Vine Point Nature Reserves
East Caicos (and nearby cays)	
Joe Grant's Cay	Unprotected
Northern coast	Unprotected in seabird areas
Marshes	Unprotected (except for small section in North, Middle and East Caicos (International Ramsar Site) Nature Reserve
South Caicos	
Long Cay, Middleton Cay, Six Hill Cay	Protected as Admiral Cockburn Nature Reserve
Other Caicos Bank cays	
Little Ambergris Cay and Fish Cays	Protected by ownership of the Turks & Caicos National Trust (a statutory independent non-profit membership conservation organization)
French, Bush and Seal Cays	Protected as French, Bush and Seal Cays Sanctuary
Grand Turk (and nearby cays)	
Salinas and wells	Unprotected
Long Cay	Protected as Long Cay Sanctuary
Penniston and East Cays	Some protection as parts of Grand Turk Cays Land and Sea National Park, but this is a recreational category, and Sanctuary status needed.
Salt Cay (and nearby cays)	
Salinas and creeks	Unprotected
Big Sand Cay Sanctuary	Sanct 23

Shearwater and White-tailed Tropicbird, nonbreeding gulls and terns, and many other features.

3. The north coastal areas of East Caicos need Nature Reserve status, as the only breeding site in TCI for Common Tern (and probably the most important site in the Caribbean), breeding Audubon's Shearwater and Least Tern, and many other features.

4. The Area of Historic Interest of Salt Works and Village in Salt Cay needs Nature Reserve status added, and the site needs to be extended to the Creeks on the eastern coast, for terns and other features of interest.

5. Penniston Cay and East Cay, within Grand Turk Cays Land and Sea National Park (a recreational category) need Sanctuary status because of their importance to many breeding seabird species.

Site protection needs to be a long-term commitment, with resources provided to the managing organization to enable effective implementation. Especially on the seabird cays, more signage, public information, warden presence, and enforcement of the ban on unlicensed access are needed to make the protection effective.

The Strategy for Action to Implement the Environment Charter for the Turks and Caicos Islands, developed by participatory processes and adopted by the TCI Executive Council in December 2003, should be implemented. The protected areas noted should be designated domestically, transferred to the ownership of a conservation body, and added to the Ramsar list of Wetlands of International Importance. Resources are needed for management of the protected areas and enforcement of protection; for additional interpretative signage and materials for a public education campaign on the importance, value to tourism, and sensitivity of breeding seabird colonies; and for the development and implementation of monitoring programs.

5

Cuba

ARIAM JIMÉNEZ, PATRICIA RODRÍGUEZ, AND PEDRO BLANCO

The Cuban archipelago is located in the western Caribbean, between North and Central America. It is bounded by the Strait of Florida, Bahamas Channel, and Atlantic Ocean in the north, Windward Passage in the east, Caribbean Sea in the south, and Yucatan Strait in the west. It consists of two main islands, Cuba (105,007 km^2) and Isla de la Juventud (former Isla de Pinos, 2,200 km^2), and 4,195 islands, islets, and cays (3,715 km^2) grouped in archipelagos: Canarreos, Sabana-Camagüey, Jardines de la Reina, and Los Colorados (maps 15–17). The landscape along the 5,746 km of coast surrounding the Cuban archipelago is diverse. There are extensive areas of sandy beaches and swamps along the coast, where the important mangrove ecosystems have developed. Rocky coasts are also frequent; they can be low or high and usually alternate with sandy regions.

In Cuba, as in the rest of the West Indies, ornithological studies have been focused mainly on landbird fauna. Remoteness and inaccessibility of the vast cay territory and marine coast areas, as well as lack of resources for research, have hindered systematic and long-term studies of seabird species that breed in the country. Until recently there has been little research that offers information about population sizes and trends, selection of breeding habitats, or breeding success, among other topics. However, a significant group of researchers and workers from protected areas all over the country has now carried out studies and made focused observations on seabird populations that are presented in this chapter.

Methods of Survey

Seabird nesting data were collected by personnel from several Cuban institutions: Instituto de Ecología y Sistemática (IES), Empresa Nacional para la Protección de la Flora y la Fauna (ENPFF), Universidad de La Habana (UH), Centro Nacional de Áreas Protegidas (CNAP), Centro de Investigaciones de Ecosistemas Costeros (CIEC), and Centro de Investigaciones y Servicios Ambientales (CISAM). All data were collected between 1980 and 2004.

Complete colony counts was the census method used in the localities where estimates of pairs of nesting seabirds existed. Ground-nesting colonies (terns and gulls) with more than 100 nesting pairs were subdivided into nest aggregation sections, and teams of 3–5 people walked through the nesting areas, noting the positions of the adults and searching for evidence of nesting (nest, eggs, or chicks). A limited search time of 15–20 minutes for each nest aggregation was set to reduce disturbance. Tree-nesting colonies (pelicans and frigatebirds) were generally visited by boat. Nesting pairs estimates were made from the boat or from vantage points (the top of the highest trees surrounding the colony) to avoid disturbance produced by researchers. Subsequent visits and nest monitoring were uncommon in most cases due to logistical limitations. All estimates offered are considered as a minimum number of nesting pairs.

Species Accounts

About 43 species of seabirds have been reported along Cuban coasts (Garrido and Kirkconnell 2000); 28 are considered winter residents or migrants, while 15 species breed, of which two are new records for Cuba (Rodríguez et al., in press; Barrios et al. 2001; table 5.1). The number of breeding species represents more than 71% of the seabirds that breed in the West Indies. However, it is possible that some other species may breed, such as Black-capped Petrel, most likely in Sierra Maestra (Santiago de Cuba), although there is no recent information to con-

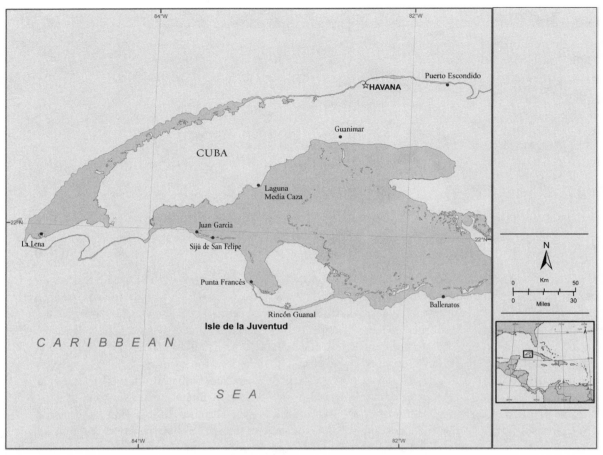

Map 15. Western Cuba and Isla de la Juventud.

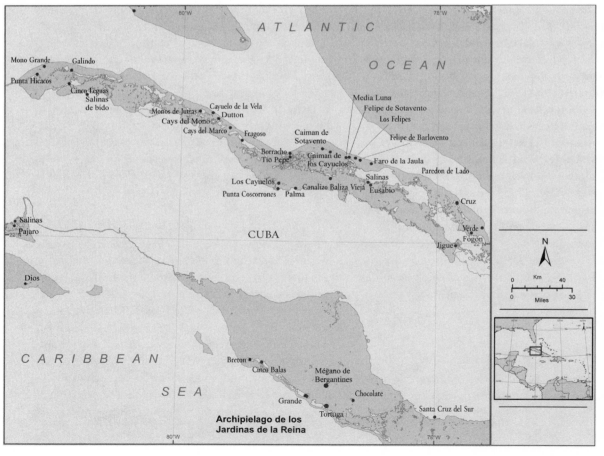

Map 16. Central Cuba and Archipelago de los Jardines de la Reina.

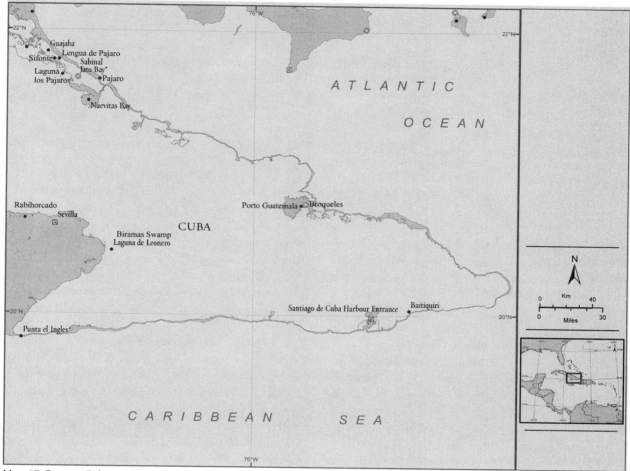

Map 17. Eastern Cuba.

firm this; the same applies to the Caspian Tern, which may breed in Las Salinas in Zapata Swamp (Garrido and Garcia 1975).

Most breeding seabirds in Cuba are migratory, arriving in early March to May and remaining during spring and summer. Mainly they come from the southern Caribbean and the coasts of Venezuela, but due to Cuba's proximity to the Bahamas and Florida, we do not rule out the possible presence of some breeding seabirds from these regions.

We could confirm from historical records that none of the breeding seabirds has disappeared from our territory. However, many colonies have declined in numbers or have disappeared from known breeding sites. That is the case of Brown Booby in Cay Mono Grande, Matanzas province, where during the nineteenth century Gundlach reported 12 pairs breeding with three other species of terns (table 5.2). In 2004 these breeding sites were still used by terns, but in the past few years no Brown Booby nests have been reported. Most of the historical breeding locations, however, still maintain breeding populations,

Table 5.1. Seabirds breeding in Cuba and minimum number of nesting pairs, 1980–2004

Common Name	Minimum number of pairs
Audubon's Shearwater	2
White-tailed Tropicbird	9
Brown Pelican	350
Magnificent Frigatebird	1,100
Laughing Gull	1,000
Brown Noddy	300
Sooty Tern	3,000
Bridled Tern	650
Least Tern	350
Gull-billed Tern	70
Roseate Tern	42
Common Tern	100
Royal Tern	40
Sandwich Tern	150

Table 5.2. Historical records of seabird breeding species in Cuba

Sites	Species	Year	Reference
Cay Piedras and Cay Galindo	Least Tern	1850	Lembeye, 1850
Cay Mono Grande	Bridled Tern, Sooty Tern, Brown Noddy, Brown Booby	1846–87	Gundlach, 1893
	Bridled Tern, Sooty Tern, Brown Noddy	1959	Bauza Collection
Punta Inglesa, Cape Cruz	White-tailed Tropicbird	1857	Gundlach, 1893
Cay La Vela	Roseate Tern	1963	García and Garrido, 1965
Punta Hicacos	Least Tern	1958–59	Bauza Collection
Guanimar	Least Tern	1959–60	Bauza Collection
Cay Caimán de los Cayuelos	Brown Noddy, Laughing Gull	1960	Bauza Collection
Cays of Felipe	Bridled Tern, Sooty Tern	1960	Bauza Collection
Cay Monitos de Jutía	Bridled Tern	1963	IES Collection
Cay Los Ballenatos	Bridled Tern, Laughing Gull, Royal Tern, Sandwich Tern	1965	García and Garrido, 1965

and in some the number of species and of breeding pairs has increased. In Cay Galindo, Lembeye (1850) reported a breeding population of Least Tern. At present, there is information about two other species breeding in this area (Laughing Gull and Royal Tern). The same phenomenon has occurred in colonies on Cays of Felipe in Ciego de Ávila and Cay la Vela in Villa Clara.

More recent ornithological studies carried out from 1980 to 2004 show the existence of 64 seabird breeding sites in 9 of the 14 provinces of the country. Of these, 28 are mixed breeding colonies that include two to six taxa.

The breeding site with the most seabird diversity is Cay Felipe de Barlovento, where six species of larids and Audubon's Shearwater have been reported. Four other cays are home to breeding populations of up to five species of terns: Cay Ballenatos in the Isla de la Juventud, Cay Faro de la Jaula, Cay Paredón de Lao in Ciego de Ávila, and Cay La Vela in Villa Clara. The biggest breeding colony in the country is located in Cay Mono Grande, in Matanzas province, where 2,334 pairs of four species of tern bred in 2004 (Bridled, Sooty, and Roseate Tern and Brown Noddy; C. Pérez, unpubl.). In addition, it is the oldest known colony and one of the best studied. Other cays with significant breeding seabird populations are Cay Felipe de Barlovento (465 pairs), Cay Faro de la Jaula (378 pairs), Cay Felipe de Sotavento (200 pairs), Cay Paredón de Lao (284 pairs), and Cay La Vela (200 pairs). Additional sites with more than 100 pairs are at Cay Ballenatos, Cay Monos de Jutía and Cay Caimán de Sotavento in Villa Clara, and Cay Sabinal in Camagüey.

The Sabana-Camagüey archipelago is the area with the highest concentration of breeding sites, species richness, and breeding individuals. The biggest archipelago in Cuba, it stretches 465 km along central-north Cuba from Punta Hicacos, Matanzas province, to Nuevitas

Bay, Camagüey province, comprising 2,517 cays, which vary in distance from the main island (17–30 km). The archipelago contains 60% of all Cuban cays and is characterized by a great diversity of habitats, including swamps, beaches, and rocky coasts. It is one of the most important systems of coastal wetlands in the country (GEF/PNUD 1999), a complex network of bays and internal macro lagoons between the archipelago and the north coast of Cuba. This complex of physico-geographical factors guarantees the existence of a great number of isolated and well-preserved potential breeding sites that foster the establishment of seabird colonies. Fourteen of the 15 seabird species breed in this region, and every year this site is home to more than 5,000 pairs of breeding seabirds.

Procellariiformes are rare coastal seabirds in Cuba. Most of the eight species reported are accidental sightings; therefore evidential records of their presence in our territory are limited. Although rare, the Black-capped Petrel was considered a summer resident of the southeast region of the country, where some authors have mentioned that it bred in Sierra Maestra (Bond 1978, 1985; Halewyn and Norton 1984), but Lee and Viña (1993) did not find evidence of breeding in Cuba.

Audubon's Shearwater

This is the only procellarid species for which breeding patterns are documented. In June 2002 two pairs were found breeding in Cay Felipe de Barlovento (22° 36' 41" N, 78° 37' 27" W), located north of Cay Guillermo in the Sabana-Camagüey archipelago (Rodríguez et al., in press). Two chicks, only a few weeks old, were found in nests located in cliffs of the highest coast of the cay. This is the first and only documented case of breeding of this species, which had been considered vagrant on Cuban coasts (Garrido and Kirkconnell, 2000).

Table 5.3. Breeding sites and minimum number of nesting pairs of Brown Pelican in Cuba, 1989–2004

Breeding Site	Year	Pairs	Reference
Cays Sevilla, Gulf of Guacanayabo	1989	> 100	García et al., 1989
	1998	60	O. Labrada, unpubl.
Cay Broqueles, Nipe Bay	1998	100	C. Cuadrado, unpubl.
Cay Bretón	1998	-	A. Parada, unpubl.
Jigüe Bay	1998	-	GEF-PNUD, 1999
Nuevitas Bay	1998	-	
Canalizo Baliza Vieja, Punta Alegre	1998	-	
Cay Guajaba	1998	-	
Cay Los Cayuelos, Los Perros Bay	1998	-	
Cay Pájaro, North of Cay Sabinal	1998	-	
Cay Salina, South of Cay Coco	1998	-	
Jato Bay, Cay Sabinal	1998	-	
Punta Coscorrones	1998	-	
Alcatraz small cays, Cay Sabinal	2001	10	Barrios et al., 2001
Salto del León, Cay Sabinal	2001	15	
Santa Cruz del Sur	2002	20	CIMAC, Camagüey
Cay Sifonte	2002	6	A. Jiménez, unpubl.
Fauna Refuge Río Maximo	2002	36	
	2003	16	
Cay Fragoso	2003	25	E. Hernández, unpubl.
	2004	35	
Cay Los Pájaros	2004	30	L. Cotayo, unpubl.

White-tailed Tropicbird

A rare summer resident in Cuban waters. It is concentrated in two territories of the southeast region: Baitiquirí, in Guantánamo province, and Punta Inglés, in Cape Cruz, Granma; the latter has been known since the late nineteenth century (Gundlach 1893). Currently the population estimate is around 9 to 14 pairs (E. Palacios, pers. comm.). Inaccessibility of the breeding sites either by the sea or by land has prevented getting more breeding data.

Brown Booby

An uncommon permanent resident along Cuban coasts, with little known about population status or distribution of breeding colonies. In the late nineteenth century Cay Mono Grande had a small breeding population of about 12 pairs (Gundlach 1893), and there was at least one nest in 1986 (O. Torres, pers. comm.); currently there is no evidence of breeding. In 1988 and 1991, two sightings of a second breeding colony together with three tern species were reported on a southwestern cay, Cays of Dios, South Zapata Swamp (L. Cotayo, pers. comm.). It was a huge colony with more than 1,000 individuals and population density of 10 nests/m².

Brown Pelican

A very common resident, breeding widely in coastal zones and isolated cays. Generally breeding dates have been reported from March to September (García et al. 1989; Garrido and Kirkconnell 2000), but recent studies confirm the presence of active colonies from November to May (A. Jiménez, unpubl.). It appears that the breeding cycle in Cuba is either irregular or extends throughout the year. The breeding population is estimated as 300–350 pairs. Currently, 19 breeding colonies have been identified in seven provinces of the central and eastern regions of the country, but population estimates refer to only nine (table 5.3). Generally colony size ranges from 6 to 36 pairs, with the highest estimates in eastern Cuba, but in 1989 a colony with more than 300 individuals (most of them breeding) was documented in Cay Sevilla, in the Gulf of Guacanayabo in the province of Granma (García et al. 1989). Almost 10 years later it was confirmed that the colony was still being used by approximately 60 pairs. Another colony of approximately 100 pairs was located in Cay Broquelis, Nipe Bay, in the province of Holguín in 1998.

There are reports of some other breeding sites of this species in Jobabo in the province of Las Tunas north of

Table 5.4. Breeding sites and minimum number of nesting pairs of Laughing Gull in Cuba, 1989–2003

Breeding site	Pairs	Year	Reference
Cay Borracho	2	1989	Blanco et al., 2001
Las Salinas, Zapata Swamp	23	1994	
Cay Caimán de Sotavento	50	1989	
Cay Mégano de Bergantines	-	1998	A. Parada, unpubl.
Cay Tortuga	-	1998	
Cay Sabinal	92	2000	Barrios et al., 2001
	60	2002	O. Barrios, unpubl.
Rio Máximo	12	2001	J. Morales, unpubl.
Cay Faro de la Jaula	70	2002	P. Rodríguez, unpubl.
Cay Felipe de Barlovento	250	2002	
Cay Felipe de Sotavento	90	2002	
Cay Fogón	10	2002	
Cay Guajaba	6	2002	
Cay Paredón de Lao	200	2002	
Cay Cinco Leguas	5	2002	P. Blanco, unpubl.
Cay Galindo	4	2002	
Cay Ballenatos	80	2003	
Ciénaga de Biramas	50	2003	

Villa Clara, and in the south of Pinar del Río, but this information awaits confirmation. The nests are built at least 3 m from the ground on the black mangrove (*Avicennia germinans*), usually very close to each other, about 1–2 m apart (Garcia et al. 1989; A. Jiménez, unpubl.). There are no reports of breeding on the ground, an observation recorded by Gundlach (1893). Brown Pelican are frequently found breeding in mixed colonies, with Double-crested Cormorant and Magnificent Frigatebird. There are usually three eggs in the nest.

Magnificent Frigatebird

This is a common resident on the coasts and cays of Cuba. Breeding begins in January with courtship and extends for about 14 months. Frigatebirds usually breed in mixed colonies, near cormorants and pelicans. They can parasitize these species for material to build nests and for food for chicks. During nest building, the sexes have different roles: females provide materials and males build the nest (Morales et al. 1991). Nests are located at different heights in the mangrove; however, there seems to be a preference for high places. There are eight breeding sites in Cuba but population estimates from only four.

The largest colony is located in Cay Rabihorcado, south of Cay Coco, Ciego de Ávila. In March 1988, 875 nests were counted, but a year later this number decreased to 628 (Morales et al. 1991). In 1998 it was confirmed that the breeding colony was still active, but there was no nest count. South of Cay Coco, in Cay Eusebio del Oeste, a breeding colony of 88 nests was found in 2002.

In Cay Sifonte, in the north of Camagüey, the existence of a breeding population of at least 60 pairs has been confirmed. Close by, in a brackish lagoon at the fauna refuge Río Máximo, a colony of about 40 pairs attempted to breed on small cays of black mangrove in 2001, but a severe wet season dramatically affected breeding success that year and the site has not been used since. There are no estimates of four other breeding colonies, located in Cay La Leña, Guanahacabibes, and Laguna Media Caza, in Los Palacios in Pinar del Río; and Cay Cinco Balas and Cay Chocolate in Jardines de la Reina archipelago (A. Parada, unpubl.).

Laughing Gull

A common resident in coastal areas throughout the year and the only representative of this genus to breed in Cuba. It uses a great variety of habitats—small rocky cays in the sea, shallow lagoons, and swamps—building nests on the ground, on vegetation, or in holes on the rocks, and it uses plant material for this purpose. The clutch size is 1–3 eggs. A total of 17 breeding sites have been identified from historic times, most concentrated in the cays on the north coast of the central region of Cuba (table 5.4). Most colonies are mixed with other species of terns, such as Bridled Tern, Sooty Tern, and Brown Noddy. Generally, monospecific colonies are small, as in Cay Fogón and Río Máximo. The largest colonies, comprising most of the breeding population of 500–700 pairs, are in the north of Ciego de Ávila, in the Cays of Felipe, Faro de la Jaula, and Paredón de Lao, which are part of the great Sabana-Camagüey archipelago. Other

Table 5.5. Breeding sites and number of nesting pairs of (1) Brown Noddy, (2) Sooty Tern, and (3) Bridled Tern in Cuba, 1988–2005

Location	Number of pairs			Year	Reference
	1	2	3		
Cay de Dios	?[a]	?	?	1988, 1991	L. Cotayo, pers. comm.
Cay Borracho	3	14	-[b]	1989	Blanco et al. 2001
Cay Caimán de Sotavento	30	-	40	1989	
Cay Monos de Jutía	-	102	42	1989	
Cay La Vela	120	-	68	1989	
Cay Faro de la Jaula	25	200	75	2002	P. Rodríguez, unpubl.
Cay Felipe de Barlovento	20	50	130	2002	
Cay Felipe de Sotavento	10	75	50	2002	
Cay Paredón de Lao	10	30	34	2002	
Cay Ballenatos	-	-	20	2003	P. Blanco, unpubl.
Cay Mono Grande	51	2,223	49	2004	C. Pérez, unpubl.
Cay Dutton, Los Pajonales.	-	-	121	2004	E. Hernández, unpubl.
Cays de Marco	-	-	30	2005	
Cays del Mono	-	-	?	2005	

a. unknown number of breeding pairs

b. not present

significant colonies are in Cay Los Ballenatos (80 pairs), Cay Caimán de Sotavento (50 pairs), and Cay Sabinal (92 pairs). Considering current data, the total breeding population is estimated at more than 1,000 pairs.

Brown Noddy, Sooty Tern, and Bridled Tern

These three species breed in large mixed colonies. This association is very common and it has been reported in some other Caribbean islands (Chardine et al. 2000a). These species are considered common by local residents. From March to April, they breed on the north and south coasts of Cuba; the breeding peak is from April to May for Bridled and Sooty Tern and from May to June for Brown Noddy. Fourteen nesting sites have been located and nine were multispecies colonies (table 5.5). The most important colonies are at Cay Mono Grande (2,323 pairs, of which 2,000 pairs were Sooty Tern; plate 30), Cay Faro de la Jaula (300 pairs), Cays Felipe de Barlovento (200 pairs), and Sotavento (135 pairs), all in the Sabana-Camagüey archipelago. Hundreds of individuals of these species have been documented in Cay Mono Grande since 1846 (Gundlach 1893). Sooty Tern is one of the commonest seabird species in the West Indies (200,000–300,000 pairs; Saliva 2000a) and in the world (Gochfeld and Burger 1996). It has the largest breeding population of the three species, with an estimated population of 3,000 pairs; that of the Bridled Tern is estimated at 650 pairs and the Brown Noddy at 300 pairs (table 5.5).

The three tern species breed in rocky cays, which are usually located off the coast and where coastal vegetation is very limited. Bridled and Sooty terns lay only one egg, rarely two, and usually on rocky or sandy substrate. In some cases, Bridled Tern may use gravel, shells, or some remains of grass, but it does not build a nest as such. The Brown Noddy usually lays only one egg and builds a nest with branches, seaweed, and remains of shells generally placed on bushes or on rock mounds.

Least Tern

A common summer resident, breeding on the coasts of mainland Cuba and the surrounding cays, mainly on the north coast. Among terns, this species had the greatest number of breeding sites registered from the nineteenth century (Gundlach 1893) to the present (a total of 18 breeding localities), mainly concentrated in the Sabana-Camagüey archipelago, in the south of the western provinces, and the Isla de la Juventud.

Colonies are generally small, from 2 to 20 pairs (table 5.6). The largest are located in Cay Fragoso, with 50 nests in 2003, 67 in 2004, and 81 in 2005; Estero de Caza, south of the Isla de la Juventud, with 34 nests (Berovides and Smith 1983); in cays Juan García and Siju, Cays of San Felipe, in the province of Pinar del Río, with 30 and 32 nests each in 2001; in Cays Tío Pepe, with 30 nests in 2003; and Cay Sabinal, with 21 nests in 2000 and 33 in 2001 (Barrios et al. 2001). Considering current data, the breeding population of this species in Cuba is estimated at more than 350 pairs.

The breeding season is from April to July. The Least Tern breeds in a great variety of habitats: cays, beaches, swamps and rocky surfaces in some shallow lagoons, al-

Table 5.6. Breeding sites and minimum number of nesting pairs of Least Tern in Cuba, 1980–2005

Breeding Site	Pairs	Year	Reference
Rincón Guanal	34	1980	Berovides and Smith, 1983
Cay Monos de Jutía	40	1989	Blanco et al., 2001
Cay La Vela	8	1989	
Cay Grande	-	1998	A. Parada, unpubl.
Cay Sabinal	33	2001	Barrios et al., 2001
Cay Guajaba	2	2002	P. Rodríguez, unpubl.
Cay Verde	3	2002	
Cay Galindo, Matanzas	6	2002	P. Blanco, unpubl.
Cay Cruz	20	2002	
Bay of Nuevitas	10	2002	
Cay Ballenatos	11	2003	
Cay Tío Pepe	30	2003	
Salinas de Bido	10	2004	
Cay Sijú, San Felipe	6	2004	V. Berovides, pers. comm.
Las Salinas, Zapata Swamp	17	1994	Blanco et al., 2001
	25	2004	L. Cotayo, pers. comm.
Laguna de Leonero, Birama Swamp	25	2003	A. Jiménez, unpubl.
Cay Juan García, San Felipe	30	2003	V. Berovides, pers. comm.
Cay Fragoso	50	2003	E. Hernández, unpubl.
	67	2004	
	81	2005	

though sometimes sandy substratum is preferred. It generally breeds in monospecific colonies but sometimes with other species, like Laughing Gull and Common and Bridled Tern. Clutch size is 1–3 eggs laid in a small depression on the sand or in a hole on the rocks, where shells, gravel, or dry vegetative residues could be found (Berovides and Smith 1983; Blanco et al. 2001). In many colonies breeding success is low, due mainly to flooding and to predation by rats, cats, crabs, and Laughing Gull. Late in June 2004, in the Cay Siju colony south of Pinar del Río, 30 nests experienced predation probably by the Cuban iguana (*Cyclura nubila;* K. Berovides, pers. comm.); and in 2001, in Cay Sabinal, the nests were lost due to a rise in the sea level (O. Barrios, unpubl.).

Gull-billed Tern

Sometimes breeds in the Caribbean and the approximate population was estimated at 100–150 individuals breeding at 5–7 sites (Chardine et al. 2000a). In Cuba, Garrido and Kirkconnell (2000) reported the status of this species as a rare winter resident and a migrant in the coastal regions. It breeds at two sites in Cuba. The first documented breeding was of 48 pairs in 2001 (Barrios et al. 2001) in Ensenada del Jato, Cay Sabinal, in the province of Camagüey; in 2004, numbers increased to 70. A smaller breeding colony, with only 8 breeding pairs, was located in Cay Sifontes (P. Rodríguez, unpubl.), also part of Sabana-Camagüey archipelago. The number of breed-

ing pairs in Cuba is estimated at between 70 and 80. This species breeds in areas with low vegetation, near the coast. It builds nests in holes on the rocks or on the sand, and uses small pieces of stone and plant material like leaves of red mangrove (*Rhizophora mangle*), *Sesuvium portulacastrum,* and *Talassia testudinum* (P. Rodríguez, unpubl.). It lays 1–2 eggs.

Roseate Tern

Populations of this species are decreasing alarmingly in various territories of the world (Gochfeld 1983). The status of this species in the West Indies is not very clear and because of the lack of information, population estimates are not exact. It is a rare summer resident, and there is little information about the location of its breeding sites, populations, or breeding patterns. It is known that it breeds in small colonies located mainly in the north coast cays, from May to July. It lays one or two eggs in slight depressions of the terrain or in rock cavities (Valdés 1984). Four breeding sites have been located. Cay La Vela, north of Villa Clara, was the first site where breeding was documented in Cuba (4 pairs), when three eggs were collected with two females that had eggs in the oviduct (May 15, 1963: García and Garrido, 1965). In 1989 four nests were found at this same site (Blanco et al. 2001). The other sites were Hicacos Peninsula, where 27 pairs were found in 2001; Cay Mono Grande, with 11 pairs in 2004; and Cay Ballenatos in the southeast of the

Isla de la Juventud, where there were no counts. Nesting population of Roseate Tern in Cuba is estimated at between 40 and 50 pairs.

Common Tern

An uncommon resident on Cuban coasts; only two breeding colonies have been found. The first documented was located in Rincón Guanal, in the south of the Isla de la Juventud, in June 1980, where 62 pairs nested with some pairs of Least Tern (Berovides and Smith 1983). In July 2005 a total of 43 pairs were breeding in a mixed colony with Bridled and Sandwich terns in Cays del Mono, situated in the protected area Lanzanillo-Pajonal-Fragoso in the Sabana-Camagüey archipelago (plate 30). The Common Tern breeds on sandy-rocky coasts, usually from April to July, usually nesting in the rocks, using dry plant stems and small shells. It lays only one egg, rarely 2 (Berovides and Smith 1983; Valdés 1984). The Cuban breeding population of Common Tern was estimated to be at least 100 pairs.

Royal Tern

A common resident in the coasts and cays of Cuba, breeding from March to July. It usually breeds in mixed colonies, located mainly in rocky cays, off the coast. Breeding colonies with Sandwich Tern are very common. This species does not build a nest; it usually lays only one egg in a slight depression on the sand or on the rocks (Blanco et al. 2001; P. Rodríguez, unpubl.). Eleven breeding sites have been identified; usually the number of pairs does not exceed 10. In 1989, 4 nests were located in Cay Caimán de Sotavento, in the north of Villa Clara; in 2002, 5 nests were found in Cay Felipe de Barlovento, 8 in Faro de la Jaula, and 10 in Cay Paredón de Lao, in the north of Ciego de Ávila; in 2003, in Cay Los Ballenatos and Biramas Swamp, 5 nests were reported; and in 2005, 2 nests were found in Cay Fragoso. There are no records of the breeding population in the rest of the identified sites at Cay La Vela, Cay Palma, Cay Galindo, and Cay Cinco Leguas. The estimated breeding population of this species is about 40 pairs but may be higher because Royal Tern is one of the most common species of tern in Cuba.

Sandwich Tern

Part of the population lives permanently in Cuba, where it is common in some regions of the country, especially in the summer, with the support of migrant individuals. The breeding season is from March to July, usually in colonies with Royal Tern, in cays or islets off the coast. Eggs are laid in a slight depression on the sand (Valdés

1984; Blanco et al. 2001). Five breeding sites have been identified: Cay Los Ballenatos in Los Canarreos archipelago (1965–2003), where approximately 22 pairs were documented in 1965 (García and Garrido 1965), which increased to 77 in 2003; Cay Tortuga in Jardines de la Reina archipelago in 1998 (number of nests was not estimated); Cay Felipe de Barlovento north of Cay Guillermo in 2002, with 11 pairs; and Cays de Marco and Cays del Mono in the protected area Lanzanillo-Pajonal-Fragoso, where 14 and 34 nests were observed, respectively. Using the current data we estimated a minimum of 150 nesting pairs.

In 2002, among 11 nests in Cay Felipe de Barlovento was one of the South American race, the Cayenne Tern. It is the first and only breeding report of this subspecies in Cuba (Pérez Mena et al. 2005) and is the most northerly point in its West Indian breeding range (see Buckley and Buckley 1984; Norton 2000). Some authors consider this subspecies a different species, but it has been reported to hybridize in some mixed colonies on certain Caribbean islands (Norton 1984).

Threats

Impact of Tourism Development

The greatly increased development of tourism in coastal regions and in the most important cays of the country constitutes one of the most serious threats to breeding seabirds in Cuba. In some territories, like the Sabana-Camagüey archipelago, where tourism development has increased rapidly, environmental management plans have become inadequate and are not keeping pace (GEF/PNUD 1999). This situation has caused loss of breeding sites due to habitat destruction to create new infrastructure. For example, in 1990–1992, 160 pairs of Laughing Gull, Bridled Tern, Sooty Tern, and Brown Noddy nested in the Media Luna colony. However, in 1995 the colony was extirpated because of human disturbance during the construction of hotels (Blanco et al. 2001).

Tourism development in the northern part of the Sabana-Camagüey archipelago has included the construction of two riprap causeways between the main island and the cays. These highways extend for more than 17 km and facilitate access to distant cays by cars and buses. The causeways contain bridges and canals approximately every 300–400 m to allow water flow. Nevertheless, changes in water flow have been detected and have resulted in sediment deposition, changes in water depth, and increasing salinity in some areas. These variations in the macro-lagoon hydrology have caused damage in mangrove islands and consequently the loss of potential breeding sites for tree-nesting species, such as frigatebirds and pelicans.

The prevailing state of disturbance in the colonies as a result of tourist visits and increased boating activities is one of the main threats, causing birds to desert nests and resulting in increased predation and death of young.

Collecting of Eggs and Unfledged Young

In some regions of the country, collecting eggs and unfledged young is still a common practice among fishermen and the local population. Some of the sites are important for nesting colonial seabirds, including Roseate Tern. Cay Borracho, Cay La Vela, Cay Mono Grande, Cay Fragoso, and Cay Los Ballenatos are among the places where this practice has become more frequent. It affects breeding success of the colonies not only because of the direct impact in removal of eggs but also through disturbance.

Hunting or fishing for terns with a hook to collect the metal banding rings has been a hobby for teenagers and children in some northern regions of the country, especially in Caibarién, Isabela de Sagua, and Cárdenas.

Predation by Introduced Animals

Predation is one of the most important causes of nest loss in seabird colonies. Although there are many natural predators of eggs and chicks (crabs, ants, birds of prey, and gulls), feral and domesticated animals such as rats, dogs, and cats introduced into these areas are a more serious problem. Causeways built to facilitate access to cays and islands and support development have been used as access routes and have provoked an increase in the population of many vertebrate land animals considered significant egg and bird predators, most notably rats and feral cats. The development of coastal regions has also increased the presence of dogs.

Conservation

Forty-four of the identified seabird breeding colonies are located in areas that are part of the National System of Protected Areas. There are 14 colonies in national parks, 26 colonies in fauna refuges, and four in ecological reserves. Most of the important colonies (in terms of size and number of species) and rare or endangered species have some kind of protection.

The biggest breeding site in the country, Cay Mono Grande (more than 2,000 pairs of Bridled Tern, Sooty Tern, Brown Noddy, and Roseate Tern), is located in the Varahicacos-Galindo Ecological Reserve. Other impor-

tant sites like Cays Caimán de Sotavento, Felipe Grande, and Felipe Chico, where more than six species of terns breed, are inside the Santa María–Los Caimanes National Park. The two breeding sites of the Roseate Tern, one of the rarest species in Cuba, and the historical colony of White-tailed Tropicbird located in Cape Cruz are also protected. In general, at least one important breeding site of each species is protected by the National System of Protected Areas.

Seabird nesting colonies located in protected areas benefit from actions taken under the management plans for these conservation units. Management plans in marine protected areas usually involve actions directed toward protection of nesting localities and censuses during the breeding season. Wardens patrol the access to cays by boat, avoiding potential human predation on eggs or other disturbances produced by fishermen visiting seabird breeding sites. Some places, such as Cay Guajaba and Cay Sabinal, have permanent stations close to the nesting areas, which enhance the surveillance system during the most critical periods of seabird breeding. Nesting seabird censuses and monitoring are carried out by personnel in protected areas. Nevertheless, generally these actions are not systematic because time and resources are limited. Protected areas also have an important role in environmental education of coastal communities. Management plans incorporate public and school education focusing on wetland ecosystems and biodiversity.

Other international conservation categories protect many of the seabird breeding areas. For instance, most regions of the Sabana-Camagüey archipelago are included in the proposal for nine Important Bird Areas (IBAs). Other territories, such as Los Canarreos, Zapata, and Biramas Swamp, were also included in this proposal. Many seabird colonies are located in the six Wetlands of International Importance (Ramsar sites): Buenavista (313,500 ha., 22° 27' N, 078° 49' W), Ciénaga de Lanier y Sur de la Isla de la Juventud (126,200 ha., 21° 36' N, 082° 48' W), Ciénaga de Zapata (452,000 ha, 22° 20' N, 81° 22' W), Gran Humedal del Norte de Ciego de Ávila (226,875 ha., 22° 19' N, 078° 29' W), Humedal Delta del Cauto (47,836 ha., 20° 34' N, 077° 12' W), and Humedal Río Máximo-Cagüey (22,000 ha., 21° 43' N, 077° 27' W).

Research Needs

There are still gaps in understanding breeding colonies in the country. Many breeding areas considered important for seabirds need to be inventoried and to have a monitoring system established, especially in Los Canarreos and Jardines de la Reina, coastal regions in the south of Pinar del Río, Zapata Swamp, and the east of Cuba. Research should focus on location and mapping of nesting sites, a study of population status and trends, breeding success of nesting species, and matters that affect adult and chick survival. Funding to improve infrastructure and technical training of personnel in marine protected areas is essential, as is design of a single methodology for all future research and periodic monitoring.

6

The Cayman Islands

PATRICIA E. BRADLEY

The Cayman Islands, 270 km² in size, are situated in the extreme western Caribbean (19° 20'–19° 43' N, 79° 50'–81° 21' W). They comprise three islands and several small cays: Grand Cayman is about 130 km southwest of Little Cayman and Cayman Brac, which are separated from each other by a channel 7 km wide (maps 18–20). The Cayman Islands are some 700 km south of Miami, 280 km northwest of Jamaica, and 240 km south of Cuba. The Yucatan Peninsula of Mexico is the closest landfall with continental America. Each of the Cayman Islands lies on an east-west axis and is of low relief, with the maximum elevation of 46 m reached on Cayman Brac. Extensive mangrove wetlands, which cover 35–40% of Grand Cayman and Little Cayman but only 3% of Cayman Brac, are associated with coastal lagoons and breeding seabird sites (Brunt 1994; Bradley 1994).

Christopher Columbus is credited with discovery of the Cayman Islands in 1503, the only island group in the West Indies never to have had permanent settlement by the pre-Columbian Taíno people of the Greater Antilles (Fewkes 1922; Stokes and Keegan 1993). Although an important provisioning stop for European ships, the islands remained uninhabited for a further 240 years until the first permanent settlers arrived on Grand Cayman in the 1730s and on Little Cayman and Cayman Brac in the 1830s.

In 2005, the GNP reached US$2 billion, tourists numbered around 2 million (90% from cruise ships), and the total population increased from 16,677 in 1979 to 32,800 in 1989 and about 50,000 in 2005 (Cayman Islands Information Service 2005).

Seabird fossils and subfossils from the late Pleistocene to late Holocene (14,000–4,500 YBP to present) from Cayman Brac contained only two species of seabirds, and abundant deposits of subfossils and well-preserved feathers indicated nesting: White-tailed tropicbird, the first fossils of this species in the West Indies, and Audu-

bon's Shearwater (Morgan 1994). There is no historical record of the shearwater, and Morgan (pers. comm.) thought it was extirpated early in the nineteenth century by predation of visiting seafarers, who most likely introduced rats and cats before the permanent settlers arrived. C. B. C. Cory sent the first ornithologist, W. B. Richardson, to the Cayman Islands in 1886 (Cory 1886a). The history of Cayman Islands ornithology with records of seabirds prior to 1975 is given in Bradley (2000).

Six species of seabird breed in the Cayman Islands: three are resident—Brown Booby, Red-footed Booby, and Magnificent Frigatebird; and three are migrants absent for part of each year—White-tailed Tropicbird, Bridled Tern, and Least Tern. Estimates of the total number of pairs in 2003–2004 are shown in table 6.1.

Methods of Survey

There have been three counts of the Red-footed Booby: an estimated 2,700 pairs in July 1975 (Diamond 1980); about 2,618 pairs in 13.8 ha in January 1986 (Clapp 1987); and 4,839 pairs in February 1997 (Burton et al. 1999; counts by quadrant extrapolated for total colony area of 16.5 ha; see species account). Direct counts of occupied nests were made for the three subpopulations of Brown Booby on Cayman Brac, Magnificent Frigatebird on Little Cayman, and Least Tern on the three islands; Bridled Tern on Grand Cayman were counted as they entered nest burrows, and some young were counted in burrows. The population of White-tailed Tropicbird on Grand Cayman was counted entering nest sites; on Cayman Brac, totals were estimated from flying birds and those entering nest sites when the population was > 100, while counts were only of birds entering nest sites around the bluff when the population fell below 50 pairs.

Population trends since 1983 are mixed. On Little Cayman, the Red-footed Booby has shown an increase

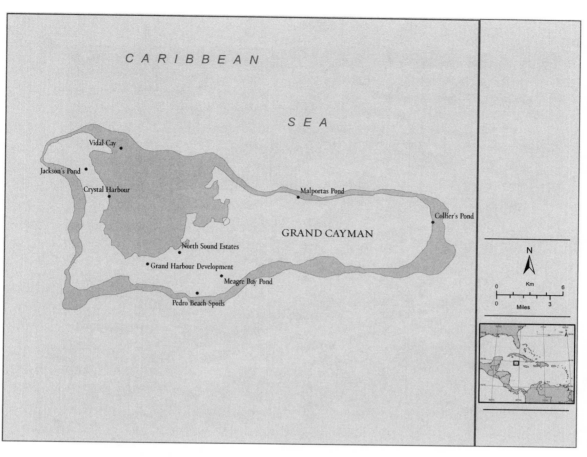

CARIBBEAN

SEA

Vidal Cay

Jackson's Pond

Crystal Harbour

Malportas Pond

Collier's Pond

GRAND CAYMAN

North Sound Estates

Grand Harbour Development

Meagre Bay Pond

Pedro Beach Spoils

N

Km
0   6

Miles
0   3

Map 18. Grand Cayman, Cayman Islands.

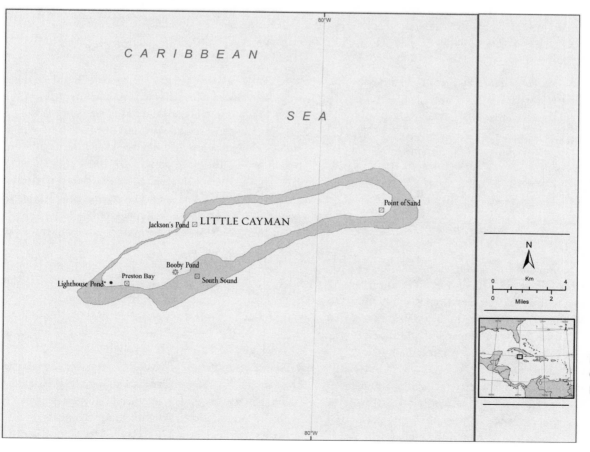

80°W

CARIBBEAN

SEA

Point of Sand

Jackson's Pond   LITTLE CAYMAN

Booby Pond

Lighthouse Pond   Preston Bay   South Sound

80°W

N

Km
0   4

Miles
0   2

Map 19. Little Cayman, Cayman Islands.

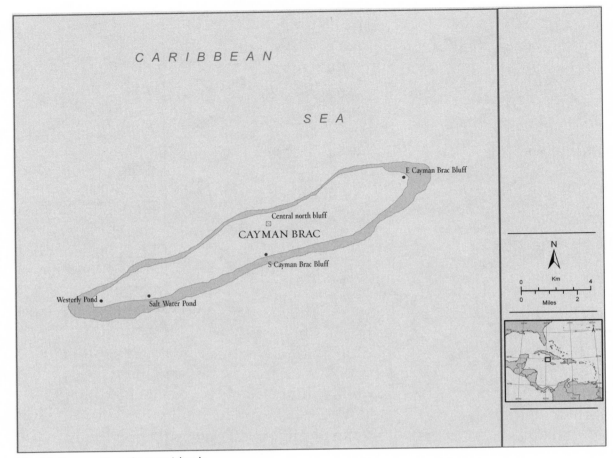

Map 20. Cayman Brac, Cayman Islands.

Table 6.1. Estimates of seabird pairs breeding in the three Cayman Islands, 2003–2004

Species	Total (pairs)
White-tailed Tropicbird	120
Brown Booby	110
Red-footed Booby	3,824–5,854
Magnificent Frigatebird	227
Bridled Tern	16
Least Tern	84

and the Magnificent Frigatebird population ranged from a mean of 150 pairs (1984–1986) to a mean of 307 (1995–1998, with a maximum of 410 nests in 1997) to 140 in 2001 and to 227 in 2004. The high counts for these two species on Little Cayman contrast with the lowest counts ever for the Brown Booby and White-tailed Tropicbirds on Cayman Brac. On Cayman Brac, the White-tailed Tropicbird declined sharply from a peak of 230 pairs in 1985 to a low of 25 in 1997, recovering to 110 pairs in 2003 (anecdotal evidence suggests that this species and the Brown Booby have declined throughout the twentieth century; Bradley 2002). The small Grand Cayman tropicbird population declined from 15–20 pairs in the 1980s to remain stable around 5–10 pairs since 1995.

The four censuses of the Least Tern in the Cayman Islands show a sharp decline, due partly to cessation of breeding on Little Cayman in 2003, 2004, and 2005 and on Cayman Brac in 2003 and 2005; three pairs nested on Cayman Brac in 2004, but no young fledged. The small Bridled Tern population has ranged from 16 to 21 pairs in the five counts since first confirmed breeding on a cay off Grand Cayman in 1995.

Grand Cayman

Grand Cayman (197 km² in area) is the largest and most westerly of the Cayman Islands; it is 35 km long and about 8 km wide (map 18). It supported 96% of the total human population of 50,000 in 2005, the majority in the western half of the island. Fringing reefs backed by shallow marine sounds encircle all but its western side, with the largest, North Sound (90 km²), enclosing several cays, of which only Vidal Cay has breeding seabirds.

Table 6.2. Status of seabird pairs breeding on Grand Cayman, 1985–2004

Species	Total (pairs)	Year
White-tailed Tropicbird	5	2004
	10	2003
	9	2000
	10	1997
	10	1996
	15	1985
Bridled Tern	16	2004
	20	2002
	21	1997
	19	1996
	17	1995
Least Tern	81	2004
	14	2003
	35	1998
	109	1997
	115	1996
	122	1995

Three species breed, all migrants: White-tailed Tropicbird, Bridled Tern, and Least Tern (table 6.2).

White-tailed Tropicbird

Migrant. A small colony breeds in holes in the 12 m high bluff from west of Pedro St. James along 5 km east to Beach Bay, 1984–2004. Extreme migrant dates 21 December–24 September.

Breeding pairs: 15 in 1985, 15–20 in 1986, 10 in 1996 and 1997, 9 in 2000, 10 in 2003–2004. Nests with young: One at Bat's Cave, 7 May 1984, first breeding record (David Wingate *in* Bradley and Rey-Millet 1995); seven along the Pedro bluff in 1996 and eight in 2000.

Bridled Tern

Summer migrant. A small colony, maximum 20 pairs (1995–2004), breeds on Vidal Cay (0.1 ha) off Barkers headland from late May to July, where the nests were in deep burrows under the tussock vegetation; otherwise this species is a rare casual visitor.

Breeding pairs: 17 on July 1995, first breeding record for the Cayman Islands (Bradley 1995); 19 in July 1996 (Bradley 1996); 21 in 1997; 20 in 2002; 16 in 2004.

Least Tern

Summer migrant, breeding on rock outcrops in lagoons, on fresh and old dredge spoil, secondary swamp, and previously on sand beaches. Extreme migrant dates 14 April–9 October; breeding May to August with the majority of young fledged by late July. The population has declined since 1995. Small numbers breed on protected ponds (Meagre Bay Pond and Collier's Pond), and occasionally on Malportas Pond and Barkers wetland. Greater numbers breed on spoil banks at large development sites on infilled mangrove; these change as the sites are converted to urban areas. Nesting success is often low or fails due to ongoing development, predation, and drowning of the chicks in the May rains; drowning and land crab predation were commented on by English (1916), who estimated 150 birds and 40 nests in 1913.

Breeding pairs: 104 in 1983 (Bradley 1986a); 43 in 1986, main colony at Jackson Pond, West Bay; 122 in 1995 (Bradley 1996), main colony at North Sound Estates development; 115 in 1996, and 109 in 1997, main colonies at Red Bay development; 35 in 1998, of which 10 were in protected areas and 25 at Jackson's Pond; no counts 1999–2002; 14 in 2003, six at Meagre Bay Pond and four at Malportas Pond; total 81 pairs (max. counts) in June 2004 with 9–13 pairs (7 young) at Meagre Bay Pond, 29–32 pairs (14 young) at a new development phase at Grand Harbour (beside Red Bay Estates), 5 pairs at the Ritz Carlton, and 30–31 pairs at Jackson's Pond.

Little Cayman

Little Cayman (28 km² in area) is 16.3 km long and 1–3 km wide; the human population is 150 (map 19). In 1888 Maynard first collected Red-footed Booby on a cay in South Sound, when he estimated 10,000 birds (Cory 1889a; Maynard 1889a; see Bradley 2000 for the history of the colony). In 1911, W. W. Brown (Bangs 1916) first collected Least Tern on Little Cayman. Three seabirds breed on the island: resident Red-footed Booby and Magnificent Frigatebird and migrant Least Tern (table 6.3).

Table 6.3. Status of seabird pairs breeding on Little Cayman, 1984–2004

Species	Total (pairs)	Year
Red-footed Booby	3,824–5,854	1997
	2,618	1986
Magnificent Frigatebird	227	2004
	141	2001
	307	1995–98
	150	1984–86
Least Tern	0	2004
	0	2003
	10[a]	2002
	10[a]	2000
	54	1997
	60	1996
	57	1995

a. no young fledged.

Red-footed Booby

Abundant resident, breeding in the Booby Pond Nature Reserve. This reserve has the greatest protection of any site in the Cayman Islands: it is a Ramsar site and an Animal Sanctuary under local legislation, owned by the National Trust and protected under National Trust Law (plate 33). The 1997 estimate of 5,000 pairs (approx. 20,000 birds) made it the largest known colony in the region, with 30% of the entire Caribbean population (Burton et al. 1999; see Hispaniola, this volume, for counts on Navassa). Adults are dimorphic (90% brown morphs, 8% white morphs, 2% intermediate; Diamond 1980). Breeding is from late September/early October to June with peak laying varying (Oct–Jan); onset of breeding has become earlier since 1996.

Breeding pairs: There have been three censuses since 1975: estimated 2,700 pairs in July 1975 (Diamond 1980); about 2,618 pairs in 13.8 ha in January 1986 (Clapp 1987); 4,839 pairs (range 3,824–5,854) in an area of 16.5 ha in February 1997 (293 nests/ha; C/1, n = 500+, and B/1, n = 290; Burton et al. 1999). Nests are 1.5–4 m above ground in bushland close to the edge of the pond (*Rhizophora*, *Laguncularia*, and *Conocarpus* spp.) and 2.5–5 m above ground in dry forest behind the bushland (*Bursera*, *Thespesia*, *Cordia*, and *Plumeria* spp.). Since Hurricane Ivan in 2004, the vegetation on the southern edge of the colony along Booby Pond has degraded, and some birds have dispersed northward closer to the designated airport site. Estimates of birds flying back into the colony at night suggest that numbers are lower than in 1997–2002, though no surveys have been conducted; a new survey is planned for 2009.

Magnificent Frigatebird

Common resident. Breeding together with Red-footed Booby in a compact colony in low mangrove and bushland on the northern landward edge of Booby Pond; the colony is protected in the Booby Pond Nature Reserve. The number of breeding pairs in January ranged from 140 to 410 (1983–2001). Resident, not breeding, on Grand Cayman and Cayman Brac, although there are historical reports of breeding up to the 1950s on both islands. Flying birds were estimated at 450 in 1983–1986; there were no counts in 1987–1994; in 1994 aerial counts indicated that the population had increased substantially, estimated at 600–700 birds; aerial counts in 1996 and 1997 gave a minimum estimate of 800 birds.

Breeding pairs: Counts of active nests gave a January mean of 150 in 1984–1986 and mean 307 in 1995–1998,

with 281 in 1995, 317 in 1996, 410 in 1997, and 220 in 1998. The count fell to 140 pairs in 2001 but increased to 227 pairs in 2004. In January 1997, 170 immature were counted, and in March 1997 the count was 224.

Least Tern

Summer migrant. Extreme dates April to October, but often leave by August, especially if breeding has failed. Breeding has been recorded at Jackson's Pond, Preston Bay westerly ponds, Lighthouse Pond, and Booby Pond; bred at Point of Sand, East End, until 1997.

Breeding pairs: Total of 14 (at Jackson's Pond, only breeding site on the island) in 1985; 57 in 1995; 60 in 1996 (Bradley 1997); 54 in 1997 (30 at westerly ponds and 24 at Jackson's Pond). Mean 10 in 2000 and 2002, when no young fledged; no birds observed in 2003; 3 birds seen but no breeding sites located in 2004–2007.

Cayman Brac

Cayman Brac (38 km² in area) is 20 km long and 1–3 km wide, with the majority of the human population of 1,600 in the west and along the northern coastal shelf (map 20). The Brac is dominated by the bluff plateau that outcrops in the west and slopes upward toward the east, terminating in 46 m high cliffs. Three seabird species breed: resident Brown Booby and migrant White-tailed Tropicbird and Least Tern (table 6.4). There is no confirmed breeding of the Masked Booby (*contra* Schreiber 2000b).

Table 6.4. Status of seabird pairs breeding on Cayman Brac, 1983–2004

Species	Total (pairs)	Year
White-tailed Tropicbird	110	2003
	35	2000
	25	1997
	28	1996
	208	1985
Brown Booby	110	2003
	49	2000
	30	1997
	32	1996
	170	1983
Least Tern	3[a]	2004
	0	2003
	15[a]	2002
	20[a]	2000
	45	1997
	27	1996

a. no young fledged.

White-tailed Tropicbird

Migrant. Breeding in caves and holes in the bluff from Stake Bay on the north coast eastward around the entire eastern bluff and west to Bat Cave on the south coast. Adults arrive from December, the majority of young fledge in July, and birds depart from mid-August to September. Common to the mid-1980s, the population declined sharply between 1983 and 1996.

Breeding pairs: Maximum of 208 in 1984–1985, the majority on the bluff face north of Spot Bay and on the southeast bluff. By 1994 the population had crashed: 28 pairs in 1996, 25 in 1997, and 35 in 2000, and pairs became widely distributed. In 2003, a maximum of 110 pairs was estimated, mainly at Spot Bay, Stake Bay, and the south bluff.

Masked Booby

A pair was first observed on the southern bluff in January 1984 (Bradley 1984) and continuously until 1994, but no breeding activity was noted; the pair roosted on the bluff face with the Brown Booby colony close to the rock outcrop Little Cayman Brac. After 1995, only one bird was observed until 2003 (*contra* Schreiber 2000b, 2–8 pairs in 1997); it was not observed in 2004–2006. In 2001, 2002, and 2003, this single Masked Booby was photographed attending a nest with a Brown Booby female; each year the nest contained a single egg that failed to hatch, and each nest was abandoned.

Brown Booby

Common resident. There are three subpopulations. The first breeds in caves, holes, and ledges on exposed faces of the northeastern bluff and on 400 m along the top of the bluff close to the cliff edge (plate 34). Breeding ceased here in 1985–1999, resuming in 2000, coinciding with a sharp population increase (Bradley 2002). The second subpopulation breeds along 5 km of the bluff edge on the south coast, and the third breeds on the extreme southeast bluff and in caves. Up to 1999 breeding extended from October to July with peaks (Nov.–Jan.); since 2000 breeding has continued throughout the year with small peaks (Oct.–Dec. and Mar.–May).

The sharp decline in the breeding population after 1985 was partly due to three factors: increased human disturbance when the first road was built to the eastern bluff, predation by increased numbers of rats and feral cats, and predation by Peregrine Falcon (*Falco peregrinus*). The falcon had been absent since the early 1970s, but an elderly resident stated that it had been a major predator of this species and the tropicbird from the early part of the century up to the 1950s (Bradley 2002).

Breeding pairs: About 170 in 1983 (140 partially fledged young counted); 32 in 1996; 30 in 1997; 49 in 2000; 110 in 2003. Eggs C/1 (n = 53), C/2 (n = 42), November–February 1982–1984.

Least Tern

Summer migrant. Nests at two sites: on the northern edge of the most westerly pond and on rock outcrops in Salt Water pond (a protected site) in the southwest wetlands.

Breeding pairs: 16 in 1984 (Bradley 1986a); 11 in 1986; 27 in 1996 (Bradley 1997); 45 in 1997; 20 in 2000 and 15 in 2002, but no young fledged in either year due to drowning of chicks in May and predation by dogs. No birds were observed in 2003; 3 pairs at the westerly ponds in June 2004 but no young fledged; a few birds observed in 2006 and 2007 did not breed.

Threats

Seabird diversity has declined in 22 years due mainly to habitat loss, human disturbance, and predation.

Habitat Loss and Insufficient Protected Areas

Habitat loss due to ongoing rapid development throughout the coasts and wetlands of the three islands is the main threat. Its intensity varies by locale (see Impacts by Island). Protected areas are urgently needed to secure the breeding sites of four species: Brown Booby, White-tailed Tropicbird, Least Tern, and Bridled Tern. In 2006 only the Red-footed Booby and Magnificent Frigatebird had adequate protected breeding habitat, owned and monitored by the National Trust; additional habitat to act as a buffer between the colony and a proposed airport has been secured.

Least Tern breed minimally in a few protected sites, but the main colonies locate on spoil/development sites, which vary from year to year and are subject to human disturbance, flooding, and introduced predators.

Human Disturbance

Although all seabird species are protected by law, there is no enforcement of the Animals Law, and seabirds receive no active protection under this law despite being legally protected species. As a result, recreational boating and predation by dogs from leisure craft are the main threat to the Bridled Tern on Vidal Cay. Hiking, climbing, and caving are threats to Brown Booby and White-tailed

Tropicbird on Cayman Brac. Visitors are not allowed into the National Trust–operated Red-footed Booby and Magnificent Frigatebird breeding areas on Little Cayman, but fishing lines and hooks are frequently observed on birds in this colony.

Predation

Rats, feral cats, and dogs are the main predators at most seabird colonies, taking eggs, young, and adults, as is underscored in the following discussion by island.

Illegal hunting is not a threat to seabirds. Collecting of eggs and unfledged young was common up to the early 1980s, but the practice has virtually died out due to increased prosperity, the inaccessibility of the majority of Brown Booby and tropicbird nests for the increasingly elderly collectors, and recent conservation efforts in public education.

Oil pollution of inshore waters is also a lesser threat than it once was. It was a problem in the 1980s when oil was trans-shipped off Cayman Brac; oil pollution from the bilges of cruise ships and trawlers was also a problem until the mid-1990s, when tighter international enforcement reduced the threat.

Impacts by Island

On Grand Cayman, development has impacted seabirds dramatically due to the human population increase from 14,000 in 1979 to 50,000+ in 2006. Tropicbirds have ceased breeding on 50% of bluff habitat on the south coast due to house building on the cliff edge. Least Tern ceased to breed on beaches after 1983 due to house building and increased tourism; nests on spoil banks at wetland development sites meet the hazards of disturbance and predation by dogs and raptors, and the addition of spring flooding means entire subpopulations often fail to raise young. Because Vidal Cay is popular with leisure boaters, the single Bridled Tern colony suffers considerable human disturbance.

Although 85% of Little Cayman remains undeveloped, increased tourism has brought a new airport along the northern boundary of the Red-footed Booby colony, which stands to become surrounded by development on all sides. No environmental impact study has occurred for the airport, and the scope of this development is of great concern; plans for road access and runway lighting have not been made public, and storm damage to nesting vegetation fringing Booby Pond (causing birds to nest farther inland) intensifies the concern. Least Tern ceased breeding on beaches after 1997 due to human disturbance. Predation by rats and birds of prey and spring flooding of nest sites have meant no young have fledged

since 1997, and breeding ceased in 2003; a few birds were present in 2004 and 2005 but did not breed.

Cayman Brac's Brown Booby nesting areas have been impacted by urban development on the southern bluff edge and by increased tourism, including recreational caving and climbing along the northeastern bluff edge. Predation by rats, feral cats, and migrant falcons is a significant threat to the fragile populations of all seabirds on the Brac; a feral cat and rat control program is sporadic.

Conservation

The Animals Law (2007 Revision) and Regulations protect all species of seabirds. The National Trust for the Cayman Islands Law (1987 Revision) and Regulations protect the land and the flora and fauna on all National Trust property. The Ramsar, Bonn, Biodiversity, and CITES conventions have been adopted by the Cayman Islands, with the implementation of necessary local legislation.

The National Conservation Law for the Cayman Islands, proposed since 2000 and promised every year since, remains on the table. It is urgently needed to allow a legal framework for the government to create and manage protected areas, to control invasive species and prevent their importation, and to establish the proposed Environmental Fund for purchase of land including seabird habitat for conservation. The new law would have implemented regulations to allow for wardens and enforcing officers and to impose significant penalties for infringement.

Sites Protected and Requiring Protection

The Cayman Islands have four protected sites locally classified as Animal Sanctuaries: Meagre Bay Pond and Collier's Pond in Grand Cayman; Salt Water Pond in Cayman Brac; and Booby Pond Nature Reserve in Little Cayman. Booby Pond is also a Ramsar site, an Important Bird Area (IBA), and a National Trust property protecting nesting Red-footed Booby and Magnificent Frigatebirds (Bradley et al. 2006).

In 2004, after representations had been made, developers agreed to cease construction at tern nesting sites on private land at Grand Harbour, Grand Cayman, to allow Least Tern young to fledge. Other sites urgently in need of protection are:

1. The bluff cliffs on the south coast from Pedro St. James to Bodden Town, Grand Cayman.
2. The Central Mangrove Wetland and Malportas

Pond, an Important Bird Area (IBA), Grand Cayman.

3. Vidal Cay, Grand Cayman.
4. All government-owned wetlands on Little Cayman to protect Least Tern (and all waterbirds, including West Indian Whistling-Duck); an IBA (Bradley et al. 2006).
5. The entire bluff face and the bluff edge breeding sites on the northeast and south coast of Cayman Brac, to protect Brown Booby and White-tailed Tropicbird, as proposed in the Management Plan (Bradley 2002).

Airport Environmental Impact Study

Any management plan for the new airport on Little Cayman must address disturbance to the adjacent Red-footed Booby colony. There must be strict controls on overflying the sulid colony in the Ramsar site, banning of all jet flights to the island, and banning of night flights. The type of airport lighting should be chosen with care to cause minimum impact to the booby colony and nest-ing turtles and should be used only in an emergency—the airport should not remain lit during the night. The Cayman Islands Government should establish a buffer zone with the northern boundary of the Red-footed Booby colony.

Seabird Management Plan

Funding for a management plan for seabirds should include provision for:

Monitoring of the six breeding seabird populations every two years.

Closing the nesting sites during the breeding season to prevent human disturbance.

Public education on the sensitivity of breeding seabird colonies to human and habitat disturbance and the importance to the Cayman Islands of conserving these colonies.

Control programs for rats and cats on all three islands.

Inclusion of seabird protection in the duties of marine enforcement officers.

7

Jamaica and Pedro and Morant Cays

ANN M. HAYNES SUTTON

Jamaica lies approximately 145 km south of Cuba and 161 km west of Haiti in the Greater Antilles (maps 21–23). The archipelagic state of Jamaica, with its 350 km limit, administers an extensive area of sea. The coastal shelf and proximal banks occupy an area of 4,170 km^2, while the Pedro Bank encompasses an area roughly equivalent to the land area of Jamaica. There are four groups of cays—the Pedro and Morant groups offshore and the Port Royal and Portland Bight cays inshore. A fifth group, the Seranilla Cays, was ceded to Colombia in the 1970s, but the surrounding waters are administered as a Joint Regime Area with Colombia.

Fourteen species of seabirds are known to breed in Jamaica (table 7.1). One species, the endemic Jamaica Petrel (*Pterodroma caribbaea*), may be extinct. Seven species are regular winter visitors, and a further 10 species are rare vagrants or transients. Little is known of population sizes, distribution, or trends of seabirds in Jamaica. Islandwide surveys by Sutton in 1997 and surveys at the Pedro Cays in 2005 (Hay 2006) confirmed breeding and provided some overall population estimates (table 7.1). Audubon's Shearwater and Black Noddy have not been confirmed as breeding. Only White-tailed Tropicbird, Magnificent Frigatebird, and Least Tern nest on the mainland. The largest concentrations of nesting terns and sulids nest offshore, on the sparsely vegetated Morant and Pedro cays. A few terns breed inshore on the Portland Bight Cays and the Port Royal Cays. There is considerable concern regarding the apparent fall in populations of Masked Booby, Brown Booby, Bridled Tern, and Sooty Tern (admittedly in incomplete surveys) on the Pedro Cays in 2004–2005. There were no post-2000 data from the Morant Cays.

Nesting habitats for seabirds in Jamaica can be broadly categorized into three groups: mainland (on the island of Jamaica), inshore cays (cays within 10 km of the mainland, including the Port Royal and Portland

Bight cays), and offshore cays (more than 10 km from the mainland—the Morant and Pedro Cay groups).

Mainland Jamaica

Seabird breeding colonies on the mainland are restricted to remote, inaccessible, or inhospitable areas—cliffs, remote mountains, and the margins of salt ponds. Mainland habitats are more exposed to humans and to predation by invasive species than are habitats on the cays. There have been no studies of seabird colonies on the mainland or threats to their survival except in the case of the Least Tern, for which the most frequently documented cause of nest failure is flooding (Fletcher 1979a; Fletcher 1981a; J. Fletcher, pers. comm., 1997). All seabirds are fully protected, but there are no specific seabird conservation areas on the mainland except within the Portland Bight Protected Area.

Jamaica Petrel

This may have been an abundant breeding species in the Blue Mountains of eastern Jamaica until the early nineteenth century. It nested in burrows and was susceptible to non-native mammalian predators: humans, feral dogs and pigs, and the small Indian mongoose (*Herpestes auropunctatus*). By the end of the nineteenth century petrel numbers were severely reduced (Imber 1991). The possibility that the species might still survive in remote locations inspired several searches in the 1960s, 1970s, and 1990s, but no evidence of its survival has yet been found (Douglas and Zonfrillo 1997; Douglas 2000a), possibly extinct.

White-tailed Tropicbird

There have been no comprehensive surveys of tropicbird breeding sites in Jamaica, but reports suggest that small breeding colonies may occur on the mainland wherever

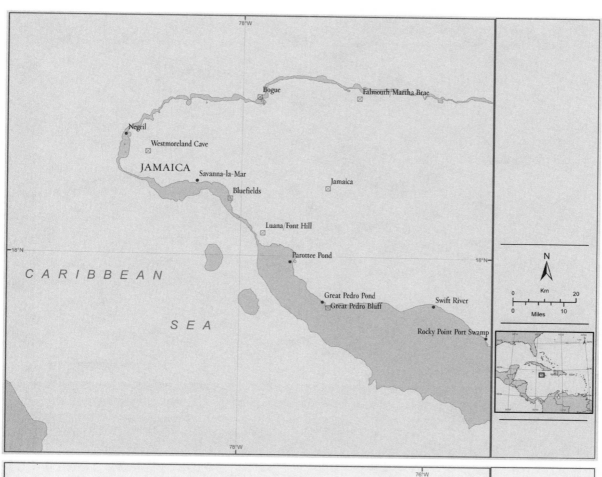

Map 21. Western Jamaica.

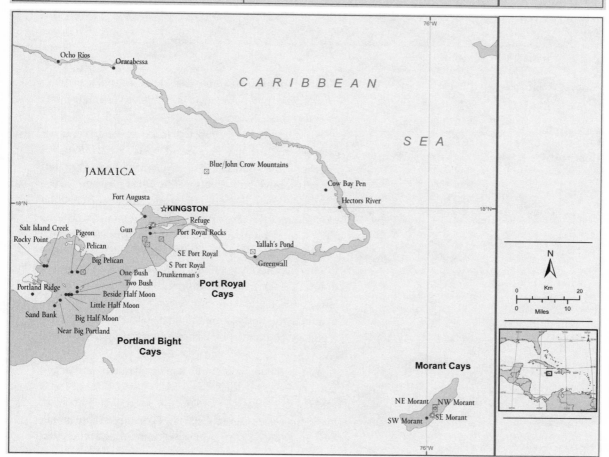

Map 22. Eastern Jamaica and Morant Cays.

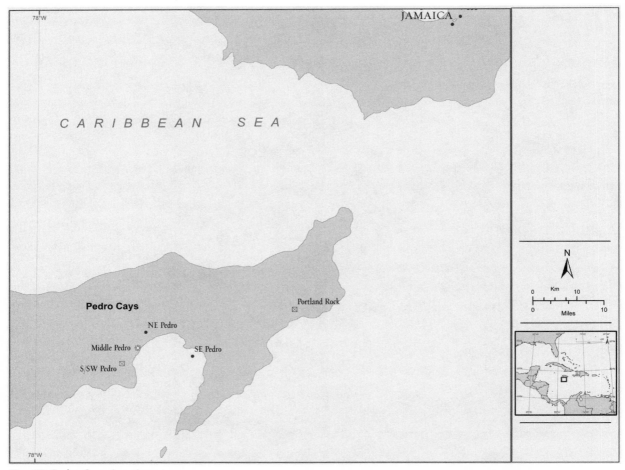

Map 23. Pedro Cays, Jamaica.

Table 7.1. Estimates of seabird pairs breeding in Jamaica, 2003–2005

Species	Estimate of breeding pairs
Jamaica Petrel	Possibly extinct
White-tailed Tropicbird	> 100
Masked Booby	267–400
Brown Booby	500–1000
Brown Pelican	150
Magnificent Frigatebird	315–345
Laughing Gull	> 14
Brown Noddy	500–2000[b]
Sooty Tern	> 50,000[b]
Bridled Tern	> 4[a]
Least Tern	< 50
Roseate Tern	> 2
Royal Tern	> 10[b]
Sandwich Tern	> 6

a. count incomplete, 2005.

b. estimated based on previous figures. There have been no recent counts.

there are suitable sea cliffs or sea caves to serve as nesting habitat. The total population is difficult to estimate but is probably more than 100 pairs.

Nesting has been reported in coastal Portland, for example at Cow Bay Pen (Scott 1891a; Smith 1970a, b; Fletcher 1981b) and Hector's River (Maddison 1977 and many recent verbal reports); at St. Mary Oracabessa (C. B. Lewis quoted in Smith 1970a) and Black Sands in 2004 (A. Sutton and B. Hay, pers. obs.); St. Ann at Ocho Rios cliffs near Plantation Inn and Jamaica Inn (Ewen 1982; Downer 1987); Westmoreland, Negril cliffs (Barneveld 1993); Clarendon, Portland Ridge (C. B. Lewis quoted in Smith 1970a); and St. Thomas at Greenwall near Yallahs in 1982 (A. Haynes-Sutton, pers. obs.). The presence of adults and nests along the northeastern coastline was regularly confirmed by casual observations 2000–2005 (A. Sutton, pers. obs., various dates).

White-tailed Tropicbirds usually arrive in Jamaica in January (e.g., Maddison and Maddison 1977a, b; Ewen 1982) or rarely as early as November (Downer 1987). Active nests have been reported in February (Scott 1891a), March (Smith 1972), and April (Fletcher 1981b), and adults and juveniles may be observed from the coast until June (Smith 1970a; Downer 1987). The largest number of active nests reported from one colony is 14 at Hector's River, 14 March 1977 (Maddison 1977). Most reports and observations are of lower numbers (e.g., Smith 1972a; Fletcher 1981b).

Brown Pelican

Brown Pelican are more numerous on the south coast where the island shelf is wide and fish are more abundant. There are no recent reports of nesting on the mainland (but see later section on Port Royal Cays); historically they roosted and nested in coastal woodlands and mangroves, for example on Pedro Bluff (Gosse 1847) and until the 1970s near a cave in Westmoreland (R. Sutton, pers. comm.). More recently colonies were reported from Manchester at the mouth of the Swift River about 1980 (A. Haynes-Sutton, pers. obs.); St. Thomas at Yallahs Pond, 59 on a roost, 28 April 1982 (Fletcher 1982a); and Salt Island Creek in 1997 (A. Haynes-Sutton, pers. obs.). There are also unconfirmed verbal reports of other roosting or breeding sites, including near Savanna-la-Mar in Westmoreland.

Pelicans are common around the coast all year round. The population appears to consist of residents augmented by winter migrants from North America in unknown proportions. Only two Brown Pelicans banded in Florida have ever been recovered in Jamaica (Office of Migratory Bird Management, pers. obs.).

Magnificent Frigatebird

Magnificent Frigatebirds are omnipresent in coastal Jamaica—hovering over beaches, especially fishing beaches, around the island. Known nest and roost sites are mainly on the inshore and offshore cays, but several males in breeding plumage were seen roosting at Parottee Pond in St. Elizabeth in October 1996 and may have been nesting there (A. Haynes-Sutton, pers. obs.).

Least Tern

Least Terns are uncommon but widely distributed along Jamaican shores. The mainland nesting population is probably less than 50 pairs (assuming there are several uncounted colonies). Historically there were probably many small breeding colonies, for example in Kingston Harbour at Port Henderson at the end of Hunt's Bay causeway, 6–8 nests, one downy chick (Kerr-Jarrett 1972); St. Elizabeth, Parottee Pond, 1 nest, 3 April 1971, and 25 present with 3 nest hollows, May 1976 (Witt et al. 1977). More recent records are Pedro Pond (R. Sutton, pers. comm.), 1 nesting in May 1996 (R. and A. Sut-

ton, pers. obs.), 1 nesting in 2004 (B. Hay and A. Sutton, pers. obs.); St. James, 1 nest with egg, 3 May 1991 (Moody 1991); Montego Freeport, downy chick being fed, 20 July 1971 (Bray 1972a); St. Thomas, Yallahs Pond, 50–80 nesting between 1978 and 1980 (Fletcher 1979a, 1980, 1981a). This site may have become unsuitable due to inundation of the nesting area.

No nests were observed in 1997 (J. Fletcher, pers. comm.). Nesting occurs between April and August (Kerr-Jarrett 1972; Fletcher 1979a, 1980, 1981a, 1982b, 1991). Research including an islandwide survey, monitoring of known colonies, habitat protection, and management should be considered for this species.

Inshore Cays—Palisadoes and Port Royal Cays

The area is situated to the southeast of Kingston, between 17° 57' and 76° 75' N and 76° 00' and 76° 20' W. The Palisadoes peninsula is a long narrow spit of land formed from a series of limestone islets linked by sand and gravel deposits, enclosing the eastern side of Kingston Harbour. To the south there are eight coralline cays, the largest of which is Lime Cay at about 2.6 ha (Wells 1988). The main habitats are beach pioneer, strand dune, thorn scrub, strand woodland, and mangroves (Asprey and Robbins 1953; Adams 1969). Introduced predators and excessive egg collection are thought to have resulted in the extirpation of breeding seabirds from North West Cay between 1987 and 1997 (Haynes-Sutton, pers. obs.).

Brown Pelican

The only recently documented nesting colony in Jamaica is on Refuge Cay, where the population in 2002–2003 was more than 150 pairs, with nesting occurring year round (P. Lindo, pers. comm.). However, the vegetation was badly damaged by Hurricane Ivan in September 2004 and showed little sign of regeneration by December 2005; the effects on nesting may have been severe but are yet to be assessed (A. Sutton, pers. obs.). Other known threats include human predation, especially harvesting of chicks, and taking of adults on hooks for sport. Historically, colonies have been reported from various of the Port Royal group of cays, including Drunkenman's Cay (Scott 1891b), South Cay (Morris 1967; Haynes 1987), Gun Cay (Haynes 1987), Refuge Cay, 24 July 1992 (Fletcher 1982a; P. Lindo, pers. comm. 2005); Kingston Harbour, near Fort Augusta (A. Downer, pers. comm.).

Magnificent Frigatebird

Historical nesting and roosting sites included the Drunkenman's Cay (Field 1894) and probably South Cay,

August 1967 (Morris 1967). There are no recent observations of breeding.

Bridled Tern

Observed nesting on South Cay (Scott 1891b; Morris 1967) and on a small exposed rocky area between South Cay and Drunkenman's Cay (Field 1894); 40 pairs probably nested there in 1997 and on an unnamed rocky shoal and South East Cay (Haynes-Sutton, pers. obs). No recent observations of breeding.

Least Tern

Nesting of about 4 pairs in 1997 was unconfirmed on South Cay and a small cay to the south of it (Haynes-Sutton, pers. obs.).

Roseate Tern

Nested on South Cay in the 1960s, where 70 nests were reported to be present at the end of July 1967 (Morris 1967). On a reconnaissance visit on 14 August 1997, 10 unidentified terns, tentatively identified as Roseate Tern, were seen on South Cay; their behavior suggested that they might have had nests, but no sign of nests, eggs, or chicks could be found (Haynes-Sutton, pers. obs.). No recent observations.

Inshore Cays—Portland Bight Cays

The Portland Bight Cays lie between 17° 40' and 17° 55' N and 77° 00' and 77° 10' W. The group consists of about 12 coralline islands. The main vegetation types include beach pioneer communities, strand dune, thorn scrub, strand woodland, and mangroves (Adams 1969; Stoddart and Fosberg 1991). The cays were badly damaged by Hurricane Ivan in September 2004, which caused loss of vegetation and reduced the size of many cays (A. Haynes-Sutton, pers. obs.). Effects on breeding populations were evaluated in 2005 (B. Hay, unpubl.). There is increasing interest in ecotourism and this might affect some seabird colonies.

Hurricane Ivan in 2004 brought a storm surge that overwashed most of the cays and seriously damaged the vegetation, killing some trees and washing others away. Threats to seabird colonies include rats, cats and dogs, pollution from Kingston Harbour, oil spills, boat traffic, power stations, and proposed heavy industry.

Magnificent Frigatebird

The breeding colony on Two Bush Cay is constantly occupied by 200–300 individuals (A. Haynes-Sutton, pers. obs., 1996–2005), but due to its inaccessibility, counting

the number of nests has been impossible. The nesting population is estimated at about 100–150 pairs. The mangrove trees on which the birds nest were badly damaged by Hurricane Ivan in 2004, but whether this affected the number of nesting pairs is not known.

Brown Noddy

Nest on Little Half Moon Cay and previously on Big Half Moon Cay. The number of breeding pairs on Big Half Moon Cay has declined from 306 pairs in 1996 to none in 2004 and 2005, while the number on Little Half Moon increased from 228 pairs in 2003 to 479 in 2004 (A. Haynes-Sutton, pers. obs. 1996–2005). It is not known whether the presence of a cat on the larger cay has contributed to the decline. Brown Noddies also nest on Sand Banks Cay (A. Haynes-Sutton and B. Hay, unpubl.).

Bridled Tern

Previously reported to nest on Pelican Island (Field 1894; and possibly so, 23 May 1993, by Richardson 1993b) and Pigeon Island (Field 1894; I. Goodbody, pers. comm.). This colony was not seen in 1996, but previously unrecorded colonies were discovered on 11 June 1996 on Sand Banks Cay (20 birds and at least one nest) and reconfirmed on 2 July 1997 (more than 30 individuals, at least one nest); on 2 July 1997 on Sandy (One Bush) Cay (20 individuals with at least six nests); and possibly other cays nearby. Breeding was confirmed in 2005 (Haynes-Sutton, pers. obs.), but no estimate of numbers was made.

Least Tern

A possible nesting colony was observed near Big Portland Cay in 1997 (A. Haynes-Sutton, pers. obs.).

Roseate Tern

Seen (possibly nesting) from Pelican Cay, 23 May 1993 (Richardson 1993a). Eight adults seen on Sand Bank Cay, Portland Bight, 11 June 1996, seemed to have established territories, but no nests were found (A. Haynes-Sutton, pers. obs.); none were seen in the same area, 2 July 1997 (Haynes-Sutton, pers. obs.).

Offshore Cays— Pedro Cays and Bank

Pedro Cays lie between 16° 57' and 17° 32' N and 77° 46' and 77° 51' W, and Portland Rock is at 17° 6' N, 77° 27' W. There are three coralline islands and a rocky shoal on the edge of Pedro Bank, about 93 km from Jamaica. The largest is South West (Bird) Cay, at 15 ha, its highest point about 5 m above sea level, followed by Middle Cay. Portland Rock is an isolated limestone outcrop between Pedro Cays and the mainland (0.7 ha, elevation 9 m; Zans 1958). Vegetation consists of low scrub including *Sesuvium*, *Tribulus*, *Portulaca*, *Argusia*, *Suriana*, *Cyperus*, *Paspalum*, and *Cordia* spp. The islands are managed by the Fisheries Division under the Morant and Pedro Cays Act. The Jamaica Defence Force Coastguard established a command post on Middle Cay in 1997. There has been little research into the birds of the islands. A planned survey in 2004 had to be aborted due to a hurricane (Haynes-Sutton, pers. comm.). Surveys were carried out in April, July, September, and November 2005 as part of an integrated project to assess the ecology and conservation needs of the cays, implemented jointly by the Nature Conservancy and government of Jamaica with funding from the National Fish and Wildlife Foundation (Hay 2006). Human activities had extirpated breeding seabirds from North West Cay before 1987 (Hay 2006; Haynes 1987).

Masked Booby

Estimated at 267–400 pairs in 2005. Numbers may have been as high as 1,000 pairs on the two cays, 1986–1997, taking into account that a complete survey was never made and breeding occurs year round. Further research is urgently needed to confirm if the low counts in 2005 on South West Cay are replicated in subsequent years. The only nesting colonies in Jamaica are on Middle and South West cays (plates 35, 36; Haynes 1986a, b; Downer 1990a; Haynes-Sutton, unpubl.). The number of nests observed on Middle Cay varies from about 200 pairs (Zans 1958) to more than 400 pairs (Haynes 1986). In 2005 about 150 pairs were present on Middle Cay in April; 281 adults and juveniles in September; and 117 pairs in November (including 56 nests with eggs, 20 nests with chicks, and 41 nests with adults but no eggs or chicks). About 200 pairs also bred on South West Cay in 1997 (Haynes-Sutton, unpubl.; Douglas et al. 1998). In September 2005 there were 76 individuals on South West Cay, where they appear to breed year round (Hay 2006).

Brown Booby

Brown Boobies nest on South West (Bird) Cay, where counts of 2,000 active nests were recorded in February 1998 (Douglas et al. 1998) and between 500 and 1,000 nests in July 1997 (Haynes-Sutton, unpubl.). Numbers were much lower in July 2005, when nests with chicks were noted, and also in April and July, but no counts were made. Flocks of juveniles were observed in April

but not July, September, or November; in September 2005, 119 adults and juveniles were counted (Hay 2006).

The low numbers in 2005 are cause for concern, and further research is urgently needed to establish the status of this large colony and whether breeding peaks have shifted or whether other factors such as impacts of hurricanes in 2004–2005 have affected the breeding population temporarily or permanently. The nesting season appears to be extended or multimodal, perhaps with a peak early in the year, but with some activity all year round. Band recoveries show that Brown Boobies move among the islands and they are the most likely booby to be observed from the mainland. One bird banded in the Virgin Islands on 15 January 1987 was recovered at Pedro Cays on 29 March 1987.

Magnificent Frigatebird

The largest known breeding colony in Jamaica is on South West Cay, where there may have been up to 1,000 active nests in July 1997 (Haynes-Sutton, unpubl.). The total population of Pedro Cays may have been more than 4,000 individuals (Haynes-Sutton, unpubl.), and breeding may be spread out over several months (Haynes 1986). There were about 1,500 individuals in all stages from adults to downy young, 23–25 February 1998 (Douglas et al. 1998). In 2005 there were 115 unfledged juveniles in April, a few downy chicks in July, and 50–100 nests with eggs and downy young in September, but surprisingly there were no active nests or fledglings in November, possibly indicating nest failure (Hay 2006).

Laughing Gull

A total of 233 adults and 14 chicks observed on South West Cay in 2005; a minimum of 14 pairs estimated (Hay 2006).

Brown Noddy

Once found on all cays (Zans 1958) but by 1997 they were restricted to South West Cay, where the estimated population was about 3,000 individuals (Haynes-Sutton, unpubl.) In July 2005 there were at least 13 active nests without eggs or chicks, nine nests with eggs, one nest with a chick, and 20 adults; the survey was incomplete (Hay 2006). The species may nest on Portland Rock, but this has not been confirmed.

Black Noddy

The first record for this species in Jamaica was made on South West Cay in July 1997 (Haynes-Sutton, unpubl.). One individual was observed. Breeding was not confirmed.

Sooty Tern

In the mid-nineteenth century, Sooty Terns were hugely abundant, numbering hundreds of thousands at the Pedro Cays (Gosse 1847). They bred on all three cays (Zans 1958) and Portland Rock, but by 1997 there was no suggestion that they used either of the two inhabited cays; there are no data about when breeding ceased. On South West Cay about 1,000 Sooty Terns were present at the end of the nesting season in 1997, and there was suitable nesting habitat with depressions resembling nest scrapes but no sign of nesting (Haynes-Sutton, unpubl.). In 2005 they were not nesting in April, although about 20 birds were seen; in July 4,000–5,000 adults were present, but there was no sign of nesting or nest failure. One unfledged chick was observed in September and none in November. It is difficult to account for the large numbers of birds observed and the lack of evidence of nesting (Hay 2006).

Bridled Tern

More abundant than Sooty Tern on South West Cay on 22 July 1997, when 1,500–2,000 individuals were estimated; the habitat was suitable for nesting and they were probably breeding (Haynes-Sutton, unpubl.). On 13 July 2005, about 60 adults were seen and 4 chicks, but the count was incomplete (Hay 2006).

Roseate Tern

On 22 July 1997, 18 adults and two chicks were counted on South West Cay (Haynes-Sutton, unpubl.); two chicks and seven adults were found on 13 July 2005 (Hay 2006).

Royal Tern

Twenty-five adults with 10 flightless but mobile chicks were seen on 22 July 1997 at South West Cay (Haynes-Sutton, unpubl.). One chick and two adults were observed in July 2005 (Hay 2006).

Sandwich Tern

Breeding has been documented in Jamaica only at South West Cay. Twenty-five adults and twelve chicks were counted on 22 July 1997 (Haynes-Sutton, unpubl); on 13 July 2005 there were two adults and six chicks (Hay 2006).

Offshore Cays—Morant Cays and Bank

The Morant Cays lie between 17° 23' and 17° 26' N and 75° 58' and 76° 00' W. There are four coralline islands at the center of the Morant Bank, about 60 km from Jamaica. The highest point is 2.71 m above mean sea level. One of the four cays is inhabited by several hundred fishermen. Common plants include *Sesuvium, Tribulus, Portulaca, Argusia, Suriana, Paspalum, Ipomoea* and *Cakile*. There have been no surveys in recent years; new surveys followed by monitoring and conservation measures are needed.

Audubon's Shearwater

There were no reported observations of this species in or near Jamaica until, on 3–4 December 1997, a team searching for the Jamaica Petrel encountered 10–14 individuals at night, possibly prospecting for nest sites on South East Cay (Douglas and Zonfrillo 1997). Breeding has not been confirmed.

Laughing Gull

The species has long been established on the Morant Cays (Scott 1891b; Haynes 1987). The population on South East Cay was 7–22 breeding pairs, 1982–1987 (Haynes-Sutton 1995, 1996). Nesting occurs in May–June.

Brown Noddy

In 1996 the population at Morant Cays was estimated at about 4,500 breeding pairs, and a further 500 were thought to nest on South West Cay (Haynes-Sutton 1996). The breeding season is similar to that of Sooty Tern—late April–June.

Sooty Tern

Breed on South East and South West cays in middle to late April through June. Conservation measures implemented in 1982 coincided with an increase in populations (e.g., Gochfeld et al. 1994; Haynes-Sutton 1995) from about 23,000 breeding pairs in 1982 to about 132,000 in 1986 and about 100,000 in 1997 (Haynes-Sutton, unpubl.).

Bridled Tern

Nests mainly on South West Cay (Haynes 1987); nesting is assumed to coincide roughly with that of the Sooty Tern, but there have been no detailed surveys and the estimate of 1,000 pairs in 1987 was based on numbers of adults.

Royal Tern

The maximum number of breeding pairs between 1978 and 1987 was 58 (Haynes-Sutton 1995). The breeding season is May–July.

Threats to Seabirds and Their Habitats

Breeding seabirds continue to be at risk in Jamaica despite legal protection of all species. Their habitats are inadequately protected and managed. The introduction of rats, cats, mice, and dogs to new islands, egg collection, and the expansion of human habitation are the major threats at present and are increasing in geographical area and intensity. There are no data about the impacts of pollution or fishing practices such as long-lining.

Human predation has been identified as the most important historical factor contributing to the decline in Jamaican seabird populations (e.g., Haynes 1987; Haynes-Sutton 1987). All tern eggs (especially Sooty Tern and Brown Noddy eggs) and tropicbird eggs are taken from time to time, but sulid eggs are not popular. Chicks and adult tropicbirds and pelicans are sometimes collected (Haynes 1987; Haynes-Sutton 1987, 1995), but there are no data about the numbers of people or birds involved.

Natural predators on seabird eggs and chicks include Laughing Gulls, Ruddy Turnstones, Magnificent Frigatebirds, and ghost crabs (*Ocypode* sp.; Haynes-Sutton 1995). A Peregrine Falcon was seen at Pedro Cays in 1989 and up to six in 2005 (Hay 2006), and local fishermen reported that they took adult and juvenile birds (Haynes-Sutton, pers. obs. 2005).

Rats, mice, dogs, cats, and pigs on the mainland, inhabited cays, and some uninhabited cays have depleted or destroyed many colonies; there have been no efforts to eradicate invasives. Trial eradications and prevention measures are needed, for example, on the Half Moon Cays of Portland Bight and Middle Cay, Pedro (Hay 2006).

Although it is not known whether the availability of nest sites is a limiting factor for seabirds on Jamaican cays, suitable habitats are scarce, and it seems logical to assume that any reduction in the amount of good nesting habitat is potentially a source of stress. Factors that appear to be reducing the amount of habitat suitable for seabird nesting in Jamaica are the increasing development of south coastal beaches and wetlands for tourism, industry, housing, and sand mining; increasing use of inshore and offshore cays by fishermen; sea level rise, hurricanes, and storms; and pollution by oil and solid wastes. It is very important to ensure that human habitation is not allowed to spread to uninhabited cays, in particular to South East or South West cays (Morant group) or South West Cay (Pedro group). The regionally important Masked Booby colony on Middle Cay, Pedro group, is under severe pressure from a squatter settlement and planned construction (plates 35, 37) as well as from expansion of a dumping area for solid wastes.

Oil and solid waste pollution are increasing on Jamaica's coasts but so far do not appear to constitute a major threat to seabirds. Jones and Bacon (1990) found that more than 60% of 26 Jamaican beaches showed signs of oil pollution. Oil was regularly encountered on South East Cay but not in sufficient quantities to affect nesting, although some nesting birds showed signs of oil. Solid waste (mainly glass and plastic) was abundant on the beaches but did not interfere with Sooty Tern nesting at Morant Cays (A. Haynes-Sutton, pers. obs. 1982–1987).

Coastal habitats, especially those on the south coast, are susceptible to flooding and changes in topography as a result of hurricanes and storms. Observations at South East Cay, Morant group, and cays in Portland Bight confirm that flooding occurs in heavy weather and that the shape and area of sandy cays change markedly from year to year (Haynes-Sutton 1995; A. Haynes-Sutton, pers. obs. 1995–1997). Even heavy rain associated with tropical waves has been associated with mortality of Sooty Tern adults at the Morant Cays (Haynes-Sutton 1995).

Storm damage may have contributed to the abandonment of Drunkenman's Cay, Port Royal group, by nesting pelicans (Haynes-Sutton, pers. obs. 1997). Jamaica tends to be affected by a serious storm or hurricane about once every 10 years (Government of Jamaica 1995). Global warming and the associated projected sea level rise and increase in severity of storms are likely to reduce the area of actual or potential habitats, affect vegetation, and increase the risk of flooding. The majority of Jamaican nesting and roosting colonies are less than 3 m above mean sea level at the highest point and therefore particularly vulnerable to these threats.

Tern colonies have great potential interest for tourists, and investigation of the possibility of tourism at the cays has been suggested (Halewyn and Norton 1984; Haynes-Sutton and Aiken 1992; Haynes-Sutton 1995), but this would have to be done under strictly controlled circumstances. Similarly, researchers visiting the cays need to be provided with a code of conduct so that their effects on nesting birds can be minimized. Increasing interest in ecotourism could potentially result in an increase in the numbers of visitors on the Port Royal and Portland Bight cays, with severe negative implications for nesting seabirds. The Morant and Pedro cays are important for turtle nesting and could be used for other types of research. It is important that efforts should be coordinated to ensure that the various research efforts complement each other.

There are no data about areas of special importance for foraging seabirds. There appears to be an upwelling area associated with a countercurrent system to the east of Jamaica, and concentrations of seabirds have been seen there (I. Goodbody, pers. comm.). Small feeding flocks of terns have been observed at several locations along the south coast, including near Yallahs Ponds, and in coastal wetlands (especially Pedro and Parottee ponds, Jacksons Bay, and several locations in Portland Bight). Threats include fish kills and pollution from agriculture, industry, domestic wastes, and oil.

Little is known about the effects of disease, parasitism, or other causes of death at Jamaican seabird colonies. Disease and parasitism do not appear to be important causes of mortality among Sooty Terns at South East Cay. There have been few deaths that could not be attributed to predation or exposure to rain. However Sooty Terns at South East Cay are infested with ticks (*Ornithodorus taljei*) that are closely related to *O. capensis*, which transmit arboviruses in the Seychelles and can lead to declines in some tern populations (Feare 1976a, b; Bourne et al. 1977).

Jamaica's fishery is mainly artisanal and there is no evidence of competition with birds. Rather, seabirds enhance fisheries by helping fishermen to locate schools of fish and to find their way to and from the fishing grounds (Haynes-Sutton 1987). However illegal long-liners are increasingly entering Jamaican waters and pose a threat to marine life.

Conservation and Recommended Action

In Jamaica attempts to manage seabirds, seabird colonies, and associated resources go back more than 140 years (Haynes-Sutton 1987; Haynes-Sutton 1995). Yet continuing weaknesses in local laws include low penalties for infractions and a lack of clarity about whether the Fisheries Division or the National Environment and Planning Agency has ultimate responsibility for management of seabirds and cays, complicating the protection of species.

Success at South East Cay has demonstrated that habitat protection is an essential ingredient in seabird conservation in Jamaica. Several other seabird habitats are currently protected, but enforcement is lacking. The Nature Conservancy is implementing a comprehensive conservation project for Pedro Cays (N. Zenny, pers. comm.).

National Law and International Treaties

Ambiguity arises about responsibility for control of egg collection because seabirds are managed as a fisheries resource under the Morant and Pedro Cays Act (administered by Fisheries Division, Ministry of Agriculture) but also as a protected species under the Wild Life Protection Act (administered by the National Environment and Planning Agency, Ministry of Land and Environment). For effective species protection and research, the ambiguity should be resolved by placing responsibility clearly with the National Environment and Planning Agency, through the Natural Resources Conservation Authority Act.

Two international treaties potentially provide protection for seabirds and habitats at the regional level: the Cartagena Convention (1983) and the Convention on Biological Diversity (known as the Biodiversity Treaty, 1992). The Protocol concerning Specially Protected Areas and Wildlife (SPAW Protocol) to the 1983 UNEP Convention for Protection and Development of the Marine Environment of the Wider Caribbean Region (Cartagena Convention) aims to encourage nations to protect and conserve the marine environment through regional initiatives to protect and manage ecosystems as well as species. Jamaica has yet to ratify this protocol. The protocol has three annexes:

Annex I: List of marine and coastal flora protected under Article (11)(a). This includes species of plants that require international protection and management.

Annex II: List of species of marine and coastal fauna protected under Article 11(1)(b). This includes species of animals that require international protection and management, including Audubon's Shearwater, Roseate Tern, Least Tern, and Brown Pelican. Masked Booby should be recommended for inclusion on Annex II.

Annex III: List of marine and coastal flora and fauna protected under Article (11)(c) for sustainable management. No seabirds are currently listed in this annex. Sooty Tern and Brown Noddy should be recommended for inclusion in Annex III.

The formation in 1997 of a Caribbean Working Group for Seabirds by the Society of Caribbean Ornithology (now the Society for the Conservation and Study of Caribbean Birds) has helped to promote international cooperation and stimulate research and conservation in Jamaica.

Seabird Management Plans

A management plan has already been developed for Sooty Tern and Brown Noddy in Jamaica (Haynes-

Sutton 1996). This should be revised. An overall seabird management plan (which would include all Jamaican species) is urgently needed. Special attention should be paid to Roseate Terns, Least Terns and Masked and Brown Boobies.

Seabird Research

Well-designed and properly implemented research and monitoring activities are essential components of an effective conservation program. Although there have been some efforts at research and monitoring at South East Cay, Morant group, their effectiveness has been limited by the inaccessibility and expense of access to the colonies (making standardized methods of data collection difficult to implement). Research should include a national survey of the status and distribution of seabird populations, routine monitoring of seabird populations at selected colonies using standard methods (including South East Cay, Morant group; Middle and South West cays, Pedro group; and Big and Little Half Moon and Sand Banks cays, Portland Bight), collection of basic ecological information related to nesting habitat quality, studies of the effectiveness of measures intended to improve nesting habitat, and an intensive banding program.

Portland Rock has not been surveyed since the 1940s and needs to be reassessed. Morant Cays need to be resurveyed to update information from the 1990s. Efforts should also be made to gather data about seabirds at sea (including sea watches and data collection by volunteers and the Jamaica Defence Force Coast Guard) and to conduct further searches for the Jamaican Petrel. Assessments of the status of and threats to tropicbird and Least Tern colonies are needed.

Reasons for the lack of research into seabirds in Jamaica include lack of awareness of their importance, lack of funds for research generally, and the logistical difficulty and expense of reaching the colonies.

Habitat Protection and Management

Introduced predators, egg collection, fishing camps on cays, and other forms of habitat disturbance have been identified as the main threats to Jamaican seabirds. Effective protection of nesting habitat and removal of introduced predators are the most important actions required to ensure seabirds' long-term survival. Protection of foraging habitat is also important, although its importance is hard to quantify, and implementation will require international cooperation.

However, the management of protected areas for a single species has led to problems in the past. It is pref-

erable to manage for an entire landscape (Duffy 1994). Most seabird colonies in Jamaica are also important for other wildlife. Most are used by sea turtles, and some are habitats for other rare, possibly endemic species of reptiles. The surrounding waters of most seabird colonies include seagrass beds and coral reefs—key areas for fish nurseries, lobsters, and conch—and all are used intensively by fishermen. Many areas also have historical remains (Haynes-Sutton and Aiken 1992). The multiple conservation values of these areas strengthen the case for developing and managing them as protected areas and indicate the need for multipurpose management. Unfortunately there is no simple recipe for this, and each case requires a unique approach (Duffy 1994).

The success of the habitat protection at Morant Cays has demonstrated the importance of habitat protection. Currently there is no legal protection for seabird habitats, although it could be offered under the Natural Resources Conservation Authority Act through the creation of protected areas and marine parks (Appendix II), the Wild Life Protection Act (Game Sanctuaries), and the Beach Control Act (Marine Protected Areas). The seasonal protected area previously operated at South East Cay by the National Environment and Planning Agency was not established under any law.

The plan for a system of protected areas for Jamaica (Haynes-Sutton and Aiken 1992) identified six areas of importance for seabirds as priority areas for protection: Blue Mountains–John Crow Mountains, Morant Cays, Pedro Cays, Port Royal (including Port Royal Cays), Black River (including Luana–Font Hill and Parottee Pond), and Portland Bight (including Portland Bight Cays). The Blue Mountain–John Crow Mountain National Park, Montego Bay Marine Park, Portland Bight Protected Area, and Port Royal and Palisadoes Protected Area are areas of actual or potential importance to seabirds that have been declared under the Natural Resources Conservation Authority Act, but levels of management and enforcement are generally low. A new plan for a system of protected areas is in preparation.

In 1997 the Jamaica Defence Force Coast Guard established a permanent base on Middle Cay, Pedro. This has improved law enforcement and facilitated research. The facility was expanded in 2006, and it is hoped that this will create an opportunity to provide protection for South West Cay. This would be a valuable refuge for terns and sulids, especially needed for Sooty Terns (Hay 2006). The Nature Conservancy is taking an active role in promoting conservation of the Pedro Cays, including monitoring and conservation of seabirds. A similar approach is needed for Morant Cays.

Area-specific management plans or operation plans will be required for each area that is brought into the protected area system (Government of Jamaica 1995). Conservation of seabirds should be addressed in the broader context of protection of the ecosystems in which they live. In developing management systems it is crucial that all stakeholders are given a chance to participate in management of tern habitats. This should be achieved through formal and informal discussion and circulation of relevant documents, which is an important part of the public education process (see later discussion). Removal of introduced predators and the prevention of their introduction to new areas will be important in any management plan. Trial eradications should be implemented at selected cays in Portland Bight.

Sustainable Use of Eggs, Chicks, and Adults

Consumption of "booby" eggs was once part of Jamaica's cultural tradition, and there is still great nostalgia for them in Kingston. However the practice of commercial egg collection has apparently died out at Morant Cays (Commander Innes, pers. comm.). A few eggs are still collected by fishermen at Pedro for subsistence. Jamaican fishermen do not usually exploit seabird chicks or adults.

Tourism and heritage value

While there is some potential for tourism, the inaccessibility of most sites and their ecological sensitivity restricts the potential for tourism. Great care should be taken before embarking on any initiatives to expand tourism, and this should be allowed only within guidelines developed for the relevant protected area.

Public education

Public awareness and understanding are essential for the success of any conservation program, including protection of seabirds at Morant Cays (Haynes-Sutton 1996). If protection of seabirds is to be extended to other cays and broadened, there will have to be a great deal of discussion and work with interest groups in order to ensure that conservation measures are workable and are supported by the users.

There are no local resource materials about seabird conservation. Two types are needed—"need to know" items that aim to increase awareness of and compliance with laws and regulations (e.g., pamphlets, posters, newspaper articles, and news items on television and radio about prosecutions); and "nice to know" more general information that helps to win support by increasing understanding of seabirds and why they should be conserved (e.g., school programs, slide shows, guided tours of seabird habitats, nesting colony surveys, dramatic presentations). The Society for Conservation and Study of Caribbean Birds recently published field guide cards and a poster on Caribbean seabirds that help to address these gaps.

Participation in development of management plans and regulations is another very important educational process—for the public and planners alike. Because Jamaica is a primarily aural society, emphasis should be placed on spoken and visual approaches, which are likely to be more effective than the written word. A plan to educate fishermen (Hay 2006) should be developed and implemented.

Acknowledgments

I wish to thank the Natural Resources Conservation Authority (now the National Environment and Planning Agency), Jamaica Defence Force Coast Guard, South Coast Conservation Foundation, Caribbean Coastal Area Management Foundation (specially D. Brandon Hay), Centre for Marine Sciences at the University of the West Indies, and the Nature Conservancy for assistance with the fieldwork and research that formed the basis for this chapter. I thank David Lee and the Society for Conservation and Study of Caribbean Birds for providing inspiration and support for my attendance at the workshop in Aruba. Leo Douglas also provided important and useful information. The National Fish and Wildlife Foundation and USAID provided funding for seabird surveys in 2004. The students of the Field Natural History Courses (2002–2005) of the Northern Caribbean University and community members from Cockpit, Clarendon, also assisted with field surveys. Patricia Bradley's support and encouragement through the long process of preparing the chapter are also much appreciated.

8

Hispaniola

Haiti and Dominican Republic, and Navassa Island (U.S.)

ALLAN KEITH

The island of Hispaniola (77,800 km²) is the second largest in the West Indies, lying in the north-central Caribbean Sea just east of Cuba (maps 24, 25). The independent nations of Haiti and the Dominican Republic (DR) divide the island between them, about 38% and 62% respectively. Hispaniola has a large and diversified known avian fauna, which includes 36 species that can be considered seabirds: four shearwaters, two storm-petrels, two tropicbirds, three boobies, one pelican, one frigatebird, and 23 jaegers, gulls, and terns. Of these, 14 have been documented to have bred in the past or do so currently. Included in this chapter are data from Navassa Island (5.2 km²), a U.S. possession administered by the U.S. Fish and Wildlife Service as Navassa Island National Wildlife Refuge, about 55 km due west of the western-most point of Haiti.

There have been relatively few documented visits to Hispaniola's seabird colonies. The first was surely that of Christopher Columbus to Alto Velo in 1494; the tern colony there is believed to have existed for at least 1,300 years, based on the discovery of indigenous people's tools of that age found there. In the period 1732–1978, there were 50 known collecting or other scientific expeditions to Hispaniola, when several visits were made to satellite islands, sometimes to more than one such island during a single expedition. The number of known such visits to each satellite island are: Ile de la Tortue (5), Ile de la Gonave (5), Cayos Siete Hermanos (4), Isla Beata (4), Ile-a-Vache (4), Isla Saona (4), Grand and/or Petite Cayemite (2), Navassa Island (2), Isla Catalina (1), and miscellaneous small islets (4). The full list of expeditions and the locations visited is included in Keith et al. (2003).

With few exceptions, seabirds nest mainly on Hispaniola's satellite islands, primarily the smaller ones without full-time human inhabitants. These islands vary greatly in size, from Ile de la Gonave, Haiti (658 km²), to tiny cays in Los Haitises National Park, DR. Maximum elevations of these islands also vary widely, from Gonave's 755 m to several islets among the Cayos Siete Hermanos, DR, of only a meter or so. The island with the largest breeding seabird colonies is Alto Velo (1 km²) off the south coast of the DR, which rises to an elevation of 152 m. Other islands hosting breeding colonies are Ile de la Tortue off the northwest coast of Haiti, 37 km long, 5 km wide and reaching an elevation of 325 m; Isla Beata (47 km²) near Alto Velo off the south coast, with an elevation of 100 m; and Isla Saona off the southeast corner of the DR, 22 km long, 3–5.5 km wide, and with an elevation of only 35 m. Navassa Island (5.2 km²) is an uninhabited, unincorporated U.S. territory and administered as a federal wildlife refuge.

Species Accounts

The following accounts provide each species' present status (table 8.1) and distribution, together with any threats that can be identified. The historical status of each species is not described in detail; for much more information on this subject, the reader is referred to Keith et al. (2003). Data from Navassa Island are included because it is faunistically part of Hispaniola.

Unfortunately, none of the breeding sites mentioned has been censused regularly, and some have not been visited in many years. The estimated total numbers in table 8.1 are highly speculative and are derived from the species accounts, which list almost all known visits to each breeding locality (Keith et al. 2003; A. Keith, pers. comm. to eds.).

Black-capped Petrel

At present this species is known to breed only in national parks in the mountains of southern Haiti and at one site in the Dominican Republic (plate 4). Specifically, nests

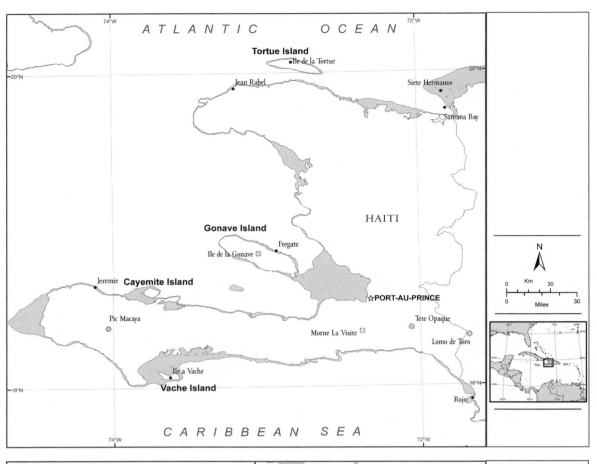

ATLANTIC OCEAN

Tortue Island
• Ile de la Tortue

Jean Rabel

Siete Hermanos
•

Samana Bay

HAITI

Gonave Island

Ile de la Gonave ⊠   Fregate

Jeremie Cayemite Island

Pic Macaya ✿

☆ PORT-AU-PRINCE

Tete Opaque
✿

Morne La Visite ⊠   Lomo de Toro

Ile a Vache

Vache Island

Rojo
•

CARIBBEAN SEA

Map 24. Haiti, Hispaniola.

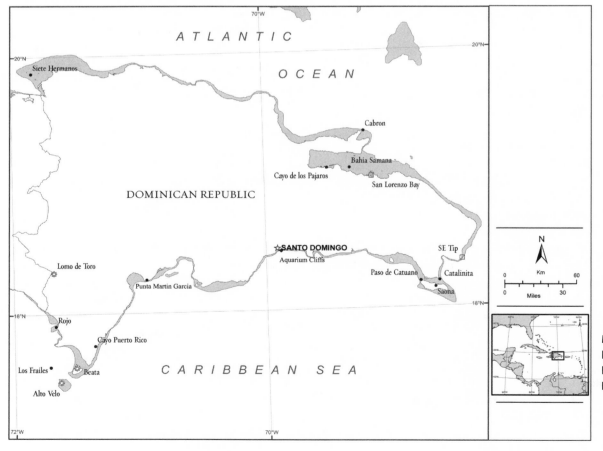

ATLANTIC

OCEAN

Siete Hermanos
•

Cabron
•

Bahia Samana

Cayo de los Pajaros
•   San Lorenzo Bay

DOMINICAN REPUBLIC

☆ SANTO DOMINGO   SE Tip ⊠

Lomo de Toro
✿   Aquarium Cliffs
Paso de Catuano   Catalinita
Punta Martin Garcia   Saona

Rojo
•
Cayo Puerto Rico
•
Los Frailes •   ✿
Beata

Alto Velo ✿   CARIBBEAN SEA

Map 25.
Dominican
Republic,
Hispaniola.

Table 8.1. Estimates of seabird pairs breeding in Hispaniola, 1992–2003

Species	Estimated total (pairs)
Black-capped Petrel	>2,000
White-tailed Tropicbird	500
Brown Booby	600 (+?)
Red-footed Booby	2,500
Brown Pelican	100–250
Magnificent Frigatebird	250–300
Laughing Gull	100
Brown Noddy	50–200
Sooty Tern	80,000
Bridled Tern	150–350
Least Tern	50–150
Royal Tern	10–20
Sandwich Tern	30–40

have been found at 1,500–2,000 m elevation in the Massif de la Selle and Massif de la Hotte in Haiti and on one peak in the Sierra de Bahoruco in the Dominican Republic near the Haitian border. The size of the breeding colonies has never been determined precisely, due to the difficulty of even reaching the breeding areas and the steepness of the slopes on which the colonies are located. Based on the number of birds making courtship calls near the nest cliffs at night, a most imprecise method to be sure, the number of birds was estimated between 4,000 and 25,000 pairs at the Morne la Selle ridge (Wingate 1964a), anywhere between extremes of 600 and 4,000 at two peaks in two national parks in the Massif de la Hotte (Collar et al. 1992); and 20–40 at the site in Sierra de Bahoruco (Lee and Viña 1993); Lee (2000a) estimated a total of less than 2,000 pairs. There are no recent total estimates.

Birds are usually present at the breeding sites between late October and early June. During this period, especially when the adults are feeding young, reasonable numbers of birds can be found just offshore, usually just out of sight from land, all along the south coast of western Dominican Republic and southern Haiti. With a good telescope, it is not unusual to be able to see a few birds from land at Punta Salinas, or from such localities as Enriquillo, Paraiso, or Cabo Rojo in southwestern Dominican Republic. Outside the breeding season, birds from the Hispaniola colonies are thought to wander widely in the eastern Caribbean and north along the eastern U.S. coast in the Gulf Stream.

While most of the breeding population nests at such inaccessible locations as to be safe from direct human threats, the Haitian national parks are increasingly being invaded by squatters, who are cutting the forest. In time this habitat degradation will have an adverse effect on the birds. In addition, some birds are lost each year by being attracted to small fires set intentionally by squatters to lure in the birds at night. While the number lost by this means each year is probably small, over time the impact on the population could be serious, especially as the number of squatters grows. Mongoose predation of young in nests is probably also a factor in some colonies. Legal protection would be desirable in Haiti, but that would not help much if the regulations are not vigorously enforced, which seems unlikely at present. As for the small colony in the Dominican Republic, there is no recent information about its status, but there is a telecommunications tower with stay wires on the mountain just above the colony, which is a threat to birds coming in at night.

White-tailed Tropicbird

This species is a relatively common breeding resident year-round at selected coastal cliff localities both on the main island and on several of its satellites. It is also regularly noted along parts of the coast, where it is thought not to breed, and at sea. Historically, nesting colonies have been documented at Cabo Rojo and on the low cliffs within the National Aquarium in Santo Domingo, DR; and at Jeremie, Jean Rabel, and Ile de la Tortue, Haiti. Large numbers of birds have also been recorded during breeding season at Punta Martin Garcia and at Isla Alto Velo, DR, where nesting was probably occurring. At least five pairs have recently been recorded nesting at Navassa Island (J. Schwagerl, pers. comm.). The present breeding population for all of Hispaniola and its satellites could be as high as 500 pairs, but the estimate of 1,000 pairs by Walsh-McGehee (2000:32) seems too high. Aside from the risk of occasional mongoose predation of nest cavities, there seem to be few threats to this species at Hispaniola.

Brown Booby

A regular and moderately common resident around most of the coast of the island, especially eastern Dominican Republic and western Haiti. Eastern DR birds probably come primarily from the known colonies on Mona and Monita islands, Puerto Rico. The species roosts regularly on Isla Saona and Isla Beata, DR, though it is thought not to breed there. Thought to breed on Isla Alto Velo, where hundreds have been seen in April (Wiley and Ottenwalder 1990); Schreiber (2000b:50) thought a few were breeding on small islands off the north and northeast coast of DR; and perhaps as many as 30–50 pairs apparently nest at Los Frailes, a group of rock outcroppings just west of Alto Velo, DR (E. M. Fernandez, pers. comm.). Birds seen in western Haiti waters are thought to come from the colony on Navassa Island, where the species has apparently bred continuously for over 70 years (Ekman 1929); at least 20 pairs were believed to be nesting there out of "several hundred" present recently (J. Schwagerl, pers. comm.). Total current breeding population may be as many as 200 pairs. Three birds banded at colonies in the Lesser Antilles have been recovered in southwestern Dominican Republic.

Red-footed Booby

Uncommon resident around the coast of the island. Birds found in eastern Dominican Republic waters probably come from the breeding colonies on Mona and Monita islands in the Mona Passage, and birds in western Haiti waters are thought to come from the colony on Navassa Island. The Red-footed Booby is rarely seen elsewhere, though more work at sea might show it to be more common than now supposed. The colony at Navassa was recently estimated at "several hundred" pairs nesting (J. Schwagerl, pers. comm.), little changed from an estimate of 100–150 pairs in July 1977 (Keith et al. 2003), and probably a little fewer than "hundreds" of pairs there in 1930 (Wetmore 1932a). However, the recent estimate may be low, since a recent high count of about 5,000 birds has been recorded (J. Schwagerl, pers. comm.). The most recent frequent visitors to the island are fishermen from Haiti, who are known to harvest eggs and chicks when they are available, but the extent of this illegal predation is unknown.

Brown Pelican

Moderately common resident along most of the coast of Hispaniola and at many satellite islands. Individuals in Haiti waters are thought to come from the colony on Navassa Island. Brown Pelican numbers appear to have declined modestly during the last 50 years due to disturbance of its nesting colonies and some degrading of the coastal environment. Over the last 100 years, successful nesting has been recorded at six sites, the colonies ranging in size from 25 to 150 pairs. Though some of these sites may have been active for a decade or more, none of the larger colonies has been recorded during the last 20 years. It is suspected that an important portion of the birds seen recently is either too young or too old to breed. Any guess at the current breeding population size is necessarily speculative, but it seems most likely to be in the 100–250 range, rather than the 500+ pair esti-

mated by Collazo et al. (2000:42). The most important risk to the species at present is from human disturbance of breeding and roosting sites as the coastline becomes more and more heavily populated.

Magnificent Frigatebird

Moderately common resident along the entire coast of the main island and its satellites, though perhaps a bit less common in Haiti. The population has declined significantly since the late 1800s (Wetmore and Swales 1931). There appear to be only two recent known breeding sites: Isla Saona in Del Este National Park, DR (about 200 pairs in 1996), and Fregate Island off the east end of Gonave Island, Haiti (about 15–25 pairs?, 1927). In addition, there may be as many as 25–40 pairs nesting on Navassa Island out of at least 100 birds present recently (J. Schwagerl, pers. comm.), some of which surely range to the western Haiti shoreline regularly; 35–60 pairs at Paso de Catuano near Isla Saona, DR (E. M. Fernandez, pers. comm.); and 50–75 pairs at Cayo de los Pajaros and other small cays in Los Haitises National Park, DR (E. M. Fernandez, pers. comm.). In all, the breeding population is probably in the range of 250–300 pairs, including those on Navassa, or somewhat more than the 150+ given by Lindsay et al. (2000). In addition, the birds range widely in the West Indies, as shown by a band return in the Dominican Republic from the very large colony on Barbuda.

Laughing Gull

This gull is a moderately common year-round resident and transient and a regular visitor from the North American mainland in winter. It is found routinely at lowland coastal ponds and lakes as well as the oceanfront. Its numbers appear to have increased since the 1930s, probably due to an increase in the North American mainland populations. Recent peak counts have been as high as 100 in a day. Only two breeding sites have been documented recently, both in the Dominican Republic: Isla Saona (27 nests in 1976) and Cayo Puerto Rico in Laguna de Oviedo (25 nests in 2003; E. M. Fernandez, pers. comm.). Some may also nest at Navassa Island (Chardine et al. 2000a), but that is not confirmed. The most important threat to Hispaniolan breeding birds is egg robbers.

Brown Noddy

Common around the coasts of the island, particularly during breeding season, but stays well offshore out of sight from land for the rest of the year. Some birds from colonies on Mona and Desecho Island also are thought to visit Dominican Republic waters during the breeding season. First discovered nesting near Isla Beata in 1931 and still there in 1977. Also breeds at Cayos Siete Hermanos, but the colony was regularly harvested by egg robbers until 2003. Recent observations have documented 5–10 pairs nesting at Navassa Island (J. Schwagerl, pers. comm.). Birds have been found at Isla Alto Velo and at Isla Catalinita near Isla Saona during or just after breeding season and probably nest there, though confirmation is lacking. Total estimated number of breeding pairs is speculative but is probably in the range of 50–200 pairs. The biggest risk to this species is continued egg predation by humans.

Sooty Tern

A common species in inshore waters during the breeding season, particularly near breeding sites. Spends the rest of the year well out to sea. Some birds also surely come to Dominican waters from the colonies on Mona and Desecho islands just to the east of Hispaniola. The colony on Isla Alto Velo was estimated in 1950 at 175,000 pairs, which had dropped to an estimated 40,000–50,000 pairs by 1980. There was an increase to 80,000 in 2001 (E. M. Fernandez, pers. comm.). The cause of this decline had been systematic large-scale egg robbing by humans. A colony of several hundred pairs on Cayos Siete Hermanos in 1952 was also completely robbed of its eggs but has been protected during breeding season from 2003. The Sooty Tern is also suspected of nesting at Isla Catalinita near Isla Saona in recent years (E. M. Fernandez, pers. comm.).

Bridled Tern

Resident in the ocean around the island, usually remaining offshore outside the breeding season and thus seldom seen at that time. General numbers appear to be little changed since the 1930s, though exact numbers are uncertain because visits to breeding sites have been infrequent in the last 70 years. Appears to have nested on the Cayos Siete Hermanos off Monte Cristi, Dominican Republic, for all of that period, though the colony suffered illegal predation by egg robbers regularly until 2003, when national park and naval guards began to be posted from mid-May until mid-July. Recent observations at Navassa Island have documented 5–10 nesting pairs. Also known or suspected to nest on Isla Beata, Isla Alto Velo, Isla Catalinita near Isla Saona, and two cays off the Samana peninsula. Total breeding population is at best a guess but is probably in the range of 150–350 pairs (J. Schwagerl, pers. comm.). The biggest threat to

this species is continued egg robbing of the colonies by humans.

Least Tern

Regular and moderately common spring and fall migrant from North American mainland breeding sites and a local breeder at a few places along the coast. Apparently the species was moderately common in the 1930s and is still so today, being recorded nesting at one site in Haiti and at least four sites in Dominican Republic, including Las Salinas and Lago Enriquillo. The number of breeding pairs surely varies from year to year; and this species probably also nests at sites that have not yet been reported, especially on satellite islands that are seldom visited. Therefore, any estimate of breeding pairs is speculative but probably ranges between 50 and 150 pairs islandwide. The principal threat to the species is predation by mongoose on the main island and egg robbing elsewhere.

Roseate Tern

Uncommon but regular spring and fall transient and former local breeder. So far it has been recorded only from the coast. It is known to have bred at two Dominican Republic localities in the 1927–1931 period: Isla Beata and San Lorenzo Bay. However, there are no documented breeding records since. There are 18 known band returns at Hispaniola from sites between Nova Scotia and New York in North America.

Royal Tern

A small colony of this species was recently confirmed on Cayo Puerto Rico in the southwest portion of Laguna Oviedo in southwestern DR, the first documented breeding of this species on Hispaniola. Though probably present for quite a few years, the colony was unknown to the ornithological community until mentioned by a local park guard in late 2003. A rough guess at the number of pairs present is 10–20 (E. M. Fernandez, pers. comm.).

Sandwich Tern

A colony was confirmed on Cayo Puerto Rico in Laguna Oviedo in 2003, the first confirmed breeding of this species on Hispaniola. The number of pairs present was estimated at 30–40 (E. M. Fernandez, pers. comm.).

Threats and Conservation

Seabirds, and most other birds, have regrettably little effective protection in Hispaniola. As far as international treaties are concerned, the Dominican Republic has been a signatory to CITES since 1987, but Haiti is not. The only designated Ramsar Convention site on the entire island is the Jaragua-Bahoruco-Enriquillo Biosphere Reserve, a nearly 500,000 ha sanctuary in southwest DR that includes mountains where a few Black-capped Petrels nest; an inland salt lake visited by a few species of seabirds, though none nest there; and two offshore islands. Both Haiti and DR became parties to the Convention on Biological Diversity in 1996. The DR joined the Specially Protected Areas and Wildlife (SPAW) Protocol of the Cartagena Convention in 1998, but Haiti has not yet joined. The DR has signed most protocols of the 1973 International Convention for the Prevention of Pollution from Ships (MARPOL), but Haiti has not.

National wildlife protection legislation has a spotty history in both countries. Haitian decrees in March 1971 and October 1978 are supposed to control hunting and list protected species, none of which are seabirds. In the DR, Article 1 of Decree No. 801–02 purports to protect all wildlife, including birds, "their eggs, nests and feathers," except for five land bird species considered pests and ten game-bird species, primarily ducks, which may be hunted for sport. A new Biodiversity Law is intended to replace this decree and has been approved. Various national and regional parks, natural monuments, and species management areas have been designated on pa-

per in both countries (EarthTrends 2003). More history of conservation legislation, principally in the DR, can be found in Keith et al. (2003:22–23, 59–62).

However, none of the laws, regulations, or protected area designations, either international or national, has much impact in a practical sense since there is no enforcement at all in Haiti and not much in the DR. Nearly all seabird colonies located anywhere near human populations continue to be regularly robbed of eggs, even at Beata and Alto Velo islands, DR, which are in the Ramsar Biosphere Reserve and designated a DR national park. Given the sorry condition of the economies of both countries, the likelihood of reduced pressure on such potential food sources or of better law enforcement seems remote.

Acknowledgments

The following persons contributed greatly to the information in this chapter: Dennis G. "J. R." Crouse Jr. for Haitian records, Eladio M. Fernandez for very important recent distributional data, Jose A. Ottenwalder for information on DR protection, Joseph Schwagerl for data on Navassa species, Jean André Victor for information on Haitian protection legislation, and David Wege for data on international protocols.

9

Puerto Rico and Its Adjacent Islands

JORGE E. SALIVA

Puerto Rico is the easternmost and smallest of the Greater Antilles, situated 1,600 km southeast of Florida, between the Caribbean Sea and the Atlantic Ocean (18° 15'N, and 66° 30' W), 110 km east of the Dominican Republic, and about 37 km west of the U.S. Virgin Islands. It was discovered by Christopher Columbus during his second voyage to the New World in 1493. The Taíno Indians, who came from South America, inhabited the island when the Spaniards arrived. The current population of Puerto Rico is close to 4 million people.

Puerto Rico is roughly 8,960 km², with a maximum length from east to west of 180 km (Punta Puerca to Punta Higuero), and a maximum width from north to south of 65 km (Isabela to Punta Colón). Over 70% of Puerto Rico's terrain is mountainous, with a central mountain chain transecting the island from east to west, coastal lowlands on the north and south, and a karst region in the northwest consisting of rugged limestone formations.

The main island of Puerto Rico is surrounded by many groups of small islands and cays (maps 26, 27), and the following harbor one or several species of seabirds: Northwest Cays (0.5 km off the north coast, between Quebradillas and Manatí); Cordillera Cays (about 2 km east of Las Cabezas de San Juan, between Fajardo and the Culebra Archipelago); Culebra Archipelago (about 17 km east of Fajardo); Vieques (about 14 km southeast of Naguabo); Cayos Fríos (about 2 km south of Ponce); Caja de Muertos (about 9.6 km south of Ponce); Cayo Guayanilla (about 5 km south of Guayanilla); Montalva Cays (20–300 m south of Guánica); Parguera Cays (3–6 km south of Lajas); Mona and Monito (about 80 km west of Cabo Rojo); Isla Ratones (about 500 m west of Cabo Rojo); and Desecheo (about 19 km west of Rincón). Several areas within the main island of Puerto Rico or close to its shore are also important breeding sites for seabirds: Northwest Cliffs (between Aguadilla and Camuy); Cueva del Indio (Camuy); Isla del Frío (off Ponce); Laguna de Las Salinas (Ponce); La Jungla Salt Flats (Guánica); Cabo Rojo Salt Flats (Cabo Rojo); and Boquerón Natural Reserve (Cabo Rojo).

Deep ocean waters fringe Puerto Rico: the Mona Passage to the west, between Puerto Rico and the Dominican Republic (about 1,000 m deep), the Puerto Rico Trench lying 120 km to the north (about 8.5 km deep), and to the south the sea bottom descends to the 5 km Venezuelan Basin. Pelagic seabirds travel to these areas to feed on fish attracted to the deep, rich upwelling waters. The Puerto Rico Bank rises from deep waters on the north and south. This platform or bank interrupts deep, cold water currents laden with nutrients from the Basin and forces them up through the shallower water creating opportunities for the food chain to interact, including near-shore and off-shore seabird species.

Methods of Survey

Species accounts were obtained through colony surveys, interviews with fishermen and local residents, and discussions with field biologists conducting research on different seabirds and landbirds in or around seabird colonies. Ground, air, and boat surveys were conducted. Colonies on islands where landing by boat was feasible were surveyed on foot and all visible nests were counted (e.g., Parguera Cays) or estimated using random plot sampling (e.g., Sooty Terns on Culebra). When seas did not allow landing, or conditions to land were too dangerous, surveys from a boat were conducted to obtain colony estimates (e.g., Lobito Cay, Culebra Archipelago). Only colonies where 90% or more of the nesting birds could be observed were surveyed. Conversely, when only a small portion of the colony was visible from a boat, this was noted and the area would only be marked as a nesting area for the species observed.

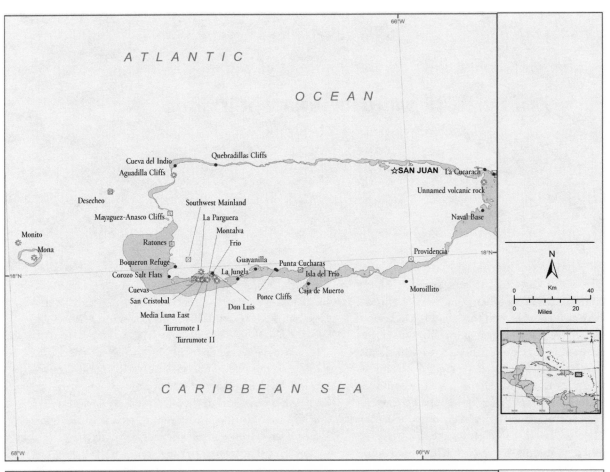

ATLANTIC

OCEAN

Quebradillas Cliffs

Cueva del Indio
Aguadilla Cliffs

☆SAN JUAN   La Cucarach

Unnamed volcanic rock

Desecheo

Mayaguez-Anasco Cliffs

Southwest Mainland

La Parguera

Naval Base

Monito

Montalva

Mona

Ratones

Frio

Providencia

18°N

Boqueron Refuge

Guayanilla

Punta Cucharas

Corozo Salt Flats

La Jungla

Isla del Frio

Cuevas

Ponce Cliffs

Caja de Muerto

Moroillito

San Cristobal

Don Luis

Media Luna East

Turrumote I

Turrumote II

16°N

CARIBBEAN SEA

N

Km
0   40
Miles
0   20

Map 26. Puerto
Rico and Mona
Island.

68°W

66°W

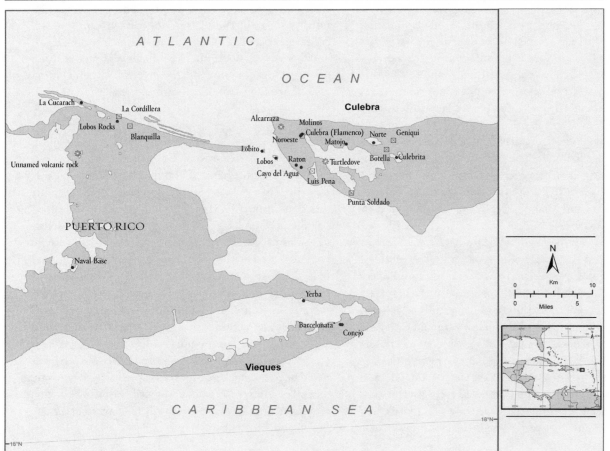

ATLANTIC

OCEAN

La Cucarach

La Cordillera

Culebra

Lobos Rocks

Alcarraza

Molinos

Blanquilla

Noroeste

Culebra (Flamenco)

Norte

Geniqui

Unnamed volcanic rock

Lobito

Matojo

Lobos

Raton

Turtledove

Botella

Culebrita

Cayo del Agua

Luis Pena

PUERTO RICO

Punta Soldado

Naval Base

Yerba

Barcelonata"

Concejo

Vieques

CARIBBEAN SEA

N

Km
0   10
Miles
0   5

Map 27. Culebra
and Vieques,
Puerto Rico.

18°N

16°N

Some colonies were surveyed by plane (180–200 m AGL, 80–90 knots) because boat landings and walking through the islands were too treacherous (e.g., Alcarraza Island in the Culebra Archipelago, Navassa Island), or as part of islandwide population surveys (e.g., Brown Pelican). During aerial surveys, two experienced biologists plotted the colony locations on a map and counted all visible nests while the airplane circled overhead, and a consensus on the number of nesting pairs was reached.

Species Accounts

Sixteen species of seabirds breed in Puerto Rico and its adjacent islands (table 9.1). Five species are resident throughout the year: Brown Booby, Red-footed Booby, Masked Booby, Brown Pelican, and Magnificent Frigatebird. Eleven species are migrants absent for part of each year: Audubon's Shearwater, White-tailed Tropicbird, Red-billed Tropicbird, Laughing Gull, Brown Noddy, Sooty Tern, Bridled Tern, Least Tern, Roseate Tern, Royal Tern, and Sandwich Tern and Cayenne Tern. Although Royal and Sandwich terns are found throughout the year, apparently most of the individuals observed outside the breeding season are transient birds (banding reports from these birds show that they were trapped near North Carolina).

Puerto Rico (Main Island)

Although the main island has a variety of habitats, ranging from wet montane forests to dry coastal scrub, mangrove lagoons, and salt ponds, only three species of seabirds nest within the main island of Puerto Rico: White-tailed Tropicbird, Brown Pelican, and Least Tern. There are no historical records of other seabird species nesting on the main island, even in coastal areas that appear suitable.

White-tailed Tropicbird

This migratory species may first appear near breeding areas as early as January, but larger numbers of adults in courtship flights arrive in February. Nesting occurs in ocean-facing crevices and caves, mostly on inaccessible cliff areas within the Northwest Cliffs and Cueva del Indio. A few (up to five) adult pairs have also been observed circling cliffs on the south coast (Ponce), which suggests that nesting may occur. The population appears stable with estimated pairs as follows: less than 100 in early March 2000; 400 in mid-February 2002; 150 in early March 2003; and 100 in late February 2004. Moni-

Table 9.1. Status of seabirds breeding in Puerto Rico and adjacent islands, 2004

Species	Nesting pairs
Audubon's Shearwater	25–40
White-tailed Tropicbird	500–525
Red-billed Tropicbird	20–30
Masked Booby	175–225
Brown Booby	1,650–1,700
Red-footed Booby	3,000–3,025
Brown Pelican	265–290
Magnificent Frigatebird	500–550
Laughing Gull	1,300–1,400
Brown Noddy	1,230–1,300
Sooty Tern	40,500–40,600
Bridled Tern	235–250
Least Tern	135–150
Roseate Tern	935–1,000
Royal Tern	10–25
Sandwich Tern[a]	675–700
Cayenne Tern[a]	5–10

a. One species, two subspecies counted separately.

toring of nesting success is nearly impossible, except at Cueva del Indio, due to location of nesting areas on sheer cliffs. Fledglings do not remain near colony sites after they fledge; thus, successful reproduction can only be determined by observing fledglings offshore during aerial surveys, or by rock climbing down to crevices and caves to record nest contents (none of which has been performed).

Brown Pelican

Three sites have records of nesting Brown Pelican: the Northwest Cliffs (only the cliffs of Aguadilla), a section of the west coast between Mayagüez and Añasco, and Isla del Frío off the southeast coast of Ponce. Pairs select forested areas with tall trees (over 5 m high). Nesting may occur throughout the year, but most nesting activity appears to occur twice a year. The timing of peak breeding activity may vary, possibly in relation to variations in feeding resources, from late July to November and/or January to early June. The Mayagüez-Añasco coast has been used only sporadically since 1990, and since 2000 nesting has been reported only once in 2002 (less than five nests). Brown Pelican activity (foraging and roosting) near the colony site at the Northwest Cliffs has been observed every year, but inaccessibility of the colony on the cliff makes aerial surveys the only effective way of monitoring breeding. Between 2000 and 2004, nesting has only been observed in 2000 (12 pairs) and 2003 (17 pairs). Brown Pelican had regularly been observed roosting with Cattle Egret (*Bubulcus ibis*) at Isla del Frío (a small mangrove cay), but nesting had only recently been reported in 2002 (small number of pairs) and in 2003 (26 pairs).

Although fledging success at these colonies is not known, chicks at various stages have been seen, suggesting successful fledging to some extent. Low nesting activity in the Mayagüez-Añasco coast may be related to human intrusion, since nesting occurs on trees (*Casuarina equisetifolia*) on a beach next to a residential area. Low nesting activity at the Northwest Cliffs, however, does not appear to be related to human activities, since the steep terrain prevents easy access to the colony site.

Bridled Tern

These terns arrive for breeding in late April and begin nesting in early to mid-May. They usually select nest locations where an overhang of vegetation or rock provides shelter for the nest, or inside crevices and caves. Young fledge in early to mid-August. They have been observed circling the Northwest Cliffs, exiting and entering cave formations, which suggests that nesting occurs. Nesting has been confirmed inside Cueva del Indio. An estimated 15–25 pairs may have been nesting at these locations since 2000 (based on aerial observations); however, no systematic surveys have been conducted at this location due to rough seas and inaccessibility of cliff crevices.

Least Tern

Adults may appear in mid-April but begin nesting in early May. Usually adults depart breeding areas with their young immediately after fledging in late June to early July. Nesting occurs in sparsely vegetated salt flat areas and mud flats, primarily at the Cabo Rojo Salt Flats, La Jungla Salt Flats, Boquerón Natural Reserve, and adjacent to the Laguna de Las Salinas pond. Since 2000, these areas have supported 20–50 pairs in any one year, but due to frequent colony-site switching and colony abandonment early in the breeding season, monitoring nesting success has not been possible.

Sporadic nesting has also been reported in mud flats on the east-northeast coast near Carolina and the east coast in Ceiba (3–10 pairs). Fledging Least Tern have been observed, accompanied by adults, staging at the Isla Grande Airport in San Juan (north), and although the origin of these birds is not known, their appearance suggests that successful nesting does happen on the north coast. Low hatching and fledging success appears to be directly related to flooding, predation by dogs, cats, mongoose, and raptors, as well as disturbance from humans trampling nests or human activities near the nesting areas.

Northwest Cays

These volcanic rocks and cays (14) are frequently overwashed by heavy north swells; jagged depressions on the rock provide nesting habitat for some seabird species. Vegetation is found only on the larger cays (> 0.5 ha). A few of these are connected to the main island through a thin strip of volcanic material. The cays that are used by seabirds, however, are separated from other land, and access is difficult unless sea conditions allow climbing over the jagged edge. Two species of seabirds nest there: Bridled Tern and Roseate Tern. Brown Noddy has been observed roosting on these cays in the summer, but no nesting has been reported.

Bridled Tern

A few pairs (not more than 5) have been observed between late May and early June on one of the Northwest Cays where Roseate Tern also nest. Although breeding has not been confirmed, the presence of Bridled Tern on the cay and the availability of suitable habitat for this species strongly suggest that nesting does occur in small numbers every year.

Roseate Tern

Arrive on the breeding areas in early May and nesting begins in mid- to late May. They shift colony sites among years but generally always use 1–3 particular cays for breeding. Young fledge in mid-July and leave the breeding areas with their parents in late July or early August. Population estimates from aerial surveys show a steady increase in colony size from 75 pairs before 2000 to close to 200 pairs in 2004. These colonies have not been visited late in the breeding season to estimate fledging, but marine biologists working offshore observed flocks of adults and young foraging offshore in early August 2003, which suggests that colonies in the Northwest Cays are fledging successfully.

Cordilla Cays

The cays and rocky outcrops in this string vary in size from a few square meters to 5 ha; some contain abundant vegetation and small salt ponds. Five seabird species nest: Brown Booby, Laughing Gull, Brown Noddy, Sooty Tern, and Sandwich Tern; nesting is on three of these cays, La Blanquilla, La Cucaracha, and an unnamed cay. Brown Pelican and Magnificent Frigatebird regularly roost on some of these islands, but no nesting has been observed. Only Brown Booby colony estimates have been conducted between 2000 and 2004. Reproductive performance of seabirds has not been monitored at any of these sites.

Brown Booby

A large colony (estimated 600 pairs) has been observed repeatedly at an unnamed cay since 1991. The cay is practically devoid of vegetation and soil, and the boobies nest on the hard surface of jagged volcanic rock. Aerial surveys have shown that the area occupied by nesting booby has not changed significantly; therefore, number of nesting birds between 2000 and 2004 resembles that of earlier years (i.e., close to 600 pairs). Apparently size of the island and nearest neighbor distance prevents expansion of this colony. Young at various stages, including fledglings, have been observed, indicating successful reproduction.

Laughing Gull

This is the only *Larus* species that nests in the Caribbean. Laughing Gulls nest at La Cucaracha, a dome-shaped cay with relatively short vegetation covering at least 75% of its surface. The gulls nest among dense vegetation. Rangers from the Puerto Rico Department of Natural and Environmental Resources patrolling the Cordillera Cays report that Laughing Gull have continued to nest on this island, but there are no breeding estimates. Fledgling Laughing Gulls have been observed west of the colony site, suggesting that successful reproduction has occurred. However, mixing of fledglings from the Culebra Archipelago to the east may confound these observations.

Brown Noddy

Small numbers (estimated 40 pairs) were seen nesting at La Blanquilla in the mid-1990s on the top of shrubs such as *Suriana maritima*. Several Brown Noddy carcasses were observed at La Cucaracha, suggesting that a raptor species may have been preying upon them at La Blanquilla. The colony has not been monitored at the end of the breeding season; therefore, the degree of reproductive success cannot be estimated with the available information. The presence of rats (*Rattus rattus*) on such a small island with scarce food resources may be affecting the breeding success and potential future increment of Brown Noddy at La Blanquilla.

Sooty Tern

Close to 300 pairs were estimated nesting under the dense vegetation at La Blanquilla in the mid-1990s. Although this colony has not been surveyed between 2000 and 2004, rangers from the Puerto Rico Department of Natural and Environmental Resources have indicated that the number of breeding pairs appears smaller than what they remember previously. The colony has not been monitored at the end of the breeding season, hence the degree of reproductive success cannot be estimated. Rats on this small island may be affecting breeding success and potential future increment of Sooty Terns at La Blanquilla.

Sandwich Tern

Observed nesting at La Blanquilla on only one occasion in the mid-1980s, when at least 250 pairs nested; but breeding has not been observed since. La Blanquilla is covered primarily by short scrubs and herbaceous plants (90%), but Sandwich Tern congregated on the sparsely vegetated areas. The presence of rats on this island may have prevented recolonization by Sandwich Terns.

Culebra Archipelago

The Culebra Archipelago contains 24 islands, cays, and rocky outcrops: Culebra Island, Alcarraza Island, Isla Culebrita, El Mono, Piedra Stevens, and Cayos Ballena, Botella, Botijuela, del Agua, Geniquí, Lobo, Lobito, Luis Peña, Matojo, Molinos, Noroeste, Norte, Pelá, Pelaíta, Pirata, Ratón, Sombrerito, Tiburón, and Yerba. One or more species of seabirds nest on 14 of these islands. Most of the islands were formed from pillow lava that emerged from volcanic eruptions, making them quite unstable and easily subjected to erosion despite the presence of dense vegetative cover on most. Culebra Island, the largest in the archipelago, is the only inhabited island, with a population of about 2,500.

The Culebra Archipelago was used extensively as a bombing range by the U.S. Navy from the 1940s until military activities ceased in 1975. The smaller cays and the northwest peninsula of Culebra Island were used as targets for military practices, and although impacts from these activities on nesting seabirds were not measured, colonies were affected by direct ordnance hits or subsequent fires that spread through nesting areas. The presence of unexploded ordnance and restrictions on access to some of the cays have prevented monitoring of nesting between 2000 and 2004 for many species, including sulids, tropicbirds, and terns. Most of the land used by the navy was transferred to the U.S. Fish and Wildlife Service to be managed as a wildlife refuge. Except for Cayo Norte, which is privately owned, the rest of the cays are managed as bird sanctuaries. Unexploded ordnance remains in most of the islands used as targets; access is therefore limited to authorized USFWS personnel who administer these areas.

Thirteen species of seabirds nest in the Culebra Archipelago: Audubon's Shearwater, Masked Booby, Brown Booby, Red-footed Booby, White-tailed Tropicbird, Red-billed Tropicbird, Laughing Gull, Brown Noddy, Sooty Tern, Bridled Tern, Roseate Tern, Royal Tern, Sandwich Tern, and Cayenne Tern. Brown Pelican and Magnificent Frigatebird regularly visit and roost within the archipelago all year round, but no nesting of these species has been observed. Small numbers of Black Noddy have also appeared frequently to join Brown Noddy during the breeding season, but no nesting or attempts to nest have been observed so far.

Some other seabird species occasionally visit the archipelago and surrounding waters at different times of the year, such as Herald's Petrel (*Pterodroma arminjoniana*), Great Shearwater (*Puffinus gravis*), Manx Shearwater (*P. puffinus*), Wilson's Storm-Petrel (*Oceanites oceanicus*), Leach's Storm-Petrel (*Oceanodroma leucorhoa*), Double-crested Cormorant (*Phalacrocorax auritus*), Common Tern (*Sterna hirundo*), Arctic Tern (*S. paradisaea*), Least Tern (*S. antillarum*), and Pomarine Skua (*Stercorarius pomarinus*).

Audubon's Shearwater

Audubon's Shearwater in the Culebra Archipelago nest under some type of shelter (boulders or vegetation), or they excavate burrows near thick vegetation or large rocks. Colonies are scattered and consist of one to five pairs per cay. Nesting has been confirmed at six cays: Alcarraza Island and Cayos del Agua, Yerba, Lobito, Luis Peña, and Matojo. Evidence of nesting activity (excavated soil, loose feathers, and/or excrement in the burrows), strongly suggests that Audubon's Shearwaters also nest at Cayo Lobo, Cayo Ratón, and Isla Culebrita. Potential habitat exists at Cayo Norte, but this cay has not been surveyed for this species. The secretive and nocturnal habits of Audubon's Shearwaters and their selection of deep burrows for nesting make it difficult to ascertain their nest sites and breeding period. Evidence of nesting activity suggests that nesting may begin as early as February and may extend to late July, when the last chicks fledge.

This species shows strong site fidelity, adults usually returning to previously occupied nest sites year after year. However, the nature of Audubon's Shearwater nest sites in the Culebra Archipelago results in many being modified, eroded, or destroyed during storms and telluric movements and subsequently being abandoned by the adults. The current population of nesting Audubon's Shearwater in the Culebra Archipelago is probably not more than 20–25 pairs. It is not known whether pairs faced with destruction of their historical nest sites have moved to other cays that have not yet been surveyed.

White-tailed Tropicbird

Similar to Red-billed Tropicbird in nesting habits and nest site selection (sheltered sites under boulders or inside caves and crevices); however, nests have not been found under vegetation. White-tailed Tropicbirds engage in fierce intraspecific and interspecific battles over nest sites. In the Culebra Archipelago, White-tailed Tropicbirds nest on five cays: Cayos Luis Peña, Noroeste, del Agua, and Molinos and near Punta Soldado (Culebra Island). Individuals have also been observed circling the cliffs of Cayo Lobo, Isla Culebrita, and Cayo Norte, suggesting that nesting has been attempted or occurs in these islands; however, it has not been confirmed.

This species shows strong site fidelity, with adults returning to previously occupied nest sites year after year. Their breeding season overlaps with that of the Red-billed Tropicbird, but most pairs are observed around February and March, and the last chicks usually fledge by the end of August or early September. Boat surveys around some of the nesting areas have detected an apparent decrease in numbers of White-tailed Tropicbird circling potential nest sites (from an estimated 75–100 pairs around 2000). The presence of rats at the largest colony in Cayo Luis Peña may be affecting breeding success and population recruitment. Young at various stages, including fledglings, have been found, indicating successful reproduction.

Red-billed Tropicbird

The Culebra Archipelago is the most westerly breeding location for this species in the Caribbean. At Culebra Red-billed Tropicbirds nest in a variety of sheltered habitats—in caves and crevices and under boulders and vegetation. They often use abandoned White-tailed Tropicbird nest sites or engage in fierce intraspecific and interspecific battles over sites. In the Culebra Archipelago Red-billed Tropicbirds nest in Alcarraza Island and Cayos Luis Peña, Ratón, Yerba, Geniquí, Molinos,

Lobito, and Matojo. Individuals have also been observed circling the cliffs of Cayo Lobo and Cayo Norte, suggesting that nesting has been attempted or occurs in these islands; however, nesting has not been confirmed there.

This species shows strong nest site fidelity, with adults returning year after year to previously occupied sites. Their breeding season overlaps with that of the White-tailed Tropicbird, but most pairs are observed near the end of May. The last chicks usually fledge by the end of August or early September. Boat surveys around some of the nesting areas have detected an apparent decrease in numbers of Red-billed Tropicbird circling potential nest sites, from 30–50 pairs estimated in 2000 to 20–30 pairs in 2004. Rats at the largest colony in Cayo Luis Peña may be affecting breeding success and population recruitment. Young at various stages, including fledglings, have been found, indicating successful reproduction.

Masked Booby

Similar in nesting habits to Brown Booby. Masked Boobies are resident year round at the Culebra Archipelago, only on Alcarraza Island, where they nest on the ground in open spaces among vegetation (*Cyperus* sp.). In the archipelago they are non-synchronous breeders, with nests at any stage of development found throughout the year. Peak incubation may vary from year to year; the largest number of breeding pairs has been observed during the months of January through March. Alcarraza became increasingly difficult to access after the early 1990s, when hurricanes eroded part of the island, rendering landing and climbing to the top of the cay particularly treacherous. Additionally, the presence of unexploded ordnance, and concomitant access restrictions, prevented monitoring of nests for this species and the Brown Booby between 2000 and 2004. Numbers of nesting pairs fluctuate drastically: some years as few as five pairs, other years as many as 75 (2004 aerial survey). Young at various stages, including fledglings, have been found, indicating successful reproduction.

Brown Booby

Resident year round at the Culebra Archipelago, where it nests on the ground in open spaces among vegetation (*Cyperus* sp.) on Alcarraza Island and Cayos Geniquí, with the majority (95%) concentrating on Cayos Geniquí. Cayos Geniquí are two volcanic cays lined east to west and joined by a strip of rocks overwashed during strong northern swells. Brown Booby in the archipelago are non-synchronous breeders, with nests at any stage of development found throughout the year. Peak incu-

bation may vary by year; the largest number of breeding pairs is usually observed from December through March. Numbers of nesting pairs have not increased dramatically since 2000, with an estimated 200–250 from aerial surveys in 2004.

Red-footed Booby

Adults and young can be observed year round in the archipelago, and pairs usually nest between February and June. Although appropriate habitat is present on many of the cays, Red-footed Booby nest only on Cayos Geniquí in some years. Nests are built on top of the few *Ficus* trees that grow on the eastern portion of these cays; however, hurricanes easily damage their canopies, and the unstable substrate provides little support to the trees. Not more than 10 pairs have ever been observed nesting at any one time, and only 3 pairs were seen during an aerial survey in 2004. Nevertheless, young Red-footed Booby at various stages have been observed, suggesting some degree of successful reproduction at Cayos Geniquí.

Laughing Gull

Selects nest sites near or under shelter of vegetation and boulders at Cayo Lobito, Cayo Matojo, and Cayos Geniquí. Nesting was reported once on the northeast coast of Culebra Island (west of Playa Zoní) in the mid-1990s, but this gull has not nested there again. Laughing Gulls arrive around mid-April to pair up and establish territories, and egg laying begins in mid-May. Most individuals depart the archipelago between late August and mid-September. Boat survey estimates suggest that population numbers have been stable or slightly increasing to close to 1,000 pairs. Although reproductive success has not been monitored, some nests have been found with three fledgings, indicating that some pairs attain 100% fledging success. Recruitment into the population should therefore be expected.

Brown Noddy

Arriving in mid- to late April, Brown Noddies quickly settle down near their prospective nest sites, where they begin courting and defending the site. Although different habitats are used for nesting, such as cliff ledges, on the ground, or over vegetation, nests are invariably located on the periphery of the nesting cay (not near the center, like Sooty Tern nests). By far, most nests are located on cliff ledges in Alcarraza and Cayos del Agua, Ratón, Yerba, Noroeste, Molinos, and Geniquí. Interestingly, despite availability of vegetation potentially suitable for nesting, only a handful of pairs nest on top of vegetation, in only one site (Cayos Geniquí).

This species shows strong nest site fidelity, adults returning year after year to previously occupied sites. Egg laying begins in early May, and chicks fledge close to eight weeks later in early to mid-August. Both adults and young remain near the archipelago after fledging, departing sometime in late August or early September. Although direct noddy nest counts have not been conducted in all nesting areas between 2000 and 2004, boat surveys around the colonies suggest that the number of breeding pairs is stable or slightly increasing, estimated as at least 800 pairs.

Sooty Tern

Large flocks arrive to the offshore waters of the Culebra Archipelago as early as late March, but they do not come in to land until late April. Most pairs begin laying a few days after the flocks settle in the nesting areas in early May. Nests are invariably located under dense vegetation, and avoidance of open spaces is the norm. Chicks take an average of eight weeks to fledge, but adult and young Sooty Tern do not leave the archipelago until late August or early September. They nest under dense vegetation at Cayos Yerba, Noroeste, and Molinos, at Alcarraza, and on Culebra Island (northwest tip of Peninsula Flamenco). Local fishermen indicate that before bombing activities began in the 1940s, Sooty Tern also nested at Cayo Botella and Cayos Geniquí, but they have not nested in these two cays ever since.

This species shows strong nest site fidelity. Although the presence of unexploded ordnance and restricted access prevented monitoring in some areas, nest counts have been conducted at the Sooty Tern colonies of Cayo Yerba, Cayo Noroeste, and Culebra Island's northwest tip, and boat surveys have shown that nesting continues at Alcarraza and Cayo Molinos. Estimates from these surveys suggest that the population of Sooty Tern is stable at Cayo Yerba and increasing at the northwest tip, with a total estimate for the archipelago of close to 40,000 pairs.

Bridled Tern

Arrive from migration in mid- to late April and, unlike Sooty Tern, they quickly settle down near their prospective nesting territories, where they begin courting and defending the territory. Nests are located near some type of shelter—caves, boulders, crevices, vegetation, discarded tires, or manmade structures—in Alcarraza and Cayos del Agua, Ratón, Yerba, Lobito, Noroeste, Molinos, and Geniquí. Adults return to previously oc-

cupied nest sites year after year. Egg laying begins near mid-May, and chicks fledge close to eight weeks later in early to mid-August. Both adults and young depart the archipelago soon after fledging.

Although the Bridled Tern is the most widespread seabird nesting in the Culebra Archipelago, colonies are small (average of 5–10 pairs), except at Cayo del Agua, where up to 130 nests have been found in a breeding season. In the early 1980s, close to 500 pairs of Bridled Tern nested in the archipelago; however, numbers steadily decreased to fewer than 200 pairs by 2000. Boat surveys around some of the nesting areas have detected an apparent decrease in numbers, particularly at the largest breeding colony in Cayo del Agua. Overall, the number of Bridled Terns in the archipelago is estimated at 75–100 pairs. The possible presence of rats on Cayo del Agua (due to its proximity to Cayo Luis Peña, which has rats) may be affecting breeding success and population recruitment. Additionally, the presence of Peregrine Falcon (*Falco peregrinus*) and Red-tailed Hawk (*Buteo jamaicensis*) during the period of colony site selection in late April (possibly attracted by the large masses of arriving Sooty Tern) may deter Bridled Tern from nesting or result in mortality of adult birds.

Roseate Tern

Arrive in the Culebra Archipelago from migration in late April and begin nesting in mid- to late May. They have nested at Cayo Ratón, Cayo Yerba, Cayo Molinos, and Culebra Island (Punta Soldado), but since 2000 Cayo Molinos has been the only cay used by Roseate Tern. Most nest sites at Cayo Ratón and Cayo Yerba are close to vegetation (*Cyperus* sp.), whereas nest sites at Cayo Molinos and Culebra Island are on volcanic rock with no vegetative cover. Although Roseate Terns arrive around the archipelago every year, they have not nested there in consecutive years since the mid-1990s. They do not show strong nest site fidelity. Adults may arrive at potential breeding sites but may abandon these shortly thereafter. The reasons for colony abandonment are not clear, but the presence of Peregrine Falcon (*Falco peregrinus*) and Red-tailed Hawk (*Buteo jamaicensis*) during the period of colony site selection in early May (possibly attracted by the large masses of Sooty Tern that arrive in late April) may deter Roseate Tern from nesting. If successful breeding occurs, adult and young Roseate Terns depart Culebra around late July.

The number nesting in the archipelago has been steadily declining from a high of over 300 pairs in 1988 to an average of 15–25 pairs in the mid-1990s. Between 2000 and 2004, Roseate Tern estimates from boat surveys have not surpassed 15 breeding pairs. Previous observations of Roseate Terns banded at Culebra but breeding in the Virgin Islands suggest that the Culebra population may have shifted to the larger colonies of the Virgin Islands.

Royal Tern

Nesting activity in the Culebra Archipelago begins in mid-May and extends through late July, when fledglings and adults migrate, possibly to the north coast of South America. However, migrants from North America begin arriving around September and remain until early April, when they are joined by breeding birds. Royal Tern nest at Cayo Lobito and Cayo Matojo, selecting nesting areas with sparse, short vegetation or devoid of vegetative cover, and always among nesting Sandwich Tern.

Once a fairly common nesting migratory seabird, with breeding pairs numbering up to 200, the Royal Tern has declined sharply in the Culebra Archipelago to the point of no nesting activity in consecutive years during the 1990s. A few pairs nested between 2000 and 2004, but nest counts were not conducted because counts risk Laughing Gull predation on eggs while adults leave nests unattended. Boat survey estimates suggest that a high of 5–10 pairs may have nested during this period. The fate of these nests is unknown, and no evidence of fledging activity was observed between 2000 and 2004. Harassment of nesting pairs and predation by neighboring Laughing Gull, coupled with the encroachment of nesting habitat by vegetation, may have played a significant role in the reduction of nesting activity of Royal Tern in the archipelago.

Sandwich Tern

Nesting activity in the Culebra Archipelago begins in mid-May and extends through late July, when fledglings and adults migrate, possibly to the north coast of South America. Migrants from North America begin arriving around September and remain until early April, when they are joined by breeding birds. Sandwich Terns nest at Cayo Lobito and Cayo Matojo, where they select nesting areas with sparse, short vegetation or devoid of vegetative cover, sometimes among nesting Royal Tern. Like Royal Tern, Sandwich Tern regularly nested in the archipelago, but numbers declined sharply to the point of no nesting activity in consecutive years during the 1990s. Only a few pairs nested between 2000 and 2004, when nest counts were avoided because they create the risk of Laughing Gull predation on unattended eggs. Boat survey estimates suggest that a high of 15–25 pairs may have nested during this period. The fate of these nests

is not known; no evidence of fledging was observed in 2000–2004. Vegetation encroachment and Laughing Gull predation and harassment of nesting pairs and vegetation encroachment may have roles in reducing Sandwich Tern nesting.

Cayenne Tern

A South American race of the Sandwich Tern, the Cayenne Tern has nested at Cayo Lobito on a few occasions (two nests), and only single individuals on nests have been observed. It is not known whether the other member of each pair was a Cayenne or Sandwich Tern. They presumably arrive at the nesting areas with Sandwich Tern, and occupy territories within this species' colony. Between 2000 and 2004, no Cayenne Tern was observed around the Culebra Archipelago.

Vieques Island

Vieques Island is about 135 km² in area, 34 km long, and 5 km wide. It lies some 13 km from the southeast coast of Puerto Rico. Its current population is about 10,000 people, and until recently about 70% of Vieques Island was owned by the U.S. Navy. The easternmost section of the island was used as a bombing range and for small arms operations, air and sea to ground combat, and amphibious attacks. After using the island for more than 60 years as a military training ground, the U.S. Navy left Vieques in 2003. Due to Navy bombing activities, the Brown Pelican colony was not monitored between 2000 and 2004; the impact of military exercises on other nesting seabirds also was not monitored.

Fourteen small islands and cays are found relatively close to the coast of Vieques Island (primarily on the south coast), but only one, Cayo Conejo, harbors seabird species. Brown Pelican, Least Tern, and Roseate Tern are the only seabird species confirmed to nest on Vieques Island. Red-billed Tropicbird have been observed flying near the cliffs of the northeast coast, but the typical repeated circling that suggests nesting activity has not been observed. Most likely, at least a few pairs nest on these cliffs. Brown Boobies are also seen roosting on Cayo Conejo, but no nesting has been observed.

Brown Pelican

Found year round feeding off the coast of Vieques Island. The second most important nesting area of Brown Pelican in Puerto Rico is Cayo Conejo, a small cay (less than 1 ha) located less than 2 km from the southeast coast of Vieques Island. Vegetation covers most of the cay; Brown Pelicans nest on top of short (less than 2 m high) woody vegetation such as *Coccoloba uvifera*. Nesting may occur throughout the year, but most nesting activity appears to occur in two peaks. The timing of peak breeding activity may vary, possibly in relation to variations in feeding resources, from late July to November and/or January to early June.

Aerial surveys conducted around Cayo Conejo showed little Brown Pelican activity, including roosting. Nesting was observed only once in 2000, when 18 pairs were recorded nesting at Cayo Conejo. Sporadic observations during this period revealed downy chicks on the cay, suggesting some level of fledging success may have occurred. Although Brown Pelican may have not been directly affected by bombing activities, disturbance caused by training exercises (particularly low overflights and explosions) may have resulted in adult pelicans leaving nests unattended and susceptible to predation by hermit crabs (*Coenobita clypeatus*).

Least Tern

Nesting activity in Vieques appears to be sporadic and has not been monitored. Between 2000 and 2004, small groups of Least Tern (5–10 individuals) were observed in the summer months fishing the inshore waters of Vieques Island, albeit not every year. Potential nesting habitat is available, particularly on the easternmost section of Vieques and an unnamed small sandy cay to the northwest. Nesting activity was reported on the sandy shore west of Blue Beach in early July 2002. It is not known how many pairs nested, but apparently the number was small (possibly 5 or fewer pairs), and both eggs and downy chicks were observed. During a subsequent visit no young or adult terns were seen, suggesting that no chicks fledged.

Roseate Tern

Roseate Terns are not common nesters in Vieques Island, where they usually appear in small foraging flocks on the southeast coast in late May. Their breeding activities around Vieques Island are not well documented because nesting occurred at the easternmost tip of the island, where military activities precluded monitoring. Although reports indicate that Roseate Tern nested in Vieques Island prior to 1990, it was not until 2001 when up to 10 pairs were reported nesting at the easternmost point in mid-July on jagged volcanic substrate without vegetation cover. Since Roseate Tern in the Caribbean are notorious colony shifters, it is possible that these late nesters were birds that had abandoned a nesting area in Culebra (Punta Soldado) in late June. This colony, however, was abandoned shortly thereafter, and the species has not been observed nesting on Vieques Island again. It is not known to what extent bombing practices around the time when Roseate Tern are selecting nest sites (late April–early May) have deterred adults from selecting Vieques for nesting.

Caja de Muertos

Located off the south coast of Puerto Rico (9.6 km south of Ponce), Caja de Muertos is approximately 2.75 km wide by 1.85 km long, with a total area of 202 ha. The vegetation is typical of a semiarid climate, with thorny shrubs and cactus predominating. About 200 m west of Caja de Muertos lies a small cay, Cayo Morrillitos, which is vegetated primarily with exotic grasses, *Coccoloba uvifera*, and *Opuntia* sp. Caja de Muertos is a Natural Reserve administered by the Puerto Rico Department of Natural and Environmental Resources, and it has no permanent inhabitants. Two species of seabird nest in Caja de Muertos: White-tailed Tropicbird and Brown Pelican. Several species of tern (Royal, Sandwich, and Least Tern) and boobies (*Sula* sp.) roost and forage near Caja de Muertos and Cayo Morrillitos, but no nesting has been observed.

White-tailed Tropicbird

Small numbers (not more than 5 pairs) nest in crevices and caves of a rocky outcrop on the westernmost tip of Caja de Muertos. Breeding success of these pairs has not been determined. Other potential nesting habitat is found on the mountain ridge that traverses the island from east to west, but nesting activity there has not been confirmed.

Brown Pelican

Although adults and immatures regularly forage in the vicinity of Caja de Muertos, nesting activity has not been recorded in Caja de Muertos since the mid-1990s, when 40+ pairs nested on top of *Coccoloba uvifera* at Cayo Morrillitos and chicks of various ages were observed, suggesting some level of fledging success. As Cayo Morrillitos has changed little since the mid-1990s, and human activity is not frequent, it is not clear why Brown Pelican have not continued to breed at this site.

Cayo Guayanilla

A section of the Unitas Reef on the south coast emerged to form "Cayo Guayanilla," a small coralline and sandy island about 1 km east of Punta Verraco, between Guayanilla and Tallaboa. The composition and size of Cayo

Guayanilla change every year, depending on storms and heavy surf that erode this small island, making it an unstable substrate for nesting seabirds. Barely above sea level, the island would sometimes submerge completely for months at a time and reemerge later. Vegetation (grass) grew on this island until 2003, when erosion caused by heavy surge removed most of it. By the summer of 2004 the island had been reduced to a few square meters with no vegetation.

Three species of seabirds have nested at Cayo Guayanilla: Least Tern, Roseate Tern, and Sandwich Tern. Although Brown Pelican, Royal Tern, Common Tern, and Laughing Gull commonly visit Cayo Guayanilla early in the breeding season (early May), these species have never nested on this island. Other species, such as American Oystercatcher (*Haematopus palliatus*), Wilson's Plover (*Charadrius wilsonia*), and Bahama Ducks (*Anas bahamensis*), have also nested on this island.

Least Tern

Arrive at Cayo Guayanilla in late April but do not begin laying eggs until the first week of May. They select open areas with no cover, usually close to some type of ocean debris. As many as 120 pairs have nested on Cayo Guayanilla in the 1990s, but the number has been steadily declining: 75–100 pairs (2000), 2 pairs (2001), 5–10 pairs (2003), and 5 pairs (2004). This reduction may be linked to the steady erosion of this island, overwashing of nests by heavy surf, and egg predation by Ruddy Turnstone (*Arenaria interpres*) and American Oystercatcher (*Haematopus palliatus*). It is possible that the increment of nesting Least Tern at the nearby mud flats of Punta Gotay (about 4 km east) reflect colony shifting from Cayo Guayanilla. Since American Oystercatchers nest on this island, their presence among nesting Least Terns may result in predation of eggs and young, disruption of incubation, and colony abandonment to areas not visited by oystercatchers (such as Punta Gotay).

Roseate Tern

Nesting activity of this species at Cayo Guayanilla is similar to that of Sandwich Tern. They arrive in early May and egg laying begins around mid- to late May. Usually, eggs are laid on fine coralline substrate, with or without nearby vegetation and coral rubble. Colony numbers are relatively small (high of 20 pairs in 1997), but only one pair nested between 2000 and 2004. Shifting of colony sites between birds from the Parguera Cays and Cayo Guayanilla is evident from observations of Roseate Tern banded in La Parguera nesting at Cayo Guayanilla. The reason for such low Roseate Tern nesting activity at Cayo

Guayanilla is not clear; however, the diminishing size of the island may play a role in the selection of larger breeding areas in La Parguera.

Sandwich Tern

Arrive at Cayo Guayanilla in late April to early May, when they begin courtship displays and mating on the shoreline of the island. By mid-May they have formed a tightly packed colony or several nesting subgroups farther inland, depending on the availability of appropriate substrate (small coralline pebbles interspersed with larger coral rubble or short vegetation). Sandwich Tern nesting activity at Cayo Guayanilla has varied dramatically during the 1990s, from as few as 5 pairs to as many as 100–200 pairs. Between 2000 and 2004, however, no Sandwich Tern nested at Cayo Guayanilla. Fledging success has not been monitored there. Most likely, the diminishing size of the island and composition change (less coral rubble) deterred the birds from continuing to nest at Cayo Guayanilla. Shifting of colony sites between Sandwich Tern from the Parguera Cays and Cayo Guayanilla may be occurring.

Montalva Cays

This group of 15–20 small (0.5–1 ha) scattered mangrove cays lies within Montalva Bay, at a distance of 10–300 m off the south coast of Guánica. The Brown Pelican is the only seabird nesting on these cays.

Brown Pelican

Nest throughout the year (mostly between January and July) on two of the Montalva Cays: Cayo Frío and Cayo Don Luis. Both islands are formed by the accumulation of large pieces of coral colonized by red mangrove (*Rhizophora mangle*). Mangroves reach up to 16 m in height, and the majority of Brown Pelican nests are located on the top of the canopy. However, some nest sites are as low as 3 m from sea level. Nests at that low level have not been successful at producing young.

Cayo Don Luis is the most important nesting area for Brown Pelican in Puerto Rico. Up to 250 nests have been reported there in one nesting period. Cayo Frío, a much smaller island, has not supported more than 20 nests in a given breeding period. Nesting attempts and breeding success, however, can vary sharply among years on both cays. Nest abandonment is common, and sometimes large colonies of more than 100 nests may be reduced to 5 active nests or less. Fledging success may be low some years (e.g., 5% in 2001) and high in others (e.g., 60% in 2003). Monitoring of Brown Pelican breeding activity at both cays showed 42 active nests in 2001 and 71 active nests in 2003. The number of Brown Pelican nesting in the Montalva Cays between 2000 and 2004 appears stable at 150–200 pairs, with high yearly fluctuations in the number of nesting pairs and nesting success.

The reason for this yearly variation is unknown but may be associated with fluctuations in prey availability, high winds or storms, and predation. Starvation of young has been commonly observed. Strong winds result in chicks falling from nests and getting entangled on tree branches. Peregrine Falcon (*Falco peregrinus*), Yellow-crowned Night-Heron (*Nyctanassa violacea*), and rats (*Rattus rattus*) have been seen at the colony, but the extent of their impact on nesting Brown Pelican has not been monitored. Hermit crabs (*Coenobita clypeatus*), which prey upon unguarded young pelicans at Cayo Conejo in Vieques, are abundant on these cays, but no evidence has been found of crabs climbing up to pelican nests.

Parguera Cays

The Parguera Cays are an array of more than 20 islands between 5 m and 3 km off the south coast of Lajas and Cabo Rojo. These islands are from 0.5 to several hectares in size, composed mostly of red mangrove (*Rhizophora mangle*) and coralline deposits (although the larger ones have volcanic substrate). Two species breed: Roseate Tern, Sandwich Tern, and Cayenne Tern nest on five of the smaller, low-lying, and sparsely vegetated cays: Cayos Turrumote I, Turrumote II, Media Luna East, Media Luna West, and San Cristóbal. Although Brown Pelican and Magnificent Frigatebird were reported nesting on a few of these cays around the 1950s, they have not nested there since the 1970s. Brown Booby, Red-footed Booby, Laughing Gull, Royal Tern, Common Tern, Brown Noddy, and Black Noddy commonly visit the Parguera Cays between May and August, but nesting has not been observed. Occasionally, small numbers of Sooty Tern, Black Tern (*Chlidonias niger*), and Greater Shearwater (*Puffinus gravis*) have been observed or collected on these cays.

Roseate Tern

Nesting activity at Parguera Cays is similar to that of the Sandwich Tern. They arrive in late April to early May and egg laying begins around mid- to late May. Usually, eggs are laid on fine coralline substrate, with or without nearby vegetation and coral rubble. Colony abandonment is very common at Parguera Cays, and Roseate Terns may switch colony locations within a breeding season. Colony switching may be linked to overwashing of nests by heavy surf and tropical storms and to egg predation by Ruddy Turnstone (*Arenaria interpres*) and American Oystercatcher (*Haematopus palliatus*). Ruddy Turnstones constantly patrol colonies, and working in pairs or trios, opportunistically harassing adult terns off nests and then cracking and eating eggs. The larger American Oystercatchers nest on the cays; undeterred by mobbing or by incubating adult terns, they walk through the colony and snatch eggs at leisure. Their presence among nesting terns and predation on eggs and young likely cause disruption of incubation and eventual colony abandonment.

Nesting activity at the Parguera Cays has varied dramatically: colony counts revealed 731 pairs in 2000, 249 pairs in 2002, and 752 pairs in 2003. Although no counts were conducted in 2001 and 2004, nesting Roseate Terns were observed at Cayo Turrumote II in 2001, and several hundred pairs were estimated from boat observations in 2004. Fledging success was not monitored between 2000 and 2004 at Parguera Cays, but large flocks of fledgling Roseate Tern accompanying their parents at the end of the breeding season (mid- to late July) suggest that fledging success may be high. The population of Roseate Terns appears stable or slightly increasing and is estimated at 700 pairs.

Sandwich Tern

Arrive at the Parguera Cays in late April to early May, when they begin courtship displays and mating on the cays' shorelines. By mid-May they either form one large, tightly packed colony on one of the cays or separate into smaller nesting subgroups on two or three different cays. In the Parguera Cays, Sandwich Tern colony site selection appears to be directly related to that of Roseate Tern, since Sandwich Terns are always accompanied by Roseate Terns (the opposite has never been observed). As in the Guayanilla Cays, Sandwich Terns select nesting areas with small coralline pebbles interspersed with larger coral rubble or short vegetation. Although colony abandonment does not appear to be common, Sandwich Terns may switch colony locations every year (perhaps following the shifting movements of Roseate Tern). Sandwich Tern nesting activity at the Parguera Cays has varied dramatically. Colony counts revealed 586 pairs in 2000, 53 pairs in 2002, and 770 pairs in 2003. No colony counts were conducted in 2001 and 2004, but several subgroups were observed at Cayo Turrumote II in 2001, and several hundred pairs were estimated from boat observations in 2004. Fledging success has not been monitored, but large crèches of young Sandwich Terns, as well as flocks of fledglings at the end of the breeding season (mid- to late July), suggest that fledging success may be high. The Sandwich Tern population at Parguera Cays appears stable or slightly increasing and is estimated at 600–650 pairs.

Cayenne Tern

The Cayenne Tern closely follows Sandwich Tern in breeding behavior and nest site selection. Variability in bill coloration has been observed, from totally dull yellow to less than half the bill yellow (usually the distal portion). Some Cayenne Terns show streaks of yellow in an otherwise black bill. Their presence at the Parguera Cays is not regular; in some years up to 5 individuals have nests, whereas in other years no nesting pairs have been detected. Between 2000 and 2004, no more than three pairs of Cayenne Tern nesting among Sandwich Tern were observed.

Isla Ratones

This small island (0.43 ha) is about 500 m from the west coast of Cabo Rojo and is managed by the Puerto Rico Department of Natural and Environmental Resources as a recreational area. The island is partially forested with introduced and native vegetation (primarily trees). Only one seabird species, Brown Pelican, has been observed nesting at Isla Ratones.

Brown Pelican

Although unconfirmed anecdotal information indicates that Brown Pelican nested on Isla Ratones prior to 1990, it was not until June 2004 that two nests were discovered on top of Australian pine (*Casuarina equisetifolia*) at some 12–13 m. One nest contained two large downy chicks, while the other seemed to have eggs or very young chicks (adults were tending the nest). Apparently closure of the island to public visiting for about two years allowed Brown Pelican to breed; they are shy when incubating or tending very young chicks and are easily disrupted by human approach. Usually, the adults do not return to tend their nests until human activity nearby ceases, rendering eggs and young chicks susceptible to overheating. Recent reopening of the island to visitors may prevent Brown Pelican from returning to Isla Ratones to nest.

Mona and Monito

Mona and Monito Islands are about 80 km from the western coast of Puerto Rico. Mona is about 11 km long and 6 km wide, with an approximate area of 5,455 ha (twice as large as Isla Culebra). Their climate is classified as semi-arid and subtropical, with temperatures fluctuating from 28°C to 35°C all year long. Mona and Monito are located close to the deepest ocean trench of the Atlantic Ocean: the Puerto Rico Trench. Between Mona and Puerto Rico, ocean depths reach over 1,000 m. Ocean depths close to Mona are 30 m, and Monito's cliffs are more than 30 m high. The islands are a Natural Reserve and have no permanent inhabitants except Puerto Rico Department of Natural and Environmental Resources personnel (on Mona) who manage the reserve.

Mona has more than 32 km of coast, 90% of which consists of abrupt cliffs of over 60 m high rising vertically from the ocean and riddled with caves. About 2% of the surface is formed by caverns, penetrating horizontally from 45 m to 250 m inside the limestone. The highest elevation is about 90 m above sea level. Coral reefs surround the south coast of Mona, where a myriad of cays protect more than 8 km of sandy beaches.

Monito is a small, relatively inaccessible, limestone island that lies about 5 km north-northwest of Mona. It is basically an irregular plateau surrounded by cliffs, and its total area is approximately 16 ha. The southern and western portions are relatively flat and the highest elevations are toward the northeast, with a maximum of 63 m near the northeastern corner. A north-south fissure extends through the lowlands on the south side. The island is covered by low shrubby vegetation dominated by *Capparis flexuosa* with some small emergent trees of *Ficus citrifolia*, *Pithecellobium unguis-cati*, and *Guapira discolor*. The many seabirds nesting on the island no doubt contribute substantial nutrients for the plants.

Seven species nest on the two islands: White-tailed Tropicbird, Brown Booby, Red-footed Booby, Laughing Gull, Brown Noddy, Sooty Tern, and Bridled Tern. Masked Booby and Magnificent Frigatebird nest only on Monito. Royal Tern and Brown Pelican regularly visit Mona and Monito but have never nested on the islands. Migrants, such as Wilson's Storm-petrel (*Oceanites oceanicus*) and Leach's Storm-petrel (*Oceanodroma leucorhoa*) have been observed in the waters surrounding Mona and Monito.

Historic accounts of Mona indicate that Audubon's Shearwater nested on Mona and possibly Monito, and although flocks of Audubon's Shearwater have been observed foraging in the Mona Passage between the Dominican Republic and Puerto Rico, no evidence has been found of any nesting activity since 1981. However, since surveys of potential Audubon's Shearwater nest sites have not been conducted between October and April, there is a possibility that this species may be nesting during this period. If nesting occurs, predation by rats and feral cats may be affecting Audubon's Shearwater breeding on Mona. Cats are not present on Monito, and a rat eradication program established in the mid-1990s by the reserve personnel has eradicated rats from Monito.

White-tailed Tropicbird

White-tailed Tropicbird on Mona and Monito nest inside caves and crevices; previously occupied nest sites are used year after year, suggesting strong site fidelity. Pairs can be observed circling potential nest sites as early as February, and the nesting season extends into late August. Monitoring of nesting success is nearly impossible (except for a few accessible pairs), due to location of nesting areas on sheer cliffs. Fledglings do not remain near colony sites after they fledge, thus successful reproduction can only be determined by observing fledglings offshore during aerial surveys, or by rock climbing down to crevices and caves to record nest contents (none of which has been performed). Aerial surveys over Mona and Monito between 2000 and 2004 have not detected an appreciable increase or decrease in population numbers from previous years, suggesting a stable population of 100–200 pairs, 75% of which are on Mona. The impact of predation by rats and feral cats at Mona has not been quantified and may be affecting tropicbird breeding success and recruitment. With the eradication of rats on Monito, the number of breeding pairs for the two islands may balance out.

Masked Booby

Nests on Monito, with nesting habits resembling those of Brown Booby: they nest on the ground in open spaces among herbaceous vegetation or exposed in areas of jagged volcanic rock; they are non-synchronous breeders; and peak incubation appears to be between December and March. With the eradication of rats from Monito, the number of breeding pairs appears to have increased slightly between 2000 and 2004; estimated at 100–150. Although breeding success on Monito has not been monitored, young Masked Booby at various stages have been observed, suggesting some degree of successful reproduction.

Brown Booby

Resident year round on Mona and Monito, nesting on the ground in open spaces among herbaceous vegetation or exposed in areas of jagged volcanic rock. Brown Booby on Mona and Monito are non-synchronous breeders, with nests at any stage of development found throughout the year, primarily between December and March. With the eradication of rats from Monito, numbers of breeding pairs appear to have increased slightly between 2000 and 2004; estimated at 700–800. Breeding success has not been monitored, but young Brown Booby at various stages have been observed, suggesting successful reproduction on Mona and Monito.

Red-footed Booby

This species is the most abundant seabird nesting on Mona and Monito, in a large scattered colony near the edge of Mona's northwestern cliffs and extending several kilometers inland, and throughout the plateau of Monito. Red-footed Booby nest throughout the year on a variety of tree species (particularly *Bursera simaruba*, *Pisonia subcordata,* and *Ficus citrifolia*), but peak nesting activity appears to be between February and June. Although breeding success at these colonies has not been monitored, young at various stages have been observed, indicating successful reproduction. Aerial surveys over Mona and Monito between 2000 and 2004 suggest that the colonies have not expanded or diminished appreciably from previous surveys. The breeding population appears stable at 2,000–3,000 pairs.

Magnificent Frigatebird

The only extant colony in Puerto Rico is on Monito Island, where frigatebirds nest on a variety of vegetation species (1–5 m in height) between December and May. Nesting is somewhat synchronous, although eggs and chicks of various stages may be observed throughout the breeding season. The breeding population may be stable or slightly increasing at 400–500 pairs. The presence of nearly fledged chicks indicates some level of fledging success. Although the impact of rats on nesting Magnificent Frigatebird is not known, if rats were preying upon eggs or young chicks, their eradication from Monito would allow recruitment of new breeding birds into the population.

Laughing Gull

These gulls nest on both Mona and Monito, selecting sites near or under shelter of vegetation and boulders or on boulders. As in other areas around Puerto Rico, they arrive around mid-April to pair up and establish territories, and egg laying begins in mid-May. Although rats and feral cats are present on Mona, Laughing Gulls are inaccessible to these predators because nests are located on large boulders that have detached from the cliff face. On Monito breeding success should have improved with eradication of rats. Thus cat and rat predation should not be limiting this species on Mona or Monito. Fledglings have been observed on the beaches of Mona at the end of the breeding season, indicating that some pairs have attained fledging success. Recruitment into the population should be expected, and the population is estimated at 75–100 pairs.

Brown Noddy

Nesting on Mona and Monito is on narrow cliff ledges between May and August (estimated 200–300 pairs). Although seemingly suitable vegetation for nesting is found throughout the cliffs on both islands, Brown Noddy do not nest in the vegetation. The vertical cliff walls where they nest make it difficult for cats to prey on this species. Enterprising rats may impact Brown Noddy nests but presumably go for easier targets, such as Sooty Tern and boobies. Since the Brown Noddy colonies on Mona and Monito have not been monitored at the end of the breeding season, the degree of reproductive success cannot be estimated.

Sooty Tern

On Mona this tern nests on the ground under or close to vegetation. However, unlike in other sites around Puerto Rico, many Sooty Tern pairs at Mona nest under less than 50% vegetation cover, or even out in the open, and they shift colony sites in some years. Abandonment of Mona colony sites has been reported for Sooty Tern nesting on the plateau (as opposed to on rocks that have fallen from the cliff face); colony shifting and abandonment may be related to disturbance and mortality caused by introduced cats, rats, goats, and pigs on Mona. Sooty Tern nesting on fallen rocks do not experience mammalian predation, but the small number of suitable rocks for nesting may limit colony size increments on Mona. Although Sooty Tern nesting had been reported on Monito prior to 1976, they never nested there again; the heavy infestation of rats up to the mid-1990s may have deterred repeat nesting. Colonies on Mona and Monito have not been monitored at the end of the breeding season; the degree of reproductive success therefore cannot be estimated. Colony size has been decreasing between 2000 and 2004, and the current estimated number of nesting Sooty Tern on Mona is 200 pairs.

Bridled Tern

Selects caves and crevices of any size, which are common throughout the cliffs of Mona and Monito, nesting between May and August (last adults observed). Although nesting habitat appears to be plentiful, the number of pairs nesting on both islands is relatively small. The somewhat secretive nature of Bridled Tern and the inaccessibility of nesting areas make it difficult to ascertain population numbers, which are estimated at not more than 100 pairs. Bridled Tern apparently disperse soon after fledging, making it difficult to determine if successful fledging has occurred.

Desecheo Island

Desecheo is a small, mountainous island of about 150 ha in the Mona Passage, approximately 21 km west of Punta Higüero, Puerto Rico. Offshore rocks, abrupt coastal cliffs, limited landing sites, and steep, rocky topography restrict human use of the island. A high evaporation rate, combined with rapid runoff due to the steep topography, results in moisture deficiencies, which are evident in the vegetation during dry periods. The island has no permanent springs, streams, or standing water. Its vegetation is a mosaic of grassy patches, scrublands, woodlands, and semideciduous forest. The grassy patches and scrublands are on exposed ridges, especially on the northern and northeastern slopes, which face the prevailing winds. The woodlands generally are found on coastal slopes and upper east- and south-facing slopes. Early naturalists reported Desecheo to be a major rookery for seabirds, resulting in its being set aside as a preserve and breeding ground by President Taft in 1912. Despite this protected status, the island has been subject to considerable disturbance and modification for croplands, cattle farming, and crabbing. It was used as a bombing, training, and gunnery range until 1966, when the U.S. Department of Health, Education, and Welfare used it to introduce a colony of rhesus monkeys (*Macaca mulatta*). In December 1976 Desecheo was transferred to the U.S. Fish and Wildlife Service, which is now responsible for its management (including control of exotic species).

Large colonies of Brown Booby, Red-footed Booby, and Magnificent Frigatebird used Desecheo for breeding until degradation of vegetation notably reduced the available nesting habitat for tree-dwelling species, and the introduced monkeys, cats, goats, and rats impacted both ground- and tree-nesting seabirds. Less than 100 pairs of nesting Brown Booby were reported by the late 1980s, and Red-footed Booby and Magnificent Frigatebird have not returned to nest there (although small numbers of both species occasionally roost on Desecheo). Bridled Tern have been observed perched on the outcrops surrounding Desecheo Island; however, nesting has not been confirmed. Although no seabirds currently breed on Desecheo, they may return to nest once the eradication of cats, monkeys and goats is completed.

Threats and Conservation

The majority of seabird colonies in Puerto Rico are located on uninhabited offshore cays and islands, most of which are designated as either federal or commonwealth sanctuaries, refuges, or reserves. Public access is restricted on most of these cays. Casual visits to the seabird colonies do happen, which may conflict with seabird breeding season. For the most part, visits appear to be short in duration, and the greatest impact may be accidental stepping on eggs. However, colony abandonment can result from repeated or lengthy visits, particularly early in the breeding season. Limited law enforcement manpower in federal and commonwealth agencies and lack of permanent posting signs at some protected areas may account for the abandonment of some traditional nesting and roosting sites (e.g., abandonment of Magnificent Frigatebird rookery off Cuevas Island, Lajas, and Brown Pelican nesting on Turrumote, Lajas), possibly due to disturbance caused by weekend picnics, an increase in boat traffic, and jet-skis driving close to the colonies.

Octopus collectors may cause disturbance at one Brown Pelican colony, due to the proximity of the colony to shallow harvesting areas; but harvesting is seasonal, and only a few skillful collectors practice it. Traditional egg collecting for human consumption was a major concern 15–20 years ago (particularly on low-profile cays), but it appears that people have today lost interest in egg collecting or have become more educated about protecting natural resources; and with economic growth, the need for seabird eggs to supplement the diet of neighboring communities may have diminished.

Currently, the main threat to nesting seabirds on offshore cays around Puerto Rico is from introduced mammals—cats, dogs, rats, pigs, goats, monkeys, and white-tailed deer (*Odocoileus virginianus*)—which may all destroy eggs, young, and adult seabirds, trample nests, or cause colony abandonment. Efforts by government agencies to control or eliminate feral animals have had mixed results. Of all seabird nesting areas in Puerto Rico, only Monito Island has had a completely successful feral animal eradication program, in which rats have been eliminated. The program to control monkeys and goats at Desecheo Island has suppressed the populations, but without complete removal of these animals, their numbers are likely to increase and they will continue to be a threat to reestablishment of seabird colonies. Hunting of pigs and goats and controlled removal of cats continue on Mona Island, but these feral animals are still abundant, primarily because bag limits have been established (except for cats). None of the other seabird breeding areas has any feral mammal control program. A more aggressive eradication program geared toward total elimination of feral animals would greatly improve the chances of more seabird breeding cays becoming free of the threat of feral mammals.

Most seabird colonies in Puerto Rico are located in federally protected or Commonwealth lands; yet no education programs geared to specifically protecting these seabird colonies from human disturbance are currently in place. Posting signs has had mixed results. Intruders rip them up to use them as improvised picnic tables, seats, or rain shelters (e.g., Parguera Cays), or signs are destroyed by high seas or strong winds (e.g., Culebra Archipelago). Outreach for public awareness and education are essential to minimize human impacts to seabird roosting and nesting colonies. Target audiences for outreach may include but are not limited to local fishermen, communities near seabird colonies, marina operators, and applicants for boat licenses. Habitat and education materials on local seabird biology should be developed for these audiences and the general public. Opportunities must be sought to inform audiences and the general public about seabirds, through the media (television, radio, and newspapers), and to ensure that up-to-date information in news releases, publications, presentations, and displays accurately portrays the status, habitat needs, and conservation problems of seabird populations in Puerto Rico.

Acknowledgments

I would like to acknowledge Miguel Canals, John Chardine, Jaime Collazo, Sergio Colón, Dennis Corales, Manuel Cruz, Glenn Cullingford, Oscar Díaz, Hector Douglas III, Steve Earsom, Héctor Horta, Nilda Jiménez, Ricardo López, Winston Martínez, Alcides Morales, Henry Morales, Silmarie Padrón, Frank Rivera, Idelfonso Ruiz, Ilse Sanders, David Shealer, Teresa Tallevast, Alexander Torres, Adrianne Tossas, Maritza Vargas, Vance Vicente, and many other biologists and volunteers who provided much-needed field assistance, seabird reports, or valuable discussions. The U.S. Fish and Wildlife Service (Ecological Services and Caribbean Islands National Wildlife Refuge) and Puerto Rico Department of Natural and Environmental Resources also provided permission, logistical support, and guidance to compile data on the seabirds of Puerto Rico.

10

United States Virgin Islands

JUDY PIERCE

The U.S. Virgin Islands (USVI) include the three main islands of St. Thomas, St. John, and St. Croix and more than 50 small cays (maps 28, 29, 30). The offshore cays of the USVI comprise about 3% of the territory's total area. Each is illustrated and described by Dammann and Nellis (1992). Thirty-two of the smaller cays are owned by the Territorial Government of the USVI and form the Virgin Islands Wildlife Refuge Complex (table 10.1). Most of the important seabird islands are located off St. Thomas and St. John, are difficult to access, and are uninhabited. Habitats on the cays are varied, but all are included in the subtropical dry forest (Ewel and Whitmore 1973).

Prior to 1975, when the Division of Fish and Wildlife began a wildlife survey of the uninhabited cays (Dewey and Nellis 1980), little was known of the breeding biology and distribution of seabird species in the U.S. Virgin Islands. The first ornithological report on seabirds breeding on the cays came from Danforth (1935a), fol-

Table 10.1. Ownership of offshore islands and cays of the U.S. Virgin Islands

Territorial Government	Federal Government	Private
Booby Rock	*National Park Service*	Cinnamon Cay
Bovoni Cay	Buck Island (St. Croix)	Current Rock
Capella Island	Cocoloba Cay	Fish Cay
Carval Rock	Hassel Island (partial)	Great St. James Island
Cas Cay	Henley Cay	Green Cay (St. Thomas) (?)
Cockroach Cay	Ramgoat Cay	Hans Lollick Island
Congo Cay	Rata Cay	Hassel Island (partial)
Cricket Rock	Trunk Cay	Inner Brass Island
Dog Island	*USFWS - NWR*	Little Hans Lollick Is.
Dutchcap Cay	Buck Island (St. Thomas)	Little St. James Is.
Flanagan Island	Green Cay (St. Croix)	Lovango Cay
Flat Cay and Little Flat Cay	*U.S. Dept. of Interior*	Mingo Cay
Frenchcap Cay	Water Island (partial)	Patricia Cay
Grass Cay	*In Dispute*	Pelican Cay
Hassel Island (partial)	Ruth Cay	Rotto Cay
Kalkun Cay		Thatch Cay
Leduck Island		Water Island (partial)
Outer Brass Island		Waterlemon Cay (?)
Perkins Cay		
Protestant Cay		
Saba Island		
Sail Rock		
Salt Cay		
Savana Island		
Shark Island		
Steven Cay		
Sula Cay		
Turtledove Cay		
Two Brothers (?)		
Water Island (partial)		
West Cay		
Whistling Cay		

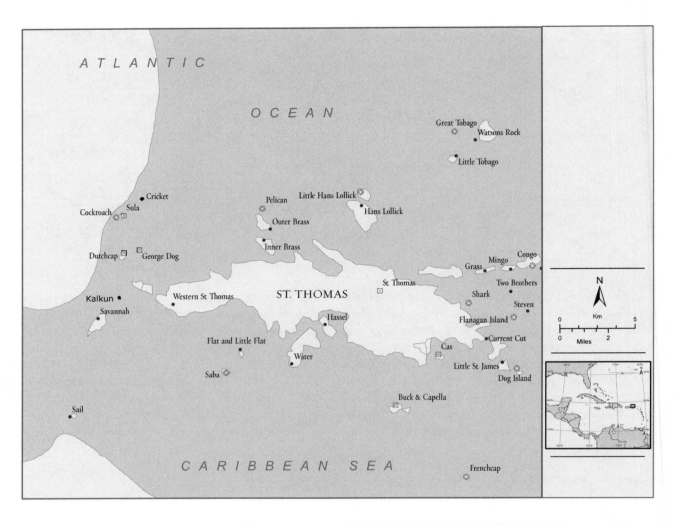

ATLANTIC

OCEAN

Great Tobago
Watsons Rock

Little Tobago

Little Hans Lollick
Cricket
Pelican
Sula
Cockroach
Outer Brass
Hans Lollick

Dutchcap
George Dog
Inner Brass

Grass
Mingo
Congo
St Thomas
Two Brothers
Kalkun
Western St Thomas
ST. THOMAS
Shark
Savannah
Steven
Hassel
Flanagan Island
Current Cut
Flat and Little Flat
Cas
Water
Little St James
Saba
Dog Island

Buck & Capella
Sail

Frenchcap
CARIBBEAN SEA

N

Km
0   5

Miles
0   2

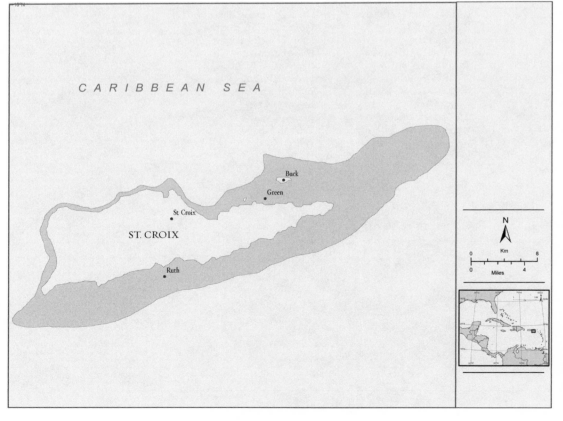

CARIBBEAN SEA

Buck

Green

St Croix
ST. CROIX
Ruth

N

Km
0   8

Miles
0   4

Above: Map 28. St. Thomas, U.S. Virgin Islands.

Left: Map 29. St. Croix, U.S. Virgin Islands.

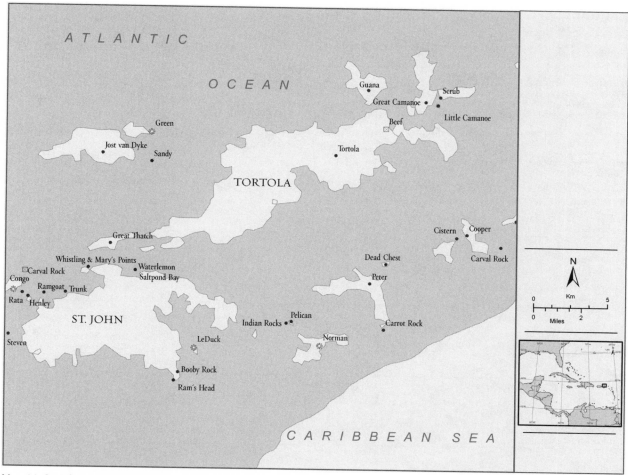

Map 30. St. John, U.S. Virgin Islands, and Tortola, British Virgin Islands.

Table 10.2. Estimates of seabird pairs breeding in the U.S. Virgin Islands

Species	Total Estimated Population
Audubon's Shearwater	20–?
White-tailed Tropicbird	30–?
Red-billed Tropicbird	225–350
Masked Booby	45–75
Brown Booby	500–1,000
Red-footed Booby	100–150
Brown Pelican	325–425
Laughing Gull	2,000–3,000
Brown Noddy	400–900
Sooty Tern	20,000–40,000?
Bridled Tern	500–1,000
Least Tern	300–600
Roseate Tern	500–2,300
Royal Tern	60–150
Sandwich Tern	100–1,000

lowed by Beatty (1941) and Nichols (1943), who both made more extensive observations of the cays. Additional contributions were made by Leopold (1963) and Kepler (1971). Since then, breeding seabirds in the USVI have been the subject of ongoing, long-term studies for several decades, primarily on the population status of breeding species (e.g., Dewey and Nellis 1980; Halewyn and Norton 1984; Pierce 1996a, b; Chardine et al. 2000a, b; Jackson 2000; Lee 2000b; Lindsay et al. 2000, Norton 2000; Saliva 2000a, b; Schreiber 2000b; and Walsh-McGehee 2000). Other studies include the distribution of Pelecaniformes at sea (Norton 1988a); the association of seabirds and game fish (Erdman 1967); breeding biology of the Red-billed Tropicbird (Pierce 1992), Brown Booby (Nellis and Pierce 1990), Least Tern (Sladen and Pierce 1988), Sooty Tern (Pierce 1996b, 1997), and Brown Noddy (Orton-Palmer 1990); cross-fostering of Masked Booby with Brown Booby (Nellis and Pierce 1991); and botulism in the Laughing Gull (Norton 1986b).

Estimates of seabird pairs breeding are given in table 10.2. With the exception of some tern species, most seabirds nest at the same colony year after year and rarely form new colonies. Due to availability of nest sites, different bird species nest on different cays. For example, Saba Island and Flat Cay harbor active rookeries during the summer months with nesting gulls and terns, while Cockroach Cay is known for its winter-nesting booby and tropicbirds (table 10.3; plate 38).

Nest sites preferred by seabirds include burrows (Audubon's Shearwater), cliffs (Brown Noddy), cliff holes (tropicbirds, Bridled Tern), trees (Brown Noddy,

Table 10.3. Number of nests of seabird species in the U.S. Virgin Islands and location of nesting colonies

	Audubon's Shearwater	White-tailed Tropicbird	Red-billed Tropicbird	Masked Booby	Brown Booby	Red-footed Booby	Brown Pelican
Booby Rock	B?						
Buck Island (St. Croix)							10–35
Buck Island (St. Thomas)	BU		<10				
Capella Island	B?		<10				
Carval Rock	B?	B?	<10				
Cas Cay		E	<5				
Cockroach Cay	5–10		100+	20–40	150–250		
Congo Cay	B?	<5	10–15				100–200
Cricket Rock	B?	B?	10–15		<5		
Current Rock							
Dog Island			<5				
15–300	25–85	100–800					
Dutchcap Cay	B?	B?	10–20		100–150	100–150	100–200
Flanagan Island	B?		<5				
Flat Cay (& Little Flat)	BU		<5				
Frenchcap Cay	BU		<5	2	200–350	BS	
Grass Cay		<5	5–10				
Great St. James Island			BU				
Green Cay (St. Croix)							25–50
Hans Lollick Island	B?	<5	10–25				BS few
Hassel Island		B?	<5				
Henley Cay							
Inner Brass Island			<10				BS
Kalkun Cay	B?		5–10		50–100		
LeDuck Island			B?				
Little Hans Lollick Island			B?				
Little St. James Island			<5				
Mary's Point, St. John							30–70
Mingo Cay		<5	15–25				
Outer Brass Island	B?	<5	5–10				
Pelican Cay	B?						
Ramgoat Cay							
Rata Cay							
Ruth Cay							
St. Croix proper							
Saltpond Bay, St. John							
Saba Island	BU		<5				
Sail Rock			B?				
Savana Island		B?	BU				
Shark Island			<5				
Steven Cay							
Sula Cay			<5	25–35	10–20		
Turtledove Cay	BU		B?				
Two Brothers			B?				
Water Island		<10	<10				
Waterlemon Cay							BS few
Whistling Cay			<5				35+
Total Population Estimate	20–?	30–?	225–350	45–75	500–1000	100–150	325–425

Notes: BU=breeds in unknown numbers, BS=breeds sometimes, B?=may breed.

Red-footed Booby, Brown Pelican, Magnificent Frigatebird), grassy flats or slopes (Brown Booby, Masked Booby, Sooty Tern, Laughing Gull), and exposed scrapes on hard soil (other terns).

Laughing Gull	Brown Noddy	Sooty Tern	Bridled Tern	Least Tern	Roseate Tern	Royal Tern	Sandwich Tern
5–20			5–20		BS		
				20–40			
100–200		BU?					
<5							
	25–75		20–40		BS 75+		
	20–40		10–30				
B?	BU		BU		BS 200–300		
	BU		BU		BS 20–150		
22+							
450+		<5			BS		
B?							
150+			B?		BS 200–1100		
217+	25–50	200–400	50–100		BS 20–200	BS	BS
<25	150–350	100–200	400+				
B?							
B?							
58+							
B?							
<10	10–20		10–20				
<5					BS 100–900		
400+		<5	<5		BS 25–1200		BS 200–700
B?							
B?							
B?							
15–20					BS 100–400	BS <5	BS 20–300
15+					BS 850+		
<5					BS 7–300		
				20–50			
				14 sites 300–600			
				BS 2–12			
100–200	100–300	20000–40000 ??	50–100			BS 20–600	
B?			BS 65–900				
<20							
407+	20–80	50–250			<20	180+	<30
			BS				
2000–3000	60–150	100–1000 (USVI only)	500–2300	300–600	500–1000	20000–40000 ??	400–900

Table 10.4. Breeding regimes of seabirds in the U.S. Virgin Islands

Species	Jan		Feb		Mar		Apr		May		Jun		Jul	
Audubon's Shearwater	X	X	X	X	X	X	X	X	X	X	X	X		
White-tailed Tropicbird			x		X	X	X	X	X	X	X	X	X	X
Red-billed Tropicbird	X	X	X	X	X	X	X	X	X	X	X	X		
Masked Booby	X	X	X	X	X	X	X	X	X	X	X	X	X	X
Brown Booby	X	X	X	X	X	X	X	X	X	X	X	X	X	X
Red-footed Booby	X	X	X	X	X	X	X	X	X	X	X	X	X	X
Brown Pelican	X	X	X	X	X	X	X	X	X	X	X	X	X	X
Laughing Gull						x	x	x	x	X	X	X	X	X
Noddy Tern									x	X	X	X	X	X
Sooty Tern							x	X	X	X	X	X	X	X
Bridled Tern									x	X	X	X	X	X
Least Tern							x	x	X	X	X	X	X	X
Roseate Tern									x	X	X	X	X	X
Royal Tern	x	x	x	x	x	x	x	x	x	X	X	X	X	X
Sandwich Tern									x	X	X	X	X	X

x = Occurrence; X = Breeding.

Methods of Survey

Methods described by Dewey and Nellis (1980) were employed for conducting censuses on the cays. All seabird islands were approached by snorkeling, except when sea conditions and an experienced boat handler permitted the occasional "bow-off." Cays with difficult access (i.e., difficulty of anchoring, landing, and climbing) were surveyed when sea conditions permitted. Population estimates were made during the breeding season for each species; however, conducting surveys during nesting peaks was not always feasible. Population estimates may be biased due to nest inaccessibility. Selected areas or species were surveyed more frequently than others due to sampling logistics and abundance of certain species.

Population estimates are expressed as pairs of breeding birds based on actual nest counts or estimates of nests observed from a boat. For Sooty Tern on Saba, transects were used to count the number of eggs; the average egg density was then multiplied by the estimated area of the colony. For species with nests that are widely scattered (Brown Noddy) or often well hidden (Bridled Tern), a combination of counts of adults and direct nest counts was used to give a rough indication of the number of breeding pairs. Censusing of densely packed tern colonies (Roseate, Sandwich, and Royal terns) was done during late incubation and during early morning hours to reduce exposure of eggs and chicks to direct sun. Since the seasonality of the booby colonies is less defined, work at these colonies was always scheduled for early morning hours in case eggs and small chicks might be present.

Species Accounts

Of 39 species of seabirds that have been recorded, 15 breed in the USVI; two of these are considered threatened (Roseate Tern) or endangered (Brown Pelican) by the U.S. Fish and Wildlife Service (USFWS), and two more are considered territorially endangered. Boobies (family Sulidae), pelicans (Pelecanidae), and frigatebirds (Fregatidae) are present year round but seasonal in their nesting activities; in contrast, shearwaters (Procellariidae), tropicbirds (Phaethontidae), and gulls and terns (Laridae) are present nearshore only during the breeding season (table 10.4).

The widely distributed Magnificent Frigatebird historically nested on Dutchcap Cay (30 pairs; Nichols 1943), but currently the only nesting colony in the region is in the British Virgin Islands (Pierce 1996a; Lindsay et al. 2000). Frigatebirds regularly forage and roost in the USVI, where they often become hooked or entangled by fishing gear.

Of ten species of jaegers and gulls, only one breeds. The widely distributed Laughing Gull routinely feeds on food discarded by humans and has thus benefited from human activities, and because gulls of this species often prey on the eggs and young of smaller tern species, including the federally threatened Roseate Tern, their burgeoning populations are of concern. The remaining species are all Nearctic migrants that rarely winter or pass through the USVI during migration.

Of 15 species of terns (family Laridae), seven are known to breed; some colony sites and populations generally fluctuate from year to year, sometimes dramati-

Aug		Sep		Oct		Nov		Dec	
								?	
X	X	x	?						
				X	X	X	X	X	X
X	X	X	X	X	X	X	X	X	X
X	X	X	X	X	X	X	X	X	X
X	X	X	X	X	X	X	X	X	X
X	X	X	X	X	X	X	X	X	X
X	X	x	x	x	x				
X	X	x	x						
X	X	x	x						
X	X	x	x						
X	x								
X	x	x	x						
X	X	x	x	x	x	x	x	x	x
X	X	x	x						

cally (Pierce 1996a, b; Chardine et al. 2000a, b; Jackson 2000; Norton 2000; Saliva 2000a, b). With the exception of the Brown Noddy, all terns in the Virgin Islands nest on the ground.

The Cayenne Tern, currently considered a South American race of the Sandwich Tern, nests in small numbers among colonies of the Sandwich Tern, with which it hybridizes; the systematic relationship between the two taxa is poorly understood (Norton 1984, 2000; Hayes 2004). Although small numbers of Royal Tern and Sandwich Tern from North American populations winter in the USVI, the remaining species depart from the USVI during winter. Current population estimates for 15 species of seabirds breeding in the USVI are given in table 10.2.

Audubon's Shearwater

Of the six species of petrels, shearwaters, and storm-petrels recorded, the territorially endangered Audubon's Shearwater is the only one that breeds in the USVI. Nesting begins in December–January, with chicks fledging during June–July. Small numbers, thought to be less than 50 pairs, currently nest on five cays off St. Thomas: Saba Island and Cockroach, Flat, Sula, and Frenchcap cays (Pierce 1996a; Lee 2000b). An abandoned egg was found on Buck Island, off St. Thomas (Pierce, unpubl.). The report by Nichols (1943) of approximately 150 pairs on Saba, where young were harvested for food by fishermen, suggests a significant decline. However, there have been no systematic searches of active nesting burrows, which are difficult to locate because the widely dispersed nests are often hidden. Nesting may be overlooked on other islands. Shearwaters are nocturnal, and nests are located in burrows or rock crevices; breeding likely occurs on all islands with suitable habitat. Peregrine Falcons are suspected of killing adults and chicks on Cockroach Cay, where they also take tropicbirds (Pierce 1996a). Disoriented fledglings have been found at the St. Thomas airport (close to Saba Island) and on the steps of a restaurant at the east end of St. Thomas.

White-tailed Tropicbird

The White-tailed Tropicbird breeds primarily on Congo Cay, Hans Lollick Island, and Water Island off St. Thomas, and several pairs nest along the south shore cliffs on St. Croix proper, where the current population is thought to number less than 50 pairs (Pierce 1996a; Walsh-McGehee 2000). However, Nichols (1943) reported 20 pairs nesting on Cas Cay, where they no longer nest, suggesting a steep decline in the USVI.

The White-tailed Tropicbird is smaller than the Red-billed Tropicbird, but nesting habits are generally similar. White-tailed Tropicbirds are more likely to be seen about the larger islands than the Red-billed Tropicbird, which shows a preference for smaller islands and cays. The breeding season occurs from April through August.

Red-billed Tropicbird

The more common Red-billed Tropicbird breeds on at least 14 cays off St. Thomas and St. John, with a current population estimate of 225–350 pairs (Pierce 1992; Pierce 1996a; Walsh-McGehee 2000).

The Red-billed Tropicbird in the USVI has an extended breeding season, starting roughly in October and lasting six months or more, with peak numbers of eggs between January and March (Pierce 1992). One egg is laid on a cliff ledge or in a rock crevice, where eggs and young are protected from extremes of temperature and weather. Many nests are inaccessible and dangerous to survey owing to their location on steep cliff faces around the edges of the islands. Aiding in detection of nesting birds in accessible areas is the tropicbird's habit of making repeated aerial approaches to the nest site before landing and disappearing into the nest crevice.

The majority of nests are found on Cockroach Cay, followed by Hans Lollick Island, Mingo Cay, Congo Cay, Kalkun Cay, and Buck and Capella islands. Inaccessible colonies on Grass Cay, Carval Rock, Inner Brass Island, Outer Brass Island, Savannah Island, and Water Island were surveyed by boat, with the number of flying adults used as the breeding population estimate. Besides the pelican colony at Mary Point, St. John, tropicbirds may be the only seabird species currently nesting on the main islands of St. Thomas and St. John, although in extremely small numbers. Individual birds have been sighted circling the cliffs on Peterborg Point, St. Thomas, and Rams Head, St. John.

Marked nests and banded birds were used to study the population on six offshore cays from 1988 to 1991 (Pierce 1992). Results of this study showed a sharp decline in the number of nests on Buck and Capella islands and Cas Cay. Peregrine Falcons were routinely seen patrolling the colonies, and numerous dead adults and nestlings were found in all the tropicbird colonies with wounds that were consistent with a falcon attack. Capella Island is a favored roost site for at least one Peregrine that was flushed on nearly every visit to the island. A falcon feather was found among the feathers of a recently killed tropicbird at the mouth of a nesting cave on Mingo Cay. On Congo Cay, a peregrine was observed to enter a tropicbird nest site (Pierce, unpubl.). Nest sites left unoccupied by the birds that died have remained unused in subsequent years, suggesting that recruitment of new birds into the population is not keeping up with the mortality rate (Pierce 1992).

Intraspecific fighting between Red-billed Tropicbirds in the nesting colonies has been observed; however, no aggression between breeding Red-billed and White-tailed Tropicbird has been observed at any of the colonies. Nest site competition may be avoided in the Virgin Islands because of different seasonality and the White-

tails' habit of nesting on the larger islands. Availability of nest sites for tropicbirds does not appear to be a limiting factor for Virgin Islands colonies.

Two episodes of avian pox virus (1988 and 1996) were observed in Red-billed Tropicbird chicks on Buck and Capella islands (Pierce, unpubl.).

Masked Booby

The Masked Booby is the least common booby in the USVI. It is the largest of the three species of sulid nesting in the Caribbean (the other two being Brown Booby and Red-footed Booby). Masked Booby are sexually dimorphic in size (females are larger than males) and voice (females honk, males whistle) but not in plumage.

The Masked Booby nests on relatively bare ground on Cockroach Cay and adjoining Sula Cay, off St. Thomas, with 45–75 pairs (Pierce 1996a; Schreiber 2000b). Being a large bird, the Masked Booby requires cleared areas in which to take off into the prevailing wind. Observations in the early 1980s suggested that vegetation encroachment was causing a gradual reduction in nest sites; however, subsequent clearing of vegetation failed to increase the breeding population (Pierce 1996a). An attempt to establish a second colony at Frenchcap Cay, off St. Thomas, began in 1981 with periodic transfer of eggs to Brown Booby nests. The cross-fostering experiment achieved limited success, with a few individuals hatched on the island returning annually to breed (Nellis and Pierce 1991; Pierce 1996a; Pierce, unpubl.).

Masked Booby in the Virgin Islands nest primarily in the winter and spring. Like the Brown Booby, they nest on the ground and lay one or two eggs but raise only one chick.

Brown Booby

The most common and widely distributed sulid in the USVI. Sexual dimorphism is evident in soft parts coloration around the bill (yellow-apricot in females, grayish green in males) as well as in vocalizations, which are similar to those of the Masked Booby (females honk, males whistle). Brown Booby are primarily inshore feeders. Like the Masked Booby, Brown Booby normally lay two eggs and raise only one chick. Brown Booby nests can be found throughout the year, the peak season being fall to winter at most colonies.

Brown Booby breeding colonies occur on five cays: Sula Island and Cockroach, Dutchcap, Kalkun, and Frenchcap cays. A few nests (< 10) have been observed on Cricket Cay and Sail Rock. The total breeding population in the USVI is estimated at 500–1,000 breeding pairs (Pierce 1996a; Schreiber 2000b). Frenchcap Cay has the largest Brown Booby colony, on average about 250 nesting pairs. The total breeding population in 1996 dropped dramatically as a result of Hurricane Marilyn, which slammed the USVI in September 1995 (Pierce 1996a).

Peregrine Falcon predation on Brown Booby chicks has been especially evident on Frenchcap Cay, a short flight from a Peregrine's roost site on Capella Island. On Frenchcap, falcons have been observed flying in a head down position, seeming to search vegetation for booby chicks. Dead booby chicks were observed during the winter months in the late 1980s with wounds to the back of the neck. Intense predation on booby chicks protracted the breeding season into late spring and summer months when adult boobies renested and Peregrines are absent from the territory. Since about 1990, peak egg laying on Frenchcap has occurred during late spring and early summer, in contrast to the usual fall–winter breeding peak.

Red-footed Booby

The smallest of the three booby species that nest in the USVI, the Red-footed Booby nests in trees, in contrast to ground-nesting Masked and Brown Booby. This species has two color morphs, brown and white: approximately 70% on Dutchcap Cay are brown morphs (Pierce, unpubl.). For both morphs, the tail is white, a diagnostic feature to distinguish this species in flight from the Masked Booby (similar to white morph) and juvenile Brown Booby (similar to brown morph). Intermediate morphs have been observed in the Virgin Islands colonies. In the Virgin Islands, this species has an annual breeding season, with nests from summer to fall, similar to the Red-footed colony on Monito, Puerto Rico (Kepler 1978).

Currently, the Red-footed Booby breeds only at Dutchcap Cay, off St. Thomas, with 100–150 breeding pairs (Pierce 1996a; Schreiber 2000b). A small colony at Frenchcap Cay (2–21 pairs) that formed in the early 1980s has been abandoned for the last few years, likely as a result of habitat loss (nesting Ficus sp. trees) due to hurricanes (Pierce, unpubl.). A former breeding colony of 30 pairs at Sula Cay (Nichols 1943) was extirpated when the nesting trees were destroyed by the U.S. military (Pierce 1996a). Red-footed Booby took over a year to return to Dutchcap Cay following Hurricane Hugo in 1989.

Brown Pelican

The federally endangered Caribbean race of the Brown Pelican breeds in the northern USVI at Congo Cay, Dutchcap Cay, Whistling Cay, and Mary Point on St. John, and on Buck Island, St. Croix. Small colonies occur sporadically on Hans Lollick Island and Waterlemon Cay and on Green Cay, St. Croix (Lombard, unpubl.). Nests may be found in any month of the year; asynchrony exists between as well as within colonies. Spatially separated subgroups show synchrony in laying within the colonies. Colonies on Congo Cay, Whistling Cay, and Mary Point, St. John, were surveyed by boat. White fluffy chicks were easily counted, while pelicans sitting in incubating positions were assumed to have eggs or small chicks.

According to Collazo and Klaas (1986), nesting populations in the USVI declined from over 475 nesting pairs during 1980 to approximately 350–400 in 1982. The current minimum breeding population of Brown Pelican in the USVI is estimated to be 325–425 pairs (Pierce 1996a; Collazo et al. 2000). Although the endangered Brown Pelican maintains a relatively stable population, in spite of having been actively engaged in nesting during the two most severe hurricanes to hit the Virgin Islands in decades, this population level does not meet the criteria to delist the species in this region under the Recovery Plan for the Brown Pelican (USFWS 1986).

Laughing Gull

The Laughing Gull is the only gull that breeds in the U.S. Virgin Islands. A common and widespread summer breeder, the Laughing Gull is the first summer migrant to reach the territory, arriving in March. During March and April large flocks of adult gulls congregate at St. Thomas harbor, at the St. Thomas landfill, and on the runway at the airport. Nesting begins in May on most of the offshore cays, when 1–3 greenish, spotted eggs are laid on the ground in a nest of woven vegetation. Most gulls depart the territory by October.

In the summer of 2000, the larger Laughing Gull colonies in the USVI were censused to get a better estimate of the total population. The largest Laughing Gull colonies occur at Dog Island, Turtledove Cay, Little Hans Lollick Island, Saba Island, Flanagan Cay, Flat Cay, and Buck Island, St. Thomas. These large colonies alone account for about 2,000 nesting pairs, with numerous smaller colonies (< 100 nests) occurring on most of the offshore cays. The estimated breeding population, therefore, is 2,000–3,000 pairs, similar to the number of nesting pairs given by Chardine et al. (2000a).

Laughing Gulls are a major predator on seabird eggs and young in the USVI and have been observed puncturing pelican and booby eggs when adults flew off the nest (Pierce 1996a); gulls have been seen carrying off Sandwich Tern eggs on Pelican Cay (the large gull colony on Little Hans Lollik is a short flight away); and they were observed consuming noddy eggs and chicks on Frenchcap Cay (Orton-Palmer 1990). Douglas (2001) reported that Laughing Gulls were "the most persistent predators" of Roseate Tern eggs and chicks on LeDuck Island, with more attacks than workers were able to record. Increasing numbers of Laughing Gull could pose a serious threat to tern productivity in the USVI. Long-term monitoring of their colonies should be done at intervals of at least every five years.

Brown Noddy

Brown Noddy arrive at the nesting colonies during late April and early May. The species is widespread and common in the USVI during the breeding season, which extends through August. An egg was observed in early August on Frenchcap Cay (Pierce 1996a). The total Brown Noddy population estimate of 400–900 breeding pairs is based on a combination of direct nest counts, numbers of adults attending colonies, and boat surveys of inaccessible sites (Pierce 1996a; Chardine et al. 2000b). The largest colonies are located on Frenchcap Cay and Saba Island.

Brown Noddy in the USVI nest in three habitat types: cliff ledges and small rock outcroppings, trees (*Ficus* sp.), and on the ground. Cliff-nesting noddies on Frenchcap had the highest nest success due to the mobbing behavior of adults in response to predators (Orton-Palmer 1990). Brown Noddy exhibit year-to-year site and mate tenacity (Morris and Chardine 1992).

Sooty Tern

The most abundant seabird breeding in the USVI as well as in the wider Caribbean region. Sooty Tern in the Virgin Islands nest under vegetation (Pierce 1996b, 1997), in contrast to most other tropical nesting sites, where they prefer to nest in the open, even when vegetation is available (Ashmole 1963a; Feare 1976c; Harrington 1974).

Sooty Tern nest at four locations in the USVI. Saba Island, the largest colony, supports about 30,000 breeding pairs (Pierce 1996b; Saliva 2000a). On Saba, eggs are laid in late April or early May. The first birds land on the western slope of Saba, with birds gradually occupying nesting territory eastward. Accurately estimating numbers of breeding Sooty Tern on Saba Island is difficult because of the extremely varied habitat and tremendous range in egg densities throughout the island and from year to year. For example, more eggs were laid in 1994, during an extremely dry year. During 1995 birds arrived late, and counts of eggs along transect lines were almost half that of the previous year. In 1996 counts returned to about the level seen in 1993 (Pierce 1996b). Saba Island is one of the most accessible offshore cays. In 1977 two fishermen were convicted in federal court for taking 1,600 Sooty Tern eggs from Saba Island (Dewey and Nellis 1980).

Smaller colonies of 50–200 breeding pairs are found on Flat Cay, Frenchcap Cay, and Turtledove Cay. One Sooty egg was found on Dog Island in 1993 and 1994, the first Sooty Tern breeding record for that island. A single egg was found in the Laughing Gull colony on Little Hans Lollik in 2000, and an adult was heard during a census of the Laughing Gull colony on Buck Island, St. Thomas, in 2003 (Pierce, unpubl.). The interval between nesting at Saba and at the smaller colonies is about 7 to 10 days.

There is evidence of population mixing of Sooty Tern by the exchange of banded birds with other Caribbean archipelagos. An immature bird banded on Saba Island was found breeding off Aruba, suggesting that Saba may be an important source of recruits for other colonies in the Caribbean (Report to Bander, Bird Banding Laboratory 1988). In Culebra, Furniss (1983) found evidence of intercolony shifts within Culebra as well as intermixing of birds with colonies as far away as the Dry Tortugas, Florida. During intense banding efforts on Saba Island in the early 1980s, Division of Fish and Wildlife staff recaptured breeding birds that were banded in Culebra (Norton 1985).

Bridled Tern

There is a close physical resemblance between the Bridled Tern and the Sooty Tern, but breeding regimes are much different. Bridled Tern nest in small, loose aggregations and conceal their nests under low vegetation or boulders and in cliff holes, making them difficult to census. The reproductive cycles of Bridled Tern are poorly documented.

The species is widespread in the USVI, nesting on many of the small offshore cays with suitable habitat. The two largest colonies of Bridled Tern occur on Saba Island and Frenchcap Cay. A total of 500–1,000 pairs probably nest in the USVI (Chardine et al. 2000a), but more intense surveys are needed to verify the accuracy of this estimate.

Least Tern

The territorially endangered Least Tern depends on beaches and salt flats for nest sites. The species nests on St. Croix and two of its offshore cays, with an estimated population of 300–600 pairs (D. B. McNair and C. Lombard, unpubl.). In recent years a few have nested at Salt Pond Bay on St. John (L. Brannick-Trager, pers. comm.). Available data suggest that the population has suffered a serious decline in St. Croix (Sladen and Pierce 1989), primarily due to human disturbance and problems with a number of exotic mammalian predators, which are harder to control on the larger islands.

Least Tern first arrive in mid-April. Nesting begins in early May and continues into August. Adults and juveniles congregate on staging grounds in September. The last sighting is in late September or early October. The birds have been recorded nesting at 26 sites on St. Croix. This includes the dry bed of coastal salt ponds, beaches, a dredge spoil pile, a gravel parking lot, and the containment areas around storage tanks, road, and parking lots at the Hess Oil of the Virgin Islands facility (HOVIC).

The USVI Division of Fish and Wildlife and North Carolina State University have launched a cooperative study (Lombard and Collazo, principal investigators) to assess the status of the species in St. Croix, including breeding productivity, survival of nestlings, and a test of mammalian predation schemes aimed at reducing egg and chick losses.

Roseate Tern

The Caribbean population of the Roseate Tern is federally listed as threatened (U.S. Fish and Wildlife Service 1987). A portion of this listing is based on the biological evidence that about half of the western Atlantic breeding population nests in the Virgin Islands (Gochfeld et al. 1998; Saliva 2000b; Pierce 2001); that breeding populations are apparently declining (U.S. Fish and Wildlife Service 1993); and that juveniles and possibly adults breeding here are taken for food and/or feathers in South America (Nisbet 1980; Hays et al. 1997). Manque Seco, Brazil, appears to be an important nonbreeding area for Caribbean Roseate Tern (Hays et al. 1999).

Egg laying occurs from mid-May to early June; typically clutches have 1–2 eggs. Eggs are laid directly on the ground, rock, or vegetation, with little or no nest material added. The more exposed nest sites of the Caribbean birds make eggs and young chicks vulnerable to predators when the parents are off the nest. Roseate Tern colonies in the USVI are particularly vulnerable because the nesting populations are often precariously situated on islands that are located near heavily used tourist areas or that are subject to predation from other animals. These colonies are readily accessible to illegal egg collecting, which often results in colony abandonment.

In contrast to most breeding seabirds in the USVI, Roseate Tern may choose a suitable nesting location in one year and ignore it in other years, or they may choose the same islands in successive years. The large year-to-year variation in numbers of nests at colonies in the USVI led to the idea that exchange of breeders occurs between the USVI, British Virgin Islands, and Puerto Rico (Pierce 2001). Nest counts at colonies in the British Virgin Islands and Puerto Rico are therefore added to USVI nest counts whenever possible to get a more accurate population estimate. The total Roseate Tern breeding population in the U.S. and British Virgin Islands is about 2,500 pairs (Halewyn and Norton 1984; Saliva 2000b; Pierce 2001).

In the USVI, certain offshore cays tend to be favored, such as Kalkun Cay and Shark Island, possibly because of the proximity of bait fish aggregations used for food. Since 1987, none of the 17 breeding sites recorded in the USVI has been used in every year (Pierce 2001). Such unpredictable and sporadic use of nesting colonies hinders attempts to manage them.

Colonies range in size from less than 100 birds to more than 1,000 (Pierce 2001). Large colonies tend to be more successful than smaller colonies, likely as a result of more effective mobbing behavior toward aerial predators. In 1998, Roseates nested for the first time on rat-infested Congo Cay (273 nests); all the eggs were promptly depredated by rats within three days. Colonies are vulnerable to predation by Laughing Gull, Red-tailed Hawk (*Buteo jamaicensis*), Yellow-crowned Night-Heron (*Nycticorax violacea*), fire ants (*Solenopsis* spp.), land crabs (*Geocarcinus ruricola*), and hermit crabs (*Coenobita clypeatus*) and on low-lying cays by shorebirds (Ruddy Turnstone, *Arenaria interpes*, and American Oystercatcher, *Haematopus palliates*).

Royal Tern

The Royal Tern is the only tern that can be seen in the territory year round. Recaptures of banded Royal Tern outside the breeding season have been migrants from northern colonies.

Nesting habits and fledging periods are similar to those of the Sandwich Tern. This species often breeds in association with Sandwich Tern, where eggs are densely packed into tight colonies. Royal Tern nest counts have fluctuated year to year, from a low of 65 to a high of 150.

Sandwich Tern

Like the Roseate Tern, Sandwich Tern may nest on different islands in successive years, but Dog Island, Turtledove Cay, and Pelican Cay have supported most of the breeding populations of Sandwich Tern and Royal Tern in the USVI. The two species tend to nest together on grassy or rock flats, usually in close proximity to nesting Laughing Gull. Cayenne Tern are occasionally found breeding with Sandwich Tern (Norton 1984; Hayes 2004).

The number of nesting Sandwich Tern in the USVI colonies is highly variable, from as few as 28 nesting pairs on Flat Cay to about 800 nesting pairs on Dog Island (Pierce 1996a). The total USVI breeding population is probably no more than 1,000 pairs.

Threats

Despite the relative inaccessibility of nesting sites on offshore cays to humans and mammalian predators, the breeding seabird populations of the USVI remain threatened by a variety of factors. Excessive human disturbance results in overheating of eggs and small chicks, sometimes provoking abandonment by adults. The Division of Fish and Wildlife has maintained sanctuary signs on the important seabird cays to limit foot traffic into the seabird colonies and to inform the public of conservation restrictions, but their effectiveness is questionable.

Seabird eggs, mistakenly referred to by locals as "booby eggs," were sold openly in Charlotte Amalie, St. Thomas, a few decades ago (Lamb 1957). Although federal and local legislation prohibit the activity in the USVI, egging has been a serious problem for open ground nesters such as Sooty Terns and Roseate Terns, and some egging probably still occurs.

The effect of predation by other birds, such as the Laughing Gull and Peregrine Falcon, may pose a serious threat to reproductive success and should be evaluated. Other potential predators of local seabirds include Red-tailed Hawk, Yellow-crowned Night-Heron, Ruddy Turnstone, and land and hermit crabs. Short-eared Owl (*Asio flammeus*) have been reported preying on terns in Puerto Rico (J. Saliva, pers. comm.). Fire ants are found on all the offshore cays and can enter pipped eggs or kill newly hatched chicks. With the exception of rats, introduced mammals are not a major threat to seabird breeding success in the USVI.

The threat of introduced plants and animals to the cays is ever present. Boats frequently run aground during storms, potentially introducing rats to the cays. Predation by introduced rats has been implicated in the decline of seabirds in the USVI (Campbell 1991). The Division of Fish and Wildlife (DFW) eliminated rats on Dog Island, Stevens Cay, and Kalkun Cay in the 1980s (Boulon and Nellis 1985). Rat eradication efforts are ongoing at Saba Island, Dutchcap Cay, Congo Cay, Buck

Island (St. Thomas), Capella Island and Green and Ruth Cays off St. Croix. The Indian mongoose (*Herpestes auropunctatus*) is not known to be on any of the islands; it has been recently eradicated from Buck Island.

Goats thrive on Inner and Outer Brass Islands, Little Hans Lollick Island, Mingo Cay, and Grass Cay, where they are periodically hunted. Goats were recently eradicated on Dutchcap Cay through a joint effort by DFW and USDA–Wildlife Services. Yet another potential threat is the introduction of exotic plant species, for which impacts on wildlife are poorly known.

The entanglement of seabirds in fishing line, especially on the breeding grounds, is a threat that often goes undetected because the breeding areas are not visited on a regular basis. Fishermen who catch seabirds while trolling often do not take the time to unhook the bird properly and instead cut the line. The returning bird trails yards of fishing line, further entangling other birds at the breeding colony. At the frigatebird colony in the British Virgin Islands we counted 46 dead birds entangled in fishing line, which snared them as they landed in the nesting trees. Young boobies and pelicans are especially vulnerable to getting snared in monofilament fishing line.

Major storms, such as Hurricanes Hugo (1989) and Marilyn (1995), have had profound direct and indirect effects on seabirds. Periodic hurricanes and tropical storms pose a threat to the cays by damaging or destroying trees, including nest sites for seabirds, and by increasing erosion. Catastrophic storms alter nesting habitat in the colonies by uprooting trees and ground cover, destroying nests, and killing adult and immature birds.

Other threats include declining fish stocks due to pollution and overfishing.

Conservation

In 1973, the government of the U.S. Virgin Islands set aside Flat Cay, Little Flat Cay, Saba Island, and Turtledove Cay as wildlife reserves, affording some protection from the poaching of seabird eggs and from habitat deterioration. Some cays, including Bovoni Cay and Cas Cay, were subsequently donated to the government. Additional legislation has been promulgated to designate all offshore cays owned by the territorial government (or government-owned sections of them) as wildlife reserves. The Commissioner of the Department of Planning and Natural Resources (DPNR) is charged with the governmental responsibility of protecting and managing these cays. Within the DPNR, the DFW is the agency responsible for the assessment of marine and wildlife resources. Current funding levels at DFW are limited and no local funds are provided to support wildlife conservation. The Bureau of Wildlife consists of one wildlife chief and one wildlife biologist for St. Thomas and St. John and one wildlife biologist for St. Croix.

Because funding for the DFW is derived exclusively from federal grants, which prohibit law enforcement, the DFW depends on other federal and territorial government agencies for enforcing laws impacting wildlife. However, enforcement of these laws has been lax and remains a major impediment to effective management and conservation of wildlife resources (Platenberg et al. 2005). Routine patrols at the important breeding sites when colonies are most vulnerable are badly needed.

All federally owned cays are protected within Virgin Islands National Park, Hassel Island National Monument, or Buck Island National Monument or as national wildlife refuges.

Acknowledgments

Seabird surveys were funded by the U.S. Fish and Wildlife Service Wildlife Restoration Grants W5 and W11, administered by Region 4 Federal Aid, Atlanta, Georgia, to the Government of the Virgin Islands, Department of Planning and Natural Resources, Division of Fish and Wildlife. I would like to thank Carol Baum, Ruth Gomez, Kevin Haddox, Daniel Nellis, Jorge Saliva, David Shealer, and Doug Teitge for assistance in the field. Thanks also to Larry Aubain, Ruth Gomez, and the Division of Environmental Enforcement, especially Robert Danet (retired), for assistance with boat transportation to the islands.

11

British Virgin Islands

E. A. SCHREIBER AND JUDY PIERCE

The British Virgin Islands (BVI) consist of about 60 islands, islets, and cays located 160 km east of Puerto Rico (maps 30–32). The total land mass is 153 km² and other than the flat Anegada, all the islands rise significantly from the sea (maximum height 500 m). Only 16 islands are inhabited; the total population is about 25,000. But most of the others are frequently visited by boaters (both tourists and locals) so that none is undisturbed. Development of all accessible islands has restricted seabirds to nesting on remote, small islands, often with inappropriate habitat in which the birds do not have highly successful reproduction. The long history of human persecution has led to the loss of many seabird nesting colonies and of at least two, if not four, nesting species.

The Caribbean is considered one of the world's "biodiversity hotspots." A hotspot is defined as an area of the planet that is critical to preserving the diversity of life on earth. Conservation International (Washington, D.C.) has designated 25 threatened regions in the world as hotspots of biodiversity. These areas, while representing only 1.4% of the land surface of the earth, hold 60% of all plant and animal species. Five of the regions named are tropical archipelagos, pointing out the severe conservation problems that islands suffer today.

The published record of the seabird biodiversity of the BVI is incomplete, even for species as visible as these. Because of this, our knowledge of current population sizes and trends is minimal, and our ability to propose appropriate conservation action is hindered. There are indications that numbers of seabirds are greatly reduced today from historical levels. Essentially all accounts by early explorers discuss the consumption of seabirds by local inhabitants (Wetmore 1918; Brodkorb 1963; Halewyn and Norton 1984), consumption that is believed to have begun with the first Indian inhabitants over 2,000 years ago. This consumption continues today, mainly of eggs.

Species Accounts

Seventeen species of seabirds bred in the British Virgin Islands 100 years ago. Today, probably 14 to 16 do (table 11.1). Masked Booby is now extirpated (table 11.2; Halewyn and Norton 1984), and Audubon's Shearwater and Red-footed Booby may be (Lee 2000b; Schreiber 2000b). Of the known breeding species, one is listed as endangered (Brown Pelican) and one as threatened (Roseate Tern) in the adjacent territory of the U.S. Virgin Islands by the U.S. Fish and Wildlife Service. An assessment of breeding seabird subspecies in the West Indies (Schreiber and Lee 2000a) also lists four species as vulnerable (Red-billed Tropicbird, White-tailed Tropicbird, Least Tern, Sandwich Tern), and two as threatened (Audubon's Shearwater, Magnificent Frigatebird). Our best assessment of the status of the species from the

Table 11.1. Status of seabird pairs breeding in the British Virgin Islands

Species	Nesting pairs
Audubon's Shearwater	0–20
White-tailed Tropicbird	60–80
Red-billed Tropicbird	80–100
Brown Booby	170–275
Red-footed Booby	1
Brown Pelican	300–400
Magnificent Frigatebird	400–800
Laughing Gull	1,000–2,000
Brown Noddy	100–300
Sooty Tern	100
Bridled Tern	150–250
Least Tern	100
Gull-billed Tern	0–4
Roseate Tern	600–2,000
Royal Tern	Breeds
Sandwich Tern	120

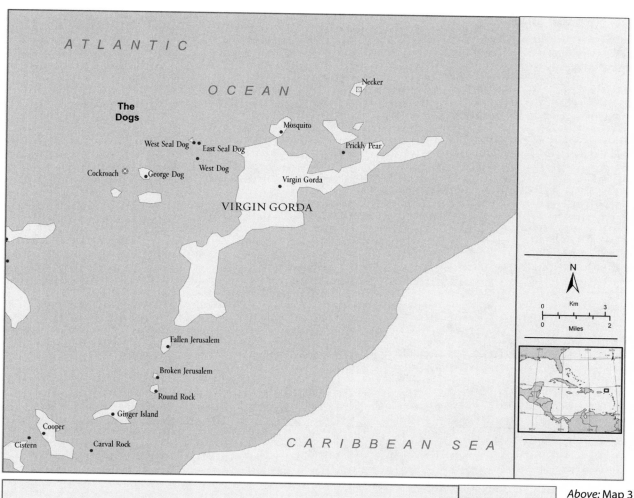

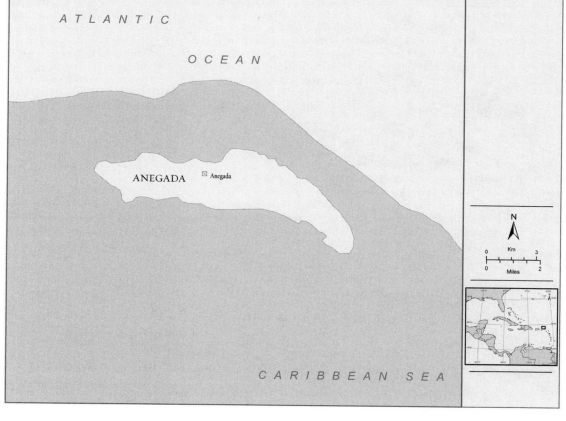

Above: Map 31. Virgin Gorda, British Virgin Islands.

Left: Map 32. Anegada, British Virgin Islands.

Table 11.2. Number of nests of seabird species in the British Virgin Islands, location of nesting colonies and time of egg laying (months when eggs are present)

Location	Audubon's Shearwater Dec–Feb	White-tailed Tropicbird May–Aug	Red-billed Tropicbird Oct–Feb	Brown Booby Sept–Dec; Yr. round	Red-footed Booby Sept–Apr	Brown Pelican Apr–May; Aug–Oct	Magn. Frigatebird Aug–Nov
Anegada	E?						E
Beef Is.	B?		B?				
Camanoe Isl.		B?	2				
Carrot Rock		Bu	4				
Carval Rock		Bu	4	10			
Cooper Is.[b]	B?						
Cockroach[a] & Dog Isles	B?	B?	Bu				
Dead Chest		B?	B?				
Fallen Jerusalem[a, c]		Bu	Bu				
Ginger	Bu	B?	Bu	10		E?	
Great Thatch	B?	B?	B?				
Great Tobago[a]	B?	5–12	10–30	120–200	1s		400–500
Little Tobago[a]	B?		Bu	50–75		50–75	
Green Cay			Bu				
Guana Is		4–8	6–15			50–100	0–30
Indian Rocks							
Mosquito Is		Bu					
Necker Is		3	B?				
Norman Is		Bu	Bu			150–200	
Pelican Is							
Peter Is		Bu	Bu				
Prickly Pear							
Scrub Is		Bu					
Round Rock		B?	B?				
Sandy Cay			2				
Seal Dog Is.		B?	5				
Tortola		5Å	Bu				
Virgin Gorda		2	B?				
Watson's Rock							
Yost van Dyke		Bu					
Total Observed	B	60–80	80–100	170–275	1	300–400	400–800
Min-Max.	0–20	14–20	10–50	150–275	0–1	280–355	400–800

Notes: Bu = breeds in unknown numbers; Bs = breeds in some years; B? = may breed; E=extirpated.
a. These islands are designated as National Parks (in Dog Islands, only West Dog).
b. Includes birds that breed on Cistern Rock just off Cooper Is.
c. Includes birds that breed on offshore rock called Broken Jerusalem.

literature and from our fieldwork is given in the following accounts.

Methods

In order to determine which species currently breed and to assess population levels so that conservation action plans may be developed, a series of surveys was conducted between 1992 and 2003. Historical data from the literature are also included. Field surveys were conducted by the authors (some with the assistance of J. Saliva) in October 1995, May 1996, October 1997 and 1998, and at least once each summer between 1992 and 2003 (except for 2002). Data for some islands are better than others owing to accessibility: some islands could only be observed from a boat.

There are essentially two breeding seasons for Caribbean seabirds, winter and spring. Gulls and terns nest mainly May through August, while shearwaters and Pelecaniforms nest mainly October through May. This requires that surveys be made in most months of the year to monitor the birds. Generally only one visit was made to a colony during a year. Because pairs or whole colonies could have failed before or after that visit, we are

Laughing Gull May–Jul	Brown Noddy May–Jul	Sooty Tern May–Jul	Bridled Tern May–Jul	Least Tern Apr–Jun	Gull-billed Tern May–Jul	Roseate Tern May–Jun	Royal Tern May–Jul	Sandwich Tern May–Jun
175–245				42	4	E	B?	60–80
	Bs			15s				B?
20								
0–50			Bs			0–20s		
Bu	10[4]	B?[1]	25					
			Bu			0–200s		
Bu			Bu			0–600s		
22								
150–300		0–50	4–10			0–20s		
Bs	37–75	30–50	5–20					
				25				
> 50			Bu			0–1700s	Bs	0–211
						E		
> 10			3–4			0–20s		
Bu								
0–40			0–10			0–15s		
> 20			E					
			2					
			E?					
Bu				Bu				
	15	0–50	5			0–150s		
Bu			< 10					
> 50			14–17			0–500s		
Bu								
			1					
	40		5			Bs		
Bu								
1000–2000	100–300	100	150–250	100	0–4	600–2000	Bs	120
130–200				67	0–4	350–1755		100–300

unable to make any estimates of reproductive success. Also, if nesting began late, birds could have laid after our survey and not been counted; thus our estimates should be considered a minimum. Because there are no long-term data, we do not know if colonies are continuing to decrease in size or not. We do know they are frequently disturbed by pleasure boaters and fishermen who land and go ashore.

Table 11.2. summarizes the data from these surveys and from the literature and provides estimated numbers of nesting pairs in the BVI, the islands on which nesting occurs, and the breeding season.

Audubon's Shearwater

Audubon's are the only Procellariiformes currently reported to nest in the BVI. It is likely that there were other species during the earlier years of human habitation, but being ground nesters, shearwaters are particularly susceptible to mammalian predators. They may still nest on Anegada (unlikely), Cooper Island, and Ginger Island, but there have been no searches for them in recent years. C. Petrovic (pers. comm.) heard shearwaters at night at Ginger Island and Cistern Point (off Cooper Island) in October and November 1995. J. Rowan Roy (pers.

comm.) reported 26 Audubon's Shearwater rafting, one possibly a juvenile, in the water 350 m north of Great Tobago in May 1995.

White-tailed Tropicbird

We estimate 60–80 White-tailed Tropicbird pairs nest in the BVI (table 11.1). Since they nest in highly inaccessible rock crevices, surveys are difficult to carry out. As with the Red-bills, a good census requires observing rock faces for days at a time to see birds flying into crevices. They nest on Carrot Rock, Carval Rock, Fallen Jerusalem, Ginger Island, Great Tobago, Guana Island, Mosquito Island, Norman Island, Peter Island (?), Round Rock (?), Scrub Island, Seal and Dog Islands, Tortola, Virgin Gorda, and Jost Van Dyke (our surveys; Mirecki 1976; Halewyn and Norton 1984; Walsh-McGehee 2000, this study).

The breeding season is similar to that of the USVI and Puerto Rico, where they nest between March and September (Schaffner 1988). Like the Red-bills, they probably have little problem with predation, except by Peregrine Falcon or rats.

Red-billed Tropicbird

This species is difficult to census, generally nesting in hard-to-find and inaccessible crevices in rocks. A few nest in more open situations between rocks or under a dense shrub, but this is uncommon. We estimate the total number of Red-billed Tropicbird nests to be about 80–100 (table 11.1).

A good census requires observing rock faces for days at a time during the breeding season, waiting for birds to fly into crevices. Nesting sites listed in table 11.1 have mostly been determined in this manner. They nest on Cockroach, Dog Islands, Fallen Jerusalem, Great Tobago, Little Tobago, Green Cay, Guana Island, Norman Island, Peter Island, and Round Rock (Mirecki 1976; Halewyn and Norton 1984; Walsh-McGehee 2000, this study). There may be small groups on other islands, and a more thorough census is needed.

The breeding season is between October and May. Red-bills are somewhat susceptible to rat predation and are taken by Peregrine Falcons. The finding of a Peregrine feather inside a crevice with a tropicbird nest in it indicates that the falcon will go into crevices to get a meal.

Brown Booby

Great Tobago and Little Tobago are the only sites of Brown Booby nesting in the BVI (table 11.2). About 120–200 pairs nest on Great Tobago and 50–75 more on Little Tobago. Brown Booby may have nested on the cliff face on the north side of Guana Island in the 1980s (J. Lazell, pers. comm.), but this is unconfirmed. Mirecki (1976) reported 120 birds on Guana, but these were probably roosting and not nesting. Generally, Brown Boobies in the Caribbean lay in September–October. On Great Tobago nests with eggs are present year round. This is unusual and could be caused by goats destroying nests and birds re-laying. The well-used goat trails make good flat nesting sites for the boobies on a steep, rubbly island. None of the birds we encountered was banded, so it was not possible to determine what percentage of nests is from re-laying birds that lost a nest. The nesting number and reproductive success on Great Tobago should be monitored. In three separate visits to the island during 1995–1997, the few chicks present appeared healthy. Rats are also present on the island and most likely eat some eggs. Efforts began in 2000 to clear the island of goats.

Red-footed Booby

We found one nest with a chick on Great Tobago in February 1992 among nesting frigatebirds. No confirmed nests have been recorded since. The closest Red-footed colony is on Dutchcap Cay in the USVI, about 12 mi southwest of Tobago. The Red-footed Booby is the only locally breeding booby that nests in trees, although some nest on the ground (Schreiber et al. 1996).

Brown Pelican

There are approximately 300–400 pairs of Brown Pelican in the BVI: Guana Island (85–100), Norman Island (150–200), and Little Tobago Island National Park (50–75; table 11.1.). This subspecies is endemic to the Caribbean. The two breeding peaks are in August–October and April–May, with some eggs found in all months (Collazo et al. 2000). Pelicans are mainly a tree-nester in the Caribbean, but will nest on the ground.

The Guana population is well protected since this is a private island with an active predator control program. The pelicans nest in small subgroups around the perimeter of the island, 13–33 m inland, on the slopes. On Norman Island pelicans nest up on hillsides along the rough southern point. Both areas are essentially inaccessible to boaters, rendering the pelicans fairly well protected from disturbance. On Little Tobago they nest on the flat top of the island. We were able to land only once on the island (1995), which has very step cliffs. On Norman and Little Tobago goats periodically trample or eat the eggs in the few pelican nests that are on the ground. Additionally, goats limit tree regeneration for future nesting habitat.

A privately funded goat removal project is ongoing on Norman Island (J. Lazell, pers. comm.). The West Indian population is listed by the U.S. Fish and Wildlife Service as endangered in Puerto Rico and the U.S. Virgin Islands.

Magnificent Frigatebird

There is one colony of Magnificent Frigatebird in the BVI (table 11.1): an estimated 400–800 pairs nest on Great Tobago each year, making up about 15% of the West Indian population (plate 39). Mirecki (1976) reported a small number of frigatebirds breeding off Anegada, but in June 1996 no nesting was observed. Reports of nesting on George Dog are unconfirmed; birds there were only roosting during our June surveys.

Females probably breed every other year, since incubation and chick rearing take about a year or more (Diamond and Schreiber 2002). Males desert the colony when chicks are 3–4 months old, leaving females to finish raising the young. A few males bred every year in the Barbuda colony (W. Trivelpiece, pers. comm.) and may do so here. The nesting number in the BVI could well be limited by the size of the available nesting habitat. Trees in the nesting area on Great Tobago are completely full of nests during the season. Adults on a nest actually brush against neighboring birds when they turn around on the nest.

They lay in August–October. Eggs are laid in a very restricted season but because incubation lasts 60 days and the chick rearing period takes 9–11 months, there are birds present in the colony year round. The presence of many fledglings flying around the BVI in each of the past five years indicates that many nests have been successful.

Laughing Gull

Laughing Gulls are the only breeding gulls in the Virgin Islands and are a common breeder on low, flat islands. Mirecki (1976) and Halewyn and Norton (1984) reported gulls nesting on Anegada in small numbers. Currently they nest on Carrot Rock, Carval Rock, Cockroach Island and the Dogs, Fallen Jerusalem, Ginger Island, Green Cay, Mosquito Island, Necker Island, Norman Island, Prickly Pear, Sandy Cay, Seal and Dog Islands, Tortola, and Jost Van Dyke. They lay primarily in May–July. In contrast to the USVI, there are no large colonies. We estimate the number of nests to be 1,000–2,000 from year to year (table 11.1). Laughing Gulls sometimes take eggs and chicks of smaller terns nesting in more open situations (Saliva 1995; Douglas 2000; Pierce 2001) as well as nestlings of other waterbirds, such as the White-cheeked

Pintail (*Anas bahamensis*, W. Coles, pers. comm.), a locally protected duck species.

Brown Noddy

Approximately 100–300 pairs nest in the BVI (table 11.1). Mirecki (1976) found small colonies of Brown Noddies on Carval Rock and Ginger Island. They still nest in both those locations as well as on Round Rock, Cooper Island, and probably in other locations with Bridled Terns, as the two species often nest together. They lay eggs mainly in late spring to early summer.

Sooty Tern

Sooty Terns have been extirpated from several historic breeding colonies in the Caribbean (Halewyn and Norton 1984; Saliva 2000a). A few small colonies may still exist in the BVI; we found birds acting as if they were nesting on several islets on which we could not land (Broken Jerusalem, Ginger Island, and Round Rock), and they appear to shift among islands between years. They used to breed on Carval Rock (Mirecki et al. 1977), and Norton et al. (1989) reported a small colony on Fallen Jerusalem. Currently there may be up to 100 pairs nesting on Broken Jerusalem, Ginger Island, and/or Round Rock (Saliva and Pierce 1996). The West Indian population was between 200,000 and 300,000 (Saliva 2000a). They lay in late spring to early summer.

Bridled Tern

Bridled Terns breed in small loosely organized colonies on smaller islands such as Carrot Rock, Seal and East Dog islands, Carval Rock, West Dog Island, Cockroach Island, Cooper Island (Cistern Point Rock), Fallen Jerusalem, Ginger Island, Green Cay, Round Rock, and Sandy Cay (Chardine et al. 2000a). Other sites with recorded breeding from earlier surveys are Necker Island, Norman Island, and Peter Island (Mirecki 1976). We did not find birds nesting on Norman, Necker, or Carval during our surveys. These terns' solitary and secretive nesting habits (laying in rock crevices, under boulder edges, or under low vegetation) make them easy to overlook during a survey. The total population for the BVI is unknown but is probably between 150 and 250 pairs. About 4,000–6,000 nested in the West Indies (Chardine et al. 2000a). They lay from early June through July.

Least Tern

We estimate the Least Tern population of the BVI to be up to 100 pairs (table 11.1). They breed in only a few places in the BVI. Nests may be found on the larger islands on dry salt ponds and, secondarily, on beaches. They are particularly good at camouflaging eggs on sandy beaches or flats and take flight when humans are some distance away, making nests hard to locate. Mirecki (1976) reported several large breeding colonies on extensive areas of dried-up mangrove lagoons, plus 30 pairs on Beef Island and 50 pairs on Anegada. During our surveys we found about 25 pairs at the salt pond on Great Thatch in 1996 and 1997, 42 nests at Flamingo Pond on Anegada in 2001, and a few nests at the newly built airport extension on Beef Island (C. Petrovic, pers. comm.). A nesting area may not be used every year as the small colonies move about. There are about 300 pairs in the U.S. Virgin Islands that move about among 20 different locations from year to year (Sladen and Pierce 1988). Movement among nesting sites by terns appears to be common and may occur owing to flooding, predation by exotic and feral animals, or human disturbance.

Gull-billed Tern

A small number of Gull-billed Tern were reported breeding on Anegada in the 1970s and in 1982, among Sandwich Terns (Mirecki 1976; R. Norton, June 1982, 5 nests, pers. comm.), but we did not find any breeding there. Two to four pairs nested on Anegada in 2005 (McGowan et al. 2006b). Careful surveys of other tern nesting populations often reveal some nests of Gull-bills among them. As Gull-billed Terns are estimated at only 100–500 pairs in the West Indies (Chardine et al. 2000a), it is important to assure that adequate, safe habitat (predator and disturbance free) exists for them to breed.

Roseate Tern

An estimated 4,000–6,000 pairs of Caribbean Roseate Terns nested in the West Indies, and the largest colonies occur on the Puerto Rico Bank, to the west of the BVI (Gochfeld et al. 1998; Saliva 2000b). We estimate that between 600 and 2,000 pairs breed in the BVI (table 11.1), with numbers varying each year as the birds shift around. Recent annual surveys of Roseate Terns have shown that they regularly shift colony sites between the U.S. Virgin Islands and the BVI (Pierce 2001). This means the BVI birds are part of a metapopulation including the U.S. Virgin Islands, Culebra, and Puerto Rico. Based on 10 years of data, the total population on the Puerto Rico Bank was estimated at 2,000–2,500 breeding pairs (Saliva 2000b).

Certain offshore cays in the BVI tend to be favored (table 11.1), but none of the breeding sites recorded over the past 10 years has been used in every year. The largest and most accessible breeding has occurred on Green Cay: 650–750 nests in 1993, 1,060 in 1994, 347 in 1995, and 1,755 in 1996 (Saliva and Pierce 1996). Smaller numbers sometimes nest on Carrot Rock, Cockroach Island, Cooper Island (Cistern Point Rock), off Fallen Jerusalem on Broken Jerusalem, Green Cay, one of the Indian Rocks, Round Rock, and Seal and Dog Islands. Norton et al. (1989) reported breeding on Anegada but no nest numbers or locations were given. We found no evidence of breeding there in 1996. Mirecki (1976) found 30 pairs breeding on Guana Island, 10 pairs on Cooper Island, plus 20 birds roosting or nesting on Cockroach Cay.

Egg laying commences in mid- to late May and may extend through June. There are no data on nest success, but large colonies appear to be more successful than smaller ones (Pierce, unpubl.). Roseate Tern eggs are favored by locals and the illegal harvest continues today. Accessible colonies are vulnerable to human disturbance from tourists, which often results in colony abandonment, especially if it occurs early in the egg-laying stage.

Royal Tern

Historic colonies of Royal Terns in the BVI are not well documented. It is thought they once bred on Anegada (Mirecki 1976) but we did not find any colonies during our surveys. If Royal Terns are nesting in the BVI, they probably do so on Anegada or with the Sandwich Tern colonies that appear sporadically. They commonly nest with Sandwich Terns. Chardine et al. (2000a) estimated 450–800 pairs in the whole West Indies.

Sandwich Tern

We estimate that at least 120 Sandwich Terns nest in the BVI (table 11.1). Mirecki (1976) reported two colonies on Anegada consisting of up to 150 birds but gave no number of nests present. Norton et al. (1989) reported 80 nests in 1982 and 41 in 1983. About 60 pairs nested in the Flamingo Pond area on Anegada in 2001 during our surveys, and 20–25 pairs nested there in 2005 (McGowan et al. 2006b). The number of pairs nesting on Green Cay was 211 in 1994, 54 in 1995, and 57 in 1996 (on a grassy area adjacent to the Roseate Tern colony). Neither Sandwich Terns nor Roseate Terns have been observed nesting on Green Cay since 1996. These terns appear to shift nesting sites from year to year, and with 1–2 surveys per year, nesting could go undetected on several of the small islets where suitable nesting habitat exists. Approximately 5% of the West Indian population (2,100–3,000) nested in the BVI (Norton 2000).

Threats

Audubon's Shearwaters are one of the favored eating species in the Caribbean, where large nestlings seem to be preferred. Given the few remaining pairs in the BVI, eating of the birds may no longer occur here. There is appropriate nesting habitat to support populations of shearwaters and petrels, though some islands have potential predators that need to be eradicated, such as rats. Surveys of current known and potential nesting sites are badly needed. A good census would require spending the night at possible colonies to hear the vocalizations of this burrow nester, using call-playback to induce birds to call.

The presence of goats on Great Tobago has threatened the large Magnificent Frigatebird colony there, the only place they nest in the BVI. Goats destroy regenerating bushes and trees, on which the frigatebirds depend for nest sites. Goats also trample nests of Brown Boobies on Great Tobago, causing reproduction to fail for large numbers of pairs. Another threat to frigatebirds is entanglement in monofilament fishing line. Birds readily dive on trolling bait or lures and get caught by the hook. Fishermen cut the line and the bird flies off, trailing yards of fishing line. Back in the nesting colony the line gets caught in branches, ensnaring the bird and killing it (generally from starvation). In June 2001 we found 46 dead frigatebirds in the nesting colony caught in monofilament line, and 32 were found in October 2007.

There are two major threats to nesting gulls and terns in the BVI: the harvest of eggs by local people for eating and rat predation on eggs and young (Halewyn and Norton 1984). The potential exists to increase tern productivity greatly by eradicating rats and by protecting some colony areas and patrolling them frequently during the nesting season to stop poaching and human disturbance.

The BVI is increasingly being promoted as a yachting destination, and each year more yachters tour through the islands. The numerous uninhabited islands and islets in the BVI constitute the few remaining places where seabirds can nest—but are also ideal sites for yachts to stop by to let people go ashore to explore (Woodfield 1999). Disturbance by boaters in many of the colonies in the BVI during the breeding season is thought to cause frequent nesting failures. When adult birds are disturbed off nests in the heat of the day, eggs and small chicks are killed by the hot sun. Exposed eggs and small chicks become easy prey for predators such as gulls, hawks, falcons, and dogs. Small chicks may run from intruders and get lost, unable to reconnect with parents. People still talk of egging in the BVI, and we believe some eggs are still taken from colonies each year. In 1997 we found 250 tern eggs piled up on the Seal/Dog Islands as though someone were getting ready to take them and left at our approach.

The BVI has small gull and tern populations compared to the U.S. Virgin Islands, where colonies are monitored and protected. Nesting areas are spread about the smaller offshore cays and on salt flats on Anegada. Nesting sites may change from year to year, which is common for some tern species. While most terns nest on sandy beaches or flat, open, grassy areas, terns in the Caribbean have been forced, in many places, to nest in inaccessible sites in order to have a successful nesting season. Many now nest on ledges of steep cliffs (Sooty Terns, sometimes Roseate Terns), in rock crevices (Brown Noddies, Bridled Terns), and on top of high, inaccessible islands, making accurate surveys difficult. Colony failure owing to human disturbance is a common problem as boaters land on islands and walk around, picnic, and play.

Pollution of the sea and oil spills are a concern in the Caribbean. There are few to no data on heavy metal or PCB levels in the birds today (Custer et al. 1983), meaning that increases in these cannot be documented in the future. Research and monitoring of seabirds are badly needed for the BVI to be able to maintain its populations of these wonderful birds.

Preservation of Seabird Biodiversity

Consistent monitoring of seabird colonies is a vital part of conservation, a fact that cannot be overemphasized. As with most local governments, the most immediate need is for government to set up a monitoring program for seabirds. Steps should then be taken to post some of the more important colony sites to prohibit entry, followed by enforcement and fines for illegal entry. The Ministry of Natural Resources and Labour and the Conservation and Fisheries Department should encourage research on seabirds as a way to assist in their conservation.

Environmental education programs in the schools can be an effective method of promoting conservation (Geoghegan et al. 1991), and many organizations provide educational material for these. In fact, organizations and government departments worldwide provide assistance with conservation issues, and these should be explored.

Seabirds are a valuable component of natural resources; bird-watching is an immensely popular hobby, and the number of participants is growing each year.

Organized birding tours could provide added income to the government and attract more tourists. They could also help pay for patrolling the colonies, since the presence of a warden with a group of tourists at a colony would prevent illegal landing. Guided visits to colonies would offer people the opportunity to enjoy the birds and learn about them, while still protecting them. Supervised visits to colonies can be conducted safely if visitors are not allowed to go into the colony but observe from a distance.

Conservation

Government Actions to Protect Seabirds

The Conservation and Fisheries Department of the Ministry of Natural Resources and Labour is the arm of the government responsible for bird conservation in the BVI. This agency is in charge of environmental planning, monitoring, patrolling and enforcement of regulations, reviewing development plans, environmental education, and fisheries management. The National Parks Trust (established in 1961) is a statutory body under the Ministry of Natural Resources and Labour that is responsible for managing 20 national parks, including marine and terrestrial areas, a number of conservation programs, historical preservation, and marine habitat protection.

The National Parks Trust is working with the Royal Society for the Protection of Birds to develop a conservation policy for the BVI (Georges 2002), and they have made excellent recent progress on seabird conservation issues. Several areas where seabirds breed have recently been designated as national parks: Great Tobago, Little Tobago, Fallen Jerusalem, West Dog, Prickly Pear, and Dead Chest. Proposed national parks include Sandy Cay, Green Cay, Sandy Spit, Great Thatch, Great Dog, George Dog, Seal Dog, Cockroach Island, the Caves, the Indians, and Pelican Island.

Great Tobago and Little Tobago National Parks are actively managed by the BVI National Parks Trust. The Trust has been working on eradicating goats from Great Tobago. But there has been a recent resurgence in the number present, and they are still causing great damage. In 2003 the Trust constructed two artificial nesting platforms of green wire mesh for frigatebirds, providing additional nesting habitat during the interim period while trees and other vegetation regenerate following goat removal. While goats do not directly affect frigatebirds, they do prevent new trees from growing. Nesting frigatebirds destroy trees over time with guano and by plucking twigs for nest material. They are dependent on new trees growing for nesting habitat as the ones they are using get destroyed. The frigatebird colony has expanded somewhat since the goat removal project began in 2000, with some birds now nesting in low bushes and shrubs. During 2004 there were an estimated 700–800 nests. The Trust is seeking funding for a rat eradication project on the island, based upon the success of a similar privately funded project on Sandy Cay.

Introduced goats are being removed from Great Tobago and Norman Islands, as are rats from Sandy Cay. The BVI government is negotiating with private owners to purchase Sandy Spit and Green Cay to prevent development on these islands. Privately owned Guana Island has been actively managed for wildlife for over 25 years and provides an excellent example of what can be accomplished when introduced species are removed from islands.

The Wild Bird Protection Ordinance as amended in 1980 allows for the designation of bird sanctuaries. The flamingo breeding area on Anegada and Fat Hog's Bay on Tortola are protected under this ordinance. Other declared bird sanctuaries include most of the seabird breeding islands in the BVI: Cockroach, Cooper, Dead Chest, Fallen Jerusalem, George Dog, Ginger, Great Dog, Great Tobago, West Dog, Little Tobago, Mosquito, Necker, Peter, Prickly Pear, Round Rock, Saba, St. Eustacia, and the Seal Dog islands. Currently there is essentially no active protection of the islands owing to lack of funds, equipment, training, and staff to carry this out.

The Protection of Trees and Conservation of Soil and Water Ordinance (1954) and the draft Coastal Conservation and Management Act (1991, not passed) seek to prevent deforestation of land on steep slopes and the resultant soil erosion and pollution of water supplies, and to preserve coastal areas. Both of these ordinances could help preserve reefs surrounding the islands and thus could also protect the feeding grounds of seabirds.

As a U.K. Overseas Territory, the BVI is included in the United Kingdom's ratification of several international agreements that affect conservation in the islands:

Convention Concerning the Protection of the World Cultural and Natural Heritage (World Heritage Convention)

Convention on Wetlands of International Importance especially as Waterfowl Habitat (Ramsar Convention)

Convention on International Trade in Endangered Species of Wild Fauna and Flora (CITES)

Convention on the Conservation of Migratory Species of Wild Animals (Bonn Convention)

Convention on Biological Diversity (CBD)

International Convention on the Regulation of Whaling

Convention for the Protection and Development of the Marine Environment of the Wider Caribbean Region (Cartagena Convention)—Protocol on Specially Protected Areas and Wildlife

Some of the wetlands on Anegada, where an introduced colony of flamingos now breeds, have been declared a Ramsar site (Flamingo Point, Bones Bight Pond, and Red Pond; Woodfield 1999). Ramsar assists governments in designating and protecting wetland areas. There are many important wetlands in the BVI that are vital for seabirds as well as supporting other significant flora and fauna, and some of those need to be added to the protected sites. Preservation of wetlands and seagrass beds should be a priority in the BVI, not only for protecting seabirds but for the production of fish and crustaceans.

None of the nesting seabirds of the BVI has been designated as endangered by the local government. The Caribbean subspecies of the Brown Pelican is on the U.S. federally endangered list and the Roseate Tern is on the U.S. federally threatened list. Several other species are considered endangered or threatened in the West Indies (Schreiber and Lee 2000b), and the BVI government should consider special protections for all of these species.

Summary of Conservation Needs

Systematic surveys and counts are badly needed in order to determine the size of the bird populations, to assess whether they are reproducing successfully, and to track what conservation measures can be effective once instituted (Croxall et al. 1984; Schreiber 2000a). The numerous uninhabited islands and islets in the BVI offer ideal nesting sites for many seabirds, but they have to be protected from disturbance and poaching by posting, fencing, and frequent patrols. In terms of importance to seabirds, the following islands are possibly the top five in need of protection and management: Cockroach Cay and the Dogs, Green Cay, Great Tobago, Little Tobago, and Norman Island. The National Parks Trust is working on Great and Little Tobago, and Norman Island is being actively preserved by private individuals.

Needed Actions

1. Monitor the colonies on a regular basis. During 3–4 visits per year to each seabird colony, record numbers of nests and chicks.

2. Make efforts to educate fishermen about removing hooks from birds and freeing them from all the fishing line, so that the birds do not fly back to the colony and become entangled in trees, killing themselves. Remove fishing line from the frigate-bird colony on Great Tobago on a regular basis.

3. Carry out a public information campaign that promotes people's desire to preserve and protect breeding sites.

4. Examine and strengthen current legislation protecting seabirds.

5. Enforce legal protections of areas and species by consistent patrolling and fines. The National Parks Trust updated its primary ordinance in the 2004 Draft National Parks Act, still pending government approval. Regulations under this legislation will address the enforcement needs within the system of parks and protected areas, but funding is a continual problem.

6. Post signs at protected sites.

7. Develop education and conservation programs on seabirds, and birds in general, for the schools as a part of the elementary and junior high school curriculum.

8. Develop a training program for people working in conservation departments or send them to one of the existing training programs (such as that carried out by the Smithsonian Institution).

9. Set up a program of ecotourism to help people learn more about the wildlife and to help bring dollars into the economy from wildlife.

10. Encourage research on the seabirds by scientists in order to help the BVI develop conservation plans and monitoring programs for the birds and to learn what perturbations they are undergoing. This could provide some excellent data at no cost to the government.

Acknowledgments

E. A. Schreiber thanks the Falconwood Foundation, H. and G. Jarecki, and J. Lazell for their generous assistance with research in the BVI. J. Pierce thanks J. Saliva of the U.S. Fish and Wildlife Service, D. Corales, P. Bailey, T. Smith, and N. Woodfield for assistance. The Conservation and Fisheries Department of the British Virgin Islands Government kindly allowed access to the islands. Both authors are grateful to J. Rowan Roy and C. Petrovic for providing unpublished data, and to the BVI National Parks Trust for providing access to Great Tobago.

12

Anguilla

STEVE H. HOLLIDAY AND KARIM V. D. HODGE

The Anguilla archipelago of islands is the most northerly of the Leeward Islands and lies at the northeastern corner of the Lesser Antilles, where the Caribbean Sea meets the Atlantic Ocean (map 33). The main island is 26 km long, 5 km at its widest point, and approximately 91 km² in area. The islands are a U.K. Overseas Territory. The population is 11,400 (2001 census), supplemented by 100,000 visitors a year; tourism is the most important economic activity on the island.

The islands lie within the tropics at 18° N, 63° W, and have a sunny climate year round, with temperatures averaging 27°C. The wet season extends from June to November, although most of the island's average rainfall of 970 mm can fall within a few weeks, causing localized flooding in low-lying areas. Anguilla is periodically hit by hurricanes, such as Luis in 1995 and Lenny in 1999, bringing extensive wind damage, torrential rain, and flooding.

Anguilla and its many outer islands and cays are low-lying and mostly rocky, with limestone, corals, and sandstones predominating. The mainland and a few of the offshore islands have extensive picturesque beaches, clear seas, and inshore coral reefs, providing rich natural resources and a basis for tourism and a fishing industry. Porous rocks capture rainfall as groundwater, and these have traditionally provided the island's water resources, although recent concerns over water quality have led to the development of a new desalination plant. Anguilla and three of the larger islands have brackish coastal lagoons, and a few ponds on the mainland are fed by springs from the water table.

Strategic land planning is difficult on Anguilla with just 5% of land in government ownership and 95% privately owned. To date there are no designated national parks or protected areas, although draft legislation to create protected areas has been prepared. Pressure for tourism developments and new housing to meet the needs of a growing population are placing increasing demands on land and natural resources. The government of Anguilla retains environmental expertise within relevant departments and provides support for the Anguilla National Trust (ANT). The ANT was established in 1988 and is Anguilla's lead organization in conserving and promoting the island's natural, historical, and cultural resources and heritage.

Offshore lie several smaller uninhabited islands and cays, of which the seven that follow are the most important for seabirds.

Anguillita (4.4 ha): A small island 350 m southwest of the western point of Anguilla, consisting of a low shelf of rock with a small sand bar on its eastern flank.

Dog Island (207 ha): A low rocky island, it is 13 km northwest of Anguilla and has three smaller cays off the west and north coasts. The cliffs and inland areas of scrub are home to Anguilla's largest seabird colonies. The coastline has low cliffs interspersed with five sandy beaches. Weathered limestone rocks reach sea level on parts of the west and northeast coast. Two large ponds lie behind beaches at Spring Bay and Stoney Bay. The center of the island is covered in impenetrable low, thorny scrub and thousands of prickly pear cacti. A small herd of about 30 feral goats is a remnant of former more extensive grazing by livestock.

Little Scrub (4.5 ha): A small rocky, limestone island, it is 800 m off the northwestern point of Scrub Island. It has low cliffs, bare areas of rock, and two small areas of vegetation on the east side and at the southwest tip, where prickly pear cactus dominates.

Prickly Pear East (31 ha): A low rocky limestone island, it is 10 km northwest of the Anguilla mainland. Beaches on the north and east shores attract tourists, and a restaurant has been built behind the north beach on a sheltered bay. The rocks form a low platform that is mostly vegetated except for a bare strip around the

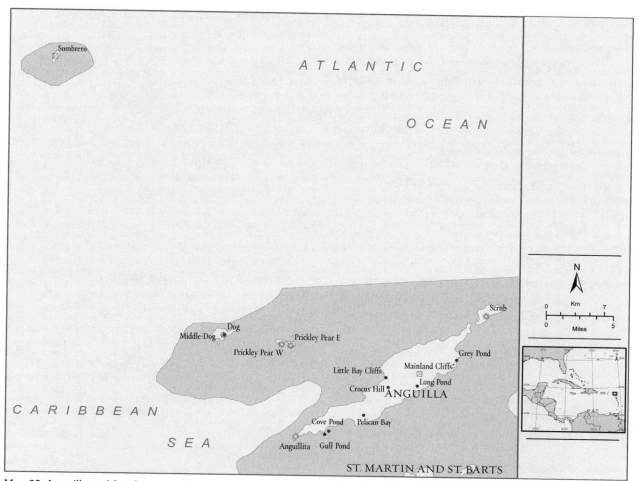

Map 33. Anguilla and Sombrero.

southern coast. Extensive areas of low scrub cover the center of the island, and there is a small pond behind the beach on the northern shore.

Prickly Pear West (32 ha): A low rocky island 11 km northwest of Anguilla, it is separated from Prickly Pear East by a channel 150 m wide. The coast has low, heavily fissured cliffs except for a small sandy bay in the north. A narrow coastal strip of bare rock surrounds the patchily vegetated island center, with areas of low scrub with a few bushes. The island is difficult to land on and as a consequence is little visited.

Scrub Island (343 ha): This is the largest of Anguilla's outer islands, separated from the mainland at its northeastern corner by a channel 500 m wide. The island is low, with a rocky, fractured limestone coast punctuated by four sandy beaches, the eastern beaches attracting breeding terns. Scrub Island has a large pond on the western side and a complex of four ponds and lagoons on the eastern side. The ponds are lined in places by mangroves and low trees. The center of the island is largely scrub,

stretching to the coastline of heavily fissured limestone and low rocky cliffs. The island is uninhabited; windblown remains of a former tourism development persist in the east and in the center is a wide grassy former airstrip. Large numbers of goats on the island are part of a project managed by Anguilla's Department of Agriculture.

Sombrero (38 ha): The only remote island in the Anguilla group, it is a flat-topped rocky outcrop lying on its own rock shelf 65 km to the northwest. The cliffs and rocky areas are home to a large seabird colony and an endemic ground lizard. The island is currently stark and bare following damage by Hurricane Luis in 1995, when large areas of cacti and other plants were destroyed. Remains of industrial buildings persist from the extensive mining of phosphate deposits in the nineteenth and early twentieth centuries, which left the surface pitted with craters up to 10 m deep. A manned lighthouse with associated buildings was in use until 2002, when it was replaced with an automated light.

Methods of Survey

The historical presence of seabirds on Anguilla is well known, but information was largely anecdotal until recently, with few quantitative records available. Lack of information on numbers of breeding seabirds presented problems in the late 1990s when trying to assess the environmental impacts of a proposed rocket launching station on Sombrero. This lack of population data has recently been partly addressed by breeding season surveys carried out as part of the Environmental Impact Assessment (EIA) for launch proposals on Sombrero and through a series of surveys undertaken by the Anguilla National Trust and the Royal Society for the Protection of Birds (RSPB), a British environmental NGO.

The seabird population data are still incomplete, and to date there has been no complete baseline census. Further surveys are required to determine population trends and to provide a more accurate assessment of the booby populations with their extended breeding season. The initial surveys have enabled Anguilla to be assessed for global and regional Important Bird Areas coordinated by Birdlife International.

Population estimates in table 12.2 include data from a range of surveys utilizing several survey methods. In 1999 surveys were undertaken by ICF Consulting, and methodologies are set out in an EIA report for all the surveys. Sombrero received an extensive study over eight days, and other seabird breeding islands received one-day visits. All surveys involved mapping of colonies. The booby colonies were counted by mapping the count areas and carrying out preliminary visual surveys, followed by counts made on walks through the colony. Terns were counted by both preliminary visual surveys and walks through the colony to flush birds that were then counted in the air.

In 2000 surveys were carried out by three teams of observers from RSPB and the ANT. These surveys were limited by the amount of time available and were all undertaken on single days. Where possible, surveys visited all suitable breeding habitats and counted actual nests. All booby colonies were counted on a walk through the colony, and some included preliminary visual counts. Terns were mostly surveyed by visual point counts from a suitable vantage point. The Sooty Tern colony on Dog Island initially was estimated by counting birds in the air over the colony when the birds were disturbed. The 2004 survey of Sooty Terns on Dog Island by Environmental Protection in the Caribbean (EPIC) was the first to map the nesting area of the colony using GIS and to estimate

the population by counting actual occupied nests in a series of sample plots.

Species Accounts

At least 15 species of seabirds currently breed on Anguilla, with a further three species reported as former or possible breeding species. Total breeding population estimates are given in table 12.1 and the distribution of breeding pairs in table 12.2.

Current breeding species: White-tailed and Red-billed Tropicbird; Masked, Brown and Red-footed Booby; Brown Pelican, Magnificent Frigatebird, Laughing Gull, Brown Noddy; Sooty Tern, Bridled Tern, Least Tern, Roseate Tern, Royal Tern and Sandwich Tern.

Former or possible breeding species: Audubon's Shearwater, Common Tern and Black Noddy.

Anguilla's seabirds mostly breed on the seven small uninhabited islands earlier named. These are all easily accessible from the mainland except for the remote rocky outcrop of Sombrero. The mainland currently holds small populations of White-tailed and Red-billed tropicbirds nesting in holes on low cliffs and several colonies of Least Terns breeding around coastal lagoons and ponds.

Audubon's Shearwater

There are unconfirmed reports of breeding in the past on Dog Island and Sombrero, and burrows were found on Dog Island in 2000. There are no recent sightings of this species to suggest it may still be present.

White-tailed Tropicbird

A few pairs breed on cliffs or among rocks at a single site on the Anguilla mainland, with 1–2 pairs at Little Bay in 2000–2001 at least. The earliest sighting is on 21 March and display has been seen at this site in April. On the offshore cay of Prickly Pear East, two pairs were found breeding in July 1999, the only record for that site to date.

Red-billed Tropicbird

This species is resident, and small numbers breed on cliffs and among boulders on the Anguilla mainland and four offshore islands. Recent records suggest a population of around 21 pairs: Anguilla (10 pairs), Dog Island (5 pairs), Prickly Pear East (2 pairs) and West (1 pair), and Scrub Island (3 pairs). Individuals were seen on nests among rocks on Dog Island in both January and April 2000.

Table 12.1. Estimates of total seabirds breeding (nests) in Anguilla in 1999, 2000, and 2004

Species	Total nests	Survey years
White-tailed Tropicbird	3–4	1999, 2000
Red-billed Tropicbird	21	1999, 2000
Masked Booby	57	2000
Brown Booby	1,965	1999, 2000
Red-footed Booby	1–2	1999, 2000
Brown Pelican	21	2004
Magnificent Frigatebird	142	2000
Laughing Gull	2,618	1999, 2000, 2004
Brown Noddy	946	1999, 2000
Sooty Tern	52,295	1999, 2000, 2004
Bridled Tern	403	1999, 2000
Least Tern	290–345	1998, 1999, 2000
Roseate Tern	210	2000
Royal Tern	155	1999, 2004
Sandwich Tern	172	1999, 2004

Note: The figures are based on minimum numbers of nests at each site in the year when the highest numbers were present at that site.

Table 12.2. Distribution of breeding seabirds on Anguilla and adjacent islets, 1998–2004

Species	Mainland	Angui-llita	Dog Is	Prickly Pear East	Prickly Pear West	Scrub & Little Scrub	Sombrero	Total
White-tailed Tropicbird	1–2			2				3–4
Red-billed Tropicbird	10		5	2	1	3		21
Masked Booby			30				27	57
Brown Booby			1,267	75	237		386	1,965
Red-footed Booby					2			1–2
Brown Pelican					21			21
Magnificent Frigatebird			142					142
Laughing Gull				2,500		100	18	2,618
Brown Noddy			111	85		400	350	946
Sooty Tern			52,000	2		3	290	52,295
Bridled Tern			8	90		35	270	403
Least Tern	209–259		10			65–70	6	290–345
Roseate Tern						210		210
Royal Tern		40				115		155
Sandwich Tern		60				112		172

Masked Booby

Small numbers breed among colonies of Brown Booby on flat, bare areas of rock on Dog Island, including Middle Cay, and on Sombrero. This species has been surveyed regularly in recent years: 30 pairs were found breeding on Dog Island and the small offshore rock stack of Middle Cay, and at least 27 pairs on Sombrero. The extended breeding season for this species and the Brown Booby suggests that these counts are minima. Visits to Sombrero in the period 1999–2002 found adults on apparently occupied nests in most months from November to at least July, suggesting breeding can take place at any time of the year with a peak in March to July. In April 2000, 10 pairs on Dog Island and 16 of 21 pairs on Sombrero were feeding single chicks.

Brown Booby

Widespread, this species breeds on four uninhabited rocky islands and cays where access remains difficult: Dog Island (1,267 pairs), Prickly Pear East (75 pairs) and West (237 pairs), and Sombrero (386 pairs). Breeding appears to take place at any time of the year but with a peak in March to July.

Red-footed Booby

A rare breeding species found only on Prickly Pear West, where nesting is in low trees. The first breeding record was of two pairs in June 1999, when both pairs had single chicks. A single adult in April 2000 was apparently incubating.

Brown Pelican

A few pairs breed sporadically on the mainland, with the last nests reported at Crocus Hill and Pelican Bay in February 1996. Brown Pelicans have recently been found breeding on Prickly Pear West, with 21 nests in 2004. There are unconfirmed reports of breeding on Sombrero in the past.

Magnificent Frigatebird

A scarce breeding species found only on Dog Island, although there was breeding on Sombrero as recently as 1985. The single colony has been little visited to avoid disturbance. A crèche of at least 142 unfledged juveniles was present in April 2000 and around 200 displaying adults were seen in December 2003.

Laughing Gull

A regular breeding species, it nests on rocky shores and in low vegetation on three uninhabited islands. This species is widespread among the islands but breeds only on Prickly Pear East (2,500 pairs), Scrub Island (100 pairs), and Sombrero (18 pairs). This species arrives in mid-April and mostly leaves in September and October.

Brown Noddy

A regular visitor, it breeds on rocky areas and sea cliffs on the outer islands in four main colonies: Dog Island (111 pairs), Prickly Pear East (85 pairs), Little Scrub (400 pairs), and Sombrero (350 pairs). An occasional pair also breeds on Scrub Island. This species arrives in mid-April and leaves by September. Recent surveys in 2004 and 2007 suggest the population on Little Scrub has declined or is much lower.

Black Noddy

Two birds were present on Sombrero in 1989 (Norton 1989) but were not seen to breed, and this remains the only record to date.

Sooty Tern

A regular visitor, this species is concentrated on Dog Island, where large numbers breed in dense low scrub in the center of the island. An estimated 20,000 birds were seen in the air above the colony in June 2000, and sample plots and colony mapping in 2004 suggest that 52,000 pairs were present. (A further survey in 2007 with increased sample plots put the population around 113,000 pairs—data not included here.) Smaller numbers breed on Sombrero (290 pairs), Prickly Pear East (2 pairs), and Scrub Island (3 pairs). This species arrives in mid-April and leaves by September.

Bridled Tern

A regular visitor breeding on outer islands with four breeding colonies: Dog Island (8 pairs), Prickly Pear East (90 pairs), Scrub Island (35 pairs), and Sombrero (270 pairs). This species arrives in mid-April and leaves by September.

Least Tern

A regular visitor breeding on coasts and lagoons on the mainland and on outer islands. Breeding has recently taken place around several ponds on the mainland including Cove, Long, Grey and Gull ponds, with 209–259 pairs present in June 2000. Further colonies are found on Dog Island (10 pairs), Scrub Island (65 pairs), and Sombrero (6 pairs). This species arrives in mid-April, with most of the population leaving by September.

Roseate Tern

A scarce visitor; the single breeding colony is on a sandy spit at the eastern end of Scrub Island. At least 210 pairs were present in June 2000. Former breeding records are for Sombrero, where it was reported in 1964 and 1985.

Common Tern

A scarce visitor; a few adults were seen with Roseate Terns on the mainland in July and August 2005, suggesting there may be a small breeding population, with Scrub Island the most likely location.

Royal Tern

A scarce breeding species with colonies found on the low-lying islands of Anguillita (40 pairs) and Scrub Island (115 pairs). It formerly occurred on Sombrero, where it was last reported breeding in 1985. The breeding season extends from April to July with birds present year round along the coast of the mainland.

Sandwich Tern

A scarce visitor with breeding colonies among coastal sand and rocks on Anguillita (60 pairs) and the northeastern coast of Scrub Island (112 pairs). This species arrives in mid-April and mostly leaves by September.

Threats

Tourist facilities increasing access and disturbance on Prickly Pear East and low-level disturbance on Dog Island, Anguillita, and Scrub Island during the main tourism season from December to June are the main threat to easily accessible nesting sites. The offshore islands and the mainland breeding sites, with the exception of Little Scrub Island and Sombrero, are privately owned with no formal protection or management.

Rats, well known for their devastating effects on seabird colonies, have recently been seen on Dog Island, Prickly Pear East, and Scrub Island. Any proposed development on Sombrero or the remaining uninhabited islands would create disturbance and enable the introduction of predators such as rats. Least Tern breeding sites on the mainland are threatened by tourism and development on coastal lagoons and salt ponds.

The current increased development phase on Anguilla has included outline proposals for the outer islands, and although no development has taken place to date, the seabird populations remain vulnerable to any development or increased access.

Conservation

A management plan for breeding seabirds is needed for the mainland sites and the offshore breeding islands. It should control visitor access during the breeding season and provide conservation information and signs. Management of the breeding habitat on Sombrero, Dog Island, and Prickly Pear East and West is required to prevent scrub encroachment of the booby nesting areas. Protected area status should be pursued for Little Scrub Island and Sombrero, which are government owned.

Opportunities for tourism initiatives to raise awareness of the seabird colonies and their importance should be considered and evaluated to help underpin their conservation. Owners on privately owned islands should be asked to prevent access during the seabird breeding season.

Feasibility studies into rat eradication should be undertaken on the three islands where they are currently known to be present.

The main Least Tern breeding sites on the mainland at Cove, Gull, Grey, and Long ponds should be protected both from development and unintentional disturbance.

A baseline breeding survey and agreed monitoring program are required for subsequent surveys of the seabird populations.

13

The Netherlands Antilles I

St. Maarten, Saba, and St. Eustatius

NATALIA COLLIER AND ADAM BROWN

The northern Netherlands Antilles include part of St. Maarten together with the islands of Saba and St. Eustatius (maps 34, 35, 37). Recent data on this region are limited and primarily focused on determining population estimates. The following species are or have been recorded breeding in the northern Netherlands Antilles: Audubon's Shearwater, White-tailed Tropicbird, Red-billed Tropicbird, Brown Booby, Brown Pelican, Laughing Gull, Brown Noddy, Sooty Tern, Bridled Tern, Least Tern, and Roseate Tern.

Unless otherwise noted, the methods in surveys conducted by Environmental Protection in the Caribbean (EPIC) were visual counts either from land or boat using binoculars and/or spotting scopes. When possible, adults or chicks in the nest were counted. If nests were not present or clearly visible, all adults were counted. Methods were not reported from other sources.

St. Maarten

St. Maarten (18.3° N, 63.7° W) is a condominium belonging to France (52 km²) and the Netherlands (33 km²; map 34). The center of the island is composed of mountainous areas rising to 425 m. The coastal areas are low hills or flat, punctuated by numerous ponds, primarily of high salinity. Shorelines are characterized by sand or rock beach with interspersed cliffs. Simpson Bay Lagoon, one of the largest lagoons in the Lesser Antilles, is a dominant feature of the island and a major yachting center. The vegetation is thorny woodland. The human population is 39,000 on Dutch St. Maarten. However, the population increases greatly during the influx of seasonal visitors and tourists, the base of the economy.

Presently nine of the ten following species are breeding on Netherlands St. Maarten (table 13.1).

Audubon's Shearwater

Suspected of breeding at Pelikan Key in unknown numbers due to the presence of fledglings in March and May (Voous and Koelers 1967). No recent records.

White-tailed Tropicbird

Up to 15 pairs reported as breeding at Cupecoy Bay cliffs (Hoogerwerf 1977; Voous 1983). Five pairs were recorded at Cupecoy Bay cliffs in 2001–2002 (Collier et al. 2002). Surveys in 2003 and 2004 recorded only one pair (pers. obs.). In 2002, nesting occurred despite the presence of a cliffside bar and timeshare above the nest site. Three pairs were historically recorded at Cole Bay and at Maho Bay but have not been observed recently (Hoogerwerf 1977; pers. obs. 2004).

Red-billed Tropicbird

Previously nested in unknown numbers at Maho Bay and Mary's Point, but there are no recent observations (Voous 1983; Collier et al. 2002; pers. obs. 2004). Two pairs were seen entering crevices at Molly B'day in 2001–2002 (Collier et al. 2002).

Table 13.1. Estimates of seabird pairs breeding on Netherlands St. Maarten, 2002–2004

Species	Counts (pairs)
White-tailed Tropicbird	1–5
Red-billed Tropicbird	2
Brown Booby	5
Brown Pelican	26–79
Laughing Gull	100
Brown Noddy	15
Bridled Tern	21
Least Tern	10
Royal Tern	47

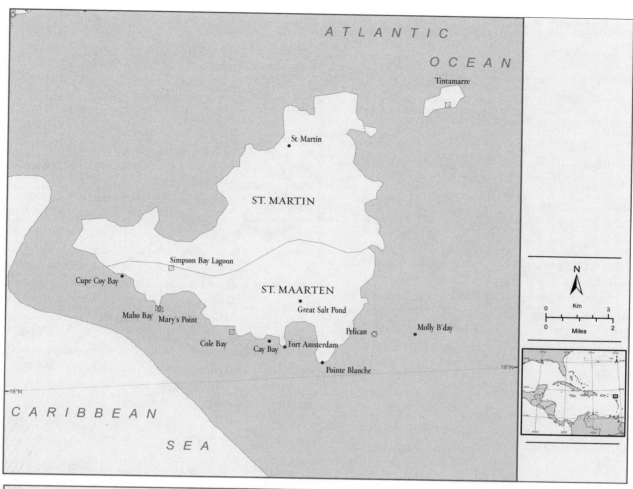

ATLANTIC

OCEAN

Tintamarre

St Martin

ST. MARTIN

Simpson Bay Lagoon

Cupe Coy Bay

ST. MAARTEN

Maho Bay   Mary's Point

Great Salt Pond

Cole Bay

Cay Bay   Fort Amsterdam

Pelican

Molly B'day

Pointe Blanche

18°N

18°N

CARIBBEAN

SEA

N

Km
0   3
0   2
Miles

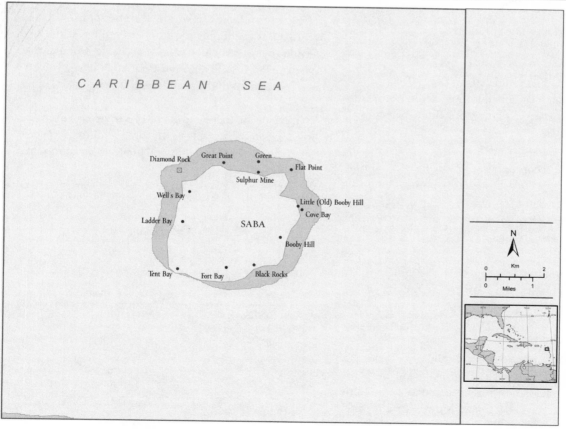

CARIBBEAN   SEA

Diamond Rock   Great Point   Green

Flat Point

Sulphur Mine

Well's Bay

Little (Old) Booby Hill
Cove Bay

Ladder Bay

SABA

Booby Hill

Tent Bay   Fort Bay   Black Rocks

N

Km
0   2
0   1
Miles

Above: Map 34. St. Martin, French Antilles, and St. Maarten, Netherlands Antilles.

Left: Map 35. Saba, Netherlands Antilles.

Brown Booby

Five chicks were seen at Molly B'day, but the number of nests is unknown (pers. obs. 2004).

Brown Pelican

Thirty-five nests counted on Pelikan Key (Voous 1983) and 19 there in 2002 (Collier et al. 2002); 60 nests at Fort Amsterdam in 2001 (Collier et al. 2002) and seven in 2004 (pers. obs.).

Laughing Gull

Great Salt Pond, where the landfill is located, is a major staging area where almost 3,000 individuals were recorded at the beginning of the breeding season and about half that number during the breeding season, presumably to forage on refuse (pers. obs. 2004). However, nesting has only been recorded on Pelikan Key, where 100 breeding pairs were counted (Voous 1983; pers. obs. 2004).

Brown Noddy

Fifty nests estimated at Point Blanche cliffs (Voous 1983); although only six nests were observed there in 2004, a total of 15 were estimated based on the number of sites not visible due to overhang (pers. obs.). Reported as breeding but numbers unknown at Pelikan Key (Voous 1983; Hoogerwerf 1977). None recorded during a land-based survey in June 2004 (pers. obs.).

Bridled Tern

In June 2004, 15 nests estimated, and eggs observed, on Pelikan Key based on number of adults calling. Six adults were seen entering crevices on Molly B'day (pers. obs.).

Least Tern

Up to ten nests recorded at Simpson Bay Lagoon on dredge spoil near Princess Juliana Airport, where most nests suffered predation, probably by feral dogs (pers. obs. 2004). This site is slated for an airport expansion project. It is now a parking lot.

Royal Tern

In June 2004, 47 nests with eggs and 90 individuals observed at Pelikan Key (pers. obs.).

Threats and Conservation

St. Maarten is a major tourism destination. It has experienced dramatic population growth and development and hence human disturbance and loss of seabird habitat. Introduced predators are a threat and include dogs, cats, rats (*Rattus* sp.), mice (*Mus musculus*), and mongoose (*Herpestes auropunctatus*). Groups of African green monkey or vervet (*Cercopithecus aethiops*), likely originating from St. Kitts or Nevis, have been observed in the higher mountainous areas and could expand to lower elevations, as has occurred in St. Kitts. Levels of egging and hunting are unknown, but the subsistence lifestyle has generally been phased out with the increase in tourism sector employment.

The Netherlands Antilles has signed various international conventions to protect wildlife, but there is no local legislation to allow implementation on St. Maarten, Saba, or St. Eustatius. The nature ordinance states that one cannot destroy valuable flora and fauna, but there is no list of species considered valuable. New nature protection legislation has been drafted and is pending government approval. However, awareness of environmental issues is on the increase due to the work of local organizations and the conspicuous loss of natural areas and wildlife. A marine protected area has been established and boat moorings have been installed, although securing park funding has been problematic.

Saba

Saba (17.38° N, 63.13° W; 13 km²) is an extinct volcanic peak, rising steeply to 887 m with a coastline dominated by agglomerate cliffs (map 35). The interior is scrub and grassland transitioning to secondary rainforest and tree fern brake at middle elevations and elfin woodland at the peak (Stoffers 1956; Augustinus et al. 1985). The human population of the island is 1,200 individuals (Rojer 1997a).

Three of the following seven species were confirmed breeding on Saba (table 13.2); three additional species are reported breeding but no population counts are available.

Table 13.2. Estimates of seabird pairs breeding on Saba, 2002–2004

Species	Counts (pairs)
Audubon's Shearwater	n/e[a]
White-tailed Tropicbird	<5
Red-billed Tropicbird	750–1,000
Brown Noddy	30
Sooty Tern	30
Bridled Tern	30

a. n/e =no estimates of breeding pairs, 2003.

Audubon's Shearwater

Saba has been a major nesting site for Audubon's Shearwater for at least several thousand years. Excavations at Plum Piece, Saba, dating to 3,000 years before present, uncovered "large quantities" of seabird bones, almost exclusively those of Audubon's Shearwater (Hofman and Hoogland 2003). Humans are suspected of having used Saba as a worksite during the shearwater nesting season. The easily captured, protein-rich shearwaters and land crabs provided an abundant food source, enabling people of a subsistence culture to focus on nonhunting activities such as boat building (Hofman and Hoogland 2003). The use of shearwaters as a human food source may currently persist on Saba.

Audubon's Shearwater, locally known as "Wedrego," is the Saban national bird and is represented on the seal of the island. However, many residents are no longer familiar with the species (pers. obs.). The peak breeding period on Saba is unknown. Specimens have been collected from Saba during December and January (Voous 1955a). One shearwater was found on an egg near Sulphur Mine in February 2002. No calls were heard during 10 hours of nocturnal observations in February (Collier et al. 2002). In April 2004, two hours of nocturnal callplayback resulted in one response by a shearwater near The Bottom. In May 2004, four hours of nocturnal callplayback resulted in three responses near The Bottom and 15–20 responses at Sulphur Mine. It is possible there is no peak in breeding activity, resulting in a protracted nesting period, which would hinder population estimates. The steep topography limits accurate nest counts as well, although numbers of flying or calling adults may be used (pers. obs.). The only existing island estimate, which is based on potential habitat, places the population at a minimum of 1,000 breeding pairs (Lee 2000b). If this estimate is accurate, Saba harbors a significant portion of the total West Indian population of Audubon's Shearwater.

White-tailed Tropicbird

Recent estimates place the population at 50–100 pairs. They are found less frequently than Red-billed Tropicbird (Walsh-McGehee 2000). A few pairs of White-tailed Tropicbirds were observed entering crevices near Booby Hill in February 2002 (pers. obs.).

Red-billed Tropicbird

Recent estimates place the population at 750–1,000 pairs (Walsh-McGehee 2000). This species nests at virtually all seaside cliffs on Saba (pers. obs.). A multiyear nest productivity and site/mate fidelity study has recently been completed at a colony near the landfill. EPIC will continue periodic checks on the colony and banded individuals.

Brown Booby

This species was reported breeding in June and July on Diamond Rock by Voous (1955a). Breeding status was considered unknown (Halewyn and Norton 1984). In 2004, Brown Booby was reported as a nonbreeder, although it is frequently seen at Green Island, including juveniles believed to originate from nesting sites on other islands (M. Walsh-McGehee, pers. comm.). Booby roosting on Green Island have been observed flushing as planes fly in to land at the airport, which opened for commercial flights in 1963 (pers. obs.). Increasing frequency of flights over the decades may have increased disturbance levels, ending any possible previous nesting.

Brown Noddy

Reported as breeding in unknown numbers (Chardine et al. 2000b; Halewyn and Norton 1984). Breeding on Diamond Rock and Green Island; an estimate of 30 pairs is based on island size (M. Walsh McGehee, pers. comm. 2004).

Sooty Tern

Breeding on Diamond Rock; an estimate of 30 pairs is based on island size (M. Walsh McGehee, pers. comm. 2004).

Bridled Tern

In May 1972, 25 pairs of Bridled Terns were observed nesting on Diamond Rock (Voous 1983). Reported as breeding (Halewyn and Norton 1984). Breeding on Green Island and Diamond Rock; an estimate of 30 pairs is based on island size (M. Walsh-McGehee, pers. comm. 2004).

Threats and Conservation

Shearwaters and tropicbirds are threatened by introduced predators including dogs, cats, rats, and mice and by goat trampling of burrows. Human disturbance may be of concern as outdoor tourism activities such as hiking and rock climbing expand. Tropicbirds nest near the entrance to the island garbage burning site as well as a quarry and harbor/coastal fortification project.

Saba maintains a marine park that supports the diving industry, a major contributor to the economy. The Saba National Park provides support to the economy as well through popular and well-maintained hiking trails.

A feral cat sterilization program has sterilized at least 200 cats thus far and a government-sponsored rodent control program is in effect in localized areas (Sally Lynn, pers. comm. 2004). The government has begun to enforce laws requiring the registration and confinement of livestock in order to reduce the environmental impacts of feral animals.

St. Eustatius

St. Eustatius, or Statia (17° 46 ' N, 62° 98 ' W; 21 km²), is composed of a denuded volcano in the northwest and a young volcano in the southeast, known as the Quill (601 m) (map 37). Between these two formations is a low sloping plain with a sand beach on the northeast and a rocky beach on the southeast (Rojer 1997b). The remainder of the coastline is steep cliffs or xeric vegetated slopes. The interior vegetation is composed primarily of thorn woodland but also secondary evergreen forest (Stoffers 1956; Augustinus et al. 1985). The human population is approximately 2,700 (Rojer 1997b).

One of the following four species, Red-billed Tropicbird, was confirmed breeding on St. Eustatius in 2003.

Audubon's Shearwater

In 1955, Voous reported that Audubon's Shearwater was found "commonly at the rocks and cliffs south of Tumble Down Dick Bay." However, this site was severely altered by the oil terminal built in the bay in 1982 (Rojer 1997b). Gallows Bay is a suspected breeding site due to the presence of the slaughtered carcasses of Audubon's Shearwaters found there in May 1972 (Voous 1983). In 2003, a resident reported that shearwaters are still heard calling as they pass over the lowlands at certain times of year, although less frequently than in the past; he was unsure of the time of year the calling occurred (Collier and Brown 2003).

White-tailed Tropicbird

Van Halewyn and Norton (1984) reported the status as breeding. Walsh-McGehee (2000) reported less than 10 pairs. None were seen during a 2003 seabird survey, although the more inaccessible portions of the island were not visited (Collier and Brown 2003).

Red-billed Tropicbird

Past estimates have placed the population at "somewhat more" than 20 pairs (Voous 1983). In 2002, 250 pairs were estimated to nest on Statia (M. Walsh McGehee, pers. comm. 2004). In 2003, the population was conservatively estimated at 100–200 breeding pairs, although a significant portion of suitable habitat was not surveyed due to time limitations (plate 40; Collier and Brown 2003).

Sooty Tern

Reported breeding prior to 1950 but no population estimate given (Saliva 2000a). No known recent sightings have been reported.

Threats and Conservation

Overgrazing is a serious problem, resulting in denuded and eroded landscapes, and goats continue to roam freely in legally protected areas, possibly trampling tropicbird and any existing shearwater burrows. Island garbage is deposited in a ravine, or *ghaut*, on Zeelandia Beach, where tropicbirds nest. During storm surges and high winds, this trash is dispersed over the coastal zone, possibly resulting in entanglement or consumption of debris such as plastics by seabirds and other marine life. Oiling of wildlife is a threat to seabirds during spills from the oil transfer station. Introduced predators that threaten seabirds include dogs, cats, rats, and mice.

The St. Eustatius Marine Park protects a strip from the high water line to a 30 m depth and provides income through dive tourism. National parks have been created to protect the volcano called the Quill and the northern hills, known as Boven Subsector. The government has recently begun to enforce laws requiring the registration and confinement of livestock.

14

The French Antilles I

Guadeloupe and Islands, St. Martin, and St. Barthélemy

GILLES LEBLOND

The French Antilles discussed here include two island groups: the northern Windward Island group and the southern Leeward Island group (maps 34, 36, 38). The Windward group comprises St. Martin (5,200 ha), Tintamarre (1,200 ha), and St. Barthélemy (St. Barts, 2,100 ha). The Leeward group comprises Guadeloupe (Basse-Terre, 84,800 ha and Grande-Terre, 59,000 ha), Marie-Galante (15,800 ha), La Desirade (2,000 ha), Petite Terre (1,700 ha), and Les Saintes (1,300 ha). The total human population is about 430,000.

Historical data on seabird populations are lacking, and a species by species comparison of breeding phenology, intra-island nesting distribution, and species composition needs to be conducted to provide a baseline for future evaluation.

Methods of Survey

Censuses of the 14 species breeding in the major two island groups have been undertaken since 1999 under the Regional Directorate of the Environment of Guadeloupe (DIREN). Counts of the majority of nesting pairs of seabirds were made on land by surveys of the entire breeding site; where this was not possible, counts of breeding populations were made from boats.

The estimated total population counts on Guadeloupe and its out-islands and St. Martin and St. Barts in 2002 are shown in table 14.1. These modern surveys do not reflect population trends for these island groups, an analysis that still needs to be done.

Three tables provide more detailed breakdown of

Table 14.1. Estimates of seabird pairs breeding on Guadeloupe, St. Martin, and St. Barthélemy, 2002

Species	Total pairs on Guadeloupe & out-islands	Total pairs on St. Martin and St. Barthélemy
Audubon's Shearwater	n/e[a]	n/e[a]
White-tailed Tropicbird	44–90	4–6
Red-billed Tropicbird	235–430	180–330
Brown Booby		150–175
Red-footed Booby	<10	
Brown Pelican		0
Laughing Gull		440–450
Brown Noddy	380–510	203–250
Sooty Tern	3,050–4,000	150–300
Bridled Tern	240–310	80–110
Least Tern	45–80	75–85
Roseate Tern	10–30	
Common Tern		0
Royal Tern		30–50

a. n/e Breeding, no estimates.

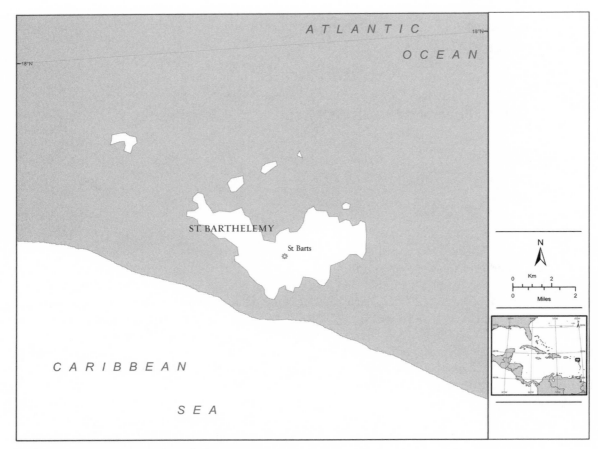

Map 36. St. Barthélemy, French Antilles.

breeding seabirds for Guadeloupe (Basse-Terre and Grande-Terre, table 14.2; Marie-Galante, table 14.3; and Les Saintes, La Desirade and Petite Terre, table 14.4). Counts for the 13 species breeding on St. Martin (and Tintamarre) and St. Barts in 2002 are in tables 14.5 and 14.6.

Species Accounts

Throughout the islands of Guadeloupe and St. Martin, the most frequent species of seabirds are Red-billed Tropicbird, Sooty Tern, and Brown Noddy (table 14.1). The islands of St. Barthélemy and Marie-Galante have the greatest numbers and species diversity.

In 2000–2002, the French Antilles gained one species, Red-footed Booby on Les Saintes, and lost one species, Sandwich Tern (and possibly also Brown Pelican and Common Tern). Since the studies of Bénito-Espinal (1990) and Bénito-Espinal and Hautcastel (2003), several species have ceased breeding, mainly on the most developed islands of St. Martin, Guadeloupe, Islet Vieux Fort on Marie Galante, and Les Saintes. Only one small

colony of Common Tern remained on Basse-Terre from the six islands listed in Bénito-Espinal (1990).

Audubon's Shearwater

A migratory breeder on St. Barts, St. Martin, and Guadeloupe, including its out-islands Marie-Galante, Les Saintes, and Desirade but not Petite Terre (Bénito-Espinal 1990). In 2000–2002, present in unknown numbers on Tintamarre (the only site for St. Martin and St. Barts), Falaises Nord-est only on Marie Galante and Desirade; presence questionable on Les Saintes and Islet Vieux Fort on Marie Galante. Absent from Guadeloupe.

White-tailed Tropicbird

A migratory breeder on St. Barts, St. Martin, and Guadeloupe, including its out-islands Marie-Galante, Les Saintes, and Desirade but not Petite Terre (Bénito-Espinal 1990). Similar distribution in 2002.

Red-billed Tropicbird

A migratory breeder at St. Barts, St. Martin, and Guadeloupe, including its out-islands Marie-Galante, Les

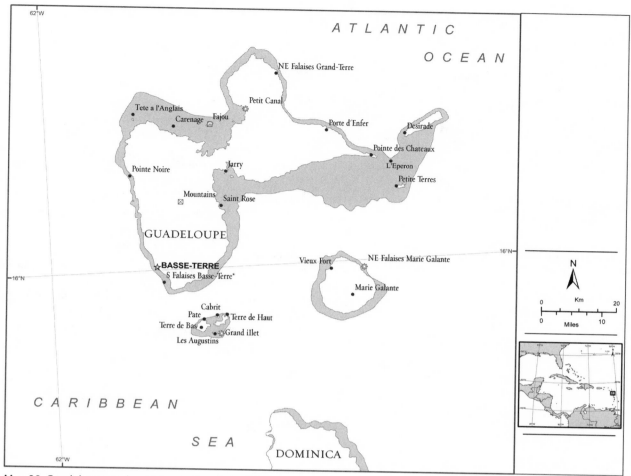

Map 38. Guadeloupe and out-islands, French Antilles.

Table 14.2. Estimates of seabird pairs breeding on Basse-Terre and Grande-Terre, Guadeloupe, 2002

Species	Basse-Terre			Grande-Terre	
	Falaise sud	Ilet Tête a l'Anglais (island)	Zone industrielle de Jarry	Falaises NE	Point de Chateaux
White-tailed Tropicbird	5–10			5–10	5–10
Red-billed Tropicbird				40–70	25–35
Brown Noddy		50–60		30–60	10–20
Sooty Tern		500–700			1,500–2,000
Bridled Tern		50–60		10–20	50–60
Least Tern.			10–30		20–30
Roseate Tern	10–30				

Table 14.3. Estimates of seabird pairs breeding on Marie-Galante, Guadeloupe, 2002

Species	Islet Vieux Fort	Falaises Nord-est
Audubon's Shearwater	?	Present
White-tailed Tropicbird	5–20	
Red-billed Tropicbird	150–300	
Brown Noddy	200–220	
Sooty Tern	600–700	300–400
Bridled Tern	40–50	10–20

Table 14.4. Estimates of seabird pairs breeding on Les Saintes, La Desirade, and Petite Terre, Guadeloupe, 2002

Species	Les Saintes	Désirade	Petite Terre
Audubon's Shearwater	?	Present	
White-tailed Tropicbird	20–30	4–10	
Red-billed Tropicbird	5	15–20	1
Red-footed Booby	<10		
Brown Noddy	50–100	40–50	
Sooty Tern	150–200		
Bridled Tern	40–50	40–50	
Least Tern			15–20

Table 14.5. Estimates of seabird pairs breeding on St. Martin, 2002

Species	Estimated Range
Audubon's Shearwater	Present (Tintamarre)
White-tailed Tropicbird	4–6
Red-billed Tropicbird	40–50
Brown Noddy	105–130
Bridled Tern	5–10
Least Tern	60–65

Table 14.6. Estimates of seabird pairs breeding on St. Barthélemy, 2000 and 2002

Species	Estimated Range
Red-billed Tropicbird	140–280
Brown Booby	150–175
Brown Pelican	18 in 2000; 0 in 2002
Laughing Gull	440–450
Brown Noddy	98–120
Sooty Tern	150–300
Bridled Tern	75–100
Least Tern	15–20
Roseate Tern	30–50 in 2000; 0 in 2002
Common Tern	30–35 in 2000; 0 in 2002
Royal Tern	30–50

Saintes, Desirade, and Petit Terre (Bénito-Espinal 1990, Leblond 2003a, b).

Brown Booby

Resident breeder on St. Barts; suspected breeder at St. Martin (Voous 1983) and on Guadeloupe, including its out-island Les Saintes (Bénito-Espinal 1990). In 2002, breeding only on St. Barts. Not breeding on St. Martin, Guadeloupe, or Les Saintes.

Red-footed Booby

Not recorded as a breeder at St. Barts, St. Martin, or Guadeloupe or its out-islands (Halewyn and Norton 1984; Bénito-Espinal 1990). In 2002, fewer than 10 pairs were

estimated at Les Saintes off the southern tip of Guadeloupe, a distribution expansion of this uncommon sulid.

Brown Pelican

An erratic breeder on St. Barts and possibly St. Martin, and on Guadeloupe only on its out-island Les Saintes (Bénito-Espinal 1990). In 2000, the only record was of 18 pairs breeding on St. Barts, but breeding was not observed in 2002.

Magnificent Frigatebird

An erratic breeder on St. Barts and St. Martin (Bénito-Espinal 1990), although Voous (1983) had no earlier data to corroborate breeding on St Martin. No recent breeding records.

Laughing Gull

A migratory breeder on St. Barts and St. Martin (Bénito-Espinal 1990). In 2002, bred only on St. Barts.

Brown Noddy

A migratory breeder at St. Barts, Tintamarre, St. Martin, and Guadeloupe, including its out-islands Marie-Galante, Les Saintes, and Desirade but not Petite Terre (Bénito-Espinal 1990). In 2002, similar records.

Sooty Tern

A resident breeder on St. Barts, St. Martin, and Guadeloupe, including its out-islands Marie-Galante, Les Saintes, and Desirade but not Petite Terre (Bénito-Espinal 1990). In 2002, results were similar except there was no breeding on St. Martin or Desirade.

Bridled Tern

A migratory breeder on St. Barts, St. Martin, and Guadeloupe, including its out-islands Marie-Galante, Les Saintes, and Desirade but not Petite Terre (Bénito-Espinal 1990). Records were similar in 2002.

Least Tern

A migratory breeder on St. Barts, St. Martin, and Guadeloupe (Bénito-Espinal 1990). In 2002, breeding on St. Barts and St. Martin, on Basse-Terre (Jarry and White islet), and on Désirade with a new colony on the out-island of Petite Terre.

Roseate Tern

A migratory breeder on St. Barts, St. Martin, and Guadeloupe, including its out-islands Marie-Galante, Les Saintes, and Desirade but not Petite Terre (Bénito-Espinal 1990). Bred on St. Barts in 2000 but not in 2002; absent from St. Martin. Basse-Terre had the only colony on Guadeloupe and its out-islands.

Common Tern

A migratory breeder on St. Barts, St. Martin, and Guadeloupe, including its out-island Marie-Galante (Bénito-Espinal 1990). Bred on St. Barts in 2000 but no records in 2002; absent from St. Martin; possibly breeding on Basse-Terre in 2002, but no recent records and no records for the out-islands.

Royal Tern

A migratory breeder on St. Barts (Bénito-Espinal 1990); a small population continued to breed on St. Barts in 2002.

Sandwich Tern

A migratory breeder at St. Barts and Guadeloupe (Bénito-Espinal 1990). Not breeding in 2002.

Threats

Apart from the islets of Tête à l'Anglais (Basse-Terre) et La Roche (Pointe des Châteaux), the seabird populations of Guadeloupe have declined in species diversity and population size due to the absence of any functional protection and to human exploitation of the littoral areas. White-tailed Tropicbirds recorded nesting on the western coast of Basse-Terre by Pinchon (1976) had deserted the sites, and only a few pairs breed in the south of Basse-Terre. The cliffs of Basse-Terre are generally less steep and therefore more accessible for building development. The seabird population density on the cliffs of Grand-Terre compared poorly with that of Marie-Galante, having a ratio of five times fewer birds: 1.9–3.3 pairs/km on Grande-Terre compared to 10.7–21.4 pairs/km on Marie-Galante (Leblond 2003a, b, 2005).

Six species of seabird breed regularly on Marie-Galante, where protection of the cliffs has allowed thriving populations of Red-billed Tropicbirds to breed in the crevices in the cliff and Sooty Tern to nest on exposed rocks at the base of the escarpment. A nature reserve is being established to include the cliffs and the islet of Vieux Fort. An additional two species, Common Tern and Roseate Tern, are irregular breeders; both were present in 2000 but not in 2002. They and the Least Tern are threatened by the loss of breeding habitat on sand banks and altered salinas and probably also by pollution of coastal seas.

The threats to seabirds on Guadeloupe are similar to those on other Caribbean Islands (table 14.7):

- Human exploitation of the shoreline, house construction, the development of windmills on the cliff tops, and agriculture and livestock close to the cliff edges.
- Leisure activities and disturbance at nesting sites during the breeding season, including various forms of boat traffic (jet-skis, kayaks).
- Taking of eggs, young, or adults at some sites.
- Lack of enforcement.

Conservation

While French legislation in theory protects seabirds from human depredation (all seabirds are protected, and capture of birds and taking of eggs are illegal), there is little enforcement or protection for colonies outside the boundaries of established reserves. Some of the islands and beaches are privately owned, principally in St. Barthélemy, which may provide some protection from trespassers. Five of the 44 seabird breeding sites (11%) are Nature Reserves with effective protection by wardens; 13 of the sites (28%) have lesser protection and no wardening under Forêt domaniale du littorale (FDL), Conservatoire de l'Espace, Littoral et des Rivages Lacustres (CERL), Loi Littorale, and 50 pas géometriques legislation.

Protective legislation for two more areas is at the planning stage: a decree under Guadeloupe's prefecture for Protection de Biotopes (APB) should allow protection of the salinas on St. Martin and thus protection for the breeding sites of Least Tern; and a nature reserve is proposed on Marie-Galante combining its cliffs and the islet of Vieux Fort.

Applicable statutes in Guadeloupe create three kinds of protection. The highest level of protection for both

Table 14.7. Threats to seabird colonies on the archipelago of Guadeloupe, St. Martin, and St. Barthélemy

Islands	Sites	Habitats	Eoliennes	Agriculture	Loisirs	Braconnage
Desirade	Falaises Desirade			x	x	
	Petite Terre					
Grande Terre	Pointe des Chateaux				x	x
	Falaise Nord Grande-terre		XX	XX		
Basse Terre	Jarry	XX				
	Ilet et Tête à l'Anglais				X	X
	Falaise SE	XX				
Les Saintes	Terre-de-Bas	X	X			?
	Terre-de-haut				X	?
	Ilots				X	?
Marie Galante	Illet Vieux Fort				X	?
	Falaise NE	X		X		X
Saint Barthélemy	Failaises St Barthélemy	X				X
	Ilots			X	X	X
	Salines	XX			X	?
St Martin	Tintamarre				XX	?
	Falaises	XX	X		X	
	Salines	XX				

Notes: X = existing threats; XX = major threats; Eoliennes—Windmills; Loisirs—Human recreational activities; Braconnage—Human predation on seabirds.

habitats and fauna is the designation *Réserve naturelle*. There are four in Guadeloupe: Grand Cul-de-Sac Marin, Petite Terre, St. Barthélemy, and St. Martin. Affecting fauna only is the Arrêté national du 17 février 1989, a ministerial decree listing all birds as protected in Guadeloupe, including seabirds. Protection for habitat derives from the following laws and regulations:

Arrêté de Protection de Biotopes (APB): Regulates human activities on small areas in order to protect threatened plant and animal species' habitats.

Sites Classés (SC): A statute of classified sites to protect, conserve, and manage habitats characteristic of regions, scientific sites, etc.; certain activities, particularly construction, are regulated.

Sites Inscrits (SI): Registered sites have legislation similar to classified sites but more permissive.

Conservatoire de l'Espace Littoral et des Rivages Lacustres (CERL): A statutory body to protect littoral areas and lakeshores. Acquired lands can be managed as reserves or by local communities and remain open to the public.

Forêt Domaniale du Littoral (FDL): State-administered property with littoral forests and mangrove managed by the forestry department (ONF).

50 pas géométriques: The "King's Steps" legislation inherited from the monarchy refers to land up to 81.2 m from the sea edge. It aims to prevent urbanization, although some lands are privately owned

(ceded by the state) or belong to the community. It applies to all the communes in Guadeloupe except St. Barthélemy (where construction is close to the edge of the sea and is a major threat to cliff nesting seabirds). The shoreline of St. Martin has mostly been sold for private development.

Loi littorale: Act passed in 1986 to regulate construction on the coast.

Recommendations

To establish valid priorities for the study and conservation of seabirds it is important to know the degree of threat to their status in Guadeloupe and the wider Caribbean. Using indices based on Schreiber (2000a), the species most at risk in Guadeloupe are, in order of threat, Common Tern, Brown Pelican, Royal Tern, Roseate Tern, Red-footed Booby, and White-tailed Tropicbird. Following the study of seabirds in Guadeloupe and recommendations (Leblond 2003a, b), the directives entailed in Orientations Régionales de Gestion et de Conservation de la Faune sauvage et de ses habitats (ORGFH) have been approved.

Recognition of Seabird Colonies

Lack of knowledge of the status and importance of seabirds along the coastal areas and shores has led to their specific needs not being taken into consideration in regional development plans. The release of this study should make up for this omission and define management requirements by the organizations involved: ONF, national parks, CERL, the Regional Directorate of the Environment of Guadeloupe (DIREN), and decision makers in local government and community associations.

Providing Specific Protection

Since the seabird studies mentioned, certain colonies have benefited from strengthened protection (Arrêté de Biotope, arrêté préfectoral, etc.) that has limited access to breeding sites during the nesting season.

Further Monitoring and a Database

This proposal would allow the production of an atlas of breeding seabirds and monitoring the status of the colonies at least every five years. It should be done in collaboration with the nature reserves and managers of the areas concerned.

Regional Cooperation

The results of the study show that the conservation needs of seabirds, with their large biogeographic ranges, make international cooperation essential. This would be the only effective means to acquire the necessary regional research and continued monitoring. With the participation of the SCSCB, it could be undertaken through CAR-SPAW—the program for Caribbean Specially Protected Areas and Wildlife under the Cartagena Convention—especially for those species considered under threat in the West Indies.

Saint Christopher (St. Kitts) and Nevis

NATALIA COLLIER AND ADAM BROWN

The Federation of Saint Christopher and Nevis consists of volcanic islands about 3 km apart in the eastern Caribbean. They were among the earliest to be colonized by Europeans, who arrived during the 1620s.

Saint Christopher (St. Kitts)

Saint Christopher (St. Kitts) lies at 17 ° 19 ' N, 62 ° 45 ' W and is 176 km² in area (map 37). At the moist north end is the dormant volcano Mt. Liamunga (1,156 m), which is forested at the upper elevations, while the lower slopes are primarily sugar cane. The northern coastline is primarily cliffs (Steadman et al. 1997). The southeast is composed of low hills and thorn woodland vegetation along a tapering peninsula used for grazing livestock and for tourism development. The southern coastline is characterized by sand or rock shores with six coastal saline ponds. The human population is approximately 30,000. Booby Island (1 ha) is a rocky, vegetated islet approximately 40 m high and located about halfway between St. Kitts and Nevis.

Unless otherwise noted, methods used in surveys conducted by Environmental Protection in the Caribbean (EPIC) were visual counts either from land or boat using binoculars and/or spotting scopes. Where possible, adults or chicks in the nest were counted. If nests were not present or clearly visible, all adults were counted. Steadman et al. (1997) used personal sight records as well as museum specimens. Methods were not reported from other sources but are primarily sight records.

Eight of the following species are breeding on St. Kitts and the majority breed on Booby Island. Counts for seven species breeding in 2004 are given in table 15.1.

Red-billed Tropicbird

In late May 2004, two individuals were observed entering crevices at Booby Island (pers. obs.).

Brown Pelican

In July 1985, 56 Pelican nests with chicks were observed at Nag's Head (Arendt 1985). Reported to nest on Booby Island, between St. Kitts and Nevis (Burdon 1920), where a few individuals were noted in 2004 (J. Johnson, pers. comm.).

Magnificent Frigatebird

In July 1985, nine Frigatebird nests with chicks were observed at Nag's Head (Arendt 1985). No recent data.

Laughing Gull

In late May 2004, 100–150 pairs were estimated for Booby Island (pers. obs.).

Brown Noddy

In late May 2004, 6–10 pairs were estimated for Booby Island (pers. obs.).

Sooty Tern

The island breeding population is estimated at 50–100 pairs, based on observations in the mid-1990s (Saliva 2000a). In late May 2004, 200–250 nests were estimated for Booby Island (pers. obs.).

Bridled Tern

In late May 2004, 50–75 nests were counted on Booby Island (pers. obs.).

Least Tern

In June 1935, 30 pairs were observed on eggs and chicks at Greatheeds Pond (Danforth 1936a). None were seen at Greatheeds Pond in 2004. However, the shoreline from Greatheeds Pond to Barker's Point held approximately 30 pairs, and it is likely this is the colony to which Danforth was referring (pers. obs.) In July 1985, prior to the con-

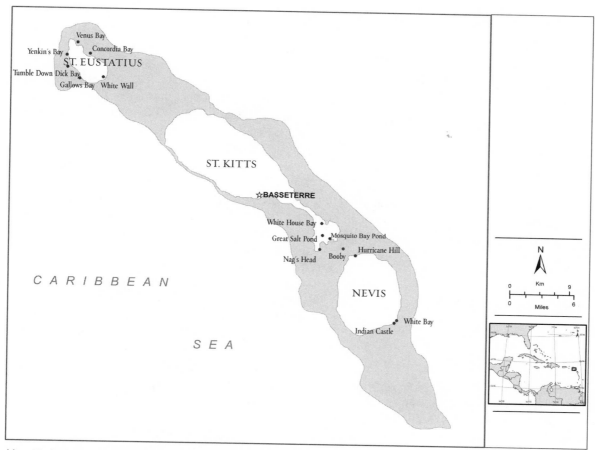

Map 37. St. Eustatius, Netherlands Antilles, and St. Christopher and Nevis.

struction of the southeast peninsula road, five nests with eggs were observed at Little Salt Pond, one nest at Mosquito Bay Beach, 16 pairs at Cockleshell Bay, and four pairs at Major's Bay (Arendt 1985). Twenty individuals, including juveniles, were observed in July 1988 on the southeast peninsula. In late May 2004, there were five nests and 20 adults at Mosquito Bay pond and five nests and 27 adults at the northeast end of Great Salt Pond. No Least Terns were observed at the remaining ponds or Cockleshell and Major's bays. All ponds are heavily frequented by cattle; tern nests are among manure piles and risk being trampled (pers. obs.).

Roseate Tern

In July 1988, 12 Roseate Terns (including juveniles) were observed at White House Bay. The island breeding population is estimated at 100–200 breeding pairs, based on observations in the mid-1990s (Saliva 2000b). In late May 2004, six pairs were recorded on Booby Island. None were seen at White House Bay, but the entire headland was not surveyed (pers. obs.).

Table 15.1. Estimates of seabird pairs breeding on St. Kitts, 2004

Species	Counts (pairs)
Red-billed Tropicbird	2
Laughing Gull	100–150
Brown Noddy	6–10
Sooty Tern	200–250
Bridled Tern	50–75
Least Tern	10–20
Roseate Tern	6

Nevis

Nevis (17 ° 10 ' N, 62 ° 35 ' W; 93 km²) is an extinct volcano rising to an elevation of 985 m (map 37). Vegetation is similar to that of northern St. Kitts. The human population is estimated at 10,000.

Three of the following four species, Magnificent Frigatebird, Laughing Gull, and Least Tern, were reported breeding in 2004, but no population counts are available. No information on survey methods was available.

Magnificent Frigatebird

Reported to nest in the Hurricane Hill–Newcastle area in unknown numbers (Hilder 1989; J. Johnson, pers. comm. 2004).

Laughing Gull

Reported nesting in the Hurricane Hill-Newcastle area in unknown numbers (Hilder 1989; J. Johnson, pers. comm. 2004).

Least Tern

Breeding was suspected (Halewyn and Norton 1984); this species is confirmed breeding at the north end of White Bay (J. Johnson, pers. comm. 2004; Hilder 1989).

Roseate Tern

Breeding is suspected but not confirmed (Saliva 2000b; Halewyn and Norton 1984), with recent sightings near Indian Castle (J. Johnson, pers. comm. 2004).

Threats and Conservation

The planned tourism development of the St. Kitts southeast peninsula will likely have an adverse impact on nesting pelicans and frigatebirds around Nag's Head and on terns around salt ponds. Currently, the only protected areas on the peninsula are slopes highly susceptible to erosion and the beaches. Grazing on the southeast peninsula creates a high risk of trampling of Least Tern nests. Introduced predators in both St. Kitts and Nevis include dogs, cats, rats, mice, mongoose, and the African Green Monkey.

A boat charter operator reported that egging of Laughing Gulls (locally called boobies) continues on a small scale. Rats were not observed during one visit to Booby Island, and no fishing settlements were present, making introduction unlikely.

There are no known officially protected areas in Nevis. St. Kitts has one protected area, the Brimstone Hill Fortress National Park. The Forestry Ordinance of 1904 protects areas above 300 m (Towle et al. 1986). The Wild Birds Protection Ordinance of 1913 prohibited or regulated hunting of 27 species. The National Conservation and Environment Protection Act (NCEPA) of 1987 enables further protection for approximately 90 avian species. An NCEPA amendment in 2000 provided Protected Area status to all South East Peninsula beaches and selected mainland beaches. It is recommended that (1) Booby Island be given protected status for its key role as the main seabird nesting for St. Kitts and Nevis and (2) grazing should be restricted at Least Tern breeding sites on the southeast peninsula. However, in 2007 a significant portion of the Southeast Peninsula had been slated for development as part of the Christophe Harbor resort, including a mega yacht marina, golf course, hotels, restaurants, and shops.

Plate 1. A 10-day-old Bermuda Petrel chick removed from a nest burrow as part of a chick growth rate study throughout the 90-day fledging period. Chicks are banded before departing to sea, returning after four years to choose nest sites and mates. Photographer Jeremy Madeiros.

Plate 2. An endangered adult Bermuda Petrel removed for banding (ringing) and a check of body condition and weight on a nesting islet in Castle Harbour Islands Nature Reserve. Photographer Jeremy Madeiros.

144

Plate 3. Nesting and prospecting adult Bermuda Petrels fly in acrobatic courtship displays over a nesting island in Castle Harbour, Bermuda, during November. The estimated 2007 population was 300 birds, with 80 active nest sites. Photographer Jeremy Madeiros.

Plate 4. An endangered Black-capped Petrel foraging off the coast of South Carolina. Copyright © Harold Stiver/VIREO.

Plate 5. Adult Audubon's Shearwater. Photographer David Lee.

Plate 6. Audubon's Shearwater chick. Photographer David Lee.

Plate 7. An adult White-tailed Tropicbird brooding in a natural cliff cavity on Nonsuch Island, Bermuda. A total of 2,000 pairs nest, with up to 600 on the Castle Harbour Islands Nature Reserve (including Nonsuch Island). Photographer Jeremy Madeiros.

Plate 8. A pair of Red-billed Tropicbirds in a cavity nest. Photographer Judy Pierce.

Plate 9. Adult Masked Booby on Middle Cay, Pedro Cays, Jamaica. Copyright © The Nature Conservancy, photographer Donovan Brandon Hay.

Plate 10. An adult Brown Booby with an eight-week-old chick on the edge of the bluff, Cayman Brac. Photographer Patricia E. Bradley.

148

Plate 11. Juvenile Brown Booby on Cayo de Agua Cay, Los Roques Archipelago National Park, Venezuela. Photographer Juan Papadakis.

Plate 12. Adult Red-footed Booby (dark phase), Booby Pond Nature Reserve, Little Cayman. Photographer Patricia E. Bradley.

Plate 13. Adult Brown Pelican in Dos Mosquises Sur Cay, Los Roques Archipelago National Park, Venezuela. Photographer Juan Papadakis.

Plate 14. Female Magnificent Frigate-bird with chick on a nest in mangrove, Booby Pond Nature Reserve, Little Cayman. Photographer Patricia E. Bradley.

Plate 15. Male Magnificent Frigatebird flying with gular sac extended, Little Cayman. Photographer Patricia E. Bradley.

Plate 16. Magnificent Frigatebird entangled in fishing line in the breeding colony on Great Tobago Cay, British Virgin Islands. Photographer Judy Pierce.

151

Plate 17. Laughing Gull in breeding plumage. Photographer Eladio Fernandez.

Plate 18. Laughing Gull nest with chick and eggs on Pelona Cay, Los Roques Archipelago National Park, Venezuela. Photographer Juan Papadakis.

Plate 19. Brown Noddy. Photographer Bruce Hallett.

Plate 20. Sooty Tern in breeding plumage. Photographer Rodrigo Lazo.

Plate 21. Bridled Tern in breeding plumage. Photographer Eladio Fernandez.

Plate 22. Least Tern in breeding plumage. Photographer Eladio Fernandez.

Plate 23. Gull-billed Tern in breeding plumage. Photographer Yves-Jacques Rey-Millet.

Plate 24. Roseate Tern in breeding plumage. Photographer Yves-Jacques Rey-Millet.

Plate 25. Common Tern in breeding plumage. Photographer Bruce Hallett.

Plate 26. Royal Tern in breeding plumage. Photographer Bruce Hallett.

Plate 27. Royal Tern in nonbreeding plumage. Photographer Bruce Hallett.

Plate 28. Sandwich Tern in breeding plumage. Photograph courtesy of the Division of Fish and Wildlife, U.S. Virgin Islands.

Plate 31. The artificial nest burrow for the Bermuda Petrel constructed with a 180 cm concrete entrance tunnel leading to an underground nest chamber 45 cm × 45 cm. A 10 cm lidded hole in the top allows observation or removal for banding. Photographer Jeremy Madeiros.

Plate 32. White-tailed Tropicbirds in artificial "igloo" nests constructed of compressed polystyrene strengthened with fiberglass. The nests are cemented into place on cliff edges and seaside terraces and camouflaged with natural rocks, Nonsuch Island, Bermuda. Photographer Jeremy Madeiros.

Plate 33. Aerial of the Booby Pond Nature Reserve, Little Cayman, with colonies of Red-footed Booby and Magnificent Frigate-bird on the landward side (left) of the pond. Photographer Patricia E. Bradley.

Plate 34. The limestone plateau of the eastern bluff, Cayman Brac, supporting Brown Booby and White-tailed Tropicbird colonies. Photographer Patricia E. Bradley.

Plate 35. Aerial of Middle Cay, Pedro Cays, Jamaica, with over 50% of the cay occupied by dwellings, confining the Masked Booby colony nests to disturbed vegetation in the northwest segment. Copyright © The Nature Conservancy, photographer Donovan Brandon Hay.

Plate 36. Aerial of South West Cay, Pedro Cays, Jamaica. The cay is uninhabited, except for fishermen, and supports booby, frigatebird, and tern colonies. Copyright © The Nature Conservancy, photographer Donovan Brandon Hay.

Plate 37. Masked Booby showing the close proximity to human settlement, Middle Cay, Pedro Cays, Jamaica. Photographer Ann Haynes Sutton.

Plate 38. Aerial of Cockroach and Sula cays, U.S. Virgin Islands. Photograph courtesy of the Division of Fish and Wildlife, U.S. Virgin Islands.

Plate 39. The Magnificent Frigatebird colony breeds in seagrape trees on the shoreline of Great Tobago Cay, British Virgin Islands. Photographer Judy Pierce.

Plate 40. A Red-billed Tropicbird flies above the rocky hills at Fort Royal, St. Eustatius, where numerous nesting sites are located. Photographer Natalia Collier.

Plate 41. Pinnacle Rock, Montserrat, is a small offshore stack off the northeastern coast. It is free from non-native species and has colonies of Brown Pelicans and Magnificent Frigatebirds. Photographer Richard Allcorn.

Plate 42. The St. Giles Islands, taken from Flagstaff Hill, Tobago, lie 0.4 km offshore to the east-northeast and have breeding colonies of Audubon's Shearwater, Red-billed Tropicbird, Brown Booby, Red-footed Booby, Magnificent Frigatebird, and Brown Noddy. Photographer Floyd Hayes.

164

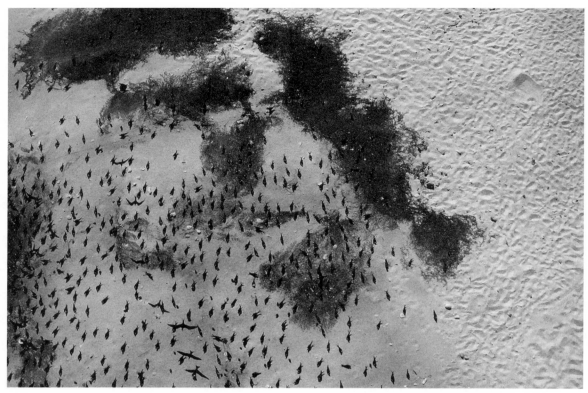

Plate 43. Aerial of a Sooty Tern colony, estimated at 12,000 pairs in 2007, taken from a kite on Aves Island, Venezuela. Photographer Rodrigo Lazo.

Plate 44. Brown Noddy colony, estimated at 5,500 pairs, nesting on sea purslane on Aves Island, Venezuela. Photographer Rodrigo Lazo.

16

Montserrat

RICHARD I. ALLCORN AND J. "SCRIBER" DALEY

Montserrat is one of the Leeward Islands lying in the middle of the Lesser Antilles in the eastern Caribbean Sea, situated at 16° 45' N, 62° 12' W. It is a single island, 11 km wide by 18 km long (198 km²), located 39 km southwest of Antigua and 64 km northwest of Guadeloupe (map 39). The Puerto Rico Bank, approximately 426 km to the WNW, is the nearest large landmass. Montserrat is entirely volcanic and very mountainous, consisting of three volcanic upwellings lying on a north-south axis.

The oldest part of the island is the Silver Hills in the north (1 million years old), while the Soufrière Hills complex in the south is only 170,000 years old and currently active. The Centre Hills (0.5–1 million years old) form the topography in the middle of the island. These mountains rise up to 900 m above sea level. They are typically heavily vegetated with cloud-, elfin and rainforest and cut through with steep valleys (locally known as *ghauts*) that run down to the sea. The coastal areas of the island below 100 m, and the drier north where not developed, are dominated by xeric acacia scrubland. The coastline, of which there is approximately 40 km, is extremely rugged, much of it made up of medium height cliffs (up to 70 m); there are no natural all-weather anchorages.

A fluctuating population of both Arawak and Carib peoples sporadically inhabited Montserrat in pre-Columbian times. Columbus "discovered" the island in 1493 but did not land on Montserrat, and the island remained free of European influence until 1632, when it fell under British control following the arrival of mainly Irish religious fugitives from Nevis and St. Christopher. It remained a British Colony for the next 300 years, developing the traditional West Indian slave-driven plantation economy. The majority of the forested land was cleared for agriculture, the main crops being sugar, cotton, and citrus fruits. The island is now a U.K. Overseas Territory.

The island was hit by two major natural disasters in the last two decades of the twentieth century. Hurricane Hugo struck Montserrat with full force in September 1989, damaging over 90 percent of the structures on the island. The tourist trade upon which the island depended was nearly extinguished and to date has not really recovered. In July 1995 the Soufrière Hills volcano, dormant throughout recorded history, rumbled into life and began an eruption that eventually buried the island's capital, Plymouth, in more than 10 metres of mud and rendered the southern half of the island, including the airport and dock facilities, uninhabitable. More than two-thirds of the 13,000 inhabitants evacuated the island, and the population now stands at around 4,500 people (Foreign and Commonwealth Office 2005).

There are no protected areas on Montserrat, although a terrestrial national park is being created in the Centre Hills (RSPB/Darwin project 2005). Work is also under way with the aim of creating a marine protected area, but no date for designation or detail of location is currently obtainable. Environmental management is retained within the Ministry for Agriculture, Housing, Land and the Environment (MAHLE) but is heavily dependent on external expertise from the United Kingdom and United States. The Montserrat National Trust (established in 1970) is the lead organization in conserving and promoting the island's cultural and environmental heritage.

Methods of Survey

While some seabirds breed throughout the year, including the Brown Booby, most species in the Caribbean nest between May and August. Ideally, breeding surveys should be undertaken toward the end of the egg-laying period, but for logistical reasons the first survey of Montserrat seabirds, in 1999, was undertaken in August.

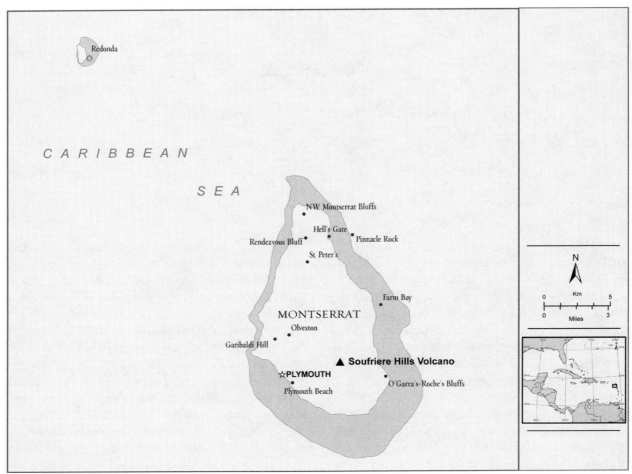

Map 39. Montserrat and Redonda.

For consistency, the repeat survey in 2005 was likewise performed toward the end of the breeding season.

With small scattered breeding populations on Montserrat, as opposed to extensive colonies, and with no potential inland breeding sites, the most effective way to survey the entire Montserrat coast in a single day is by boat. Due to prevailing wind and sea conditions, the survey progressed from the west of the island around the southern tip and along the windward eastern coast. The locations of all sightings of seabirds were recorded on an island map and the GPS position taken. Where possible the age, sex, and behavior of the individual birds were also recorded. As the survey time was near the end of or after the main breeding season, identifying active breeding sites was not possible. Instead, the locations of plausible Apparently Occupied Sites (AOS) were recorded. Although survey design was not ideal to obtain exact population and breeding data, the repetitive nature of the survey should at least provide a useful indicative trend of the status of the small seabird populations on Montserrat.

Seabirds on the Island

Eight species of seabird, of which four are known to breed on the island, were recorded during the two surveys undertaken in 1999 and 2005 (table 16.1), with another nine species seen in the surrounding seas. Montserrat does not currently hold any regionally significant seabird populations.

Montserrat's seabirds mostly breed on the cliffs that form much of the rugged coastline of the island. There is one rocky stack, Pinnacle Rock (approx. 15 m^3; plate 41) on the northeast coast, which holds breeding Magnificent Frigatebird. Since there are no coastal lagoons or ponds nesting opportunities for non-cliff-nesting species such as terns are limited, although there are reports that some tern species have been using the newly created volcanic fans on the east coast for nesting. The nearby uninhabited island of Redonda, 18 km to the north, holds substantial numbers of breeding seabirds (C. Bowden, RSPB, pers. comm.) and many birds seen offshore of Montserrat may well originate from there.

Table 16.1. Estimates of seabird pairs breeding on Montserrat, 1999 and 2005

Species	Breeding pairs	
	1999	2005
Red-billed Tropicbird	16	11
Brown Booby	22	9
Brown Pelican	15	14
Magnificent Frigatebird	21	27

The historical presence of seabirds on Montserrat is unrecorded. An out-of-breeding-season boat survey of the cliffs was undertaken in August 1999, and the Royal Society for the Protection of Birds (U.K.) Montserrat Oriole Programme staff undertook a repeat survey in August 2005. These will hopefully form the basis for regular surveys to provide population trends and inform conservation action on the island. Due to ongoing volcanic activity in the south, it is logistically difficult to follow up sightings or undertake cliff surveys from the land.

Species Accounts

Four resident species are known to breed: Red-billed Tropicbird, Brown Booby, Brown Pelican, and Magnificent Frigatebird. One migrant, Royal Tern, is thought to have colonized recently, and there are unconfirmed reports of Caspian Tern breeding (two juveniles were seen fishing with adults in Fox's Bay in August 2005, possibly suggesting a small local population). There are no historical records for Audubon's Shearwater breeding, although remains of this species were found in archaeological excavations at Trants (Reis and Steadman 1999).

Red-billed Tropicbird

Small colonies of this species breed in holes in the cliffs around the island. The main concentrations are on North-West Bluff and beneath the South Soufrière Hills between O'Garra's and Roche's Bluff. Pairs presumed to be breeding have also been recorded below Olveston and near Hell's Gate. Breeding pairs: 16 in 1999, 11 in 2005.

Brown Booby

Common resident and regularly encountered offshore all around Montserrat. Nesting is restricted to the sheltered cliff ledges on the northwest, with the largest colony located just north of the port on Rendezvous Bluff. A large population (150+) was recorded on Redonda in 2001. Breeding pairs: 22 in 1999, 9 in 2005.

Brown Pelican

Common resident. Found around the island in sheltered bays and inshore waters but more common on the leeward western side. Confirmed locations for breeding include Pinnacle Rock, St. Peter's, and Garibaldi Hill. Local reports suggest numbers have been increasing since 2002. Breeding pairs: 15 in 1999, 14 in 2005.

Magnificent Frigatebird

A common resident and visible around the entire coastline. The only breeding colony appears to be offshore on Pinnacle Rock (plate 41). At least 100 pairs were thought to be breeding on Redonda in 2001. Breeding pairs: 21 in 1999, 27 in 2005.

Royal Tern

Reports of breeding on the recently created pyroclastic fans in Farm Bay remain unconfirmed; Plymouth beach appears to support a few pairs. A juvenile Royal Tern seen in 2005 would suggest that this species does breed on island.

Threats

Seabirds on Montserrat are not under any immediate high-level threat, but due care should be taken to ensure that the small numbers occurring on island will persist. There are currently no protected areas on Montserrat, and addressing this situation in conjunction with the proposed development of a marine reserve would be highly beneficial. Clifftop residential developments continue along the western coast of Montserrat, especially in Woodlands, Olveston, and Old Towne, and their impact, including habitat destruction and increased disturbance, should be investigated and monitored.

A suggestion was made post-1997 to collapse the cliff face at Little Bay to create a breakwater for the new port. This would have destroyed the main Brown Booby site on the island as well as the only known remaining roost for the bat (*Brachyphylla cavernarum*) (S. Pederson, South Dakota State University, pers. comm.) and Caribbean Martin nest sites. Although this scheme has not progressed, vigilance is needed to ensure that such environmentally catastrophic proposals do not proceed in the future. Southern nest sites are at continued risk from pyroclastic activity, although as they survived the main eruptions, it is hoped that they will survive future volcanic activity.

Egg collecting and hunting may have been a problem in the past (as it was with forest bird species and sea turtles). This appears to have declined or stopped completely, but again vigilance on this potential problem should be maintained. Predation by rats, feral cats, and possibly feral pigs may continue to pose a significant problem. These species have been identified as problems at seabird colonies globally and may explain the low numbers of many seabird species on Montserrat and why the Magnificent Frigatebirds only nest offshore on Pinnacle Rock.

There is presumably little doubt that Montserrat formerly had far more seabirds than there are now, and their disappearance must be largely due to non-indigenous pressure, especially from cats, rats, and humans. The absence of shearwaters is almost certainly due to predation by introduced mammals. It is also probable that predators currently limit the range, and probably the numbers, of seabirds by restricting their breeding opportunities to the offshore stacks and the few less accessible cliffs. These sites may be unproductive, due to predation or poor habitat quality, and without a proper investigation of breeding success, there is the risk that the surviving populations are, at best, stable, or possibly population sinks driving a continued decline.

Conservation

There is no law in place on Montserrat that specifically addresses seabirds or their habitats. Given the birds' low numbers and probable low regional importance, this is not a high priority. All species of seabirds are afforded all-year protection from hunting or harvesting under the Forestry, Wildlife, National Parks and Protected Areas Act 1996, wherein all the known species, and all migratory terns and gulls, are listed as First Schedule (Section 31): Protected Wildlife. While there is no evidence that this law is currently being contravened, there is concern because monitoring and enforcement are so slight that any infringement would not be detected.

Montserrat has no protected sites. Sites potentially requiring protection are: (1) the cliffs of North-West Bluff and Rendezvous Bluff, (2) Pinnacle Rock, and (3) South Soufrière bluffs.

These sites, unsurprisingly, overlook many of the important inshore marine habitats, especially coral reefs and the tidal swellings where currents meet. Conservation and protection of both the cliffs and the water beneath them would be highly beneficial to local biodiversity and to the local economy through fisheries and tourism.

Further actions required are as follows:

Regular monitoring of seabird sites and numbers, especially in the breeding season.

Investigation into the effects of feral animals (especially rats, cats and pigs) on ground-nesting seabirds and development of appropriate control programs.

Maintaining vigilance to ensure the integrity of current nesting areas.

It is worth noting that almost nothing is known concerning the breeding phenology of seabirds in Montserrat. This is a crucial issue for tropical seabirds, because the breeding season can be locally variable, protracted, or even bimodal. Counts can seriously underestimate local population sizes and trends if they are undertaken at the wrong time of year, or even if done only once in a protracted season. This could well be the case for the limited data collected for seabirds on Montserrat; care should be taken in making assumptions based on these numbers. Both surveys described in this chapter were conducted in August, and, as noted, this is likely to have been late in the breeding season if not outside it for most of the species observed.

Acknowledgments

The authors would like to thank Phil Atkinson (who undertook the first survey) and the RSPB, especially Geoff Hilton and Chris Bowden, for their contributions to the surveys. Bryan Cunningham from Seawolf Diving was instrumental in the logistical completion of the second survey. Thanks also to Calvin Fenton and the Montserrat Forestry staff for their time and contributions.

Antigua-Barbuda-Redonda and Selected Offshore Islands

INGRID SYLVESTER, VICTOR JOSEPH, JUNIOR PROSPER, SHANEE PROSPER, AND BRANDON HAY

Antigua, Barbuda, and Redonda form a tripartite state, located 400 km southeast of Puerto Rico in the Lesser Antilles. Antigua is located at 17° 10' N, ° 40' W, and Barbuda is 45 km north of Antigua at 17° 35' N, 61° 48' W. Redonda, which lies closer to the island of Montserrat, is max. 39 km west-southwest of Antigua (maps 39, 40).

The islands of Antigua and Barbuda are populated, whereas Redonda is completely uninhabited. The total population stands at about 78,580, of which 1,200–1,600 are resident in Barbuda (Statistics Division, pers. comm. 2003). The island of Redonda is currently devoid of residents; however during the guano mining operation between 1895 and 1914, more than 130 persons, consisting of a labor force primarily from Montserrat, lived and worked on the island in shifts. Redonda remains remote and difficult to access and thus acts as a haven for nesting and migrant seabirds.

The 51 offshore islands of Antigua and Barbuda include Rabbit, Redhead, Lobster, and Great Bird islands in the North Sound area; Green and York in the east, and Five Islands in the west. All are uninhabited with the notable exception of the second largest of these, Long Island, which has been transformed into a major resort and area of luxury homes.

Topography

The topography of Antigua is diverse, and the island is characterized by three general geological regions. The northern and eastern portion is made up of hard and soft limestone deposits; the central plain is a mixture of agglomerates, tuffs, and conglomerates mixed with cherts and limestone. The south and southwestern portion of Antigua is of volcanic origin dating to the Upper Oligocene some 30–40 million years ago, having hard igneous rocks on the uplands and sedimentary deposits in the

valleys. This area has "light soils over calcareous sandstones and heavier soils over calcareous grits and deeper well-drained clays over marls" (Howell 1991). The central plain is found between the limestone and volcanic zones and consists of flood plains and low elevation hills. The volcanic zone in the south features small alluvial valleys and peaks; Boggy Peak is the highest point at 400 m.

The offshore cays of Antigua are relics of coral reefs; individual, or joined by a sand bar in the case of Great Bird Island, or artificially formed (e.g., Maiden Island) by the U.S. Navy with dredge spoil. Those in the northeast are characterized by limestone cliffs covered by dry scrub vegetation and surrounded by mangrove and coral reef systems, which provide valuable resources to the avifauna.

Barbuda (161 km²) is 23 km long by 8 km wide. It is a low-lying, coralline island, rising to a maximum of 31 m at the Central Highlands, which form a plateau in the north-central part of the island. It is divided into three geological zones: the highlands area, which is made up of hard limestone and solution holes; the Codrington Limestone region, which is composed of sandy and fossiliferous sediments; and the Palmetto region, composed of beach sand and shelly marine deposits. The only settlement is the town of Codrington on the western end of the island on the shore of the Codrington Lagoon (Danforth 1935b). The lagoon, the site of the frigate bird colony, is a mangrove-sheltered water body about 3 km wide, lying parallel to the sea but separated by a spit. The lagoon has a shallow bottom and extensive seagrass beds.

Redonda is the extinct cone of a volcano, approximately 1.6 km long by 0.8 km wide with cliffs of 278 m in altitude. The island is completely bounded by steep cliffs; a single beach and a plateau are the only sites accessible by boat and air.

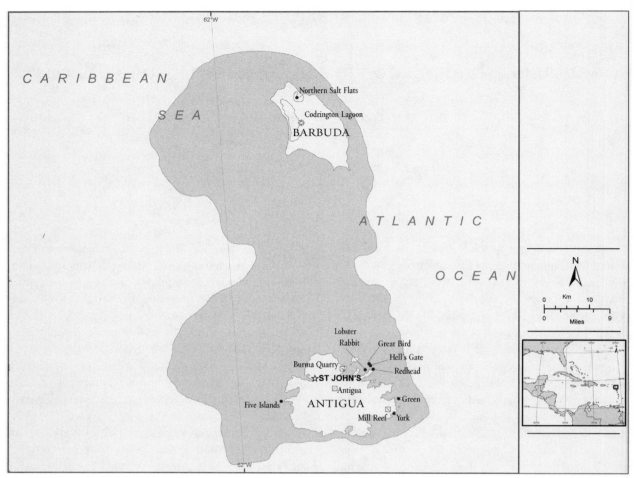

Map 40. Antigua and Barbuda.

Vegetation

The principal vegetation types on Antigua are ever-green deciduous forest in the southwest and evergreen woodland in the northeast. Barbuda is covered with xerophytic, dry woodland attributed to shallow soils, low rainfall, and the presence of grazers. Vegetation species that dominate the interior of the islands include black willow (*Capparis cynophallophora*), dogwood (*C. flexuosa*), wild eggplant (*Solanum toruum*), century plant (*Agave karatto*), prickly pear (*Opuntia dillenii*), and organ pipe cactus (*Pilosocereus* spp). Codrington Lagoon is lined by black mangrove (*Avicennia germinans*), red mangrove (*Rhizophora mangle*), white mangrove (*Laguncularia racemosa*), and buttonwood (*Conocarpus erectus*) (Howell 1991). At present Redonda is sparsely vegetated, but the species present include *Ficus citrifolia* and purslane (*Portulaca oleracea*); (Lindsay and Horwith, 1997a), and unidentified grasses.

The offshore islands are composed of sparsely to densely vegetated, consolidated or unconsolidated material. Since the eradication of rats on several islands, there have been observations that the vegetative cover has increased. Great Bird Island and Green Island were the only study sites having sand dunes with herbaceous vegetation, as *Ipomoea pes-caprae–Canavalia rosea* association (Lindsay and Horwith 1997a). Several of the islets are fringed by mangrove species—Great Bird, Rabbit, Redhead, Galley, Lobster, and Green islands.

Survey Sites

The seabirds of Antigua and Barbuda have not been studied using consistent methodology on a long-term basis; however, there have been occasional reports and studies over many years. One study, initiated by the Islands Resources Foundation from April to July, 1996, was limited to Antigua only. The Environmental Awareness Group (EAG) has been conducting regular surveys and monitoring of nesting seabirds on Antigua's offshore cays since 2000. Counts are of nests on the ground and/ or vegetation. Surveys are currently being conducted on five of the offshore islands—Rabbit, Redhead, Lobster, Great Bird (North Sound area), and Green islands—generally on a monthly basis, when flying birds are counted visually. The aim is to update the species inventory and determine population estimates, in order to provide the baseline for future research and area management and justify the establishment of species-specific protective legislation.

A grant from the National Fish and Wildlife Foundation funded studies on seldom visited islands—York, Five Islands, and Redonda. Funding did not include Barbuda, for which a literature search was conducted. Redonda is characterized by sheer cliffs and steep inclines; hence an aerial survey by helicopter was attempted and the coastal areas to the south and southwest were surveyed on foot.

Species Accounts

The ornithological history, although sporadic, is rich and dates to the period of Cyrus Winch's voyage to the region to collect specimens for Cory's catalogue of birds of the West Indies (Cory 1891a). Paleo-ornithologists and cultural archaeologists have contributed important information on the status of seabirds on Barbuda and Antigua. Their investigations are cited in the following accounts, as are recent surveys by short and long-term visitors who collected specimens or recorded species habits and phenology.

The offshore islands of Antigua provide refuges, foraging areas, and nesting sites for a wide diversity of species. There were 10 species found breeding in 2004: Red-billed Tropicbird, Brown Booby, Red-footed Booby, Brown Pelican, Magnificent Frigatebird, Laughing Gull, Brown Noddy, Sooty Tern, Roseate Tern, and Sandwich Tern The population estimates of breeding pairs in August 2004 are shown in table 17.1. The study was conducted during the chick stage for some species and at the end of the breeding season for other species.

Audubon's Shearwater

Known from midden material at Mill Reef, Antigua (Wing et al. 1968). Steadman and Olsen (in Pregill et al. 1988) identified fossil evidence of this species in a quarry fissure, suggesting that the species once nested on Antigua. They further speculate that material recovered from Barbuda (Brodkorb 1963) suggests this shearwater was more widespread as a nesting species. Indeed, the islets such as Great Bird or Hell's Gate would seem to provide

Table 17.1. Estimates of seabird pairs breeding on Antigua, Redonda, and offshore islands, August 2004

Species	Minimum Breeding pairs
Red-billed Tropicbird	3
Brown Booby	12
Red-footed Booby	60
Brown Pelican	53
Magnificent Frigatebird[a]	25
Laughing Gull	70
Brown Noddy	140
Sooty Tern	514
Bridled Tern	16
Roseate Tern	4
Sandwich Tern	7

a. Counts do not include species on Barbuda where the large frigatebird colony was estimated at 2,000 pairs (Lindsay et al. 2000).

suitable habitat. Audubon's Shearwater should be looked for on Redonda for possible breeding (Horwith and Lindsay 1997). There is no confirmation of breeding.

White-tailed Tropicbird

Recorded from vertebrate bone material at Mill Reef midden (Wing et al. 1968) and also reported from Barbuda as fossil material.

Red-billed Tropicbird

Danforth (1933; 1934a) reported three individuals observed at Great Bird Island on 3 August 1933. A local observer, Mr. Box, informed Danforth that in May there were large numbers breeding on the cliffs. Until this period, the species had not previously been recorded from Antigua. Holland and Williams (1978) reported that this species was common flying in and out of the sea cliffs at Great Bird Island from 1972 to 1977. A winter count of this species (2) was reported in 1977 at Barbuda (J. Marshall, pers. comm.). Varnham (2001) reported Red-billed Tropicbird with young on Green Island in May 2001. Survey work in 2004 at Green Island noted 3–4 pairs.

Masked Booby

Reported as a possible breeder at Redonda (Halewyn and Norton 1984). Birds were observed on Redonda in August 2004, including immatures, but it was too late in the season to confirm breeding.

Brown Booby

Specimen recorded by Cory (1891a) from Antigua in July. Breeding was suspected but not confirmed on Five Islands in 2004. A minimum of 12 pairs nested on Redonda in 2004.

Red-footed Booby

Estimates of this species are problematic since they breed on Redonda, where terrestrial surveys are difficult. Halewyn and Norton (1984) estimated around 1,000 pairs. Recent survey in 2004 recorded approximately 60 pairs in August.

Brown Pelican

Specimen was recorded by Cory (1891a) from Antigua in July. A few occur regularly around the coast, but they are not known to breed in Antigua; Danforth (1934a) observed them at Fort James, Long Bay, Old Road, Indian Creek, Rabbit Island, Hell Gate Island, and Long Island. A winter period count at Barbuda recorded 54 birds in 2005 (J. Marshall, pers. comm.). Green Cay may have breeding birds (Varnham 2001), but this needs to be monitored. Recent survey work indicates a few small groups totaling 53–55 pairs are nesting off Antigua at Five Islands, Rabbit, Redhead, and York Island. Additional surveys are warranted during optimal breeding season.

Magnificent Frigatebird

Danforth (1934a) reported them as common residents, but not breeding, around the coasts of Antigua, including Gunthorpe Reservoirs, Rabbit Island, Great Bird Island, and Long Island. The large colony at Barbuda was noted to have nestlings in October in 1948 (Bond 1965a). In 1971 the colony was estimated to consist of about 2,500 pairs (Howell 1991). A 1977 winter count at Barbuda put the number at 3,500 birds (J. Marshall, in litt.). E. A. Schreiber counted about 2,000 also in 1977. Barbuda, with approximately 40% of the region's breeding birds, has the most important breeding colony in the West Indies (Lindsay et al. 2000). Following Hurricane Luis in September 1995, a survey was conducted in 1996 and the colony was estimated at 1,500–2,000 pairs (Schreiber 1996); it could now be up to 2,500 nests. Ten pairs noted at York Island in 2004 warrant confirmation. An estimated 25 pairs were observed on Redonda in 2004.

Laughing Gull

Specimen recorded by Cory (1891a) from Antigua in July. Wing et al. (1968) found remains of this species at Mill Reef midden. Holland and Williams (1978) found this species common on the offshore islands of Antigua and recorded over 400 individuals during an April feeding frenzy at McKinnon's salt pond. Recent survey work in 2004 noted about 80 pairs at Great Bird (60–70) and York islands (10).

Brown Noddy

Holland and Williams (1978) reported that several hundred were found breeding at Great Bird Island, Antigua, in late May 1977. Approximately 140 pairs nested at Great Bird (20–25), Green (100), and Rabbit islands (20) in 2004, which suggests sustained breeding, a possible result of the rodent eradication program.

Sooty Tern

Reported nesting on North Sound islands (Holland and Williams 1978) and more recently by Horwith and Lindsay (1997). The 500 pairs noted on Green Island in the 2004 survey suggest a population increase, a possible result of the rodent eradication program; also on Great Bird Island (10–15 pairs) and Redonda (4 pairs).

Bridled Tern

Bred in scattered, small groups on the islets surrounding Antigua (Horwith and Lindsay, 1997). Up to 16 pairs were noted in 2004: Five Islands (7), Great Bird Island (3), and Redonda (6).

Least Tern

Specimen was recorded by Cory (1891a) from Antigua in July; a fairly common breeder in Antigua from April to September (Holland and Williams 1978). The species' nesting habits on Antigua are scattered and opportunistic. In the mid-1990s about 20 pairs nested at the Darkwood mangroves, habitat now gone. Also known to nest at McKinnon's salt pond when it is dry, and in small numbers at other dry ponds (Horwith and Lindsay 1997). No 2004 breeding records.

Gull-billed Tern

Although reported during summer months near Hodges Bay (Holland and Williams 1978), breeding has not been confirmed. This species nests in small groups at inland salt pond edges and may suffer from predation and disturbance.

Roseate Tern

Specimen was recorded by Cory (1891a) from Antigua in July. Found breeding in May at York Island near Mill Reef (Holland and Williams 1978), where more than 100 birds were counted in successive years. Recent survey work in August 2004 may have missed the breeding season as this species tends to nest from late May to July, although 4 pairs were counted at Green Island.

Common Tern

Reported to nest at Codrington Lagoon, Barbuda, in 1996 (Horwith and Lindsay 1997). Continued monitoring at Barbuda is warranted, especially among Roseate Tern colonies.

Royal Tern

Not confirmed as a breeder by Holland and Williams (1978) from 1972 to 1977, although present in small numbers in summer. Not noted in August 2004 survey.

Sandwich Tern

Specimen recorded by Cory (1891a) from Antigua in July. Apparently not found breeding by Holland and Williams (1978), but seven pairs were noted at Five Islands in the August 2004 survey.

Threats

Anthropogenic activities and natural disasters are some of the threats facing Antigua's seabirds. Historically, the islands have been visited by egg collectors and boaters, and they now attract ecotourists and scientific investigators.

Despite being a signatory to international conservation conventions, Antigua has no legislation affording direct protection for specific seabirds, and existing legislation protecting biodiversity is ineffective and/or not enforced. Antigua is working to fulfill its obligations, but scarcity of information, inadequate legal protection, and increased human traffic through the islands result in a combination of factors that could undermine previous research activities, restoration efforts, and public awareness programs. The categories of threats so far recognized are itemized along with any current or future activities to reduce them. Recommendations are given to ensure a rational approach to the conservation and management of seabird nesting areas.

Invasive species

The species that pose the most significant threats to breeding seabirds are the black rat (*Rattus rattus*), brown rat (*R. norvegicus*), goat, mongoose (*Herpestus auropunctatus*), and to some degree dogs that visitors bring to the offshore islands. On Barbuda, Redonda, and the mainland, several invasive species still abound. Barbuda's lack of pelicans, boobies, herons, and egrets was

attributed to predation on the birds by invasive species (Schreiber 1996).

Human Disturbance

Direct disturbance by recreational visitors, fishermen, loggers, hunters/egg gatherers, researchers, and construction activities is the second greatest concern on the breeding offshore islands. In the late 1970s to early 1980s, the harvesting of eggs was an obvious practice by older fishermen (Lindsay and Horwith 1997b). Recently egg collection has been on the decline as younger resource users replace the fishermen. The Environmental Awareness Group also carries out a public awareness program to emphasize the relationships between human behavior, nesting seabirds, and eco-tourism, aiming to persuade all users, owners, and stakeholders to become more environmentally responsible.

Habitat Loss

The third most significant threat is habitat loss: direct destruction of mangrove swamps, coral reefs, seagrass beds, and other sensitive seabird feeding areas as a result of human activities is a concern. Examples include filling for construction and recreation, dredging that results in silting, dumping of waste, use of explosives in fishing, and breaking and damaging of live coral by anchoring and fishing. Additionally, the loss of important nesting sites can have potentially negative impacts on breeding success of several species. Currently, the Forestry Department of the Ministry of Agriculture, Marine Resources, Lands, Environment, Agro-industry and National Parks actively discourages people from removing trees, soil, and sand from potential seabird nesting areas; however, no mechanism is currently in place for consistent monitoring and apprehending of persons who engage in these activities.

Natural Disasters

Impacts from natural disasters can be substantial: Antigua falls in the direct path of hurricanes that affect the region and result in the death of seabirds and habitat destruction. Drought spanning several years has also potentially affected populations of birds indirectly through a reduction of vegetative cover. The removal of foliage and soil has exacerbated the effects of hurricanes on avian populations.

Uncontrolled Fishing

Lack of regulation is a concern. The North Sound area is proposed as a national park with multiuse zones, but currently there is uncontrolled fishing by recreational and commercial fishermen. Fish catches are not limited by species type and size and are largely unregulated by the Fisheries Division due to their limited resources.

Pollution

The threat of pollution from dumping of waste, including agrochemicals, on offshore islands, in the sea, and in feeding areas such as mangroves is a great concern. Runoff from anthropogenic activities and industries can have negative effects on populations of seabirds that forage close to runoff sources or feed on fish that have bioaccumulated toxins; the immune system response of birds can be altered by petrochemicals (Schreiber 2000a; Island Resources Foundation 1996). There is a shortage of knowledge regarding chemicals (type and quantity) entering fishing zones around Antigua and Barbuda, which are reported to be a leading importer of agrochemicals in the eastern Caribbean (Howell 1991).

Conservation

To date no serious study has been done to identify and quantify the threats to seabirds or to measure the success of invasive species eradication in Antigua. In recent years, the Environmental Awareness Group has made a concerted attempt to gather data on nesting seabirds in Antigua and its offshore islands in order to develop management and conservation strategies as well as to influence policy makers with respect to the conservation of avifauna.

The monitoring of biodiversity has been identified by EAG as an important activity, as the current information bank is inadequate for providing effective support for policy decisions and enforcement. There are plans by government to redraft acts and create structures that will provide for the management of wildlife in Antigua and Barbuda (Index to the Laws of Antigua and Barbuda (Revised Edition) 1992; National Coordinating Mechanism for Environmental Conventions NCM-7, Environment Division, Ministry of Tourism and the Environment 2002; Proposal for Additional Funding of a Biodiversity Enabling Activity, 2003).

The proposed Environmental Management Bill would afford protection to habitats and seabird species in Antigua and its territories. Relevant stakeholders affected by the bill have been identified as tourism operators, private and public sector institutions, fishermen and community groups, chemical importers, etc.

Rehabilitation Activities

The EAG is maintaining a black rat eradication program on six of the islets on which seabird nesting activity has been documented. This exercise was initiated in 1995 and entails the placement of the rodenticide Klerat (Varnham 2001). Prior to the rat eradication program, no detailed study was made of nesting seabird populations of the offshore islands. However comparing present seabird populations with historical anecdotal accounts, the eradication work has been hugely successful, with no re-invasion by the rat; a noticeable increase in seabird populations, especially Sooty and Bridled terns; and the recovery of habitats (V. Joseph, pers comm.).

Legislation for Protection of Seabirds and Nesting Areas

Antigua is a signatory to a number of environmental agreements, including the Convention on International Trade in Endangered Species of Wild Fauna and Flora, or CITES (1997), Convention on Biological Diversity (2000), Protocol Concerning Specially Protected Areas and Wildlife (SPAW) to the Cartagena Convention (1990), Convention for the Protection and Development of Marine Environment of the Wider Caribbean Region (1983), Protocol Concerning Pollution from Land Based Sources and Activities in the Wider Caribbean Region (1999), and the Stockholm Convention (2003). In order to ratify the provisions of these treaties, legislation such as the Environmental Management Act has been drafted. However, there are a number of legislative instruments in existence for the protection of wildlife in Antigua, although with regard to seabirds, none of these pieces of legislation is enforced.

Legislation pertinent to seabird protection is found in the Wild Birds Protection Act (1913). The act prohibits the catching and taking of specified categories of birds and their eggs and prohibits the hunting of others except in the open season. The Protection of Animals Act (1935) provides protection to all animals, including wild birds, through the confiscation of ill-treated animals and imposition of penalties or imprisonment. In addition, the Barbuda (Shooting and Fishing) By-Law (1959) exists for seabird protection.

Other pieces of legislation that provide indirect protection of key habitats and/or species include the proposed Development Control Act (2003), Marine Areas (Preservation and Enhancement) Act (1972), National Parks Act (1985), Mongoose Prohibition (Barbuda) Act, Fisheries Act (1983), Public Health Act (1957), Litter Act (1983), and the Pesticides Control Act (1973).

Recommendations

1. Policy, Legal, and Institutional Arrangements

Increase institutional capacity of governmental agencies with a mandate for management of avifauna.

Deploy government wildlife officers in enforcement.

Update legislation to include implementation and enforcement regulations for the establishment and management of protected areas not limited to:

- Inclusion of offshore islands and wetlands as protected areas.
- Establishment of no-anchoring and no-fishing zones in protected areas.
- Restriction of access to seabird colonies during the breeding season.
- Declaration of seabird nesting areas that occupy Crown and some private lands as protected areas.
- Designate the North Sound area, and Green, York, and Redonda islands as protected areas.
- Institutionalize systems for collection of material, information sharing and intellectual rights.

2. Conservation and Research Activities

Identify and quantify the impact of goats and mongoose on nesting seabirds and habitats.

Undertake feasibility studies and develop an invasive species eradication program for other offshore cays including Redonda.

Create and implement a monitoring program on Barbuda and Redonda during the breeding seasons.

Deploy a volunteer conservation and research program.

Train authorized researchers in survey and monitoring.

3. Education and Public Awareness Activities

Increase knowledge of decision makers, policy makers, all users of offshore cays, and the general public about seabirds.

18

The French Antilles II

Martinique

VINCENT LEMOINE, LIONEL DUBIEF, AND VALÉRIE GENESSEAUX

Martinique is the most southerly of the French islands, in the middle of the Lesser Antilles arc, flanked to the north by Dominica and to the south by Saint Lucia, at 14° 30 ' N and 61° W (map 41). At 1,100 km² Martinique is one of the smallest French Departments with a total human population of about 400,000. The tropical climate is hot (year round average temperature of 26°C) and wet (humidity of 80% in March–April and 87% in October–November).

The land is mountainous in the north, dominated by the Carbet peaks (1,207 m) and Mt. Pelée (1,397 m), still an active volcano and one of the most observed in the world. In the rest of the island, the relief consists of hillocks (called *mornes*) that can reach a height of about 500 m (Vauclin's Mountain and in Diamant). The largest mangrove wetland (12 km²) in Martinique, also one of the largest in the Lesser Antilles, is situated in a central plain between the mountains and hills. The coast has many sand beaches and stretches of rocky cliffs. The beaches seem to receive too much human use to allow seabirds to breed, but the rocky cliffs are favorable for small seabird colonies and isolated pairs.

Several uninhabited islets lie off Martinique, of which the following are the most important for seabirds:

Sainte-Anne's Islets are part of Sainte-Anne's town, in the south of Martinique; there are six islets, of which four (Hardy, Percé, Poirier, and Burgaux) form a national nature reserve for seabirds (total area 5.5 ha).

Diamant's Rock (6 ha) is part of Diamant's town, in the southwest of Martinique.

Boisseau and Petit-Piton islets (0.5 and 0.6 ha) are part of Robert's town, lying off the middle of the Atlantic coast.

Sainte-Marie Islet (4 ha) and Pain de Sucre (sugar loaf, 2.1 ha) are part of Sainte-Marie's town off the northeast Atlantic coast.

Caravelle's Rock (1.1 ha) is a part of Trinité's town off Caravelle's peninsula in the middle of the Atlantic coast.

Table du Diable (devil's table, 0.4 ha) is a rock near the famous Saline's beach, a part of Sainte-Anne's town.

Species Accounts

Historical data on seabird populations are scarce. There are only few references: Pinchon (1976), Bénito-Espinal (1990), and Bénito-Espinal and Haucastel (2003). Further surveys are required to determine population trends. Merging past and current population data is awkward with older information largely anecdotal and with few quantitative data available. However, under the management of the Regional Natural Park of Martinique (PNRM) and French Environment Ministry, surveys have been undertaken since 1997 on the nature reserve of Sainte-Anne's Islets, on one of the four islets (Brithmer 2002; Brithmer and Pascal 2001; De Mercey 1997, 1998a, 1998b; De Mercey and Jérémie 1999; Jérémie 2003, 2005; Jérémie and Brithmer 2005), and one survey was carried out on Diamant's Rock in 2003 (Lévesque 2004). In 2006, new counts of the Roseate Tern population by L. Dubief showed greatly increased numbers of breeding pairs for Martinique.

Methods of Survey

The counts of most surveys involve flying birds and/or birds on the ground. The number of individuals is divided by two, to give number of pairs. On Sainte-Anne's Islets, the number of Audubon's Shearwater and Red-billed Tropicbird was determined from the number of nests with one fledgling and also by the number of ringed adults for Audubon's Shearwater.

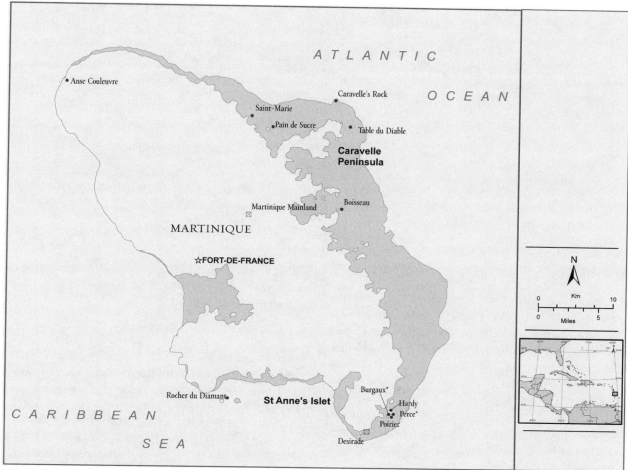

Map 41. Martinique, French Antilles.

Seven species of seabird currently breed on Martinique: Audubon's Shearwater, White-tailed Tropicbird, Red-billed Tropicbird, Brown Noddy, Sooty Tern, Bridled Tern, and Roseate Tern. Estimates of the breeding populations (pairs) in 2001–2005 are in table 18.1. The counts and distribution of pairs, 1997–2005, are shown in table 18.2.

Audubon's Shearwater

A migratory breeder on three islets of Sainte-Anne—Hardy, Percé, and Burgaux—with an estimated 50–80 pairs in 2005 (Brithmer 2002; Brithmer and Pascal 2001; De Mercey 1997, 1998a, 1998b; De Mercey and Jérémie 1999; Jérémie 2003, 2005; Jérémie and Brithmer 2005).

White-tailed Tropicbird

A migratory breeder with one pair on Diamant's Rock in 2003 (Lévesque 2004) and up to five pairs on several

Table 18.1. Estimates of seabird pairs breeding on Martinique, 2001–2005

Species	Total
Audubon's Shearwater	50–80
Red-billed Tropicbird	35–61
White-tailed Tropicbird	2–9
Brown Noddy	330–1,020
Sooty Tern	1,100–12,000
Bridled Tern	160–410
Roseate Tern	50–100

rocky cliffs on the mainland (L. Dubief, S. Jérémie, V. Lemoine, S. Raigné, pers. obs. 2004, 2005). Up to four bred on Caravelle's Reserve in 1994, but there are no recent confirmations (Barré et al. 1996; Bulens et al. 1994; L. Dubief, V. Lemoine, J. C. Nicolas, pers. obs). According to these incomplete data the population was estimated at 2–9 pairs in 2005.

Table 18.2. Distribution of breeding pairs of seabirds on Martinique, 1997–2005

	St.-Anne Islets	Diamant's Rock	Boisseau, and Petit-Piton Islets, Pain de Sucre Peninsula	Mainland and other islets	Caravelle's Reserve	Table du Diable's rock	Total
Audubon's Shearwater	50–80						50–80
Red-billed Tropicbird	10–11	15–20		8–25	2–5		35–61
White-tailed Tropicbird		1		1–5	0–3		2–9
Brown Noddy	40–570	200–250		40–80	20–50	30–70	330–1,020
Sooty Tern	1,100–12,000						1,100–12,000
Bridled Tern	20–150	100–120		10–40	30–100		160–410
Roseate Tern			50–100		?		50–100

Red-billed Tropicbird

A migratory breeder on the Sainte-Anne's islet of Hardy with 10–11 pairs (Brithmer 2002; Brithmer and Pascal 2001; De Mercey 1997, 1998a, 1998b; De Mercey and Jérémie 1999; Jérémie 2003, 2005; and Jérémie and Brithmer 2005), 15–20 pairs on Diamant's Rock (Lévesque 2004); and 8–25 pairs on several rocky cliffs on the mainland (L. Dubief, V. Lemoine, pers. obs. 2004, 2005). A few pairs (2–5) breed on Caravelle's reserve (Barré et al. 1996; Bulens et al. 1994; L. Dubief, V. Lemoine, pers. obs. 2004, 2005). According to these incomplete data the population was estimated at 35–61 pairs in 2005.

Brown Noddy

A migratory breeder with 40–570 pairs on Sainte-Anne's Islets, according to an estimation based on incomplete data from 1998 to 2005 (Brithmer 2002; Brithmer and Pascal 2001; De Mercey 1997, 1998a, 1998b; De Mercey and Jérémie 1999; Jérémie 2003, 2005; Jérémie and Brithmer 2005); 200–250 pairs on Diamant's Rock (Lévesque 2004); 20–50 pairs on Caravelle's islets in 2004–2005 (Barré et al. 1996; Bulens et al. 1994; L. Dubief, V. Lemoine, pers. obs., 2004, 2005); 30–70 pairs on Table du Diable (L. Dubief, V. Lemoine, pers. obs. 2004, 2005); and 40–80 on the mainland and several other islets (L. Dubief, V. Lemoine, J. C. Nicolas, pers. obs. 2004, 2005). From the incomplete 2001–2005 data, the population was estimated at 330–1,020 pairs in 2005.

Sooty Tern

A migratory breeder on Sainte-Anne's islets of Hardy, Percé, Poirier, and Burgaux, where the population fluctuated from 1,100 in 2001 to 12,000 in 2004 (Brithmer 2002; Brithmer and Pascal 2001; De Mercey 1997, 1998a, 1998b; De Mercey and Jérémie 1999; Jérémie 2003, 2005;

Jérémie and Brithmer 2005). A colony was breeding on Caravelle's islets in 1994 but no survey has been made since (Bulens et al. 1994).

Bridled Tern

A migratory breeder with 20–150 pairs on Sainte-Anne's Islets, according to an estimation based on incomplete data from 2001 to 2005 (Brithmer 2002; Brithmer and Pascal 2001; De Mercey 1997, 1998a, 1998b; De Mercey and Jérémie 1999; Jérémie 2003, 2005; and Jérémie and Brithmer 2005); 100–120 pairs on Diamant's Rock (Lévesque 2004) and on several other islets (L. Dubief, V. Lemoine, pers. obs. 2004, 2005). Between 30 and 100 pairs bred on Caravelle's islets 2004–2005 (Bulens et al. 1994; L. Dubief, V. Lemoine, J. C. Nicolas, pers. obs. 2004, 2005). Between 10 and 40 on the mainland and several other islets (L. Dubief, V. Lemoine, pers. obs. 2004, 2005). Based on the incomplete data of 2001 to 2005, the population was estimated at 160–410 pairs in 2005.

Roseate Tern

A migratory breeder each year on Pain de Sucre Peninsula and/or Robert's Boisseau Islet, Petit-Piton Islet, or Sainte-Marie's Islet. In 2005, the population was estimated at 50–100 pairs in Robert's Boisseau Islet, but no survey was made on Pain de Sucre Peninsula (L. Dubief, pers. obs. 2005). A few individuals were also observed off Anse Couleuvre at Prêcheur's town (L. Dubief, V. Lemoine, pers. obs. 2004, 2005). A few pairs were breeding on Caravelle's islets in 1994, but no survey has been conducted since (Barré et al. 1996; Bulens et al. 1994). New counts in 2006 gave c. 250 pairs at Pain de Sucre (Sainte Marie) and c. 150–200 in Islet Petit-Piton, a minimum of 400 pairs, the largest count outside the Puerto Rican Bank (L. Dubief, in prep.).

Possible Additional Breeding Species

Breeding has not been confirmed for any of the following species.

Brown Booby

Suspected breeder on Diamant's Rock (Lévesque 2004) and Caravelle's Rock. A few individuals may have bred on Caravelle's islets in 1994 (Barré et al. 1996; Bulens et al. 1994). Since that time, several individuals have been observed around the mainland during breeding season.

Magnificent Frigatebird

Observed throughout the year around Martinique, sometimes in roosts of 50–100 individuals (Lévesque 2004; L. Dubief, V. Lemoine, pers. obs. 2004, 2005). It is a suspected breeder on Caravelle's Rock (L. Dubief, V. Lemoine, pers. obs. 2004, 2005).

Least Tern

Observed around Martinique in very small numbers. A survey of individuals observed in April, needed to determine breeding status, has not yet been undertaken (L. Dubief, V. Lemoine, F. Martail, pers. obs. 2004, 2005).

Common Tern

Breeding has not been confirmed since 1994. A few are observed during the breeding season around Martinique, but breeding of up to three pairs was recorded only in Caravelle's reserve in 1994 (Barré et al. 1996).

Royal Tern

Observed during the breeding season around Martinique in small numbers, sometimes in a group of 10 individuals. Several pairs may breed on islets or on rocky coastline (L. Dubief, V. Lemoine, F. Martail, J. C. Nicolas, S. Raigné, pers. obs. 2004, 2005).

Sandwich Tern

Observed during the breeding season around Martinique in small numbers, sometimes in a group of 10 individuals (L. Dubief, V. Lemoine, pers. obs. 2004, 2005). An adult feeding a juvenile was seen on a Sainte-Marie beach in August 2004 (V. Lemoine, pers. obs. 2004, 2005).

Threats

Urbanization of the coast on some of Robert's and François's islets.
Human disturbance due to leisure activities (hiking, yachting, jet-skis, kitesurfing) on Sainte-Anne's Is-

lets, Boisseau and Petit-Piton islets, other islets, and the mainland).
Poachers may still take some eggs.
Predation by migrant Peregrine Falcon, which attacks nesting seabirds, sometimes provokes the departure of an entire tern colony.
Predation by rats, well known for their devastating effects on seabird colonies (Sainte-Anne's Islets, Pain de Sucre Peninsula, Boisseau and Petit Piton islets, and most of the other sites).

Conservation

All the species mentioned have been protected in Martinique by a ministerial decree since 1989. Sainte-Anne's Islets have been protected since 1995 as a national nature reserve. Landing is forbidden except for scientists carrying out studies for the Regional Natural Park of Martinique, which administers this area. Elimination of rats (*Rattus rattus*) succeeded on Sainte-Anne's Islets after three years of trapping in 1999–2002 by PNRM guards. Diamant's Rock is protected since 1994 by a decree of Martinique's prefecture (Arrêté Préfectoral de Protection de Biotope), which forbids landing between 1 January and 31 August, during the breeding season. Boisseau Islet has been protected since 2002 by a decree of Martinique's prefecture that prohibits landing between September and December. Pain de Sucre has been protected by a decree of Martinique's prefecture since 1999. Caravelle's peninsula has been protected since 1976 as a national nature reserve (370 ha) administered by PNRM.

In spite of these legislative protections, the surveillance on breeding sites remains insufficient to protect seabirds because of the lack of enforcement by environmental managers and wardens. There is a need for more local scientists and ornithologists to monitor seabirds and make new surveys, and for scientific training of local bird-watchers, voluntary workers, and dynamic conservation associations.

Recommendations

Rat eradication should be undertaken on islets where rats are known to be present.
The need to monitor colonies during each breeding season is urgent.
Communication with the inhabitants is essential, especially with fishermen and tourists, to create an understanding of the importance of protecting breeding seabirds.

An overall survey should be undertaken to identify breeding species and breeding sites, as proposed by the conservation organization Société pour l'Etude, la Protection et l'Aménagement de la Nature en Martinique (SEPANMAR).

Protection of all major breeding sites should be pursued.

A management plan is needed for all sites.

Acknowledgments

SEPANMAR and the authors wish to thank all the birdwatchers and organizations who provided data used to write this chapter.

19

Saint Lucia

DONALD ANTHONY AND ALWIN DORNELLY

St. Lucia (661 km^2) lies in the Leeward Islands in the Lesser Antilles, between Martinique 30 km to the north and St. Vincent 31 km to the south (map 42). The island is volcanic and mountainous with a maximum elevation of 950 m. There are 20 small islands and cays close to the shoreline, 16 off the eastern coast and four off the northwest coast. The human population is approximately 167,000 (Towle and Towle 1991).

The Maria Islands lie approximately 1 km off the southeast coast of St. Lucia and comprise two small islets, Maria Major (10.2 ha) and Maria Minor (2.2 ha), and a single emergent rock (0.04 ha). The vegetation of Maria Major is stands of dry scrub woodland, grasses, and cacti. A trail running along the eastern edge of the islet begins at the coast and climbs at a steep gradient. The trail starts in low grasses near the coast, traverses a white cedar (*Tabebuia pallida*) forest, and passes through organ pipe and prickly pear cacti to reach a maximum elevation of 100 m. Maria Minor is similar with grasses and less dry scrub woodland; the maximum elevation is 24 m. The islands are protected as the Maria Islands Nature Reserve, managed by the National Trust. Every year between March and July, seabirds congregate on these twin islands to nest at all elevations and on all vegetation types, including on exposed rocks and among cacti. Such nesting activity would appear to indicate absence of natural avian predators on the islands.

Methods of Survey

The 2002 survey of Maria Major and Maria Minor, undertaken jointly by the Forestry Department and the National Trust (South), sought to continue documenting the seabird populations to determine trends since the 2000, 1992, and 1983 surveys (table 19.1). Tour guides from the National Trust also received training in seabird survey techniques during this exercise. At least five species were recorded during the survey period, although only two, Sooty Tern and Roseate Tern, were confirmed nesting (table 19.2). On Maria Major, the xerophytic vegetation made a normal line transect difficult; instead the established trail was used as the main transect line, with secondary trails off the main trail as secondary transects. All eggs within 1 m on either side of the trail from the center were counted, with one egg considered to represent one nesting pair. The population estimate was derived by extrapolation of the calculated result over an area of 2 ha. On Maria Minor, the circular sample plot method, based on Feare (1976c), was applied in seven circular plots each with a 2 m radius. All eggs and nests within the perimeter were counted. The density of nests was also calculated for the entire sample, and the results were extrapolated for the entire island to estimate the population.

Other poorly studied breeding sites include Anse Chastanet, Cape Moule à Chique, and Louvet Beach on the mainland; on the islands L'Islet, L'Islet à Ramier, Praslin, Frigate, Dennery, Fous, and Lapins; and Burgot Rocks (Keith 1997). Counts from these sites are visual estimates of pairs at nest sites.

Table 19.1. Estimates of seabird pairs breeding on St. Lucia, 2000 and 2002

Species	Estimates (pairs)
White-tailed Tropicbird	1–10
Red-billed Tropicbird	22–27
Magnificent Frigatebird	50–100
Brown Noddy	10
Sooty Tern	38,147
Bridled Tern	70
Roseate Tern	10–75

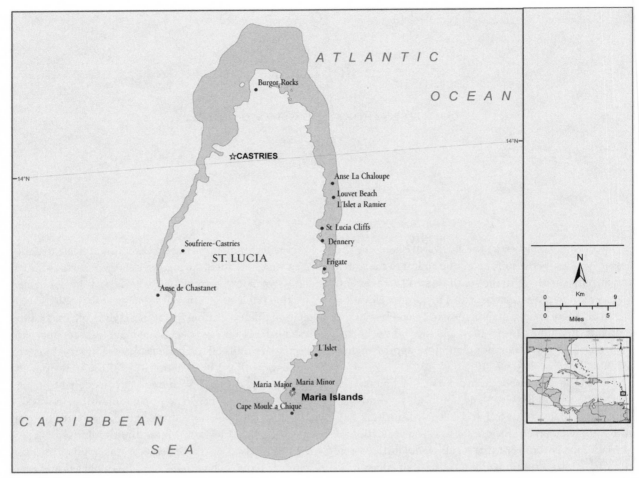

Map 42. St. Lucia.

Species Accounts

Seven species of seabirds are known to breed on St. Lucia, six with estimates of breeding pairs (table 19.1). Some records of nesting seabirds for St. Lucia are as recent as the 1970s, with later records from sporadic surveys in the 1980s and 1990s (Burke 1992a; Raffaele et al., 1998a).

The most comprehensive surveys have been on the Maria Islands (tables 19.2, 19.3), with few counts at breeding sites on the mainland or other offshore islands and keys. Brown Booby is yet unconfirmed as breeding on Fous and Lapin islands and Burgot Rocks (Keith 1997). Obviously, more work needs to be done.

Records indicate an upward trend in the overall seabird population at the Maria Islands from the early 1980s to the present, due to a sharp increase of Sooty Terns between 1992 and 2002 (table 19.3). Saliva (2000a) reported an increase in breeding pairs of Sooty Terns for Culebra, Puerto Rico, for recent years and suggested that such an increase might be due to recruitment of birds from abandoned colonies at other sites. There is a downward

Table 19.2. Counts of seabird pairs breeding on Maria Islands, St. Lucia, 2002

Species	Maria Major	Maria Minor	Total (pairs)
Red-billed Tropicbird	(6)	12	12
Brown Noddy	(10)	0	(10)
Sooty Tern	32,867	5,280	38,147
Bridled Tern	(10)	0	(10)
Roseate Tern	0	10	10

Note: Numbers in parentheses are of individual flying birds known to breed prior to 2002.

Table 19.3. Counts of seabird pairs breeding on Maria Islands, St. Lucia, 1983–2000

Species	1983	1992	2000
Red-billed Tropicbird			12
Brown Noddy	100	100	~10
Sooty Tern	100	600	35,000
Bridled Tern	210	150	~70
Roseate Tern	Several pairs	75	75

trend for Roseate Tern, Bridled Tern, and Brown Noddy for the same period since Burke (1992) reported 75 pairs, 150 pairs, and 100 pairs respectively. Perhaps such reductions are due to the sampling technique and the difficulty in accessing cliff edges during counts.

White-tailed Tropicbird

Breeds in small numbers on the mainland on the cliffs at Anse de Chastanet; no counts are available (pers. obs.). Suspected breeding reported here and between Soufrière and Castries (Keith 1997).

Red-billed Tropicbird

Six birds observed in flight on Maria Major in 2002 were presumed to be nesting; 8–12 pairs have nested regularly (pers. obs.). Breeds around the cliffs on the mainland: 15 pairs established for 20 years at Cape Moule à Chique, and a few north of Louvet Beach (Keith 1997).

Magnificent Frigatebird

Resident. Around 50–100 pairs breed on Frigate Island (pers. obs.; Keith 1997).

Brown Noddy

Ten birds were recorded in flight on Maria Major in 2002, and although no nests were located, they were presumed breeding. In 1983 and 1992, the total counts for the Maria Islands were 100 pairs; in 2000 the count fell to 10 pairs. In 1986 breeding was noted at Frigate Island (18 pairs) and Dennery Island (20–30 pairs) and was considered probable at Burgot Rocks (Keith 1997). In 1987 and until at least 1995 there was breeding at Anse la Chaloupe (Keith 1997).

Sooty Tern

In 2002 this was the only species observed nesting on Maria Major: a total of 1,272 eggs were counted, which when extrapolated over an area of 24,281.22 m^2 gave an estimate of 32,867 nesting pairs. The average number of eggs was 1.57, and average egg density of the entire sample was 0.15 eggs/m^2, or an estimated 3,300 nesting pairs or, with standard deviation, 5,280 for the island. On Maria Minor, eggs (n = 11) were counted in four out of the seven plots: 7 in plot 2; no eggs were found in plots 4, 5, and 6. In 1983 the total counts for the Maria Islands were 100 pairs, in 1992 there were 600 pairs (Burke 1992), in 2000 the count was 35,000, and in 2002 it was 38,147.

Bridled Tern

Ten birds were observed in flight on Maria Major in 2002, but nests were not located in the transects; in 2000, around 70 pairs were counted, a decline from 150 pairs in 1992 (Burke 1992) and 200 pairs in 1983, when 20 pairs were confirmed on Maria Minor (Keith 1997).

Roseate Tern

First recorded in 1970 (Keith 1997). Ten pairs were confirmed nesting on Maria Minor in 2002. In 1992 and 2000, 75 pairs were counted, but none were present in 1983, when several pairs nested on Maria Major. In 1986, 25 pairs nested at L'Islet and 30 pairs at L'Islet à Ramier (Keith 1997).

Threats

Coastal development on the mainland linked to the rapid growth in tourism has impacted habitats that were formerly relatively safe nesting sites for seabirds. This and the presence of predators such as rats, mongoose, and feral cats are the major threats. Collecting eggs remains a problem on the mainland but is now something of the past on the offshore islands, although there may still be some sporadic incidents. The regular presence of humans on the many offshore islands during the nesting season disturbs nesting seabirds and causes nest failure. This situation, if not addressed urgently, will lead to a dramatic decline in the overall seabird population on the islands. Of all indications, the decline of seabird populations in the Caribbean region appears to be due, to a great extent, to the growing tourism industry. Regular censusing and monitoring are essential to record noticeable trends; data for many species are not available due to a lack of proper monitoring and scant long-term records.

Conservation

All seabirds are protected, and offenders proven guilty can face a $5,000 fine or one year in prison. The St. Lucia Forestry Department has the legal mandate for protection and conservation of the avifauna. The Maria Islands, Frigate Island, and some other offshore islands are protected under the jurisdiction of the St. Lucia National Trust. The Maria Islands Nature Reserve is closed to the public during the seabird nesting season.

20

Barbados

MARTIN D. FROST

Barbados, 430 km² in area, is the easternmost island of the Lesser Antilles, lying at 13° 10' N and 59° 31' W (map 43). Consisting predominantly of coral limestone strata of Pleistocene age, the island is an uplifted ridge atop folded beds of "oceanics" from the sea floor, produced by ancient volcanic activity related to subduction of the Caribbean plate.

The land is hilly and rocky with limited terrestrial biodiversity by virtue of its thin mosaic of arable soils and distance from large land masses. The limestone and coral subsurface is overlain with a veneer of organic soil measuring on average less than 36.0 mm to hardly more than 1 m at the deepest point. The highest point of the island, Mt. Hillaby, reaches 336 m. The climate is moderated by the northeast trade winds, and mean temperatures range from a low of 15.6°C during the winter months, December–March, to 33.0°C in the summer, May–June. Precipitation averages 152.4 mm per year with two discernable periods, a dry season occurring in winter to late spring, and a wet season during June to December, when 75 percent of precipitation occurs. Rainfall yields 200+ mm in the highland areas to 110+ mm in the lowland south.

The island's indigenous people came from Venezuela by dugout canoe. By 1625 Barbados had been visited by the Spanish and Portuguese and claimed by the British. British settlement took hold by 1630 with the introduction of sugar cane, and Barbados remained under British authority until 1966, when it received its independence. The capital city, Bridgetown, was named "Indian Bridge" for a rudimentary footbridge the natives had made to cross a river. When the bridge was replaced after 1654, the city was renamed.

Despite the marginal soil conditions, Barbados produced sugar cane of quality for more than a century, and diverse agriculture is sustained to this day. Between 1630 and 1846 Barbados had 491 sugar plantations with 506 windmills. The plantation economy was heavily supported by both indentured servants and slaves. Today the population of Barbados is one of the densest in the region and boasts the third oldest uninterrupted parliamentary government in the world. The demand for housing and sustainable tourism are becoming increasingly important and are limiting the amount of open space for agriculture. Future housing needs conflict with the need to allow agricultural areas to regenerate natural vegetation that could benefit the native biodiversity and reduce soil depletion through runoff.

The island has a wide range of ecosystems dependent upon the sparse soil and variable precipitation. Among its unique ecosystems is vast underground maze of rivers, caves, and lakes, providing a source of potable water. Some fresh basins and brackish water are exposed at the surface in swamps and backwaters.

The swamps of Barbados are in the south and southwest of the island. They are the major wetlands of Barbados, supporting an assemblage of plants and animals forming an important link in the food chain of offshore fish and birds. The renowned Graeme Hall Swamp, located in the parish of Christ Church, is the largest expanse of inland water in Barbados, and the swamp's red and white mangrove trees provide habitat for several local species of birds. In addition the swamp is a temporary home for a large number of migrant and wintering waterbirds and shorebirds.

The Barbados coast is not all sandy beaches. Besides mangrove swamps, there are cliffs, tide pools, and areas where beds of low-lying coral rock, sandstone, clay, or shale reach out to the sea. Tidal flats and wave ridges occur mostly off the east coast within eroded limestone plateaus and other low-lying rock formations. On the south and southwest coasts are many tide pools, an important ecological resource, acting as nurseries for juvenile fish important to seabirds of the region.

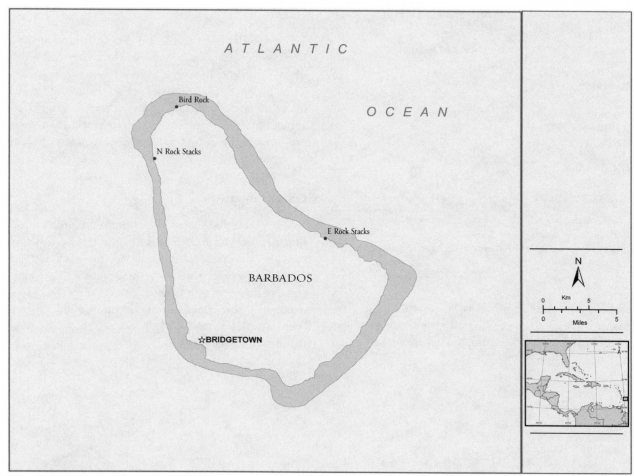

Map 43. Barbados.

Species Accounts

The island's only breeding seabird is Audubon's Shearwater. Brown Pelican was reported breeding shortly after colonization of the island (Colt 1631) but must have ceased to breed here within a relatively short time thereafter. There is no evidence to suggest that any other seabird species nests or nested on Barbados.

Audubon's Shearwater

Known only to breed at Bird Rock, a small rock stack about 100 m offshore from Cluffs (13° 20′ N, 59° 27′ W), St. Lucy, on the north coast. There are other rock stacks on the northern and eastern coasts that could be suitable nesting sites, but these have not been thoroughly investigated.

An estimated 50 to 100 pairs nest on Bird Rock based on recent visual counts of up to 114 birds returning to the rock stack after sunset in January 2000. Hughes (1750:251), who was the first to refer to breeding birds at Bird Rock, noted "to be seen at most times of the year, a great many of their nests and eggs." Feilden (1889a:503) stated similarly that shearwaters "bred in considerable numbers this year." His report of "twenty-four young . . . and a single egg" taken from Bird Rock a few hours prior to his visit there (Feilden 1889b:62) is a rare quantitative assessment. Based on the limited historical data and particularly the rock stack's small size, it is likely that the population size has not changed significantly since the mid-eighteenth century.

The limited data available suggest that the peak breeding season occurs from January to May. However, the presence of birds at Bird Rock during other months (table 20.1)—specimens collected from burrows in July (American Museum of Natural History) and October (University Museum of Zoology Cambridge)—suggests that breeding, or possibly roosting, may occur throughout the year. Egg and specimen data obtained by H. W. Feilden include 7 "deeply incubated" eggs collected on 22 March 1889 and three young taken on 9 May 1888. Two

Table 20.1. Estimates of Audubon's Shearwater on Bird Rock, Barbados, 1996–2003

Date	Number of birds counted
April 1996	c. 24
May 1996	c. 15
June 1996	c. 10
Late November 1996	c. 10
Mid-January 1997	c. 40
March 22, 1997	52
March 28, 1997	106
March 7, 1998	10
January 8, 2000	114
December 20, 2003	41

Notes: Observations of varying duration made from adjacent cliff between 18:30 and 20:00h. A light beam is shone out to sea to lee of Bird Rock and birds are counted as they cross the light beam on approach to Bird Rock.

of these young are described as "mainly still in nestling down," while the third was "in partial nestling down." No data on hatching and fledgling success are available.

Threats

Future development of the cliff line surrounding Bird Rock could create disturbances, which may make this isolated, offshore nesting site less attractive. A recent attempt to construct a house below the cliff line within 400 m of Bird Rock was halted by the authorities, an encouraging sign. Harvesting of birds, particularly young, was practiced in the distant past but is not known to occur at present.

Conservation

This is a protected species under the Wild Birds Protection Act (1978), which makes unauthorized possession of feathers, skins, or live birds illegal. There is a need for the planning authorities to be made aware of the existence of this nesting location. Further study is required to obtain a more complete understanding of this species' breeding cycle on Bird Rock, including subspecific identity of the population.

21

Saint Vincent, the Grenadines, and Grenada

MARTIN D. FROST, FLOYD E. HAYES, AND ANN M. HAYNES SUTTON

St. Vincent, the Grenadines, and Grenada make up an archipelago of more than 30 volcanic islands in the southern Lesser Antilles (maps 44, 45). St. Vincent, a larger island and most northerly of the island chain, is separated from the smaller Grenadine islands to the south by a narrow trough exceeding 500 m in depth. The Grenadines are collectively situated upon a shallow shelf less than 100 m deep and are separated from Grenada, a larger island to the south, by a narrow trough about 200 m deep. Some upwelling of deeper ocean waters is thought to occur along the eastern edge of the insular shelf, which potentially provides nutrients for seabirds and their food supply (Anonymous 1991a, b).

Species Accounts

Of the 15 seabird species that are reported to have bred in the archipelago, 10 species were confirmed breeding in 2004 (table 21.1). Surprisingly little is known about the breeding seabird fauna of St. Vincent, the Grenadines, and Grenada. Although the smaller uninhabited islands of the Grenadines provide ideal habitat for nesting seabirds, only a few of the breeding colonies have been visited by ornithologists. Most of the published information on breeding seabird populations dates from the early part of the twentieth century or before and is partially anecdotal, derived from secondhand accounts; however, some is included here due to the paucity of breeding data (Wells 1887, 1902; Clark 1905a; Devas 1943; Bond 1950a; see review by Hayes 2002). Given the antiquity of published data, some authors concluded that the major seabird colonies had been extirpated (e.g., Schreiber and Lee 2000a). However, a recent at-sea survey by Hayes (2002) revealed high densities of potentially breeding seabirds within the archipelago, including large numbers of boobies flying in the direction of suspected colonies,

findings confirmed in brief surveys conducted during summer 2004 by M. Frost and R. W. Burke and by A. Sutton and B. Hay in this chapter. This chapter presents the results of the 2004 surveys; reviews the breeding seabird fauna of the archipelago, including the Grenadine islands belonging to Grenada; and emphasizes the urgent need for further exploratory surveys. Frost and Burke or Sutton and Hay citations without dates in the species accounts are all observations from the 2004 surveys.

Audubon's Shearwater

Known to have nested in the Grenadines and on islets around Grenada. "Well-known nester on certain small rocky islets" in the St. Vincent Grenadines with no further information provided as to the exact locations (Thayer 1925). In the Grenada Grenadines, Wells (1902) reported nesting "on most of our little islets" around Carriacou and specifically mentioned Bonaparte Rocks as "a favorite abode." Known to breed around Grenada on Green Island and Sandy Island off the north coast (Devas 1943, 1954) and Labaye Rock, about 2 km off Grenville (Wells 1902). Within the archipelago are many rock stacks, which could be suitable nesting sites.

No recent data from known breeding locations. Recent at-sea observations in small numbers in December (Wells and Wells 2000) and March (T. Blunden, pers. comm.) suggest that breeding still occurs in the region. The historical information contains no quantitative assessments but suggests that the species was common to abundant. Thayer (1925) noted that in the St. Vincent Grenadines it was "fairly common," whereas Wells (1902) stated "very numerous" for Carriacou and surrounding islets, and around Grenada, Devas (1954) described this species as "by no means uncommon."

Breeding data: The limited data available suggest that breeding occurs from March to May. Devas (1954) stated:

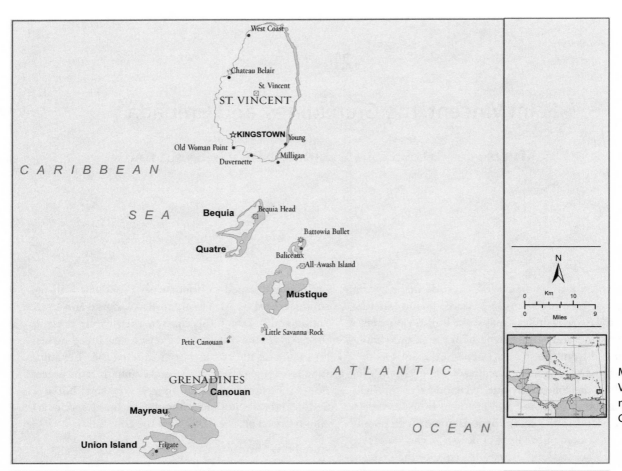

Map 44. St. Vincent and northern Grenadines.

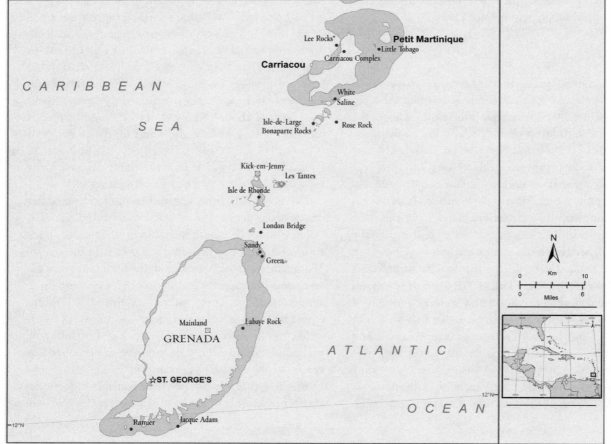

Map 45. Grenada and southern Grenadines.

Table 21.1. Estimates of seabird pairs breeding on St. Vincent and the Grenadines and Grenada, 2004

Species	Breeding 2004
White-tailed Tropicbird	Confirmed
Red-billed Tropicbird	Confirmed
Brown Booby	>315
Red-footed Booby	>3,500
Laughing Gull	>22
Brown Noddy	>145
Sooty Tern	>2,500
Bridled Tern	Confirmed
Roseate Tern	>15
Sandwich Tern	Confirmed

"They breed locally (April to May)." Wells (1902) found three burrows with one young, an adult and one young, and an adult with a highly incubated egg on Labaye Rock on April 2, 1888.

White-tailed Tropicbird

Known to have nested "along leeward [west] coast of main island of St. Vincent" (Thayer 1925). Devas (1954) reported a breeding colony at Old Woman Point on St. Vincent's south coast and suggested possible breeding colonies at Young Island and Duvernette Island off St. Vincent's south coast.

Recent observations of small numbers along the leeward coast of St. Vincent (Wells and Wells 2000), around the cliffs near Old Woman Point (R. W. Burke, pers. comm.), and around Young and Duvernette islands (E. B. Massiah, pers. comm.) suggest that these traditional locations are still being used. Thayer (1925) recorded: "Six or seven colonies of from five to twenty or more pairs each. . . . Disappeared in September (?), began to reappear about Dec. 22. . . Do not find this species in Cays [i.e., St. Vincent Grenadines], where *aethereus* is common, and vice versa." Similarly, Devas (1954) commented: "It is not to be seen off Grenada, or among the Grenadine Islands, but in St. Vincent. . . . There I had the pleasure of watching numbers of them." Thus it appears that its population size has not changed significantly.

Breeding data: "Eggs taken in April" (Thayer 1925) appears to be the only available data, but see breeding data for Red-billed Tropicbird.

Red-billed Tropicbird

Known to have nested in the Grenadines. Clark (1905a) reported breeding colonies from Bequia Head (on Bequia), Battowia, Baliceaux, Frigate Island, Rose Rock, Kick-'em-Jenny, and Les Tantes. Devas (1943, 1954) reported nesting on Lea Rocks and suggested tropicbirds

might breed on Saline Island, Isle de Rhonde, and other island rocks in the vicinity of Les Tantes. Thayer (1925) listed "Little Shimminee (Little Savanna Rock)" as a location where he retrieved a bird from a rock hole.

The status of this species on mainland St. Vincent and Grenada is unclear. Clark (1905a) gave its status on St. Vincent: "There is a considerable colony of them near Old Woman's Point, just west of Kingstown, and another at Layou." For St. Vincent, interestingly, Clark does not list White-tailed Tropicbird, which is known to nest at Old Woman Point; he may have confused the two species. Thayer (1925) wrote "not found (?) about St. Vincent mainland." Clark's (1905a) statement "is locally common about the cliffs" of Grenada is suggestive that breeding occurred on the Grenada mainland.

Recent data from known breeding locations include a March 1993 estimate of a few pairs at the Bequia Head colony (T. Blunden, pers. comm.), four individuals at Battowia in June 2004 (M. Frost and R. W. Burke), three and two individuals at Kick-'em-Jenny and Les Tantes respectively, and about a dozen individuals each at Frigate Island and an adjacent rock between Frigate Island and Rose Rock in August 2004 (A. Sutton and B. Hay). The historical information contains no quantitative assessments but suggests that the species was common to abundant. Wells (1887) reported it as "abundant amongst the small islands between this [Grenada] and Carriacou" and Devas (1943) noted "you will be astonished to spy numbers of them" in referring to the Les Tantes colony. Thayer (1925) stated that in the St. Vincent Grenadines it was "Common. . . . Does not appear to have migration away from Cays, as *americanus* [*lepturus*] has away from St. Vincent coast."

Breeding data: The limited historical data available suggest that breeding occurs during April and May, although recent data suggest this may be extended until August. Devas (1954) stated "during the breeding season (April to May)" and one was taken from a nest on Les Tantes in April (Wells 1887). A. Sutton and B. Hay observed birds entering and leaving crevices in August 2004. Clark (1905a) reported breeding February to April, but as discussed under range, it is not certain whether these observations pertain to this tropicbird species.

Masked Booby

Known to have nested on Battowia Bullet (off Battowia) and All Awash Islet (Thayer 1925). This species was not seen on Battowia Bullet or on All Awash Islet in June 2004, although a subadult was observed south of Bequia in 2004 (M. Frost and R. W. Burke). At least one adult was identified among 10 white *Sula* feeding near

Kick-'em-Jenny in August 2004 (A. Sutton and B. Hay, pers. obs.). Very few, usually of unstated age, have been reported in recent visits to the area (Smith and Smith, unpubl.; Wells and Wells 2000; Hayes 2002; E. B. Massiah and R. W. Burke, pers. comm.), making it difficult to assess whether there is a continued breeding presence.

The historical information contains no quantitative assessments but suggests that the species was never common. Thayer (1925) reported nesting on Battowia Bullet "in considerable numbers" and commented: "Highly local and on whole uncommon in region. Must eat fish eastward at sea, because not seen among other species attending fish-swarms in the channels among the Cays [St. Vincent Grenadines] or about St. Vincent." Devas (1954) noted that "it is very rare."

Breeding data: No data available.

Brown Booby

Known to have nested in the Grenadines at Bequia Head (on Bequia; T. Blunden, pers. comm.), Sail Rock, Les Tantes, and The Sisters in 2004 (A. Sutton and B. Hay), and on Battowia and Kick-'em-Jenny (Clark 1905a). In addition, a colony on Little Tobago (off Petit Martinique) was reported to Clark (1905a). Thayer (1925) noted "nests on most of the rocky Cays [St. Vincent Grenadines]" without citing specific locations and continued: "Probably a few pairs nest on wilder parts of St. Vincent mainland coast."

Recent data from known breeding locations include large numbers in March 1993 at the Bequia Head colony (T. Blunden, pers. comm.); 100 nests with chicks estimated in August 2004 at Sail Rock, with about five nests each on Les Tantes, The Sisters, and Kick-'em-Jenny (A. Sutton and B. Hay); and 200 nests estimated in June 2004 on Battowia (M. Frost and R. W. Burke). The historical assessments of "Hundreds . . . nest at Battowia and Kick-'em-Jenny" (Clark 1905a) and "nests . . . in some places in considerable colonies" (Thayer 1925) suggest that the species was common to abundant, which still seems to be the case. This is the only one of the *Sula* species that may be regularly observed from the shores (particularly the leeward coast) of mainland St. Vincent and Grenada. Clark (1905a) noted that on the leeward coast of St. Vincent, this species begins "to fly down the coast at about three in the afternoon, making for Battowia, which island is the favorite roosting place of all the sea birds in the region."

Breeding data: Clark (1905a) stated that "the breeding season is from February to May," although recent data show this is extended until August. Nests with no eggs, freshly laid eggs, recently hatched chicks, and large downy chicks acquiring feathers were observed in late June 2004 (M. Frost and R. W. Burke), and up to three incubating birds and many nests with chicks in late August 2004 (A. Sutton and B. Hay).

Red-footed Booby

Known to have nested in the Grenadines at Bequia Head (on Bequia; T. Blunden, pers. comm.), on Battowia (Thayer 1925), on Les Tantes and The Sisters in 2004 (A. Sutton and B. Hay), and on Kick-'em-Jenny (Wells 1902; Clark 1905a). Thayer (1925) reported nesting "on some few other smaller Cays [St. Vincent Grenadines] which have trees and bushes," without citing specific locations.

Recent data from known breeding locations include small numbers in March 1993 at the Bequia Head colony (T. Blunden, pers. comm.); a conservative estimate of 3,000 nests on Battowia in June 2004 (M. Frost and R. W. Burke); more than 500 nests on Les Tantes; and several nests on The Sisters and 15 nests on Kick-'em-Jenny in August 2004 (A. Sutton and B. Hay).

Historical assessments of "An immense colony in Battowia (perhaps 3 or 4 or more thousand)" (Thayer 1925), "large numbers . . . inhabit Kik-en-jenny" (Wells 1902), and "nests in numbers on Kick-'em-Jenny" (Clark 1905a) suggest that the species was the most abundant of the *Sula* species, which still seems to be the case. The decline in numbers on Kick-'em-Jenny is intriguing. Smith and Smith (unpubl.) observed thousands in late May 1998 near that island, where they presumably bred. Clark (1905a) and Thayer (1925) commented that the white-tailed brown phase predominated, which still seems to be true at present (Hayes 2002; M. Frost and R. W. Burke; A. Sutton and B. Hay).

Breeding data: No historical data appear to be available. Thayer (1925) called this booby "a tree-nester and tree-rooster par excellence." Nests in late June were at various stages from under construction through fully developed chicks (M. Frost and R. W. Burke); A. Sutton and B. Hay found nests with chicks in late August 2004. Locals on Bequia advised that this species could be found breeding on Battowia at all times of the year (M. Frost and R. W. Burke).

Brown Pelican

Known to have nested "on a few remote cays" in the St. Vincent Grenadines (Thayer 1925); he did not cite specific locations. Ober (1880) stated: "breeds on the rocks north of Grenada, as well as through the Grenadines," apparently based on secondhand accounts. This assessment was questioned by Clark (1905a), who found no evidence of nesting despite "careful search and exhaustive inquiry." Wells (1887) noted that "they are supposed to breed on some of the isolated rocks" but later was of the opinion that they did not breed in the area (Wells 1902).

The recent data suggest that the species is uncommon to common between Canouan and Carriacou but rarer outside these central Grenadine islands (Smith and Smith, unpubl. 1998; Wells and Wells 2000; Hayes 2002; E. B. Massiah and R. W. Burke, pers. comm.). This species was considered uncommon around the St. Vincent coast (Clark 1905a; Thayer 1925) but common to numerous at certain times of the year in the Grenadines and around Grenada (Wells 1887, 1902; Clark 1905a). Although a few birds are present all year round in the latter locations, most of the birds leave the area by February and only begin to return in early summer, May or June (Wells 1902; Clark 1905a; Devas 1943; Groome 1970).

It is possible that some of the birds observed during the winter months may be referable to the North American race, *Pelecanus occidentalis carolinensis*, which has been recorded on Trinidad and Venezuela (ffrench 1991; Meyer de Schauensee and Phelps 1978). Based on their long-term persistence in the area and scarcity in neighboring islands, Hayes (2002) suspected that a small breeding population exists, possibly on Pelican Cay.

Breeding data: A male in which "testes were enormous" collected in early January (Thayer 1925) suggests that breeding occurs in the early part of the year; this appears to be the only available data.

Magnificent Frigatebird

Known to have nested in the Grenadines at Battowia (Clark 1905a; Thayer 1925) and Kick-'em-Jenny (Wells 1887, 1902). Devas (1943) suggested breeding might occur at London Bridge.

There were 119 individuals, of all ages and both sexes, counted in June 2004 at a favored roost on Battowia, appropriately called Man O'War Hole; however, there was no evidence of nesting (M. Frost and R. W. Burke). Our guide, as well as locals on Bequia, advised that this roost site was used year round but that the species had never bred there in living memory. Ten individuals were observed roosting on Sail Rock and a smaller roost site at The Sisters in August 2004; neither location had any sign of nesting activity, but this species was not observed on Kick-'em-Jenny (A. Sutton and B. Hay). Recent observations at different times of the year show this species to be widespread in small numbers throughout the

region (Smith and Smith, unpubl.); Wells and Wells 2000; Hayes 2002; E. B. Massiah and R. W. Burke, pers. comm.), with the 2004 surveys suggesting that these refer to nonbreeding individuals, which may roost at a few locations in the area. Thayer (1925) observed "a splendid colony (of a thousand or more) in Battowia . . . which furnishes I think all the wandering Frigate Birds of these waters for many miles around," but Wells (1902) did not offer a quantitative assessment of the colonies nesting at Kick-'em-Jenny.

Breeding data: Wells (1887) found nests with young in May, which seems to be the only available data.

Laughing Gull

Known to have nested in the Grenadines, on the islets around Grenada, and on the Grenada mainland. Clark (1905a) reported nesting "on the small islets about Carriacou, and rather generally on the more isolated keys all through the Grenadines," with Isle-de-Large being named as especially important by Wells (1902). Devas (1943) listed Les Tantes as a breeding location. Wells (1887) reported nesting on the ledges of cliffs on the Grenada mainland, and Danforth (1936a) noted a breeding colony at Glover Island, off Grenada's south coast. Thayer (1925) noted "nests . . . on smaller Cays" in the St. Vincent Grenadines but only specifically listed Petit Canouan.

This species was present on most islands during an August 2004 survey of the southern Grenadines, but the only evidence for nesting was on Petit Canouan, where an estimated 10 pairs successfully nested (A. Sutton and B. Hay). Although there were around 400 individuals on Battowia in June 2004, observers found only one chick and approximately 12 nests, presumed to belong to this species. The nests, however, had no egg, egg shell or chick in the nest vicinity, possibly suggesting that this site had suffered from egg taking (M. Frost and R. W. Burke).

Other recent observations suggest that this species is common throughout the Grenadines during summer months (Smith and Smith, unpubl.; E. B. Massiah and R. W. Burke, pers. comm.) and indicate that it still nests there. Historical assessments suggest that this species was common to abundant throughout the area from March to August, when numbers start to decline, and by October they have disappeared (Wells 1887; Clark 1905a; Thayer 1925; Devas 1954). This suggests that there has been no significant population change.

Breeding data: Wells (1902) noted that breeding occurred in the months of May and June, and Thayer (1925) found many eggs in the first days of June on Petit Canouan, with those opened fresh or little incubated. Danforth (1936a) observed a large nesting colony in late July on Glover Island. The presence of a chick on Battowia in late June 2004 (M. Frost and R. W. Burke) and juveniles in late August 2004 on Petit Canouan (A. Sutton and B. Hay) is consistent with the historical assessment of egg laying toward the end of May and early June.

Brown Noddy

Known to have nested in the Grenadines at West Cay (off Bequia), White Island, Isle de Large, Rose Rock, and Lee Rocks (Wells 1887, 1902; Clark 1905a); at Petit Canouan, The Sisters, and Kick-'em-Jenny in August 2004 (A. Sutton and B. Hay); and on the St. Vincent mainland at Chateau Belair (Lowe 1909; Bond 1928a). Devas (1943) suggested Les Tantes as a breeding location, whereas Thayer (1925) noted breeding on "several of the Cays [St. Vincent Grenadines], larger and smaller" but gave no specific locations.

Nesting activity was observed in August 2004 on Petit Canouan, The Sisters, and Kick-'em-Jenny, with estimates of 100, 10, and 10 pairs, respectively; nesting probably occurs on Sail Rock, where 200 individuals were seen with hundreds more at sea. Concentrations of around 100 individuals at Les Tantes and islets around Carriacou suggest nesting there, although very few were noted around Isle de Large and Rose Rocks (A. Sutton and B. Hay). Ten pairs estimated each on Battowia and All Awash, with fewer pairs on the Pillories (M. Frost and R. W. Burke).

Historical assessments indicate that this species was abundant throughout the Grenadines but less common off the coasts of Grenada and St. Vincent (Wells 1887, 1902; Clark 1905a; Devas 1954). Indeed, Thayer (1925) noted: "The most abundant seabird in the Cays. Holds its own even where other species disappear, owing to its English-sparrow-like versatility of . . . nesting habits. Thousands on each of several of the Cays." This species is only present during the summer breeding months, probably March to September, but exact details of arrival and departure dates do not appear to be available.

Breeding data: Wells (1887, 1902) found nests at Isle de Large, Rose Rock, and Lee Rocks in May and noted: "The eggs are usually placed in a hole or depression in the rock, [which] contain from two to three eggs." Thayer (1925) did not note the time of year when breeding occurred but stated: "Nests indifferently in crevices and small caves of the sea cliffs, in grass, in bushes, in trees (with a nest almost like a crow's nest); on rocks; in cactus." Chicks and recently fledged juveniles were observed in late August 2004 (A. Sutton and B. Hay).

Sooty Tern

Known to have nested in the Grenadines at Isle de Large, Bonaparte Rocks, Kick-'em-Jenny, Isle Ronde, and Lee Rocks as well as on some of the smaller islets, particularly between Carriacou and Grenada (Wells 1887, 1902; Clark 1905a). Nesting observed on Sail Rock and Petit Canouan (A. Sutton and B. Hay). Thayer (1925) suggested that breeding occurred in the more northern Grenadines, but no specific localities were given.

Recent observations at sea during late May and late July–early August suggest that this species is common throughout the Grenadines, particularly around Kick-'em-Jenny (Smith and Smith, unpubl; E. B. Massiah and R. W. Burke, pers. comm.). More than 1,000 and 3,000 individuals (adults and chicks) were observed on Sail Rock and Petit Canouan respectively in late August 2004, but very few were observed between Carriacou and Kick-'em-Jenny apart from an estimated 50 pairs at Frigate Island (A. Sutton and B. Hay). Late June 2004 estimates were 500 pairs on All Awash and 15 pairs on Battowia Bullet (M. Frost and R. W. Burke).

Historical assessments indicate that this species was abundant in the southern Grenadines, less common in the northern Grenadines, and only occasionally seen in waters around mainland St. Vincent and Grenada (Wells 1887, 1902, Clark 1905a; Thayer 1925; Devas 1943). This species is only present during the summer breeding months, probably March to September, but exact details of arrival and departure dates do not appear to be available.

Breeding data: The only available data appear to be incubation observed in June 2004 (M. Frost and R. W. Burke) and chicks and fledglings in August 2004 (A. Sutton and B. Hay).

Bridled Tern

Known to have nested in the Grenadines and on Grenada. Wells (1887, 1902) and Clark (1905a) reported colonies at White Island, Rose Rocks, and Lee Rocks, and Devas (1954) noted breeding on the Grenada mainland, Les Tantes, Green Island, and "elsewhere."

Recent observations at sea during late May and late July–early August suggest that this species is common throughout the Grenadines, particularly around Kick-'em-Jenny (Smith and Smith, unpubl. 1998; E. B. Massiah and R. W. Burke, pers. comm.). June 2004 estimates were 50 birds at All Awash and 5 pairs at the Pillories, with suspected nesting in small numbers on Battowia Bullet (M. Frost and R. W. Burke). Few were observed in late August 2004 in the southern Grenadines, suggesting that the majority of birds had already dispersed; evidence of nesting activity was found only on Les Tantes (A. Sutton and B. Hay). The historical assessments given to this species were "Abundant in Cays [St. Vincent Grenadines], almost rivaling *fuscata*" (Thayer 1925), "abundant among the islets" (Wells 1887), and "common about the southern Grenadines, nesting abundantly . . . single birds or pairs are frequent in the northern Grenadines and about the shores of St. Vincent and Grenada" (Clark 1905a). This species is only present during the summer breeding months, probably March to September, but exact details of arrival and departure dates do not appear to be available.

Breeding data: Limited data are available. Wells (1887, 1902) found nests at Lee Rocks and Rose Rock in May, with a clutch size of two eggs, and stated that "they hardly make any nest, a tuft of grass, or a depression in the rock serving as a place for depositing its eggs." Thayer (1925) observed: "Nests in rock-crevices and holes more than on grassy flats and open ground as *fuscata* does." Clark (1905a) reported that the White Island colony was "in the midst of a rookery of several hundred Noddies [*Anous stolidus*]."

Roseate Tern

Known to have nested in the Grenadines and on Grenada and possibly on St. Vincent. Wells (1902) and Clark (1905a) reported breeding near Carriacou at Frigate Island and Rose Rock and that a colony at Isle Jacques Adam had been abandoned. Wells (1887) reported breeding at Lee Rocks and on the Grenada mainland. Devas (1954) listed Les Tantes and Green Island as nesting places, and Danforth (1936a) cited Glover Island. Thayer (1925) indicated "small colonies scattered throughout the Grenadines" but gave no specific locations and noted: "I believe on 'Milligan Cay' close to S. coast St. Vincent proper."

In August 2004 observers found a maximum of 15 pairs at Mabouya Island, with smaller numbers of adults and chicks at The Sisters, Sandy Island, and Jack Adam Island, and observed this species around most islands between Carriacou and Kick-'em-Jenny (A. Sutton and B. Hay). About 12 individuals each at Semples Cay and Syrup Cay to the south of Bequia were presumed to be nesting, and about 20 individuals around Battowia and Battowia Bullet may also have been nesting there in June 2004 (M. Frost and R. W. Burke). The historical assess-

ments suggest that the species was "fairly common" in the Grenadines and around Grenada but less so around St. Vincent (Wells 1887, 1902; Clark 1905a; Danforth 1936a; Devas 1943), with the only quantitative assessment of nesting colonies being provided by Thayer (1925) who noted "from four to fifteen or twenty pairs each." This species is a summer visitor, being present from April to September but then vacating the area (Devas 1954).

Breeding data: The limited data available suggest that the breeding season occurs from May to August. Wells (1887) found "nests with two eggs each at Lee Rocks in May" and (1902) stated: "I have taken their eggs there [presumably Frigate Island and/or Rose Rock] in May. . . . The eggs are two in number, generally laid on the bare ground, but sometimes in a grass tuft." Danforth (1936a) observed a large nesting colony on Glover Island in late July. Chicks were observed in late August 2004 (A. Sutton and B. Hay).

Royal Tern

Reported to have nested "on the islets" and "on the rocks," presumably referring to those around the Grenada mainland and Carriacou, respectively (Wells 1887, 1902); Wells did not specifically name a location and was unsuccessful in procuring eggs.

Recent data from several months of the year suggest that this species is uncommon (Smith and Smith, unpubl.; Wells and Wells 2000; Hayes 2002; A. Sutton and B. Hay; E. B. Massiah and R. W. Burke, pers. comm.), which corresponds closely to the historical assessment (Wells 1887, 1902; Clark 1905a; Thayer 1925; Devas 1943). This tern's presence in the region throughout the year suggests that breeding in small numbers may occur. Thayer (1925) noted that it seemed "to be the only Laridae which is not absent from these waters for several months after nesting season," although it is possible that the individuals present in the summer months disperse and are replaced by wintering North American birds.

Breeding data: Wells (1887) noted that breeding occurred "in April and May," which appear to be the only available data.

Sandwich Tern

Known to have nested at Jack Adam Island in 2004 (A. Sutton and B. Hay). Reported to have nested in the Tobago Cays (Bond 1950a). It is unclear whether this was in error as no further reference to this species breeding in the Grenadines is found in Bond's later publications.

Recent observations suggest that this species is rare to uncommon throughout the region (Smith and Smith, unpubl.; Hayes 2002; E. B. Massiah and R. W. Burke, pers. comm.). Its occurrence in late May and late July–early August suggested that breeding might occur, and this was confirmed by Sutton and Hay in late August 2004.

Breeding data: Flightless chicks noted in late August 2004 (A. Sutton and B. Hay).

Threats

Poaching of eggs was practiced in the past, with "boatloads of eggs collected annually, and sometimes even sold in Kingstown" (Thayer 1925). In addition, people harvested young Audubon's Shearwater in large numbers—and probably of other species (Wells 1902; Thayer 1925). The extent to which these practices occur at present is unknown, but egg taking still occurred on islets off north Grenada in the early 1990s (R. Miller, pers. comm.) and still occurs in the Grenadines (A. Sutton and B. Hay; H. Belmar, pers. comm.). Uncontrolled development and unregulated use of terrestrial and marine habitats and resources within the Grenadine islands, which are viewed as having high potential for foreign exchange earnings through tourism and associated development, could lead to (and in some instances have already led to) problems with overfishing, nearshore habitat destruction and degradation, sedimentation, and recreational abuse of coral reefs (R. Mahon, pers. comm.). These matters could in the long term affect the size and viability of nesting seabird populations within the region.

Conservation

Several marine protected areas have been established or have been identified as desirable within the Grenadines, but progress has been slow in implementation of the management plan and enforcement of regulations within these protected areas (R. Mahon, pers. comm.). Surveys of the isolated islets within the archipelago, especially those where seabirds have previously been reported to breed, are urgently needed to document the breeding seabird fauna and to determine what steps need to be taken to preserve them.

22

Trinidad and Tobago

FLOYD E. HAYES AND STEFAN BODNAR

Perched on the continental shelf of northeastern South America between the Caribbean Sea and Atlantic Ocean, the Republic of Trinidad and Tobago comprises an archipelago of two large continental islands and numerous smaller islands (map 46). The archipelago's marine environment (see reviews by Kenny and Bacon 1981; Agard and Gobin 2000) is influenced primarily by the Guyana Current, a derivative of the westward-flowing South Equatorial Current, which is deflected northwest toward Trinidad and Tobago by South America's east coast. The island of Trinidad splits the Guyana Current in two: part of it enters the Gulf of Paria, which separates Trinidad from the Venezuelan mainland, and the rest flows through Tobago Sound, which separates Trinidad and Tobago. The currents rejoin to the north, forming the northward flowing Antillean Current.

Salinity in nearshore waters, especially in the Gulf of Paria, is lowered by large volumes of fresh water discharged from several major rivers on the South American continent, including the Orinoco River just south of the archipelago. Marine productivity in the region is high due to elevated nutrient levels transported by rivers and vertical mixing caused by bathymetrical irregularities.

The region's marine ecosystems support many breeding seabird colonies, which are generally restricted to the smaller, uninhabited satellite islands off the coasts of Trinidad and Tobago, especially the latter. A wealth of published information documents the seabirds breeding at various colonies within the past half century, but few reports contain precise information on population size, and most reports are limited to a few well-known colonies (see reviews by ffrench 1973a, 1991a). Here we review the status of breeding seabird fauna of Trinidad and Tobago, augmented with recent observations by ourselves and others.

Methods of Survey

We reviewed the published literature on breeding seabird populations in Trinidad and Tobago. We also opportunistically visited various seabird colonies in Trinidad and Tobago to assess their breeding bird populations. Off Trinidad, a suspected colony at Gasparillo was censused in situ by Hayes on 18 October 1996 and from a boat on 16 February 1997; a suspected colony at Huevos was censused from a ship by Hayes on 27 June 1999, 15 July 2001, 1 August 2001, and 26 October 2001; a suspected colony on an islet at Petite Tacarib Bay was censused from Trinidad by Martyn Kenefick on 11 May 2002; and a former colony at Soldado Rock was censused from a boat by Hayes and colleagues on 22 April 2001.

Off Tobago, the colony at St. Giles Islands was censused in situ and from a boat by Bodnar during 2–3 May 2000 and from a boat by Hayes et al. on 1 April 1998 and 8 October 2001; the colony at Little Tobago was censused in situ by Bodnar on 7 May 2000; the colony along cliffs of northeastern Tobago was censused from a boat by Hayes et al. on 1 April 1998 and 8 October 2001; the colony at Smith Island was censused from Tobago by Hayes on 1 April and 11 May 1998; and the colony on a small islet off Courland Point was censused from Tobago by Hayes on 24 May 2001. Although some were direct counts, most were estimated; the number of pairs present was estimated by dividing the total number of individuals observed by two.

Trinidad

Situated 19.4 km from the Venezuelan mainland, Trinidad (10° 30'N, 61° 20' W, 4,520 km^2) consists of coastal lowlands and broad valleys sandwiched between three mountain ranges rising up to 925 m. The native terres-

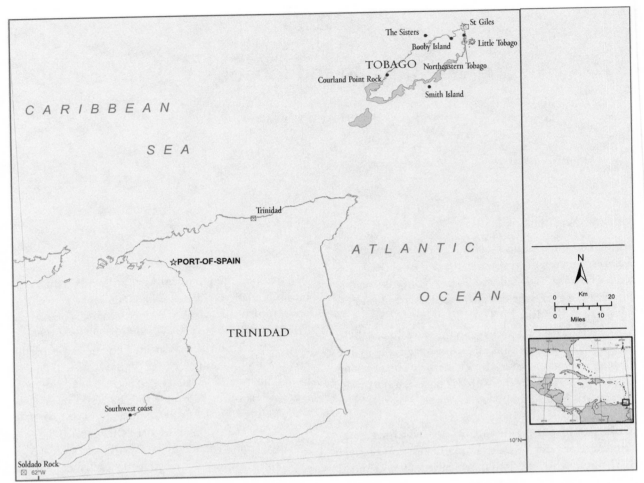

Map 46. Trinidad and Tobago.

trial vegetation varies from tropical rainforest at higher elevations to seasonal forest, tropical savanna, mangrove swamp, and littoral woodland at lower elevations. The coasts are characterized by sandy beaches alternating with rocky headlands, with extensive mangrove swamps and tidal mud flats occurring along portions of the west coast. Major ports are all located on the west coast (Port of Spain, Port Lisas, San Fernando, and Point Fortin). The human population in 2000 was 1,208,282.

Trinidad has two major breeding seabird colonies: Soldado Rock (0.8 ha, 35 m high), located 10.0 km west of Icacos Peninsula in the southwest; and Saut d'Eau Island (15 ha, 107 m high), 0.4 km off the north-central coast. The Soldado Rock colony may have been abandoned (see Threats and Conservation). A small seabird colony was recently reported on a small rocky islet off Petite Tacarib Bay along the north coast (M. Kenefick, pers. comm.), and other colonies may occur on simi-

lar islets along the north coast (e.g., Hayes and Samad 2002).

Seven species of seabirds have been confirmed breeding since 1947, but only the Roseate Tern was a confirmed breeder on Trinidad between 2001 and 2002.

Brown Pelican

Breeding January–April at Saut d'Eau Island, where an estimated 150 nests were reported by Brown (1947). Brown Pelican were also reported to nest occasionally in mangrove swamps of Trinidad (Belcher and Smooker 1934; Herklots 1961; ffrench 1973a, 1991a), but no details are provided and there are no recent breeding records. In the Bocas Islands off northwest Trinidad, Hayes and Samad (2002) suspected nesting of small numbers at traditional roosts on the southwest side of Gasparillo Island and on a large rock on the north side of Huevos Island (not confirmed); at the latter locality, up to 130 were viewed repeatedly from a ferry during 1999–2002.

Magnificent Frigatebird

Up to 500 roost at Soldado Rock but only "a few nests" were found in February 1973 (John Saunders, *in* ffrench 1990), and two eggs that "may well have been of this species" were found in October 1983 (A. W. Diamond, *in* ffrench 1990). However, none were found by ffrench (1973a, 1990, 1991a), who visited the island 29 times from 1960 to 1982. About 120 frigatebirds were seen on 22 April 2001, but there was no sign of nesting (F. E. Hayes).

Brown Noddy

Observed March–July at Soldado Rock, where 3,000–5,000 bred during 1960–1982; egg dates ranged from 18 March to 9 July (ffrench 1973a, 1990, 1991b). None were present on 22 April 2001 (F. E. Hayes).

Sooty Tern

Breeds March–May at Soldado Rock, where up to 10,000 were estimated breeding on 27 April 1958 (Herklots 1961). However, ffrench (1973a, 1990, 1991a) estimated the breeding population at 5,000 individuals, suggesting that Herklots's numbers were overestimates. Egg dates ranged from 4 March to 27 May (ffrench 1973a, 1990). None were present on 22 April 2001 (F. E. Hayes).

Roseate Tern

About 50 adults were seen nesting on a vegetated islet off Petite Tacarib Bay, on the north coast, on 11 May 2002 (M. Kenefick, pers. comm.). Ten terns thought to be this species and seen flying near Huevos Island on 27 June 1999 may have been nesting on a rock off the north coast (Hayes and Samad 2002).

Royal Tern

At Soldado Rock, 14 eggs were found in June 1962, another 14 in June 1966, and a small nestling was found on 15 June 1963; apparently none survived (ffrench and Collins 1965); none were found breeding in subsequent years (ffrench 1973a, 1990, 1991a). None were present on 22 April 2001 (F. E. Hayes).

Sandwich Tern

At Soldado Rock, four eggs were found on 10 June 1962, and a pair of adults was seen feeding a young bird on 15 June 1963 (ffrench and Collins 1965); none were found in subsequent years (ffrench 1973a, 1990, 1991a). The adults were of the South American race *eurygnatha*, which may

be a distinct species (see Hayes 2004). None were present on 22 April 2001 (F. E. Hayes).

Tobago

Tobago (11° 15' N, 60° 40' W, 306 km²) is located 19 km northeast of Trinidad and 118 km from the Venezuelan mainland. A mountain ridge up to 576 m high forms the island's backbone. The native terrestrial vegetation is similar to that of Trinidad. The coasts are characterized by sandy beaches alternating with rock headlands except at the western tip, where a mangrove lagoon is situated behind an extensive shallow coral reef formation. The major port, Scarborough, is on the south coast, and the minor port of Charlotteville on the north coast. The human population in 2000 was 54,084.

The three major breeding seabird colonies in Tobago are the St. Giles Islands (27 ha, 114 m high), located 0.4 km offshore at the northeastern tip (plate 42); nearby Little Tobago (113 ha, 137 m high), located 1.6 km offshore; and Smith's Island (1 ha, 20 m high), 0.5 km south of Pinfold Bay in south-central Tobago.

Five additional minor colonies have been reported around the Tobago coast: a sandbar at Buccoo Reef (0.01 ha, 1 m high), off Pigeon Point in the southwest; a rocky islet off Courland Point (0.01 ha, 10 m high), also on the southwest coast; Sisters Rocks (2 ha, 15 m high), off Bloody Bay in north-central Tobago; Booby Island (0.3 ha, 25 m high), off Cambleton and Man-o-War Bay in the northeast; and rocky headlands along the northeastern tip of Tobago. Seabird nesting probably occurs on privately owned Goat Island (5 ha, 46 m high) at the northeastern tip, but no details have been published.

Thirteen species of seabirds have been confirmed breeding since 1958, and of these 12 were still breeding in 1997–2001, although no counts of the Brown Pelican were available (table 22.1).

Table 22.1. Estimates of seabird pairs breeding on Tobago, 1997–2001

Species	Estimated Pairs
Audubon's Shearwater	>500
Red-billed Tropicbird	52
Masked Booby	5
Brown Booby	84
Red-footed Booby	465
Magnificent Frigatebird	800
Laughing Gull	258
Brown Noddy	500
Sooty Tern	>500
Bridled Tern	50
Roseate Tern	55

Audubon's Shearwater

Breeds January–April in burrows on St. Giles and Little Tobago. "Hundreds" were thought to breed on the St. Giles Islands during 1958–1968 (Dinsmore and ffrench 1969), and an estimated 1,000 bred at Little Tobago during 1965–1966 (Dinsmore 1972). Two nestlings were noted on the St. Giles Islands during 2–3 May 2000, and five nestlings were banded on Little Tobago during May–June 2000, undoubtedly representing a small proportion of the breeding population (S. Bodnar). The population estimate is more than 500 pairs.

White-tailed Tropicbird

This species was first observed at Little Tobago on 29 December 1983 (ffrench 1991a) but not seen subsequently until 1 April 1988 (White and Hayes 2002). Since 1988 a pair has been seen repeatedly at Little Tobago and nearby Goat Island. Breeding on Little Tobago was suspected for several years. In 2003 an individual thought to be nesting was seen at the same spot on the ground for several weeks and consistently pointed out to ecotourists through a telescope, but no eggs or nestlings were ever seen (D. Rooks, pers. comm.).

Red-billed Tropicbird

Breeds November–April on St. Giles, Little Tobago, and Smith's Island. An estimated 200 bred on the St. Giles Islands during 1958–1968 (Dinsmore and ffrench 1969). "Some tens" were seen but not observed nesting in 1971 (Spaans 1973), but only three adults and no young were noted during 2–3 May 2000 (S. Bodnar). An estimated 500 bred on Little Tobago during 1965–1966 (Dinsmore 1972), but only 100 adults were present during a survey on 7 May 2000 (S. Bodnar). No estimates have been published for Smith's Island (ffrench 1973a, 1991a). A few individuals flying about steep coastal cliffs of northeastern Tobago on 1 April 1998 may have been breeding (F. E. Hayes).

Masked Booby

This species was first reported from the St. Giles Islands on 29 September 1994, when three adults were found (R. ffrench *in* Hayes and White 2000). Numbers gradually increased, peaking at 60 on 13 January 1999 (D. Finch *in* White and Hayes 2002). About 10 adults were present, and one was seen feeding one of four young, on 25 April 2000 (S. Bodnar *in* White and Hayes 2002), providing the first confirmation of breeding.

Brown Booby

Breeds June–March on northeastern Tobago, St. Giles Islands, and Little Tobago. On the St. Giles Islands, Dinsmore and ffrench (1969) reported "many" breeding from 1958 to 1968, 100 nests were estimated in 1971 (Spaans 1973), and a survey on 2–3 May 2000 produced 17 young and 74 adults (S. Bodnar). The population of Little Tobago was estimated to be 300 during 1965–1966 (Dinsmore 1972) but only 100 during 1975–1976, when nesting was monitored for 71 pairs (Morris 1977a, 1984). A survey of Little Tobago on 7 May 2000 revealed 18 young and 75 adults (S. Bodnar). About 10 nests were seen on cliffs of northeastern Tobago in April–May 2000 (S. Bodnar) and on 8 October 2001 (F. E. Hayes).

Red-footed Booby

Breeds August–April on the St. Giles Islands, with numbers during 1958–1968 estimated from "several hundred" (Dinsmore and ffrench 1969) to "perhaps 1,500" (ffrench 1973a, 1991a). A "few hundred nests" were seen in 1971, with the population estimated at 750 pairs (Spaans 1973). During 2–3 May 2000, 402–419 young were counted and 900 adults were estimated on the St. Giles Islands (S. Bodnar). Breeding has occurred annually on Little Tobago since about 1990 (D. Rooks, pers. comm.). A census of Little Tobago on 7 May 2000 revealed 12 young and an estimated 30 adults (S. Bodnar).

Brown Pelican

Small numbers reported to breed "on remote rocks on Tobago" but no details provided (ffrench 1973a, 1991a). Bond (1970) reported: "It is said that there is or was a nesting colony on 'The Sisters' off the north coast, but this has not been confirmed."

Magnificent Frigatebird

Breeds December–April on the St. Giles Islands, where up to 2000 "nest or roost" (Dinsmore and ffrench 1969). A survey on 2–3 May 2000 revealed 108 young and 1,600 adults (S. Bodnar).

Laughing Gull

Breeds April to June on Little Tobago, where up to 750 bred during 1965–1966 (Dinsmore 1972). During 1976, 187 nests were monitored, which were thought to comprise only 25–30% of those present (Morris 1984), providing an estimate of 623–748 pairs. A survey of Little Tobago on 7 May 2000 found 50 young and 517 adults (S. Bodnar). Breeding was suspected but no eggs were found on the St. Giles Islands, where 400 were noted on 4 May 1966 (Dinsmore and ffrench 1969; Rooks 1988); and a small group was noted in 1971 (Spaans 1973) and only 25 during 2–3 May 2000 (S. Bodnar). Nesting was also suspected along the north coast of Tobago (ffrench 1973a, 1991a).

Brown Noddy

Breeds February–July on the St. Giles Islands, Little Tobago, and Smith's Island. During 1958–1968, an estimated 1,000 bred on the St. Giles Islands (Dinsmore and ffrench 1969), and "several thousands" were estimated in 1971 (Spaans 1973), but only 15 adults were present during 2–3 May (S. Bodnar). An estimated 1,200 bred on Little Tobago during 1965–1966 (Dinsmore 1972); 125 nests were monitored during 1976 (Morris 1984); but only 10 young and 70 adults were present on 7 May 2000 (S. Bodnar). None were seen during surveys of both islands during 2–7 May 2000 (S. Bodnar). Up to 1,000 birds on Smith's Island in 1973; hundreds appeared to be breeding there when viewed through a telescope on land on 11 May 1998 (F. E. Hayes). Also reported breeding along the "leeward coast" of Tobago (Belcher and Smooker 1935), with no details provided. The population estimate is more than 500 pairs.

Sooty Tern

Breeds February–June at Little Tobago and Smith's Island, with an estimated 2,100 on Little Tobago (Dinsmore 1972) and 1,000 on Smith's Island (ffrench 1973a, 1991a). In 1976, 109 nests were monitored on Little Tobago (Morris 1984). Although none were seen at Little Tobago during 2–7 May 2000 (S. Bodnar), fair numbers were seen later in the season and in other recent years (F. E. Hayes). Hundreds appeared to be breeding on Smith's Island when viewed through a telescope from land on 11 May 1998 (F. E. Hayes). Nesting was suspected on St. Giles Islands (Dinsmore and ffrench 1969, Spaans 1973) and along the north coast of Tobago (Belcher and Smooker 1935), but no nests have been found. The population estimate is more than 500 pairs.

Bridled Tern

Breeds April–June on Little Tobago, with an estimated 150 during 1965–1966 (Dinsmore 1972) and 86 adults found on 7 May 2000 (S. Bodnar). Also reported breeding on Smith's Island in July 1958 (Snow in Herklots 1961), but no further details were provided. Several were noted flying about Smith's Island and presumed to be breeding when viewed through a telescope from land on

11 May 1998 (F. E. Hayes). Nesting suspected on the St. Giles Islands, where "several" were seen on 4 May 1966, immatures were noted on 21 August 1968 (Dinsmore and ffrench 1969), "some tens" were seen in April 1971 (Spaans 1973), and eight adults were seen during 2–3 May 2000 (S. Bodnar), but no nests have been found.

Roseate Tern

Breeds May–June on rocks along the north coast of Tobago. On 2 June 1966, 200 adults were seen in a colony with eggs and downy young on a rocky slope of northeast Tobago, just opposite the St. Giles Islands (Dinsmore and ffrench 1969). About 10 pairs nested on Booby Island in May and June 1986 and 1987 (Rooks, pers. comm. 1988). On a small rock just offshore from Courland Point, B. Goodwin (in litt.) reported a colony of about 100 Common Terns (*Sterna hirundo*) breeding in May 1997; however, the identity of these birds as Roseate Terns was confirmed on 24 May 2001, when 111 incubating adults and two small chicks were observed (F. E. Hayes).

Royal Tern

While fishing from a boat, Rooks (pers. comm. 1988) observed many breeding on Sisters Islands, with "nest being visible from the sea" (Rooks, pers. comm. 1988). Nesting also suspected on the St. Giles Islands, but no nests observed (Rooks 1988).

Threats and Conservation

The major seabird colonies are legally protected as wildlife sanctuaries (Bacon and ffrench 1992). These include Soldado Rock and Saut d'Eau Island off Trinidad and Little Tobago and St. Giles off Tobago. Yet despite legal protection of seabirds within the wildlife sanctuaries, law enforcement is lax and poaching still occurs. The Division of Forestry needs more resources to enforce wildlife laws effectively.

Trinidad Colony Abandoned

In Trinidad, the major seabird breeding colony at Soldado Rock, which formerly hosted up to 10,000 Sooty Tern and Brown Noddy, plus smaller numbers of other seabirds, appears to have been abandoned (table 22.1.), possibly due to extensive degradation of marine habitat in the Gulf of Paria (Agard and Gobin 2000). No nesting seabirds were present when the island was circled closely by boat on 22 April 2001 or when examined more distantly by telescope from Icacos Peninsula on 26 May 2002 (F. E. Hayes et al., pers. obs). Colony abandonment may have been caused by a decline in fisheries production in the southern Gulf of Paria, perhaps due to increased sedimentation from the Orinoco River, overfishing, or excessive pollution.

Further evidence of marine habitat degradation is provided by the dramatic decline of wintering Common Tern in the region. In the early 1980s, up to 2,000 regularly wintered along the Icacos Peninsula of southwestern Trinidad, where they were attracted to the fishing industry but were malnourished and frequently captured by hand by fishermen (Blokpoel et al. 1982, 1984; Morris et al. 1982). Very few terns were present in 1993–2002, with a maximum count of 34 on 23 June 2002 (F. E. Hayes et al., pers obs.), suggesting that the available food supply could no longer support a large population of wintering terns and, by deduction, breeding terns. Alternatively, the undocumented poaching of adults, chicks, and eggs of breeding seabirds may have caused or contributed to abandonment of the colony.

Poaching in Tobago

In Tobago, the major seabird colonies on the St. Giles Islands, Little Tobago, and Smith's Island still host large populations of all previously reported breeding species. Although scanty, historical data suggest that several seabird species may be declining (the data are most compelling for Brown Booby), while the Laughing Gull, which probably benefits from human activities (e.g., scavenging for food scraps), appears to be increasing (table 22.1).

Despite official protection of the St. Giles Islands and Little Tobago as wildlife sanctuaries (Dinsmore and ffrench 1969; Bacon and ffrench 1972), poaching of seabird eggs has been a major problem. Morris (1977a, 1984) attributed the decline in breeding Brown Boobies at Little Tobago to poaching, although he did not personally witness this. Morris (1984:7) stated that "while evidence was circumstantial, I suggest that human poaching of both eggs and chicks occurred at the booby colonies" and "while I was unable to confirm it directly, the practice appears to be an annual event related to local harvest festivities." Diamond (1983) reported finding "four or five piles of frigatebird wings and other remains" of "at least one hundred individuals" of Magnificent Frigatebird on the St. Giles Islands on 22 May 1983. Diamond (1983) noted: "Poaching, especially of Brown Boobies but probably of terns and gulls and their eggs as well, for 'Booby meat' for village harvest festivals on Tobago, is reportedly a serious problem."

Such poaching still occurs, as evidenced by 150 Red-footed Booby and 15 Magnificent Frigatebird carcasses, plus piles of wings from previous years, found on the St.

Giles Islands in May 2000 (S. Bodnar). The greatest concentration of Red-footed Booby carcasses and the lowest density of young birds were in the more accessible lower slopes, where trees were typically 2–2.5 m high; these areas appeared abandoned as breeding areas, although the guano indicated previous use. The young boobies were concentrated in higher trees (up to 7 m) on the steeper slopes of the island. More efficient law enforcement is needed to protect breeding seabirds, which attract large numbers of ecotourists and provide a significant economic resource for the local human population.

Other Risk Factors

With the exception of a few man-made structures and heavy use of trails by ecotourists on Little Tobago, the terrestrial habitat on all known seabird breeding colonies in Trinidad and Tobago remains relatively pristine. Other than a small population of feral red junglefowl (*Gallus gallus*) established more than a century ago on Little Tobago (Dinsmore 1972), no exotic animals are currently known to exist on the islands. There have been no attempts to control predators within seabird colonies. Rats (*Rattus* spp.), however, are notorious predators of eggs and chicks of the smaller seabird species and may well exist undetected in seabird colonies. Searches should be conducted for rats, which should be eradicated if found.

A few other factors may adversely affect breeding seabird populations. Although no data are available, pollutants biomagnified through the food chain may adversely affect the health of seabirds, and overfishing may reduce the seabirds' food supply. Incidental by-catch of seabirds by fishermen is clearly a threat to Magnificent Frigatebirds and probably to other seabirds as well. In May 2000, S. Bodnar observed many live frigatebirds on the St. Giles Islands that were either ensnared or hooked with fishing line.

Surveys Are Needed

Although 15 species of seabirds have been reported nesting in the archipelago, breeding of the Sandwich Tern was limited to a few birds and has not been reported since 1963. It is uncertain whether the Royal Tern still breeds. The Masked Booby and White-tailed Tropicbird appear to be recent colonists, the former first confirmed nesting in 2000 and the latter probably nesting in 2003. While there have been several studies on the breeding biology of seabirds in Trinidad and Tobago (Dinsmore 1972; ffrench 1991b; Morris 1977a, 1984), much remains to be learned about the impact of potential threats on seabirds.

Given the scanty information available on extant breeding seabird populations, surveys are urgently needed throughout the archipelago, including isolated rocks that may shelter previously unreported breeding colonies, to document the current status of breeding seabird populations better, to evaluate the quality of breeding habitat, and to assess any steps that need to be taken to preserve the integrity of marine and terrestrial ecosystems.

Acknowledgments

Our observations of seabird colonies were supported financially by Blue Waters Inn, Caribbean Union College, and the University of the West Indies. We thank the Coast Guard of Trinidad and Tobago and the Division of Forestry in Tobago for providing transportation to various islands. We thank Newton George, Brian Goodwin, Martyn Kenefick, and David Rooks for kindly sharing their observations with us.

23

The Netherlands Antilles II

Lago Reef, Aruba

RUUD VAN HALEWIJN

Aruba is a 193 km² island situated on the outer edge of the continental shelf of Venezuela (map 47). On clear days, the Venezuelan Peninsula de Paraguaná 29 km away is visible from Aruba. The island is located in an arid zone that extends along the north coast of South America from the Goajira peninsula of Colombia through Trinidad. Long-term averages for Aruba are 425 mm in annual precipitation and an annual evaporation rate of 3,000 mm. Politically, Aruba has been an autonomous entity in the Kingdom of the Netherlands since 1986. The island is densely populated, with 102,000 inhabitants (2006) and some 642,000 visitors annually (2002, 2003). Tourism, offshore banking, and the oil industry are the economic mainstays.

A broken coral shore reef parallels Aruba's lee shoreline at 200 to 1,000 m offshore. Four small sand and coral shingle keys that constitute the southeast end of the reef are collectively known as Lago Reef or the San Nicolas Bay keys (see description in van Halewijn 1988; de Kort 1995). Lying opposite San Nicolas and the oil refinery, the keys of Lago Reef annually harbor a large and varied larid seabird breeding population. The westernmost of the four seabird keys lies immediately opposite and in the lee of the refinery. Here, air, soil, and water are very heavily polluted, vegetation is lacking, and there is no benthic life at all. Conditions at the two easternmost keys are much better; both have vegetation of herbs and low shrubs and lie in relatively clean water with seagrass beds, live corals, reef fish, and sea turtles. The four keys are under the jurisdiction of the government of Aruba.

Seabirds

Lago Reef constitutes the major seabird breeding site in any of the six Caribbean islands that form part of the Kingdom of the Netherlands (the others being neighboring Curaçao and Bonaire, and the three Windward islands of St. Martin, Saba, and St. Eustatius, almost 1,000 km to the northeast). Lago Reef is especially valuable since it harbors the largest known Cayenne Tern breeding colony, with about 3,500 pairs in good years (see Hayes 2004 for a recent discussion of systematics and taxonomy of Cayenne Tern). Local breeding populations of Black Noddy, Common Tern, and Roseate Tern, though relatively small 20–50, 40, and >60 pairs, respectively), are valuable when considered in an overall Caribbean perspective. The remaining six species are all larids with an extensive breeding distribution.

Lago Reef is one of very few seabird breeding sites in the Caribbean where the historical record—though with hiatuses—can be traced back into the late nineteenth century (Halewijn 1988). In the years 1892 (Hartert 1893) and 1961 (Voous 1963) small numbers of nests of Roseate and Bridled terns were found, and ornithologists visiting Lago Reef prior to the 1970s also found just two tern species nesting.

Total estimates of seabirds breeding in Aruba are given in table 23.1. A summary of results of breeding seabird surveys at Lago Reef in the past 30 years is presented in table 23.2. A notable increase in diversity and abundance of the local larid breeding population occurred from the 1970s through the 1990s, with the first breeding records of six species as follows: Cayenne Tern (1970–71), Sooty Tern (1976), Laughing Gull (1976–79), Brown Noddy (1983), Black Noddy (1992) and Royal Tern (1998). What factors triggered the establishment of additional tern species is unknown. Circumstantial evidence suggests that the major colony of Cayenne Terns moved first from Curaçao to Bonaire (late 1960s) and then from Bonaire to Aruba. The presence of a large and conspicuous Cayenne Tern colony on Lago Reef may subsequently have attracted other tern species and the Laughing Gull.

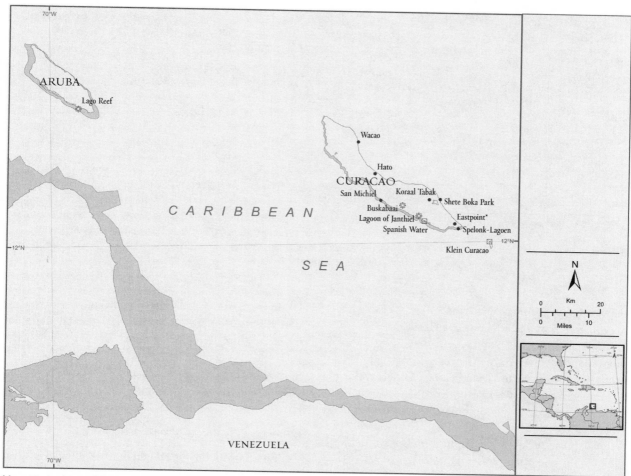

Map 47. Aruba and Curaçao, Netherlands Antilles.

Table 23.1. Estimates of seabird pairs breeding on Aruba, 1999–2001

Species	Counts (pairs)
Laughing Gull	350
Brown Noddy	164
Black Noddy	48
Sooty Tern	6,650
Bridled Tern	122
Least Tern	55
Roseate Tern	52
Common Tern	143
Royal Tern	1–2
Cayenne Tern	3,582

In recent years, Lago Reef has harbored a total of about 10,000 pairs of ten larid seabird species, dominated by Cayenne Tern and Sooty Tern. Tern and gull nests are to be found on each of the four keys each year, but the distribution of nests and colonies in a given year is unpredictable. This applies especially to Cayenne Tern colonies.

Three of the 10 species nest elsewhere in Aruba as well. Small numbers of Cayenne and Common terns also breed on small keys of the northwest end of the reef, opposite the capital, Oranjestad. Least Tern is almost ubiquitous along the coastline, where the total breeding population of Aruba is estimated at about 200 pairs (*cf.* chapter 24).

Synchrony

For a tropical locality, the high degree of intra- and inter-specific synchronization of egg laying in the seabird community is remarkable. Each year, most laying occurs in the first three weeks of May in all species. Synchronization probably results from frequent intra- and inter-specific interactions prior to egg laying. However, ultimate factors determining synchrony are unknown. It is unlikely that there is a predictable annual flush of food for larids in these tropical waters. Furthermore, the various larid species not only have differing feeding methods whereby they exploit different staple foods—

Table 23.2. Survey results of seabird breeding populations, Lago Reef, Aruba, 1974–2002

	1974–1983	1984–1990	1991–1998	1999–2002
Laughing Gull	4–5 (1979)	58 (1990)	47 (1991)	350 (2001)
Brown Noddy	2–5 (1983)	13 (1987, 1988, 1990)	43–45 (1994)	164 (2001)
Black Noddy	Individuals present in 1979 & 1980; no nests	Present annually, number of individuals increased; no nests	13–20 (1992, 1993, 1994)	48 (2001)
Sooty Tern	60–150 (1983)	3,200 (1990)	4,200 (1995)	6,650 (1999)
Bridled Tern	20 (1979, 1983)	52–59 (1986)	57 (1994)	122 (1999)
Least Tern	"a few" (1979)	95+ (1988)	89 (1993)	55 (2001)
Roseate Tern	50 (1979)	112 (1989)	64 (1994)	52 (2001)
Common Tern	70 (1978)	36 (1984)	38 (1994)	143 (1999)
Royal Tern		Individuals present, no nests	1 (1998)	1–2 (1999, 2000, 2001)
Cayenne Tern	2,500 (1977), 3,000 (1979)	3,300 (1988), 3,500 (1984)	3,400–3,750 (1991–95)	3,226 (1999), 3,582 (2001)

Sources: For 1974–1983, sources detailed in Table 1, p. 44 in van Halewijn 1988. For 1984–1990, Ruud van Halewijn (Utrecht, Netherlands). For 1991–1998, Klaas Bakker (Bonaire); Karel Beylevelt (Haarlem, Netherlands); Roeland de Kort (Aruba); Claudia Wilds † (DC, USA); no data for 1996 and 1997; minimal data for 1998. For 1999–2002, Adrian Del Nevo (CA, USA); for 1999, unpublished, in Debrot (this vol.).

Notes: Maximum number of nests is given; date of the count is given in parentheses.

they also exploit different marine zones: species forage mainly in the coastal, offshore, or pelagic zones.

There are indications that when Sooty Terns became more abundant breeders than Cayenne Terns (as of 1990), sooties gradually started laying earlier. Observations in 2004 suggest that sooties may have been incubating eggs as early as late March (Mlodinow 2004). This phenomenon deserves to be studied in detail. The gradually increased spread of laying has implications for wardening, signposting, and other conservation-oriented activities.

Threats

Close proximity to sites of heavy industry and growing tourism development place these seabird nesting sites at considerable risk.

The Oil Refinery

The principal towns of San Nicolas and Oranjestad and the main tourist area of Aruba are all located on the southwest-facing lee shoreline. Initial economic prosperity at Aruba was due to the establishment in 1929 of an oil refinery, the Lago Oil and Transport Company. It was closed down by Exxon in 1985 but reopened in 1991 as Coastal Aruba Refining Company, an El Paso Corporation entity. In March 2004, when the refinery was producing about 225,000 barrels a day, El Paso sold it to Valero Energy Corporation. Soon afterward, the Valero Aruba Refinery announced that it would invest more than $100 million over five years to reduce emissions of sulphur dioxide from refinery stacks by about 80%.

The large oil refining plant was and is responsible for chronic and severe oil, tar, air, auditory, and visual pol-lution of marine and terrestrial biota and—until the last port engineering project in 1969—for habitat alteration by blasting and dredging. Paradoxically, expansion of the larid seabird breeding population at Lago Reef occurred in spite of the adverse impacts of a variety of threats, all of which continue to exert an influence up to the present.

Other Significant Disturbances

Conservation action focuses on the first two and last two factors listed.

Egg collecting is still practiced by a few local fishermen.

Human disturbance involving recreational boaters, jet-skis, and researchers is on the rise; there has been a marked increase in recreational activities on San Nicolas Bay, resulting in more people visiting the seabird keys; most mean no harm but nevertheless disturb the birds.

Pollution includes oil, tar, and smoke; many birds are found with oil on their plumage, especially Cayenne Terns.

Predation mainly involves Laughing Gulls (see The Gull Problem) and to a lesser extent the occasional rat and various other birds, reptiles, and invertebrates.

Kleptoparasitism mainly by the Laughing Gull but also by Magnificent Frigatebird and jaegers.

Flooding occasionally affects nests of Bridled, Cayenne, and Common terns, at least.

Disease and mortality incidents have disturbed colonies: gull mortality from botulism proven; mortality of adult breeding Common Terns from botulism likely but unproven; occasional die-offs of adult breeding Cayenne and Sooty terns recorded, cause(s) unknown; concentrations of heavy metals in corpses not high.

Enforcement of extant laws protecting birds is non-existent.

No official formal protection specifically for Lago Reef has been implemented (see De Kort 1995).

Development

The coastline opposite the seabird keys—where until recently public access was restricted—is an attractive area for developers. Minimum distance between the keys and the coastline of San Nicolas Bay is no more than 600 m. This makes the tern breeding sites on the keys extremely vulnerable. Since 1990, there have been various plans for local development of tourism and/or recreation, the 2002 plan encompassed the construction of two luxury hotels.

In 2004 the Aruban Ministry of Tourism contracted for a tourism master plan for this area with the American firm Sasaki of Boston, which produced plans in the 1980s for the "tourist corridor" in northwest Aruba. Master plan presentation to government provided an opportunity for conservation NGOs to review it for adverse impacts on the seabird breeding sites on the keys.

Permanent structures on the keys of Lago Reef would be fatal for the local seabird breeding population. This type of development has already occurred in two localities elsewhere on Aruba's reef, and the consequences were devastating (disappearance of a Brown Pelican breeding colony and Magnificent Frigatebird roost). Development therefore constitutes a serious potential threat.

The Gull Problem

Since Laughing Gulls first nested on Lago Reef in the 1970s, the gull breeding population has steadily expanded. The intensity of gull predation on Cayenne Terns increased concurrently. Gulls take Cayenne Tern eggs and small, unguarded wandering Cayenne Tern chicks. My estimates of gull predation in various years (1984–1990) range between 20 and 50% of all Cayenne Tern eggs laid. Gulls also kleptoparasitize adult Cayenne Terns approaching the colony with fish in the bill. As of 1987, gulls have also been observed preying on eggs of Sooty Terns. For a gull, it costs less energy to obtain a Sooty Tern's egg than a Cayenne Tern's. This is a consequence of behavioral differences between Cayenne and Sooty terns when incubating: upon disturbance, Cay-

enne Terns are much more reluctant to abandon their egg than are sooties.

There does not seem to be a straightforward management strategy to reduce the adverse impact of gulls on terns. Whether all predatory gulls are local breeders (as opposed to nonbreeding adult and subadult loafers) is questionable. Therefore, elimination of gull eggs, nests, and/or breeding birds is expected not to result in a significant reduction of gull predation on terns.

Conservation-oriented measures that directly or indirectly stimulate growth of the local gull breeding population (like distributing nest-boxes intended for Bridled Terns) must be avoided.

Conservation

All species nesting on Lago Reef are formally protected by laws dating back to the 1930s. Egg collecting and even "disturbing" breeding birds are illegal, but enforcement of these laws is the exception rather than the rule. A seabird conservation project including censusing of seabird breeding populations started in 1983 as a joint Aruban-Dutch project, involving the Aruban conservation NGO called FANAPA and the Dutch chapter of Birdlife International (Gochfeld et al. 1994; Del Nevo 2001). It has continued—with varying intensity—to the present.

As part of this project, conservation-oriented action was undertaken at the height of the breeding season (May–June), especially during 1983–1991, including signposting and wardening of the keys and educational publicity in local media (newspapers, television). The major aims of these activities were to reduce egg collecting, to prevent visits to the keys by people unaware of the birds' life requirements, and to inform the general public of the value and vulnerability of Lago Reef as a seabird breeding site, including the request to stay away from the keys from May through July.

Vegetation manipulation was implemented in the mid- and late 1990s. This involved removal of patches of sea purslane (Sesuvium portulacastrum), and to a lesser extent of buttonwood shrubs (Conocarpus erectus), in order to create more bare sandy ground attractive for nesting Cayenne and Common terns. In 1999, 247 artificial nesting sites in the form of nest-boxes, chick-boxes, and "wigwams" were distributed over the keys, intended to stimulate Bridled Tern breeding. Most of the occupied boxes, unfortunately, were used by Laughing Gulls. Despite that setback, the project has provided models for subsequent monitoring.

The call to protect breeding habitat has not yet found legislative support. In spite of many serious attempts to convince local politicians of the value and vulnerability of the Lago Reef seabird colonies, the four small keys still lack formal protected status. Several politicians and other influential Arubans who visited the keys to view the seabirds and their nests at close range admitted to being deeply impressed. However, this sentiment has not led to tangible results in the form of new legislation. Indeed, all that is needed to ensure a future for the Lago Reef seabird colonies is officially prohibiting people from setting foot on the four seabird keys between the beginning of April and the end of July.

Signposting, wardening, and educational publicity, mainly during 1983–1991, undoubtedly have had positive effects, but it must be noted that the increase of the local seabird breeding population occurred in the course of three decades, from the 1970s through the 1990s. The number of Arubans familiar with the Lago Reef as a valuable seabird breeding site is still very small. The long-term survival of the valuable Lago Reef seabird breeding population can be ensured only through a comprehensive conservation program implemented by Arubans. This program should include signposting, wardening, and surveying (all during April–July); educational activities (local TV, newspapers, leaflet, booklet); and political pressure in order to obtain a formal protected status for the Lago Reef seabird keys. This inclusive activity is particularly urgent in light of development plans being made for this part of Aruba.

Acknowledgments

For generously providing unpublished observations, I thank Adrian Del Nevo and Roland de Kort. My work in Aruba, 1984–1990, would not have been possible without the contributions of Roy Alderlieste, Klaas Bakker, Egbert Boerstra, Herny Coffi, and Arie Spaans.

24

The Netherlands Antilles III

Curaçao and Bonaire

ADOLPHE O. DEBROT, COEN BOOGERD, AND DIETER VAN DEN BROECK

The islands of the Leeward Netherlands Antilles (Aruba, Curaçao, and Bonaire, the ABC islands) lie next to each other off the north coast of Venezuela in the southern Caribbean Sea, just downstream of one of the most productive upwelling areas of the Caribbean (Sturm 1991; maps 47, 48). These islands have long been recognized as regionally important breeding sites for several tern species (Voous 1983; Halewyn and Norton 1984). While Aruba has had a sovereign status within the Kingdom of the Netherlands since 1986, Curaçao and Bonaire form part of the Netherlands Antilles, together with Saba, St. Eustatius, and St. Maarten, three islands separated from the Leeward group by about 900 km of open sea.

In contrast to the large tern nesting colonies of Aruba, numbering in the thousands and fairly well studied in recent years (Halewijn 1985, 1986, 1988, in press; Gochfeld et al. 1994; Del Nevo, in prep.), little recent information is available for Bonaire (Del Nevo, in prep.; J. V. Wells and A. Childs Wells, in prep.), and none is available for Curaçao.

Curaçao (444 km^2) lies about 70 km from the Venezuelan mainland and has approximately 130,000 inhabitants. The highest point is 375 m above sea level. The island consists of a volcanic core rimmed by coastal limestone formations. Rainfall averages 550 mm per year and the vegetation is generally xerophytic, with landscapes dominated by cactus and thorn scrub. Approximately 10 km to the east lies a small (1.3 km^2), flat offshore reef island named Klein Curaçao, which is under Curaçao jurisdiction. Terns nest in coastal areas of both islands as well as on small islets in the inland lagoons of the main island of Curaçao.

Bonaire (288 km^2) lies about 40 km to the northeast of Curaçao. Its highest point is 241 m and total inhabitants number about 14,000. As in Curaçao, the island consists of a volcanic core rimmed by limestone formations.

Rainfall averages 450 mm a year and the vegetation is similar to that of Curaçao. Bonaire has an offshore island named Klein Bonaire that falls under Bonaire jurisdiction. Klein Bonaire (6 km^2) is a flat, completely calcareous island located about 1.5 km off the west coast of the main island. Terns nest in coastal areas of both islands as well as on small islets in the inland lagoons of the main island of Bonaire.

The objectives of the study presented in this chapter were to provide comprehensive tern nesting surveys for both Curaçao and Bonaire so as to update tern species nesting status for these islands, identify key breeding areas for conservation, and make conservation recommendations.

Methods of Survey

In 2002 all coastal and lagoon areas falling under Curaçao and Bonaire jurisdiction were surveyed at least three times by two persons working together. The Curaçao coastline and Klein Curaçao were surveyed in the last weeks of May, June, and July, while the Bonaire coastline and Klein Bonaire were surveyed in the first weeks of June, July, and August. Lagoons were surveyed from vantage points, while coastal areas were largely surveyed by jeep or boat. We used Minolta 7 × 35 wide-angle field glasses and a Nikon Spotter XL spotting scope. Once birds were detected, they were identified and counted. Often, brooding birds (Laughing Gull, Common Tern) or flocks of chicks (Royal Tern and Cayenne Tern) could be individually counted. However, for the Least Tern this was generally not possible. In the case of the Least Tern, the birds were flushed and estimated once in the air. The number of birds was then divided in half to provide a rough estimate of the number of breeding pairs. The estimates provided are judged to err on the low side

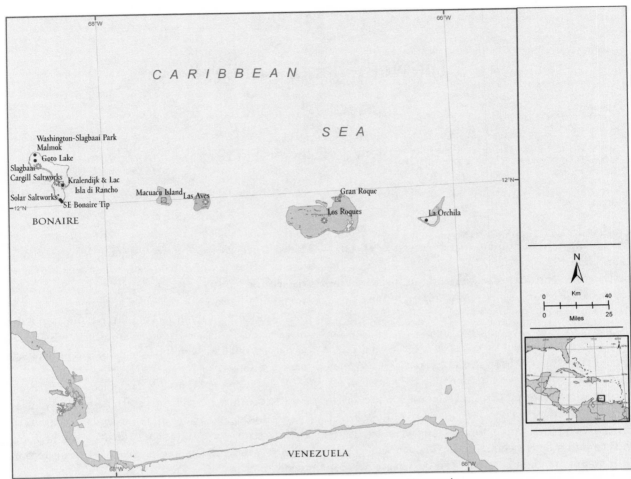

Map 48. Bonaire, Netherlands Antilles, and Los Roques, La Orchila, and Las Aves, Venezuela.

and hence to be indicative of minimum population estimates.

Table 24.1 provides a summary of results in terms of seabird nesting for the Curaçao and Bonaire jurisdictions in the year 2002. Breeding locations for the main islands and their satellites are given in tables 24.2 and 24.3.

Species Accounts

In 2002 one species of gull, Laughing Gull, and two species of tern, Common Tern and Least Tern, nested on Curaçao (table 24.1) at a total of 18 locations (table 24.2), two of which were missed in 2002 but "rediscovered" in 2004. Species that have nested on Curaçao in the twen-

tieth century but not in recent decades are Roseate Tern, Royal Tern, and Cayenne Tern (Voous 1983).

On Bonaire four species of terns and one species of gull nested (table 24.1). The number of pairs per site at a total of 49 locations is given in table 24.3. The only species documented in the past but not found nesting in recent years on Bonaire is the Roseate Tern. Possible nesting by small numbers of Audubon's Shearwater and Magnificent Frigatebird in Bonaire has never been confirmed (Voous 1983; Halewyn and Norton 1984).

Laughing Gull

Voous (1983) listed this species as only incidentally nesting on Bonaire and possibly nesting on Klein Curaçao and Aruba. In the meantime, the species has been found

Table 24.1. Estimates of seabird pairs breeding on Curaçao and Bonaire, 2002

	Laughing Gull	Least Tern	Common Tern	Royal Tern	Cayenne Tern
Curaçao	3	619+	133+		
Bonaire	60	792+	39	85	180

Table 24.2. Estimates of seabird pairs at breeding sites on Curaçao, summer 2002

Site #	Location	Laughing Gull	Common Tern	Least Tern	Disturbance/ Predation
1	Boka Bartol			50, c	
2	Playa Grandi, N side			25, c	
3	Playa Grandi, S side			100+, c	
4	Saliña Rif-St. Marie			4, d[a]	
5	Shingot, 1 km W			75+, e[a]	
6	Saliña St. Michiel		15, c		
7	7th windmill			6, d	
8	3d windmill			1, d	
9	Ser'i Kueba, coast			5, d	
10	St. Jorisbaai, W side			50+, e	By dogs
11	Isla di Makuaku		3, c		
12	Saliña Janthiel	3, c	75, c	9, d	
13	Ser'i Boka, E side			4, d	
14	West of Pos # 2			100, e	
15	Punt Kanon			12, d	
16	Klein Curaçao			143+, e	
17[b]	Islands in Buskabaai		40+, c, e	20+, c	
18[b]	W shore Buskabaai			15+, e	
	Curaçao totals	3	133+	619+	

a. Evidence for breeding: d = defense, e = eggs, c = chicks.

b. Sites 17 and 18 were missed in 2002, data are from 25 May and 2 June, 2004.

nesting annually and in steadily increasing numbers on Aruba (Gochfeld et al. 1994). In this study we further document its repeated nesting on Curaçao and a significantly increased nesting aggregation on Bonaire. This species was often seen marauding in tern colonies in Curaçao and Bonaire (Cayenne and Common terns) and is a potential threat to these endangered tern species. Its population expansion in the ABC islands should be a matter of concern.

On Curaçao three pairs of Laughing Gulls nested on the tern island in the lagoon of Janthiel in 2002, in association with nesting Common Tern and nesting Black-winged Stilt (*Himantopus himantopus*). In 2003, the gulls were present again (two pairs and one chick, 23 June 2002); they harassed Common Tern chicks and probably fed upon the chicks and eggs.

On Bonaire Laughing Gulls nested at two locations (table 24.3). They nested together with Cayenne Terns and Common Terns on an island in Goto Lake (several chicks on 1 July 2002), and they nested on the dams of condenser C-3 in the Cargill saltworks area (flying chicks, 12 July 2002). Total numbers for the saltworks area are about 50 pairs (R. St. Jago, pers. comm.).

Least Tern

While Voous (1983) and van Halewyn and Norton (1984) indicated that total numbers of nesting Least Tern may approach 1,000 pairs for the ABC islands, few attempts

have been made to provide comprehensive estimates. The Least Tern nests in many types of coastal areas and is known for asynchronous breeding. This makes counts tedious, and the chance of missing small colonies is high. In this species territorial buzzing of intruders to a site by single adult birds or jointly by pairs was a common behavior and was considered to be evidence of recent or imminent nesting, allowing such sites to be included as nesting sites.

In July 2001, Wells and Childs Wells (in prep.) surveyed tern nesting on Bonaire (and Klein Bonaire) and documented some 360 adult birds or 180 pairs at some 13 sites. However, their survey was late in the season and did not include the extensive grounds of the Cargill saltworks. In late June 1999, Del Nevo (in prep.) did a more extensive survey and documented at least 450 pairs nesting at 37 locations on the island; his survey was also relatively late in the season and did not include the island of Klein Bonaire. As a consequence he considered his to be minimum estimates (Del Nevo, in prep.). In contrast, the Least Tern estimate of 85 pairs for Aruba (Del Nevo, in prep.) was from early in the season and is likely accurate, though results by van Halewijn (1985, 1986) for Aruba were significantly higher (1984: 155+ pairs; 1985: 140 pairs).

In the present study we made three surveys of Curaçao and Bonaire and included all coastal areas of the islands, and yet the estimates obtained likely err on the low

Table 24.3. Estimates of seabird pairs at breeding sites on Bonaire, summer 2002

Site #	Location	Laughing Gull	Least Tern	Common Tern	Royal Tern	Cayenne Tern	Comments
1	Island Goto Lake	10, c		5, c		180, c	at viewpoint park
2	Island Saliña Slagbaai		87, c	4, c			at viewpoint park
3	Boka Bartol		3, d				
4	Malmok		10, e				
5	Seru Meimei		8, d				
6	Playa Macoshi		10, d				
7	Boka Chikitu, W side		30+, e				
8	Boka Chikitu, E side		8, d				
9	E of Boka Chikitu		50+, d				
10	Morotin		8, d				
11	Pos di Punta		5, d				
12	Boka Onima, W side		3, d				
13	Boka Onima, E side		15, d				
14	W of Boka Onima		6, d				
15	W of Fontein		1, d				
16	W of Pos Roshikiri		1, d				
17	E of Kueba Roshikiri		15, d				
18	W of Suplado		1, d				
19	W of Boka Kanoa		10, d				
20	W side Punta Spelonk		10, d				
21	S side Punta Spelonk		10, d				
22	S of Lighthouse		3, c				
23	S of location # 22		10, d				
24	N side Boka Chikitu		40, d				
25	S side Boka Chikitu		10, d				
26	S of Boka Chikitu		15, d				
27	N of Pos Kurá		10, c				
28	Lagun, N side		15, d				
29	road to Lagun		3, e				
30	Lagun S side		30, c				
31	S of Boka Washikemba		5, c				
32	Roi Lamunchi		10				
33	road to Cai		2				
34	bahia Cai		4				
35	Cai		2				
36	Marcultura-Intake[a]		111+, c, e				
37	Intake-Lacre Punt		10, d				
38	Witte Pan		5, c				
39	Condenser[b] C-5		30	5			
40	island Condenser C-8		50+				
41	islands Condenser C-9		5				site later flooded
42	Condenser C-2a		50+				
43	S of Condenser C1–d				85, c		
44	island N side Cond. C-5			20, c			dog tracks nearby
45	S dike Cond. C-4			5			
46	Cristallizer[c] F-3		30, d				
47	dams Condenser C-3	50, c					30 (+ 20,pers. comm. St. Jago)
48	S side Klein Bonaire		1, d				
49	W saliña Klein Bonaire		50+, e				cat seen
	Bonaire totals	60	792+	39	85	180	

Note: Evidence for breeding: d = defense, e = eggs, c = chicks.

a. Intake = seawater intake canal for solar saltworks.

b. Condenser = expansive shallow pond for solar evaporation to form concentrated brine.

c. Crystallizer = shallow pond for salt precipitation and harvest.

side (smaller aggregations were undoubtedly missed and the number of birds in large aggregations was estimated conservatively). For Curaçao the total breeding population is estimated at 619 pairs, while for Bonaire the total is estimated at about 792 pairs. Our survey yields a total breeding population of some 1,400 pairs for Curaçao and Bonaire combined, which amounts to more than 20% of the total Caribbean breeding population estimate by van Halewyn and Norton (1984).

By mid-May most birds were not yet nesting but were assembling on the breeding sites and starting courtship behavior. Bird numbers peaked by late May and early June. The earliest eggs we documented were 16 May at Wacao, on Curaçao; the latest eggs observed were on 12 July 2002 on Klein Bonaire and the road to Lagoen, Bonaire, and 13 July at Malmok, Bonaire. Large, almost fully feathered fledglings were seen on 8 June on the south side of Lagoen.

On Curaçao, Least Tern were the most numerous species, amounting to some 619 pairs and nesting at 16 of the 18 tern breeding sites located. Most nesting took place along the barren wind-exposed coast of the islands. The largest breeding aggregations were at the plantations of Wacao (sites 1–3), at Hato (site 5), Koraal Tabak (site 10), Eastpoint (site 14), and Klein Curaçao (site 16).

For the most part these are regular breeding sites. Wacao is visited annually (R. Finies, pers. comm.); Koraal Tabak had 100+ breeding pairs with chicks and eggs on 3 June 1996 (A. Debrot, pers. obs.); the Eastpoint site is a traditional breeding site (confidential source); and Klein Curaçao is also visited annually (A. Debrot, pers. obs.). Other sites in Curaçao with recent larger breeding aggregations of Least Terns, but not intensively used in 2002, were a coastal site just east of Boka Tabla in the Shete Boka Park (30+ pairs, W. Sambo, pers. comm.); a site at Boka Patrick (20+ pairs, 2003, I. Nagelkerken, pers. comm.); Kabes di Mangusá, Groot St. Joris (C. Schmitz, pers. comm.); and a site on the shore of Janthielbaai (many birds in 1989, Debrot and de Freitas 1991; 100+ pairs, May 1996, A. Debrot and B. de Boer; 6 pairs, May 2004, A. Debrot and T. Ryan). The earliest eggs we documented were 16 May 2002 at Wacao. Feeding by adults took place in the rough waters of the exposed northeast coast, just off the breeding site.

On Bonaire, Least Terns were also the most numerous nesting species, amounting to some 792 pairs, nesting at 44 of the 49 breeding sites located. Most nesting took place along the barren wind-exposed coast of the island, and adults generally fed in the rough waters just off the breeding sites. Nesting was much more widely spread and colonies were much more open and dis-

persed than on Curaçao. Areas with the largest breeding aggregations on Bonaire were the north coast of the Washington-Slagbaai Park (sites 4–9); the coast between Spelonk and Lagoen (sites 21–28); the southeastern tip of the island (site 36); and the solar saltworks area (sites 39–42, 46). One site not visited in the present study due to inaccessibility but known to have served as a breeding site in the past is Isla di Rancho at Lac. Between 1994 and 1996, upwards of 20 pairs of Least Terns were observed nesting there one year but were not seen the subsequent two years (E. Newton, pers. comm.)

Voous (1983) and van Halewyn and Norton (1984) believed the majority of Least Tern breeding to be taking place on Bonaire. Our results confirm this. We suggest (as does Del Nevo, in prep.) that the paucity of birds on Aruba may due to the extreme human disturbance. All breeding habitat along the north coast of Aruba lies close to a particularly intensively used tourist route (A. Debrot, pers. obs.). In contrast, on Curaçao and Bonaire several of the large traditional breeding sites are in relatively inaccessible areas or on private property where disturbance is limited.

A notable contrast between Curaçao and Bonaire is that on Curaçao, nesting appears to be much more concentrated into larger aggregations than on Bonaire (tables 24.2, 24.3). The abundance of Sparrow Hawks (*Falco sparverius*) on Curaçao and their absence from Bonaire may contribute to this evident difference in nest site dispersion (Del Nevo, in prep.). It may be that breeding site selection for this species is partly dictated by nearby food availability.

Roseate Tern

No Roseate Tern nesting was documented in the present study for either Curaçao or Bonaire, whereas the species formerly nested at several sites on both islands (Ansingh et al. 1960; Voous 1963, 1983). Voous (1963) pointed out that the species never formed breeding colonies of its own but always joined other species. This would suggest that when large colonies of other species are disrupted (as they have been), the Roseate Tern will be one of the first species to stop nesting. Hence, it could be that this species may be particularly vulnerable to local extirpation due to declines in other species.

Common Tern

Ansingh and Koelers (1957) and Voous (1965, 1983) mention the presence of four nesting sites for the Common Tern in Curaçao: Isla di Makuaku in the St. Jorisbaai, "islets in Schottegat harbor" (specifically in Buskabaai), Janthiel, and Spaanse Water. We also documented four nesting sites in Curaçao, the most important of which are at Buskabaai and Janthiel. Voous (1965) indicated only 14 nesting pairs from Buskabaai, but the current numbers (40+) are considerably higher. Ansingh et al. (1960) found no nesting of Common Terns at Janthiel, which in the present study is documented as an important breeding site for this species. For Isla di Makuaku, Voous (1965) estimated 5 pairs, similar to our findings. For Spaanse Water, Voous (1965) indicated 10–15 pairs. However, this site has had no breeding since 1992.

Both in Curaçao and Bonaire, this species showed a great preference for nesting on islets and in aggregations of 20 or more pairs. Current totals for Curaçao (133 pairs), Bonaire (39 pairs), and Aruba (143 pairs, Del Nevo, in prep.) mean that, as previously indicated by van Halewyn and Norton (1984), the Leeward Dutch Antilles continue to be a critical breeding area for this species in the Caribbean.

On Curaçao, the Common Tern was the second most abundant breeding species in 2002. It was found at three sites, Janthiel (75 pairs), St. Michiel (15 pairs), and Isla Makuaku (3 pairs). In 2004 a traditional breeding site of importance was rediscovered (table 24.2). The site had simply been missed in the 2002 survey and amounts to more than 40 pairs on an island in Buskabaai, in the contaminated harbor of Willemstad. According to Refineria Isla, breeding had occurred there every year for at least five years (R. Rhuggenaath, pers. comm.). Last documented breeding at a traditional site in Spaanse Water was 1 pair on the island of Willemsberg with chicks on 3 June 1992 (A. Debrot, pers. obs.). Almost all feeding by the Common Tern colonies of Janthiel and Buskabaai throughout the breeding season takes place inside the highly contaminated Schottegat harbor (A. Debrot, pers. obs. 2002–2004). As a consequence many of the breeding Common Terns are soiled by oil.

For Bonaire, Del Nevo (in prep.) found Common Terns at two sites in 1999. We documented them from three locations inside the Cargill saltworks area, from Goto, and from Slagbaai. In June 1998, 3–4 active nests were seen at Slagbaai (J. Ligon, pers. comm.).

Royal Tern

Voous (1983) indicated only small numbers of nesting birds from Bonaire and Curaçao. However, Del Nevo reported a nesting colony of some 87 birds from a confidential nesting site (saltworks area) in 1999 on Bonaire. Our results for 2002, and those by Del Nevo for 1999 (in prep.) indicate repeated nesting by larger numbers of Royal Terns in the saltworks area of Bonaire, as hinted at by Voous (1983) but only now confirmed. Breeding has not been confirmed on Curacao. About 200 adult birds were first noticed on 31 May in the Cargill saltworks area. The birds were again seen on 1 July 2002 (A. Debrot and A. Del Nevo, pers. obs.), but no nesting could be confirmed. However, on 12 July 2002, 50+ well-fledged chicks were observed at the same location, confirming that nesting had occurred. Our estimate stands at 85 pairs in concordance with the count by Del Nevo in 1999.

Cayenne Tern

This species did not nest in Curaçao in 2002, nor in recent years, having disappeared since the early 1960s, when they nested at several sites in Curaçao, numbering upward of 1,000 pairs (Ansingh et al. 1960; Voous 1983). Most birds fed at sea off the north coast of the island, although the lagoon of Eastpoint is also specifically mentioned (Ansingh et al. 1960). All three former breeding sites of the Cayenne Tern experience heavy recreational disturbance. Their former main site, Janthiel, is frequented daily for recreation, jogging, and horseback riding. Only Least and Common terns hang on at this site. In the last two decades the other lesser site in the Spaanse Water has been crowded by sprawling marinas nearby, with intense disturbance by sailing, motor boating, jet-skis, and campers trespassing onto the former nesting islands (Willemsberg, Penso, Chikitu, and Meeuwtje) where the Cayenne Terns (and Common Terns up till 1992) formerly nested. The species has also not nested in recent years on Klein Curaçao.

However, on Bonaire they continue to breed, albeit in much reduced numbers compared to as recently as 1982, when 600 pairs nested at Goto, or 1969, when 3,000–4,000 nested in the saltworks area (Voous 1983). A colony estimated at about 150 pairs was found on an island on the west side of the Goto Salt Lake on 8 June 2002. By 1 July, 170–190 large chicks were counted and the estimate was increased to 180 pairs (A. Debrot and A. Del Nevo, pers. obs.). The adult birds all flew off and on, bringing food from a westerly direction and evidently feeding off the western side of the island. Del Nevo (pers. comm., 2003) reported a colony of 170 birds nesting at a confidential site (in the Cargill saltworks area) on Bonaire in 1999. No birds were observed nesting in Goto Lake by Del Nevo in 1999 (in prep.), and it may be that the same flock had simply moved breeding locations.

Conservation

Ironically, the appeal of these islands for outdoor recreation has resulted in sufficiently heavy tourist use of seabird breeding sites to place at risk the birds that are part of the islands' appeal.

Legislation and Protection

By means of national ordinances of 20 July 1926 (PB 1926, No. 60) and 28 September 1931 (PB 1931, No. 59), all species in question are legally protected in the Netherlands Antilles. The Cayenne Tern was added to the list of protected species in 1955 (PB 1955, No. 86), while all other terns breeding on these islands were added in 1960 (PB 1960, No. 102; Timmers 1979). The birds may not be taken, their eggs may not be taken, and their nests may not be disturbed (Timmers 1979). To our knowledge, "disturbance" of tern nests has never been legally defined or tested in a court of law. However, research evidence from tern colonies in the United States would appear to recommend a minimum nondisturbance distance of about 150 m around the nesting site (T. Ryan, pers. comm.).

Within the jurisdiction of Curaçao, most of the breeding sites fall inside the boundaries of conservation areas as designated by the Island Development Plan (Eilandelijke Ontwikkelingsplan; AB 1995, No. 36) as ratified in 1997. Only three important nesting sites do not fall inside legally designated conservation areas. One of these is the Least Tern site of Klein Curaçao (site 16; 100+ pairs), where Cayenne Terns and probably Laughing Gulls have also nested in the recent past (Voous 1983), and which remains an important sea turtle nesting island (Debrot et al. 2005). The other sites not legally designated as conservation areas, and therefore more at risk of disturbance, are the small island on the west side of Buskabaai and the western shore of Buskabaai, in the oil-polluted Schottegat harbor of Willemstad. Notwithstanding a high level of private land ownership on Curaçao, many important sites further lie on public land. These are Hato (#5), St. Michiel (#6), Isla di Makuaku (#11, DROV, 1985), Eastpoint (#13; DROV, 1985), Klein Curaçao (#16), and Buskabaai (#17, #18).

Within the jurisdiction of Bonaire, the majority of the nesting sites fall inside protected zones as defined in the Bonaire nature policy plan (Natuurbeleidsplan 1999–2004), as ratified by the Island Council in June 1999. Private land ownership is much less common in Bonaire and only affects the coastal Least Tern sites

between Lagoen and Lac (#30–#35). Even most of the industrial saltworks area is government land granted in lease (E. Newton, pers. comm.).

While there is some scope for exercising conservation measures, at present Bonaire has no enforcement of applicable laws and no wardening.

Disturbance

Recreational disturbance is the single most serious and pervasive threat to the future of seabird nesting in Curaçao and Bonaire (Debrot and de Freitas 1991; Debrot and Sybesma 2000) and requires concerted action. Most public wilderness areas remain unmanaged, while interest in outdoor recreation has grown dramatically in recent years, particularly in Curaçao. There is no closed season in the colonies during breeding, and in most areas in Curaçao, colonies are disturbed daily by joggers, sightseers, organized nature trail walks, and/or people taking dogs for a stroll.

The Janthiel and Spaanse Water sites already mentioned are examples of the damage that uncontrolled recreational access can have. Another is the Common Tern breeding site of the islet Isla di Makuaku in St. Jorisbaai. This was the first site in Curaçao designated as a seabird sanctuary area (DROV 1985). All that presently remains are the concrete posts of the sign (announcing the reserve) that stood there years ago. This remote island is named after the frigatebirds that traditionally roosted there. However, since 2001 the birds have been chased off by recreational wind- and kite-surfers and by police helicopters conducting practices nearby (C. Schmitz and M. Martina, pers. comm.). For now the age-old late-afternoon sight of circling frigatebirds is a distant memory, preserved for posterity only in the poem "Isla di Makwakoe" by the well-known Dutch writer Boeli van Leeuwen (1947).

With the growing popularity of outdoor and nature-related recreation, even the most remote areas of the island are being seriously disturbed, and measures are urgently needed to keep seabird sites off limits to the public. Until the recent past, the small island of Klein Curaçao (1.7 km[2]), known as an important seabird nesting site since the early seventeenth century (Eeuwens 1926), was visited only by small numbers of boaters and fishermen. However, in the last ten years recreational visitors have swelled to several hundred people a week, and this is causing heavy disturbance to the Least Tern breeding colony.

On Bonaire, human disturbance is much less acute

than on Curaçao. Nevertheless, several important breeding sites inside or bordering the Washington-Slagbaai Park lie particularly close to routes open to vehicles and accessible to the public (e.g., Least Tern nesting sites at Boka Chikitu and the tern islands of Slagbaai and Goto Lake). The National Park Foundation (STINAPA Bonaire) could implement measures to keep such sites closed to the public during the breeding season from April through August.

Egg Collection

While collection of eggs is practically a thing of the past in both Curaçao and Bonaire, legal instruments have as yet translated into little actual protection of nesting sites. Boiled tern eggs (especially from the Aves Islands; Boeke 1907) were regularly sold from large baskets by street vendors in Willemstad until the 1930s and 1940s. Collection of tern eggs was done by first removing and destroying all eggs from the nesting site and then returning at two-day intervals to reap the fresh eggs (A. Debrot Sr., pers. comm.; e.g., Eeuwens 1926). In 2004 a single instance of egg collection was documented. In mid-May the management of the Isla Refinery was asked by an employee for permission to collect tern eggs for "potency." Permission was granted, and 31 eggs were collected from sites 17 and 18 (R. Rhuggenaath, pers. comm.). Since being informed of the protected status of these birds, refinery personnel have promised full cooperation for seabird protection, including information to employees, closure of the areas during the breeding season, and placement of poisoned bait against stray dogs (R. Rhuggenaath, pers. comm.).

Oil Pollution

Oil pollution is of particular concern in Curaçao considering that the birds in the two main Common Tern colonies at risk feed almost exclusively in the oil-contaminated Schottegat harbor. This underscores the need to continue with efforts to clean up this harbor, which—despite the contamination—is an important feeding area visited by large numbers of seabirds and shorebirds. Studies to assess and monitor the levels and effects of contamination in these birds are recommended.

Predation

Feral cats take large numbers of prey and are a recognized exotic pest in the island ecosystem (Churcher and Lawton 1989; Garcia et al. 2001; Nogales et al. 2004). On Klein Curaçao predation by feral cats on terns was observed and formed a significant threat (A. Debrot, pers. obs.). However, on 6 October 2001, five of the six cats

present on the island (4 females, 1 male) were exterminated using the pesticide Temik-10 mixed in canned cat-food. A lone male cat in poor condition escaped extermination and was reported still alive (May 2004, G. van Buurt, pers. comm.).

Feral cats are particularly abundant on Bonaire and were observed, for instance, on the Least Tern nesting colony of Klein Bonaire. We strongly recommend measures to control and/or exterminate cats from parks and tern breeding areas (as do Wells and Childs Wells, in prep.) to the maximum extent possible. For dogs, use of poisoned baits places at points of passage and sheltered against nontarget scavengers is more effective than shooting (A. Debrot, pers. obs.).

A matter of concern, especially on Bonaire, is the large increase of nesting by Laughing Gulls. The adult birds harass the tern colonies, taking tern eggs and young, especially when the gulls are raising their own young (Del Nevo, in prep.). Field measures that have been used in the past are to "prick" or shake eggs to prevent hatching of the gull chicks (Del Nevo, in prep.) and use of poisoned bait to kill adult nesting birds (R. van Halewijn, pers. comm.). However, in some cases it appears that nonbreeding "loafing" subadults can cause more disturbance and conduct more predation than breeding gulls, and certain measures could even aggravate the situation (R. van Halewijn, pers. comm.).

Artificial Nest Islands

One of the key waterbird and tern breeding areas of Bonaire is the expansive saltworks area, which covers approximately 27 km^2 on the southern part of the island. The Flamingo sanctuary lies inside the saltworks area and is actively managed for optimal breeding of the Flamingo (*Phoenicopterus ruber*). However, aside from keeping the public out, no specific measures are being taken to protect or stimulate tern breeding. Most of the dikes in the saltworks area are subject to low yet disruptive levels of industrial traffic. In addition, dikes are only second-rate breeding sites, as most of the large tern species prefer to nest on small islands (as in Aruba; see van Halewijn 1986; Del Nevo, in prep.). However, islands are exceedingly scarce in the constructed saltworks.

The saltworks area has grown significantly in recent years, but few areas have been added that are of any real nesting value to most tern species. Therefore, we recommend the construction of a number of low artificial islands inside the large evaporating ponds to improve nesting habitat availability and help restore and increase tern nesting to its historic levels in this key seabird area. In the United States many management techniques have been developed to help increase or restore tern populations (Wells and Child Wells, in prep.; Kress 1998), including use of decoys to attract birds to new or prior breeding sites.

Acknowledgments

This study would not have been possible without the generous assistance of several individuals and organizations. Our colleague Leon Pors prepared the figures, while George Saragoza, July-Ann Frans, Edwin Domacassé, and Fernando Simal of STINAPA Bonaire provided logistical assistance on Bonaire, both on land and at sea. Thanks are due to Jack Chalk of Habitat Bonaire for providing a luxurious apartment during our visits to the "Flamingo island." We further thank Jan Gielen and Rudi St. Jago of the Cargill saltworks of Bonaire, and N. Chaclin and R. Rhuggenaath of Refineria Isla (Curazao) SA for their cooperation with this study. Reviews by R. van Halewijn and E. Newton provided numerous important improvements to the manuscript. Principal funding for this study was by the Carmabi Foundation based on annual general subsidies by the Central Government of the Netherlands Antilles and the Island Government of Curaçao. Additional funding was provided as student grants to the junior authors by the Hogeschool INHOLLAND Delft in the Netherlands.

25

The Islands of Venezuela

DIANA ESCLASANS, MIGUEL LENTINO, ALEJANDRO LUY, AND CARLOS BOSQUE

The Venezuelan coastline is approximately 3,964 km long. Off the coastline, from the Gulf of Venezuela in the west to the Gulf of Paria in the east, extends a series of islands that are all Venezuelan territory except for Aruba, Curaçao, and Bonaire. The islands of Margarita, Coche, and Cubagua make up the State of Nueva Esparta, and the rest make up the Federal Dependencies, a group of approximately 311 islands, cays, and small barren islets with an estimated area of 316 km^2 (maps 48, 49, 50). These islands host important colonies of seabirds and 14 endemic subspecies of landbirds.

Study of the birds of Venezuelan islands began in the early twentieth century (Ferry 1908; Cory 1909; Lowe 1911a). Initial investigations consisted mostly of inventories of species, but authors occasionally added comments on the activity of colonies seabirds. The most important bird inventories were made during the 1940s and 1950s, and until now they have been the main source of information on bird diversity of the islands (Fernández 1945; Phelps Jr. 1945, 1948; Phelps and Phelps Jr. 1950, 1957, 1959a, 1959b; Ginés and Yépez 1956, 1960; Yépez 1963a, 1963b, 1964a, 1964b). In later years fewer studies on island birds have been conducted, particularly on the most remote islands; nonetheless, a few described aspects of the biology of some marine species (LeCroy 1976) and made reliable estimates of colony sizes in some islands, such as Isla Aves (Lazell 1967; Gremone and Gómez 1983) and Los Roques Archipelago (Guzmán and Schreiber 1987; Luy 1997; Bosque et al. 2001; Esclasans 2003).

The only counts of breeding seabirds since 1996 were from Los Roques and Aves Island (table 25.1); a list of all known breeding species is given in table 25.2. Subsequent information refers only to the string of islands that lie parallel to the mainland coast: Margarita, Coche, Cubagua, La Orchila, La Tortuga, La Blanquilla, and Aves, and the archipelagos Los Monjes, Las Aves, Los Roques, Los Hermanos, Los Frailes, and Los Testigos. Table 25.3

shows the location of these islands and their most important habitat types. The richest islands or groups of islands in terms of number of breeding seabirds are Los Roques Archipelago (15 species), Las Aves Archipelago (11 species), La Orchila Archipelago (8 species), and Los Hermanos Archipelago (7 species; table 25.2). Detailed studies on these islands are few, and for some locations we can report only the presence (or absence) of species. For three localities we provide nest counts (breeding pairs): Marites Lagoon, Los Roques Archipelago, and Las Aves (table 25.2).

The most important finding in this chapter are that one of the largest Caribbean breeding populations of Masked Booby was found on Los Monjes Archipelago in 1996 (Ricardo Muñoz Tebar pers. comm.), and the largest colony of Brown Noddy remains on Las Aves (Rodrigo Lazo, pers. comm.). Significant numbers of Black Noddy (the largest colony in the Caribbean) breed in Los Roques Archipelago. In addition, we point out that populations of several species of seabirds are seemingly in decline. Our review shows that current knowledge of

Table 25.1. Counts of seabird pairs breeding on Los Roques Archipelago, 2001–2002 (the only post-1996 counts in Venezuela)

Species	Number of pairs
Brown Booby	474
Red-footed Booby	1,113
Brown Pelican	491
Laughing Gull	544
Brown Noddy	313
Black Noddy	52
Sooty Tern	5
Bridled Tern	418
Least Tern	205
Common Tern	104
Royal Tern	25
Cayenne Tern	75

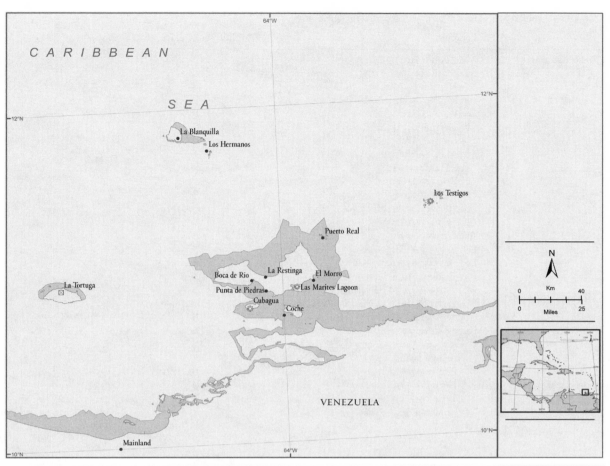

Map 49. La Blanquilla, Los Testigos, Los Hermanos, Coche, Cubagua, and La Tortuga, Venezuela.

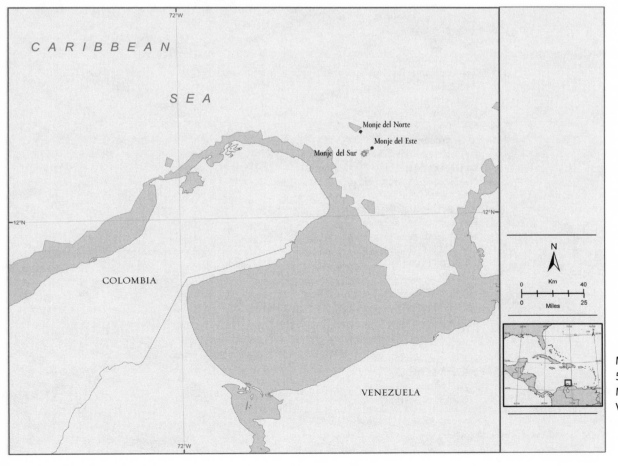

Map 50. Los Monjes, Venezuela.

Table 25.2. Counts of seabird pairs breeding in the Venezuelan islands and archipelagos

Species	Location	Number of Pairs
Audubon's Shearwater	Los Roques Archipelago	B[a]
	La Orchila Island	B
	Los Hermanos Archipelago	B
Red-billed Tropicbird	Los Monjes Archipelago	B
	Los Roques Archipelago	B
	Los Hermanos Archipelago	B
Masked Booby	Los Monjes Archipelago	200[d]
Brown Booby	Los Monjes Archipelago	200[d]
	Aves Archipelago	B
	Los Roques Archipelago	474[f]
	La Orchila Island	B
	Los Hermanos Archipelago	B
	Los Testigos Archipelago	B
Red-footed Booby	Aves Archipelago	B
	Los Roques Archipelago	1,113[f]
	Los Hermanos Archipelago	B
	Los Testigos Archipelago	B
Brown Pelican	Margarita Island, La Restinga Lagoon	B
	Margarita Island, Las Marites Lagoon	291[c]
	Coche Island	B
	Cubagua Island	B
	Los Roques Archipelago	491[f]
	La Tortuga Island	B
	Los Frailes Archipelago	B
Magnificent Frigatebird	Los Hermanos Archipelago	B
	Los Testigos Archipelago	B
Laughing Gull	Coche Island	B
	Aves Archipelago	B
	Los Roques Archipelago	544[f]
	La Orchila Island	B
	Los Hermanos Archipelago	B
	Los Testigos Archipelago	B
Brown Noddy	Aves Archipelago	B
	Los Roques Archipelago	313[f]
	La Orchila Island	B
	Los Hermanos Archipelago	B
	Aves Island	5,000[g]
Black Noddy	Aves Archipelago	B
	Los Roques Archipelago	52[f]
Sooty Tern	Los Monjes Archipelago	B
	Aves Archipelago	B
	Los Roques Archipelago	5[e]
	La Orchila Island	B
	Los Hermanos Archipelago	B
	Aves Island	12,000[g]
Bridled Tern	Aves Archipelago	B
	Los Roques Archipelago	418[f]
	Aves Island	B
Least Tern	Los Roques Archipelago	205[f]
	La Orchila Island	B
Roseate Tern	Aves Archipelago	B
	Los Roques Archipelago	E[b]
Common Tern	Aves Archipelago	B
	Los Roques Archipelago	104[f]
	La Orchila Island	B
Royal Tern	Aves Archipelago	B
	Los Roques Archipelago	25[e]
	La Orchila Island	B
Cayenne Tern	Aves Archipelago	B
	Los Roques Archipelago	75[e]

a. Breeds in unknown numbers, no recent counts.

b. Breed historically, extirpated; no recent data.

c. Guzmán and Schreiber (1987).

d. Ricardo Muñoz Tebar, pers. comm. (data from 1996).

e. Bosque et al (2001).

f. Esclasans (2003).

g. Rodrigo Lazo (2007, unpublished data).

Table 25.3. Location, area, topography, and habitat types of Venezuelan islands and archipelagos

Island or archipelago	Location	Area (km²)	No. islands or keys	Habitat/vegetation types	Physiognomy and Topography
Margarita Island	10°51' 11°10' N 63°46' 64°24' W	933.80	1	Semiarid thorn scrub, mesophytic vegetation.	Formed by two large hilly portions joined by narrow sandy isthmus.
Coche Island	10°44' 10°49' N 63°53' 64°00' W	43.09	1	Xerophytic and halophylous vegetation. Cacti (*Opuntia* sp., *Melocactus* sp.), dominant.	Has a smooth relief, slanting from north to south, Elevations below 50m.
Cubagua Island	10°47' 10°51' N 64°08' 64°14' W	22.44	1	Xerophytic and halophylous vegetation. Cacti (*Opuntia* sp., *Melocactus* sp.).	Smooth relief shaped by rounded hills, not higher than six meters.
Los Monjes Archipelago	12°22' 12°21' N 70°55' 70°53' W	0.2	5	Rocky shores, grasses.	Formed by three groups of islands, Northern Monjes (6 islands), Southern Monjes (2 islands) and Eastern Monjes (1 island). Monje Grande, in the Southern Monjes, 600 m long, 350 m wide, and 70 m highest elevation.
Las Aves Archipelago	12° N 12° N 67°25' 67°40' W	3.4	8	*Batis maritime* dominant along beaches. Dunes covered by herbaceous veg. Large mangrove stands, *Rhizophora mangle* and *Avicennia germinans*.	Formed by two growing atolls of islets and coral reefs.
Los Roques Archipelago	11°44' 11°58' N 66°32' 66°52' W	40.6	58	Mangroves, herbaceous "prairies," halophylous vegetation along shorelines, thorn scrub, rocky cliffs, storm terraces, sea grass bottoms (*Thalassia testudinum*).	Mostly sandy keys of coralline origin and a large number of sandbanks, all together in an oval shape around a shallow lagoon (1–10 m deep). Largest island, Gran Roque, to the north, has rocky cliffs.
La Orchila Island	11°47' 11°49' N 66°6' 66°13' W	40	7	Mangroves, xerophytic vegetation, cacti, spinescent shrubs, and herbs.	This archipelago includes sandy keys and emerged coral reefs to the northwest. La Orchila Island is mostly flat with a single elevation of 150 m.
La Tortuga Island	10°57' N 65°19' W	156.6	18	Mangroves, xerophytic vegetation, cacti, spinescent shrubs, and herbs.	Nearly flat, reaches 40 m high toward the center.
La Blanquilla Island	11°50' N 64°35' W	64.5	1	Mangroves, xerophytic vegetation, cacti, spinescent shrubs, and herbs.	Nearly flat, reaches less than 40 m high.
Los Hermanos Archipelago	11°45' N 64°25' W	2.1	7	Xerophytic vegetation, cacti dominant.	Formed by seven islets having steep rocky slopes, no sandy beaches.
Los Frailes Archipelago	11°11' 11°14' N 63°42' 63°46' W	1.9	8	Xerophytic veg., cacti dominant: *Cereus veriabilis*, *Opuntia wentiana*, *Melocatus caesius*, and *Cenchrus echinatus*.	Largest island is Puerto Real, 2.2 km long and 0.75 km²; highest elevation 90 m.
Los Testigos Archipelago	11°20' 11°25' N 63°02' 63°09' W	6.5	15	Xerophytic vegetation, shrubs and mid-size trees present, e.g., *Hippomane mancinella*. No mangroves.	Testigo Grande, largest island, about 5 km long. Maximum elevation about 150 m.
Aves Island	15°40' N 63°36' W	0.035	1	Halophylous litoral "prairies," e.g., *Sesuvium portulacastrum* and *Portulaca aleracea*	Low and flat; formed by calcareous sand and coral conglomerates laid on the rocky platform.

Venezuelan seabirds is very poor, and that only at Los Roques Archipelago and Aves Island have recent counts of breeding pairs been conducted (Bosque et al. 2001; Esclasans 2003; Rodrigo Lazo, pers. comm.).

Description of the Islands

Most of the islands lie between 150 and 200 km to the north of the mainland, forming a more or less parallel rosary along the coastline; the exception is Aves Island, about 500 km north (table 25.3). These islands originated in the early Cretaceous and consist of surfacing igneous-metamorphic rocks. On some of them the rocky plinth is covered by substantial calcareous deposits that form extensive coralline archipelagos, such as at Los Roques and Las Aves. The islands are quite arid, annual precipitation generally averaging less than 100 mm, and their average yearly ambient temperature is above 28°C. Evaporation is high, and humid northeast trade winds sweep the islands continuously. These conditions shape the predominant vegetation types of the islands: mangroves, thorny scrub, halophytic savannas, and patches of xerophytic scrub (Fontana 1993).

These islands and cays host a diverse avifauna of some 123 species, 70 aquatic and 53 terrestrial. Of the 32 species of seabirds known for Venezuela, 17 have breeding colonies in the islands (table 25.2). Six are resident (Red-billed Tropicbird, Masked Booby, Brown Booby, Red-footed Booby, Brown Pelican, and Magnificent Frigatebird); three are migratory (Audubon's Shearwater, Brown Noddy, and Black Noddy); and eight have resident and migratory populations (Laughing Gull and Sooty, Bridled, Least, Roseate, Common, Royal and Cayenne terns).

Methods of Surveying the Colonies

In this review, we report estimates of breeding pairs and colony sizes from information in the literature or from our field studies, where indicated. In general the method employed on a majority of the islands was a direct count of each colony. Bosque et al. (2001) and Esclasans (2003) used a combination of census methods to count the number of breeding pairs on Los Roques Archipelago (map 48). On smaller cays, the total number of birds or pairs was counted, while on larger islands subsamples were taken along predetermined transect and the total number of nests or pairs was estimated by considering the area where the main breeding colony occurred on a given island.

Counts of Bridled Terns were made by the flush-counting method (Burger and Lawrence 2000), to provide a rough indication of the numbers of breeding pairs. The ratio was determined depending on the area of the rocky section, the preferred site for nesting. Red-footed Booby on Los Bobos Cays was sampled from boats along the coastline when breeding in mangrove swamps.

Margarita, Coche, and Cubagua Islands

The islands of Margarita, Coche, and Cubagua are located north of Araya Peninsula (Sucre State), off the eastern coast of the country and making up the State of Nueva Esparta. Table 25.2 shows reports of breeding colonies in Coche, Cubagua, and two localities on Margarita Island: La Restinga and Las Marites Lagoon.

Overall, 15 species of seabirds are known from Margarita Island, and Coche and Cubagua host eight and seven species respectively (Yépez 1963a, 1964a; Bisbal 2001). Of these, only two species breed: Brown Pelican and Laughing Gull. The current knowledge of sizes of the colonies is sparse. Brown Pelican were reported to be very common (Yépez 1963b), but it was not until 1983 that population estimates were made. Guzmán and Schreiber (1987) reported 291 nests in Las Marites Lagoon (table 25.2) and estimated a population of about 743 individuals in the islands, while Bisbal (2001) observed 800 individuals of Brown Pelican resting in Punta Arena, Cubagua. Therefore, there are not sufficient data to indicate if the population of Brown Pelican has diminished or increased in these islands.

Los Monjes Archipelago

Los Monjes Archipelago is a set of small barren islets located to the northwest of the Gulf of Venezuela, near the western limit of the country. All the islands have meager vegetation, grasses and lichens being dominant (Williams 1980).

Four species breed on this archipelago (Red-billed Tropicbird, Masked Booby, Brown Booby, and Sooty Tern). The Masked Booby population numbered approximately 500 individuals or an estimated 200 pairs in 1996, making it the largest colony in Venezuela; the estimate for Brown Booby was 200 pairs; there are no post-2000 counts (Ricardo Muñoz Tebar, pers. comm.; table 25.2). Red-billed Tropicbird and Sooty Tern also bred, but the size of the colonies was not estimated (Ricardo Muñoz Tebar, pers. comm.). Between 1995 and 1998 the southern islets of Los Monjes were linked by a man-made isthmus with the purpose of constructing a port and a military base. It seems probable that this construction has had a negative effect on the population of Masked Boobies, but no study has yet been done. The position of the Los Monjes Archipelago likely makes these islands essential in the migratory route of many bird species, but again no assessment has been made.

Las Aves Archipelago

Two reef complexes known as Las Aves Windward (three islands) and Las Aves Leeward (five islands) make up the Las Aves Archipelago. The islands are located about 160 km north of the mainland (map 48). Vegetation of the islands is halophytic-xerophytic (Williams 1980).

Eleven species breed in these islands, two sulids and eight larids (table 25.2). The initial observations were made in 1958 and 1959. In 1958 between 1,800 and 2,000 individuals of Brown Booby were recorded on Bubí Cay, in the northern sector of Las Aves Windward (Werf et al. 1958). In 1959 a flock of 300 to 400 individuals of Red-footed Booby was recorded on Tesoro Island, located on the western part of Las Aves Windward; additionally, 200 nests were noted in a patch of black mangrove (*Avicennia germinans*) on the same island (Ginés and Yépez 1960). Van Halewyn and Norton (1984) in their review of the status of Caribbean birds estimated the population of Brown Booby at 1,000 birds and that of Red-footed Booby at 1,200 individuals. The latter figures suggest that populations of Brown Booby have declined while those of Red-footed Booby have increased since the 1950s, but there are no recent reports to support this indication of an increase.

Los Roques Archipelago

Los Roques encompass most of the typical coastal ecosystems of Caribbean shorelines, including sandy beaches, shallow lagoons, brine ponds, grass prairies, mangroves, storm terraces, and rocky cliffs (map 48). Most of the knowledge of birds inhabiting cays and islands of Los Roques is due to the studies and explorations made by the Phelpses (1950, 1959b). Several later workers have studied some of these islands and their species composition (Lentino et al. 1994; Lentino and Rodner 2003), in some cases estimating population sizes (LeCroy 1976; Guzmán and Schreiber 1987; Luy 1997; Bosque et al. 2001).

Twenty-two species of seabirds have been reported on the archipelago, of which 15 species breed, including Red-billed Tropicbird (for which there are no counts),

with breeding unconfirmed for Roseate Tern. Bosque et al. (2001) and Esclasans (2003) made recent counts of breeding pairs for 11 species of seabirds that breed in the archipelago (tables 25.1, 25.2). Those counts represent minimum numbers of breeding pairs present in the archipelago, because we were unable to count all the colonies on larger islands and unable to visit the southern cays (Gresqui, Sal, and Maria Uespen cays).

Populations of Brown Pelican, Bridled Tern, and Least Tern seem to have diminished in the last decade, since more recent estimates of their populations (Luy 1997; Bosque et al. 2001) are substantially lower than those reported by van Halewyn and Norton (1984). The latter authors estimated for Los Roques a population of 2,000 Brown Pelican. In 1992, 310 nests of this species were noted on Los Canquises, and their total population on Los Roques was estimated at 923 birds (Luy 1997), with at least 491 pairs in 2002 (Esclasans 2003), seemingly a declining trend for this species.

Phelps and Phelps Jr. (1959b) pointed out the presence of several individuals of Masked Booby and reported nesting on two islands, Gran Roque and Selesquí. Van Halewyn and Norton (1984) indicated that this species was scarce on Los Roques, and reported no more than 15 individuals there. Luy in September of 1992 registered a nest of this booby on Selesquí, and Bosque et al. (2001) reported just one Masked Booby on Selesquí; there was no evidence of breeding on this island or in any other of the islands of the archipelago (Esclasans 2003). Masked Boobies have always been rare on Los Roques, but the nearly total lack of recent reports suggests that they are now disappearing.

In contrast, numbers of Brown Booby, Laughing Gull, Royal Tern, and Common Tern seem to have increased, when comparing recent figures to those of van Halewyn and Norton (1984). The Brown Booby colony has increased to 474 pairs. Recent estimates of Laughing Gull were of at least 1,200 individuals (544 pairs) (table 25.1), substantially higher than the earlier estimate of 100 individuals (Halewyn and Norton 1984). Red-footed Booby (1,113 pairs) and Brown Noddy (313 pairs) have maintained large breeding colonies on Los Roques (table 25.1), likely comparable in numbers to those initially observed by Phelps and Phelps Jr. in the 1950s.

The Black Noddy is considered a rare species throughout the Caribbean, its total population for the whole region being estimated at 10–100 pairs (Chardine et al. 2000b). Luy in 1992 observed several tens of this species on Los Roques but did not record any nests. Esclasans (2003) counted 52 breeding pairs on Los Roques (table 25.1), where the species commonly nests in small colonies within stands of black mangrove on several islands.

It is important to emphasize that our counts show legally protected cays hosting the largest breeding colonies, such as Brown Pelican, Brown Booby, and Red-Footed Booby (resident species) on Los Canquises cay and the archipelago's largest colony of Red-Footed Booby on Los Bobos cay. Both of these sites are within the restricted use zones (Integral Protection Zones) of a national park.

Roseate Terns were reported nesting on four islands in the archipelago by Phelps and Phelps Jr. (1959b), but neither Bosque et al. (2001) nor Esclasans (2003) found any nests of this species.

La Orchila Archipelago

This small archipelago consists of La Orchila Island and a group of sandy cays and emergent coralline reefs. Phelps and Phelps Jr. (1959a) reported 11 species of seabirds for La Orchila, and Lentino et al. (1994) added two species to the list, Yellow-billed Tern and Cayenne Tern, bringing the total number of species to 13.

Eight species are known to breed: Audubon's Shearwater, Brown Booby, Laughing Gull, Brown Noddy, Sooty Tern, Least Tern, Common Tern, and Royal Tern (table 25.2), although there are no recent population data. Nonetheless, Meyer de Schauensee and Phelps Jr. (1978) noted that the populations of Sooty Tern had diminished considerably by the time of their publication.

La Tortuga Island

La Tortuga is the second largest Venezuelan island after Margarita. Seven species of seabirds have been recorded, but only Brown Pelican were ever reported breeding in a large colony (Cory 1909). Later studies have not recorded any breeding colonies (Fernández 1945; Phelps Jr. 1945; Guzmán and Schreiber 1987).

La Blanquilla Island

Vegetation on this island includes columnar cacti at higher elevations, the salt-loving grass known as turtle-weed (*Batis maritima*), and mangrove stands dominated by the same species as those of Los Roques and La Orchila. Phelps Jr. (1948) listed three species of seabirds: Brown Pelican, Brown Booby, and Magnificent Frigatebird. Lentino et al. (1994) added six more species: Audubon's Shearwater, Red-billed Tropicbird, Masked Booby,

Brown Booby, Laughing Gull, and Royal Tern—bringing the total observed to nine species. There is no information about breeding colonies on this island.

Los Hermanos Archipelago

Los Hermanos is located north of Margarita Island. Seven species are known to breed (table 25.2): Audubon's Shearwater, Red-billed Tropicbird, Brown Booby, Red-footed Booby, Magnificent Frigatebird, Brown Noddy, and Sooty Tern (Phelps Jr. 1948). There are no data on colony sizes.

Los Frailes Archipelago

Los Frailes is formed by seven small islands, five small barren islets, and numerous cays positioned in two parallel rows about 2 km apart and scattered in an area not greater than 14 km^2. Knowledge on the birds of Los Frailes is mostly due to observations by Phelps Jr. (1945), who listed four species of seabirds: Brown Pelican, Brown Booby, Magnificent Frigatebird, and Laughing Gull. Yépez (1963b) indicated the existence of a breeding colony of Brown Pelican (table 25.2), but there is no recent information on the breeding status of these species.

Los Testigos Archipelago

Rainfall on Los Testigos (approx. 400 mm per year) is considerably higher than on the rest of the islands, and its vegetation is more lush (Williams 1980). Five species of seabirds have been recorded at Los Testigos, three of them breeding: Red-footed Booby, Brown Booby, and Magnificent Frigatebird (table 25.2). There are no data on their current colony sizes.

Aves Island

Isla Las Aves is the island farthest from the Venezuelan mainland, located some 500 km north of Margarita. Its climate is rigorous, and frequent hurricanes limit the development of vegetation. Two prostrate species, *Sesuvium portulacastrum* and *Portulaca oleracea*, are prominent (Gremone and Gómez 1983).

Three species of seabirds breed on Las Aves: Bridled Tern, Sooty Tern, and Brown Noddy. The Sooty Tern colony, estimated by Zuloaga (1955) at 500,000 individuals, occurred with a smaller number of Brown Noddy. Lazell (1967) recorded three species of terns nesting, and estimated 4,000–5,000 nests of Sooty Tern;

about 1,000 nests of Bridled Tern; and 10,000–12,000 nests of Brown Noddy (table 25.2). In 1982, 250,000 individuals of Sooty Tern and 60,000 individuals of Brown Noddy were recorded by Gremone and Gómez (1983). Rodrigo Lazo (2007, unpublished data) estimated 5,509 breeding pairs of Brown Noddy and 12,182 pairs of Sooty Tern, the largest colony in Venezuela. Although the population of Sooty Tern has declined in recent years, Aves Island continues to be one of the most important sites in the Caribbean for this species. To date, it remains an important nesting site for Sooty Tern and Brown Noddy although the number of breeding pairs can be highly variable from year to year due to the passage of hurricanes. Large numbers of green turtles (*Chelonia mydas*) also lay their eggs there, and the island was declared a wildlife refuge in 1972.

Threats

In general, marine birds inhabiting Venezuelan islands have been well protected due to their remoteness or through law enforcement, and their nesting habitats have been relatively safe, but there are disturbance and egg collecting issues. We have no information about predation by feral cats, rats, snakes, or invasive species.

Human Disturbance and Habitat Loss

Human intervention has become more extensive on Los Roques Archipelago, Margarita, Coche, and Tortuga islands, where tourist activity has increased considerably during the last decade. The remoteness of Los Roques and the protection of certain cays (e.g., Los Canquises and Los Bobos) have safeguarded the breeding colonies for more than 40 years.

In contrast, the colonies of Least Tern and Laughing Gull are at risk on cays that have no legal protection, such as Los Noronquises, due to disturbances in the breeding colonies. We consider investigations of the impact of tourism on breeding sites and populations of seabirds at these islands to warrant a high research priority. Likewise, the potential impact of the construction of a fishing port in Los Monjes has yet to be evaluated. The need to perform accurate and regular population surveys on Venezuelan islands to determine seabird population trends is urgent.

Egg Taking

Egg taking is an important threat, particularly impacting colonies that nest in the ground. This threat has been documented in past surveys in the Los Roques Archipelago and in our 2001 and 2002 surveys (Bosque et al. 2001; Esclasans 2003), when we noted egg taking for Least Tern, Common Tern, and Laughing Gull in Los Noronquises cays, areas that have important colonies for these species but with recreational zone classification, where use is not restricted.

Conservation

Efforts are geared toward enhancing the security of existing protected areas and promoting additional monitoring of colonies and public awareness about the needs of seabirds.

Protected Areas

Several of the Venezuelan islands are protected under different legislative regimens. Las Aves was declared a wildlife refuge in 1972. Los Roques Archipelago became a national park in 1972 and a Ramsar site in 1996. On Margarita Island there are two protected areas: Las Marites Lagoon, declared a natural monument in 1974, and La Restinga Lagoon, a national park since 1974.

We consider that protected islands have contributed significantly to the preservation of seabirds; for example, on Los Roques Archipelago, the largest colonies of resident species are located on islands with restricted use zones (Integral Protection Zones; Bosque et al. 2001; Esclasans 2003).

Need for Monitoring and Surveys

We urgently need to conduct surveys to provide up-to-date data because the bulk of information was collected prior to the 1980s. We have recent information only for the Los Roques Archipelago, with its important seabird colonies, particularly of Brown Pelican and Black Noddy—considered critically endangered and endangered, respectively (Schreiber 2000a). The Venezuelan islands host major seabird breeding colonies and represent important areas for the conservation of seabirds in the Caribbean. New census data are essential for estimating overall Caribbean seabird populations.

For resident species, we also need information on patterns of local movements between islands and the mainland. Apparently several species that are common on the islands, as well as along or just off the mainland coast, form large breeding colonies only on the islands. Examples include terns, sulids, and Magnificent Frigatebird. It was discovered, for example, that Cayenne Tern individuals inhabiting the Orinoco Delta, in extreme eastern Venezuela, had fledged from the colony of San Nicholas, Aruba (Lentino 2004).

Third, there is an urgent need to recognize precise

patterns of species population trends and hold periodic censuses for both resident and migratory species in the Venezuelan islands. Some of what appear to be tendencies toward population decline—or increase—of the resident species discussed may be due, at least partially, to periodic local movements. For instance, numbers of Laughing Gulls on Los Roques increase sharply from May to July during breeding but are negligible during the earlier part of the year. Similarly, Brown Pelican numbers reach a maximum around November and a minimum near February.

Public Education and Awareness

Fundación Científica Los Roques (FCLR) is conducting an education project with the students of the school on Gran Roque Cay, Los Roques. The objective of this project is to create awareness of the need for conservation of the birds of the archipelago, and plans are to create an ecological brigade for monitoring and conservation of the natural resources in the archipelago (Bladimir Rodriguez, pers. comm.). Our collaboration with the project consists of providing courses on identification and surveys and explaining the importance of participation by the local population in the conservation of the seabird colonies.

Acknowledgments

We wish to thank the Instituto de Tecnología y Ciencias Marinas (INTECMAR) of University Simón Bolivar for support and financing for the 2001 surveys on the islands of Los Roques Archipelago, and we thank the Instituto de Recursos Naturales Renovables (IRNR) and Agencia Española de Cooperación Internancional (AECI) for support and logistical assistance for the 2002 surveys. Warm and heartfelt thanks go to Toribio Mata, Federico Pizanni, Gianni Papadakis, and Carlos Aurrecoechea for their help with surveys on Los Roques. Thanks also go to Robin Restall for his help with the manuscript.

26

Colombia

The Archipelago of San Andrés, Old Providence, and Santa Catalina

MARION HOWARD, MARIA ISABEL MORENO, PAUL SALAMAN, AND MARTHA INÉS GARCÍA

The San Andrés Archipelago is in the western Caribbean. It includes three small inhabited islands and a number of uninhabited cays and atolls (maps 50, 51). The territorial waters are about 300,000 km², nearly 10% of the Caribbean Sea. The largest island, San Andrés, is 800 km northwest of Colombia, 150 km east of Nicaragua, and 725 km south of Grand Cayman. Old Providence and Santa Catalina, which are separated by a 155 m wide channel, are 80 km north of San Andrés. Corals, mangroves, and seagrass beds surround the inhabited islands. The archipelago's coral reef ecosystems are among the healthiest in the Americas and include two barrier reefs, five atolls, and less well defined coral banks stretching more than 500 km along the Nicaraguan rise.

The entire archipelago is now the Seaflower Biosphere Reserve, which was declared a member of the World Network of Biosphere Reserves by UNESCO's Man and the Biosphere Program in 2000. It is part of both the Caribbean Terrestrial Hotspot and the Western Caribbean Coral Reef Hotspot, which is considered one of the world's ten regions exceptionally rich in marine species and facing extreme threat. The Seaflower Biosphere Reserve is classified as a secondary Endemic Bird Area and has been declared an Important Bird Area by BirdLife International (Moreno et al. 2003). Breeding colonies of seabirds have been reported on Old Providence and on the cays of Roncador, Serrana, and Serranilla in the archipelago's northern region.

Seabirds

Little ornithological information is available, which is not surprising given that the San Andrés Archipelago is one of the least studied and remotest areas in the Caribbean Sea. Existing data are primarily notes on the presence of species. A census of the archipelago's seabirds has not been done and nor have major surveys or regular monitoring.

Information published on seabird colonies was found in Ortega (1941), Bond and Meyer de Schauensee (1944), Bond (1950b), Wetmore (1965), Ben-Tuvia and Ríos (1970), Chiriví (1988), Díaz et al. (1996), and Raffaele et al. (1998a, b). Chiriví's work (1988) was based on visual surveys and specimens gathered in 1975. Recently more information has been collected in the Northern Cays. These data were found in unpublished reports—primarily from CORALINA, the environmental authority for the archipelago—and include McCormick (1999), García (2005a, 2005b), and T. McNish (unpubl. 2001). Surveys were done in April and May 2005 in two joint expeditions by CORALINA and the Christian University of San Andrés, with the collaboration of the Colombian navy (García 2005a). Because financial resources have been unavailable for major surveys or monitoring, recent visits have been brief and have involved only visual surveys.

Seven species of seabirds have been confirmed breeding in the San Andrés Archipelago since 1941: Audubon's Shearwater, Masked Booby, Brown Booby, Magnificent Frigatebird, Brown Noddy, Sooty Tern, and Royal Tern (table 26.1, 26.2). All except Audubon's Shearwater and Masked Booby have been confirmed breeding since 1999. An additional species, Laughing Gull, has been sighted with reproductive plumage on cays far from documented colonies, but nests have not been observed. It is possible that nests were located in the same atolls on cays where researchers were unable to land.

San Andrés Island

San Andrés (12° 29'–12° 36' N, 81° 41'–81° 43' W) is a low coral and limestone island with an elevation of 90 m. It

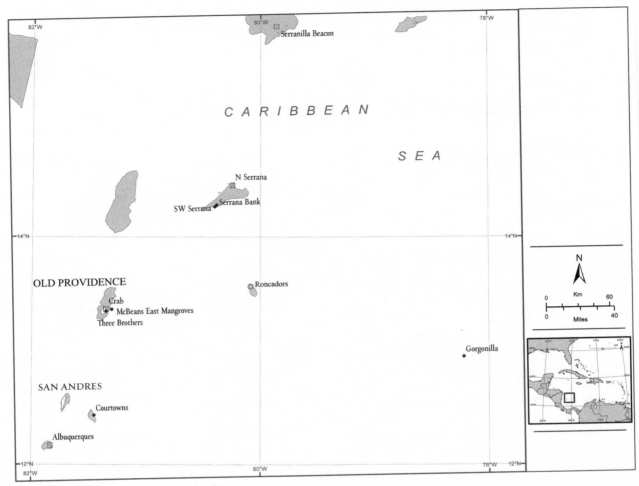

Map 51. San Andrés Archipelago, Colombia.

Table 26.1. Counts of seabird pairs breeding on the San Andrés Archipelago, 1999–2003

Species	Estimated pairs
Brown Booby	100–300
Brown Noddy	>250
Sooty Tern	>1000

is the archipelago's largest and most populated island, with an area of 27 km^2 and a population of about 70,000. Economic activities are tourism, commerce (dependent on tourism), government employment, artisanal fishing, and small-scale agriculture. There are also relatively large informal and black market economies.

The environment and economy have suffered from the high human population density. At more than 2,500 people per km^2, San Andrés has the highest population density of any oceanic island in the Americas and one of the highest in the world. The population increased rapidly because of internal migration following declara-

tion as a free port in 1953, growing from 5,675 in 1950 to 23,000 in 1973 (Bent 2000). By 1985 population was 42,000, and only 15 years later it was 70,000 (World Gazetteer 2002; Howard et al. 2003). Virtually all immigrants were from the Colombian mainland.

The island is very urbanized, with human settlements spreading. Mature forest remains on only 5% of the island (Toro et al. 1999). Vegetation cover is mainly cultivated or scrub: coconut palms, mixed-crop agriculture, fruit trees, and ornamentals. Five mangrove swamps cover a total of 161 hectares. The largest stand of mangroves, Hooker Bight–Honda Bay, is a regional park. No seabirds are known to breed in San Andrés.

Old Providence

Old Providence (13° 19' 23"–13° 23' 50" N, 81° 21' 08"–81° 23' 58" W) was formed by an extinct Miocene volcano and is mountainous with a maximum elevation of 380 m. It has an area of 18 km^2 and a population of about 5,000.

Table 26.2. Distribution of seabird colonies breeding on the San Andrés Archipelago, 1941–2005

Species	Site	Year breeding confirmed	Source
Audubon's Shearwater	Providence	1948	Bond 1950b
Sula sp.	Serrana	1995	Díaz et al. 1996
Masked Booby	Serranilla	1998	Raffaele et al. 1998a, b
		1975	Chiriví 1988
Brown Booby	Roncador	1941	Bond & Meyer de Schauensee 1944
		2005	García 2005a
		1999	McCormick 1999
	Serrana	1975	Chiriví 1988
		1969	Ben-Tuvia & Ríos 1970
	Serranilla	1941	Ortega 1941
		1975	Chiriví 1988
Magnificent Frigatebird	Providence	1941	Bond & Meyer de Schauensee 1944
		2004	García 2005b
		1948	Bond 1950b
	Roncador	1941	Bond & Meyer 1944
		1999	McCormick 1999
	Serrana	2003	García 2005b
		1995	Díaz et al. 1996
	Serranilla	1975	Chiriví 1988
Laughing Gull	Serrana	2003	García 2005b
	Serranilla	2005	García 2005a
Sterna spp.	Serrana	1995	Díaz et al. 1996
Sooty Tern	Roncador	1975	Chiriví 1988
	Serrana	2005	García 2005a
		2003	García 2005b
		1999	McCormick 1999
		1975	Chiriví 1988
	Serranilla	1975	Chiriví 1988
Brown Noddy	Roncador	1975	Chiriví 1988
	Serrana	2005	García 2005a
		1975	Chiriví 1988
		1965	Wetmore 1965
	Serranilla	1975	Chiriví 1988
Royal Tern	Serrana	1999	McCormick 1999

The economy depends on ecotourism, government employment, cottage industries, and artisanal fishing and farming. The Old Providence barrier reef is 32 km long with an area of 255 km^2, making it one of the largest barrier reefs in the Americas (Geister and Díaz 1996).

Old Providence has an unusually well-preserved tropical transitional forest (Gentry, field notes) and healthy mangroves covering 54 hectares. With an area of 30 hectares, the Oyster Creek mangroves are the largest and most productive and are part of the archipelago's only national park, Old Providence McBean Lagoon.

Two colonies of seabirds have been recorded in Old Providence but only one, Magnificent Frigatebird, still exists. Audubon's Shearwater has not been recorded since 1950.

Audubon's Shearwater

In 1948 a small colony was observed nesting on Crab Cay, an islet in the Old Providence lagoon (Bond 1950b). No nests have been recorded since that time. Crab Cay is heavily visited by locals and tourists, making it unlikely that breeding would resume.

Magnificent Frigatebird

A nesting colony is located in the Oyster Creek mangroves on the east coast of Old Providence (Bond and Meyer de Schauensee 1944; Bond 1950b; Archibold, pers. comm. 2004, cited in García 2005b). Recently several nests were also found on the Three Brothers Cays, south of Crab Cay (Archibold, pers. comm. 2004, cited in García 2005b). No population numbers or characteristics have been recorded.

Santa Catalina

This small island (13° 23' N, 81° 22' W) has an area of 1 km² with a population of less than 200 people. It is separated from Old Providence by a narrow seagrass-lined channel 155 m across (Howard et al. 2003). The island is densely wooded and has one mangrove swamp. There is no evidence of breeding seabirds.

Roncador Bank

Roncador (13° 34' N, 80° 05' W) is an atoll 222 km northeast of San Andrés. It measures 15 km by 7 km, with a 12 km reef to windward. There is one cay made of coral rubble and other marine debris that has an area of 72,556 m² (CORALINA GIS) and an elevation of 4 m. It is rocky with sparse vegetation and a single small beach.

Roncador has been visited by the archipelago's artisanal fishermen for centuries and is still frequented by them. The United States controlled the atoll in the mid-1900s. It was returned to Colombia in 1981 when the United States relinquished its claim (Quita Sueño Treaty). A lighthouse was built in 1978 on the northernmost end of the reef. Roncador is under the jurisdiction of Colombia's maritime authority, the Direccíon General Marítima (DIMAR), and there is a small naval outpost. Permission from the navy is required for landing.

Four species of seabirds have been confirmed breeding in Roncador (Brown Booby, Magnificent Frigatebird, Sooty Tern, and Brown Noddy). Only Brown Booby and Magnificent Frigatebird have been confirmed breeding since 1999.

Brown Booby

A nesting colony of 600 to 800 individuals with eggs and fledglings was reported in May 1975 (Chirivi 1988) and again in 1999 (McCormick 1999). In 2005, a colony of 200 or more adults with fledglings was observed (García 2005a). Chirivi (1988) reported nests on the intertidal area of the beach and in sandy areas inland. García reported nests only in sandy inland areas with sea purslane (*Sesuvium portulacastrum*). No nests were observed in rocky areas.

Magnificent Frigatebird

A nesting colony was reported in 1999 (McCormick 1999).

Brown Noddy

Fledglings were observed in May 1975 and breeding was reported, with numbers unknown (Chirivi 1988). Nests were found on the ground in sand and rocks, with or without vegetation. Nests had no particular structure and were 30 cm to 50 cm apart.

Sooty Tern

Nesting was reported in 1975, associated with Brown Noddy (Chirivi 1988). The nests were described as shallow depressions in sand or rock with no nesting material. Nests were scattered and separate.

Serrana Bank

Serrana (14° 17' N, 80° 23' W) is an atoll 244.5 km north northeast of San Andrés and is 36 km long and 15 km wide, with a complex coral reef system 37 km by 30 km. Six cays are located on the reef. Seabird colonies have been recorded on two—Southwest Cay and North Cay. The largest and most densely vegetated is Southwest Cay, which has an area of 278,093 m² (CORALINA GIS). Low-growing maritime vegetation like lavender (*Tournefortia* sp.), bay cedar (*Suriana maritima*), and sea purslane (*Sesuvium portulacastrum*) is abundant. This is the archipelago's largest sand cay, with dunes over 10 m high. North Cay has an area of 5,221 m² and is low, with an elevation of 1.5 m (CORALINA GIS). It is made of coral rubble, sand, and other marine debris. Vegetation, primarily lavender and bay cedar, is sparse (Milliman 1969; García 2005b).

Serrana has been the site of traditional fishing by islanders from San Andrés and Old Providence since the 1600s and is now visited by both artisanal and industrial fishing boats. Artisanal fishermen use mainly North Cay. Guano was extracted in the past, as were seabird and turtle eggs. In 1981 the United States also recognized Colombia's sovereignty over this atoll. Since that time, Serrana has been under the jurisdiction of DIMAR. A lighthouse administrated by the maritime authority is located on the west end of Southwest Cay. There is also a naval outpost on Southwest Cay, and permits are required to land or stay on any of the cays.

Magnificent Frigatebird, Brown Noddy, Sooty Tern, and Royal Tern have been confirmed breeding in Serrana since 1995; of these the Magnificent Frigatebird, Sooty Tern, and Brown Noddy were breeding in 2003 (García 2005a). There was no evidence that the once large colony of Brown Booby still existed in 2003. A sulid colony and a larid colony were seen in 1995 identified by genus only (Díaz et al. 1996). In 2003, Laughing Gulls were sighted on North Cay with reproductive plumage, but no nests were observed (García 2005b). It is possible that this species was breeding on one of the atoll's other cays.

Sulids, *Sula* sp.

A breeding colony of *Sula* sp. was seen on Southwest Cay in 1995 (Díaz et al. 1996). Fifty-four individuals were photographed (Díaz et al. 2000), but the species is not identifiable in the photo.

Brown Booby

A breeding colony of 15,000 individuals was recorded and photographed on Southwest Cay in 1941 (Ortega 1941). A photograph showing 33 individuals was taken in August 1969 on Southwest Cay (Ben-Tuvia and Ríos 1970).

Magnificent Frigatebird

A nesting colony was reported on North Cay in 1995 (Díaz et al. 1996) and 2003 (García 2005b). Díaz reported nests on coral boulders.

Larids

A breeding colony of terns was observed nesting in the vegetation of Southwest Cay in 1995 (Díaz et al. 1996). Species were not identified.

Brown Noddy

A large breeding colony for the species was reported in 1965 (Wetmore 1965) and 1975 (Chiriví 1988). Chiriví characterized the nests as similar to those on Roncador: on the ground in sand or rocks, irrespective of vegetation; unstructured, and spaced 30 to 50 m apart. In 2005, a colony of at least 500 individuals (estimated 250 pairs) with fledglings was observed (García 2005a).

Sooty Tern

There is a major colony in Southwest Cay, breeding year round. According to Chiriví (1988), in 1985 nesting was associated with Brown Noddy. This colony was observed again in 1999 (McCormick 1999) and 2003 (García 2005b). In 2005, a breeding colony of over 500 individuals (estimated to be as large as several thousand) was seen (García 2005a). These researchers described the nests as shallow depressions in sand, coral rubble, or on boulders, regardless of vegetation cover. No nesting material was used, and the distance between nests was about 50 cm.

Royal Tern

In 1999, this species was reported to be using the dunes of Serrana as a breeding site (McCormick 1999).

Serranilla Bank

Serranilla Bank (15° 47' N, 79° 50' W) is 444.5 km north-northeast of San Andrés and is 45 km long and 37 km wide. There are three cays, East, Middle, and Beacon. Breeding colonies have been recorded only on Beacon Cay, which is the largest with an area of 51,476 m² (CORALINA GIS). Dominant vegetation includes lavender (*Tournefortia* sp.), bay cedar (*Suriana maritima*), sea purslane (*Sesuvium portulacastrum*), and coastal spurge (*Euphorbia mesembrianthemifolia*) (Chiriví 1988; García 2005b).

This bank is shared with Honduras except for Beacon Cay and an area of 12 nautical miles around this cay, which are solely under Colombian control. Serranilla, like the other Northern Banks, is under the jurisdiction of DIMAR; there is a naval station on Beacon Cay, and permission is required for any landing or stay. Industrial fishing is carried out by fleets from the mainland of Colombia and Honduras. Because of the distance from the islands and predominance of industrial vessels, artisanal fishermen rarely visit this bank.

Colonies of Brown Booby, Masked Booby, Magnificent Frigatebird, Brown Noddy, and Sooty Tern were known to breed (Chiriví 1988). There are no recent confirmations of breeding. Although Laughing Gulls with reproductive plumage were sighted on Beacon Cay in 2005, no nests were seen (García 2005a). There is no evidence indicating whether there were nests on outlying cays because researchers were not permitted to land.

Masked Booby

A breeding colony was first reported in 1941 (Bond and Meyer de Schauensee 1944). In 1975 a small breeding colony with 30 nests, each with 2 eggs, was observed on Beacon Cay. A female with an egg in its oviduct was also collected (Chiriví 1988). Chiriví described the nests as depressions in sand surrounded by abundant pieces of dead coral. Unstructured nests were also found on the ground in an inland meadow of coastal spurge (*Euphorbia mesembrianthemifolia*). Raffaele et al. (1998a, b) also reported a breeding colony in Serranilla.

Brown Booby

Bond and Meyer de Schauensee (1944) reported the existence of a breeding colony on Beacon Cay in 1941.

In 1975, 1,600 to 2,000 individuals were recorded, with incubation in February and March (Chiriví 1988). Nests were found on the top of bay cedar shrubs (*Suriana maritima*), in sites where natural thickets of branches could support chicks without any additional nest structure. Nests were also located in sandy soil in coastal spurge (*Euphorbia mesembrianthemifolia*). No nests were sited near beaches or rocks (Chiriví 1988).

Magnificent Frigatebird

A large nesting colony was located on Beacon Cay in 1975. Nests were in bay cedar shrubs (*Suriana maritima*) only on branches with setting fruit and were 80 cm to 1 m off the ground. Reproduction began in early May (Chiriví 1988).

Brown Noddy

A breeding colony was recorded in 1975 on Beacon Cay (Chiriví 1988). Similar to nests of this species in Roncador and Serrana, nests were on the ground in sand or rocky substrate, regardless of vegetation. Nests were unstructured and 30 to 50 cm apart (Chiriví 1988).

Sooty Tern

A breeding colony was observed in 1975 (Chiriví 1988). No details or characteristics were described.

Threats

The breeding colony of Magnificent Frigatebirds in Old Providence is little threatened because of the protected status and strict management of the Oyster Creek mangroves, which are part of the national park. The only airport in Old Providence is adjacent to this site and, at present, the island is served by small aircraft from San Andrés, with a maximum of a few trips a day. If the airport was enlarged to accommodate larger aircraft and jets or if air traffic substantially increased, the breeding colony could be impacted by noise and habitat destruction. The Three Brothers Cays are also in the national park and are well protected. There are no known threats to nests.

The situation in the Northern Cays is quite different. Although the cays and banks are protected, seabird colonies in Roncador, Serrana, and Serranilla face many threats, and lack of management puts their survival at risk. A traditional threat is harvesting of booby eggs, considered a delicacy. They have been gathered by artisanal fishermen visiting the cays for as long as anyone can remember. Historically nests were raided by fishermen from farther away as well. Barriga reported that Jamaican fishermen raided nests from June through August (Barriga et al. 1985). Eggs are also gathered by naval personnel.

Threats are posed by the naval outposts. Habitat destruction and fragmentation threaten survival of colonies. Naval personnel have altered the cays' fragile ecosystem and fragmented habitat by collecting material, cutting paths, and creating small parks. Rocks, shells, boulders, and coral rubble have been gathered and used to build walls, line paths, define parks, and construct ornamental displays. Rock walls have been built on beaches and coastlines, and paths have been cut through vegetation and nesting habitat.

Few animals are found on these cays. The presence of rats threatens the colonies' survival. Dogs have occasionally been brought to the cays by naval personnel, as on Serrana's Southwest Cay. Although there are no feral animals, domestic animals pose an obvious threat to chicks and nesting birds, especially those nesting on the ground.

Occasional threats to adult birds have been observed. Artisanal fishermen have reported seeing seabirds hooked by long-lines and tangled in fishing gear. There have also been reports that personnel stationed on the cays shoot seabirds for sport, although these reports have lessened in recent years. Random acts of vandalism and careless behavior by naval personnel, fishermen, and other visitors also disturb nesting.

Conservation

Significant marine and coastal ecosystems in the San Andrés Archipelago are protected, including those that offer habitat for seabirds. Mangroves have been fully protected by congressional law since 1994 (Law 136), and mangrove forests are recovering and increasing in area in San Andrés and Old Providence. Coral reefs, banks, and cays were designated special management areas by the Minister of Environment in 1996 (Resolution 1426). The national park, Old Providence McBean Lagoon, was established in 1995 (Resolution 1021). This park includes the Oyster Creek mangroves, Crab Cay, and Three Brothers Cays, all of which are seabird habitat. In 1998, all beaches were declared special conservation zones by CORALINA (Resolution 151).

CORALINA is the representative of Colombia's National Environment System (SINA) in the San Andrés Archipelago and is the government agency responsible for environmental enforcement, planning, management, and education throughout the territory (Law 99). This agency was created by law in 1993 and began operations in 1995. To support and strengthen management, CORALINA has set up the Seaflower Biosphere Reserve, designated by UNESCO in 2000, and the Seaflower Marine Protected Area (MPA), declared by the Ministry of Environment, Housing, and Territorial Development in 2005 (Resolution 107). All seabird habitat in the archipelago, with the exception of Serranilla Bank, is included in the 65,000 km^2 of the Seaflower MPA.

Although the sites where seabirds nest have been included in conservation legislation, the remoteness of the Northern Banks has made implementation and enforcement virtually impossible. CORALINA does not have financial resources or equipment (including a vessel) to visit the Northern Cays. Recent work has mostly been carried out by brokering space in other expeditions. Another major challenge is that naval personnel, all of whom are from mainland Colombia, are stationed on the cays for only about 40 days each. The constant influx of new people and their lack of familiarity with the region have made it very difficult to create awareness about seabirds, to build their capacity to support surveying and monitoring, or to involve them in conservation.

In 2004, CORALINA promoted an agreement with DIMAR to collaborate for the first time on work related to the presence of sea turtles and seabirds in the banks. As part of this agreement, arriving navy personnel were trained in seabird biology and conservation, and the maritime authority transported researchers to the cays and facilitated permits for the surveys in April and May 2005. The establishment of the MPA and formal agreements between the maritime authority and the environmental authority now provide a framework for conservation and management of the remote cays and banks.

The executive director of CORALINA announced in June 2005 that conservation of the outlying cays is an MPA management priority and that work will begin with stakeholders—including institutions and user groups—to agree on and implement conservation actions. To support this goal, Colombia's national climate change project (INAP), which is funded by the Global Environment Facility (GEF) and implemented by the World Bank, includes activities to improve management of the cays and banks.

Recommended Actions

A Sea and Shorebird Species Conservation Plan has been completed for the San Andrés Archipelago (García 2005b). This document is currently under review and will be incorporated into the Seaflower MPA integrated management plan. A number of actions are recommended, including:

1. Research

- Complete baseline research including gathering information on species, distribution, abundance, characteristics, behavior, presence of disease, etc.
- Identify and analyze threats.

2. Management

- Implement ongoing monitoring, surveillance, and enforcement, including brokering agreements between CORALINA, DIMAR, other institutions, and stakeholders to share responsibility for monitoring and enforcement.
- Protect and recover breeding habitat.
- Eradicate rats and other introduced species.
- Require environmental authorization for activities carried out in the cays.
- Implement alternatives to reduce pollution and improve solid and liquid waste disposal in the cays; for example, install composting toilets.
- Set up mechanisms to ensure collaboration, information sharing, and management support that involve all stakeholders including authorities, user groups, and NGOs.

3. Regulation

- Prohibit construction of any more permanent structures in the Northern Banks.
- Prohibit the introduction of plant and animal species; including pets and other domestic animals.
- Prohibit actions that threaten seabird survival, including gathering eggs; disturbing colonies or nests; destroying, fragmenting, or altering habitat; and feeding, capturing, or killing adults and juveniles.

4. Capacity building

- Educate and create awareness in the general public, user groups, authorities, and other institutions.
- Train naval personnel en route to the cays during stopovers in San Andrés.
- Carry out "training of trainers" courses with user groups and the maritime authority, working together to set up a program to ensure long-term multiplication of training to all personnel stationed on the cays.

27

A Geographic Information System (GIS) of Breeding Sites

WILLIAM A. MACKIN

The GIS for seabirds of the Caribbean, Bahamas, and Bermuda is a database for the historic and current nesting sites of seabirds in the wider Caribbean with the aim of monitoring long-term changes in populations. The database now lists 805 sites where nesting by seabirds has been documented. Of those sites, 108 (13.4%) are known to be extirpated or severely depleted, 589 (73.1%) are of moderate or unknown status, and 107 (13.3%) contain more than 5% of the estimated population of one or more species in the West Indies. The median number of species per colony is 2, and the most diverse assemblage on a single island was 16 species on Sombrero Island in the Lesser Antilles, although Venezuela's Los Roques Archipelago harbors 18 species. The Bahamas has the most nesting sites with 217, while Cuba is second with 70.

This chapter identifies 25 of the most important and 25 of the most endangered sites in the West Indies in terms of the percentage of the total known population that each site holds. It also specifies the most poorly known regions in terms of the average date of the last survey and the range of minimum and maximum estimates for the total population. These data are accessible online and are updated regularly for the use of scientists and conservation authorities at www.wicbirds.net.

The Database

The known breeding sites for seabirds in the Caribbean and West Indies were entered into a database and used to produce maps for Schreiber and Lee (2000a) from the latitude and longitude coordinates for the sites (Mackin 2000). The system tracks the past, present, and future status of the colonies, including threats to the populations and estimates of the numbers of breeding pairs. Since 2000, the number and precision of records has increased so that most colonies are mapped to a specific area of large islands or to specific small cays. This im-

provement should be attributed to the Schreiber and Lee (2000a) book, several individuals in the field who have submitted records, and the researchers who collected and contributed the data for this volume. At the time of writing the database includes 3,103 surveys of 805 locations from 64 contributors and 85 scientific papers. Its Web site includes maps and summary data based on updated information, and instructions for requesting and submitting records are available. The SCSCB Web site (www.scscb.org) provides a link to the database through the seabird working group page.

Three longstanding issues with the database continue. As noted in Mackin (2000), contributors often failed to provide the latitude and longitude coordinates for sites, and some locations could not be verified. Common names were often ambiguous or did not appear in the NIMA Geonames server (a gazetteer of geographic place names). In some cases, coordinates were found using Google Earth© software, and the reference points are given in the text. Some sites that were found in the Geonames server are slightly off the actual islands on the Nature Conservancy's basemaps, but we have corrected those errors that were detected and will gradually fix others.

When the identity of the island was unclear, I chose a site to the best of my ability and marked the colony name with an asterisk (34 sites). Most of these were fixed during the editing of the book, but there will always be room for improvement. Thus, the data should be used with the knowledge that sites could be off from their actual locations, and corrections from contributors and knowledgeable locals are encouraged and appreciated. A second issue is that authors vary in the precision with which they report breeding sites. Great progress has been achieved in listing sites by the precise area of the island where the colony occurs, rather than in estimates that cover entire islands or groups of islands, and this trend should con-

Table 27.1. Population totals of Caribbean seabirds

Code	Common Name	Islands	2006 Population	Estimate	Major Site	Pairs/Site
1	Bermuda Petrel	2	71	71	71	286
2	Black-capped Petrel	7	2,000	1,315	1,000	0
3	Jamaica Petrel	1	0	0	0	24
4	Audubon's Shearwater	113	2,676	1,582	800	13
5	White-tailed Tropicbird	198	4,050	2,258	650	20
6	Red-billed Tropicbird	136	1,730	1,861	150	23
7	Masked Booby	30	750	580	200	395
8	Brown Booby	93	6,980	8,663	1,267	59
9	Red-footed Booby	37	14,600	13,718	4,832	75
10	Brown Pelican	102	2,400	2,609	491	25
11	Magnificent Frigatebird	104	6,100	6,447	2,000	87
12	Laughing Gull	141	12,200	11,738	2,000	7
13	Brown Noddy	184	37,192	42,951	11,000	17
14	Black Noddy	6	100	96	48	36
15	Sooty Tern	165	315,942	439,508	80,000	202
16	Bridled Tern	198	8,900	7,197	2,000	1915
17	Least Tern	160	4,410	4,135	420	45
18	Gull-billed Tern	35	250	241	70	9
19	Roseate Tern	150	3,605	5,412	700	17
20	Common Tern	38	627	731	200	28
21	Royal Tern	71	645	1,147	270	25
22	Sandwich Tern	63	1,605	2,943	400	154
23	Cayenne Tern	25	3,840	3,766	3,226	24

Note: Columns present (left to right) the code that identifies each species in table 27.5, common name, number of islands where it has been reported, estimate of 2006 population by the authors of this book, sum of the most recent lowest estimates from the database, major breeding site, and mean number of pairs that nest at each site.

tinue as more surveys are published or submitted to the database. For the database to track population changes, it is necessary to have the exact locations.

The last issue is that contributors often use different methods to estimate population sizes or do not provide estimates. High and low estimates and the methods used to acquire them (e.g., count, random plot census, line transect, boat estimate, etc.) and comments about the colony are helpful. The database is designed to build on previous work by keeping all data that are submitted for historical comparison. Even if no count is made, a general guess of the number of breeding pairs (0–10, 10–50, 50–100, 100–500, etc.) is superior to a listing as "breeding" because it enables colonies to be grouped and compared to later years when more precise measurements are made. Updated copies of all the tables in this chapter appear on the Web site.

Total Populations in the Caribbean

The database tracks the total population by recording low and high estimates from each survey of an island.

Low estimates are used for estimates in this volume because counts tend to overestimate the number of actual breeding pairs, as opposed to birds present at the colony, and many species shift between islands in different years.

Many of the surveys (645 of 1,936) indicate only that a species breeds at the site. For these sites, an estimate of 1 to 10 pairs was entered. Similarly, if the contributor suspected breeding by the species (112 of 1,936 surveys), then an estimate of 0 to 10 pairs was entered. These estimates are the best available data but should improve with future research. Regionwide estimates of the population were produced from the lowest and highest estimates from the most recent surveys at each colony (table 27.1).

In addition, the total estimates made by the authors in this book are included as a separate field (2006 population, table 27.1) for each species. Their estimates incorporate local information better than the database does, particularly for the terns, which tend to shift locations frequently. However, the two types of data complement each other well and produced similar estimates for the populations.

Breeding Sites

The maps in this book were created from the database by Mike Palmer of the Nature Conservancy. The colonies are organized in appendix A by the island code number, which also appears next to each colony on the maps. The species column lists all the species that occur or have occurred on an island by their code numbers from table 27.1.

Any point on the maps can be cross-referenced to table 27.5, which summarizes the data for all 800 breeding sites. Table 27.5 is organized by the chapter of the book in which each island is covered and, alphabetically, by the name of the site. The table includes an estimate of the total number of breeding pairs of all species, codes for the nesting species (see table 27.1), the most recent year of reporting, and one of the recent contributors for the site. The table also gives a ranking of status. The three ranks of status signify the size and health of the population (0 = extirpated or declining, needs intervention; 1 = less than 5% population; 2 = contains more than 5% of the breeding pairs in the region). Extirpated or declining colonies are marked with an *X* on the maps. Islands with 5% or more of the population are marked with an asterisk on the maps; an asterisk also marks the species that has the significant population listed in the Species Code column of table 27.5.

Contributors

The database includes the source that submitted each survey as the contributor. If the data were from a published paper, the reference is added to the reference table. Contributors are all denoted by a three-letter code. The amount of work necessary for acquiring these records through research and field work was impressive, and I thank each of the contributors (in alphabetical order of their code): R. I. Allcorn and J. S. Daley (ALD); Anne Haynes Sutton (ASU); Sandy Sprunt (AXS); Betty Ann Schreiber (BAS); Stefan Bodner (BNR); James Bond (BON; submitted by David Lee); Elwood Bracey (BRC); Bruce Hallett (BRH); P. Blanco, B. Sanchez, and A. Hernandez (BSH); Bailey Smith (BSM); Don Buden (BUD); J. Rothchild and L. Roth (CR2); Jaime Collazo (CZO); A. Debrot, C. Boogerd, and D. van den Broeck (DEB); D. Anthony and A. Dornelly (DOA); Larry Dougan (DOU); David Lee (DSL); Eric Carey (ECA); Erica Gates (EGA); Floyd Hayes (FLH); Martin Frost (FST); Fred Schaffner (FWS); Jon Gerwin (GER); Gilles Leblond (GLB); Bill Hayes (HAY); Steve Holliday (HDA); B. Horwith and K. Lindsay (HOL); Island Conserva-

tion Fund (ICF); Jorge Saliva (JES); Jerry Jackson (JJA); Jeremy Madeiros (JLM); Jim Parnell (JPA); Judy Pierce (JPI); A. Jiménez, P. Rodríguez, and P. Blanco (JRB); J. and R. Morris (JRM); Allen Keith (KTH); Jim Kushlan (KUS); V. Lemoine, L. Dubief, and V. Genesseaux (LGD); Miguel Lentino (LTO); E. Massiah and M. Frost (MAF); Andrew McGowan et al. (MGO); M. I. Moreno and P. Salaman (MOS); Mandy Walsh-McGehee (MWM); Natalia Collier (NAC); Luis Naranjo (NAR); Rob Norton (NOR); Patricia Bradley (PEB); Mike Pienkowski (PNK); Randolph Winston (RAW); Chris Rimmer (RIM); Rob Pagliaro (RPG); Ingrid Sylvester et al. (SYL); J. Tunnell and B. Chapman (TCH); Tony White (TOW); R. van Halewyn and R. Norton (VHN); K. H. Voous (VOO); Will Mackin (WAM).

Most Important Colonies

The database can track the number of species in each colony and produce answers to basic questions. Table 27.2 includes the 25 most important colonies in the region for the 23 species covered by the database. Importance was defined as the highest ratio of the remaining population that the island holds for any one species.

Most Endangered Colonies

The most endangered colonies are those that are experiencing declines but retain high ratios of the remaining pairs of a species in the West Indies (table 27.3). Three colonies are known to be declining but hold 5% of the remaining population of one species. The most endangered site is the large Gull-Billed Tern colony at Salt Pond on Rum Cay in the eastern islands of the Bahamas. Rats have been eating the tern eggs and preventing reproductive success (Buden 1990a). Sombrero Island north of Anguilla is the next most threatened cay, with important Brown Booby and Bridled Tern populations. The island has invasive mammals and had been proposed as a site for a rocket launch facility (J. Pierce, pers. comm.). South West Cay in the Pedro Cays of Jamaica (S/SW Pedro in the table) holds 5% of the remaining pairs of Masked Boobies and important Magnificent Frigatebird and Brown Booby populations. Haynes Sutton (this volume) reports rats on the cay causing declines in all species there. Table 27.3 represents the kinds of problems that we know about in the West Indies and Caribbean, and it should be an effective benchmark for identifying islands that need the most urgent conservation actions.

One area where the database should expand in the future is in providing information about threats from

Table 27.2. Most important colonies

Order	Common Name	Name Group	Island	Site Estimate	2006 Population	Ratio
1	Bermuda Petrel	Nonsuch	Bermuda	71	71	1.00
2	Cayenne Tern	Lago Reef	Aruba	3,226	3,840	0.84
3	Black-capped Petrel	Pic Macaya	Massif de la Hotte	1,000	2,000	0.50
4	Black Noddy	Lago Reef	Aruba	48	100	0.48
5	Black Noddy	Los Roques	Los Roques	44	100	0.44
6	Royal Tern	Middle Caicos	Middle Caicos	270	645	0.42
7	Magnificent Frigatebird	Codrington Lagoon	Barbuda	2,000	6,100	0.33
8	Common Tern	Northern Coast	East Caicos	200	627	0.32
9	Audubon's Shearwater	Long Cay	Exumas	800	2,676	0.30
10	Brown Noddy	French	Caicos	11,000	37,192	0.30
11	Gull-billed Tern	Sabinal	Camaguey	70	250	0.28
12	Masked Booby	Monje del Sur	Los Monjes	200	750	0.27
13	Sooty Tern	Alto Velo	Dom. Rep.	80,000	315,942	0.25
14	Sandwich Tern	Dolly's Rock	South Andros	400	1,605	0.25
15	Red-footed Booby	Booby Pond	Little Cayman	3,824	16,590	0.23
16	Bridled Tern	Penniston	Turks	2,000	8,900	0.22
17	Sooty Tern	SE Morant	Morant Cays	70,000	315,942	0.22
18	Brown Pelican	Los Roques	Los Roques	491	2,400	0.20
19	Roseate Tern	La Parguera	Lajas	700	3,605	0.19
20	Brown Booby	Dog Cay	Anguilla	1,267	6,980	0.18
21	Red-footed Booby	Battowia Bullet	Grenadines	3,000	16,590	0.18
22	Royal Tern	Scrub Cay	Anguilla	115	645	0.18
23	Common Tern	Los Roques	Los Roques	110	627	0.18
24	Laughing Gull	Prickly Pear E	Anguilla	2,000	12,200	0.16
25	Brown Noddy	Long Cay	Turks	6,000	37,192	0.16

Note: Ratio is the proportion of the 2006 population that occurs on the island.

introduced predators, development, harvesting of eggs, and other data for each of the colonies. That information is tracked in the current system and I encourage submission of reports about specific threats.

Regions in Need of Surveys

Future surveys could target areas that either have not been surveyed in a number of years or have large ranges of population estimates per number of colonies in the region. Table 27.4 lists 20 regions in order of the mean most recent survey. The Windward Islands, particularly Grenada, the Grenadines, and St. Vincent, have not been surveyed recently. The Colombian islands in the Western

Caribbean have an average survey date of 1987. Bermuda's populations are well documented. The Morant and Pedro banks have the highest range per known colony. Surveys in such areas should provide the most information per unit of investment in censuses.

Acknowledgments

Thanks go to Michael Palmer and the Nature Conservancy for producing the maps; to all the contributors earlier listed; to David Lee, Haven Wiley, Patricia Bradley, Ann Haynes Sutton, Jeremy Baggish (for help with queries), and Amy Mackin; and to the United States National Fish and Wildlife Foundation for funding.

236

Table 27.3. Most endangered colonies

Area	Island Name	Species	Breeding Pairs	Ratio	Year	Contributor
Rum Cay	Salt Pond	Gull-billed Tern	14	0.056	1989	BUD
Anguilla	Sombrero	Brown Booby	386	0.055	2005	HDA
Jamaica	S/SW Pedro	Masked Booby	38	0.051	2005	ASU
St. Thomas	Dutchcap	Brown Pelican	100	0.042	1996	JPI
Tobago	St. Giles	Audubon's Shearwater	100	0.037	2000	BNR
Venezuela	Aves	Sooty Tern	10,000	0.032	2005	LTO
Anguilla	Sombrero	Bridled Tern	270	0.030	2005	HDA
Martinique	Mainland	Red-billed Tropicbird	50	0.029	1998	DSL
Venezuela	Aves	Cayenne Tern	100	0.026	1999	BAS
Puerto Rico	Culebra (Flamenco)	Sooty Tern	8,000	0.025	2005	JES
Cuba	Sevilla	Brown Pelican	60	0.025	1998	JRB
Dom. Rep.	San Lorenzo Bay	Magnificent Frigatebird	150	0.025	1962	DSL
Tobago	St. Giles	Red-footed Booby	402	0.024	2000	BNR
Rum Cay	Carmichael Pond	Gull-billed Tern	6	0.024	1989	BUD
St. Thomas	Dutchcap	Brown Booby	150	0.021	1996	JPI
St. John	Carval Rock	Roseate Tern	77	0.021	1992	JPI
Jamaica	S/SW Pedro	Magnificent Frigatebird	115	0.019	2005	ASU
Exumas	Allan's	Audubon's Shearwater	50	0.019	2003	WAM
Tobago	St. Giles	Magnificent Frigatebird	108	0.018	2000	BNR
British V.I.	Anegada	Gull-billed Tern	4	0.016	2005	MGO
British V.I.	Anegada	Sandwich Tern	25	0.016	2005	MGO
Jamaica	S/SW Pedro	Brown Booby	100	0.014	2005	ASU
Antigua	Burma Quarry	Roseate Tern	50	0.014	1999	JES
Antigua	Antigua	Roseate Tern	50	0.014	1984	VHN

Note: Ratio describes the proportion of the population of the listed species that occurs on the threatened island.

Table 27.4. Regions in need of surveys

Region	Year	Colonies	Lowest Estimate	Highest Estimate	Range	Range/Colony
Windward Islands	1968	53	39,235	52,869	13,634	257.2
Southern Bahamas	1992	27	1,464	2,008	544	20.1
Western Caribbean	1993	6	212	2,084	1,872	312.0
Hispaniola	1993	27	133,175	135,897	2,722	100.8
Little Bahama Bank	1994	24	248	590	342	14.3
Great Bahama Bank	1995	129	11,597	16,391	4,794	37.2
Morant Bank	1995	4	76,125	88,044	11,919	2979.8
Jamaica	1995	40	950	1,320	370	9.3
Cay Sal Bank	1996	7	18,472	19,220	748	106.9
Cuba	1997	70	5,750	7,229	1,479	21.1
Eastern Bahamas	1998	29	2,219	2,478	259	8.9
Central Caribbean	1999	12	15,513	21,293	5,780	481.7
Pedro Bank	2000	5	489	5,323	4,834	966.8
Leeward Islands	2000	202	96,893	150,098	53,205	263.4
Cayman Islands	2001	23	5,730	6,880	1,150	50.0
Coastal S. America	2001	44	16,933	23,455	6,522	148.2
Turks Bank	2001	10	54,790	55,632	842	84.2
Caicos Bank	2001	23	26,954	27,387	433	18.8
Puerto Rico	2001	53	48,765	51,740	2,975	56.1
Bermuda	2005	18	888	1,241	353	19.6

Note: Regions of the West Indies are listed in order of the average year of last survey for colonies. Estimates are for numbers of breeding pairs. Range shows the range between highest and lowest estimates, and Range/Colony indicates the average uncertainty per known nesting colony in a region.

Table 27.5. Year and species of seabirds nesting in the Caribbean, Bermuda, and the West Indies

Chapter 2

Island Name	Island Group	Region	Rank	Total Pairs	Contributor	Last Survey	Species Codes
Admiralty House Park*	Pembroke Parish	Bermuda	1	1	JLM	2005	5
Astwood Park*	Warwick Parish	Bermuda	1	1	JLM	2005	5
Bermuda Mainland	Bermuda	Bermuda	0	0	JLM	2005	1, 4, 17, 19
Castle Harbour Islands	Bermuda	Bermuda	2	651	JLM	2005	5*, 20
Daniel's Head	Somerset Island	Bermuda	1	1	JLM	2005	5
Ely's Harbour Island	Sandys Parish	Bermuda	1	2	JLM	2005	5, 20
Ferry Point Park	St. George's Island	Bermuda	1	1	JLM	2005	5
Great Head Park	St. David's Island	Bermuda	1	1	JLM	2005	5
Great Sound	Warwick Parish	Bermuda	1	1	JLM	2005	20
Hamilton Harbour	Paget Parish	Bermuda	1	1	JLM	2005	20
Harrington Sound	Hamilton Parish	Bermuda	1	2	JLM	2005	5, 20
Mangrove Bay	Sandys Parish	Bermuda	1	1	JLM	2005	20
Nonsuch	Bermuda	Bermuda	2	71	JLM	2006	1*
Railway Trail Park	Somerset Island	Bermuda	1	1	JLM	2005	5
South Shore Park*	Warwick Parish	Bermuda	1	1	JLM	2005	5
Southampton High Point	Bermuda	Bermuda	1	150	JLM	2005	5
Spittal Pond	Smiths Parish	Bermuda	1	1	JLM	2005	5
Wreck Hill Estate	Sandys Parish	Bermuda	1	1	JLM	2005	5

Chapter 3

Island Name	Island Group	Region	Rank	Total Pairs	Contributor	Last Survey	Species Codes
Abner	Berry Islands	Great Bahama Bank	1	0	KUS	2002	17, 19
Abraham's Bay	Mayaguana	Southern Bahamas	1	3	BRH	1999	17
Acklins	Acklins	Southern Bahamas	0	2	VHN	1998	5, 17, 19
Alder	Berry Islands	Great Bahama Bank	2	400	KUS	2002	13, 15, 16, 19*
Allan's	Exumas	Great Bahama Bank	0	50	WAM	2003	4
Alligator	Exumas	Great Bahama Bank	1	100	DSL	1994	13
Anguillas	Cay Sal	Cay Sal Bank	2	95	BRH	1996	19*, 22
Atwood	Samana Cay	Southern Bahamas	1	34	BRH	1999	4, 5, 11, 13, 15, 16
Battleship	Exumas	Great Bahama Bank	1	150	WAM	2003	13, 15
Berries	Berry Islands	Great Bahama Bank	0	0	TOW	1999	5
Bight of Acklins	Acklins	Southern Bahamas	1	1	AXS	1984	12
Bimini	Bimini	Great Bahama Bank	0	5	VHN	1984	11, 13, 15, 16, 17, 19
Bird Rock	Crooked	Southern Bahamas	1	0	NOR	1979	22
Boat House Rock	Rum Cay	Eastern Bahamas	1	26	BUD	1989	16, 17
Booby	Conception	Eastern Bahamas	1	2	BRH	1984	13, 15
Booby	Mayaguana	Southern Bahamas	0	71	BON	1998	5, 8, 11
Brine Pond	Cat Island	Great Bahama Bank	2	12	BUD	1986	18*
Buena Vista	Ragged Islands	Great Bahama Bank	1	10	BRH	1999	5, 12, 15, 18, 19
Bushes	Berry Islands	Great Bahama Bank	1	1	KUS	2002	19

Cape Verde Cliffs	Long Island	Great Bahama Bank	0	0	BUD	1990	8
Carmichael Pond	Rum Cay	Eastern Bahamas	0	17	BUD	1989	17, 18, 19
Castle	Acklins	Southern Bahamas	1	1	BRH	2005	15
Cat	Berry Islands	Great Bahama Bank	1	0	KUS	2002	18
Cat's East Coast	Cat Island	Great Bahama Bank	1	1	BUD	1982	5
Catto	San Salvador	Eastern Bahamas	1	312	HAY	2003	4, 8, 9, 11, 13, 15, 16, 19, 21
Cay Lobos	Ragged Islands	Great Bahama Bank	2	144	ECA	1998	15, 17, 19, 22*
Cay Sal	Cay Sal	Cay Sal Bank	1	150	AXS	1996	12, 17
Cay Verde	Ragged Islands	Great Bahama Bank	2	616	ECA	1998	4, 5, 8*, 11, 12, 13, 15, 16
Channel	Exumas	Great Bahama Bank	2	250	WAM	2002	4*, 13, 15
Channel Rocks	Little Bahama Bank	Little Bahama Bank	1	1	AXS	1984	16
Chub	Berry Islands	Great Bahama Bank	1	2	KUS	2002	17
Clarence Town Harbor	Long Island	Great Bahama Bank	1	3	AXS	1984	16, 29, 22
Columbus Point	Cat Island	Great Bahama Bank	1	10	BUD	1986	13
Conception	Conception	Eastern Bahamas	1	75	AXS	1998	4, 5, 16
Conch Shell Point	Great Inagua	Southern Bahamas	1	1	TOW	2005	5
Crab Rock	Abaco	Little Bahama Bank	1	20	TOW	2001	19
Crooked	Crooked	Southern Bahamas	1	2	AXS	1998	5, 13
Cut	San Salvador	Eastern Bahamas	1	1	HAY	2003	4
Damas	Cay Sal	Cay Sal Bank	2	6075	WAM	1996	13, 15, 16*
Danger	Exumas	Great Bahama Bank	1	250	WAM	2006	13, 15
Deep Lake	Long Island	Great Bahama Bank	1	2	BUD	1990	17
Dog Rocks	Cay Sal	Cay Sal Bank	2	6075	WAM	1996	13, 15, 16*
Dolly's Rock	South Andros	Great Bahama Bank	2	477	NOR	1984	15, 16, 21*, 22*
Don't Rock	Abaco	Little Bahama Bank	1	17	BRC	2003	13, 19
Double-headed Shots	Cay Sal	Cay Sal Bank	1	1	AXS	1984	4
Duck	Exumas	Great Bahama Bank	1	127	BSM	1999	12, 13, 15, 16
Duck	Exumas	Great Bahama Bank	1	101	BSM	2000	12, 17
Duncan Town	Ragged Islands	Great Bahama Bank	1	6	BRH	1999	18
East of Channel	Exumas	Great Bahama Bank	1	15	BRH	2000	19
East Pimlicos	Exumas	Great Bahama Bank	1	15	WAM	2002	4, 5
East Plana	Plana Cays	Southern Bahamas	1	2	BUD	1998	4, 5
Elbow	Abaco	Little Bahama Bank	1	1	VHN	1998	5, 17
Elbow	Exumas	Great Bahama Bank	1	10	WAM	2005	5
Elbow	Cay Sal	Cay Sal Bank	1	1	BRH	2005	4, 8
Eleuthera	Eleuthera	Great Bahama Bank	0	2	VHN	1999	4, 17, 18
Emerald Rock	Exumas	Great Bahama Bank	1	50	WAM	2006	13, 15
Exuma Bridge	Exumas	Great Bahama Bank	1	1	BSM	2001	17
Exuma Ferry Cays	Exumas	Great Bahama Bank	2	33	BSM	2001	5, 12, 16, 21*
Fernandez Bay	Cat Island	Great Bahama Bank	1	4	BUD	1986	16
Fernandez Cays	Cat Island	Great Bahama Bank	1	18	BUD	1986	16, 19
Finley	Eleuthera	Great Bahama Bank	1	1	AXS	1984	15
Fish	Abaco	Little Bahama Bank	1	17	VHN	1998	4, 5, 15, 19
Flat Top Rock	Exumas	Great Bahama Bank	1	10	CR2	2000	12
French Wells Sandbar	Crooked	Southern Bahamas	1	1	NOR	1997	19, 22
Frozen	Berry Islands	Great Bahama Bank	1	1401	KUS	2002	13, 16, 17, 19
Ft. George*	Bahamas	Great Bahama Bank	1	1	JJA	1999	17

Table 27.5.—Continued

240

Island Name	Island Group	Region	Rank	Total Pairs	Contributor	Last Survey	Species Codes
Galliot	Long Island	Great Bahama Bank	2	152	BUD	1991	13, 19*, 22
Gambier Lake	Cat Island	Great Bahama Bank	2	77	BUD	1986	17, 18*, 21*
Gaulin	San Salvador	Eastern Bahamas	1	267	HAY	2003	4, 13, 15, 16, 19
Gaulin	Exumas	Great Bahama Bank	1	3	BSM	2000	5
Glass Window Cliffs	Eleuthera	Great Bahama Bank	1	0	DSL	1999	5
Goat	Little San Salvador	Great Bahama Bank	1	19	AXS	1984	5, 13, 15, 16, 19
Gold Rock	Acklins	Southern Bahamas	1	50	TOW	1997	13
Goulding	New Providence	Great Bahama Bank	1	250	BRH	2003	13, 15, 16
Goulding	San Salvador	Eastern Bahamas	1	15	HAY	2003	4, 16
Graham's Harbour	San Salvador	Eastern Bahamas	1	26	HAY	2003	4, 5
Grassy	Exumas	Great Bahama Bank	1	271	BSM	2000	13, 15, 16, 19, 22
Grassy Creek	South Andros	Great Bahama Bank	1	4	AXS	1998	5, 13, 15, 16
Great Guana	Abaco	Little Bahama Bank	1	1	DSL	1998	5
Great Lake	Long Island	Great Bahama Bank	1	3	BUD	1990	18
Great Lakes	San Salvador	Eastern Bahamas	1	5	HAY	2003	18
Green	San Salvador	Eastern Bahamas	1	308	HAY	2003	4, 13, 15, 16, 19
Green	South Andros	Great Bahama Bank	0	1	DSL	1884	4
Grog Pond	Exumas	Great Bahama Bank	1	5	WHI	1997	17
Guana	Cat Island	Great Bahama Bank	1	77	BUD	1986	13, 16
Guana*	Berry Islands	Great Bahama Bank	1	0	KUS	2002	18
Gun Bluff	Crooked	Southern Bahamas	1	1	DSL	1998	5
Halls Pond	Exumas	Great Bahama Bank	1	1	DSL	1998	5, 19
Hawksbill	Exumas	Great Bahama Bank	1	58	BUD	2000	5, 19, 21, 22
Hawksbill Rock	Exumas	Great Bahama Bank	1	1	BRH	1984	19
High	Berry Islands	Great Bahama Bank	1	22	KUS	2002	13, 16
High	South Andros	Great Bahama Bank	1	1	AXS	1984	13
High	San Salvador	Eastern Bahamas	1	124	HAY	2003	4, 17, 19
Hogsty Reef	Inagua	Southern Bahamas	2	150	NOR	1979	22*
Hole-in-the-Wall	Abaco	Little Bahama Bank	1	10	DSL	1998	5
Hurricane Hole	Abaco	Little Bahama Bank	1	1	DSL	1998	5
Inland Areas*	Great Inagua	Southern Bahamas	2	263	JPA	2000	17*, 18, 21
Jumentos	Ragged Islands	Great Bahama Bank	1	1	DSL	1998	5
Jump Off Rocks	Walker's Cay	Little Bahama Bank	1	1	AXS	1984	15
Landrail Point	Crooked	Southern Bahamas	1	1	DSL	1998	5
Liberty Rock	Rum Cay	Eastern Bahamas	1	1	BUD	1989	5
Lightning Rocks	Exumas	Great Bahama Bank	1	31	DSL	1994	15, 19, 22
Little Bell Island	Exumas	Great Bahama Bank	1	18	BRH	1998	5, 16, 17, 19
Little Cistern	Exumas	Great Bahama Bank	0	55	WAM	2006	4, 12
Little Elizabeth	Exumas	Great Bahama Bank	1	60	BSM	1999	17, 20
Little Green	South Andros	Great Bahama Bank	1	2	AXS	1984	15, 16
Little Harbor	Abaco	Little Bahama Bank	1	1	DSL	1998	5
Little Harbor	Long Island	Great Bahama Bank	1	2	BUD	1990	13, 15
Little Hawksbill	Exumas	Great Bahama Bank	1	1	DSL	1994	5
Little Inagua	Little Inagua	Southern Bahamas	1	126	JJA	1999	5, 17

continued

Little Pigeon	Exumas	Great Bahama Bank	2	300	BSM	1998	15, 19, 22*
Little San Salvador	Little San Salvador	Eastern Bahamas	1	4	AXS	2000	5, 15, 16, 19
Little Walker's	Walker's Cay	Little Bahama Bank	1	1	DSL	1999	4, 15
Little Whale	Berry Islands	Great Bahama Bank	1	75	KUS	2002	19
Lochabar	Long Island	Great Bahama Bank	1	200	BUD	1988	15
Long	Exumas	Great Bahama Bank	2	800	WAM	2000	4*
Long Rocks	Little San Salvador	Great Bahama Bank	1	1	AXS	1984	13
Low	San Salvador	Eastern Bahamas	1	14	HAY	2003	4, 16
Low Rock	San Salvador	Eastern Bahamas	1	30	HAY	2003	16, 19, 21
Lucaya Beach	Grand Bahama	Little Bahama Bank	1	7	EGA	2002	17
Malabars	Exumas	Great Bahama Bank	1	1	WAM	2006	4, 16
Mamma Rhoda Rock	Berry Islands	Great Bahama Bank	1	276	KUS	2002	13, 15, 16, 19, 21
Manhead	San Salvador	Eastern Bahamas	1	41	HAY	2003	4, 16
Man-o-War	Exumas	Great Bahama Bank	1	35	BSM	2000	5, 11, 15, 16
Man-o-War Bush	Abaco	Little Bahama Bank	1	1	KUS	2004	11
Mayaguana	Mayaguana	Southern Bahamas	1	1	BRH	2005	4, 5
McKenzie Pond	Long Island	Great Bahama Bank	2	15	BUD	1990	18*
Meritek Ponds	Long Island	Great Bahama Bank	0	25	BUD	1990	15, 16, 19
Moriah Harbour	Exumas	Great Bahama Bank	1	16	BSM	2000	5, 17, 18
Muertos	Cay Sal	Cay Sal Bank	2	6075	WAM	1996	13, 15, 16*
Munjack Cay Rocks	Abaco	Little Bahama Bank	1	0	BRC	2003	19
N. Channel Rocks	Exumas	Great Bahama Bank	1	18	TOW	2001	13, 15, 16, 19, 22
Nancy	San Salvador	Eastern Bahamas	1	4	HAY	2000	4
Narrow Water	Exumas	Great Bahama Bank	1	112	DSL	2006	13, 15
New Providence	New Providence	Great Bahama Bank	0	0	AXS	1984	11
Noddy	Exumas	Great Bahama Bank	2	50	WAM	2000	4*
No-name	Abaco	Little Bahama Bank	1	2	BRC	2003	16, 19
North Bimini	Berry Islands	Great Bahama Bank	1	0	BRH	1999	17
North Fish	Berry Islands	Great Bahama Bank	1	250	KUS	2002	12
North Mariah Harbour	Exumas	Great Bahama Bank	1	120	BSM	2001	15, 19
North Market Fish	Berry Islands	Great Bahama Bank	1	20	KUS	2002	12
North Point Bluffs	San Salvador	Eastern Bahamas	1	11	HAY	2000	4
North Rock	Mira-Por-Vos	Southern Bahamas	2	600	DSL	1998	8*
NW Cliffs	Long Island	Great Bahama Bank	1	5	BUD	1990	5
Old Kerrs	Abaco	Little Bahama Bank	1	29	KUS	2004	19
O'Niel's Pond	Long Island	Great Bahama Bank	2	10	BUD	1990	18*
Pee Wee Point	Rum Cay	Eastern Bahamas	1	13	BUD	1989	5
Pelican	Exumas	Great Bahama Bank	1	23	BSM	2001	13, 15, 20
Pelican	Exumas	Great Bahama Bank	1	3	BSM	2001	13, 15, 16
Pelicans	Abaco	Little Bahama Bank	1	28	RNO	2004	4, 13, 15, 16, 17, 19
Peterson	Grand Bahama	Little Bahama Bank	1	50	EGA	2004	16
Petits	Berry Islands	Great Bahama Bank	1	475	KUS	2002	12, 13, 16, 17, 19
Pigeon	San Salvador	Eastern Bahamas	1	260	HAY	2003	12
Pigeon Creek East	San Salvador	Eastern Bahamas	1	1	HAY	2003	4
Pimlico Rocks	Exumas	Great Bahama Bank	1	0	WAM	1999	4

Table 27.5.—*Continued*

Island Name	Island Group	Region	Rank	Total Pairs	Contributor	Last Survey	Species Codes
Pond NE of O'Niel's	Long Island	Great Bahama Bank	1	2	BUD	1990	17
Pond S of Gordons	Long Island	Great Bahama Bank	1	10	BUD	1990	22
Porte Howe Cliffs	Cat Island	Great Bahama Bank	1	1	BUD	1986	5
Red Pond	Cat Island	Great Bahama Bank	1	1	BUD	1986	18
Rhoda Rocks	Abaco	Little Bahama Bank	1	2	AXS	1984	15, 16
Rock South of Cistern	Exumas	Great Bahama Bank	1	20	DSL	1994	17
Rocky Dundas	Exumas	Great Bahama Bank	1	1	DSL	1994	4
Rum	Berry Islands	Great Bahama Bank	1	1200	KUS	2002	15, 16
Rum	Rum Cay	Eastern Bahamas	1	143	AXS	2000	5, 17, 18, 19, 21
S Cat Shore	Cat Island	Great Bahama Bank	1	1	DSL	2000	13
Saddle	Exumas	Great Bahama Bank	1	31	WAM	2006	13, 15, 16
Sail Rocks	Exumas	Great Bahama Bank	1	2	AXS	1984	12, 15
Salina Point	Acklins	Southern Bahamas	1	1	DSL	2000	17
Salt	New Providence	Great Bahama Bank	0	0	TOW	1998	19
Salt Lakes*	Great Inagua	Southern Bahamas	2	126	AXS	2000	19, 22*
Salt Pond	Rum Cay	Eastern Bahamas	0	33	BUD	1989	17, 18
San Salvador	San Salvador	Eastern Bahamas	1	16	JJA	1999	4, 5, 17
Sandy	Berry Islands	Great Bahama Bank	1	25	KUS	2002	12
Sandy	Exumas	Great Bahama Bank	1	20	WAM	2005	4, 5
Sandy	Exumas	Great Bahama Bank	1	1	BSM	2001	21
Sandy Point	Rum Cay	Eastern Bahamas	1	5	BUD	1989	21
Santo Domingo	Ragged Islands	Great Bahama Bank	0	0	ECA	1998	7, 8
Schooners	Eleuthera	Great Bahama Bank	1	11	AXS	1984	12, 21, 22
Seal	Ragged Islands	Great Bahama Bank	0	0	AXS	1987	5, 11
Ship Channels	Exumas	Great Bahama Bank	1	1	AXS	1984	12
Shroud	Exumas	Great Bahama Bank	1	25	WAM	2005	5
Slipper*	Acklins	Southern Bahamas	1	1	NOR	2003	10
Smiths	Exumas	Great Bahama Bank	1	2	BSM	2001	19, 22
Smokey Point Salt Pond	Cat Island	Great Bahama Bank	2	31	BUD	1986	17, 18*
South Market Fish	Berry Islands	Great Bahama Bank	1	25	KUS	2002	12, 17, 19
South Mira-Por-Vos	Mira-Por-Vos	Southern Bahamas	1	5	BUD	1987	4, 8, 13, 15, 16
South Rocks	Conception	Eastern Bahamas	1	19	AXS	1998	4, 5, 13, 15, 16, 21
South Stirrup	Berry Islands	Great Bahama Bank	1	0	KUS	2002	17
South Westridge Estate	New Providence	Great Bahama Bank	1	37	TOW	2005	17, 18
Southwest Point	San Salvador	Eastern Bahamas	1	10	HAY	1999	17
Spoil Island	Abaco	Little Bahama Bank	1	10	BRC	2000	17
Stirrup	Long Island	Great Bahama Bank	1	25	BSM	2003	19
Strachan	Long Island	Great Bahama Bank	1	1510	BUD	1990	13, 15
Tait's Pond	Long Island	Great Bahama Bank	2	3	BUD	1990	18*
Tea Bay Ponds	Cat Island	Great Bahama Bank	1	1	BUD	1982	18
Tea Table Rock	Exumas	Great Bahama Bank	1	22	WAM	2002	16, 21
Tee	Little San Salvador	Great Bahama Bank	1	1	AXS	1984	13
The Gulf Bluffs	San Salvador	Eastern Bahamas	1	24	HAY	2000	4

continued

				Total		Last	
		Region	Rank	Pairs	Contributor	Survey	Species Codes
Tilloo	Abaco	Little Bahama Bank	1	23	RPG	2004	5, 16, 17, 19
Tom Brown's	Walker's Cay	Little Bahama Bank	1	2	DSL	1984	4, 15
Twins	Exumas	Great Bahama Bank	1	1	DSL	1994	4
Two Rocks	Abaco	Little Bahama Bank	1	2	BRC	2003	16
Upper Lakes*	Great Inagua	Southern Bahamas	1	1	AXS	1984	10
Warderick Wells	Exumas	Great Bahama Bank	1	44	DSL	2005	5, 17, 18
Washerwoman	South Andros	Great Bahama Bank	1	4	AXS	1984	4, 13, 15, 16
Waters	Ragged Islands	Great Bahama Bank	1	3	BSM	2005	5, 13, 17
West Little Pigeon	Exumas	Great Bahama Bank	1	3	BSM	1998	15, 19, 22
West of North Channel	Exumas	Great Bahama Bank	2	100	BSM	1999	22*
West Pelican	Exumas	Great Bahama Bank	1	50	BSM	1998	15
West Pimlicos	Exumas	Great Bahama Bank	1	51	WAM	2002	4, 12
West Plana	Plana Cays	Southern Bahamas	1	1	DSL	1998	5
West Thunderball Rock	Exumas	Great Bahama Bank	1	50	WAM	2003	13
Whale	Abaco	Little Bahama Bank	1	21	TWH	2003	15, 16, 19
White	Berry Islands	Great Bahama Bank	1	60	KUS	2002	12, 16, 19
White	San Salvador	Eastern Bahamas	1	431	HAY	2003	7, 8, 9, 11, 13, 15, 16, 19
White	North of Plana	Southern Bahamas	0	0	DSL	1998	7, 8

Chapter 4

Island Name	Island Group	Region	Rank	Total Pairs	Contributor	Last Survey	Species Codes
Big Iguana	Caicos	Caicos Bank	1	1	DSL	1998	5
Big Sand	Turks	Turks Bank	2	44286	PNK	2002	5, 13, 15*, 16, 17
Bush	Bush & Seals	Caicos Bank	2	4525	PNK	2002	13*, 15, 16
Cotton	Turks	Turks Bank	1	1	DSL	1998	5
Dove	Caicos	Caicos Bank	1	1	DSL	1998	5
East	Turks	Turks Bank	1	194	PNK	2005	4, 12, 13, 17, 22
East Caicos	Caicos	Caicos Bank	1	2	AXS	1998	5, 8
Fish	Outer Caicos	Caicos Bank	2	350	PNK	2002	13, 15, 16, 19
Five Cays	Providenciales	Caicos Bank	1	66	PNK	2004	4, 5, 17
French	Caicos	Caicos Bank	2	11161	PNK	2002	5, 12, 13*, 15, 16
Grand Turk	Turks	Turks Bank	2	554	PNK	2004	5, 11, 12, 17*, 20, 21, 22
Highas	Middle Caicos	Caicos Bank	1	50	PNK	2002	5, 13, 16
Indian*	Bush & Seals	Caicos Bank	2	4000	PNK	2002	13*, 15
Joe Grant's	East Caicos	Caicos Bank	1	10	PNK	2004	5
Little Ambergris	Outer Caicos	Caicos Bank	2	580	PNK	2002	12, 19*, 21, 22*
Little Sand	Sand Cays	Turks Bank	1	2	PNK	2005	12, 19
Little Water	Caicos	Caicos Bank	1	10	DSL	1998	5
Long	Caicos	Caicos Bank	1	2	PNK	2005	4, 5
Long	Turks	Turks Bank	2	6063	PNK	2002	5, 13*, 16
Man-o-War Bush	Middle Caicos	Caicos Bank	1	35	PNK	2002	11
Middle Caicos	Middle Caicos	Caicos Bank	2	1862	PNK	2005	4, 5, 11, 12*, 16, 17, 18*, 21*, 22*
Northern Coast	East Caicos	Caicos Bank	2	231	PNK	2004	4, 17, 20

Table 27.5.—*Continued*

Island Name	Island Group	Region	Rank	Total Pairs	Contributor	Last Survey	Species Codes
Pear	Turks	Turks Bank	1	0	PNK	2005	5
Pear	Bush & Seals	Caicos Bank	1	50	PNK	2002	13
Penniston	Turks	Turks Bank	2	3310	PNK	2002	8, 11, 13, 16*
Pine	Caicos	Caicos Bank	1	2	JJA	1999	5, 17
Round	Gibbs Cay	Turks Bank	1	101	PNK	2002	13, 16
Salt	Turks	Turks Bank	1	279	PNK	2004	5, 12, 17, 19, 21, 22
Six Hills	South Caicos	Caicos Bank	1	13	PNK	2004	4, 5, 13, 15, 16
South Caicos	Caicos	Caicos Bank	1	1	DSL	1998	5
Stubbs	Caicos	Caicos Bank	1	1	DSL	1998	5
West Caicos	Caicos	Caicos Bank	1	0	NOR	1998	22
Whites	Outer Caicos	Caicos Bank	2	4001	PNK	2002	13*, 15, 16

Chapter 5

Island Name	Island Group	Region	Rank	Total Pairs	Contributor	Last Survey	Species Codes
Alcatraz small cays	Sabinal	Cuba	1	10	JRB	2001	10
Baitiquiri	Guantanamo	Cuba	1	1	JRB	2005	5
Ballenato	Camaguey	Cuba	2	191	JRB	2004	12, 13, 16, 17, 19, 21, 22*
Ballenatos	Isle of Youth	Cuba	1	1	JRB	2006	19
Borracho	Cuba	Cuba	1	19	JRB	1989	11, 13, 15
Breton	Cuba	Cuba	1	1	JRB	1998	10
Broqueles	Nipe Bay (Holguin)	Cuba	1	100	JRB	1998	10
Caiman de los Cayuelos	Cuba	Cuba	1	2	JRB	1960	11, 13
Caiman de Sotavento	Villa Clara	Cuba	1	124	JRB	1989	11, 13, 16, 21
Canalizo Baliza Vieja	Punta Alegre	Cuba	1	1	JRB	1998	10
Cay de Dios*	South Zapata Swamp	Cuba	1	4	JRB	1991	8, 13, 15, 16
Cayo de Piedras	Sancti Spirtu	Cuba	1	4	JRB	2005	8, 12, 17, 21
Cays del Marco	Cays del Marco	Cuba	1	64	JRB	2005	16, 22
Cays del Mono	Cuba	Cuba	2	57	JRB	2005	16, 20*, 22
Cayuelo de la Vela	Villa Clara	Cuba	1	72	JRB	2005	16, 17, 19, 21
Chocolate	Jardines de la Reina	Cuba	1	1	JRB	2005	11
Cienaga de Biramas*	Cuba	Cuba	1	55	JRB	2003	12, 21
Cinco Balas	Jardines de la Reina	Cuba	1	1	JRB	2005	11
Cinco Leguas	Matanzas	Cuba	1	6	JRB	2005	12, 21
Cruz	Cuba	Cuba	1	20	JRB	2002	17
Dutton	Los Pajonales	Cuba	1	121	JRB	2004	16
Estero de Caza	Isle of Youth	Cuba	1	34	JRB	1983	17
Eusebio del Oeste*	Ciego de Avila	Cuba	1	88	JRB	2002	11
Faro de la Juala*	Cays of San Felipe	Cuba	1	375	JRB	2002	12, 13, 15, 16, 21
Fauna Refuge Rio Maximo	Cuba	Cuba	1	68	JRB	2003	10, 11, 12
Felipe de Barlovento*	Cays of San Felipe	Cuba	1	457	JRB	2005	12, 13, 15, 16, 21, 22, 23
Felipe de Sotavento*	Cays of San Felipe	Cuba	1	225	JRB	2002	12, 13, 15, 16
Fogon*	Pinar del Rio	Cuba	1	10	JRB	2002	12

continued

Fragoso	Cuba	1	118	JRB	2005	10, 17, 21
Galindo	Villa Clara	1	11	JRB	2005	12, 17, 21
Guajaba	Cuba	1	9	JRB	2002	10, 11, 17
Guanimars	La Habana	1	1	JRB	1958	17
Jato Bay*	Sabinal	1	1	JRB	1998	10
Jigue Bay	Cuba	1	1	JRB	1998	10
Juan Garcia	Cays of San Felipe	1	30	JRB	2003	17
La Lena	Guanahacabibes	1	1	JRB	2005	11
Laguna de Leonero*	Biramas Swamp	1	25	JRB	2003	17
Laguna Media Caza	Los Palacios of Pinar del Rio	1	1	JRB	2005	11
Las Salinas	Zapata Swamp	1	48	JRB	2004	12, 17
Loma de los Chivos	Guantanamo	1	1	DSL	1998	5
Los Canarreos	Los Canarreos	1	0	NOR	1998	22
Los Cayuelos	Los Perros Bay	1	1	JRB	1998	10
Los Felipes	Ciego de Avila	1	6	JRB	2000	4, 11, 13, 15, 16
Medialuna	Ciego de Avila	1	2	BSH	1998	21, 22
Megano de Bergantines	Cuba	1	1	JRB	1998	12
Mono Grande	Matanzas	1	2336	JRB	2005	8, 13, 15, 16, 17, 19
Monos de Jutias	Villa Clara	1	104	JRB	1998	15, 16, 17
Nuevitas Bay	Cuba	1	11	JRB	2002	10, 17
Pajaro*	North of Sabinal	1	30	JRB	2004	10
Palma	Isle of Youth	1	1	JRB	2005	21
Paredon de Lado	Ciego de Avila	2	279	JRB	2002	12, 13, 15*, 16, 21
Port Guatemala*	Nipe Bay	1	30	JRB	2002	22
Puerto Escondido	Guantanamo	1	0	DSL	1962	11
Punta Coscorrones	Sancti Spiritus	1	1	JRB	1998	10
Punta el Ingles	Cabo Cruz	1	80	DSL	1984	5
Punta Hicacos	Matanzas	1	28	JRB	2001	17, 19
Rabihorcado	Ciego de Avila	2	1	JRB	1998	11*
Rincon Guanal	Cuba	2	96	JRB	1980	17, 20*
Sabinal	Camaguey	2	163	JRB	2004	11, 17, 18*
Salina	South of Cay Coco	1	1	JRB	1998	10
Salinas de bido	Cuba	1	10	JRB	2004	17
Salto del Leon*	Sabinal	1	15	JRB	2001	10
Santa Cruz del Sur	Camaguey	1	20	JRB	2002	10
Santiago de Cuba Harbour	Santiago de Cuba	0	0	DSL	1998	5
Sevilla	Golf of Guacanayabo	0	60	JRB	1998	10
Sifonte**	Camaguey	2	74	JRB	2005	10, 11, 18*
Siju de San Felipe	Pinar del Rio	1	6	JRB	2004	17
Tio Pepe	Cuba	1	30	JRB	2003	17
Tortuga	Cuba	1	2	JRB	1998	12, 22
Verde*	Camaguey	1	3	JRB	2002	17

Table 27.5.—*Continued*

Chapter 6

Island Name	Island Group	Region	Rank	Total Pairs	Contributor	Last Survey	Species Codes
Booby Pond	Little Cayman	Cayman Islands	2	4086	PEB	2001	9*, 11*, 17
Central North Bluff	Cayman Brac	Cayman Islands	0	0	PEB	2000	8
Collier's Pond	Grand Cayman	Cayman Islands	1	40	PEB	1996	17
Crystal Harbour	Grand Cayman	Cayman Islands	1	5	PEB	2004	17
E Cayman Brac Bluff	Cayman Brac	Cayman Islands	1	150	PEB	2003	8
Grand Harbour	Grand Cayman	Cayman Islands	1	138	PEB	2004	17
Jackson's Pond	Little Cayman	Cayman Islands	0	0	PEB	2003	17
Jackson's Pond	Grand Cayman	Cayman Islands	1	30	PEB	2004	17
Lighthouse Pond	Little Cayman	Cayman Islands	1	0	PEB	2003	17
Malportas Pond	Grand Cayman	Cayman Islands	1	4	PEB	2003	17
Meagre Bay Pond	Grand Cayman	Cayman Islands	1	9	PEB	2004	17
North Sound Estates	Grand Cayman	Cayman Islands	1	122	PEB	1995	18
Pedro Beach Spoils	Grand Cayman	Cayman Islands	1	10	PEB	1997	5
Point of sand	Little Cayman	Cayman Islands	0	0	PEB	1997	17
Preston Bay	Little Cayman	Cayman Islands	0	0	PEB	2003	17
S Cayman Brac Bluff	Cayman Brac	Cayman Islands	1	10	PEB	2003	8
Salt Water Pond	Cayman Brac	Cayman Islands	1	3	PEB	2004	17
South Sound	Little Cayman	Cayman Islands	0	0	PEB	2006	9
Vidal Cay	Grand Cayman	Cayman Islands	1	16	PEB	2004	16
Westerly Pond	Cayman Brac	Cayman Islands	1	45	PEB	1997	17

Chapter 7

Island Name	Island Group	Region	Rank	Total Pairs	Contributor	Last Survey	Species Codes
Beside Half Moon	Portland Bight	Jamaica	1	5	ASU	1997	16
Big Half Moon	Portland Bight	Jamaica	1	2	ASU	2004	13, 16
Big Pelican	Portland Bight	Jamaica	0	0	ASU	1996	10
Blue/John Crow Mountains	Portland	Jamaica	0	0	ASU	1998	3
Bluefields	Westmoreland	Jamaica	0	0	ASU	1991	10
Bogue	St. James	Jamaica	0	1	ASU	1997	11, 17
Cow Bay Pen	Portland	Jamaica	1	15	ASU	1981	5
Drunkenman's	Port Royal	Jamaica	0	0	ASU	1997	10, 11
Falmouth/Martha Brae	Trelawny	Jamaica	0	1	ASU	1997	11
Fort Augusta	Port Royal	Jamaica	1	1	ASU	1997	10
Great Pedro Bluff	St. Elizabeth	Jamaica	0	0	ASU	2005	10
Great Pedro Pond	St. Elizabeth	Jamaica	1	1	ASU	2004	17
Greenwall	St. Thomas	Jamaica	1	1	ASU	1982	5
Gun	Port Royal	Jamaica	1	1	ASU	1997	10
Hectors River	Portland	Jamaica	1	24	ASU	1997	5
Jamaica	Jamaica	Jamaica	0	0	ASU	1998	11
Little Half Moon	Portland Bight	Jamaica	1	489	ASU	2005	13, 16

continued

Island Name	Island Group	Region	Rank	Total Pairs	Contributor	Last Survey	Species Codes
Luana/Font Hill	St. Elizabeth	Jamaica	0	0	ASU	2005	10
Middle Pedro	Pedro Group	Pedro Bank	2	76	ASU	2005	7*, 8, 13, 15
NE Morant	Morant Cays	Morant Bank	0	0	DSL	1999	13, 15
NE Pedro	Pedro Group	Pedro Bank	1	0	DSI	1998	8, 15
Near Big Portland	Portland Bight	Jamaica	1	1	ASU	1997	17
Negril	Westmoreland	Jamaica	1	3	ASU	1993	5
NW Morant	Morant Cays	Morant Bank	0	0	ASU	1997	15
Ocho Rios	St. Ann	Jamaica	1	15	ASU	1987	5
One Bush	Portland Bight	Jamaica	1	2	ASU	2005	16, 17
Oracabessa	St. Mary	Jamaica	1	15	ASU	1970	5
Parottee Pond	St. Elizabeth	Jamaica	1	13	ASU	1996	11, 17
Pelican	Portland Bight	Jamaica	1	1	ASU	1997	16, 19
Pigeon	Portland Bight	Jamaica	1	1	ASU	1997	16, 19
Port Royal Rocks	Port Royal	Jamaica	1	15	ASU	1997	16
Portland Ridge	Clarendon	Jamaica	1	15	ASU	1970	5
Portland Rock	Pedro Group	Pedro Bank	0	100	ASU	2005	13, 15
Refuge	Port Royal	Jamaica	2	150	ASU	2003	10*
Rocky Point	Clarendon	Jamaica	1	20	ASU	1996	17
Rocky Point Port Swamp	Clarendon	Jamaica	1	1	ASU	1997	17
S Port Royal	Port Royal	Jamaica	0	21	ASU	1997	10, 11, 16, 17, 19
S/SW Pedro	Pedro Group	Pedro Bank	0	303	ASU	2005	7, 8, 9, 11, 12, 13, 15, 19, 21, 22
Salt Island Creek	Portland Bight	Jamaica	1	2	ASU	1997	10, 11
Sand Bank	Portland Bight	Jamaica	1	16	ASU	2004	13, 16, 19
Savanna-la-Mar	Westmoreland	Jamaica	1	0	ASU	2006	10
SE Morant	Morant Cays	Morant Bank	2	74525	ASU	1997	4, 12, 13*, 15*
SE Pedro	Pedro Group	Pedro Bank	0	10	ASU	1997	21
SE Port Royal	Port Royal	Jamaica	0	8	ASU	1997	10, 16
SW Morant	Morant Cays	Morant Bank	1	1600	ASU	1996	13, 15, 16
Swift River	Manchester	Jamaica	1	10	ASU	1982	10
Two Bush	Portland Bight	Jamaica	1	100	ASU	2004	11
Westmoreland Cave	Westmoreland	Jamaica	0	0	ASU	2005	10
Yallah's Pond	St. Thomas	Jamaica	0	0	ASU	1997	10, 17

Chapter 8

Island Name	Island Group	Region	Rank	Total Pairs	Contributor	Last Survey	Species Codes
Alto Velo	Dom. Rep.	Hispaniola	2	80402	KTH	2005	5, 8, 10, 12, 13, 15*, 16, 19
Bahia Samana	Dom. Rep.	Hispaniola	1	1	VHN	1984	10, 16, 19, 22
Beata	Dom. Rep.	Hispaniola	2	50652	KTH	2005	5, 8, 10*, 12, 13, 15*, 16, 17*, 18, 19
Cabron	Dom. Rep.	Hispaniola	1	20	DSL	1998	5
Catalinita	Dom. Rep.	Hispaniola	1	3	KTH	2005	10, 12, 13, 15, 16, 17, 19, 23
Cayo de los Pajaros	Los Haitises	Hispaniola	1	50	KTH	2005	11
Cayo Puerto Rico	Laguna de Oviedo	Hispaniola	1	65	KTH	2003	12, 21, 22
Fregate	Gonave	Hispaniola	1	0	WAM	2005	11

Table 27.5.—Continued

Island Name	Island Group	Region	Rank	Total Pairs	Contributor	Last Survey	Species Codes
Ile a Vache	Haiti	Hispaniola	1	1	DSL	1998	5
Ile de la Gonave	Haiti	Hispaniola	0	0	DSL	2005	4, 10, 11
Ile de la Tortue	Haiti	Hispaniola	1	1	KTH	2006	5
Jean Rabel	Haiti	Hispaniola	1	1	KTH	2006	5
Jeremie	Haiti	Hispaniola	1	1	KTH	2005	5
Lomo de Toro	Sierra de Baoruco	Hispaniola	2	5	VHN	1984	2*
Los Frailes	Alto Velo	Hispaniola	1	10	KTH	2005	8
Morne La Visite	Massif de la Selle	Hispaniola	0	10	RIM	2005	2*
Navassa	Navassa	Hispaniola	1	171	KTH	2005	4, 5, 8, 9, 11, 12, 13, 16
Paso de Catuano	Saona	Hispaniola	1	35	KTH	2005	11
Pic Macaya	Massif de la Hotte	Hispaniola	2	1000	DSL	1999	2*
Rojo	Dom. Rep.	Hispaniola	1	60	DSL	1998	5
Samana Bay	Haiti	Hispaniola	1	0	BON	1956	11
San Lorenzo Bay	Dom. Rep.	Hispaniola	0	150	KTH	2005	11, 19
Saona	Dom. Rep.	Hispaniola	1	234	DSL	1998	5, 10, 11, 12, 13, 15, 16, 17, 19
SE Tip	Dom. Rep.	Hispaniola	0	0	VHN	1984	16, 20
Siete Hermanos	Monte Criste	Hispaniola	1	3	KTH	2005	13, 15, 16
Tete Opaque	Massif de la Selle	Hispaniola	2	300	RIM	1983	2*

Chapter 9

Island Name	Island Group	Region	Rank	Total Pairs	Contributor	Last Survey	Species Codes
Aguadilla Cliffs	Aguadilla	Puerto Rico	2	101	JES	2005	5*, 10
Alcarraza	Culebra	Puerto Rico	2	8235	JES	2005	4, 5*, 6, 7*, 8, 13, 15, 16
Barcelonata*	Vieques	Puerto Rico	1	75	FWS	1997	19
Blanquilla	Fajardo	Puerto Rico	0	300	JES	2005	13, 15, 22
Boqueron Refuge	Cabo Rojo	Puerto Rico	1	20	JES	1997	17
Botella	Culebra	Puerto Rico	0	0	JES	1940	15
Caja de Muerto	Ponce	Puerto Rico	1	2	DSL	1998	4, 5
Cayo del Agua	Culebra	Puerto Rico	1	141	JES	2005	4, 5, 13, 16
Conejo	Vieques	Puerto Rico	1	29	JES	2005	5, 6, 10, 17, 19
Corozo Salt Flats	Cabo Rojo	Puerto Rico	1	20	JES	2005	17
Cueva del Indio	Puerto Rico	Puerto Rico	1	15	JES	2005	16
Cuevas	Lajas	Puerto Rico	0	0	JES	2005	11
Culebra (Flamenco)	Culebra	Puerto Rico	0	8001	JES	2005	13, 15, 22
Culebrita	Culebra	Puerto Rico	1	0	JES	2005	4
Desecheo	Mayaguez	Puerto Rico	0	1	JES	2005	8, 9, 11, 16
Don Luis	Guanica	Puerto Rico	2	130	JES	2005	10*
Frio	Montalva Cays	Puerto Rico	1	10	JES	2005	10
Geniqui	Culebra	Puerto Rico	0	187	JES	2005	4, 5, 6, 8, 9, 12, 13, 15, 16
Guayanilla	Punta Verraco	Puerto Rico	1	2	JES	2005	17, 19, 22
Isla del Frio	Southeast Ponce	Puerto Rico	0	5	JES	2005	10
La Cordillera	Fajardo	Puerto Rico	0	0	JES	2005	8

Island Name	Island Group	Region	Rank	Total Pairs	Contributor	Last Survey	Species Codes
La Cucaracha	Cordilleras	Puerto Rico	1	10	JES	2005	12
La Jungla	Guanica	Puerto Rico	1	1	JES	1997	17
La Parguera	Lajas	Puerto Rico	2	700	JES	2005	10, 11, 19*
Lobito	Culebra	Puerto Rico	1	333	JES	2005	4, 6, 12, 16, 21, 22, 23
Lobos	Culebra	Puerto Rico	1	1	JES	2005	5, 6
Lobos Rocks	Fajardo	Puerto Rico	1	6	DSL	1998	5, 12, 13, 16, 21, 22
Luis Pena	Culebra	Puerto Rico	0	30	JES	2005	5, 6
Matojo	Culebra	Puerto Rico	1	14	FWS	2005	4, 6, 12, 16, 21, 22, 23
Mayaguez-Anasco Cliffs	Puerto Rico	Puerto Rico	0	0	JES	2005	10
Media Luna East	Lajas	Puerto Rico	2	260	JES	2005	15, 19, 22*
Media Luna West	Lajas	Puerto Rico	2	260	JES	2005	15, 19, 22*
Molinos	Culebra	Puerto Rico	1	8134	JES	2005	5, 6, 13, 15, 16, 19, 22
Mona	Mayaguez	Puerto Rico	2	1805	JES	2005	4, 5, 7, 8, 9*, 12, 13, 15, 16
Monito	Mayaguez	Puerto Rico	2	2115	JES	2005	4, 5, 7*, 8*, 9*, 11*, 12, 13, 15, 16
Montalva	Guanica	Puerto Rico	0	0	JES	2005	10
Morrillito	Ponce	Puerto Rico	1	40	JES	2005	10
Naval Base	Ceiba	Puerto Rico	1	3	JES	2005	17
Noroeste	Culebra	Puerto Rico	1	8122	JES	2005	13, 14, 15, 16
Norte	Culebra	Puerto Rico	1	0	JES	2005	5, 6
Ponce Cliffs	Ponce	Puerto Rico	1	2	DSL	1998	5, 19
Providencia	Puerto Rico	Puerto Rico	0	0	NAR	2005	4
Punta Cucharas	Ponce	Puerto Rico	1	2	DSL	1998	6, 17
Punta Soldado	Culebra	Puerto Rico	0	5	WAM	2005	5, 19
Quebradillas Cliffs	Quebradillas	Puerto Rico	1	2	DSL	1998	5, 16
Raton	Culebra	Puerto Rico	1	132	JES	2005	4, 5, 6, 13, 16, 19
Ratones	Cabo Rojo	Puerto Rico	0	2	JES	2005	10
San Cristobal	Lajas	Puerto Rico	2	260	JES	2005	15, 19, 22*
Southwest Mainland	Puerto Rico	Puerto Rico	0	0	BAS	1999	11, 18, 20
Turrumote I	Lajas	Puerto Rico	2	260	JES	2005	15, 19, 22*
Turrumote II	Lajas	Puerto Rico	2	261	JES	2005	8, 15, 19, 22*
Unnamed volcanic rock	Cordilleras	Puerto Rico	2	600	JES	2005	8*
Yerba	Culebra	Puerto Rico	1	8131	JES	2005	4, 5, 13, 15, 16, 19

Chapter 10

Island Name	Island Group	Region	Rank	Total Pairs	Contributor	Last Survey	Species Codes
Booby Rock	St. John	Leeward Islands	1	17	JPI	1990	12, 16, 19
Buck	St. Croix	Leeward Islands	1	30	JPI	1996	10, 17
Buck & Capella	St. Thomas	Leeward Islands	0	55	BAS	1999	6, 12
Carval Rock	U.S. Virgins	Leeward Islands	0	122	JPI	1999	5, 6, 13, 16, 19
Cas	St. Thomas	Leeward Islands	0	5	JPI	2005	5, 6
Cockroach	St. Thomas	Leeward Islands	2	330	JPI	1999	4, 5, 6*, 7*, 8, 9, 13, 16, 21
Congo	U.S. Virgins	Leeward Islands	2	138	JPI	1999	5, 6, 10*, 13, 16
Cricket	St. Thomas	Leeward Islands	1	52	JPI	1999	5, 6, 8, 13, 16, 22

continued

Table 27.5.—*Continued*

Island Name	Island Group	Region	Rank	Total Pairs	Contributor	Last Survey	Species Codes
Current Cut	U.S. Virgins	Leeward Islands	1	100	BAS	1999	12
Dog Island	U.S. Virgins	Leeward Islands	2	343	JPI	1999	5, 6, 12, 15, 19, 21, 22*
Dutchcap	St. Thomas	Leeward Islands	0	387	BAS	1999	5, 6, 8, 9, 10, 11, 13, 16
Flanagan Island	St. John	Leeward Islands	2	304	BAS	1999	5, 6, 12, 13, 16, 19*
Flat and Little Flat	U.S. Virgins	Leeward Islands	1	501	BAS	1999	4, 6, 12, 13, 15, 16, 19, 21, 22
Frenchcap	St. Thomas	Leeward Islands	2	725	JPI	1999	4, 5, 6, 7*, 8, 9, 12, 13, 15, 16, 21
George Dog	U.S. Virgins	Leeward Islands	0	0	JPI	1998	11
Grass	St. Thomas	Leeward Islands	1	5	JPI	2005	6
Green	St. Croix	Leeward Islands	1	4	JPI	1997	5
Hans Lollick	St. Thomas	Leeward Islands	1	21	BAS	1999	5, 6, 10, 22
Hassel	U.S. Virgins	Leeward Islands	1	1	JPI	2006	5
Henley	U.S. Virgins	Leeward Islands	1	100	BAS	1999	12
Inner Brass	U.S. Virgins	Leeward Islands	1	1	JPI	2005	6
Kalkun	St. Thomas	Leeward Islands	1	135	JPI	1999	6, 8, 13, 16, 19*, 21
LeDuck	St. John	Leeward Islands	2	550	BAS	1999	12, 19*
Little Hans Lollick	St. Thomas	Leeward Islands	2	400	BAS	1999	12, 22*
Little St. James	U.S. Virgins	Leeward Islands	1	1	JPI	2005	6
Mingo	U.S. Virgins	Leeward Islands	1	19	JPI	1999	5, 6
Outer Brass	U.S. Virgins	Leeward Islands	1	3	JPI	1997	5
Pelican	St. Thomas	Leeward Islands	2	122	BAS	1999	15, 19*, 21, 22*
Ramgoat	U.S. Virgins	Leeward Islands	1	50	BAS	1999	12
Ram's Head	St. John	Leeward Islands	1	4	VHN	1999	5, 6, 20
Rata	U.S. Virgins	Leeward Islands	1	20	BAS	1999	12
Ruth	St. Croix	Leeward Islands	1	1	JPI	2006	17
Saba	St. Thomas	Leeward Islands	2	30372	JPI	1999	4, 6, 12, 13, 15*, 16, 19
Sail	U.S. Virgins	Leeward Islands	1	0	JPI	2005	6, 13
Saltpond Bay	St. John	Leeward Islands	1	2	JPI	2006	17
Savannah	U.S. Virgins	Leeward Islands	1	1	JPI	2005	6
Shark	St. Thomas	Leeward Islands	2	103	JPI	1996	6, 19*
St. Croix	St. Croix	Leeward Islands	1	300	VHN	2005	17, 20
St. Thomas	St. Thomas	Leeward Islands	0	1	BAS	1999	17, 18
Steven	St. John	Leeward Islands	1	20	JPI	2006	17
Sula	St. Thomas	Leeward Islands	0	36	JPI	2005	4, 6, 9, 13
Trunk	U.S. Virgins	Leeward Islands	1	100	BAS	1999	12
Turtledove	U.S. Virgins	Leeward Islands	2	370	JPI	1997	12, 13, 15, 16, 21, 22*
Two Brothers	St. Thomas	Leeward Islands	1	0	JPI	2005	6
Water	U.S. Virgins	Leeward Islands	1	7	JPI	1999	5, 6
Waterlemon	St. John	Leeward Islands	1	1	JPI	2006	10
Western St. Thomas	St. Thomas	Leeward Islands	1	1	DSL	1998	6
Whistling & Mary's Points	St. John	Leeward Islands	1	6	JPI	1999	5, 6, 10

Chapter 11

Island Name	Island Group	Region	Rank	Total Pairs	Contributor	Last Survey	Species Codes
Anegada	Anegada	Leeward Islands	0	91	MGO	2005	4, 11, 12, 15, 16, 17, 22
Beef	Tortola	Leeward Islands	0	2	BAS	2005	17, 22
Broken Jerusalem	Ginger	Leeward Islands	1	4	BAS	2005	4, 15, 16, 19
Carrot Rock	Peter	Leeward Islands	1	4	MGO	2005	12, 16, 19
Carval Rock	Ginger	Leeward Islands	1	5	MGO	2005	12, 13, 15, 16
Cistern	Cooper	Leeward Islands	1	2	MGO	2005	12, 19
Cockroach	Virgin Gorda	Leeward Islands	2	12	MGO	2005	6, 12, 16, 19*
Cooper	Cooper	Leeward Islands	1	4	MGO	2005	4, 16, 19
Deadmans Chest	Peter	Leeward Islands	1	1	MGO	2005	12
East Seal Dog	Virgin Gorda	Leeward Islands	1	3	MGO	2005	6, 12, 16
Fallen Jerusalem	Ginger	Leeward Islands	1	8	MGO	2005	5, 6, 12, 15, 16, 19
George Dog	Virgin Gorda	Leeward Islands	1	34	MGO	2005	5, 6, 12, 16, 19
Ginger Island	Ginger	Leeward Islands	1	5	MGO	2005	4, 12, 13, 15, 16
Great Camanoe	Tortola	Leeward Islands	1	2	MGO	2005	6, 12
Great Thatch	Tortola	Leeward Islands	1	30	JJA	1999	17
Great Tobago	Jost van Dyke	Leeward Islands	2	596	MGO	2005	4, 5, 6, 8, 9, 11*
Green	Jost van Dyke	Leeward Islands	2	449	JPI	2005	6, 12, 16, 19, 22*
Guana	Tortola	Leeward Islands	1	86	BAS	2005	5, 6, 10, 19
Indian Rocks	Norman	Leeward Islands	1	2	MGO	2005	19
Jost van Dyke	Jost van Dyke	Leeward Islands	1	2	JPI	2005	5, 12
Little Camanoe	Tortola	Leeward Islands	1	1	JPI	2006	12
Little Tobago	Jost van Dyke	Leeward Islands	1	102	JPI	2005	6, 8, 10, 13, 20
Mosquito	Virgin Gorda	Leeward Islands	1	2	JPI	2005	5, 12
Necker	Virgin Gorda	Leeward Islands	0	14	MGO	2005	12, 16
Norman	Norman	Leeward Islands	2	217	MGO	2005	5, 6, 10*, 12, 16
Pelican	Norman Island	Leeward Islands	1	1	MGO	2005	16
Peter	Peter	Leeward Islands	1	2	BAS	2005	5, 6, 16
Prickly Pear	Virgin Gorda	Leeward Islands	1	1	JPI	2005	12
Round Rock	Ginger	Leeward Islands	1	6	MGO	2005	5, 6, 13, 15, 16, 19
Sandy	Jost van Dyke	Leeward Islands	1	2	JPI	2005	12, 16
Scrub	Tortola	Leeward Islands	1	1	JPI	2006	5
Tortola	Tortola	Leeward Islands	1	2	BAS	2005	5, 12
Virgin Gorda	Virgin Gorda	Leeward Islands	1	3	MGO	2005	5
Watsons Rock	Jost van Dyke	Leeward Islands	1	2	MGO	2005	13, 16
West Dog	Virgin Gorda	Leeward Islands	1	3	BAS	2005	12, 19
West Seal Dog	Virgin Gorda	Leeward Islands	1	2	MGO	2005	12, 16

continued

Table 27.5.—*Continued*

Chapter 12

Island Name	Island Group	Region	Rank	Total Pairs	Contributor	Last Survey	Species Codes
Anguillita	Anguilla	Leeward Islands	2	100	HDA	2005	21, 22*
Cove Pond	Anguilla	Leeward Islands	1	52	HDA	2000	17
Crocus Hill	Anguilla	Leeward Islands	1	1	HDA	1996	10
Dog	Anguilla	Leeward Islands	2	32634	HDA	2005	4, 6, 7*, 8*, 11, 12, 13, 15, 16, 17
Grey Pond	Anguilla	Leeward Islands	1	52	HDA	2000	17
Gull Pond	Anguilla	Leeward Islands	1	52	HDA	2000	17
Little Bay Cliffs	Anguilla	Leeward Islands	1	1	HDA	2001	5
Long Pond	Anguilla	Leeward Islands	1	52	HDA	2000	17
Mainland Cliffs*	Anguilla	Leeward Islands	0	10	HDA	2005	5, 6, 11
Middle Dog	Anguilla	Leeward Islands	1	1	HDA	2005	7
Pelican Bay	Anguilla	Leeward Islands	1	1	HDA	1996	10
Prickly Pear E	Anguilla	Leeward Islands	2	2161	HDA	2005	5, 6, 8, 12*, 13, 15, 16, 17
Prickly Pear W	Anguilla	Leeward Islands	2	608	NAC	2004	6, 8*, 9, 10, 12, 15, 16
Scrub	Anguilla	Leeward Islands	2	1086	HDA	2005	6, 12, 13, 15, 16, 17, 19, 20*, 21, 22
Sombrero	Anguilla	Leeward Islands	0	1334	HDA	2005	4, 6, 7, 8, 10, 11, 12, 13, 14, 15, 16, 17, 18, 19, 21, 22

Chapter 13

Island Name	Island Group	Region	Rank	Total Pairs	Contributor	Last Survey	Species Codes
Cole Bay	St. Maartin	Leeward Islands	0	0	NAC	2005	5
Fort Amsterdam	St. Maartin	Leeward Islands	1	7	NAC	2004	10
Great Salt Pond	St. Maartin	Leeward Islands	1	0	NAC	2005	12
Maho Bay	St. Maartin	Leeward Islands	0	0	NAC	2004	5, 6
Mary's Point	St. Maartin	Leeward Islands	0	0	NAC	2004	6
Molly Bday	St. Maartin	Leeward Islands	1	13	NAC	2004	6, 8, 16
Pelican	St. Maartin	Leeward Islands	2	183	NAC	2004	4, 6, 10, 12, 13, 16, 21*
Pointe Blanche	St. Maartin	Leeward Islands	1	15	NAC	2004	13
Simpson Bay Lagoon	St. Maartin	Leeward Islands	0	5	NAC	2004	17
Black Rocks	Saba	Leeward Islands	1	75	MWM	1998	6
Booby Hill	Saba	Leeward Islands	1	78	NAC	2004	4, 5, 6
Cove Bay	Saba	Leeward Islands	1	76	MWM	1998	5, 6
Diamond Rock	Saba	Leeward Islands	0	31	MWM	2004	8, 13, 15, 16
Flat Point	Saba	Leeward Islands	1	76	MWM	1998	5, 6
Fort Bay	Saba	Leeward Islands	1	1	NAC	2004	4, 5
Great Point	Saba	Leeward Islands	1	75	NAC	2002	4, 6
Green	Saba	Leeward Islands	1	91	MWM	2004	6, 8, 13, 16
Ladder Bay	Saba	Leeward Islands	1	1	DSL	1998	5

Island Name	Island Group	Region	Rank	Total Pairs	Contributor	Last Survey	Species Codes
Little (Old) Booby Hill	Saba	Leeward Islands	1	75	MWM	1998	6
Sulphur Mine	Saba	Leeward Islands	1	90	NAC	2004	4, 6
Tent Bay	Saba	Leeward Islands	1	75	MWM	1998	6
Well's Bay	Saba	Leeward Islands	1	75	NAC	2004	4, 6
Cay Bay	St. Eustatius	Leeward Islands	1	1	DSL	1998	6
Concordia Bay	St. Eustatius	Leeward Islands	1	1	DSL	1998	6
Cupe Coy Bay	St. Eustatius	Leeward Islands	1	1	NAC	2004	5
Gallows Bay	St. Eustatius	Leeward Islands	1	2	NAC	2003	4, 6
Tumble Down Dick Bay	St. Eustatius	Leeward Islands	1	2	NAC	1998	4, 6
Venus Bay	St. Eustatius	Leeward Islands	1	1	DSL	1998	6
White Wall	St. Eustatius	Leeward Islands	1	1	DSL	1998	6
Yenkin's Bay	St. Eustatius	Leeward Islands	1	1	DSL	1998	6

Chapter 14

Island Name	Island Group	Region	Rank	Total Pairs	Contributor	Last Survey	Species Codes
St. Martin	St. Martin	Leeward Islands	1	214	GLB	2002	5, 6, 13, 16, 17
Tintamarre	St. Martin	Leeward Islands	0	0	NAC	2002	4
Cabrit	The Saints	Leeward Islands	1	2	GLB	1998	5
Carenage	The Saints	Leeward Islands	1	74	GLB	1998	17, 19
Desirade	Desirade	Leeward Islands	1	100	GLB	2002	4, 5, 6, 13, 16
Fajou	Grand Cul-de-Sac	Leeward Islands	0	0	GLB	2002	10
Grand illet	The Saints	Leeward Islands	2	821	GLB	1998	5, 8, 9, 10, 11*, 13, 16
Jarry	Basse-Terre	Leeward Islands	1	5	GLB	2002	17
L'Eperon*	Marie Galante	Leeward Islands	1	5	GLB	1998	6
Les Augustins	The Saints	Leeward Islands	1	456	GLB	1998	8, 10, 13, 15, 16
Marie Galante	Marie Galante	Leeward Islands	1	372	BAS	1999	5, 6, 8, 13, 15, 16, 20
Mountains	Basse-Terre	Leeward Islands	0	0	DSL	1999	2, 6
NE Falaises	Grand-Terre	Leeward Islands	1	85	GLB	2002	5, 6, 113, 16
NE Falaises	Marie Galante	Leeward Islands	2	666	GLB	2002	4, 5, 6*, 13, 15, 16
Pate	The Saints	Leeward Islands	1	120	GLB	1998	13, 15, 16
Petit Canal	Grande-Terre	Leeward Islands	2	250	GLB	1997	11*
Petite Terres	Petite terres	Leeward Islands	1	16	GLB	2002	6, 17
Pointe des Chateaux	Grande-Terre	Leeward Islands	1	1610	GLB	2002	5, 6, 13, 15, 16, 17
Pointe Noire	Basse-Terre	Leeward Islands	1	2	GLB	1997	10
Porte d'Enfer	Basse-Terre	Leeward Islands	1	12	GLB	1998	6
S Falaises*	Basse-Terre	Leeward Islands	1	5	GLB	2002	5
Saint Rose	The Saints	Leeward Islands	1	150	GLB	1997	11
St. Barts	St. Bartholomew	Leeward Islands	2	1158	VHN	2002	4, 6*, 8, 10, 12, 13, 15, 16, 17, 19, 21
Terre de Bas	The Saints	Leeward Islands	1	138	GLB	1998	5, 6, 8, 13, 15
Terre de Haut	The Saints	Leeward Islands	1	19	GLB	1998	5, 13
Tete a l'Anglais	Basse-Terre	Leeward Islands	1	610	GLB	2002	13, 15, 16, 19
Tillet	Basse-Terre	Leeward Islands	1	1900	GLB	1998	8, 11, 13, 15, 16
Vieux Fort	Marie Galante	Leeward Islands	1	640	GLB	2002	4, 15, 16

continued

254

Table 27.5.—*Continued*

Chapter 15

Island Name	Island Group	Region	Rank	Total Pairs	Contributor	Last Survey	Species Codes
Booby	St. Kitts	Leeward Islands	1	420	NAC	2004	6, 10, 12, 13, 15, 16, 19
Great Salt Pond	St. Kitts	Leeward Islands	1	5	NAC	2004	17
Hurricane Hill	Nevis	Leeward Islands	1	2	NAC	2004	11, 12
Indian Castle	Nevis	Leeward Islands	1	0	NAC	2004	19
Mosquito Bay Pond	St. Kitts	Leeward Islands	1	5	NAC	2004	17
Nag's Head	St. Kitts	Leeward Islands	1	10	NAC	1988	11, 17
White Bay	Nevis	Leeward Islands	1	1	NAC	2004	17
White House Bay	St. Kitts	Leeward Islands	1	1	NAC	1988	19

Chapter 16

Island Name	Island Group	Region	Rank	Total Pairs	Contributor	Last Survey	Species Codes
Farm Bay	Montserrat	Leeward Islands	1	1	ALD	2005	21
Garibaldi Hill	Montserrat	Leeward Islands	1	1	ALD	1999	10
Hell's Gate	Montserrat	Leeward Islands	1	1	ALD	2005	6
NW Montserrat Bluffs	Montserrat	Leeward Islands	1	2	ALD	2005	6, 8
O'Garra's-Roche's Bluffs	Montserrat	Leeward Islands	1	1	ALD	2005	6
Olveston	Montserrat	Leeward Islands	1	1	ALD	2005	6
Pinnacle Rock	Montserrat	Leeward Islands	1	28	ALD	2005	10, 11
Plymouth Beach	Montserrat	Leeward Islands	1	1	ALD	2005	21
Rendezvous Bluff	Montserrat	Leeward Islands	1	1	ALD	1999	8
St. Peter's	Montserrat	Leeward Islands	1	1	ALD	1999	10

Chapter 17

Island Name	Island Group	Region	Rank	Total Pairs	Contributor	Last Survey	Species Codes
Antigua	Antigua	Leeward Islands	0	51	SYL	1999	17, 19
Burma Quarry	Antigua	Leeward Islands	0	383	BAS	1999	5, 12, 15, 19
Codrington Lagoon	Barbuda	Leeward Islands	2	2163	SYL	1999	5, 6*, 10, 11*, 12
Five Islands	Antigua	Leeward Islands	1	26	SYL	2005	8, 10, 13, 22
Great Bird	Antigua	Leeward Islands	1	113	SYL	2004	6, 10
Green	Antigua	Leeward Islands	1	607	SYL	2004	6, 13, 15, 19
Hell's Gate	Antigua	Leeward Islands	1	0	SYL	2004	4
Lobster	Antigua	Leeward Islands	1	0	SYL	2004	15
Mill Reef	Antigua	Leeward Islands	0	0	SYL	2004	4, 5, 12
Northern Salt Flats	Barbuda	Leeward Islands	1	1	JJA	1999	17
Rabbit	Antigua	Leeward Islands	1	32	SYL	2005	10, 13
Redhead	Antigua	Leeward Islands	1	12	SYL	2005	10
Redonda	Redonda	Leeward Islands	2	351	SYL	2004	5, 6*, 7, 8, 9*, 11, 13
York	Antigua	Leeward Islands	1	82	SYL	2005	10, 11, 12, 19

continued

Chapter 18

Island Name	Island Group	Region	Rank	Total Pairs	Contributor	Last Survey	Species Codes
Anse Couleuvre	Martinique	Leeward Islands	1	0	LGD	2005	19
Boisseau	Martinique	Leeward Islands	1	1	LGD	2005	19
Burgaux*	Martinique	Leeward Islands	1	121	LGD	2004	4, 13, 15
Caravelle's Rock	Martinique	Leeward Islands	1	15	LGD	2004	8, 11, 13, 15, 16, 19, 20
Desirade	Martinique	Leeward Islands	0	1	LGD	2005	4, 11
Hardy	Martinique	Leeward Islands	1	1150	LGD	2005	4, 6, 11, 13, 15
Martinique Mainland	Martinique	Leeward Islands	0	100	LGD	2004	2, 5, 6, 8, 13
Pain de Sucre	Martinique	Leeward Islands	1	1	LGD	2005	19
Perce*	Martinique	Leeward Islands	1	1	LGD	2004	4, 13, 15
Poirier	Martinique	Leeward Islands	1	5000	LGD	2002	15
Rocher du Diamant	Martinique	Leeward Islands	1	3	LGD	2004	5, 6, 8, 13
Saint-Marie	Martinique	Leeward Islands	1	1	LGD	2005	19, 21
Table du Diable	Martinique	Leeward Islands	1	0	LGD	2004	13

Chapter 19

Island Name	Island Group	Region	Rank	Total Pairs	Contributor	Last Survey	Species Codes
St. Lucia Cliffs	St. Lucia	Windward Islands	1	1	DOA	2004	6

Chapter 20

Island Name	Island Group	Region	Rank	Total Pairs	Contributor	Last Survey	Species Codes
Bird Rock	Barbados	Windward Islands	1	110	FST	2005	4, 11
E Rock Stacks	Barbados	Windward Islands	1	0	FST	2005	4
N Rock Stacks	Barbados	Windward Islands	1	0	FST	2005	4

Chapter 21

Island Name	Island Group	Region	Rank	Total Pairs	Contributor	Last Survey	Species Codes
All-Awash Island	Grenadines	Windward Islands	0	526	ASU	2004	7, 8, 9, 16, 17
Baliceaux	Grenadines	Windward Islands	1	1	FLH	1905	6
Battowia Bullet	Grenadines	Windward Islands	2	3216	ASU	2005	6, 7, 8, 9*, 11, 15, 16, 19
Bequia Head	Grenadines	Windward Islands	0	12	FLH	2005	6, 8, 9, 11
Bonaparte Rocks	Grenada	Windward Islands	1	2	FLH	1902	4, 15
Carriacou Complex	Grenada	Windward Islands	1	4	FLH	2002	4, 10, 12, 15, 21
Chateau Belair	St. Vincent	Windward Islands	1	1	FLH	1909	13
Duvernette	St. Vincent	Windward Islands	1	1	FLH	2005	5
Frigate	Grenadines	Windward Islands	1	62	ASU	2004	6, 15, 19
Green	Grenada	Windward Islands	1	3	FLH	1954	4, 16, 19
Isle de Rhonde	Grenadines	Windward Islands	1	1	FLH	1954	6, 15
Isle-de-Large	Grenadines	Windward Islands	1	3	FLH	1902	11, 13, 15

256

Table 27.5.—*Continued*

Island Name	Island Group	Region	Rank	Total Pairs	Contributor	Last Survey	Species Codes
Jacque Adam	Grenada	Windward Islands	1	1	ASU	2004	19
Kick-em-Jenny	Grenada	Windward Islands	0	26	FST	2004	6, 7, 8, 9, 11, 15
Labaye Rock	Grenada	Windward Islands	1	3	FLH	1888	4
Lee Rocks*	Grenadines	Windward Islands	1	5	FLH	1954	6, 13, 15, 16, 19
Les Tantes	Grenadines	Windward Islands	2	510	ASU	2004	6, 8, 9*, 12, 16, 19
Little Savanna Rock	Grenadines	Windward Islands	1	1	FLH	1925	6
Little Tobago	Grenada	Windward Islands	1	2	FLH	1950	8, 22
London Bridge	Grenada	Windward Islands	1	0	FLH	1943	11
Mainland	Grenada	Windward Islands	0	4	FLH	1999	9, 12, 13, 15, 16, 19, 21
Milligan	Grenadines	Windward Islands	1	4	FLH	1925	19
Old Woman Point	St. Vincent	Windward Islands	1	1	FLH	2005	5
Petit Canouan	Grenadines	Windward Islands	1	1010	ASU	2004	12, 15
Ramier	Grenada	Windward Islands	1	2	FLH	1998	5, 6, 11, 19
Rose Rock	Grenadines	Windward Islands	1	4	FLH	1905	6, 13, 15, 19
Saline	Grenadines	Windward Islands	1	0	FLH	1954	6
Sandy*	Grenada	Windward Islands	1	1	FLH	1943	4
St. Vincent	St. Vincent	Windward Islands	0	1	FLH	2005	5, 6, 8, 13, 19
West Coast	St. Vincent	Windward Islands	1	1	FLH	2000	5
White	Grenada	Windward Islands	1	2	FLH	1905	13, 16
Young	St. Vincent	Windward Islands	1	1	FLH	2005	5

Chapter 22

Island Name	Island Group	Region	Rank	Total Pairs	Contributor	Last Survey	Species Codes
Booby Island	Tobago	Windward Islands	1	10	FLH	1986	19
Courland Point Rock	Tobago	Windward Islands	1	113	FLH	2001	19
Little Tobago	Tobago	South America	2	550	BNR	2004	4, 5, 6*, 8, 9, 12, 13, 15, 16, 19*
Northeastern Tobago	Tobago	South America	1	22	FLH	2005	6, 8, 10, 12, 13, 15, 19
Smith Island	Trinidad	South America	1	401	FLH	1998	6, 13, 15, 16
Soldado Rock	Trinidad	South America	0	0	FLH	2002	13, 15, 23
Southwest coast	Trinidad	South America	1	2500	VHN	1984	15
St. Giles	Tobago	South America	0	631	BNR	2004	4, 6, 7, 8, 9, 11*, 12, 13, 15, 16, 21
The Sisters	Tobago	Windward Islands	1	2	FLH	1988	10, 21
Trinidad	Trinidad	South America	0	0	FLH	2005	6, 10, 11

Chapter 23

Island Name	Island Group	Region	Rank	Total Pairs	Contributor	Last Survey	Species Codes
Lago Reef	Aruba	South America	2	10656	NOR	2002	12, 13, 14, 15, 16, 17, 19, 20*, 21, 23*

Chapter 24

Island Name	Island Group	Region	Rank	Total Pairs	Contributor	Last Survey	Species Codes
Cargill Saltworks	Bonaire	Bonaire	2	136	DEB	2002	12, 19, 20, 21,* 23
Goto Lake	Bonaire	Bonaire	2	183	DEB	2002	12, 15*, 20
Isla di Rancho	Bonaire	Bonaire	1	20	DEB	1996	17
Kralendijk & Lac	Bonaire	Bonaire	0	0	DEB	2002	11
Malmok	Bonaire	Bonaire	1	10	DEB	2002	17
SE Bonaire Tip	Bonaire	Bonaire	1	10	DEB	2002	17
Slagbaai	Bonaire	Bonaire	1	3	DEB	1998	20
Solar Saltworks*	Bonaire	Bonaire	1	10	DEB	2002	17
Spelonk-Lagoen	Bonaire	Bonaire	1	10	DEB	2002	17
Washington-Slagbaai Park	Bonaire	Bonaire	1	10	DEB	2002	17
Buskabaai	Curacao	Curacao	2	40	DEB	2002	20*
Eastpoint*	Curacao	Curacao	1	10	DEB	2002	17
Hato	Curacao	Curacao	1	1	DEB	2002	17
Klein Curacao	Curacao	Curacao	0	0	DEB	2002	23
Koraal Tabak	Curacao	Curacao	1	10	DEB	2002	17
Lagoon of Janthiel	Curacao	Curacao	2	178	DEB	2002	12, 17, 19, 20*, 23
Macuacu Island	Curacao	Curacao	0	3	DEB	2002	11, 20
San Michiel	Curacao	Curacao	1	15	DEB	2002	20
Shete Boka Park	Curacao	Curacao	1	30	DEB	2002	17
Spanish Water	Curacao	Curacao	0	0	DEB	2002	15, 20
Wacao	Curacao	Curacao	1	10	DEB	2002	17

Chapter 25

Island Name	Island Group	Region	Rank	Total Pairs	Contributor	Last Survey	Species Codes
Aves	Venezuela	Central Caribbean	0	10209	LTO	2005	6, 7, 8*, 9*, 10, 11, 12, 13, 14*, 15, 16, 19, 20, 21, 23*
Boca de Rio	Margarita	South America	1	2	LTO	2005	10, 17
Coche	Venezuela	South America	1	5	LTO	2005	10, 12, 16, 17, 19
Cubagua	Venezuela	South America	2	306	LTO	2005	8, 10*, 11, 12, 17, 20, 21
El Morro	Margarita	South America	1	3	LTO	2005	12, 15, 17
Gran Roque	Los Roques	Central Caribbean	0	0	LTO	2001	7
La Blanquilla	Venezuela	Central Caribbean	1	9	LTO	1994	4, 6, 7, 8, 9, 10, 11, 12, 21
La Orchila	Venezuela	Central Caribbean	1	13	LTO	2005	4, 6, 8, 9, 10, 11, 12, 13, 15, 17, 20, 21, 23
La Restinga	Margarita	South America	1	6	LTO	2005	10, 11, 17, 19, 21
La Tortuga	Venezuela	South America	0	5	LTO	2005	8, 10, 11, 12, 20, 21
Las Aves	Las Aves	Central Caribbean	2	356	LTO	2005	8, 9, 10, 11, 12, 13, 14*, 15*, 16, 17, 19, 20, 21, 23

continued

Table 27.5.—*Continued*

Island Name	Island Group	Region	Rank	Total Pairs	Contributor	Last Survey	Species Codes
Las Marites Lagoon	Margarita	South America	2	104	LTO	2005	10*, 11, 17, 18, 21
Los Hermanos	Venezuela	Central Caribbean	1	6	LTO	2005	4, 6, 7, 8, 9, 11, 13, 15, 21
Los Roques	Los Roques	Central Caribbean	2	3959	LTO	2005	4, 6, 7, 8*, 9*, 10*, 11, 12, 13, 14*, 15, 16, 17, 19, 20*, 21, 22, 23
Los Testigos	Venezuela	Central Caribbean	2	701	DSL	1998	6, 8, 9, 11*
Mainland	Venezuela	South America	1	2	VHN	1998	6, 8, 11
Monje del Sur	Los Monjes	Central Caribbean	2	253	LTO	2005	6, 7, 8, 10, 11
Monje del Este	Los Monjes	Central Caribbean	1	1	LTO	2005	15
Monje del Norte	Los Monjes	Central Caribbean	1	2	LTO	2005	10, 15
Puerto Real	Los Frailes	Central Caribbean	1	4	LTO	1945	8, 10, 11, 12
Punta de Piedras	Margarita	South America	1	6	LTO	2005	7, 10, 12, 17, 18, 21

Chapter 26

Island Name	Island Group	Region	Rank	Total Pairs	Contributor	Last Survey	Species Codes
Albuquerques	Colombia	South America	0	1	DSL	1998	8, 9
Colombia Coast	Colombia	South America	1	1	VHN	1998	8, 11
Courtowns	Colombia	South America	1	0	VHN	1984	11
Crab	Old Providence	Western Caribbean	0	0	MOS	2006	4
Gorgonilla	Columbia	South America	1	40	VHN	1998	7, 11
McBeans East Mangroves	Old Providence	Western Caribbean	1	1	MOS	1950	11
N Serrana	Serrana Bank	Western Caribbean	0	10	MOS	1995	9
Ron Cadors	Colombia	South America	2	1002	MOS	1999	8*, 9, 11, 13, 15
Serrana Bank	Colombia	South America	1	1	MOR	1999	21
Serranilla Beacon	Sarranilla Bank	Western Caribbean	0	0	MOS	1999	7, 8, 11
SW Serrana	Serrana Bank	Western Caribbean	1	200	MOS	1999	8, 13, 15
Three Brothers	Old Providence	Western Caribbean	1	1	MOS	2004	11

Notes: Island name, group, and region are followed by the status ranking and total number of pairs of each species, contributor of the data, and year of most recent survey. Only one contributor could be listed for each location; codes corresponding to each contributor are in table 27.1. Numerical codes for the species are listed in the chapter text. Asterisks denote island identity not certain.

28

Local, Regional, and Global Threats

ROBERT L. NORTON

Observing the astonishing bounty of Jamaican seabirds 150 years ago, Philip H. Gosse noted that the Pedro Cays, "the grand field whence this harvest is reaped . . . are the resort of thousands and tens of thousands of sea-fowl." Besides the birds crowded together in breeding colonies, he recorded that "myriads of birds are upon the wing in all directions . . . in the same dense numbers" (Gosse 1847). Today the Pedro Cays turn up among the Caribbean's most endangered seabird breeding sites.

When the long list of local, regional, and global threats is added to the region's already seemingly insurmountable problems—rapid human population growth, increased resource use, pollution of wetlands and both inshore and deep water areas, collapsing fish stocks, refugees in the northern West Indies, and the need for seabird eggs as a protein source for poor people—it is clear there is a crisis and thus a responsibility to take action now.

Major threats to seabirds as discussed in the island accounts are consolidated in the first part of this chapter to provide regionwide perspective. Later sections address global threats that will impact Caribbean seabirds and describe additional indirect hazards resulting from human activity. Although the regionwide discussion is somewhat repetitive of other workers' assessments through the years, it establishes the continued severity of these threats. With the passage of time, these qualitative assessments have shifted in their relative importance from direct exploitation to more subtle issues, such as land use decisions and the effects of waste and spoilage of human endeavors on the environment. A more "modern" threat to seabirds as well as to other species in the region is a lack of legislative support. Without legal recognition of seabirds' need for undisturbed breeding and feeding territories, and recognition of the need to enforce laws, little success can be achieved. These modern threats are depicted in several ways, including a focus on islands or subregions in the Antilles.

Local and Regional Threats to Seabirds

Researchers may have identified certain threats based on a particular species or location. The collective response to this subject in this volume shows us a geographic context, albeit imperfect. Each island account was then assessed according to the number and types of threats to the seabird biodiversity within the area shown in figure 28.1. The cumulative effect of all threat types and quantification is quite telling and points directly to potential trouble spots and areas that require immediate attention.

There are two approaches to viewing these data. The first is a qualitative grouping according to the series descriptions that follow. The second is a quantitative view ascribing a simple value to each type of threat. The objective is for results to focus future conservation efforts toward a particular location or species per location. This may be a useful tool to determine where resources and strategies can be best used to counter the loss of breeding seabirds.

Loss of Breeding Habitat

Globally, predation is considered the greatest threat to seabirds, but since the economic boom in the Caribbean in the 1990s, habitat threats have superseded those of predation. The exceptional rate of loss of seabird breeding habitat is identified as the major and most immediate threat throughout the preceding accounts. Escalating loss and degradation of breeding habitat, whether of nesting sites on the main islands (cliffs, coastal areas, and wetlands) or on the larger uninhabited cays, is impacting almost all sites as construction projects increase to provide for expanding numbers of residents and tour-

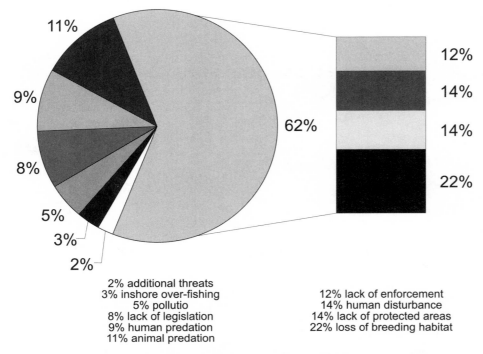

2% additional threats
3% inshore over-fishing
5% pollutio
8% lack of legislation
9% human predation
11% animal predation

12% lack of enforcement
14% human disturbance
14% lack of protected areas
22% loss of breeding habitat

Figure 28.1. Distribution of threats described by island authors for breeding seabirds.

ists. The facts are bleak. For example, the British Virgin Islands and Antigua have each lost about 80% of their wetlands. Threats to foraging areas are less well understood, especially in the open sea, and few or no data are available in the region. Soil erosion along coasts and beaches also creates incipient loss of habitat.

On islands, most human activity and associated environmental impacts are on the coasts. Tourism and new urbanlike developments direct the future of growth along low-lying areas adjacent to amenities and infrastructure. Increasingly, salt ponds, swamps, and wetlands are the areas of choice for new development, since they can be engineered into developable property. These areas have traditionally been feeding, roosting, and nesting sites for some of the region's nearshore seabirds (Laughing Gulls, Least Terns, and Gull-billed Terns). Seabird nesting habitat, whether beachfronts or offshore islets, is usurped with little regard for mitigating the losses of the original inhabitants. Far too few species have been able to adapt to nesting on rooftops, for example, in response to habitat change, loss, or predation.

Predation

Mammalian predators, invasive species, and grazing animals, whether self-introduced or aided by humans, present significant threats causing population loss and extirpation. Interference comes in many forms and initially dates from shortly after European contact in the

New World. Rats, for example, were released on the islands unintentionally or otherwise. Soon other predatory mammals, such as the small Indian mongoose (*Herpestes auropunctatus*), were brought to the islands to correct this unfortunate consequence. The European ark of domesticated animals also brought dogs, cats, goats, pigs, cattle—and birds.

All these introductions have had direct and indirect impacts on indigenous and endemic flora and fauna of the Caribbean region. Montane as well as coastal nesting sites were invaded by rats and, in some areas, by the mongoose introduced to control them—the irony being that the rat is generally nocturnal and the mongoose diurnal, a double jeopardy for ground-nesting fauna.

Human Disturbance

The second major threat is identified as human disturbance at nest sites during the breeding season, usually related to recreation, egg harvesting, and marine tourism. This has exacerbated threats to the offshore cays where boaters go ashore and disturb nesting terns, gulls, boobies, and frigatebirds.

Overfishing

This occurs in inshore waters and protected waters. Visible threats to seabirds in the region—that is, egging, tourism disturbance, and habitat destruction—have not changed much since the extensive review of threats to

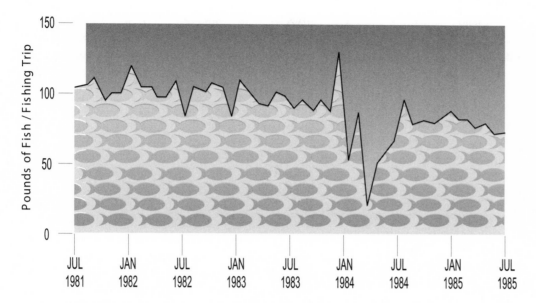

Figure 28.2. Artisanal fishery decline, July 1981–July 1985, St. Thomas, U.S. Virgin Islands.

seabirds (Burger and Gochfeld 1994). What has changed since Gochfeld et al. (1994) reviewed threats to West Indies seabirds, an interim assessment following van Halewyn and Norton (1984) and prior to Schreiber and Lee (2000a), is an emerging recognition that unseen forces have been debilitating reef and nearshore ecosystems that normally host myriad zoo- and macroplankton supporting the region's seabird ecology and biodiversity.

In spite of major areas of Puerto Rico's Culebra Archipelago being under federal ownership, with frequent monitoring and enforcement, Gochfeld et al. (1994) point out that (with the exception of an opportunistic Sooty Tern population) seabirds nesting at Culebra cays generally declined in the decade of the 1980s. The perceived Culebra decline monitored through 1989 also mirrored incipient ecological depressions eastward to the northern U.S. Virgin Islands in local fisheries and seabird biometrics (R. L. Norton, unpubl.). Fishery monitoring programs in the early 1980s surveyed artisanal catch (indigenous fish pot traps) on a weekly basis at St. Thomas (fig. 28.2) coincidentally with seabird monitoring efforts initiated in the late 1970s. During this period, the metrics of first and second eggs of offshore-feeding sulids and some sternids feeding inshore were below norm or average (Norton *in* Duffy et al. 1988). Although these depressions or deviations were considered a phenomenon related to a strong El Niño/Southern Oscillation (ENSO) at the time, they could have been a local signal of a longer-term shift in sea temperature or other reactions masked by El Niño.

Fish pot catch in pounds per trip declined steadily over a period of 48 months well in advance of the 1983–1984 ENSO event and continued declining for some time thereafter, a condition not well understood. Whether the fishery decline was an indicator of exhaustive overfishing or a response to environmental effects, or both, seabird populations in the Eastern Puerto Rico Bank were also showing signs of disruption, fragmentation, and decline. Burger and Gochfeld (1994) listed global warming as a potential threat but had not yet linked it to a discussion of large-scale, human-induced environmental change. A decade later, we may be able to draw tighter conclusions based on extensive worldwide efforts to understand global climate change and effects on seabirds (Schreiber and Schreiber 1983).

Other Regional Threats Identified

Additional issues coming up repeatedly in the island accounts are:

Lack or inadequacy of legislation to protect seabirds and their habitats is frequently mentioned by authors.

Enforcement of existing laws is commonly inadequate or nonexistent, including in designated protected areas.

Human resources for seabird management or enforcement are insufficient, and wildlife and environmental agencies do not have the financial resources to monitor and manage seabird nesting sites and important habitats. Lack of management means there are very few genuinely protected areas for seabirds, recreational boat traffic at nest sites is uncontrolled, and garbage (including plastics) is uncollected.

Local pollution involves oil, plastics, chemicals, and solid waste.

Additional threats identified, some of which are likely to increase in importance, included ambient light pollution, entanglement in fishing lines (especially boobies, pelicans and frigatebirds), ingestion of plastics, and sand mining.

Huggins et al. (2007) summarize their findings thus: "Heightening human pressures in the region are thought to be putting the biodiversity of the region under unprecedented stress. Activities include cruise ship tourism, terrestrial and marine tourism and their associated infrastructures, hydropower dams and reservoirs, canalization, freshwater withdrawals, road building, agriculture, over-fishing, introduction of alien species, sand and bedrock mining, discharge of untreated sewage and industrial waters, intensive agrochemicals use, aquaculture, over-harvesting, population growth, urban sprawl and resource extraction. These activities can lead to changes in ecological systems such as habitat fragmentation, degradation and loss, invasive species, hydrological regime change, degraded water quality, pollutant release, sedimentation, ecosystem service degradation and the resulting effects on local human communities. The cumulative impacts of all these influences on biodiversity are largely unknown. The complex mix of political and social factors exacerbates these problems and results in

the Caribbean being one of the world's most threatened places. The strategies necessary to balance sustaining the livelihoods of people and the growth of economies with the need to reduce threats and protect remaining biodiversity are complex and interrelated. Deciding how and where to act in the face of multiple, imminent threats is an increasing challenge."

Quantification of these threats attempts to indicate a focus for conservation planners and researchers to direct future efforts for seabird conservation, either locally as indicated in table 28.1 for specific threats per location or for particular species per location. For those locations that rank high in table 28.1, it is suggested that the most productive course of action is to look to stronger enabling legislation to protect seabird breeding and feeding territories, following up with mechanisms to monitor seabird populations according to methods described in this volume, and working to provide penalties to establish an enforcement presence.

Global Threats to Caribbean Seabirds

Climate change or global warming, now recognized as a near certainty (Intergovernmental Panel on Climate Change 2007), will have profound impacts on the oceans and seabirds in coming decades. Beyond the hazards of rising sea levels, other threats deriving from climate change and having widespread effects include shifts in ocean chemistry and storm behavior. A fourth suite of threats deriving at least partly from global forces, though

Table 28.1. Island accounts with greatest potential threats to local breeding seabird diversity based on cumulative threats identified by island authors

Island Account	Breeding species #s (Mackin)	Total Cumulative Threats
Antigua-Barbuda	6, 8, 9, 10, 11, 12, 13, 15, 16, 19, 22	10
Guadeloupe	3*, 4, 5, 6, 9, 13, 15, 16, 17, 19	10
St. Martin	4, 5, 6, 8, 10, 12, 13, 15, 16, 17, 21	9
Cuba	2, 4, 5, 10, 11, 12, 13, 15, 16, 17, 18, 19, 20, 21, 22	9
Hispaniola	2, 5, 8, 9, 10, 11, 12, 13, 15, 16, 17, 21, 22	9
St. Lucia	5, 6, 11, 13, 15, 16, 19	9
Bahamas	4, 5, 8, 9, 10, 11, 12, 13, 15, 16, 17, 18, 19, 21, 22	9
Cayman Island	5, 8, 9, 11, 16, 17	9
Jamaica	3*, 5, 7, 8, 10, 11, 12, 13, 15, 16, 17, 19, 21, 22	8
Trinidad & Tobago	4, 6, 7, 8, 9, 11, 12, 13, 15, 16, 19	7
Turks & Caicos	4, 5, 8, 11, 12, 13, 15, 16, 17, 18, 19, 20, 21, 22	7
Martinique	4, 5, 6, 13, 15, 16, 19	7
St. Vincent, Grenada, Grenadines	5, 6, 8, 9, 12, 13, 15, 16, 19, 22	7
Aruba	12, 13, 14, 15, 16, 17, 19, 20, 21, 23	6

Note: Species codes, see Appendix A.

* = extirpated or extinct breeding populations.

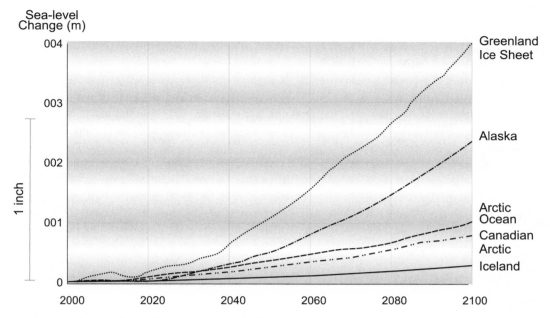

Figure 28.3. Projected contribution of arctic land ice to sea level change. Reproduced with permission from Paul Grabhorn, Grabhorn Studio, 369 Montezuma Ave., Santa Fe, NM 87501.

problems may seem local, includes worldwide impacts of pollution and overfishing (see Collateral Damage).

Climate Change and Sea Level Rise

Seabirds have responded to climate change for millennia. Since the last Ice Age, when much of the planet's fresh water was stored at the higher latitudes and released gradually over the centuries, birds with life histories dependent on the interaction of fresh and saline water have been able to adapt to the availability of this unique resource and its interface with land. About 20,000 years ago, sea level was approximately 200 fathoms or 200 meters below current elevations.

Following are a few of the specific outcomes of climate change, either as a single event or an accumulation of convergent trends. In the West Indies, white-band disease or bleaching discovered among corals in the 1980s was initially a mystery but is now widely recognized as a reaction to warmer water temperatures (Feely et al. 2004). Measurements suggest that heating penetrated more than 750 m below the surface (Hansen et al. 2005; Barnett et al. 2005). Root et al. (2003) document that even the small-scale or early signs of global warming can be seen in the increasingly early arrival dates of spring migrants, including birds, insects, and fish, as well as in the poleward or upslope shift of plant communities.

In the last 20,000 breeding seasons, various seabirds have benefited from an increase in areas covered by shallow seas and outflow conveying enormous amounts of nutrients. Similarly, some species experienced lo-

cal extirpation as a result of rising sea level (Olson and Hilgartner 1982). There is paleontological evidence that abrupt sea level rise may have been responsible for the extinction of the North Atlantic's only short-tailed albatross (*Phoebastria albatrus*) colony at the edge of the tropical North Atlantic, associated with melting of the Western Antarctic Ice Sheet. Bones of adults and young as well as eggs were found buried in sediments at Bermuda (Olson and Hearty 2003). The authors suggest as likely a sudden flooding of the colony.

Some estimates predict that sea level will rise as much as 30 cm in the present century. Global surface temperature increased 0.6°C in the last century, causing sea level to rise 10–20 cm in the last 100 years (Lovgren 2004a, b). Over the last 50 years, average temperatures in the Antarctic Peninsula have risen by 2.5°C, causing a pattern of ice shelf disintegration of the Larsen B shelf not seen in 12,000 years (Kwok and Comiso 2002). Arctic ice retreat continues (Figure 28.3) at a record rate and is likely to result in a long-term decline (Arendt et al. 2002; Overpeck et al. 2005). In fact, analysis of trapped ancient air bubbles from both the Greenland and Antarctic ice sheets indicates that atmospheric carbon dioxide today is higher than at any time on record (Siegenthaler et al. 2004). The data also show that temperature and CO_2 concentrations have risen in tandem throughout the period. Reports indicate that the higher latitudes are warming (melting) twice as fast as the rest of the planet, by as much as 20% melt since 1979. The 2002 breakup of the huge Larsen B ice shelf has accelerated West Antarctic glacier flow (Scambos et al. 2004) by releasing its massive pressure.

Responses to these impacts will depend on the local conditions and climate. Natural shoreline vegetation may adapt where sediment accretion equals sea level rise. Offshore islets may respond similarly for a time, providing some habitat for some species if the accretion and sea rise are gradual and in tandem. The current observation that sea level *is* rising as a response to accelerated release of solid water at the poles and high mountain glaciers warrants seabird biologists monitoring the effects of global warming on their species of concern, as have their terrestrial counterparts. There is little debate on the fact that sea level is changing; the debate appears to be centered on the quality and quantity of change; that is, rate and increment. The rate and increment, no matter how slight, speak directly to the impact on nesting seabirds and how quickly, if at all, various species will react to loss of habitat and water quality of nearshore feeding areas.

The southern oceans will be warmer and fresher through part of the heat transfer cycle, and that spells trouble for the Antarctic krill (*Euphausia superba*) ecosystem response (Reid and Croxall 2001). Increased levels of fresh water in the regions surrounding the Antarctic Ice Shelf portend changes in capacity of sea ice to shelter algae upon which krill feed. Reid and Croxall found that reduction in krill lowered breeding success in black-browed albatross (*Thalassarche melanophrys*), and fewer chicks reduce future recruitment and breeding success. Thomas et al. (2004) discuss extinction risk from climate change. Body condition of Magellan Penguins (*Pheniscus magalleniscus*) as evidenced by weight is enhanced during cold surface water conditions of La Niña but deteriorates when surface waters are warmed during El Niño, and under the most severe conditions, penguins starve (Boersma 1998). Analysis of a long-term data set from counts of the population suggests that the population has fluctuated, dropping precipitously after the 1982–1983 El Niño (Duffy et al. 1988) and has since then been recovering very slowly. Productivity measures among a sample of breeding seabirds in the U.S. Virgin Islands also suggested an ENSO effect likely driven by lack of rainfall and nutrient outwash (Norton *in* Duffy et al. 1988).

Sea level rise from melting glaciers, thermal expansion of tropical waters, and the potential of an increasingly active, long-term hurricane cycle beginning sooner and ending later are formidable and irrepressible challenges to both human and seabird existence in low-lying areas. Indeed, these effects are expected to impact:

- lowland inundation and wetland displacement
- shoreline erosion
- more severe storm-surge flooding
- saltwater intrusion into estuaries and freshwater aquifers
- altered tidal range in rivers and bays
- changes in beach sedimentation patterns
- reduced light penetration to benthic organisms.

Tectonic activity is also a cause of sea level rise. In the Indian Ocean, an event like the tsunami in 2004 was a precursor to sustained sea level rise related to slippage of massive tectonic plates. There may be other submerged seabird breeding sites throughout the North Atlantic rim of offshore islands and volcanic peaks, now lurking below the surface as seamounts. Limestone platforms uplifted by tectonic action in the eastern Caribbean, such as Sombrero Island in the middle of the Anegada Passage, provide superlative breeding opportunities for a large suite of seabirds.

Sombrero functions as a breeding site despite having some necessary human activity (e.g., a lighthouse) and some unnecessary activity (e.g., a rocket launch site proposal, since abandoned), but this nesting site is only a few meters above sea level. It will face hurricane assaults and results similar to those experienced by Bermuda. At least in the recent past, wherever the sea removes a habitat, it also seems to provide new opportunities elsewhere. Such is the case of Aves Island, a sand-covered hump to the west of the Lesser Antilles. This shoal provides a habitat that is in constant use by breeding Sooty Terns as well as marine turtles. But it too may be lost with a rising sea.

Changes in Ocean Chemistry

A number of complex issues are contributing to a decline and retreat in the equatorial glaciers (Mt. Kilimanjaro and the Peruvian range) since the Industrial Revolution. While these sensitive sites seem to be reacting rapidly to climate change, the polar regions may be lagging not too far behind (Arendt et al. 2002) in their decline. Other issues related to heat transfer from the southern oceans to the northern oceans suggest differential heating and cooling leading to loss of ice cover in the northern latitudes ahead of the southern latitudes. Confounding the issue of southern ocean transfer of heat to northern latitudes is the west-to-east warm and vice versa (La Niña) cold water anomaly of the El Niño/ Southern Oscillation. A sudden and long-term shift in this cycle, on the order of a decade or century, leads the global climate to *cool* significantly. The challenge is to distinguish which

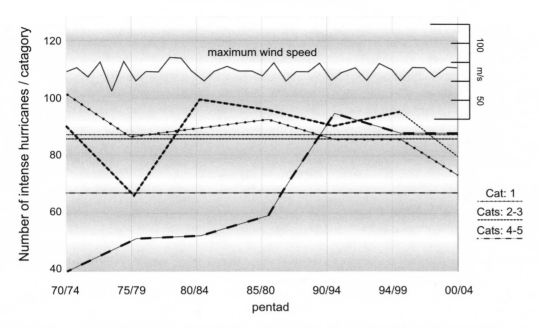

Figure 28.4. Number of severe storms in tropical North Atlantic. Reproduced with permission from AAAS "Science" 309: 1846–1848 (2005).

climate effect is actually controlling the ocean circulation system (Clement et al. 2001).

Changes in salinity are expected to alter oceanic circulation in the South Atlantic (Jacobs et al. 2002). Divergence from currently understood oceanic circulations might mean massive shifts in food chain responses for both low and high trophic-level organisms, as has occurred in the northern Pacific and the western Atlantic. Future populations of Southern Ocean seabirds could be similarly affected. Meanwhile, northern and mid-latitude seabird species could be faced with fewer nesting sites as thermal expansion and sea level claim habitats throughout the Caribbean. Viable breeding sites will be at a premium for many species that nest on the surface of cays and islets.

Additional concern is being raised regarding the capacity of the oceans to absorb carbon dioxide, produced by burning fossil fuels and other industrial processes. The oceans are recognized as an important carbon sink, but the ability to absorb CO_2 has its limits and its impacts. Excess absorption may cause shells of marine animals, including corals and plankton, to dissolve with a lower pH (Feely et al. 2004). The result is an accumulation of carbonic acid that is corrosive to shells and reefs. John Raven of Britain's Royal Society was quoted in the *New York Times* (1 July 2005) suggesting that the near surface pH of the oceans will drop from 7.7 to 7.9 by 2100; a shift of 0.1 on the pH scale is equivalent to 30%

more hydrogen ions. Raven predicts noticeable gaps in coral reefs by midcentury, because they will be weaker and prone to storm damage. There are skeptics who say corals are better suited now to building reef than in the past because warmer water dissolves calcium carbonate, and that some species will adapt to this new environment (Done 1992). However, warmer temperatures and lower pH seem to be stressing reef systems, which could affect the myriad of marine invertebrates, embryos, and larvae dependent upon a vibrant reef. The risk of extinction to reef organisms and other species associated with reef production could be significant and noticeable by 2050 (Thomas et al. 2004).

Hurricanes and Perfect Storms

Added to the concern of altered ocean chemistry impacting the food chain is the threat of increased hurricane frequency and stronger activity over the next 10 to 20 years. Over the last century, temperature has risen 0.5°C globally. The United Nations Intergovernmental Panel on Climate Change estimated in 2001 that by the end of this century, another 1.6° to 5.5°C is achievable if carbon dioxide emissions continue to rise at current rates. These results may be seen in a gradual increase in weather extremes, as predicted by Emanuel (2005) and corroborated independently by Webster et al. (2005), with climate models indicating that global warming makes hurricanes stronger (fig. 28.4).

However, another working theory is that a gradual shift is likely to result in a sudden lurch or tipping point, also known as abrupt climate change, to a long-term extreme cooling or heating of the planet. The storm seasons appear to be expanding temporally and geographically; in a first for the modern period since satellite imagery, a tropical cyclone reported in the South Atlantic off Brazil in March 2004 (NASA 2004). In another recent example, southern hemisphere storms that were remnants of Tropical Cyclone Isobel merged with a non-tropical low-pressure system to create a very large and uncharacteristically powerful storm system across Western Australia on 4 January 2007. The storm's development drew parallels with the "Perfect Storm" in the North Atlantic Ocean during October 1991. The BBC News reported very heavy rain reaching 135 mm in southern sections of Western Australia, along with winds gusting to 72 km/hr. If coral reefs are weakened by lowered pH and salinity in their environment, it could be difficult for reefs to maintain their productivity when faced with more intense storms. Indeed, sea level rise and thermal expansion will create storm surges that could result in shorelines up to 125 meters farther inland in low-lying areas (Knutson and Tuleya 2004).

At worst, the impacts of climate change in the Caribbean may be a combination of extremes: warmer surface temperatures to a depth sufficient to impact reefs, intense cyclonic activity disrupting breeding success, alternating deep dry and wet periods, and loss of shoreline to rising sea levels. Any one of these scenarios, or a coinciding of them, portends difficult conservation planning for workers concerned about even one species. Yet, the more similarity researchers can find among Caribbean seabirds' life history requirements, the better the opportunities for conservation workers to maximize their efforts.

Researchers are keenly aware of the dangers posed by intensified natural events such as hurricanes, which could potentially wipe out a local breeding colony of a rare seabird. Hurricane Fabian caused severe damage to the world's only nesting location of the Bermuda Petrel (*Pterodroma cahow*) in 2003 as result of a direct hit to the island. The overwash of sea during this event broke apart sections of the islands and otherwise flooded natural and man-made nesting burrows constructed for the purpose of increasing the survivability of a species in which numbers had been threatened by competition from tropicbirds and predation by rats. An important component of biologists' planning was moving chicks to imprint on other islets to spread the risk. This type of forward thinking and experimentation is sorely needed in other colonies throughout the region.

The overwash conditions experienced at Bermuda, and obviously at other low-lying islands, are a wake-up call to seabird and other biologists and conservation planners faced with the dilemma of rising sea level. Breeding seabirds of the region are pushed to the limits of acceptable nesting habitat each season when they return to islets, cays, and beaches now occupied by humans and their increasing demands for space. A common requirement of isolation from competing members of their species while maintaining close association for mutual benefit is creating a smaller world for seabirds.

Collateral Damage

Further complicating the lives of seabirds are hazards they face from some commercial fishing practices and from ocean pollution—hazards encountered both in the Caribbean and elsewhere during migration.

Long-Line Fishing

Seabird populations worldwide are threatened by the fishing industry and are generally characterized by the somewhat dismissive term *by-catch*. This can be described as either off-shore or in-shore incidents. Off-shore, the practice of setting out miles of specialized, baited long lines, some with small submerged, chemically generated lights attached to hooks to attract fish far off-shore, also attracts diving seabirds. Once the bill is caught in the barbed hook, the bird soon drowns. Studies on the Florida East Coast and in the Caribbean region have recently shown (Browder 2006) that no birds were lost as by-catch as a result of long-line fishing in these two regions, as opposed to the notable losses in the Pacific. The long-line effort in Florida and Caribbean waters was above the average for eight Atlantic areas studied: the Gulf of Mexico, Middle Atlantic Bight, North-Central Atlantic, Northeast Coastal, North-East Distant, Sargasso Sea, South Atlantic Bight, and the distant south off the coast of eastern South America. The study found gulls and migrant shearwaters to be the most vulnerable species. In contrast, in-shore by-catch is principally by cast-lines when fishermen throw out a line and pelicans, frigatebirds, gulls or boobies dive on the bait and get hooked. Fishermen will simply cut the line and leave the bird to succumb to entanglement and eventual death.

Lack of seabird by-catch from Florida and Caribbean waters in 1992–2005 (Browder 2006) is likely due to the relatively low marine productivity as compared to the Pacific and North Atlantic ecosystems. The tropical marine ecosystem of the West Indies may boast a wide variety of marine bird species (chapter 1, table 1.1), yet the relative abundance of these species is low as a result of the Caribbean region's low chlorophyll *a* and low levels of nutrients by comparison with the large upwelling as seen on the Pacific coast of North and South America, for example. There is some freshwater outwelling, marine upwelling, and eddy formation associated with major currents sweeping past and through the Lesser and Greater Antilles, creating localized exceptions, but the region has otherwise depauperate food sources for pelagic fisheries and birds. In contrast, the North Atlantic may have fewer marine bird species, but the number of individuals exceeds any correlates in the tropics (e.g., gannets versus boobies). Browder (2006) notes that species-specific problems could occur and go unrecognized under the current protocol, although affirming that the U.S. National Marine Fisheries Service intends to continue collecting data on seabird by-catch through observer programs and other means.

Pollution

Shipping poses another threat due both to increased cruise and commercial traffic in the Caribbean (e.g., the Cayman Islands now have 2 million cruise visitors a year) and, as the formerly common practice of dumping wastes of all types directly into the open sea, to non-biodegradable materials (plastics in particular) being ingested by pelagic species (Baltz and Morejohn 1976; Rothstein 1973), and also being used in nest decoration (Podolsky and Kress 1989).

Oil

In addition to intentional dumping of wastes (Austin and Stoops-Glas 1977), there are the unpredictable, albeit expected, oil spills that also claim many seabirds, either by direct contact with the oil slick or in time through ingestion of oiled material or tar balls. Following a spill, crude oil eventually breaks down into several different components, which cause their own problems for the environment. Heavier oil mixes with sediments on the ocean floor and turns into a thick tarlike mass that can destroy the habitat of many bottom-dwelling organisms. These tarlike clumps can also drift with tides and currents, eventually washing up on beaches far away from the spill. Evidence of oiled seabirds in the vastness of the tropical Atlantic Ocean was detected among Bermudan White-tailed Tropicbirds from 1968 to the early 1970s

(Wingate, *in* Butler et al. 1983). During this period the number of oil-fouled tropicbirds went from approximately 10% of the population in 1968 to upwards of 25% in the 1970s (Lee and Walsh-McGehee 2000). According to Wingate (*in* Lee and Walsh-McGehee 2000), oiled tropicbirds failed to breed. Oil pollution peaked in the Sargasso Sea around 1972 and began to decline as a result of new regulations on dumping oil at sea (Lee and Walsh-McGehee 2000).

The largest recorded oil spill in the West Indies occurred in 1979 off Tobago when the *Atlantic Empress* lost 257,000 tonnes, according to the Petroleum Institute. There have been other spills of lesser magnitude in the region since 1968 off Puerto Rico (21 tonnes). Following the 1995 spill at St. Lucia, West Indies, local government established a National Oil Spills Contingency Plan in August 1996. The Petroleum Institute data indicate that the loss of crude via shipping mishaps has dropped significantly since the 1960s and 1970s, reducing at least potential catastrophe over the last 20 years. For diving seabirds, oil pollution remains a threat largely undocumented or underreported in the Caribbean; there has been a noticeable improvement in oil discharge from cruise ships in the last few years.

Plastics

In the marine environment plastics create a major problem (Day et al. 1982; Moser and Lee 1992), either by ingestion directly or from secondary sources in the food chain. A list of species affected has been compiled by Laist (1997). While ingestion of plastics, primarily by Procellarid species, was studied over a period of 14 years (Moser and Lee 1992), the authors did not find sufficient evidence that seabird health was affected. Pierce et al. (2004) report cases of plastic obstruction and starvation in species that migrate through the region, and ecological correlates such as Masked Booby and Audubon's Shearwater, for example, suggest indigenous species could be as susceptible to plastic debris in the pelagic environment.

Pesticides

Wingate (1978) estimated that pesticides were responsible in part for the sharp decline in tropicbird production in Bermuda over the previous 25 years. Custer et al. (1983) investigated the potential for organochlorine compounds in Roseate Tern eggs from the Virgin Islands, as well as in northern latitude populations, and reported "none of the eggs from Dog Island contained organochlorine compounds at a concentration equal to the level of detection. This indicates that the marine environment of the U.S. Virgin Islands is exceptionally free from DDE and PCB contamination." DDE levels have decreased along the Atlantic coast since the late 1960s and early 1970s (Custer et al. 1983). Whether these statements can be extrapolated to other Antillean areas of high cruise vessel or tanker traffic during that period may be a reasonable assumption. While the Custer study was conducted more than two and half decades ago, improvement in the enforcement of regulations and standards protecting the environment from careless handling of organo-compounds and fuels suggests that these chemicals may not be a widespread "background" threat to marine birds of the region.

Based on the premise that tropical terns feed offshore, Burger and Gochfeld (1991) predicted that heavy metal accumulation in terns breeding near Puerto Rico would be lower than in more industrialized surroundings such as those in the northeastern United States. The data did not support the hypothesis, as Bridled Tern had high lead and cadmium levels, and Roseate and Sooty terns had high levels of mercury. Interspecific variability in accumulations of metals has been reported, and differences in age classes have also been detected for roseate terns; the older the chick, the lower the level of detectability through elimination of growing feathers. However, this condition prevails only through subadult stages when young birds can be more easily tested, and mercury is accumulated with age or survivorship. First laid eggs had a higher burden of contamination than succeeding eggs.

Adult survivorship of Roseate Terns on the Eastern Puerto Rico Bank was found to range from 71% to 80% (Shealer et al. 2005) by following birds banded in 1991 to 1994; this was considered low compared to other seabirds breeding in the region. Roseate Tern mortality is tied to losses during the nonbreeding season, when continental and Caribbean populations overlap (Shealer et al. 2005), increasing the risk of competition and reduced fitness.

Future of the Global Commons

All this seems to suggest a bleak future for seabirds. Climatologists struggling for more precise answers and predictions lament that they are data poor as a result of changing administrations and budget priorities. Field researchers with an understanding of ocean-atmospheric trends such as El Niño recognized in the early 1980s, through the abandonment of breeding sites in the Pacific, that a major climatic event was under way (Schreiber and Schreiber 1983). This epiphany led to an explosion of

research on the El Niño/La Niña phenomena. Researchers studying the habits of seabirds in the tropics stand at the edge of yet another monumental event—signaling the advent of sea level rise as experienced in the annual breeding cycles of seabirds. As noted, some experts predict a 30 cm increase in sea level in this century. What will this change mean to marine fauna? How will we know when it begins? (Has it already begun?) How will various species respond?

Jared Diamond (2005) cautions against group decision making by providing a roadmap, as he describes it, outlining the contributing failures in such a process: "1) a group may fail to anticipate a problem before the problem actually arrives, 2) when the problem does arrive, the group may fail to perceive it, 3) after they perceive it, they may fail even to try to solve it, and 4) they may try to solve it but may not succeed." The opposite of this trail of folly is, of course, successful decision making. We need to look carefully at what has worked for various conservation projects and apply the results to management strategies and conservation efforts for problems we perceive as threats now. We need to be very honest about where we currently are on this road map so as not to repeat steps and squander valuable time and resources.

A loose network of seabird biologists is already in place. What is needed is a concerted effort to monitor seabird behavior and productivity using similar methodology throughout the Gulf-Caribbean Basin (Schreiber and Lee 2000a). The call for this effort appeared in *Status and Conservation of the World's Seabirds* (Croxall et al. 1984), with the recognition that pollution was a ubiquitous agent affecting seabirds throughout the "global commons—our oceans." Schreiber and Lee also pointed to continued piecemeal destruction of crucial habitat in order to meet the apparent insatiable need to "improve" land for human uses.

Today we see an even larger Goliath in the form of climate change rising up over the horizon. What can be done to ensure that there is a David to take on this giant? Expanded knowledge and appreciation of all West Indian seabirds must be handed down to successive groups of resident biologists trained and ready to keep longitudinal studies active. Funding for a regional monitoring program must be secure and endowed for the future. As the alarm signals and conservation efforts described in this inventory reflect, we have largely avoided Diamond's first three contributing failures of not anticipating problems, not perceiving threats once they arise, or not even attempting to address them. We are already at number four: working for solutions. Seabird populations, particularly species groups that habituate to nearshore waters and banks such as in eastern Puerto Rico or the southern Bahamas, are somewhat symbiotic. These groups interact and respond to one another's good fortune as well as bad. Resident Laughing Gull, for example, interact with Brown Pelican; Magnificent Frigatebird react to feeding groups of three species of boobies, two tropicbird species, a shearwater, and several tern species. It may therefore be reasonable to consider all species in the region relative to each other in this tropical Western Atlantic biome as a means to determine their overall status within the region.

While banding studies have shown that representatives from each species may wander outside the Caribbean region, the 21 extant species surveyed for this volume are indigenous, and they have complementary life histories. Their individual status as species can be viewed as a part of the whole, an overarching organism responding to the conditions of its environment, its sum greater than its parts. In that light, compromising any species is at some level also a risk to them all.

29

Status of Caribbean Seabirds

PATRICIA E. BRADLEY AND ROBERT L. NORTON

Columbus provided an early description of Caribbean seabirds as flocks signaled his approach to land on 4 October 1492: "More than forty petrels came to the ship together, and two boobies. A frigate bird came to the ship, and a white bird like a gull" (*Log of Columbus* in Casas 1986). Five hundred years ago, seabirds in the Caribbean possibly numbered tens of millions. In the early twenty-first century, they appear to be continuing a long decline, with a total population numbering under 2 million.

If successful conservation strategies can be implemented in the Caribbean in the near future, it should be possible to stabilize or even increase seabird numbers and emulate Great Britain and Ireland, where, in 35 years, numbers increased from 5 to 8 million as a direct result of increased protection at breeding colonies and wintering grounds (Mitchell et al. 2004).

This is the third inventory of breeding Caribbean seabirds and the first to present inventories island by island (as opposed to species by species, as previously). It is incomplete, as many sites remain to be surveyed either for the first time or for updated data, as in the case of the Black-capped Petrel. To reduce overestimates, conservative count numbers (minimum in the range) were used for 2007 data.

Chapter 27 lists the most threatened and most important colonies as well as sites in need of surveys, and by ranking status: 13.4% of sites were shown to be extirpated or depleted; 73.1% to be of moderate or unknown status; and 13.3% to contain more than 5% of the estimated regional population of one or more species (Mackin, and maps 1–51, this volume). Colonies with 5% of the regional population qualify as international Important Bird Areas (IBAs), and those with 1% as Caribbean IBAs—all are in need of protection.

The first inventory by van Halewyn and Norton (1984) was a herculean task. In spite of the senior author's vast experience in the southern tier of continental islands and the Windwards, there was much yet unknown about the many breeding stations on offshore cays and islands of the Greater Antilles and Leeward Islands, except to egg collectors and fishermen. In 1984 van Halewyn and Norton combined their data to produce maps for each species based on field experience and historic records, despite the literature being both thin and seemingly effusive about the status of many species; they also recognized the urgency of ever-mounting threats to the survival of the region's seabirds.

Data Sets for 1984, 2000, and 2007

Counts from the three data sets (table 29.1) give estimates of breeding populations of 21 species of Caribbean seabirds at three points, 1984, 2000 and 2007, a period extending over 23 years with data for the inventories extending over 100 years.

Some indications about the reliability of estimates are in order. Estimates of breeding seabird populations are based on a number of varying factors, including accessibility to colonies and levels of disturbance species will tolerate. Given the types of constraints that researchers may have in determining a breeding population, even when the species is generally colloquial or attending nests, it may be reasonable to accept a plus or minus factor of perhaps 10%. Table 29.2 suggests that species for which estimates greatly exceed 15% and approach 50% are in need of more rigorous counting techniques or a reassessment of contributing data.

Three species that pose a particularly difficult challenge are Roseate, Royal, and Sandwich terns, populations of which appear to constitute cells of a metapopulation and do not nest consistently at a given location or remain within a given political entity, where populations can be monitored carefully using the same methodology and effort. If one is to assume that population esti-

Table 29.1. Comparison of data sets: Halewyn and Norton (1984), Schreiber and Lee (2000a), and Bradley and Norton (2007)

Species	Halewyn & Norton 1984	Schreiber & Lee 2000	Bradley & Norton 2007
Bermuda Petrel	32	N/A	71
Black-capped Petrel	25,000	2,000	No new data
Audubon's Shearwater	5,000	3,000–5,000	2,676–3,107
White-tailed Tropicbird	10,000	2,500–3,500	4,156–4,544
Red-billed Tropicbird	1,600	1,800–2,500	1,736–2,604
Masked Booby	2,500	550–650	750–972
Brown Booby	17,000	5,500–7,800	6,942–7,748
Red-footed Booby	14,000	8,200–10,000	14,585–16,691
Brown Pelican	6,200	1,500	2,412–2,849
Magnificent Frigatebird	8,000	4,300–5,300	6,099–6,926
Laughing Gull	7,000	5,000–10,000	12,222–13,791
Brown Noddy	28,000	10,000–18,000	42,192–44,083
Black Noddy	Present	<100	100
Sooty Tern	500,000	200,000–300,000	317,942–341,992
Bridled Tern	7,000	5,000–7,000	8,909–10,368
Least Tern	6,000	1,500–3000	4,410–4,985
Gull-billed Tern	Present	100–500	250–310
Roseate Tern	4,000	4,000–6,000	3,571–7,095
Common Tern	750	50–100	627–637
Royal Tern	1,400	450–800	647–840
Sandwich Tern	2,000	2,100–3,000	1,608–2,605
Cayenne Tern[a]	8,000	Combined w/ above	3,844–3,858

a. A race of Sandwich Tern.

Table 29.2. Gull and tern population estimates as spread between maximum and minimum counts and the average of the estimate

Species	Spread from Max and Min in Population	Spread/Ave in %
Laughing Gull	1,569	6.4
Brown Noddy	1,891	4.9
Sooty Tern	24,050	7.3
Bridled Tern	1,459	15
Least Tern	575	12.2
Gull-billed Tern	60	10.7
Roseate Tern	3,524	66
Common Tern	10	1.5
Royal Tern	213	28.2
Sandwich Tern	997	47.3
Cayenne Tern	14	< 1

mates (table 29.2) are correct, management approaches may have difficulty determining whether a population is stable or in serious trouble from year to year.

Comparison of the Data Sets

Data collection of Caribbean seabird populations remains very uneven, with good understanding of some species on some islands using standardized census methods but nothing comparable in other cases. Inevitably, this volume contains some of the inaccuracies inherent in the two previous major studies. Valid comparisons between the three regional data sets would require standardized methods of data collection across the range, not yet achieved in the Caribbean, an area acknowledged as biodiversity data-poor although showing rapid improvements in the twenty-first century. Thus comparisons in this case are problematic and lack scientific rigor due to the great variation in and nonstandardization of the data collection parameters (some different observers, different census methods, some different sites, seasonal variations, etc). However, a number of consistencies allowed

Table 29.3. Comparison of Caribbean data sets: Halewyn and Norton (1984) and Bradley and Norton (2007)

Species	Halewyn & Norton (1984)	Bradley & Norton to 2007	23 yr. % change in Caribbean populations
White-tailed Tropicbird	10,000[b]	4,100[b]	-59
Red-billed Tropicbird	1,600	1,800	+13
Masked Booby	2,500	750	-70
Brown Booby	17,000	7,000	-59
Red-footed Booby	14,000	14,600	+4
Brown Pelican	6,200	2,400	-61
Magnificent Frigatebird	8,000	6,100	-24
Laughing Gull	7,000	12,000	+71
Brown Noddy	28,000	42,200	+51
Sooty Tern	500,000	318,000	-36
Bridled Tern	7,000	9,000	+29
Least Tern	6,000	4,500	-25
Roseate Tern	4,000	3,600	-11
Common Tern	750[b]	630[b]	-16
Royal Tern	1,400	650	-54
Sandwich Tern[a]	10,000	5,500	-45

a. The total population of the Sandwich Tern, includes the Cayenne Tern subspecies,
b. Caribbean and Bermuda populations

limited comparisons of some taxa to be made with fair reliability between 1984 and 2007, where, for example, the majority of the same islands and major colonies were visited in 1984, 2000, and 2007 and in the same (breeding) season.

Caribbean Data Sets: Halewyn and Norton 1984, vs. Bradley and Norton 2007

The Caribbean populations of 16 taxa from the 2007 data set were compared with those of van Halewyn and Norton (1984) and included counts of the Atlantic populations on Bermuda for two species (White-tailed Tropicbird and Common Tern; table 29.3). The data set of Bradley and Norton (to 2007) was compiled from Caribbean species-country matrices (tables 29.6, 29.7) giving the range of regional populations, minimum-maximum species counts per island, breeding confirmations with no estimates (counted as 1–10), and extirpations. The Bermuda Petrel, Black-capped Petrel, Audubon's Shearwater, Black Noddy, and Gull-billed Tern were omitted from the comparison.

In 2007, four species showed increases over the 1984 figures ranging from 13% to 71%: Red-billed Tropicbird (13%), Laughing Gull (71%), Brown Noddy (51%) and Bridled Tern (29%). Eleven species showed declines ranging between 11% and 70% (White-tailed Tropicbird, Masked Booby, Brown Booby, Brown Pelican, Magnificent Frigatebird, Sooty Tern, Least Tern, Roseate Tern, Common Tern, Royal Tern, and Sandwich Tern (two subspecies; table 29.3, fig. 29.1). The White-tailed Tropic-

bird (10,000 to 4,000) and Masked Booby (2,500 to 750) showed the greatest population falls.

West Indian Data Sets: Schreiber and Lee 2000a vs. Bradley and Norton 2007

The 2007 West Indian data sets showed considerable increases in breeding populations since 2000, attributed mainly to the inclusion of new counts of colonies that were previously unknown or for which estimates were too low in 2000. Thus few of these higher estimates probably constitute a "true" increase, reinforcing the need for more and standardized methods of survey with regional training. In a comparison between the 2007 data set with those of Schreiber and Lee (2000a) from the traditional West Indian region, five species had similar counts (White-tailed Tropicbird [excluding Bermuda], Red-billed Tropicbird, Masked Booby, Brown Pelican, and Roseate Tern). Ten species showed increased counts in 2007 (Brown Booby, Red-footed Booby, Magnificent Frigatebird, Laughing Gull, Brown Noddy, Sooty Tern, Bridled Tern, Least Tern, Common Tern, and Royal Tern); one species (Sandwich Tern) showed a decline (table 29.4).

Regional Distribution of Caribbean Seabird Populations

Caribbean seabirds are discussed by species, in some cases just in a brief summary. In others, the opening material refers to Caribbean data of van Halewyn and

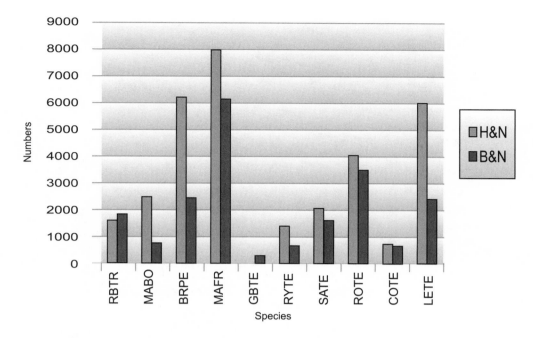

Figure 29.1. Population declines for 10 species in the Caribbean, 1984 vs. 2007.

Norton (1984) and this volume, followed by the West Indies data of Schreiber and Lee (2000a) and this volume. Minimum counts from individual islands of pairs (given in parentheses) refer to data in this volume unless otherwise indicated.

The following abbreviations are used: USVI = United States Virgin Islands, BVI = British Virgin Islands, TCI = Turks and Caicos Islands, St. Kitts = St. Christopher. All seabird numbers refer to breeding pairs.

Bermuda Petrel (Cahow)

Extirpated from the West Indies, it now exists only as a critically endangered species in the Atlantic in Bermuda, in a managed population painstakingly rebuilt by David Wingate over 30 years. Until 2004, the population was confined to four islets (0.8 ha), since which time birds have been translocated to Nonsuch Island and are establishing a successful new colony with translocated chicks returning to breed in 2008. This volume reports the 2005 population as 71 pairs, 250 individuals, the result of an intensive management program and good protection. This increase is from 18 pairs and eight fledged young in 1962, and 32 pairs in 1984 (Halewyn and Norton 1984).

Jamaican Petrel

This species is probably extinct, although a few birds may remain in the remote mountain areas.

Black-capped Petrel

This West Indian endemic race is endangered and confirmed breeding only in the southern mountain ranges of Hispaniola; its range at sea extends into southeastern U.S. waters. The total populations in Haiti and the Dominican Republic remain unknown; there are only two counts confirming the presence of birds in 2002 and 2005 that add any information to the <2000 pairs estimate by Lee (2000a). However, most authors expect that the species will continue to decline due to habitat destruction, logging, and human and introduced predators. In

Table 29.4. Comparison of West Indian data sets: Schreiber and Lee (2000a) and Bradley and Norton (2007)

Species	Schreiber & Lee (2000a)	Bradley & Norton to 2007
Brown Booby	5,500	6,800
Red-footed Booby	8,200	13,600
Magnificent Frigatebird	4,300	6,100
Laughing Gull	5,000	11,000
Brown Noddy	12,000	37,000
Sooty Tern	200,000	296,000
Bridled Tern	4,000	8,400
Least Tern	1,500	2,700
Common Tern	50	200
Royal Tern	450	534
Sandwich Tern	2,100	1,600

Haiti, where the majority of extant colonies are located, estimates declined from a possible 25,000 (Halewyn and Norton 1984) to 600 pairs in 12 colonies at the Massif de la Selle and Massif de la Hotte (Collar et al. 1992). Birds were present at the Massif de la Selle in 2005, with four to seven individuals noted between Pie la Visite and Morne Cabaio, and further degradation of the forest habitat was reported (C. Rimmer, pers. comm. to D. Wege). In the Dominican Republic in Sierra de Baoruco 65 pairs were estimated (Woods and Ottenwalder 1983), 5–40 (Lee 2000a), and 200 in 2002 (Simons et al. 2002).

This petrel is extirpated in Martinique and Guadeloupe, and probably Dominica, although a recent specimen may indicate breeding (Lee 2000a). The mountains in Cuba are thought likely to have breeding sites, but there are no breeding confirmations.

Audubon's Shearwater

The shearwater continues to breed widely throughout the Bahamas and the Caribbean, where fossils and subfossils prove it was once abundant (e.g., Cayman Islands), and where it has shown exceptional vulnerability to human and animal predation. The last known extirpation was in Bermuda by 1981. Van Halewyn and Norton (1984) estimated the Caribbean population at 5,000; this volume reports breeding on 12 islands and estimates a decline to 2,700. Reported on three of the Venezuelan archipelagos but no estimates were available. Reports by Voous (1983) of breeding in Curaçao and Bonaire have never been confirmed. The five-year study by William Mackin (Mackin 2004, 2005) of Audubon's Shearwater on Long Cay, Bahamas, is a model of its kind and needs to be repeated in the region beginning with Saba, the Turks and Caicos Islands, and Dominica to obtain more comprehensive population estimates.

Lee (2000b) estimated the West Indian population at 3,000 and this volume reports 2,700. There were only 25 pairs from Saba, where 1,000 pairs were estimated (Lee 2000b). The counts from the Bahamas showed a large increase (2,000), with breeding reported throughout the archipelago; Mackin (2004) noted 789 on Long Cay, Exumas, or 233 pairs/ha, the densest colony known. Other reports are the first breeding record for Cuba (two pairs in 2002 on the Sabana-Camagüey Archipelago), Puerto Rico (25, a recent confirmation), USVI (>20), Martinique (50), Barbados (50), and Tobago (>500). Breeding, with no estimates, was reported throughout TCI and the French Antillean islands of Tintamarre and Guadeloupe. Breeding has not been confirmed on Jamaica, BVI, Anguilla, Netherlands St. Maarten and St. Eustatius, Antigua and Barbuda, or St. Vincent, the Grenadines, or

Grenada. Breeding has never been reported from Hispaniola, possibly because of few studies on the many islands and cays of this large island.

The status of the race *P. l. loyemilleri* in the western Caribbean is unknown; it is probably extirpated in Providencia, San Andrés Archipelago, where it was once common (Bond 1950), and although reported off Venezuela, it is not breeding.

White-tailed Tropicbird

Breeding from Bermuda and through the West Indies from the Bahamas south to St. Vincent and the Grenadines. Van Halewyn and Norton (1984) estimated the Atlantic and West Indian population at 10,000 pairs. This volume reports breeding counts on 16 islands and estimates the combined total to be 4,100, including 2,000 in Bermuda, a 59% decline.

Walsh-McGehee (2000) estimated the West Indian population at 2,500; this volume estimates 2,100, with counts from the Bahamas (450), TCI (224), Cayman Islands (120), and Puerto Rico (500) and breeding confirmed on Anguilla (3–4), Jamaica (<100), BVI (60), USVI (>30), French Antilles (54), and Cuba (1–4). The estimate for Hispaniola (500) was considered by Keith et al. (2003) to be more realistic than 1,000 (Walsh-McGehee 2000). In the Netherlands Antilles in 2002, only a few pairs were observed on Saba and none on St. Eustatius, where Walsh-McGehee (2000) estimated Saba (50) and St. Eustatius (10). Breeding was confirmed with no estimates on St. Lucia and St. Vincent and the Grenadines, and on Navassa Island. There were no reports from St. Kitts–Nevis or from Antigua, where birds were breeding on Great Bird Island, 1973–1975 (Bradley, pers. obs.).

Red-billed Tropicbird

This species breeds from Puerto Rico (most westerly part of its West Indian range) through the Virgin Islands and Lesser Antilles to Tobago and the islands of Venezuela. Van Halewyn and Norton (1984) estimated the Caribbean population at 1,600 pairs, and this volume reports breeding on 17 islands and 1,800, an increase of 13%. There were no estimates for Venezuela, although breeding was confirmed on two archipelagos and La Tortuga Island.

Walsh-McGehee (2000) estimated the West Indian population at 1,800, with the largest population (750) in Saba thought to have remained relatively stable to 2003. This volume also estimates 1,800, with increases on BVI (80), St. Eustatius (100), and the French Antilles (450). There were new records for Anguilla (21), St. Kitts (2), Montserrat (11), and St. Lucia (23); breeding was confirmed on St. Vincent, Grenada, and the Grenadines; Antigua (3), Tobago (53), and Puerto Rico (20) had reduced populations.

Masked Booby

The Caribbean population was estimated at 2,500 pairs, and this booby's scarcity and loss of breeding sites were mentioned (Halewyn and Norton 1984). This volume reports breeding counts on six islands (with probable sites on two additional islands) and estimates 750 pairs, a 70% decline. There are no recent counts at two of the most important sites: in 1996, 200 were estimated on Los Monjes Archipelago, Venezuela, now a major tourist destination, and the last breeding confirmation on Serranilla, San Andrés Archipelago, was in 1975 (Chiriví 1988).

Schreiber (2000b) estimated the West Indian population at 550 pairs, and this volume estimates an identical total (550). The largest colony in the West Indies was on the Pedro Cays, Jamaica (267), where the census was incomplete. There was an increase in Puerto Rico (to 175), and a decrease on USVI (45), while Anguilla (57) remained the same. The first modern breeding record on Tobago (5) was reported. On Antigua, birds were present only on Redonda, where van Halewyn and Norton (1984) reported breeding, but breeding was not confirmed in 2004 (although birds were observed) as the trip was outside the breeding season. There was no breeding confirmation on St. Vincent, the Grenadines, or Grenada. Breeding (contra Schreiber 2000b) was not confirmed in the Bahamas or the Cayman Islands, and this sulid still breeds on Middle Cay, Jamaica.

Brown Booby

The Caribbean estimate was 17,000 (Halewyn and Norton 1984) and this volume reports breeding counts from 17 islands and estimates 7,000, a 59% decline. There were new data from Los Roques, Venezuela (474), where five additional colonies are known (no estimates), and from Roncador, Colombian archipelago (>100 in 2005).

Schreiber (2000b) estimated the West Indian population at 5,500 and this volume estimates 6,800. This was due to increased counts in the Cayman Islands (110), Puerto Rico (1,650), USVI (500), BVI (170), and Anguilla (1,965); there were decreases in the Bahamas (550) and Tobago (84). Thirteen pairs were estimated on Redonda, Antigua, Montserrat (9), and Hispaniola (600). There were new breeding data at six sites on St. Vincent, the Grenadines, and Grenada (315), confirmation of breeding on Cuba in 1991 (no estimates) and on French St. Barts. (150). In Jamaica, the high counts of

1997 (500–1,000) and 1998 (2,000 pairs) were not repeated in 2005, when an incomplete survey gave about 50 pairs. Breeding was not confirmed on TCI and St. Lucia.

Red-footed Booby

The Caribbean population was estimated at 14,000 (Halewyn and Norton 1984) and this volume reports breeding on 12 islands and estimates 14,600. There were new counts on Los Roques, Venezuela (1,113), and there was breeding on three other islands of the archipelago.

Schreiber (2000b) estimated the West Indian population at 8,200 and this volume reports 13,600. The first modern counts, with large populations, were provided for Navassa (2,500; see Hispaniola) and Grenada and the Grenadines (3,500+); increased populations on Puerto Rico (3,000) and Tobago (464); and the first breeding confirmation on Les Saintes, French Antilles (<10). Fewer than five pairs each were reported on the Bahamas and Anguilla. The population on Redonda (<60) was much reduced from 1,000 (Halewyn and Norton 1984) as the survey was late in the breeding season. Counts were lower on USVI (100). There were no new data on the Little Cayman colony (3,824–5,854), the largest in the Caribbean after 1997 (Burton et al. 1999), although a new census is planned as there are concerns numbers have declined. No colonies were reported on Jamaica, TCI, or Cuba.

Brown Pelican

The population of the Caribbean race was estimated at 6,200 pairs (Halewyn and Norton 1984) and this volume reports 2,400 pairs on 13 islands, a 61% decline. In Venezuela there were new counts on Los Roques Archipelago (about 800) and Margarita Island, and four other islands/archipelagos had (uncounted) colonies.

Collazo et al. (2000) estimated the West Indian population at 1,500 and this volume estimates a slight increase (1,630). Included are the first counts from Cuba (300 pairs at 18 colonies); the first breeding records from Anguilla (21) and Montserrat (14); increases in Jamaica (>150), Puerto Rico (265), USVI (325), and BVI (300); and an estimate for Hispaniola (100) lower than 500+ (Collazo et al. 2000). Breeding was confirmed from the Bahamas (50), Netherlands St. Maarten (26), and Antigua (53). The species was extirpated in the French Antilles and was not breeding on TCI.

Magnificent Frigatebird

For the Caribbean, van Halewyn and Norton (1984) estimated 8,000 and this volume reports breeding on 16 islands (data only from the West Indies) and estimates 6,100, a 24% decline (there was no new count on Barbuda where the 1996 estimate was used (Schreiber 1996) as local reports point to a healthy colony. Breeding was confirmed (no estimates) on Providence and Serrana, San Andrés Archipelago, and the Venezuelan islands.

Lindsay et al. (2000) estimated the West Indian population at 4,300. The 2007 counts show a 42% increase. The largest colonies were in Barbuda (2,000), where recent reports (Bradley, pers. comm.) estimate the colony size similar to the 1996 figures (Schreiber 1996), and in Cuba (1,000). Other colonies were in Puerto Rico (500), BVI (400), the Bahamas (150), Cayman Islands (227), Hispaniola (250), Anguilla (142), Redonda (100), Tobago (800), TCI (>35), Montserrat (27), and St. Lucia (50). There were no breeding colonies reported on USVI or the French Antilles. In Jamaica, 1,500 pairs were counted in 1998, falling to 315 in incomplete surveys in 2005.

Laughing Gull

Distribution of this species, the only gull native to the region, is widespread, loosely associated with nesting terns or near tern colonies. Van Halewyn and Norton (1984) estimated the Caribbean population at 7,000 and this volume reports breeding on 20 islands and estimates 12,300, a 71% increase. Numbers increased on Aruba (350) and Bonaire (60), where large tern colonies may be attracting or sustaining gull recruitment; the only counts on Venezuela were on Los Roques Archipelago (>544).

Chardine et al. (2000a) estimated the West Indian population at 5,000, and this volume estimates 11,000. There were increased populations on the Bahamas (2,000), first counts from Cuba (>1,000), Anguilla (2,600), and St Martin, French Antilles (450); also from Puerto Rico (1,300), USVI (2,000), BVI (1,000), Antigua/Barbuda (70), and TCI (170). The species is absent as a breeder from the Cayman Islands and much of the Lesser Antilles. Colonies under 10–15 pairs are not likely to persist without terneries nearby.

Brown Noddy

This species is more tolerant of intruders than many, allowing better survey results. Van Halewyn and Norton (1984) estimated the Caribbean population at 28,000 and this volume reports breeding counts from 22 islands and estimates a 51% increase to 42,200, with counts from the continental islands: Aruba (164), Los Roques and Aves Island,Venezuela (5,313) and Colombia (>250)

Chardine et al. (2000b) estimated the West Indian population at 12,000 and this volume estimates 37,000. The increase was due to increased populations on the Ba-

hamas (4,400) and Puerto Rico (1,300) and new counts on TCI (27,000), Anguilla (726), and the French Antilles (910). Other estimates were from Cuba (300), Hispaniola (50), lower numbers in Jamaica (500, down from 7,000 in 1996–1997), USVI (400), BVI (100), Antigua/Barbuda (140), Netherlands Antilles (45), St. Kitts (8), St. Lucia (5), St. Vincent and the Grenadines (145), and Tobago (500), down from 1,200 in Chardine et al. (2000b).

Black Noddy

A marginal breeder since the loss of habitat off Belize in the mid-1980s when the once large breeding colony dispersed and numbers declined to zero. Van Halewyn and Norton (1984) estimated the Caribbean population at 100, the same as Chardine et al. (2000b) and this volume, a stable trend. The only nesting sites were on the continental islands of Aruba (48) and Los Roques Archipelago, Venezuela (52), where a recent count took place.

Chardine et al. (2000b) estimated 10 in the West Indies and this volume had no reports of breeding, only reports of a few individuals from the Puerto Rico Bank, Sombrero in Anguilla, Jamaica, and Cuba.

Sooty Tern

This is the most abundant resident tern in the region. The Caribbean population was estimated by van Halewyn and Norton (1984) at 500,000 and by Saliva (2000a) at 230,000; this volume reports breeding on 22 islands and estimates 318,000, a 36% decline from the 1984 figure. The Caribbean population could still be as high as 500,000 if the large populations reported in Saliva (2000a) from Jamaica (70,000), Cuba (40,000), and Venezuela (20,000), reported as sharply reduced in this volume, were found to be extant. There are no recent counts from six previous breeding locations in Venezuela, which—despite losing almost 50% of its Sooty Tern population since 1955—had about 125,000 pairs in 1984 and 12,000 pairs on Aves Island in 2006. Other estimates were for Aruba (6,650) and Serrana, San Andrés Archipelago (>1,000).

Saliva (2000a) estimated the West Indian population at 200,000. This volume estimates 296,000, with large populations from new locations: TCI (48,300), Hispaniola (80,000), Anguilla (52,300), St. Lucia (38,000), and St. Vincent, the Grenadines and Grenada (2,500). There were estimates from the Bahamas (7,200), Cuba (3,000), Puerto Rico (40,500), USVI (20,000), BVI (100), Antigua/Barbuda (514), Netherlands Saba (30), French St. Martin (150), Guadeloupe (3,000), and Martinique (1,100), and St. Kitts (200). In Jamaica there is cause for concern: in 1997, 1,000 were estimated on the Pedro Cays and in 2005, 4,500 birds were present but none were nesting, and only one unfledged chick was seen over three visits spanning the year; counts from the Morant Cays were 23,000 in 1986, 132,000 in 1986 and 100,000 in 1997 but there are no recent data; 50,000 pairs are estimated. Their preference for nesting in large, generally open colonies on offshore islands and their laying of replacement eggs have helped to establish this species as an abundant food source.

Bridled Tern

The more secretive nesting habits of this species, with nests often hidden by vegetation, make survey difficult, suggesting that numbers in the region may be underestimated. Van Halewyn and Norton (1984) estimated a Caribbean population of 7,000 and this volume reports breeding on 22 islands and an estimate of 9,000, a 29% increase. Estimates include Aruba (122) and Los Roques, Venezuela (418).

Chardine et al. (2000a) estimated the West Indian population at 4,000. This volume estimates 8,400. There were major declines in Jamaica, where 1,030 were estimated on the Morant Cays in 1987 and 750–1,000 on the Pedro Cays in 1997, but only four active nests were located in 2005. There were increases on the Bahamas (2,200), TCI (3,333), and Cuba (650); other counts were Hispaniola (150), Cayman Islands (16), Puerto Rico (235), USVI (500), BVI (150), Anguilla (400), Antigua/Barbuda (16), northern Netherlands Antilles (51), St. Kitts (60), French Antilles (480), and Tobago (50).

Least Tern

This species prefers to nest in small to moderately high numbers (2 to 100 pairs) at saline flats, on dredge spoil, or on other disturbed sandy or rock-strewn sites, even fresh construction areas. Sites are vulnerable to predation and flooding; West Indian birds are not reported to breed on the roofs of buildings. The Caribbean population was estimated by van Halewyn and Norton (1984) at 6,000 and this volume reports breeding counts on 18 islands and estimates 4,500, a 25% decline. The highest concentrations were on the Bahamian Archipelago, the Puerto Rican bank, and the continental islands: Aruba (55), Bonaire (792), Curaçao (619), Netherlands Antilles, and Los Roques, Venezuela (205). As we were going to press a colony in St. Croix previously estimated at 300–600 pairs was found to hold 900–1,340 nests, data not included here.

Jackson (2000) estimated the West Indian population at 1,500 and this volume estimates 2,700: Bahamas (600),

TCI (640), Cuba (350), Hispaniola (100), Jamaica (<50), Cayman Islands (84), Puerto Rico (150), USVI (300), BVI (100), Anguilla (290), Netherlands St. Maarten (10), French Antilles (120), and St. Kitts (40). Numbers have fallen by around 60–70% in Jamaica and the Cayman Islands in the last 10 years. In 1997 at Codrington Lagoon, Barbuda, the number was reported to exceed 1,000, but no Least Tern were reported in recent surveys.

Gull-billed Tern

This is perhaps the least known resident tern in the region because of its apparent dependence on coastal freshwater to brackish wetlands, habitats that are especially vulnerable to development. The endemic race has always been a marginal breeder in the Bahamian archipelago and the Greater Antilles: van Halewyn and Norton (1984) offered no estimates and Chardine et al. (2000a) estimated 100 pairs. It is extirpated on Puerto Rico, USVI and Anguilla. Numbers have declined in the United States as well.

This volume reports a slightly higher estimate (250), with distribution confined to the Bahamas (100), a first estimate from Cuba (70), BVI (4), Anegada (table B.2 in appendix B) where five pairs formerly bred, and TCI (80) where numbers are likely higher, as at least two colonies of 30 and 50 pairs were located in marshes where a large area remained to be sampled and where extensive wetlands are protected under Ramsar designation. Small colonies may reach a dozen pairs in remote areas, such as Great Inagua, but do not seem to persist.

Roseate Tern

Van Halewyn and Norton (1984) estimated the Caribbean population at 4,000 and this volume reports breeding on 18 islands and estimates 3,600, an 11% decline. The only count from the continental islands was from Aruba (52); the species breeds on Aves Island, Venezuela, but there are no estimates.

U.S. authorities consider the West Indian race of this species threatened; Saliva (2000b) estimated 4,000. This volume estimates 3,550. Numbers in the Bahamas (800) and TCI (200) indicate substantial populations possibly sending recruits to Cuba (40–50). The population is centered on the Puerto Rican Bank: Puerto Rico (935); USVI (500–2,300), and BVI (600–2,000), showing wide yearly fluctuations; and Anguilla (210). Roseates were absent as breeders from Hispaniola and the Cayman Islands; there were possibly two pairs in Jamaica. In the Lesser Antilles, there were small colonies in the French Antilles (60), St. Kitts (>6), St. Lucia (10), St. Vincent and the Grenadines (15), and Trinidad and Tobago (136). This species seems to be declining in the south but its habit of shifting nesting sites with increasing levels of disturbance makes estimates difficult.

Common Tern

Literature references to breeding Common Tern may be confusing this tern and West Indian Roseate Tern, which has a slightly noticeable bi-colored bill during breeding, resembling the red-billed North American form of Common Tern. The history of this species in the Antilles is not well known and it is considered a marginal breeder (Del Hoyo et al. 1996). Van Halewyn and Norton (1984) estimated the Caribbean and Bermuda population at 750 and estimates for the last 20 years have always been low. This volume reports breeding counts from seven islands and estimates 630, with the Bermuda population—recurring breeders, with about 25 pairs since the 1960s—reduced to 8 (with no young fledged) after Hurricane Fabian in 2004. The continental islands reported: Curaçao (133), Aruba (143), Bonaire (39), Netherlands Antilles, and Los Roques, Venezuela (104), where two other locations were listed with no modern estimates.

Buckley and Buckley (2000) estimated the West Indian population at 50 and this volume reports 200, with breeding at only two (new) locations: TCI (100 on uninhabited East Caicos, extensive areas of which have been designated a Ramsar site) and Cuba (110). The last reports of breeding in the French Antilles were from Guadeloupe in 2000 and Martinique in 1994.

Royal Tern

Van Halewyn and Norton (1984) estimated the Caribbean population at 1,400, and this volume estimates 650, a 54% decrease. There was breeding in Aruba (1) and Bonaire (85), Netherlands Antilles and Los Roques, Venezuela (25).

The West Indian population is small: Chardine et al. (2000a) estimated 450, and this volume estimates 534, with counts from the Bahamas (200) and Hispaniola (10), new counts for Cuba (20), TCI (10–100 estimated), Anguilla (155), Netherlands St. Maarten (47), and French St. Martin (30). There were lower counts for Puerto Rico (10), USVI (60), and Jamaica (1). Populations are extirpated on BVI and Trinidad. Generally, Royal Terns breed in widespread small colonies with an average of 10 pairs, and colonies of up to 100 pairs may include other gregarious nesters such as Sandwich Terns; nests are subject to flooding.

Sandwich Tern

The two subspecies of the Sandwich Tern are an estimated total of 5,500 in 2007. Van Halewyn and Norton

(1984) estimated the West Indies population at 2,000 pairs and Norton (2000) at 2,100. This volume reports a reduced population (1,600). There were lower counts in the Bahamas (335), the first counts from Cuba (160), Hispaniola (30) and Jamaica (<6). The center of the population for this race is the Puerto Rico Bank (none were reported south): Puerto Rico (675), a wide range in estimates from USVI (100–1,000), BVI (100), and Anguilla (172). As with other white-backed terns, Sandwich Terns are loosely faithful to nesting islets, avoiding a densely populated site in subsequent year(s).

Cayenne Tern

First reported nesting on the continental islands of Aruba, Bonaire, Curaçao in 1984, the Caribbean population was estimated at 9,000 (Halewyn 1985), and Norton (2000) estimated about 12,000, of which 9,000 were on Aruba, Bonaire, and Curaçao, Netherlands Antilles. This volume estimates a sharp decline to 3,900: Aruba (3,600), Bonaire (180), extirpation on Curaçao (most likely due to tourist development), and Los Roques, Venezuela (75). This race has been found breeding in small numbers among *Thalasseus sandvicensis acuflavida* occasionally in the Greater Antilles and recently in Cuba, and on St. Thomas, USVI, BVI, and Anegada. Norton (2000) estimated the West Indian population at 10 and this volume estimates a similarly low number (<20) breeding at three locations: Puerto Rico (5–10), Cuba (the first record of one pair), and USVI ("occasional" breeder); there were no reports from BVI. While some experts consider Cayenne Tern a separate species, the taxonomy remains clouded since pure forms of both Cayenne and Sandwich terns have been documented attending the same nest and young (Norton 1984).

Determining Status Categories

Four different methods are extant to determine the threat status of Caribbean seabirds. Three agencies have classified their conservation status: the World Conservation Union (IUCN), U.S. Fish and Wildlife Service (USFWS), and the North American Waterbird Conservation Plan (NAWCP). Schreiber (2000a) proposed new criteria for Caribbean seabirds by modifying IUCN criteria.

The IUCN Red List (2006) recognizes three species as Globally Endangered (EN), and 19 species as Least Concern (LC). USFWS recognizes three species as Endangered (EN) and two as Threatened (T). The NAWCP criteria for endangerment focuses on North and Central America and the Caribbean islands, listing two species

Table 29.5. Comparison of status assessments from regional studies against agency evaluations and two proposed new definitions for Caribbean populations

Species	H&N[a] (1984)	S[b] (2000a)	B&N[c] (2009)	IUCN[d] 2006	NAWCP[e] (2002)	USFWS[f]
Bermuda Petrel	SC	-	EN CARS	EN	HC	EN
Black-capped Petrel	SC	CE	EN CARS	EN	HIM	
Audubon's Shearwater	SC	NT	CARS	LC	HIM	EN
White-tailed Tropicbird	NIC	V	CARS	LC	HC	
Red-billed Tropicbird	M	V	CNIC	LC	HC	
Masked Booby	SC	E	CARS	LC	HC	
Brown Booby	M	-	CARS	LC	HC	
Red-footed Booby	M	-	CINC	LC	HC	
Brown Pelican	SC	E	CARS	LC	MC	T
Magnificent Frigatebird	SC	NT	CARS	LC	HC	
Laughing Gull	NIC	-	CNIC	LC	LC	
Brown Noddy	NIC	-	CNIC	LC	LC	
Black Noddy	SC	CE	CARS	LC	MC	
Sooty Tern	M	-	CARS	LC	MC	
Bridled Tern	NIC	-	CNIC	LC	HC	
Least Tern	M	V	CARS	LC	HC	EN
Gull-billed Tern		CE	CARS	LC	HC	
Roseate Tern	SC	-	CARS	LC	HC	T
Common Tern	M	CE	CARS	LC	LC	
Royal Tern	M	E	CARS	LC	MC	
Sandwich /Cayenne Tern	M	V	CARS	LC	NC	

a. H&N (1984) SC= Special Concern, M=Monitor, NIC=No Immediate Concern.
b. S (2000a) Modified IUCN criteria. CE= Critically Endangered, E=Endangered, NT=Near Threatened, V=Vulnerable.
c. B&N (2007) EN= Globally endangered; CARS=Caribbean At-Risk Species, CNIC= Caribbean No Immediate Concern.
d. IUCN (2006) EN=Endangered, LC= Least Concern.
e. NAWCP (2002) HIM= Highly Imperiled, HC= High Concern, MC= Moderate Concern, (2002) LC= Least Concern.
f. USFWS EN= Endangered, T= Threatened.

as Highly Imperiled (HIM), 11 of High Concern (HC), 4 of Moderate Concern (MC), and 3 of Low Concern (LC). Schreiber (2000a) classified species with Caribbean populations into four categories: Critically Endangered (CE), Endangered (EN), Vulnerable (V), or Near-threatened (NT) (table 29.5).

- Twenty-one species of seabirds were inventoried out of 22 breeding in the Caribbean (there were no estimates for the Jamaican Petrel, which is likely extinct).
- IUCN lists two species as globally threatened: Bermuda Petrel and Black-capped Petrel (Jamaican Petrel is sometimes treated as a subspecies of Black-capped Petrel). Bermuda Petrel, although showing a 55% increase since 1984, depends totally on stringent management for its survival and remains globally endangered.
- Many seabird species globally listed by IUCN as of Least Concern have shown sharp declines in their Caribbean populations in 20 years. Clearly this classification is inadequate in a regional dimension. From a different perspective, BirdLife International recognizes sites holding 1% of the Caribbean population of seabirds as IBAs.
- The NAWCP classification of 11 species under threat (two as Highly Imperiled and nine as High Concern) is borne out by the population estimates in this volume and percentage declines. However, globally threatened species are not acknowledged.
- Five species listed by USFWS as endangered or threatened breed in Caribbean waters: Bermuda Petrel, Audubon's Shearwater, Brown Pelican, Least Tern, and Roseate Tern. But the listing has no legal weight outside U.S. territorial waters.
- The modification by Schreiber (2000a), applying the IUCN criteria of global threat to Caribbean populations, concluded that 15 species were threatened, which is accepted here, but using the criteria of IUCN terms for endangerment modified for the Caribbean is not. These criteria should be used only for globally threatened species.
- Two species were not inventoried in 1984 but had marginal populations in 2000 and in this volume and are at the edge of their range: Black Noddy and Gull-billed Tern.
- Population counts showed declines for 11 species between 1984 and 2007 and increases for 13 species between 2000 and 2007. Only four species showed increased counts over 1984 and 2000 figures.

Proposed Status Definitions for Use in Advocacy and Outreach

Defining threat status for Caribbean populations of seabirds is essential for implementing conservation strategies; however, the NAWCP definitions are too technical for general conservation applications by stakeholders, such as advocacy and education. It is therefore proposed that the majority of seabirds be listed as priority species to bring governments an awareness of their collective threatened status:

- The Caribbean populations of 16 species are designated as Caribbean At-Risk Species (CARS; table 29.5) to aid conservation work but not replace scientific definitions, such as those of NAWCP and IUCN. Two species are globally threatened and 14 are subject to varying degrees of regional threat: Audubon's Shearwater, White-tailed Tropicbird, Masked Booby, Brown Booby, Brown Pelican, Magnificent Frigatebird, Black Noddy, Sooty Tern, Least Tern, Gull-billed Tern, Roseate Tern, Common Tern, Royal Tern, and Sandwich Tern/Cayenne Tern.
- Five species with similar or increased counts in 2007 over 1984 and 2000 are defined as Caribbean Species of No-Immediate Concern (CNIC): Red-billed Tropicbird, Red-footed Booby, Laughing Gull, Brown Noddy, and Bridled Tern (table 29.5). Regular monitoring will remain essential as the majority of colonies are not on protected sites; sites holding significant populations for each species are or may come under threat, thus impacting the entire regional population.

This chapter offers a brief analysis of the third inventory and suggests definitions to bring the collective plight of seabirds to a wider audience. More sophisticated strategies must be applied in designating protected areas that take account of socioeconomic impacts, something beyond the scope of this book. Huggins et al. (2007) have taken these factors into accounts in the wide span of criteria assembled into a conservation-related geospatial database in order to map and model such conservation areas.

Table 29.6. Caribbean distribution and regional totals of breeding pairs, petrels to frigatebirds

Country	Bermuda Petrel	Black-capped Petrel	Audubon's Shearwater	Red-billed Tropicbird	White-tailed Tropicbird	Masked Booby	Brown Booby	Red-footed Booby	Brown Pelican	Magnificent Frigatebird
Bermuda	71	e			2000			3	50	150
Bahamas			2000–2300		450–500		550–650			35–235
TCI			1–10		224					
Cuba			2		9–14		1–10		300	1000–1100
Cayman Is					120	267–400	110	4839		227
Jamaica					100		50		150	315–365
Hispaniola		2000			500		600	2500	100–250	250–300
Puerto Rico			25–40	20–30	500–525	175–225	1650–1700	3000–3025	265–290	500–550
USVI			20	225–350	30	45–75	500–1000	100–150	325–425	
BVI				80–100	60–80		170–275		300–400	400–800
Anguilla				21	3–4	57	1965	1–2	21	142
Neth. St.M				2	1		5		26–79	
Neth. Saba			25	750–1000	1–4	5				
Neth. St.Eu				100–200	1–10					
Fr St Martin			1–10	180–330	4–6		150–175			
Fr Guadeloupe		e	1–10	235–430	44–90			10		
Fr Martinique			50–80	35–61	6					
St. Kitts Nevis				2					1–10	1–10
Montserrat				11–16			9–22		14	27
Antigua Barbuda				3			13	60	53	2100
St Lucia				22–27	1–10					
Barbados			50–100							50–100
St Vin, G,G				1–10	1–10		315	3500		
Neth. Aruba										
Neth. Bonaire										
Neth. Curacao										
Trinidad										
Tobago			500	53		5	84	465		800
Venezuelan Isls			1–10	1–10		200	674	1113	782	1–10
Colombian Arch.						1–10	100	1–10		1–10
Total	71	2000	2676–3107	1756–2604	4056–4244	750–972	6942–7748	14585–16691	2412–2849	6099–6926

Note: Where breeding is confirmed with no estimates, 1–10 pairs are estimated.

Table 29.7. Caribbean distribution and regional totals of breeding pairs, gulls to noddies.

Location	Laughing Gull	Brown Noddy	Black Noddy	Sooty Tern	Bridled Tern	Least Tern	Gull-billed Tern	Roseate Tern	Common Tern	Royal Tern	Sandwich Tern	Cayenne Tern
Bermuda									8			
Bahamas	2000–2400	4300–4500		7200–8000	2200–2500	600–650	100–150	800–900		200–250	335–360	
TCI	170	27000		48305	3333	640	80	200	100	1–10	1–10	
Cuba	>1000	300		3000	650	>350	70–80	40–50	100–110	20	160–170	1
Cayman Is	>14	500			16	84						
Jamaica	100			1	4	<50		2		1	6	
Hispaniola	100	50–200		80000	150–350	50–150				10–20	30–40	
Puerto Rico	1300–1400	1230–1300		40500	235–250	135–150	e	935–1000		10–25	675–700	5–10
USVI	2000–3000	400–900		20,000–40,000	500–1000	300–600		500–2300		60–150	100–1000	1
BVI	1000–2000	100–300		100	150–250	100	4	600–2000			120	
Anguilla	2618	726		52295	403	290–345		210		155	172	
Neth. StM	100	15			21	10				47		
Neth. Saba		30		30	30							
Neth. St.Eu												
Fr St Martin	440–450	203–250		150–300	80–110	75–85				30–50		
Fr Guadeloupe		380–510		3050–4000	240–310	45–80		10–30				
Fr Martinique		330–1020		1100–12000	160–380			50–100				
St. Kitts Nevis	100–150	6–10		200–250	50–75	10–20		>6				
Montserrat												
Antigua Barbuda	70	140		514	16			4			7	
St Lucia		10		38147	70			10–75				
Barbados												
St Vinc, Ge,Gren	>22	145		2500	1–10			>15			1	
Neth. Aruba	350	164	48	6650	122	55		52	143	1–2		3582
Neth. Bonaire	60					792			39	85		180
Neth. Curacao	3					619			133			
Trinidad								25–30				
Tobago	258	>500		>500	50			111		1–10		
Venezuelan Isds	>544	5,313	52	12000	418	205		1–10	104	25		>75
Colombian Arch.	1–10	>250		>1000						1–10		
Total	12222–13791	42192–44083	100	317942–341992	8909–10368	4410–4985	250–310	3571–7095	627–637	647–860	1608–2605	3844–3858

Note: Where breeding is confirmed with no estimates, 1–10 pairs are estimated

30

Conservation of Caribbean Seabirds

PATRICIA E. BRADLEY

The precipitous global decline of seabirds is shown in the IUCN Red List Indices (BirdLife International 2004), and Caribbean seabirds certainly reflect this decline (fig. 30.1). This volume provides interesting new data but also voices the concerns of authors throughout the region that the achievement of sustainable populations will require major increases in the attention, resources, and priority accorded their conservation. This is encapsulated succinctly in the foreword by John Croxall, one of the world's leading seabird specialists.

It is important that hemispheric, even global approaches underpin any conservation strategies because the range of seabird families extends around the world's oceans. Such proposals are already at various stages of planning and implementation. The North America Waterbird Conservation Plan (NAWCP) includes all waterbirds in North and Central America and the Caribbean (Kushlan et al. 2002); the Agreement on the Conservation of Albatrosses and Petrels (ACAP) includes the three species of Caribbean procellarid; the BirdLife International database on Important Bird Areas (IBAs, sites of international importance for birds) for the entire Caribbean will include Marine IBAs (priority sites for seabirds with breeding and foraging habitats at sea); and the Nature Conservancy report *Biodiversity Conservation Assessment of the Insular Caribbean Using the Caribbean Decision Support System* (Huggins et al. 2007), to provide systematic and strategic means to manage the region's ecosystems and human societies. The Waterbird Conservation Council (WCC), while a volunteer body, can provide guidance in determining the direction of both a hemispheric and a Caribbean strategy for conservation with the Society for the Conservation and Study of Caribbean Birds (SCSCB), for example drafting the Caribbean Waterbird Conservation Plan.

Understanding the dynamics of the Caribbean's sea-

bird populations and designing the most effective conservation responses calls, at local levels, for increased research, monitoring, surveys, training of local observers, and—more profoundly—for gaining recognition of the importance of the region's seabirds to all, not just to the few concerned specialists and observers. The difficulties facing a coordinated regional conservation effort in the Caribbean are its geographical extent (and difficulty of travel between countries), the number of political entities involved, and a lack of resources. Politically, there are 21 independent nations, three Dutch territories, three French Departments, and five British Overseas Territories, involving more than 26 million people. Considering only the countries included in this volume, seabird conservation strategy presents a formidable task. The primary threats outlined by previous authors (Halewyn and Norton 1984; Gochfeld et al. 1994; Schreiber 2000a) have not changed, but the anthropogenic threats have accelerated and expanded together with the added dimension, and international recognition, of global warming.

In this chapter, immediate actions to sustain Caribbean seabirds are proposed under the headings of capacity building, research and monitoring, conservation strategies including protected areas and management, and nature tourism, while international and hemispheric initiatives are being implemented. The appointment of a coordinator with responsibilities for seabirds is considered key, both to empower local NGOs to lead conservation efforts in their countries and to support advocacy to gain government cooperation in addressing major conservation issues for seabirds—monitoring, protected areas, legislation, enforcement, and predation control. Methods of revenue raising are suggested to support protected area land purchase and management. Conservation management must be linked to socioeconomic planning and development (fig. 30.2).

1988
1992
1996
2000
2004
0.00
-0.02
-0.04
-0.06
-0.08
-0.10
-0.12
-0.14
-0.16
Red List Index
SEABIRDS
Better
Worse
Pigeons
Waterbirds
Parrots
Raptors
Gamebirds
Seabirds

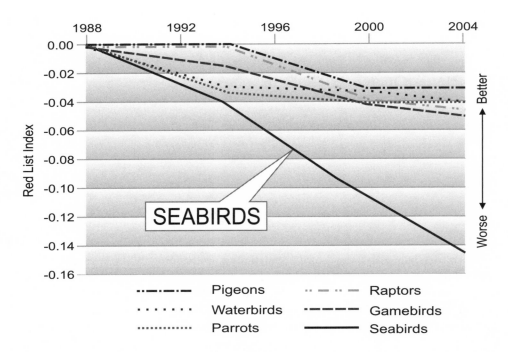

Figure 30.1. IUCN Red List indices for selected bird species groups. Reproduced with permission from BirdLife International (2004), Cambridge, U.K.: BirdLife International.

SUMMARY OF CONSERVATION ISSUES
& PROPOSALS TO INITIATE ACTIONS
CAPACITY BUILDING
1. Role of SCSCB in regional conservation
2. Advocacy: Appointment of a Caribbean Seabird Co-ordinator
3. Capacity building and public education in the region
RESEARCH AND MONITORING
4. Monitoring priority species and sites
5. Surveys of new breeding sites
CONSERVATION STRATEGIES AT BREEDING SITES
6. Protected areas: The need to protect additional breeding and foraging habitats
7. Management planning for protected areas
SUSTAINABLE NATURE TOURISM
8. Develop cooperation with regional tourism organizations and conservation NGOs
9. Ecosystem Services
10. SCSCB to develop a protocol for sustainable nature tourism

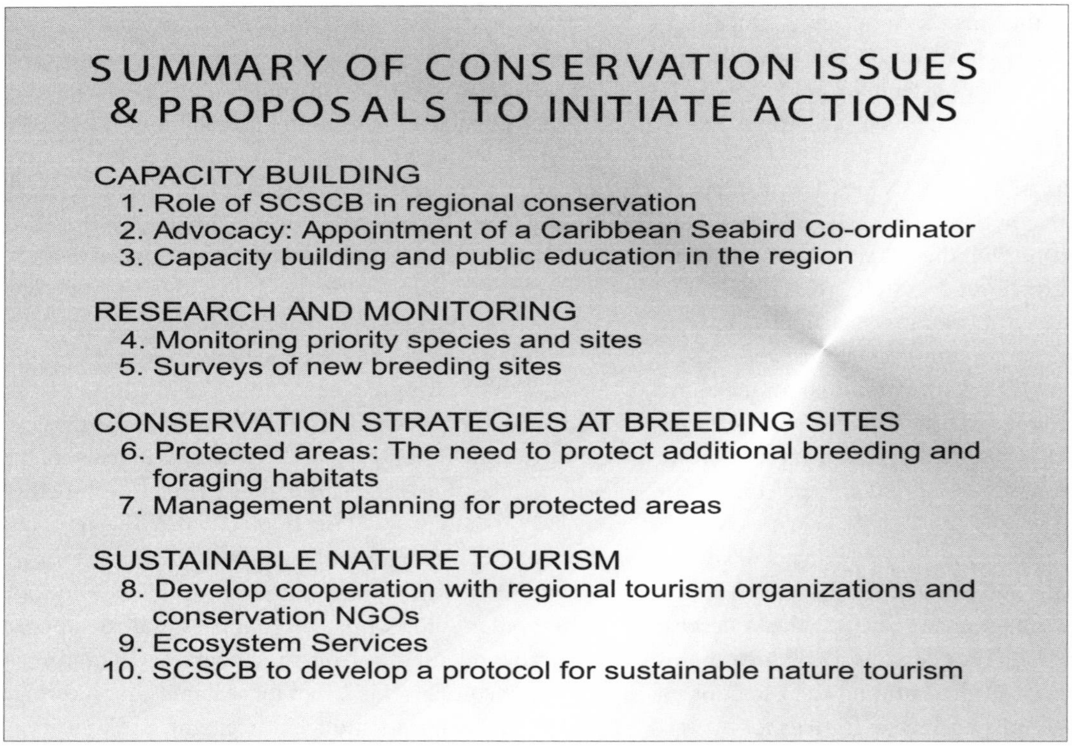

Figure 30.2. Summary of conservation issues and proposed actions.

Capacity Building

1. Role of SCSCB in regional conservation and training

SCSCB is the only regional conservation organization for birds, including seabirds, able to bring together the region's stakeholders: local NGOs, government decision makers, and some of the many authors of this volume who are already key figures in seabird conservation in their respective islands. Regional NGOs will be required to have increasing involvement in lobbying governments and working with them to achieve protection and sustain biodiversity.

Proposal: The seabird section of the Caribbean Waterbird Conservation Plan should be completed by the Seabird Working Group of SCSCB. A seabird conservation workshop should be included in all future meetings of SCSCB to provide a forum for stakeholders: to bring together conservation NGOs to empower them to spearhead conservation efforts in their countries, to address threats to seabirds, to decide future priorities for regional conservation initiatives, and to continue training government and volunteer observers.

2. Advocacy: Appointment of a Caribbean Seabird Coordinator

The appointment and funding of a regional Seabird Coordinator is proposed as the most effective way to initiate and sustain systematic outreach and advocacy with the express responsibility of leading a conservation program forward into the future. The main tasks of the Seabird Coordinator would be similar to those undertaken by the project coordinator of the West Indian Whistling-Duck Working Group (WIWDWG) but with greater emphasis on advocacy at national levels throughout the region—that is, aiming to change the political will by creating awareness of and receptiveness to seabird conservation and its important economic role in nature tourism. Thus the Seabird Coordinator would establish contacts with government ministers, political leaders, and senior civil servants heading the Departments of Environment, Tourism, Planning, and Education as well as working with community leaders, educators, and local and international conservation NGOs. The Seabird Coordinator would work to empower local NGOs and with them organize and advise on capacity building programs for teachers, including the development of resource materials and training of field officers.

Proposal: Representatives of international NGOs and funding agencies working in the region should be invited to each workshop (e.g., RARE, BirdLife International, National Audubon Society, WWFN, Royal Society for the Protection of Birds, Island Conservation, the Nature Conservancy, U.S. Fish and Wildlife Service International Division, and coordinators of the Waterbird Conservation for the Americas initiative). They should be asked to identify funding opportunities for priority seabird projects that will have an immediate impact on alleviating the major conservation threats and on developing effective site protection; they should be asked to help fund the Seabird Coordinator.

3. Capacity building and public education in the region

3a. Importance of outreach

Outreach was considered by many authors as the necessary first step to initiate conservation programs. The West Indian Whistling-Duck and Wetlands Conservation Project developed by WIWDWG of the SCSCB is the one of the most comprehensive capacity building programs in the region, having successfully raised awareness and advanced conservation for a flagship species, the West Indian Whistling-Duck, other waterbirds, and wetlands throughout the Caribbean (Sorenson and Bradley 2000; Sorenson et al. 2004, 2005). Awareness must be at two levels: "need to know," aimed at increasing awareness of and compliance with laws and regulations through news items, pamphlets, and posters; and "nice to know," aimed at increasing understanding of seabirds through interpretative material and signage at protected sites to explain their life histories and importance to communities in maintaining healthy reefs, fishing, and sustainable tourism. The SCSCB poster "Save Our Seabirds" and Caribbean seabird identification cards are effective tools, but additional resource materials, along the lines of *Wondrous West Indian Wetlands: Teachers' Resource Book*, should be written to train educators. The WIWDWG by supporting wetlands already promotes the conservation of breeding and foraging habitat of many species of seabirds.

Proposal: SCSCB should emulate the West Indian Whistling-Duck Working Group model and include a conservation program Save Our Seabirds (the title of the SCSCB seabird poster) with the development of a resource manual by the extant Seabird Working Group. While the most endangered species in the Caribbean are nocturnal procellarids, a more visible seabird, such as a tropicbird or a sulid, should be chosen as the flagship species to represent all seabirds and their habitats.

3b. Training

Training is considered an essential part of capacity building in the region; it is also included in proposals 1, 2, 4 and 7.

Proposal: Consideration should be given to funded training scholarships by governments and NGOs for students from host countries to travel to, for example, Puerto Rico, the U.S. Virgin Islands, United Kingdom, and France, to train educators, conservation managers, and wildlife officers.

Research and Monitoring

4. Monitoring priority species and sites: Defining the program

Almost all authors stress the need for seabird surveys and regular monitoring of colonies, and most acknowledge the lack of trained local observers and the need for standardization of monitoring/survey techniques to ensure the validity of data throughout the region. As resources are scarce, the priority species and sites should be chosen (the largest colonies, those with the greatest diversity, those showing the greatest decline, or those colonies already protected). Threat assessment and the response required must be addressed for each species and site in order to plan a regional conservation strategy that will benefit all species at risk. It will be necessary to distinguish between those colonies in decline but with the potential of being stabilized and, if not already protected, with the greatest of chance of gaining sustainability with management, and those colonies rating zero in the database (see chapter 27), already extirpated or are highly vulnerable and unlikely to be saved without excessively costly restoration programs. Resources should usually go to the former colonies except in the case of the Black-capped Petrel, a high-risk species in terms of gaining sustainability but, as an endemic, a candidate for extinction unless international management is forthcoming.

4a. Defining the status of Caribbean seabirds

Of the 21 seabird taxa inventoried, two species are listed as globally threatened (BirdLife International 2004), and the Caribbean populations of 14 taxa, while not globally threatened, are considered to be under regional threat. The list of 16 priority species, defined as Caribbean At-Risk Species (CARS) is not prioritized, as threat assessment for all species will change as new impacts on colonies take effect. The CARS definition does not define endangerment; instead it is intended to focus the attention of stakeholders on the need for regional and local conservation for such species. Five species, defined as Caribbean No-Immediate Concern (CNIC), while not considered to be under immediate threat, require regular monitoring to identify new threats that may impact the colonies in the future.

Proposal: To raise the profile of seabirds among stakeholders in the region, 16 species are considered priority species and defined as CARS. A report on the status of all breeding seabirds and breeding sites in need of protection should be provided to decision makers and NGOs in each nation to aid lobbying for more protected areas and management within the region.

4b. Monitoring priority species and breeding sites

Regional monitoring should be directed at 16 priority Species: two endangered species (table 30.1) and 14 CARS (table 30.2), species selected on the criteria of endemism, the GIS database results, percentage decline in 20 years, vulnerability (including lack of protected habitat), and habitat threats. A priority breeding site is perceived as one that is critical to sustaining the regional population. A short list of the islands with sites where monitoring is planned is given in table 30.3; other sites are evaluated in the GIS discussion (chapter 27).

BirdLife Partners have developed a simple but quantitative IBA monitoring framework to record "State," "Pressure," and "Response" variables for IBAs. This also provides a standardized means to monitor Marine IBAs

Table 30.1. Globally endangered priority species (CARS), priority breeding sites, and action required

Priority species globally endangered	Priority sites holding endemic species	Action required
Bermuda Petrel	Bermuda[a]	Continued conservation management
Black-capped Petrel	Hispaniola: Massif de la Selle, Massif de la Hotte (Haiti), Sierra de Baoruco (Dominican Republic).	Monitoring urgent; species in danger of extinction unless management introduced
	Cuba as possible site	Reports from Cuba need fully investigated

a. Population managed.

Table 30.2. Priority Caribbean At-Risk Species (CARS), islands with priority sites, and action required

Priority Species Caribbean (CARS) At-Risk Species	Priority sites holding the largest colonies of each species	Action required[a]
Audubon's Shearwater	Bahamas, Saba, TCI, Tobago	Establish Caribbean range beginning with Saba, TCI and include Dominica
White-tailed Tropicbird	Bermuda,[c] Bahamas, TCI, Puerto Rico,[b] Hispaniola	Monitor species on the Bahamas and TCI and Hispaniola
Masked Booby	Pedro Cays Jamaica, Los Monijes Venezuela, Serranilla San Andreas Archipelago, Puerto Rico,[b] Redonda	Monitor Serranilla and Redonda.
Brown Booby	Pedro Cays Jamaica, Puerto Rico,[b] Anguilla,[b] USVI,[b] Hispaniola	Survey Jamaica and Hispaniola
Brown Pelican	Los Roques, Cuba, USVI,[b] BVI, Puerto Rico,[b] Hispaniola	Surveys of Venezuelan islands and Hispaniola
Magnificent Frigatebird	Barbuda; Jamaica, Cuba, Puerto Rico,[b] BVI, Cayman Islands,[b] Hispaniola,	New survey essential on Barbuda
Black Noddy	Lago Reef Aruba, Los Roques Venezuela	Regular monitoring and management for the only two breeding colonies known in the Caribbean
Sooty Tern	Alto Velo Hispaniola, TCI, Maria Islands St Lucia, Anguilla, USVI,[b] Puerto Rico,[b] Pedro and Morant Cays Jamaica, Aves Island	Survey Hispaniola and Jamaica
Least Tern	Bahamas, TCI, Cuba, USVI,[b] Anguilla,[b] Bonaire,[b] Curacao,[b] Los Roques	Management needed to sustain populations, especially on private land
Gull-billed Tern	Bahamas, Cuba, TCI	Regular monitoring needed on Cuba and TCI; new surveys on Bahamas
Roseate Tern	Bahamas, TCI, Puerto Rico,[b] USVI,[b] BVI, Anguilla, Cuba	Monitor the Bahamas
Common Tern	TCI, Cuba, Curacao,[b] Aruba, Bonaire,[b] Los Roques	Further monitoring on TCI and Cuba
Royal Tern	Bahamas, Anguilla, USVI,[b] Dutch and French St. Martin, Bonaire,[b] Les Roques	Surveys needed on Bahamas, and TCI
Sandwich Tern/Cayenne Tern	Puerto Rico,[b] USVI,[b] BVI,[b] Bahamas, Anguilla, Cuba Lago Reef Aruba, Bonaire, Los Roques	Monitor the Bahamas Regular monitoring and protection for the Lago Reef

a. Actions required for Jamaica and Hispaniola are given in Table 30.3.

b. Populations monitored regularly.

c. Populations managed.

and is backed up by a database that allows national partners to analyze and respond to the monitoring data (see 6a).

Proposal: Seabird specialists from the Americas and Caribbean should be asked to form a Corps of Seabird Specialists (CSS) to advise on, assist with, or lead a regional monitoring program, beginning with priority sites and species identified in tables 30.1–30.4. Governments should offer CSS assistance with logistics and involvement of local wildlife officers during monitoring; at the same time, specialists should train local field biologists, government wildlife officers, and volunteer observers to

Table 30.3. Priority sites where monitoring is planned from 2008

Priority sites	Species involved	Action
Pedro Cays, Jamaica Haiti, Dominican Republic and satellites	Masked Booby, Brown Booby, Sooty Tern, Black-capped Petrel	Monitoring to assess changes to seabird populations Preliminary monitoring planned 2008/2010
Los Monijes, Venezuela	Masked Booby	Monitoring planned 2008/2009
Sombrero and Dog Island, Anguilla	Masked and Brown Booby, larids	Further monitoring planned together with a management strategy predator control for privately owned cays

Table 30.4. Islands requiring new breeding surveys or a modern inventory

Breeding sites	Species	Action required
St. Vincent, Grenada and the Grenadines	Red-footed Booby and all seabirds	New seabird inventories including confirmation of large sulid colony on Battowia in 2004.
Haiti and Dominican Republic	White-tailed Tropicbird, Brown Booby, Magnificent Frigatebird and all other seabirds	New seabird inventories for both Islands and satellites
Jamaica	All seabirds	Update inventory
Morant Cays	Sooty Tern	New survey in breeding season
Remote cays in northern and southern Bahamas	Larids	Completion of new surveys of the outer islands, Bahamas begun in 2006.
Redonda	Sulids	Surveys
Barbuda	Magnificent Frigatebird	New Survey
Little Cayman	Red-footed Booby	New Survey planned 2009

enable them to maintain regular monitoring programs. Funding will be required for travel, including boat hire and subsistence. This proposal should be discussed at the SCSCB workshop.

5. Surveys of islands for new breeding sites and sites that need an updated inventory

Ideally, the inventory of Caribbean seabirds, begun in Schreiber and Lee (2000a) and continued in this volume, should be completed for the entire region. While in the short term completion is probably unrealistic until internationally funded programs can be implemented, table 30.4 indicates where surveys should be directed. There remain many islands and cays that need to be surveyed for the first time in order to determine if they are priority sites holding significant populations that will require appropriate conservation action. There are other sites where the surveys require to be updated to determine the status of known colonies.

Proposal: The CSS, with the logistical support of national governments and international NGOs, should begin surveys of new potential priority sites as soon as logistics allow, beginning with islands proposed in table 30.4 and, in the case of Jamaica and Hispaniola (Haiti and the Dominican Republic), new resurveys of the complete seabird inventory. University involvement from North America and Britain could help with continuity, provide prospective seabird specialists with field experience, and allow training of local volunteers and field biologists.

Conservation Strategies at Breeding Sites

6. Protected areas: The need to protect additional breeding and foraging habitat

Most Caribbean seabirds have restricted breeding sites on wetlands, coastal areas, and small offshore keys, often of low elevation, where anthropogenic effects related to population increases and tourism are an escalating cause of their loss and decline. Almost all authors accept that the only way to protect seabirds is to create many more legally protected areas of breeding and foraging habitat, followed by effective management and enforcement.

This calls for excellent baseline information to develop the most effective strategies and recovery plans.

6a. Important Bird Areas (IBAs)

BirdLife International's IBA initiative aims to identify, monitor and protect a global network of sites for globally threatened birds, endemic birds, or significant numbers of migratory or congregatory species (such as breeding seabirds). The process of documentation of IBAs is nearing completion throughout the Caribbean, and their designation, provided they receive local support, will be critical to the long-term viability of priority bird populations across a geographic range (www.birdlife.org/datazone). A directory of sites for the U.K. Overseas Territories (UKOTs) is already published (Sanders 2006). At present in the Caribbean, regional seabird colonies that qualify as IBAs are those supporting globally threatened taxa, or more than 1% of the Caribbean population of a species, or 10,000 pairs of seabirds, thus encompassing many of the priority sites and species. IBAs in the Caribbean will provide a framework through which to lobby governments, landowners, and other stakeholders, to advocate new legislation, and to achieve priority site protection and management at a local level.

BirdLife International is in the initial stages of extending and adapting the IBA program to the marine environment, where 88 Marine IBAs (breeding colony IBAs with adjacent feeding and maintenance areas at sea) have already been identified and mapped. The development by BirdLife International of a species-specific database on the range of foraging distances of seabirds from breeding colonies will contribute to determining the seaward extension of candidate Marine IBAs. Ultimately the sites will contribute to initiatives to gain greater protection and sustainable management of the marine environment.

Proposal: SCSCB, BirdLife Partners, and other national NGOs should lobby governments and work with stakeholders throughout the region to ensure that protected status is granted to sites holding more than 1% of the regional population of seabirds together with adjacent foraging sites identified as Marine IBAs, and facilitate appropriate conservation management plans.

6b. Seabird protection in foraging areas at sea

Loss of fish stocks, legally and illegally, is a threat to seabirds, and protected areas must include foraging habitat. Too little is still known regarding seabird at-sea distribution, diet, foraging strategies, and threats in Caribbean waters. BirdLife's intention is to identify priority areas of high seas foraging sites not contiguous with breeding sites as Marine IBAs and, as well, to designate Marine IBAs with large coastal congregations of nonbreeding birds.

Studies of at-sea distribution of pelagic seabirds should continue to include assessments of their impact on commercial fisheries in the Atlantic/Gulf/Caribbean; this could be undertaken by a research department of a university (vessel-based and remote recording-satellite telemetry). By-catch has less impact in the Caribbean than other regions (Browder 2006); however, the Black-capped Petrel is at risk in the North Atlantic.

Proposal: Governments should be lobbied to support the protection of candidate at-sea Marine IBAs and incorporate them into Marine Protected Areas. The Waterbird Conservation Council should address this issue on behalf of Caribbean nations. They should also encourage local governments to train regional observers to participate in at-sea monitoring, to determine feeding grounds and foraging requirements, and to identify the effects of long-line fishing and propose methods of mitigation, such as the use of more seabird-friendly fishing gear.

6c. Criteria for national priority sites < 1% of the population

Some priority seabird sites do not meet the IBA global or 1% Caribbean population criteria but are of national importance and require protection by national governments.

Proposal: Consistent criteria at a different level to that of IBAs should be derived for the Caribbean to allow protection of nationally important sites to be linked into a recognized protected network for smaller groups of seabirds in the region.

6d. Protection of sites on government-owned land

Priority sites for seabirds on government-owned land (known as Crown land in UKOTs and ex-UKOTs) should be identified by BirdLife International in the IBA program and by local NGOs.

Proposal: Conservation NGOs should lobby their governments to grant protected status to government-owned wetlands, coastal areas, and offshore cays that are designated seabird IBAs or recognized in some other way as priority sites.

6e. Privately owned land

In many jurisdictions it is not possible to protect sites on private land without acquisition. In these cases, local planning laws should be investigated, as regulations made under the main law may allow controls on coastal areas used seasonally by breeding seabirds. Other initiatives could include getting agreement from landowners to protect sites from disturbance during the breeding season (e.g., work on construction sites was halted in the Cayman Islands to protect breeding Least Tern); instituting a form of shared responsibility (e.g., as in Martinique); exchanging the site for similar land, receiving the land as a donation, or as a last resort, raising funds with governments (see 7b, Environmental Fund) and local and international NGOs to purchase the sites.

Proposal: Conservation NGOs and wildlife officers should seek the cooperation of private landowners to permit monitoring of nesting sites on their land and should explore ways to gain protection for such sites.

7. Management planning for protected areas

Effective management strategies are essential to maintain protected areas. They should address research issues, regular monitoring of species and habitat, threat assessments, enforcement, closure during the breeding season, wardening, developing education outreach and interpretative materials, and—just as important—integrating the areas into the national socioeconomic planning framework. Models exist from the National Trusts in the Bahamas, Cayman Islands, and Turks and Caicos Islands. Multipurpose management systems include entire ecosystems (seabirds and waterbirds, other fauna and flora), all stakeholders, and historic sites. Such plans take considerable consultation and consensual agreement among all stakeholders, but they have the advantage of benefiting local economics through nature tourism and other sustainable livelihoods, and they appeal to funding organizations.

7a. The Nature Conservancy (TNC)

The Caribbean Decision Support System (CDSS; Huggins et al. 2007) is designed to approach biodiversity conservation through strategic planning linking comprehensive ecosystem and human socioeconomic data. It aims to meet the needs of resource managers in decision making on protection of the region's natural resources. The CDSS was used by TNC in a large-scale biodiversity assessment to identify target biodiversity areas in which to concentrate quantitative conservation planning.

Caribbean countries that have signed the Convention on Biodiversity are expected to provide a gap analysis stating the current level of protection for terrestrial and marine habitats and targets, including critical seabird nesting and foraging areas. Spatial data are the prime inputs for a gap analysis. Therefore it is important to maintain and update the regional spatial database on the status of seabirds in the Caribbean and to make the data readily available to national governments and NGOs for various planning activities and the development of conservation strategies. TNC has mapped Mackin's database for this volume and included the data in the CDSS.

Proposal: Data on seabirds should continue to be provided to TNC, and national governments should be supported by conservation NGOs in resource management planning involving priority species and sites. Funding should be sought to continue the compilation of the database.

7b. The need for conservation legislation and enforcement; both new legislation and enforcement of existing legislation to protect seabird habitats are needed.

New legislation: Up-to-date and comprehensive conservation legislation is lacking on many islands, and its absence limits all forms of conservation planning and management. Such legislation is essential to create and manage protected areas, control invasive species, and allow the setting up and administration of an Environmental Fund to purchase land for conservation.

Proposal: Based on the conservation laws of France and U.K. and U.S. Caribbean territories, a template should be developed to assist governments to develop conservation legislation where no such legislation exists. It must incorporate implementing regulations to protect seabirds and their breeding habitats, create buffers around breeding sites, and make breeding sites off limits to the public during the breeding season; control pollution, predation, and livestock; and install signage, introduce wardening, enforce local laws, prevent fishing in marine parks, limit aircraft flight paths over nesting sites, and control light pollution.

The legislation should allow for the creation of some form of environmental/conservation fund able to receive the proceeds of a conservation (or tourist) tax. It should be "ring-fenced" to ensure that the funds do not enter general government revenue but are managed by an appointed Conservation Board. This fund can be used to purchase land to create protected areas and for conservation management. It already works effectively in the Turks and Caicos Islands and is being implemented in the Cayman Islands.

Enforcement of existing legislation: Lack of enforcement is endemic throughout the region, especially in protected areas, even where adequate legislation and regulations already exist. Human predation, egg taking, and overfishing often go unchallenged. There is a need for conservation NGOs to lobby their governments regarding the enforcement of existing legislation and to obtain judicial support for enforcement by raising awareness of existing threats to seabirds. Here advocacy and training can play a major role in changing the situation.

Proposal: Local governments should train wildlife/ marine officers in the enforcement of laws and regulations affecting seabirds and fisheries. The Seabird Coordinator, local conservation NGOs, and international NGOs should lobby local governments on this issue, including explaining the economic value of seabird conservation for nature tourism.

7c. Predation control of introduced mammals

Globally, predation is considered the greatest threat to seabirds, and although habitat destruction is perceived as a greater threat in the Caribbean, predation undoubtedly remains the main threat at sites where human activity is reduced, such as in protected areas close to human settlement. Predator control programs should address eradication, first of rats and cats, followed by dogs, mongooses, pigs, rabbits, and monkeys on the main islands and inshore cays. Eradication is expensive and slow to bring results, therefore sites must be chosen with a high expectation of success and an intended benefit to the seabird population.

The choice of techniques (trapping, bait, shooting) is important, and the projects must be accorded a long-term commitment by governments to ensuring that sites remain predator free. To their credit, the Environmental Awareness Group in Antigua are managing successful black rat eradication on six cays; and Monito Island, Puerto Rico, is predator free after a rat eradication project. Local legislation should allow control of access to predator-free cays. For some species (e.g., Least Tern), fencing breeding sites and controlling predation have been a successful joint strategy.

Proposal: Predation control programs should be pursued by all local governments, or by NGOs, such as humane societies, working with government Departments of Public Health. International funding and expertise will also be required for Caribbean priority sites and species: Pedro Cays, Jamaica, would be an obvious candidate.

7d. International Conventions

All island nations that are signatories to international Conventions (CITES, Bonn, Ramsar, SPAW Protocol of the Cartagena Convention, MARPOL, Biodiversity Treaty) require suitable enabling local legislation to enact the international conventions. Caribbean nations should be encouraged to sign these conventions as well as the Agreement on the Conservation of Albatrosses and Petrels (ACAP), as petrels are the most endangered group of seabirds in the region. While no Caribbean nation has a major fishing fleet, the region is fished by other nations.

Proposal: Local biologists, conservation NGOs, and the Seabird Coordinator should lobby local governments to accede to treaties related to seabirds and their habitats and to enact suitable enabling legislation.

7e. Management responses to global climate changes

In the light of projected sea level rise, increasing sea surface temperatures, and increased tropical storm activity in the coming decades, management plans should include new initiatives for seabird habitat creation, restoration, and enhancement. Many small islands have a small surge envelope, and sea level rise will increase the areas of inundation, outpace the growth of coral reefs, reduce beaches, and challenge the ability of coastal mangrove to keep pace, thus impacting seabird habitat.

Innovative ways to provide more secure habitat for nesting seabirds must be planned and implemented, such as building or creating artificial islands; using clean waste construction materials to enhance nesting sites for shearwaters, gulls, and terns; and translocation and use of decoys to begin new colonies on more secure sites (Kress 1998). Such techniques and enhancement have been effectively used for the Bermuda Petrel and White-tailed Tropicbird. Restoration of wetlands and coastlines, although an expensive and long-term commitment, has great potential in the region as it adds a nature tourism dimension.

Restoration of degraded habitats can be done, and projects have been successful in Bermuda and the Bahamas (and in Mexico and Canada). A new project on St. Vincent aims to restore the wetland at Ashton Lagoon, Union Island, a failed marina site. Warming of the seas is likely in the coming decades, and management plans must therefore include foraging habitat at sea.

Proposal: SCSCB, WCC, and BirdLife International should prepare a blueprint of management plans for protected priority sites under such threats to encompass habitat creation, restoration, translocation, and enhancement and for at-sea foraging areas.

7f. Protection of inshore fish stocks

The importance of protecting local feeding habitat for seabirds is stressed throughout. Overfishing is a severe threat to seabirds both legally and illegally in protected areas, as are pollution (plastics, oil, and sewage); chemical runoff and sediment from erosion caused by overgrazing cause damage to reefs and fish stocks in inshore waters. There is a need to institute water controls to improve the quality of inshore waters. Lack of enforcement in protected areas should also be addressed.

Proposal: Through advocacy, local NGOs should encourage governments: (i) to enact legislation creating Marine Protected Areas for inshore fisheries to include replenishment zones, catch limits, closed seasons, and penalties for fishing in protected areas and for polluting sites; (ii) to ensure that marine enforcement officers are funded, trained, supplied with boats, and supported in their duties; (iii) to seek the support of local industries in joint pollution control and in setting a natural background standard for water quality for outflow systems to improve environmental conditions for seabirds (and humans).

Sustainable Tourism

Caribbean tourism is the major growth factor driving the economies of most nations. In 2005 there were 22 million stay-over visitors, 20 million cruise ship visitors, and US$ 21 billion expended. Nature tourism is a main foreign exchange earner and, in many cases, often the only viable financial solution to fund biodiversity conservation.

8. Develop cooperation with regional tourism and conservation organizations

Caribbean tourism is well organized within three large bodies: the Caribbean Tourism Association (CTO), the Caribbean Cruise Association (CCA), and the Caribbean Hotel Association (CHO). These umbrella bodies, to which all Caribbean governments and many private member organizations belong, should be lobbied to produce a best-practice protocol combining economic benefits with sustainable use of natural resources. Successful examples of nature tourism from the region should be showcased at conferences.

Proposal: With the support of SCSCB, community-based associations and conservation NGOs should take the initiative to engage with major organizations involved in Caribbean tourism to begin greater involvement and cooperation to support real sustainable tourism initiatives related to biodiversity. The umbrella organizations should be asked to provide funding to local governments specifically to train local biologists and wardens, develop management plans for protected sites, and provide en-

forcement measures to ensure that nature tourism sites are sustained in the long term.

9. Ecosystem services

The concept of ecosystem services is used to evaluate the fundamental life-supporting resources provided "free" by the natural world, including soil formation, clean water and air, food and raw materials, habitat, seed dispersal and pollination, flood and storm protection, and decomposition of waste. Globally, the services are reckoned to be worth US$ 33 trillion (Constanza et al. 1997). With international funding, ecological economists could calculate concrete values for these interconnected resources in the Caribbean (already implemented successfully in Costa Rica, where 30 criteria defining ecosystem services are extant). This would allow sound economic long-term planning by governments, the CTO, CCA, CHO, and stakeholders to limit unsustainable use of resources and negative impacts from excessive tourist growth; the issue of compensation for loss of ecosystem services due to pollution, habitat loss, and urban development could then be addressed. Compensation funds could be used as revenue toward seabird conservation including habitat restoration, the purchase of land for protected areas ,and biodiversity management. The CTO and the CHO should also define protocols that would make unacceptable the new and alarming practice by Caribbean governments of removing the protected status from conservation areas in order to allow new developments by international hotel groups; for example, at the site protecting the Grenada Dove. A further method of raising revenue method is the introduction of the "user pays" concept, that is, users should contribute to sustaining natural resources through payment of user fees. It should involve all users, including residents, cruise ships, and hotels, with the benefit that those who conserve the resource receive the money collected.

Proposal: The evaluation of economic ecosystems in the Caribbean should be explored with advice from the Ecological Society of America, and if considered feasible, funding for such a project should be sought from the World Bank.

10. SCSCB to develop a protocol for sustainable nature tourism through parnerships

Sustaining seabird tourism requires strengthening community participation by providing jobs for guides and boat operators, and on-job training that should include good management practices designed to prevent exploitation. Effective management strategies supported by political policies must be employed to ensure sustainability and to prevent the major predicament of nature tourism, where increased success equals increased human impact. Sites must have legal limits on human numbers (of both service providers and visitors) and on the permitted degree of disturbance, if they are to generate income in the long term without resulting in overexploitation, an escalation of disturbance at nest sites, and abandonment. There are already successful examples of sustainable tourism in the region, including the WIWDWG "Watchable Wildlife Ponds" concept for waterbirds and some seabirds in the Bahamas, Barbuda, and on Little Cayman and Cayman Brac.

Proposal: As nature tourism is such a major factor in the economy of the Caribbean, the SCSCB should include such a workshop in each biannual meeting and adapt as a blueprint for the Caribbean one of the protocols used to manage successful nature tourism sites in other parts of the region or the world. The SCSCB should be represented at the annual CTO meeting to promote sustainable tourism, and representatives of the CTO, CCA, and CHO should be asked to attend SCSCB workshops, as well as local NGOs from the region.

Conclusion

Conservation must be established at local and national levels before regional and global programs can be effective. Thus SCSCB should encourage local conservation NGOs to bring the recommendations in this volume to the attention of each national government. The hope is that once they are made aware of the Caribbean at-risk status of their seabirds, and of priority breeding and foraging sites, each government will respond by supporting the conservation actions proposed here and enlisting the support of international NGOs to allow effective regional programs to follow.

31

A Bibliography of Seabirds of the Caribbean Region

JAMES W. WILEY AND FLOYD E. HAYES

This bibliography contains most, but by no means all, of the literature on seabirds in the West Indies. The area covered extends beyond the Greater West Indies as defined by Bond (1980)—that is, the Bahama Islands; the Greater and Lesser Antilles, south to Barbados and Grenada; and the extralimital islands of San Andrés (St. Andrew), Providencia (Old Providence), and the Swan Islands—to include the additional islands addressed in the present volume. The listing therefore includes literature on seabirds in the Dutch islands of Aruba, Bonaire, and Curaçao; Trinidad and Tobago; several islands off Venezuela; and Bermuda. As defined for this volume by Bradley and Norton, seabirds include species in the families Procellariidae, Hydrobatidae, Phaethontidae, Sulidae, Pelecanidae, Fregatidae, and Laridae (see table 31.1). The bibliography includes references from 1526 to 2007 but excludes most of James Bond's Check-lists and Supplements; regional reports that appear in *American Birds*, *Audubon Field Notes*, *National Audubon Society Field Notes*, and *North American Birds*; and many general references for the region. Several references given are not restricted to the subject region or taxonomic group and are included because they are cited by chapter contributors. Multiple references by the same author(s) published in the same year and cited within this volume are distinguished by a letter following the year of publication (e.g., 1980a, 1980b). Over 1,500 references are included.

Acknowledgments

Many people and institutions have helped in several ways in the production of the bibliography. Several deserve special recognition for their contributions and encouragement: Lynda Garrett and Wanda Manning, Patuxent Wildlife Research Center; Jo Anne Feheley, U.S. Department of Agriculture–Forest Service, Institute of Tropical Forestry; Vivian Fuentes, Puerto Rican Agriculture Experiment Station; Dr. Eduardo Cardona, Puerto Rico Department of Natural Resources; Rodolfo Vera and Edith Aguado Figueiras, Biblioteca M. Jaume, Museo Nacional de Historia Natural, La Habana; Nancy Machado Lorenzo and Carmen Zita Quirantes Hernández, Biblioteca Nacional José Martí, La Habana; Sumithra Achuthan, Grambling State University Library; Drs. Dean Amadon, Mary LeCroy, and Rosemarie Gnam, American Museum of Natural History; Dr. Frank Gill and Christine Bush, Academy of Natural Sciences of Philadelphia; Kathy Donahue, Rare Book Collection, University of California at Los Angeles; Kimball Garrett and Betty Ann Schreiber, Los Angeles County Museum of Natural History; Lloyd Kiff, Jim Jennings, Ed Harrison, and Jon Fisher, Western Foundation of Vertebrate Zoology; Elaine Smyth, Emily Robinson, Lynne Wells, and Christina Riquelmy, Rare Book Collection, Louisiana State University; Judy Buys and Joanne Langston, Southern Science Center, National Biological Service; Janet Hinshaw and Dr. Robert Payne, University of Michigan, Ann Arbor; Catherine Levy, Gosse Bird Club; and the late Oscar T. "Bud" Owre, University of Miami, who in 1979 insisted that Wiley compile a bibliography on West Indian birds.

Table 31.1. Subjects included in the bibliography

Order	Family
Procellariiformes	Procellariidae: Shearwaters and Petrels
	Hydrobatidae: Storm-Petrels
Pelecaniformes	Phaethontidae: Tropicbirds
	Sulidae: Boobies and Gannets
	Pelecanidae: Pelicans
	Fregatidae: Frigatebirds
Charadriiformes	Laridae: Skuas, Gulls, and Terns

Finally, we thank the many authors who generously provided copies of their publications for our examination and inclusion.

Bibliography

A., J. A. 1909. Chapman on the life-histories of the booby and man-o'-war bird. *Auk* 26: 205.

Abbad y Lasierra, F. I. 1788. *Historia geográfica, civil y natural de la isla de San Juan Bautista de Puerto Rico*. Madrid, Spain: A. Espinosa.

Abbott, G. A. 1922. In Cuba. *Oölogist* 39: 173.

Acosta, M., and V. Berovides Alvarez. 1984. Ornitocenosis de los cayos Coco y Romano, Archipiélago de Sabana-Camagüey, Cuba. *Poeyana* 274: 1–10.

Acosta, M., and L. Mugica. 1994. Notas sobre la comunidad de aves del embalse Leonero, provincia Granma. *Cienc. Biol. Acad. Cienc. Cuba* 27: 169–171.

Acosta, M., M. E. Ibarra, and E. Fernandez. 1988. Aspectos ecológicos de la avifauna de Cayo Matías (Grupo Insular de los Canarreos, Cuba). *Poeyana* 360: 1–11.

Acosta, M., L. Mugica Valdés, and G. Alvarez. 1991. Ecología trófica de la principales especies de aves que afectan el cultivo del camaron blanco en Tunas de Zaza. *Pitirre* 4(2): 7.

Acosta, M., J. A. Morales, M. Gonzalez, and L. Mugica Valdés. 1992. Dinámica de la comunidad de aves de la playa La Tinaja, Ciego de Ávila, Cuba. *Cienc. Biol. Acad. Cienc. Cuba* 24: 44–58.

Acosta, M., L. Mugica, and S. Valdes. 1994. Estructura trófica de una comunidad de aves acuáticas. *Cienc. Biol. Acad. Cienc. Cuba* 27: 24–44.

Adams, C. D. 1969. A botanical description of Big Pelican Cay, a little known island off the south coast of Jamaica. *Atoll Res. Bull.* 130: 1–10.

Agard, J. B. R., and J. F. Gobin. 2000. The Lesser Antilles, Trinidad and Tobago. Pp. 627–641 *in* Shepperd, C. R. C., ed., *Seas at the millennium: An environmental evaluation,* vol. 1. Oxford, U.K.: Elsevier Science Ltd.

Agardy, T. 1982. *A preliminary report on the status of the Brown Pelican in the U.S. Virgin Islands, 1980–81.* Unpublished administrative report. St. Thomas, U.S. Virgin Islands: Division of Fish and Wildlife.

Aguayo Castro, C. G. 1937. Sobre algunas aves halladas en Cuba. *Mem. Soc. Cubana Hist. Nat. "Felipe Poey"* 11: 57–60.

Aguero Cobiellas, R., and F. Hernandez Driggs. 1988. Lista preliminar de las aves observadas en las playas de Estero y Pesquero Nuevo de la provincia de Hoguín. *Garciana* 9: 4.

Aiken, K. A. 1986. Observations on bird roosting changes at the Mona reservoir. *Nat. Hist. Notes Nat. Hist. Soc. Jamaica,* n. s., 2: 3–4.

Aitken, T. H. G., A. H. Jonkers, E. S. Tikasingh, and C. B. Worth. 1968. Hughes virus from Trinidadian ticks and terns. *J. Med. Entomol.* 5: 501–503.

Aldridge, B. M. 1987. Sampling migratory birds and other ob-servations on Providenciales Islands B. W. I. *N. Am. Bird Bander* 12: 13–18.

Alexander, W. B. 1927. Kittiwake gull in the Caribbean Sea. *Auk* 44: 241–242.

Allen, G. M. 1905. Summer birds in the Bahamas. *Auk* 22: 113–133.

Allen, J. A. 1880. List of the birds of the island of Santa Lucia, West Indies. *Bull. Nuttall Ornithological Club* 5: 163–169.

———. 1881. Supplementary list of birds of the island of Santa Lucia, W. I. *Bull. Nuttall Ornithological Club* 6: 128.

Alleng, G. 1990. Recovery of nesting sites in the Port Royal mangroves, south coast, Jamaica, following Hurricane "Gilbert." *Gosse Bird Club Broads.* 55: 5–9.

Alleng, G. P., and C. A. Alleng. 1993. Survey of Least Tern nesting sites along the south coast of Jamaica. *Pitirre* 6(1): 4.

Alleng, P., and C. A. M. Whyte-Alleng. 1993. Survey of Least Tern nesting sites on the south coast of Jamaica. *Colon. Waterbirds* 16: 190–193.

Alvarez Conde, J. 1945. *La Laguna del Tesora: Dos excursiones científicas a la Ciénaga de Zapata, costa sur de la provincia de Las Villas.* La Habana, Cuba: Impresa Monte e Indio.

American Ornithologists' Union. 1998. *Check-list of North American birds.* 7th ed. Washington, D.C.: American Ornithologists' Union.

———. 2006. Forty-seventh supplement to the American Ornithologists' Union *Check-list of North American birds. Auk* 123: 926–936.

Amos, E. J. R. 1991. *The birds of Bermuda.* Warwick, Bermuda: Corncrake Press.

Anonymous. 1891. Feilden on the domicile of the Diablotin. *Ibis* 3: 131.

———. 1963. More birds listed for Grand Bahama. *Fla. Nat.* 36: 78.

———. 1972. Breeding of the Least Tern in Jamaica. *Gosse Bird Club Broads.* 18: 18.

———. 1991a. *St. Vincent and the Grenadines: Environmental profile.* St. Michael, Barbados: Caribbean Conservation Association.

———. 1991b. *Grenada: Environmental profile.* St. Michael, Barbados: Caribbean Conservation Association.

———. 1996. *Forestry, Wildlife, National Parks and Protected Areas Act.* Plymouth: Government of Montserrat.

Ansingh, F. H., and H. J. Koelers. 1957. Common Tern (*Sterna h. hirundo*) breeding in the Netherlands Antilles. *Auk* 74: 266.

Ansingh, F. H., H. J. Koelers, P. A. van der Werf, and K. H. Voous. 1960. The breeding of the Cayenne or Yellow-billed Sandwich Tern in Curaçao in 1958. *Ardea* 48: 51–65.

Appleby, R. H., and C. R. Clark. 1974. September birdwatching in Jamaica. *Gosse Bird Club Broads.* 22: 10–14.

———. 1974. Black Tern. *Gosse Bird Club Broads.* 23: 23.

———. 1974. Ring-billed Gull. *Gosse Bird Club Broads.* 23: 23.

Arendt, A. A., K. A. Echelmeyer, W. D. Harrison, C. S. Lingle, and V. B. Valentine. 2002. Rapid wastage of Alaskan glaciers and their contribution to rising sea level. *Science* 297: 382–386.

Arendt, W. J. 1985. *Wildlife assessment of the southeastern peninsula, St. Kitts, West Indies.* Unpublished Report. Río Piedras, Puerto Rico: USDA Forest Service, Institute of Tropical Forestry.

———. 1995. *Assessment of avian relative abundance on Guana Island, British Virgin Islands, with emphasis on the Pearly-eyed Thrasher* (Margarops fuscatus). Unpublished report, Project No. IITFW-WJA59140264, to the Conservation Agency and the Guana Island Club. Río Piedras, Puerto Rico: International Institute of Tropical Forestry.

Arendt, W. J., and A. I. Arendt. 1986. Wildlife assessment of the southeastern peninsula, St. Kitts, West Indies. Unpaginated *in* Towle, E. L., A. Archer, P. J. Butler, K. E. Coulianos, M. H. Goodwin, S. T. Goodwin, I. Jackson, D. Nicholson, W. E. Rainey, J. A. Towle, W. Wernicke, and N. J. O. Liverpool, eds., *Environmental assessment report on the proposed southeast peninsula access road, St. Kitts, West Indies.* Report to U.S. Agency for International Development/USDA Forest Service. St. Thomas, U.S. Virgin Islands: Islands Research Foundation.

Ashcroft, M. T. 1965. A visit to St. Kitts, Nevis and Anguilla. *Gosse Bird Club Broads.* 4: 10–12.

Ashmole, N. P. 1963a. The biology of the Wideawake or Sooty Tern *Sterna fuscata* on Ascension Island. *Ibis* 103: 297–364.

———. 1963. Molt and breeding in populations of the Sooty Tern *Sterna fuscata. Postilla* 76: 1–18.

Asprey, G. F., and R. G. Robbins. 1953. The vegetation of Jamaica. *Ecological Monographs* 23: 359–412.

Attrill, R. 1979. Little San Salvador. *Bahamas Natur.* 4: 2–8.

Atwood, T. 1791. *The history of the island of Dominica: Containing a description of its situation, extent, climate, mountains, rivers, natural productions & c. & c. together with an account of the civil government, trade, laws, customs, and manners of the different inhabitants of that island, its conquest by the French, and restoration to the British dominions.* London: privately printed for J. Johnson, No. 72, St. Paul's Churchyard.

Augustinus, P. G. E. F., R. P. R. Mees, and M. Prins. 1985. *Biotic and abiotic components of the landscapes of Saba (Netherlands Antilles).* Uitgave Natuurwetenschappelijke Studiekring voor Suriname en de Nederlandse Antillen 115, Utrecht.

Austin, H. M., and P. M. Stoops-Glas. 1977. The distribution of polystyrene spheres and nibs in Block Island Sound during 1972–1973. *Chesapeake Science* 18: 89–92.

Austin, O. L. 1951. Group adherence in the Common Tern. *Bird-Banding* 22: 1–15.

———. 1953. The migration of the Common Tern (*Sterna hirundo*) in the western hemisphere. *Bird-Banding* 24: 39–55.

Bacon, P. R., and R. P. ffrench. 1972. *The wildlife sanctuaries of Trinidad and Tobago.* Port of Spain, Trinidad: Ministry of Agriculture, Lands and Fisheries.

Bahamas National Trust. 1986. Bahamas. Pp. 433–446 *in* Scott, D. A., and M. Carbonell, eds., *A directory of Neotropical wetlands.* Cambridge, U.K.: International Union for Conservation of Nature and Natural Resources and International Waterfowl Research Bureau (Slimbridge).

Baillie, J. E. M., C. Hilton-Taylor, and S. N. Stuart (eds.). 2004. *IUCN Red List of threatened species: A global species assessment.* Gland, Switzerland: International Union for Conservation of Nature and Natural Resources.

Balat, F. 1986. Contribución al conocimiento de comunidades de aves de la Ciudad de La Habana. *Zprávy Geografického Ustavu Csav* 23: 11–23.

Baltz, D. M., and G. V. Morejohn. 1976. Evidence from seabirds of plastic particle pollution off central California. *Western Birds* 7: 111–112.

Baltz, M. E., M. J. Burke, and P. J. Davidson. 1998. New records of Audubon's Shearwater (*Puffinus lherminieri*) breeding colonies in the Exuma Cays. *Bahamas J. Sci.* 6: 43–46.

Bangs, O. 1900. Notes on a collection of Bahama birds. *Auk* 17: 283–293.

———. 1916. A collection of birds from the Cayman Islands. *Bull. Mus. Comp. Zool.* 60: 303–320.

Bangs, O., and F. H. Kennard. 1920. A list of the birds of Jamaica. Pp. 684–701 *in* Cundall, F., ed., *Handbook of Jamaica.* Kingston: Government Printing Office.

Bangs, O., and T. E. Penard. 1919. Some critical notes on birds. *Bull. Mus. Comp. Zool.* 63: 21–40.

Bangs, O., and W. R. Zappey. 1905. Birds of the Isle of Pines. *Am. Nat.* 39: 179–215.

Bannerman, D. A. 1904. Ornithological notes made on a trip to the West Indies. *Zoologist*, ser. 4, 8: 228–230.

Barbour, T. 1923. *The birds of Cuba.* Cambridge, Mass.: Memoirs of the Nuttall Ornithological Club no. 6.

———. 1943. *Cuban ornithology.* Cambridge, Mass.: Memoirs of the Nuttall Ornithological Club no. 9.

Barlow, J. C. 1978. Records of migrants from Grand Cayman Island. *Bull. Br. Ornithol. Club* 98: 144–146.

Barnés, V., Jr. 1946. The birds of Mona Island, Puerto Rico. *Auk* 63: 318–327.

Barnett, T. P., D. W. Pierce, K. M. AchutaRao, P. J. Gleckler, B. D. Santer, J. M. Gregory, and W. M. Washington. 2005. Penetration of human-induced warming into the world's oceans. *Science* 309 (5732): 284–287.

Barneveld, R. Van. 1993. White-tailed Tropicbird. *Gosse Bird Club Broads.* 60: 29.

Barré, N., P. Feldmann, J. H. Leman, and A. M. Revel. 1996. *Suivi ornithologique de la Réserve naturelle de la Caravelle 1995-1996.* Rapport no. 13. Fort-de-France, Martinique: Association pour l'Etude et la protection des Vertébrés des petites Antilles (AEVA)–Parc Naturel Regional de la Martinique.

Barriga-Bonilla, E., J. Hernandez-Camacho, I. Jaramillo T., R. Jaramillo Mejia, L. E. Mora Osejo, P. Pinto Escobar, and P. M. Ruiz Carranza. 1969. *La Isla San Andrés: Contribución al conocimiento de su ecología, flora, fauna y pesca.* Vol. 2. Bogotá: Instituto de Ciencias Naturales, Universidad Nacional de Colombia.

Barriga, E., J. Hernández C., I. Jaramillo, R. Jaramillo, L. E. Mora, P. Pinto, and P. Ruiz. 1985. *La Isla de San Andrés: Contribución al conocimiento de su ecología, flora, fauna y pesca.* 2nd edition. Bogotá: Universidad Nacional de Colombia.

Barrios, O., R. Soriano, and G. Paneca. 2001. *Colonias de nidificación de aves acuáticas en Cayo Sabinal.* Informe Proyecto Sabana Camagüey CUB/98/G32. Camagüey, Cuba: Centro de Investigaciones de Medio Ambiente de Camagüey.

Bartsch, P. 1918. Biological explorations in Cuba and Haiti. *Smithson. Misc. Coll.* 68: 40–48.

Bautista M., E. A., T. A. Vargas Mora, G. M. Santana Z., and G. Gross. 1986. *Informe sobre estudio basico de la fauna y consideraciones ecologicas del "Parque Nacional Los Haitises": Propuesta para la elaboracion plan de manejo.* Santo Domingo, República Dominicana: Departamento de Vida Silvestre, Secretaria de Estado de Agricultura.

Beatty, H. A. 1930. Birds of St. Croix. *Journal of the Department of Agriculture of Porto Rico.* 14: 135–150.

———. 1936. New bird records for St. Croix, V. I. *Auk* 53: 456–457.

———. 1938. Notes from St. Thomas and cays, Virgin Islands. *Auk* 55: 552–553.

———. 1941. New bird records and some notes for the Virgin Islands. *Journal of Agriculture of the University of Puerto Rico.* 25: 32–36.

———. 1944. The insects of St. Croix, V. I. *Journal of Agriculture of the University of Puerto Rico.* 28: 114–172.

Beck, R. H. 1921. Bird collecting in the highlands of Santo Domingo. *Nat. Hist.* 21: 37–49.

Beebe, W. 1927. Notes on the birds of Haiti. *Bull. N.Y. Zool. Soc.* 30: 136–141.

———. 1927. List of Haitian birds observed. Appendix D. Pp. 216–224 *in Beneath tropic seas: A record of diving among the coral reefs of Haiti.* New York: G. P. Putnam's Sons.

———. 1932. *Nonsuch: Land of water.* New York: Brewer, Warren and Putnam.

———. 1935. Rediscovery of the Bermuda Cahow. *Bull. N.Y. Zool. Soc.* 38: 187–190.

Belant, J. L., and R. A. Dolbeer. 1993. Migration and dispersal of Laughing Gulls in the United States. *J. Field Ornithol.* 64: 557–565.

Belcher, C., and G. D. Smooker. 1934. Birds of the colony of Trinidad and Tobago. *Ibis* 1934: 572–595.

———. 1935. Birds of the colony of Trinidad and Tobago. Part II. *Ibis* 1935: 279–297.

Bellingham, P. 1991. Leach's Petrel. *Gosse Bird Club Broads.* 57: 18.

Bénito-Espinal, E. 1982. *Shooting in Guadeloupe.* Guadeloupe: Architecture and Environmental Regional Service Regional Delegate's Office.

———. 1990. *Oiseaux des Petites Antilles.* Saint-Barthélemy, Guadeloupe, French West Indies: Les Editions du Latanier.

Bénito-Espinal, E., and P. Hautcastel. 2003. *Les oiseaux des Antilles et leur nid: Petites et Grandes Antilles.* Les Abimes, Guadeloupe: PLB Editions.

Bent, A. C. 1921. Roseate Tern *Sterna dougalli* Montagu. Pp. 256–264 *in Bent, A. C., ed., Life histories of North American gulls and terns: Order Longipennes.* Bulletin 113. Washington, D.C.: U.S. National Museum.

———. 1922. Black-capped Petrel *Pterodroma hasitata* (Kuhl). Pp. 106–121 *in Bent, A. C., ed., Life histories of North American petrels and pelicans and their allies: Order Tubinares and Order Steganopodes.* Bulletin 121. Washington, D.C.: U.S. National Museum.

———. 1922. Yellow-billed Tropic-bird *Leptophaethon lepturus catesbyi* (Brandt). Pp. 181–187 *in Bent, A. C., ed., Life histories of North American petrels and pelicans and their allies: Order Tubinares and Order Steganopodes.* Bulletin 121. Washington, D.C.: U.S. National Museum.

———. 1922. Booby *Sula leucogastris.* Pp. 200–208 *in Bent, A. C., ed., Life histories of North American petrels and pelicans and their allies: Order Tubinares and Order Steganopodes.* Bulletin 121. Washington, D.C.: U.S. National Museum.

———. 1922. Red-footed Booby *Sula piscator.* Pp. 211–216 *in Bent, A. C., ed., Life histories of North American petrels and pelicans and their allies: Order Tubinares and Order Steganopodes.* Bulletin 121. Washington, D.C.: U.S. National Museum.

———. 1922. Brown Pelican *Pelecanus occidentalis occidentalis* Linnaeus. Pp. 294–301 *in Bent, A. C., ed., Life histories of North American petrels and pelicans and their allies: Order Tubinares and Order Steganopodes.* Bulletin 121. Washington, D.C.: U.S. National Museum.

———. 1922. Man-o'-War-Bird *Fregata magnificens* Mathews. Pp. 306–315 *in Bent, A. C., ed., Life histories of North American petrels and pelicans and their allies: Order Tubinares and Order Steganopodes.* Bulletin 121. Washington, D.C.: U.S. National Museum.

———. 1947. Cabot's Tern *Sterna sandvicensis acuflavida* Cabot. Pp. 221–227 *in Bent, A. C., ed., Life histories of North American gulls and terns: Order Longipennes.* New York: Dodd, Mead & Company.

———. 1947. Sooty Tern *Sterna fuscata* Linnaeus. Pp. 279–287 *in Bent, A. C., ed., Life histories of North American gulls and terns: Order Longipennes.* New York: Dodd, Mead & Company.

———. 1947. Bridled Tern *Sterna anaetheta* Scopoli. Pp. 287–287 *in Bent, A. C., ed., Life histories of North American gulls and terns: Order Longipennes.* New York: Dodd, Mead & Company.

———. 1947. Noddy *Anous stolidus* Linnaeus. Pp. 301–310 *in Bent, A. C., ed., Life histories of North American gulls and terns: Order Longipennes.* New York: Dodd, Mead & Company.

Bent, O. 2000. *Environmental impacts of tourism on coastal resources and ecosystems in the San Andres Archipelago.* Unpublished report, European Union INCO-DC project. San Andres, Colombia: CORALINA.

Ben-Tuvia, A., and C. E. Ríos. 1970. Report on a R/V Chocó cruise to Providence Island and adjacent banks of Quitasueño and Serrana near the Caribbean islands of Colombia. Proyecto para el desarrollo de la pesca marítima en Colombia (PNUD). *Fondo Esp.-FAO-INDERENA, Com.* 1: 9–45.

Berovides Alvarez, V., and R. Smith Canet. 1983. Aspectos ecológicos de la nidificación de *Sterna hirundo* y *S. albifrons*. *Cienc. Biol. Acad. Cienc. Cuba* 9: 128–31.

Bibby, C. J., N. D. Burgess, D. A. Hill, and S. Mustoe. 2000. *Bird census techniques, 2nd ed.* London: Academic Press.

BirdLife International. 2000. *Threatened birds of the world.* Barcelona, Spain: Lynx Editions and BirdLife International.

———. 2004. *State of the world's birds 2004: indicators for our changing world.* Cambridge, U.K.: BirdLife International.

Bisbal, F. 2001. *Inventario preliminar de los vertebrados de la isla de Cubagua.* Serie Informes Técnicos DGF/IT/411. Maracay, Venezuela: Ministerio del Ambiente y de los Recursos Naturales (MARN).

Black, A. 1969. Magnificent Frigatebird. *Gosse Bird Club Broads.* 13: 18.

———. 1972. Black Tern. *Gosse Bird Club Broads.* 18: 20.

———. 1972. Magnificent Frigatebird. *Gosse Bird Club Broads.* 19: 22.

———. 1973. Brown Pelican. *Gosse Bird Club Broads.* 20: 20.

———. 1982. Brown Pelican. *Gosse Bird Club Broads.* 39: 14.

———. 1983. Brown Pelican. *Gosse Bird Club Broads.* 40: 16.

———. 1989. Pelican. *Gosse Bird Club Broads.* 52: 12.

Black, A., and C. Black. 1981. Black Tern. *Gosse Bird Club Broads.* 37: 12.

Black, A., C. Black, A. Downer, I. Kerr-Jarrett, K. Mcmurray, S. Spence, and B. Pearson. 1973. Migrant dates. *Gosse Bird Club Broads.* 21: 11–12.

Black, C. 1966. Brown Pelican. *Gosse Bird Club Broads.* 6: 14.

———. 1966. Magnificent Frigate Bird. *Gosse Bird Club Broads.* 6: 15.

———. 1980. Magnificent Frigatebird. *Gosse Bird Club Broads.* 34: 15–16.

Blake, C. H. 1956. Some bird weights from Jamaica. *Bird-Banding* 27: 174–178.

Blanco, E. T. 1969. *Apuntes para la historia de la fauna ornitológica de Puerto Rico.* San Juan: Editorial Coquí.

Blanco, P., and H. Gonzalez. 1995. Nuevos registros de *Rynchops niger* Linneo, 1758 (Aves: Laridae) para Cuba. *Poeyana* 448: 1–8.

Blanco, P., S. Peris, and B. Sánchez. 2001. *Las aves limícolas (Charadriiformes) nidificantes de Cuba: Su distribución y reproducción.* Alicante, Spain: Centro Iberoamericano de la Biodiversidad.

Blokpoel, H., R. D. Morris, and P. Trull. 1982. Winter observations of Common Terns in Trinidad, Guyana and Suriname. *Colon. Waterbirds* 5: 144–147.

Blokpoel, H., R. D. Morris, and G. D. Tessier. 1984. Field investigations of the biology of Common Terns wintering in Trinidad. *J. Field Ornithol.* 55: 424–434.

Boeke, J. 1907. Iets over de visserij op Bonaire. *Neerlandia* 11(12): 206–207.

Boersma, P. D. 1998. Population trends of the Galapagos Penguin: Impacts of El Niño and La Niña. *Condor* 100: 245–253.

Bond, J. 1928a. On the birds of Dominica, St. Lucia, St. Vincent, and Barbados, B.W.I. *Proc. Acad. Nat. Sci. Philadelphia* 80: 523–545.

———. 1928b. The distribution and habits of the birds of the Republic of Haiti. *Proc. Acad. Nat. Sci. Philadelphia* 80: 483–521.

———. 1939. Notes on birds from the West Indies and other Caribbean islands. *Notulae Naturae, Acad. Nat. Sci. Philadelphia* 13: 1–6.

———. 1941. Nidification of the birds of Dominica, B.W.I. *Auk* 58: 364–375.

———. 1942. Additional notes on West Indian birds. *Proc. Acad. Nat. Sci. Philadelphia* 94: 89–106.

———. 1945. Identity of Catesby's Tropic-bird. *Auk* 62: 660.

———. 1946. The birds of Mona. *Notulae Naturae, Acad. Nat. Sci. Philadelphia* 176: 1–10.

———. 1950a. *Check-list of birds of the West Indies*, 3rd ed. Philadelphia: Academy of Natural Sciences.

———. 1950b. Results of the Catherwood-Chaplin West Indies Expedition, 1948. Part II: Birds of Cayo Largo (Cuba), San Andrés and Providencia. *Proc. Acad. Nat. Sci. Philadelphia* 102: 43–68.

———. 1963. Derivation of the Antillean avifauna. *Proc. Acad. Nat. Sci. Philadelphia* 115: 79–98.

———. 1965a. *Tenth supplement to the check-list of birds of the West Indies (1956).* Philadelphia: Academy of Natural Sciences.

———. 1965. A few problems concerning the bird life of Jamaica, which the amateur ornithologist may be able to clarify. *Gosse Bird Club Broads.* 4: 1–3.

———. 1967. Jamaican Black Capped Petrel. *Gosse Bird Club Broads.* 8: 15.

———. 1970. *Native and winter resident birds of Tobago.* Philadelphia: Academy of Natural Sciences.

———. 1978. *Twenty-second supplement to the check-list of birds of the West Indies (1956).* Philadelphia: Academy of Natural Sciences.

———. 1980. *Birds of the West Indies*, 4th ed. Boston: Houghton Mifflin.

———. 1985. *Birds of the West Indies*, 5th ed. Boston: Houghton Mifflin.

Bond, J., and R. Meyer de Schauensee. 1944. Results of the fifth George Vanderbilt Expedition (1941): The birds of islands of Providence and St. Andrews and the cays in the southwestern Caribbean outside of the 100 fathom line. *Academy of Natural Sciences of Philadelphia, Monograph no. 6*: 7–56.

Bond, J., and A. Moreno Bonilla. 1947. Notas ornitologicas (No. 5). *Mem. Soc. Cubana Hist. Nat. "Felipe Poey"* 19: 109–110.

Bonhote, J. L. 1899. A list of birds collected on the island of New Providence, Bahamas. *Ibis* 5: 506–520.

——. 1901. On a collection of birds made by Mr. T. R. Thompson at the Cay Lobos Lighthouse, Bahamas. *Auk* 18: 145–149.

——. 1903. Bird migration at some of the Bahama lighthouses. *Auk* 20: 169–179.

——. 1903. Field notes on some Bahama birds. Part IV. *Avicult. Mag.*, n.s., 1: 87–95.

Bon Saint Côme, M. 1989. Rapport de Mission du Comité Scientifique du Parc Régional Naturel de la Caravelle effectuée en Guadeloupe du 20 au 23 Octobre 1989 après le passage de l'Ouragan Hugo. Pp. 30–48 *in Mission d'Étude en Guadeloupe après l'Ouragan "Hugo" effectuée par le Comité Scientifique du PNRM*. Fort-de-France: Parc Naturel Régional de la Martinique.

Bosque, C., D. Esclasans, and F. Pizani. 2001. *La conservación de las colonias reproductivas de las aves marino-costeras del Parque Nacional Archipiélago Los Roques*. Caracas, Venezuela: INTECMAR, Universidad Simón Bolivar-INPARQUES.

Boulon, R. H., and D. Nellis. 1985. *Virgin Islands*. Pittman-Roberton Final Report, FW-3-IID, 1981–1985, St. Thomas, U.S. Virgin Islands: Division of Fish and Wildlife.

Boulon, R. H., R. L. Norton, and T. A. Agardy. 1982. *Status of the Brown Pelican (Pelecanus o. occidentalis) in the Virgin Islands*. St. Thomas, U.S. Virgin Islands: Department of Conservation and Cultural Affairs, Government of the Virgin Islands.

Bourliere, F. 1949. The *Ornithographia Americana* of Father Plumier, 1689–1696. *Wilson Bull.* 61: 103–105.

Bourne, W. R., J. A. Bogan, D. Bullock, A. W. Diamond, and C. J. Feare. 1977. Abnormal terns, sick seabirds and shorebirds, organochlorines and arboviruses in the Indian Ocean. *Marine Pollution Bull.* 8: 154–158.

Bowdish, B. S. 1900. Some winter birds on the island of Vieques. *Oölogist* 17: 71–74.

——. 1900. A day on De Cicheo Island. *Oölogist* 17: 117–120.

——. 1902. Birds of Porto Rico. *Auk* 19: 356–366.

——. 1918. [Letter]. *Oölogist* 35: 119.

Bracey, E. W. 2003. Breeding terns on Abaco. *Bahamas J. Sci.* 11: 32–35.

Bradlee, T. S., L. L. Mowbray, and W. F. Eaton. 1931. A list of birds recorded from the Bermudas. *Proc. Boston Soc. Nat. Hist.* 39: 279–382.

Bradley, P. E. 1984. Masked Booby (Blue-faced Booby)—*Sula dactylatra*. *Gosse Bird Club Broads.* 42: 11.

——. 1984. A bird's eye view. *Gosse Bird Club Broads.* 44: 2–4.

——. 1986a. The Cayman Islands. Pp. 468–471 *in* Scott, D. A., and M. Carbonell, eds., *A directory of Neotropical wetlands*. Gland, Switzerland: International Union for Conservation of Nature and Natural Resources.

——. 1986. Unusual sighting from Cayman. *Gosse Bird Club Broads.* 46: 5.

——. 1990. Notes on conservation in the Turks and Caicos Islands and in the Cayman Islands. *Pitirre* 3(3): 2.

——. 1994. The avifauna of the Cayman Islands: An overview.

Pp. 377–406 *in* Brunt, M. A., and J. E. Davies, eds., *The Cayman Islands: Natural history and biogeography*. Monographiae biologicae 71. Dordrecht, Netherlands: Kluwer Academic Publishers.

——. [1995]. *The birds of the Turks & Caicos Islands: The official checklist*. Grand Turk: National Trust of the Turks and Caicos Islands.

——. 1996. Cayman Islands report. *Pitirre* 9(3): 17–18.

——. 1997. *Report on the birds of Cayman Brac*. George Town, Cayman Islands: Department of the Environment, Cayman Islands Government.

——. 1999. *Report on the birds and their habitats on Little Cayman*. George Town, Cayman Islands: Department of the Environment, Cayman Islands Government.

——. 2000. *The birds of the Cayman Islands*. BOU Checklist no. 19. Tring, U.K.: British Ornithologists' Union.

——. 2002. *Management plan to conserve the Brown Booby and its habitat on Cayman Brac*. George Town, Cayman Islands: Cayman Islands Government.

Bradley, P. E., M. Cottam, G. Ebank-Petrie, and J. Solomon. 2006. Cayman Islands. Pp. 65–98 *in* Sanders, S. M., ed., *Important Bird Areas in the UK Overseas Territories: Priority sites for conservation*. Sandy, Bedfordshire, U.K.: Royal Society for the Protection of Birds.

Bradley, P. E., and Y. J. Rey-Millet. 1995. *Birds of the Cayman Islands*, 2nd ed. Italy: Caerulea Press.

Bray, D. 1972a. Least Tern. *Gosse Bird Club Broads.* 18: 20.

——. 1972. Mona Reservoir 1972. *Gosse Bird Club Broads.* 18: 9–10.

Bried, J., and M. C. Magalhães. 2004. First Palearctic record of the endangered Bermuda Petrel *Pterodroma cahow*. *Bull. Br. Ornithol. Club* 124: 202–206.

Brinsley, G. G. 1971. White-tailed Tropicbird. *Gosse Bird Club Broads.* 16: 22.

Brisson, M. J. 1760. *Ornithologie ou méthode contenant la division des oiseaux en ordres, sections, genres, espèces & leurs variétés. A laquelle on a joint une description exacte de chaque espèce, avec les citations des auteurs qui en ont traité, les noms qu'ils leur ont donnés, ceux que leur ont donnés les différentes nations, & les noms vulgaires. Par M. Brisson . . . Ouvrage enrichi de figures en taille-douce*. Paris: Jean-Baptiste Bauche.

——. 1763. *Ornithologica sive synopsis methodica sistens avium divisionem in ordines, sectiones, genera, species, ipsarumque varietates. Cum accurata cujusque speciei descriptione, citationibus auctorum de iis tractantium, nominibus eis ab ipsis & nationibusimpositis, nomi-nimbusque vulgaribus*. Paris: Theodorum Haak.

Brithmer, R. 2002. *Réserve naturelle des îlets de Sainte-Anne, suivi ornithologique, année 2001*. Unpublished report. Fort-de-France, Martinique: Association Ornithologique de la Martinique (AOMA), Parc Naturel Régional de la Martinique.

Brithmer, R., and M. Pascal. 2001. *Suiví des populations d'oiseaux sur la Réserve Naturelle des îlets de Sainte-Anne, année 2000*. Unpublished report. Fort-de-France, Martinique: Association Ornithologique de la Martinique (AOMA), Parc Naturel Régional de la Martinique.

Brodkorb, P. 1963. Catalogue of fossil birds: Part 1 (Archaeopterygiformes through Ardeiformes). *Bull. Fla. State Mus., Biol. Sci.* 7: 179–293.

———. 1967. Catalogue of fossil birds: Part 3 (Ralliformes, Ichthyornithiformes, Charadriiformes). *Bull. Fla. State Mus., Biol. Sci.* 11: 99–220.

———. 1974. Bird remains from Pre-Columbian middens in the Virgin Islands. *Q. J. Fla. Acad. Sci.* [for 1972] 35: 239–240.

Browder, J. A. 2006. *The U.S. national plan of action for reducing the incidental catch of seabirds in longline fisheries (NPOA): Its implications in the U.S. Atlantic tuna, swordfish, and shark longline fisheries.* P. 16 in Report to NOAA Fisheries National Seabird Program, NOAA Fisheries Service, Southeast Fisheries Science Center, Miami, FL Report No. PRD-05/06–21.

Brown, G. J., C. Degia, R. Williams, and D. Williams. 1992. The cays—Bushy & Maiden. *Gosse Bird Club Broads.* 59: 14.

Brown, L. 1947. *Birds and I.* London: Michael Joseph.

Brown, R. G. B. 1973. A Black-capped Petrel north of Bermuda. *Am. Birds* 27: 742.

Browne, P. 1756. *The civil and natural history of Jamaica . . . [including] birds, fishes, reptiles, and insects.* London: B. White and Son.

Bruner, S. C. 1925. The man-o'-war birds. *Nature Mag.* 6: 283–286.

———. 1934. El "Dovekie" en Cuba, un nuevo record para nuestra avifauna. *Mem. Soc. Cubana Hist. Nat. "Felipe Poey"* 8: 51–52.

———. 1938. Datos sobre la migracion de aves en Cuba. Parte I. *Mem. Soc. Cubana Hist. Nat. "Felipe Poey"* 12: 167–179.

———. 1939. Aves del bosque de la Havana. *Mem. Soc. Cubana Hist. Nat. "Felipe Poey"* 13: 331–344.

———. 1943. Notas ornitologicas: Miscelanea. *Mem. Soc. Cubana Hist. Nat. "Felipe Poey"* 17: 19–21.

———. 1943. Adiciones a las aves del bosque de la Habana. *Mem. Soc. Cubana Hist. Nat. "Felipe Poey"* 17: 135–138.

Brunt, M. A. 1994. Vegetation of the Cayman Islands. Pp. 245–283 in Brunt, M. A., and J. Davis, eds., *The Cayman Islands: Natural history and biogeography.* Netherlands: Kluwer Academic Publishers.

Bryant, H. 1859. A list of birds seen at the Bahamas, from Jan. 20th to May 14th, 1859, with descriptions of new or little known species. *Proc. Boston Soc. Nat. Hist.* 7: 102–134.

———. 1868. A list of the birds of St. Domingo, with descriptions of some new species or varieties. *Proc. Boston Soc. Nat. Hist.* 11: 89–99.

Bryer, M., I. Fisher, S. Holliday, and J. Hughes. 2000. *Birds of Anguilla and the outer islands: November 1999 to June 2000.* Sabbatical report to Royal Society for the Protection of Birds and Anguilla National Trust. Sandy, Bedfordshire, U.K.: Royal Society for the Protection of Birds.

———. 2001. *Birds and potential IBAs in Anguilla.* Sabbatical report to Anguilla National Trust. Sandy, Bedfordshire, U.K.: Royal Society for the Protection of Birds.

Buckley, P. A., and F. G. Buckley. 1970. Notes of the distribution of some Puerto Rican birds and on the courtship behavior of White-tailed Tropicbirds. *Condor* 72: 483–486.

———. 1984. Cayenne Tern new to North America, with comments on its relationship to Sandwich Tern. *Auk* 101: 396–398.

———. 2000. Breeding Common Terns in Greater West Indies: Status and conservation priorities. Pp. 96–102 in Schreiber, E. A., and D. S. Lee, eds., *Status and conservation of West Indian seabirds.* Special Publication no. 1. Ruston, La.: Society of Caribbean Ornithology.

Buden, D. W. 1987a. *The birds of the southern Bahamas: An annotated check-list.* BOU Check-list no. 8. London: British Ornithologists' Union.

———. 1987b. Birds of the Cay Sal Bank and Ragged Islands, Bahamas. *Fla. Sci.* 50: 21–33.

———. 1987. The birds of Cat Island, Bahamas. *Wilson Bull.* 99: 579–600.

———. 1990a. The birds of Rum Cay, Bahama Islands. *Wilson Bull.* 102: 451–468.

———. 1990. Report on the birds collected during the Armour-Utowana West Indian Expeditions. *Bull. Br. Ornithol. Club* 110: 14–20.

———. 1991. Bird band recoveries in the Bahama Islands. *Carib. J. Sci.* 27: 63–70.

———. 1992a. The birds of Long Island, Bahamas. *Wilson Bull.* 104: 220–243.

———. 1992b. The birds of the Exumas, Bahama Islands. *Wilson Bull.* 104: 674–698.

———. 1993. Bird band recoveries from Haiti and the Dominican Republic. *Carib. J. Sci.* 29: 179–185.

———. 1993. Summer recoveries of banded neotropical migrants in the West Indies. *Fla. Field Nat.* 21: 11–15.

Buden, D. W., and S. L. Olson. 1989. *The avifauna of the cayerias of southern Cuba, with the ornithological results of the Paul Bartsch Expedition of 1930.* Smithsonian Contributions to Zoology no. 477. Washington, D.C.: Smithsonian Institution Press.

Buden, D. W., and A. Schwartz. 1968. Reptiles and birds of the Cay Sal Bank, Bahama Islands. *Q. J. Fla. Acad. Sci.* 31: 290–320.

Buden, D. W., and A. Sprunt, IV. 1993. Additional observations on the birds of the Exumas, Bahama Islands. *Wilson Bull.* 105: 514–518.

Buden, D. W., and R. L. Wetenkamp. 1993. North American bird band recoveries from the Lesser Antilles. *Ornitol. Neotrop.* 4: 83–90.

Buffon, G. L. L., comte de. 1770–1786. *Histoire naturelle des oiseaux, avec la description du Cabinet du Roi.* Paris: Imprimerie Royale.

Buide Gonzalez, M. S., J. Fernandez Milera, O. Garcia Montaña, O. H. Garrido, H. de los Santos Izquierdo, G. Silva Taboada, and L. S. Varona Calvo. 1974. *Las especies amenazadas de vertebrados cubanos*. La Habana: Academia de Ciencias de Cuba, Instituto de Zoología.

Bulens, P. J., G. Bonet, A. Le Dru, M. Tanasi, and J. Tayalay. 1994. *Premiers résultats sur un suivi de l'avifaune de la presqu'île de la Caravelle*. Unpublished report. Fort-de-France, Martinique: Association pour l'Etude et la protection des Vertébrés des petites Antilles (AEVA)–Parc Naturel Regional de la Martinique.

Bull, J. 1978. Palearctic waders and larids in the southern Caribbean. *Ardea* 66: 121–123.

Bullock, I. D., and C. H. Gomersall. 1981. The breeding population of terns in Orkney and Shetland in 1980. *Bird Study* 28: 187–200.

Bureau, L. 1907. Monographie de la Sterne de Dougall (*Sterna dougalli*). Pp. 289–346 in Hartert, E. J. O., and J. L. Bonhote, eds., *Proceedings of the Fourth International Ornithological Congress (1905)*. London: Dulan and Company.

Burdon, K. J. 1920. *A handbook of St. Kitts-Nevis*. London: Government of St. Kitts-Nevis, West India Committee.

Burger, A., and A. D. Lawrence. 2000. Seabird monitoring techniques. Pp. 148–173 in Schreiber, E. A., and D. S. Lee, eds., *Status and conservation of West Indian seabirds*. Special Publication no. 1. Ruston, La.: Society of Caribbean Ornithology.

Burger, J., and M. Gochfeld. 1984. Comparative nest site selection in Caribbean and Hawaiian Sooty Terns. *Colon. Waterbirds Group Newsl.* 8: 37.

———. 1985. Nest site selection by Laughing Gulls: Comparison of tropical colonies (Culebra, Puerto Rico) with temperate colonies (New Jersey). *Condor* 87: 364–373.

———. 1986. Nest site selection in Sooty Terns (*Sterna fuscata*) in Puerto Rico and Hawaii. *Colon. Waterbirds* 9: 31–45.

———. 1988. Defensive aggression in terns: Effect of species, density, and isolation. *Aggressive Behav.* 14: 169–178.

———. 1988. Nest-site selection by Roseate Terns in two tropical colonies on Culebra, Puerto Rico. *Condor* 90: 843–851.

———. 1989. Response of young terns to human handling. *Pitirre* 2(2): 6–7.

———. 1990. Heavy metal levels in Culebra terns. *Pitirre* 3(3): 6.

———. 1991. Lead, mercury, and cadmium in feathers of tropical terns in Puerto Rico and Australia. *Arch. Environ. Contam. Toxicol.* 21: 311–315.

——— (eds.). 1994. *Seabirds on islands: Threats, case studies and action plans*. BirdLife Conservation Series no. 1. Cambridge, U.K.: BirdLife International.

———. 2002. Effects of chemicals and pollution on seabirds. Pp. 485–526 in Schreiber, E. A., and J. Burger, eds., *Biology of marine birds*. Boca Raton, Fla.: CRC Press.

———. 2004. Marine birds as sentinels of environmental pollution. *Ecohealth* 1: 263–274.

Burger, J., M. Gochfeld, D. J. Gochfeld, and J. E. Saliva. 1989. Nest site selection in Zenaida Doves (*Zenaida aurita*) in Puerto Rico. *Biotropica* 21: 244–249.

Burger, J., M. Gochfeld, J. E. Saliva, D. Gochfeld, and H. Mo-rales. 1989. Antipredator behaviour in nesting Zenaida Doves (*Zenaida aurita*): Parental investment or offspring vulnerability. *Behav.* 111: 129–143.

Burger, J., M. Gochfeld, J. E. Saliva, D. J. Gochfeld, D. A. Gochfeld, and H. Morales. 1991. Habitat use by nesting Zenaida Doves *Zenaida aurita* in Puerto Rico: Avoidance of islands without nesting seabirds. *Ornis Scand.* 22: 367–374.

Burke, E. 1972. Water birds. *Gosse Bird Club Broads.* 18: 20.

Burke, R. W. 1992a. *Sea bird survey, Maria Islands*. Unpublished report. Vieux Fort, St. Lucia: Caribbean Natural Resources Institute.

Burke, W. 1992. Second winter sighting of the Common Black-headed Gull (*Larus ridibundus*) in St. Lucia, Lesser Antilles. *Pitirre* 5(2): 4.

Burton, F. J., P. E. Bradley, E. A. Schreiber, G. A. Schink, and R. W. Burton. 1999. Status of Red-footed Booby *Sula sula* on Little Cayman, British West Indies. *Bird Conserv. Intl.* 9: 227–233.

Butcher, R. D. 1956. A visit to the Virgin Islands National Park. *Nat. Parks Mag.* 30: 164–168.

Butler, J. N., B. F. Morris, J. Cadwaller, and A. W. Stoner. 1983. Studies of sargassum and the sargassum community. *Bermuda Biol. Sta. Spec. Publ.* 22: 1–85.

Butler, P. J., R. E. Lewis, R. E. Turley, and I. Caffoor. 1978. *North East London Polytechnic Saint Lucia research report*. Unpublished report. London: North East London Polytechnic.

Butterfield, D. S. 1989. *Held in trust: Properties of the National Trust*. Hamilton, Bermuda: Bermuda National Trust.

Cabrales, M. 1977. "El pajaro de la bruja": Principio y fin de una leyenda. *Bohemia* (Habana) 69: 88–89.

Cairns, D. K. 1987. Seabirds as indicators of marine food supplies. *Biological Oceanography* 5: 261–271.

Campbell, E. W. 1991. The effect of introduced roof rats on bird diversity of Antillean cays. *J. Field Ornithol.* 62: 343–348.

Capstick, E. 1971. Red-footed Boobies? *Gosse Bird Club Broads.* 16: 22.

Carouge. 2005. *Suivi ornithologique sur la réserve naturelle des îlets de Sainte-Anne, année 2004*. Unpublished report. Fort-de-France, Martinique: Parc Naturel Régional de la Martinique.

Carte, A. 1866. On an undescribed species of petrel from the Blue Mountains of Jamaica. *Proc. Zool. Soc. London* 1866: 93–95.

Casas, Fray Bartolomé de las. *Historia de las Indias* [1561]. Caracas: Biblioteca Ayacucho, 1986.

Casement, M. B. 1979. Sea report sheets. *Sea Swallow* 28: 23–42.

Cassin, J. 1860. Catalogue of birds from the island of St. Thomas, West Indies, collected and presented to the Academy of Natural Sciences by Mr. Robert Swift. With notes. *Proc. Acad. Nat. Sci. Philadelphia* 13: 374–379.

Catesby, M. 1731–1743. *The natural history of Carolina, Florida, and the Bahama Islands: containing the figures of birds, beasts, fishes, serpents, insects, and plants*. London: W. Innys and R. Manby.

Cayman Islands Information Service. 2005. *Cayman Islands Annual Report*. George Town, Grand Cayman: Cayman Islands Government Information Service.

Chapman, F. M. 1894. On the birds of the island of Trinidad. *Bull. Amer. Mus. Nat. Hist.* 6: 1–86.

———. 1907. A season's field work. *Bird-Lore* 9: 256–263.

———. 1908. *Camps and cruises of an ornithologist*. New York: D. Appleton and Company

———. 1908. A contribution to the life-histories of the booby (*Sula leucogastra*) and man-of-war bird (*Fregata aquila*). Papers from the Tortugas Laboratory of the Carnegie Institution of Washington. Vol. II. *Carnegie Inst. Washington Publ.* 103: 139–151.

———. 1918. Notes from a traveler in the tropics. I: Down the coastline to Cuba. *Bird-Lore* 20: 393–397.

Chapman, S. E. 1981. Notes on seabird reports received 1979–1980. *Sea Swallow* 30: 45–67.

———. 1982. Notes on seabird reports received 1980–81. *Sea Swallow* 31: 5–24.

Chardine, J. W. 1987. Brown Noddy vocal behavior. *Auk* 104: 790.

Chardine, J. W., and R. D. Morris. 1987. Trapping and color banding Brown Noddy and Bridled Tern adults at the breeding colony. *Colon. Waterbirds* 10: 100–102.

———. 1989. Sexual size dimorphism and assortative mating in the Brown Noddy. *Condor* 91: 868–874.

———. 1997. Hurricanes and Brown Noddies. *Colon. Waterbird Soc. Bull.* 20: 65.

Chardine, J. W., R. D. Morris, and F. C. Schaffner 1985. Sexual dimorphism, reproductive success and chick growth of Brown Noddies nesting on Culebra, Puerto Rico. *Colon. Waterbirds Group Newsl.* 9: 22.

Chardine, J. W., R. D. Morris, J. F. Parnell, and J. Pierce. 2000a. Status and conservation priorities for Laughing Gulls, Gull-billed Terns, Royal Terns and Bridled Terns in the West Indies. Pp. 65–79 *in* Schreiber, E. A., and D. S. Lee, eds., *Status and conservation of West Indian seabirds*. Special Publication no. 1. Ruston, La.: Society of Caribbean Ornithology.

Chardine, J. W., R. D. Morris, and R. L. Norton. 2000b. Status and conservation needs of Brown Noddies and Black Noddies in the West Indies. Pp. 118–125 *in* Schreiber, E. A., and D. S. Lee, eds., *Status and conservation of West Indian seabirds*. Special Publication no. 1. Ruston, La.: Society of Caribbean Ornithology.

Charlevoix, P. F. X. de. 1730. *Histoire de l'isle Espagnole ou de S. Domingue: Ecrite particulièrement sur des mémoires manuscrits du P. Jean-Baptiste Le Pers, Jesuite, missionaire à Saint Domingue, & sur les pièces originales, qui se conservent au dépôt de la marine*. Paris: F. Barois.

Cherrie, G. K. 1896. Contribution to the ornithology of San Domingo. *Field Columbian Mus., Publ. 10, Ornithol. Ser.*, 1: 1–26.

Cheshire, N. G. 1993. Notes on seabird reports received in 1992. *Sea Swallow* 42: 5–15.

Chilman, P. W. G. 1979. A voyage in the Caribbean and Gulf of Mexico, April, 1977. *Sea Swallow* 28: 11–14.

———. 1984. Migrants in the Western Atlantic: Spring 1982. *Sea Swallow* 33: 61–64.

Chiriví Gallego, H. 1988. Fauna tetrapoda y algunos aspectos ecológicos de los cayos del Archipiélago de San Andrés y Providencia, Colombia. *Trianea* (Acta Cient. Tecn. INDERENA) 2: 277–337.

Christy, C. 1897. Field-notes on the birds of the island of San Domingo. *Ibis* 3: 317–343.

Churcher, P. B., and J. H. Lawton. 1989. Beware of well-fed felines. *Nat. Hist.* 7: 40–47.

Clapp, R. B. 1986. *A resurvey of the Red-footed Booby colony on Little Cayman Island*. Unpublished report. Washington, D.C.: U.S. Fish Wildlife Service, Natl. Mus. Nat. Hist.

———. 1987. Status of the Red-footed Booby colony on Little Cayman Island. *Atoll Res. Bull.* 304: 1–15.

Clapp, R. B., M. K. Klimkiewicz, and J. H. Kennard. 1982. Longevity records of North American birds: Gaviidae through Alcidae. *J. Field Ornithol.* 53: 81–124.

Clark, A. H. 1905a. Birds of the southern Lesser Antilles. *Proc. Boston Soc. Nat. Hist.* 32: 203–312.

———. 1905. The migration of certain shore birds. *Auk* 22: 134–140.

[———]. 1905. The birds of St. Vincent. *West Ind. Bull.* 5: 75–95.

———. 1911. A list of the birds of the island of St. Lucia. *West Ind. Bull.* 11: 182–193.

Clement, A. C., M. A. Cane, and R. Seager. 2001. An orbitally driven tropical source for abrupt climate change. *J. Climate* 14: 2369–2375.

Clough, G. C., and G. Fulk. 1971. The vertebrate fauna and the vegetation of East Plana Cay, Bahama Islands. *Atoll Res. Bull.* 138: 1–15.

Coblentz, B. E. 1986. A possible reason for age-differential foraging success in Brown Pelicans. *J. Field Ornithol.* 57: 63–64.

Collar, N. J., and P. Andrew. 1988. *Birds to watch: The ICBP world check-list of threatened birds*. ICBP Tech. Publ. no. 8. Washington, D.C.: Smithsonian Institution Press.

Collar, N. J., L. P. Gonzaga, N. Krabbe, A. Madrono Nieto, L. G. Naranjo, T. A. Parker, III, and D. C. Wedge. 1992. *Threatened birds of the Americas: The ICBP/IUCN Red Data Book*, 3rd ed. Cambridge, U.K.: International Council for Bird Preservation.

Collazo, J. A. 1985. *Status and population ecology of the Brown Pelican on the Puerto Rico Bank region*. Ph.D. dissertation. Ames: Iowa State University.

Collazo, J. A., and T. Agardy. 1982. Preliminary data on some aspects of the ecology of Brown Pelicans in Puerto Rico and the U.S. Virgin Islands. Pp. 101–114 *in* Nievas Rivera, L. O., and R. A. Pérez-Rivera, eds., *Memorias del Tercer Simposio sobre la Fauna de Puerto Rico*. Humacao: Universidad de Puerto Rico, Departamento de Biología.

Collazo, J. A., and E. E. Klaas. 1985. *Status and ecology of the Brown Pelican in the Greater Puerto Rican Bank region*. Final report to the Department of Natural Resources, San Juan, Puerto Rico. Ames: Iowa Cooperative Fish and Wildlife Research Unit.

———. 1986. *Recovery plan for the Caribbean Brown Pelican in Puerto Rico and the U.S. Virgin Islands*. Atlanta, Ga.: U.S. Fish and Wildlife Service, Region 4, Office of Endangered Species.

Collazo, J. A., J. E. Saliva, and J. Pierce. 2000. Conservation of the Brown Pelican in the West Indies. Pp. 39–45 *in* Schreiber, E. A., and D. S. Lee, eds., *Status and conservation of West Indian seabirds*. Special Publication no. 1. Ruston, La.: Society of Caribbean Ornithology.

Collazo, J. A., T. Agardy, E. E. Klaas, J. E. Saliva, and J. Pierce. 1998. An interdecadal comparison of population parameters of Brown Pelicans in Puerto Rico and the U.S. Virgin Islands. *Colon. Waterbirds* 21: 61–65.

Collier, N. C., and A. C. Brown. 2003. *Report to St. Eustatius National Parks: Surveys of sea and terrestrial birds*. Unpublished report. Riviera Beach, Fla.: Environmental Protection in the Caribbean.

———. 2004. *Anguilla's offshore islands: Seabird census and nest monitoring, May–June 2004*. Unpublished report to Ministry of Environment, Anguilla. Riviera Beach, Fla.: Environmental Protection in the Caribbean.

Collier, N. C., A. C. Brown, and M. Hester. 2002. Searches for seabird breeding colonies in the Lesser Antilles. *Pitirre* 15(3): 110–116.

Collins, C. T. 1969. A review of the shearwater records for Trinidad and Tobago. *Ibis* 111: 251–253.

Collins, C. T., and E. S. Tikasingh. 1974. Status of the Great Shearwater in Trinidad, West Indies. *Bull. Br. Ornithol. Club* 94: 96–99.

Colón, J. A. 1982. Notas sobre una colonia de Gaviota Chica, *Sterna albifrons*, en El Tuque, Ponce, Puerto Rico. Pp. 115–122 *in* Nievas Rivera, L. O., and R. A. Pérez-Rivera, eds., *Memorias del Tercer Simposio sobre la Fauna de Puerto Rico*. Humacao: Universidad de Puerto Rico, Departamento de Biología.

Colt, H. 1631. The diary of Sir Henry Colt 1631. *J. Barbados Mus. Hist. Soc.* 21: 5–12.

Connor, H. A., and R. W. Loftin. 1985. The birds of Eleuthera Island, Bahamas. *Fla. Field Nat.* 14: 77–93.

Constanza, R., R. D'Arge, R. S. de Groot, S. Farber, M. Grosso, B. Hannon, K. Limburg, S. Naeem, R. V. O'Neill, J. Paruelo, R. G. Raskin, P. Sutton, and M. van den Belt. 1997. The value of the world's ecosystem services and natural capital. *Nature* 387(6630): 253–260.

Cooke, M. T. 1938. Some interesting recoveries of banded birds. *Bird-Banding* 9: 184–190.

———. 1942. Returns from banded birds: Some longevity records of wild birds. *Bird-Banding* 13: 70–74.

———. 1943. Returns from banded birds: Some miscellaneous recoveries of interest. *Bird-Banding* 14: 67–74.

———. 1945. Returns from banded birds: Some interesting recoveries. *Bird-Banding* 16: 15–21.

———. 1945. Transoceanic recoveries of banded birds. *Bird-Banding* 16: 123–129.

———. 1946. Returns of banded birds: Some recent records of interest. *Bird-Banding* 17: 63–71.

Cory, C. B. 1880. *Birds of the Bahama Islands: Containing many birds new to the islands, and a number of undescribed winter plumages of North American species*. Boston, Mass.: privately published by the author.

———. 1881. List of the birds of Haiti, taken in different parts of the island between January 1 and March 12, 1881. *Bull. Nuttall Ornithological Club* 6: 151–155.

———. 1885. *A list of birds of the West Indies, including the Bahama Islands and the Greater and Lesser Antilles, excepting the islands of Tobago and Trinidad*. Boston, Mass.: Estes and Lauriat.

———. 1886a. A list of birds collected on the island of Grand Cayman, W.I., by W. B. Richardson, during the summer of 1886. *Auk* 3: 501–502.

———. 1886. *A list of the birds of the West Indies, including the Bahama Islands and the Greater and Lesser Antilles, excepting the islands of Tobago and Trinidad*, rev. ed. Boston, Mass.: Estes and Lauriat.

———. 1887. A list of the birds collected by Mr. W. B. Richardson, in the island of Martinique, West Indies. *Auk* 4: 95–96.

———. 1887. A list of the birds taken by Mr. Robert Henderson, in the islands of Old Providence and St. Andrews, Caribbean Sea, during the winter of 1886–87. *Auk* 4: 180–181.

———. 1888. The birds of the West Indies, including the Bahama Islands, the Greater and the Lesser Antilles, excepting the islands of Tobago and Trinidad. *Auk* 4: 48–92.

———. 1889a. A list of the birds collected by Mr. C. J. Maynard in the islands of Little Cayman and Cayman Brack, West Indies. *Auk* 6: 30–32.

———. 1889. *The birds of the West Indies, including all species known to occur in the Bahama Islands, the Greater Antilles, the Caymans, and the Lesser Antilles, excepting the islands of Tobago and Trinidad*. Boston, Mass.: Estes and Lauriat.

———. 1890. On a collection of birds made during the winter of 1889–90, by Cyrus S. Winch, in the islands of St. Thomas, Tortola, Anegada, and Virgin Gorda, West Indies. *Auk* 7: 373–375.

———. 1890. *Birds of the Bahama Islands containing many birds new to the islands, and a number of undescribed winter plumages to North American birds*, rev. (2nd) ed. Boston, Mass.: Estes and Lauriat.

———. 1891a. A collection of birds taken by Cyrus S. Winch in the islands of Anguilla, Antigua, and St. Eustatius, West Indies, during April, May, June, and a part of July, 1890. *Auk* 8: 46–47.

———. 1891. A list of the birds collected in the islands of St. Croix and St. Kitts, West Indies, during March and April, and in Guadeloupe during August, September, and October, 1890. *Auk* 8: 47–49.

———. 1891. A list of birds taken and observed in Cuba and the Bahama Islands, during March and April, 1891. *Auk* 8: 292–294.

———. 1891. List of birds collected on the island of Inagua, Bahama Islands, from May 1 to July 10, 1891. *Auk* 8: 351.

———. 1891. On a collection of birds made on the islands of Anguilla and Cay Sal or Salt Cay, Bahama Islands, by Mr. Cyrus S. Winch, during May, 1891. *Auk* 8: 352.

———. 1892. A list of birds taken on Maraguana, Watling's Island, and Inagua, Bahamas, during July, August, September, and October, 1891. *Auk* 9: 48–49.

———. 1892. Remarks on a collection of birds made by Wilmot W. Brown, Jr., on Mona and Porto Rico during February and a part of March, 1892. *Auk* 9: 228–229.

———. 1892. *Catalogue of West Indian birds, containing a list of all species known to occur in the Bahama Islands, the Greater Antilles, the Caymans, and the Lesser Antilles, excepting the islands of Tobago and Trinidad.* Boston, Mass.: privately published by the author, Alfred Mudge & Son, Printer.

———. 1909. The birds of the Leeward Islands, Caribbean Sea. *Field Mus. Nat. Hist., Publ. 137, Ornithol. Ser.,* 1(5): 193–255.

Courchamp, F., J.-L. Chapuis, and M. Pascal. 2003. Mammal invaders on islands: Impact, control and control impact. *Biol. Rev.* 78: 347–383.

Crombie, R. I., D. W. Steadman, and J. C. Barber. 1984. A preliminary survey of the vertebrates of Cabarita Island, St. Mary Parish, Jamaica. *Atoll Res. Bull.* 280: 1–15.

Croxall, J. P., P. G. H. Evans, and R. W. Schreiber. 1984. *Status and conservation of the world's seabirds.* ICBP Tech. Publ. no. 2. Cambridge, U.K.: International Council for Bird Preservation.

Cruz, A. 1977. The use of mangroves by birds in Jamaica. *Gosse Bird Club Broads.* 29: 4–5.

Cruz, A., and P. Fairbairn. 1980. Conservation of natural resources in the Caribbean: The avifauna of Jamaica. Pp. 438–444 *in* Sabol, K., ed., *Transactions of the Forty-fifth North American Wildlife and Natural Resources Conference.* Washington, D.C.: Wildlife Management Institute.

Cruz Lorenzo, J. de la, and R. Alayo Soto. 1984. Primeros datos sobre la nidificación del Vencejo de Collar, *Streptoprocne zonaris pallidifrons* y del Contramaestre, *Phaethon lepturus catesbyi* (Aves: Apodidae y Phaethontidae) de Cuba. P. 456 *in IV Conferencia Científica sobre Educacion Superior, 1984.* La Habana, Cuba: Universidad de La Habana.

Cruz Lorenzo, J. de la, and O. H. Garrido. 1973. Lista de los anfibios, reptiles, aves y mamiferos colectados en el Plan Jibacoa-Cayojabos. Pp. 16–25 *in* Garcia, I., R. Alyayo, N. Novoa, A. Nicholas, R. Gonzalez, L. de Armas, D. Dominguez, C. Somoza, A. de la Osa, J. de la Cruz, O. H. Garrido, J. Ramon Cuevas, and J. Fontaines, eds., *Informe del trabajo faunístico realizado en el plan Jibacoa-Cayojabos.* Serie Biologica no. 43. La Habana: Academia de Ciencias de Cuba.

Cubillas Hernandez, S. O., A. Kirkconnell, R. M. Posada Rodríguez, and A. Llanes Sosa. 1988. Aves observadas en los cayos Rosario y Cantiles, Archipiélago de los Canarreos, Cuba. *Misc. Zool., Inst. Zool. Acad. Cienc. Cuba* 38: 1–2.

Cuello, J. P. 1988. Lista de las aves fósiles de la región neotropical y de las islas antillanas. *Paula-Coutiana, Porto Alegre* 2: 3–79.

Currie, H., and R. B. H. Smith. 1992. Least Tern. *Gosse Bird Club Broads.* 59: 18.

Custer, T. W., I. C. T. Nisbet, and A. J. Krynitsky. 1983. Organochlorine residues and shell characteristics of Roseate Tern eggs, 1981. *J. Field Ornithol.* 54: 394–400.

Dammann, A. E., and D. W. Nellis. 1992. *A natural history atlas to the cays of the U.S. Virgin Islands.* Sarasota, Fla.: Pineapple Press.

Danforth, S. T. 1922. Some impressions of Porto Rican bird life. *Oölogist* 39: 10–11.

———. 1925. New birds for Porto Rico. *Auk* 42: 558–563.

———. 1925. Birds seen between Porto Rico and New York. *Wilson Bull.* 37: 76–77.

———. 1926. The Least Tern (*Sternula antillarum antillarum*), in Grenada, Lesser Antilles. *Auk* 43: 363.

———. 1926. An ecological study of Cartagena Lagoon, Porto Rico, with special reference to the birds. *J. Agric. Univ. P.R.* 10: 1–136.

———. 1928. Birds observed in Jamaica during the summer of 1926. *Auk* 45: 480–491.

———. 1928. Birds observed in the vicinity of Santiago de Cuba. *Wilson Bull.* 40: 178–182.

———. 1929. Notes on the birds of Hispaniola. *Auk* 46: 358–375.

———. 1930. Bird records from the Virgin Islands. *J. Dept. Agric. P.R.* 14: 107–134.

———. 1930. Notes on the birds of St. Martin and St. Eustatius. *Auk* 47: 44–47.

———. 1930. Bird records from the Virgin Islands. *J. Dept. Agric. P.R.* 14: 107–134.

———. 1931. Puerto Rican ornithological records. *J. Dept. Agric. P.R.* 15: 33–106.

———. 1933. A list of the birds known from Antigua, B.W.I. *Suppl. Leeward Islands Gazette,* 16 Nov.: 1–4.

———. 1934a. The birds of Antigua. *Auk* 51: 350–364.

———. 1934. Some West Indian records of Charadriiformes. *Auk* 51: 103.

———. 1935a. Supplementary account of the birds of the Virgin Islands, including Culebra and adjacent islets pertaining to Puerto Rico, with notes on their food habits. *J. Agric. Univ. P.R.* 19: 439–472.

———. 1935b. The birds of Barbuda, with notes on their economic importance, and relationship to the Puerto Rican avifauna. *J. Agric. Univ. P.R.* 19: 473–482.

———. 1935. Leach's Petrel in the West Indies. *Auk* 52: 74.

———. 1935. Investigations concerning Cuban birds, with special reference to their economic status, and consideration of those which might be desirable for introduction into Puerto Rico. *J. Agric. Univ. P.R.* 19: 421–437.

———. 1935. The birds of Saint Lucia. *Monogr. Univ. P.R., Phys. Biolog. Sci. B* 3: 129.

———. 1936a. The birds of St. Kitts and Nevis. *Trop. Agric.* (Trinidad) 13: 213–217.

———. 1936b. A bird new to the West Indian avifauna. *Auk* 53: 82.

———. 1936. New records for Mona Island, West Indies. *Auk* 53: 100.

———. 1937. Ornithological investigations in Vieques Island, Puerto Rico, during December 1935. *J. Agric. Univ. P.R.* 21: 539–550.

———. 1938. The birds of Saba. *J. Agric. Univ. P.R.* 22: 503–512.

———. 1939. The birds of Montserrat. *J. Agric. Univ. P.R.* 23: 47–66.

———. 1939. The birds of Guadeloupe and adjacent islands. *J. Agric. Univ. P.R.* 23: 9–46.

———. 1939. The birds of Montserrat. *J. Agric. Univ. P.R.* 23: 47–66.

Dathe, H., and W. Fischer. 1969. Bemerkenswerte beobachtungen auf Kuba im frühjahr 1968. *J. Ornithol.* 110: 111–112.

———. 1979. Beiträge zur ornithologie Kubas. *Beitr. Vogelkd.* 25: 171–203.

Daubenton, Edmé-L. 1765–1781. *Planches enluminées pour servir a l'histoire naturelle de M. Le compte de Buffon.* Paris: Pancoucke.

Davies, J. E. 1994. Rare and endemic plants, animals and habitats in the Cayman Islands, and related legislation. Pp. 527–541 *in* Brunt, M. A., and J. E. Davies, eds., *The Cayman Islands: Natural history and biogeography.* Monographiae Biologicae vol. 7. Dordrecht, Netherlands: Kluwer Academic Publishers.

Davis, D. E. 1941. Notes on Cuban birds. *Wilson Bull.* 53: 37–40.

Davis, S., and A. Smith. 1995. Birds at Fort Clarence Beach Park, beside the Great Salt Pond, St. Catherine. *Gosse Bird Club Broads.* 65: 15.

Day, R. H., D. H. S. Wehle, and F. Coleman. 1982. Ingestion of plastic by marine birds: A global phenomenon. Publ. abstract in *Pacific Seabird Group Bull.* 9: 77.

Dean, T. 1999. Bird sightings recorded by members of Quest Nature Tour Group February 24–March 7, 1999. Unpublished notes in Turks and Caicos National Trust files, Providenciales.

Dean, T., and D. Osborne. N.d. (1992 or later). *Checklist of the birds of North Andros Island, Bahamas.* Privately published.

Debrot, A. O., N. Esteban, R. Le Scao, A. Caballero, and P. C. Hoetjes. 2005. New sea turtle nesting records for the Netherlands Antilles provide impetus to conservation action. *Carib. J. Sci.* 41: 334–339.

Debrot, A. O., and J. A. de Freitas. 1991. *Wilderness areas of exceptional conservation value in Curaçao, Netherlands Antilles.* Amsterdam, Netherlands: Netherlands Commission for International Nature Protection Mededelingen No. 26.

Debrot, A. O., and J. Sybesma. 2000. The Dutch Antilles. Ch. 38, pp. 595–614 *in* Sheppard, C. R. C., ed., *Seas at the millennium: An environmental evaluation.* Vol. I: *Regional Chapters: Europe, the Americas and West Africa.* Amsterdam, Netherlands: Elsevier.

de Dalmas, R. 1900. Note sur une collection d'oiseaux de l'ile de Tobago. *Mem. Soc. Zool. France* 13: 132–144.

De Kort, R. E. 1995. The Larid seabird breeding populations of the San Nicolas Bay cays, Aruba. *Pitirre* 8(3): 15.

Delacour, J. 1938. Journal de Croisière (Yacht *Rosaura*, octobre 1937–janvier 1938). *Oiseau Rev. Fr. Ornithol.* 8: 541–557.

Del Hoyo, J., A. Elliott, and J. Sargatal (eds.). 1992. *Handbook of birds of the world. Vol. I: Ostrich to ducks.* Barcelona, Spain: Lynx Editions.

———. 1996. *Handbook of birds of the world. Vol. 3: Hoatzin to auks.* Barcelona, Spain: Lynx Editions.

Del Nevo, A. J. 2001. The status, distribution and conservation of terns on Aruba and Bonaire. *Pitirre* 14(3): 144.

De Mercey, P. 1997. *Inventaire, étude biologique et suiví de l'avifaune de la Réserve Naturelle des îlets de Saint Anne.* Rapport intermédiaire. Fort-de-France, Martinique: Parc Naturel Régional de la Martinique–GÉODE Caraïbe.

———. 1998a. *Etude le l'avifaune de la réserve naturelle des îlets de Sainte-Anne.* Rapport intermédiaire suite au suivi des colonies de sternes de juillet à septembre 1997. Fort-de-France, Martinique: Parc Naturel Régional de la Martinique–GÉODE Caraïbe.

———. 1998b. *Etude de l'avifaune de la réserve naturelle des îlets de Sainte-Anne.* Bilan provisoire de l'étude. Fort-de-France, Martinique: Parc Naturel Régional de la Martinique–GÉODE Caraïbe.

De Mercey, P., and S. Jérémie. 1999. *Etude de l'avifaune de la réserve naturelle des îlets de Sainte-Anne.* Diagnostic écologique et bilan de la nidification 1997, 1998, 1999. Fort-de-France, Martinique: Parc Naturel Régional de la Martinique–GÉODE Caraïbe.

Departamento de Recursos Naturales. 1985. *Evaluacion ambiental y determinacion de impacto ambiental no significativo: Reglamento propuesto para regir el manejo de las especies vulnerables o en peligro de extincion en el estado libre asociado de Puerto Rico.* San Juan, Puerto Rico: Departamento de Recursos Naturales.

Descourtilz, M. É. 1809. *Voyages d'un naturaliste, et ses observations faites sur les trois règnes de la nature, dans plusieurs ports de mer français, en Espagne, au continent de l'Amérique septentrionale, à Saint-Yago de Cuba, et à Saint-Domingue, ou l'auteur devenu le prisonnier de 10,000 noirs révoltés, et par suite mis en liberté par un colonne del'armée française, donne des détails circonstanciés sur l'expédition du général LeClerc.* Paris: Père Dufart, Libraire-Éditeur.

———. 1935. *Voyages d'un naturaliste et ses observations.* Abridged ed. Paris: Plon.

Devas, R. P. 1943. *Birds of Grenada, St. Vincent and the Grenadines.* St. George's, Grenada: Carenage Press.

———. 1954. *Birds of Grenada, St. Vincent and the Grenadines.* Port-of-Spain, Trinidad: Yuilles Printery.

Dewey, R. A., and D. W. Nellis. 1980. Seabird research in the U.S. Virgin Islands. Pp. 445–452 *in* Sabol, K., ed., *Transactions of the Forty-fifth North American Wildlife and Natural Resources Conference.* Washington, D. C.: Wildlife Management Institute.

Diamond, A. 1971. Bird Notes: Least Terns. *Gosse Bird Club Broads.* 17: 27.

Diamond, A. W. 1972. Sexual dimorphism in breeding cycles and unequal sex ratio in Magnificent Frigatebirds. *Ibis* 114: 395–398.

———. 1973. Notes on the breeding biology and behavior of the Magnificent Frigatebird. *Condor* 75: 200–209.

———. 1975. Biology and behaviour of frigatebirds *Fregata* spp. on Aldabra Atoll. *Ibis* 117: 302–323.

———. 1975. The biology of Tropicbirds at Aldabra Atoll, Indian Ocean. *Auk* 92: 16–39.

———. 1976. Subannual breeding and moult cycles in the Bridled Tern *Sterna anaethetus* in the Seychelles. *Ibis* 118: 414–419.

———. 1980. The Red-footed Booby colony on Little Cayman: Size, structure and significance. *Atoll Res. Bull.* 241: 165–170.

———. 1983. *Censusing and managing cage-birds, sea-birds, and birds harmful to agriculture in Trinidad and Tobago.* Port of Spain, Trinidad: Ministry of Agriculture, Lands and Food Production–Food and Agriculture Organization of the United Nations.

Diamond, A. W., and F. L. Filion (eds.) 1987. *The value of birds.* Technical Publication no. 6. Cambridge, U.K.: International Council for Bird Preservation.

Diamond, A. W., and E. A. Schreiber. 2002. The Magnificent Frigatebird *Fregata magnificens. In* Poole, A., and F. Gill, eds., *The birds of North America,* no. 601. Philadelphia: Birds of North America.

Diamond, J. M. 2005. *Collapse: How societies choose to fail or succeed.* New York: Penguin.

Diamond, T. 1971. Least Tern. *Gosse Bird Club Broads.* 17: 27.

Díaz, J. M., G. Díaz, J. Garzón, J. Geister, J. A. Sanchez, and S. Zea. 1996. *Atlas de los arrecifes coralinos del Caribe colombiano. I: Complejos arrecifales oceánicos.* Serie de publicaciones especiales, no. 2. Santa Marta, Colombia: Instituto de Investigaciones Marinas y Costeras José Benito Vives de Andréis (INVEMAR).

Díaz, J. M., L. M. Barrios, M. H. Cendales, J. Garzon, J. Geister, M. López, G. H. Ospina, F. Parra-Velandia, J. Pinzón, B. Vargas, F. A. Zapata, and S. Zea. 2000. *Areas coralinas de Colombia.* Serie Publicaciones Especiales no. 5. Santa Marta, Colombia: Instituto de Investigaciones Marinas y Costeras José Benito Vives de Andréis (INVEMAR).

Dinsmore, J. J. 1972. Avifauna of Little Tobago Island. *Q. J. Fla. Acad. Sci.* 35: 55–71.

Dinsmore, J. J., and R. ffrench. 1969. Birds of St. Giles Islands, Tobago. *Wilson Bull.* 81: 460–463.

Dobson, A. 2002. *A birdwatching guide to Bermuda.* Shrewsbury, U.K.: Arlequin Press.

Dod, A. S. de. 1972. Aves de nuestra pais: La Tijereta, gran volandora. *El Caribe* 2: 11–A.

———. 1973. Aves de nuestra pais: El majestuoso Pelicano. *El Caribe* 1: 11–A.

———. 1973. Aves de nuestra pais: La Gaviota dominicana. *El Caribe* 6: 11–A.

———. 1973. Aves de nuestra pais: las gaviotas son gregarias. *El Caribe* 8: 11–A.

———. 1976. Loma Jamao: en Busca del Diabliotín. *El Caribe*: 9.

———. 1979. Llegan nuevos miembros familia de gaviotas. *El Caribe*: 9.

———. 1979. Aparecen piedras volcánicas desplazadas en Jaiquí Picado. *El Caribe*: 9.

———. 1980. Colonia de *Pterodroma hasitata* en Republica Dominicana. NP-2/81 *in* Cicero, J., ed., *Naturalista Postal* 1980. Carta Ocasional del Herbario. Santo Domingo, República Dominicana: Universidad Autonoma de Santo Domingo.

———. 1981. Aparace la primera colonia de Diablotines. *El Caribe*: 25.

———. 1982. Un paseso sin suerte por la Loma de Toro. *El Caribe*: 19.

———. 1982. Sigue la mala suerte en Loma de Toro. *El Caribe*: 19.

———. 1982. Ornitólogos frustrados en Loma de Toro. *El Caribe*: 19.

———. 1982. ¡Adiós, Loma de Toro! *El Caribe*: 19.

———. 1984. El Diablotín, un ave rara y una curiosidad. *El Caribe*: 17.

———. 1985. Los Diablotines y los Lavapiés. *El Caribe*: 18.

———. 1986. Jejenes y Tijeretas en un viaje feliz. *El Caribe*: 18.

———. 1988. Los bubíes del Caribe. *El Caribe*: 18.

———. 1988. Si no son bubíes ¿qué son? *El Caribe*: 18.

———. 1992. *Endangered and endemic birds of the Dominican Republic.* Fort Bragg, Calif.: Cypress House.

Dod, A. S. de., and D. A. Siri Nuñez. 1980. Aves migratorias accidentales observados este año en Republica Dominicana. NP-39/80 *in* Cicero, J., ed., *Naturalista Postal* 1980. Carta Ocasional del Herbario. Santo Domingo, República Dominicana: Universidad Autonoma de Santo Domingo.

Dominguez Montandon, T. G., and D. Siri. 1989. Estudio preliminar de la avifauna en las lagunas Limón y Redonda, Miches. *Pitirre* 2(3): 7–8.

Donaldson, A. 1996. Birds at Middle Cay, Morant, Cays (off the south east coast). *Gosse Bird Club Broads.* 66: 29.

Done, T. J. 1992. Phase shifts in coral reef communities and their ecological significance. *Hydrobiologia* 247: 121–132.

Douglas, H. D. 2000. *Ecological and behavioral factors affecting the productivity and coloniality of Caribbean Roseate Terns.* Unpublished report. Boquerón, Puerto Rico: Caribbean Field Office, U.S. Fish and Wildlife Service.

———. 2001. *Results of Roseate Tern research and monitoring efforts at LeDuck I., U.S. Virgin Islands in 2001.* Unpublished report. Boquerón, Puerto Rico: U.S. Fish and Wildlife Service, Caribbean Field Office.

Douglas, L. 2000a. Status of the Jamaican petrel in the West Indies. Pp. 19–24 in Schreiber, E. A., and D. S. Lee, eds., *Status and conservation of West Indian seabirds*. Special Publication no. 1. Ruston, La.: Society of Caribbean Ornithology.

Douglas, L., D. Lewis, and C. Levy. 1998. Bird Notes: Masked Booby, Brown Booby. *Gosse Bird Club Broads*. 70: 20.

Douglas, L., and B. Zonfrillo. 1997. First record of Audubon's Shearwater and Black-capped Petrel from Jamaica. *Gosse Bird Club Broads*. 69: 4–6.

Downer, A. 1965. Magnificent Frigatebird. *Gosse Bird Club Broads*. 5: 20.

———. 1967. Black Tern. *Gosse Bird Club Broads*. 8: 16.

———. 1971. Herring Gull. *Gosse Bird Club Broads*. 16: 18.

———. 1973. Caspian Tern. *Gosse Bird Club Broads*. 20: 22.

———. 1974. White-tailed Tropicbirds. *Gosse Bird Club Broads*. 23: 11–12.

———. 1975. White-tailed Tropicbird. *Gosse Bird Club Broads*. 25: 19.

———. 1976. Brown Booby. *Gosse Bird Club Broads*. 26: 16.

———. 1979. White-tailed Tropicbird. *Gosse Bird Club Broads*. 32: 12.

———. 1981. Laughing Gull. *Gosse Bird Club Broads*. 37: 12.

———. 1982. Sandwich Tern. *Gosse Bird Club Broads*. 38: 13.

———. 1983. White-tailed Tropicbird. *Gosse Bird Club Broads*. 40: 16.

———. 1983. Brown Pelican. *Gosse Bird Club Broads*. 40: 16.

———. 1984. Least Tern. *Gosse Bird Club Broads*. 43: 14.

———. 1985. Least Terns and Black Terns. *Gosse Bird Club Broads*. 44: 12.

———. 1987. White-tailed Tropicbird. *Gosse Bird Club Broads*. 48: 9.

———. 1988. Ibis nesting on Refuge Cay in Kingston Harbour, May 7, 1988. *Gosse Bird Club Broads*. 51: 11.

———. 1988. Nesting colony at Parottee Pond, July 1988. *Gosse Bird Club Broads*. 51: 11.

———. 1989. Brown Pelican. *Gosse Bird Club Broads*. 53: 23.

———. 1989. Gull-billed Tern. *Gosse Bird Club Broads*. 53: 25.

———. 1990a. Trip to Pedro Cays. *Gosse Bird Club Broads*. 54: 18.

———. 1990. Bridled Tern. *Gosse Bird Club Broads*. 54: 20–21.

———. 1992. Brown Pelican. *Gosse Bird Club Broads*. 59: 16.

Downer, A., and A. Black (eds.). 1972. Breeding of the Least Tern in Jamaica. *Gosse Bird Club Broads*. 18: 18.

Downer, A., and J. Fletcher. 1980. Migrant dates. *Gosse Bird Club Broads*. 35: 10.

Downer, A., J. Fletcher, Y. Becker, and C. Levy. 1989. Least Tern. *Gosse Bird Club Broads*. 53: 25.

Downer, A., G. H. Gale, R. L. Sutton, and M. Hodgson. 1975. Herring Gull. *Gosse Bird Club Broads*. 24: 19.

Downer, A., and C. Levy. 1989. Nesting terns and noddies. *Gosse Bird Club Broads*. 53: 20–21.

Downer, A., and D. Verley. 1976. Mullion Cove. *Gosse Bird Club Broads*. 27: 12.

DROV (Dienst Ruimtelijke Ontwikkeling en Volkshuisvesting), Curaçao. 1985. *Monumenten inventarisatie*. Band IV. Willemstad, Curaçao: Natuur/Cultuurmonumenten. Irregular pagination.

Duffield, J. M., and J. E. Cardona. 1978. *Estimated avian population density and diversity indices of Vieques Island*. San Juan, Puerto Rico: Department of Natural Resources.

Duffy, D. 1994. Afterwards: An agenda for managing seabirds and islands. Pp. 311–318 in Nettleship, D. N., J. Burger, and M. Gochfeld, eds., *Seabirds on islands: Threats, case studies and action plans*. BirdLife Conservation Ser. no. 1. Cambridge, U.K.: BirdLife International.

Duffy, D., W. E. Arntz, H. T. Serpa, P. D. Boersma, and R. L. Norton. 1988. A comparison of the effects of El Niño and the Southern Oscillation on birds in Peru and the Atlantic Ocean. Pp. 1740–1746 in Ouellet, H., ed., *Proceedings of the 19th International Ornithological Congress (1986)*, Ottawa, Ontario: University of Ottawa Press.

Dugand, A. 1947. Aves marinas de las costas e islas Colombianas. *Caldasia* 4: 379–398.

Du Mont, K. 1964. Magnificent Frigatebird. *Gosse Bird Club Broads*. 3: 14.

Dumont, P. A. 1934. On the specimens of *Fregata magnificens* in the University of Iowa Museum. *Wilson Bull*. 46: 120–122.

Dunham, J. B., K. Burnett, and G. Wenz (eds.). 1990. *The birds of Lee Stocking Island and Northern Great Exuma: Records of observations from February 1987 to April 1989 by the staff of the Caribbean Marine Research Center*. Unpublished report. Lee Stocking Island, Exuma Cays, Bahamas: Caribbean Marine Research Center.

du Tertre, J. B. 1654. *Histoire générale des iles de S. Christophe, de la Guadeloupe, de la Martinique, et autres dans l'Amérique. Ou l'on verra l'establissement des colonies étrangères, & tout ce qui se passes dans les voyages & retours des Indes . . . De plus, la description de tous les animaux de la mer, de l'air, & de la terre: & vn traite fort ample des moeurs des sauvages du pays*. Paris: J. Langlois et E. Langlois.

du Tertre, L. R. P. J. 1667. *Histoire générale des Antilles habitées par les Français. Divisée en deux tomes et enrichie de cartes & de figures*. Paris: Thomas Iolly.

EarthTrends. 2003. *Earthtrends country profiles: biodiversity and protected areas—Dominican Republic*. http://earthtrends. wri.org.

Eaton, R. J. 1934. The migratory movements of certain colonies of Herring Gulls in eastern North America. *Bird-Banding* 5: 1–19.

Eeuwens, P. A. 1926. Klein-Curaçao. *West Indische Gids* 7: 401–411.

Ekman, E. L. 1929. Plants of Navassa Island, West Indies. *Ark. Bot*. 22A: 1–12.

———. 1941. Excursion botanique dans de nord-ouest de la République Dominicaine. *Rev. Soc. d'Hist. Géogr. d'Haiti* 12: 37–50.

Emanuel, K. A. 2005. Increasing destructiveness of tropical cyclones over the past 30 Years. *Nature* 436: 686–688.

English, T. M. S. 1916. Notes on some of the birds of Grand Cayman, West Indies. *Ibis* 4: 17–35.

Erdman, D. S. 1960. *Preliminary report on the sportfishery of Mona Island, with notes on the status of game birds and mammals.* Unpublished report. San Juan, Puerto Rico: Department of Natural Resources.

———. 1960. *Mona Island fish and game investigational report, May 14–22, 1960.* Unpublished report. San Juan, Puerto Rico: Department of Natural Resources.

———. 1962. *Mona Island sport fishery investigations, Oct. 11–17, 1962.* Unpublished report. San Juan, Puerto Rico: Commonwealth of Puerto Rico Department of Agriculture.

———. 1967. Sea birds in relation to game fish schools off Puerto Rico and the Virgin Islands. *Carib. J. Sci.* 7: 79–85.

Erskine, A. J. 1963. The Black-headed Gull (*Larus ridibundus*) in eastern North America. *Audubon Field Notes* 17: 334–338.

Erwin, R. M., J. A. Kushlan, C. Luthin, I. M. Price, and A. Sprunt, IV. 1984. Conservation of colonial waterbirds in the Caribbean Basin: Summary of a panel discussion. *Colon. Waterbirds* 7: 139–142.

Erwin, R. M. G., J. Smith, and R. B. Clapp. 1986. Winter distribution and oiling of Common Terns in Trinidad. *J. Field Ornithol.* 57: 300–308.

Esclasans, D. 2003. Colonias de aves marino-costeras. Pp. 120–165 in *Propuesta de lineamientos para una gestión orientada hacia la conservación del Parque Nacional Archipiélago de Los Roques.* Technical Report. Caracas, Venezuela: Instituto de Recursos Naturales Renovables (IRNR)–Agencia Española de Cooperación Internacional.

Estrada, A. R., and J. Novo Rodríguez. 1984. Reptiles y aves de Cayo Inés de Soto, Archipiélago de los Colorados, Pinar del Río, Cuba. *Misc. Zool., Inst. Zool. Acad. Cienc. Cuba* 23: 1.

Estrada, A. R., and R. Rodríguez. 1985. Lista de vertebrados terrestres de Cayo Campos, Archipiélago de los Canarreos, Cuba. *Misc. Zool., Inst. Zool. Acad. Cienc. Cuba* 27:2–3.

Evermann, B. W. 1902. General report on the investigations in Porto Rico of the United States Fish Commission Steamer Fish Hawk in 1899. *Bull. U.S. Fish Comm.* 20: 3–302.

Ewel, J. J., and J. L. Whitmore. 1973. *The ecological life zones of Puerto Rico and the U.S. Virgin Islands.* Forest Sciences Research Paper ITF-18. Río Piedras, Puerto Rico: Institute of Tropical Forestry.

Ewen, B. 1982. White-tailed Tropicbird. *Gosse Bird Club Broads.* 38: 11.

Fairbairn, P. 1979. The Natural History Society of Jamaica outing to Treasure Beach, Great Pedro Pond, Parottee Pond, Black River and Luana Point, 23–25 February, 1979. *Nat. Hist. Notes Nat. Hist. Soc. Jamaica,* n.s., 1: 1–4.

———. 1979. *Joint NRCD/Fisheries Division proposal for research on boobies (Sterna fuscata and Anous stolidus).* Unpublished memorandum. Kingston, Jamaica: Natural Resources Conservation Department.

Fairbairn, P., and A. M. Haynes. 1982. Jamaican surveys of the West Indian manatee (*Trichechus manatus*), dolphin (*Tursiops truncatus*), sea turtles (families Cheloniidae and Der-

mochelydae) and booby terns (family Laridae). *FAO Fish. Rep.* 278 (Supplement): 289–295.

Farr, T. H. 1990. Recovery of banded bird. *Gosse Bird Club Broads.* 55: 15.

Feare, C. J. 1976a. The exploitation of Sooty Tern eggs in the Seychelles. *Biol. Conserv.* 10: 169–181.

———. 1976b. Desertion and abnormal development in a colony of Sooty Terns (*Sterna fuscata*) infested by virus-infected ticks. *Ibis* 118: 112–115.

———. 1976c. The breeding of the Sooty Tern (*Sterna fuscata*) in the Seychelles and the effects of experimental removal of its eggs. *J. Zoology* (London) 179: 317–360.

Feare, C. J., and A. Haynes Sutton. 1998. Notes on the round table discussion on a scientific approach to sustainable use of birds. Abstract *in* Adams, N., and R. Slotow, eds., *Proceedings of the 22nd International Ornithological* Congress, Durban, South Africa. Johannesburg: BirdLife South Africa.

Feely, R. A., C. L. Sabine, K. Lee, W. Beralson, J. Kleypas, V. J. Fabry, and F. J. Millero. 2004. Impact of anthropogenic CO_2 on the $CaCO_3$ system in the oceans. *Science* 305: 362–366.

Feilden, H. W. 1888. Richardson's Skua in the island of Barbados. *Zoologist* 3(12): 350.

———. 1889a. On the breeding of *Puffinus audouboni* in the island of Barbados. *Ibis*, series 6, 1: 60–63.

———. 1889b. On the birds of Barbados. *Ibis* 1: 477–503.

———. 1894. The deserted domicile of the Diablotin in Dominica. *Trans. Norfolk and Norwich Naturalist Soc.* 5: 24–39.

———. 1902. Birds of Barbados. *West Ind. Bull.* 3: 333–352.

Feldmann, P., A. Le Dru, C. Pavis, and P. Villard. 1995. *Checklist of the birds of Guadeloupe, Martinique and their offshore islands.* Petit Bourg, Guadeloupe: Association pour l'Étude et la protection des Vertébrés des petites Antilles.

Feldmann, P., and P. Villard. 1993. *Oiseaux de Guadeloupe et de Martinique.* Petit Bourg, Guadeloupe: Association pour l'Étude et la protection des Vertébrés des petites Antilles.

Fernández Yépez, A. 1945. Fauna y flora Tortuguenses 1: Aves de la Isla la Tortuga. *Mem. Soc. Cienc. Nat. La Salle* 5(13): 29–31.

Ferry, J. F. 1908. A month's bird-collecting in Venezuela. *Condor* 10: 225–230.

Fewkes, J. W. 1922. A prehistoric island culture area of America. *Bur. Amer. Ethn. Ann. Rep.* 34: 49–281.

ffrench, R. P. 1961. The Red-billed Tropicbird. *J. Trinidad Field Naturalists' Club* 1961: 9–10

———. 1963. Bulwer's Petrel in Trinidad, West Indies. *Auk* 80: 379.

———. 1965. Check-list of the birds of Grand Fond Valley and Bay. *J. Trinidad Field Naturalists' Club* 1965: 37–39.

———. 1967. Checklist of the birds of Huevos and Chacachacare. *J. Trinidad Field Naturalists' Club* 1967: 25–27.

———. 1969. The avifauna of Saut D'Eau Island. *J. Trinidad Field Naturalists' Club* 1969: 16.

———. 1973a. *A guide to the birds of Trinidad and Tobago.* Wynnewood, Pa.: Livingston Publishing Company (rev. editions 1976, 1980, 1985, Newtown Square, Pa.: Harrowood Books).

———. 1973. Dubious bird records for Trinidad and Tobago. *J. Trinidad Field Naturalists' Club* 1973: 74–79.

———. 1975. A bird visitor from Finland. *J. Trinidad and Tobago Field Naturalists' Club* 1975: 85–86.

———. 1977. Some interesting bird records from Trinidad & Tobago. *Living World, J. Trinidad and Tobago Field Naturalists' Club* 1977: 9–10.

———. 1979. More records of rare birds in Trinidad and Tobago. *Living World, J. Trinidad and Tobago Field Naturalists' Club* 1978–1979: 25–26.

———. 1981. Some recent additions to the avifauna of Trinidad and Tobago. *Living World, J. Trinidad and Tobago Field Naturalists' Club* 1981–1982: 35–36.

———. 1983. Further notes on the avifauna of Trinidad & Tobago. *Living World, J. Trinidad and Tobago Field Naturalists' Club* 1983–1984: 32–34.

———. 1986. Movements of seabirds off Crown Point, Tobago. *Living World, J. Trinidad and Tobago Field Naturalists' Club* 1985–1986: 5–8.

———. 1986. Additional notes on the birds of Trinidad and Tobago. *Living World, J. Trinidad and Tobago Field Naturalists' Club* 1985–1986: 9–11.

———. 1988. *Supplement to A guide to the birds of Trinidad and Tobago.* Published by the author.

———. 1990. The birds and other vertebrates of Soldado Rock, Trinidad. *Living World, J. Trinidad and Tobago Field Naturalists' Club* 1989–1990: 16–20.

———. 1991a. *A guide to the birds of Trinidad and Tobago*, 2nd ed. Ithaca, N.Y.: Cornell University Press.

———. 1991b. Synchronous breeding and moult in the Brown Noddy tern on Soldado Rock, Trinidad. *Living World, J. Trinidad and Tobago Field Naturalists' Club* 1991–1992: 39–41.

———. 1993. Further records of birds on Trinidad and Tobago. *Living World, J. Trinidad and Tobago Field Naturalists' Club* 1993–1994: 28–31.

———. 1996. *Checklist of the birds of Trinidad and Tobago.* Arima, Trinidad: Asa Wright Nature Centre.

ffrench, R. P., and C. T. Collins. 1965. Royal and Cayenne terns breeding in Trinidad, West Indies. *Auk* 82: 277.

ffrench, R. P., and M. ffrench. 1966. Recent records of birds in Trinidad and Tobago. *Wilson Bull.* 78: 5–11.

ffrench, R. P., and F. E. Hayes. 1998. Rare bird records from Trinidad & Tobago in 1997. *Cotinga* 9: 84–85.

ffrench, R. P., and G. White. 1999. Verification of rare bird records from Trinidad & Tobago. *Cotinga* 12: 80–82.

Field, G. W. 1894. Notes on the birds of Port Henderson, Jamaica, West Indies. *Auk* 11: 117–127.

Fischer, W. 1969. Beobachtungen an Schlafplätzen des Kuhreihers auf Kuba. *Falke* 16: 220–224.

Fisher, A. K., and A. Wetmore. 1931. Report on birds recorded by the Pinchot Expedition of 1929 to the Caribbean and Pacific. *Proc. U.S. Natl. Mus.* 79: 1–66.

Fisher, D. J. 1978. First record of Black-headed Gull *Larus ridibundus* and third record of Herring Gull *Larus agentatus* for South America. *Bull. Br. Ornithol. Club* 98: 113.

Fletcher, J. 1978. Common Stilts at the Yallahs Pond. *Gosse Bird Club Broads.* 31: 3–6.

———. 1978. Least Tern. *Gosse Bird Club Broads.* 31: 11.

———. 1979. Shorebirds—& others. *Gosse Bird Club Broads.* 32: 7–8.

———. 1979a. A nesting site for Least Terns. *Gosse Bird Club Broads.* 33: 9–10.

———. 1980. Further notes on nesting Least Terns. *Gosse Bird Club Broads.* 35: 2–3.

———. 1981a. Least Tern nesting. *Gosse Bird Club Broads.* 37: 9.

———. 1981b. White-tailed Tropicbird. *Gosse Bird Club Broads.* 37: 12.

———. 1981. Laughing Gull. *Gosse Bird Club Broads.* 37: 12.

———. 1982a. Brown Pelican. *Gosse Bird Club Broads.* 39: 14.

———. 1982b. Least Terns. *Gosse Bird Club Broads.* 39: 15.

———. 1982. Brown Pelican. *Gosse Bird Club Broads.* 38: 12.

———. 1983. Black Tern. *Gosse Bird Club Broads.* 41: 18.

———. 1984. Laughing Gull. *Gosse Bird Club Broads.* 42: 12.

———. 1984. Sandwich Tern. *Gosse Bird Club Broads.* 43: 14.

———. 1986. Laughing Gull. *Gosse Bird Club Broads.* 46: 9.

———. 1987. Sandwich Tern. *Gosse Bird Club Broads.* 48: 11.

———. 1987. Gull-billed Tern. *Gosse Bird Club Broads.* 48: 11.

———. 1987. Sandwich Tern. *Gosse Bird Club Broads.* 48: 11.

———. 1988. Herring Gull. *Gosse Bird Club Broads.* 51: 14.

———. 1989. Refuge Cay visit. *Gosse Bird Club Broads.* 53: 19–20.

———. 1990. Field trips 1990. *Gosse Bird Club Broads.* 54: 7.

———. 1991. Terns. *Gosse Bird Club Broads.* 57: 21.

———. 1992. Refuge Cay, Kingston Harbour. *Gosse Bird Club Broads.* 59: 14.

———. 1994. White-tailed Tropicbirds. *Gosse Bird Club Broads.* 62: 11–12.

Fontana. 1993. Imagen Atlas de Venezuela: Una visión espacial. Pp. 237–249 *in* Petróleos de Venezuela S.A (Ed.) Caracas, Venezuela.

Foreign and Commonwealth Office (FCO, U.K.). 2005. Country Profiles. www.fco.gov.uk.

Friedman, R. 1948. Black Skimmer and White Pelicans in the Bahamas. *Auk* 65: 142.

Fuller, M. R., H. H. Obrecht, III, C. J. Pennycuick, and F. C. Schaffner. 1989. Aerial tracking of radio-marked White-tailed Tropicbirds over the Caribbean Sea. Pp. 133–138 *in* Amlaner, C. J., Jr., ed., *Biotelemetry X: Proceedings of the Tenth International Symposium on Biotelemetry.* Fayetteville: University of Arkansas Press.

Furniss, S. 1981. *Birds of Puerto Rico and the U.S. Virgin Islands.* Unpublished checklist. Boquerón, Puerto Rico: U.S. Fish and Wildlife Service, Caribbean Islands National Wildlife Refuge.

———. 1983. Status of the seabirds of the Culebra Archipelago, Puerto Rico. *Colon. Waterbirds* 6: 121–125.

Furniss, S., and J. Collazo. 1983. Recent avian records for the

Culebra Archipelago, Puerto Rico. Pp. 115–121 *in* Pérez-Rivera, R. A., L. O. Nieves-Rivera, and E. Ortiz-Corp's, eds., *Memorias del Cuarto Simposio sobre la Fauna de Puerto Rico y el Caribe.* Humacao: Universidad de Puerto Rico.

Furniss, S., J. Taylor, and M. Griffen-Taylor. 1984. Preliminary report on the nesting biology of White-tailed Tropicbirds at Cayo Luis Peña, Puerto Rico. *Colon. Waterbirds Group Newsl.* 8: 38.

García, I., R. Alayo, N. Novoa, A. Nicholas, R. Gonzalez, L. F. de Armas, D. Dominguez, C. Somoza, A. de la Osa, J. de la Cruz, O. H. Garrido, J. Ramon Cuevas, and J. Fontaines. 1973. Lista de los anfibios, reptiles, aves y mamiferos collectados en el Plan Jibacoa-Cayajabos. Informe del Trabajo faunístico realizado en el plan Jibacoa-Cayajabos. *Serie Biol., Inst. Zool., A.C.C.* 43: 1–25.

García, M. A., C. E. Diez, and A. O. Alvarez. 2001. The impact of feral cats on Mona Island wildlife and recommendations for their control. *Carib. J. Sci.* 37: 107–108.

García, M. E., A. Torres, R. Abreu, and J. de la Cruz. 1989. Datos sobre la nidificación de *Pelecanus occidentalis, Phalacrocorax auritus* y *Nycticorax nycticorax* (Aves: Pelecanidae, Phalacrocoracidae, Ardeidae) en Cayos Sevilla, Cuba. *Cienc. Biol. Acad. Cienc. Cuba* 21–22: 179–181.

García, M. I. 2005a. *Memorias censo de aves marinas y playeras en las islas menores del archipiélago.* Memorandum of Agreement—CORALINA/Christian University of San Andres, Armada Nacional. San Andrés: CORALINA.

———. 2005b. *Plan de acción de conservación de las aves playeras y marinas del Archipiélago de San Andrés, Providencia y Santa Catalina.* Technical report. GEF project, Caribbean Archipelago Biosphere Reserve: Regional Marine Protected Areas. San Andrés: CORALINA.

Garcia Montaña, F., and O. H. Garrido. 1965. Catálogo de las aves de Cuba. *In* Catálogo de la fauna cubana. XIII. *Trab. Divulg. Mus. "Felipe Poey," Acad. Cienc. Cuba* 27: 82.

Garcia Montaña, F., and O. H. Garrido. 1965. Nuevos registros de nidificacion de aves en Cuba. *Poeyana* 9: 1–3.

Gardener, A., S. Bingham, and M. Bingham. 1995. Birds at Malvern, St. Elizabeth. *Gosse Bird Club Broads.* 64: 17–18.

Garrido, O. H. 1973. Anfibios, reptiles y aves del Archipiélago de Sabana-Camagüey, Cuba. *Torreia* (Havana), ser. nueva, 27: 1–72.

———. 1973. Anfibios, reptiles y aves de Cayo Real (Cayos de San Felipe), Cuba. *Poeyana* 119: 1–50.

———. 1980. Adiciones a la fauna de vertebrados de la Península de Guanahacabibes. *Misc. Zool., Inst. Zool. Acad. Cienc. Cuba* 10: 2–4.

———. 1980. Los vertebrados terrestres de la Península de Zapata. *Poeyana* 203: 1–49.

———. 1985. Cuban endangered birds. Pp. 992–999 *in* Buckley, P. A., M. S. Foster, E. S. Morton, R. S. Ridgely, and F. G. Buckley, eds., *Neotropical ornithology.* Ornithological Monograph no. 36. Washington, D.C.: American Ornithologists' Union.

———. 1988. *La migración de las aves en Cuba.* Sevilla, Spain: Graficas Mirte S.A., Publicaciones de la Asociacion de Amigos de Doñana.

———. 1988. Nueva gaviota (Aves: Laridae) para Cuba. *Misc. Zool., Inst. Zool. Acad. Cienc. Cuba* 37: 3–4.

Garrido, O. H., and F. Garcia Montaña. 1965. Aves nuevas para Cuba. *Poeyana* 10: 1–6.

———. 1967. Nuevo *Oceanodroma* (Aves: Hydrobatidae) para las Antillas. *Trab. Divulg. Mus. "Felipe Poey," Acad. Cienc. Cuba* 48: 1–4.

———. 1968. Nuevos reportes de aves para Cuba. *Torreia* (Havana), ser. nueva, 4: 3–13.

———. 1975. *Catálogo de las aves de Cuba.* La Habana: Academia de Ciencias de Cuba.

Garrido, O. H. and A. Kirkconnell. 2000. *Field guide to the birds of Cuba.* Ithaca, N.Y.: Cornell University Press.

Garrido, O. H. and A. Silva Lee. 1990. Seabirds nesting in southern Cuba. *Pitirre* 3(3): 7.

Garrido, O. H. and A. Schwartz. 1968. Anfibios, reptiles y aves de la península de Guanahacabibes, Cuba. *Poeyana* A 53: 1–68.

———. 1969. Anfibios, reptiles y aves de Cayo Cantiles. *Poeyana* A 67: 1–44.

Garrido, O. H., A. R. Estrada, and A. Llanes Sosa. 1986. Anfibios, reptiles y aves de Cayo Guajaba, Archipiélago de Sabana-Camagüey, Cuba. *Poeyana* 328: 1–34.

GEF/PNUD [Global Environmental Facility/Programa de las Naciones Unidas para el Desarrollo]. 1999. *Protección de la biodiversidad y desarrollo sostenible en el ecosistema Sabana-Camagüey.* Alcolado, P. M., E. E. García, and N. Espinosa, eds. Madrid: CESYTA.

Geister, J., and J. M. Díaz. 1996. *Field guide to the oceanic barrier reefs and atolls of the southwestern Caribbean.* Santa Marta, Colombia: INVEMAR.

Geoghegan, T., Y. Renard, and A. Smith 1991. Community participation in protected area management: Some cases from the Caribbean. Pp. 53–59 *in* Cambers, G., ed., *Proceedings of the Regional Symposium public and private co-operation in national park development,* 23–25 August 1991. Tortola: British Virgin Islands National Parks Trust.

Georges, E. 2002. Bird conservation planning in the British Virgin Islands. In Ralph, C. J., G. Hunt, J. Piatt, and M. Raphael, eds., *Bird conservation implementation and integration in the Americas: Conference Program and Abstracts of the Third International Partners in Flight Conference,* March 20–24, 2002, Asilomar, Calif. Gen. Tech. Rep. PSW-GTR-191. Albany, Calif.: Pacific Southwest Research Station, Forest Service, U.S. Department of Agriculture.

Gibbs, R. G. 1973. A note on pesticide residues in Great Shearwater. *J. Trinidad Field Naturalists' Club* 1973: 80.

———. 1975. Observations of jaegers and terns from N. E. Trinidad. *J. Trinidad and Tobago Field Naturalists' Club* 1975: 82–83.

Gibbs-Williams, E. 1999. *Bird records from the Caicos Islands, Turks and Caicos, February–April 1999.* Unpublished report.

Providenciales, Turks and Caicos Islands: Turks and Caicos National Trust.

Ginés, H., and G. Yépez T. 1956. Avifauna de las Islas. Pp. 68–78 in Venegas F., P., ed., *El Archipiélago de los Roques y La Orchila*. Caracas, Venezuela: Sociedad de Ciencias Naturales. La Salle, Editorial Sucre.

———. 1960. Aspectos de la naturaleza de las Islas Las Aves, Venezuela. *Mem. Soc. Cienc. Nat. La Salle* 20(55): 5–53.

Gochfeld, M. 1983. The Roseate Tern: World distribution and status of a threatened species. *Biol. Conserv.* 25: 103–125.

Gochfeld, M., and J. Burger. 1996. Family Sternidae (Terns). Pp. 624–667 in del Hoyo, J., A. Elliot, and J. Sargatal, eds., *Handbook of the birds of the world. Vol. 3: Hotzin to auks.* Barcelona, Spain: Lynx Editions.

Gochfeld, M., J. Burger, A. Haynes-Sutton, R. van Halewyn, and J. E. Saliva. 1994. Successful approaches to seabird protection in the West Indies. Pp. 186–209 in Nettleship, D. N., J. Burger, and M. Gochfeld, eds., *Seabirds on islands: Threats, case studies and action plans.* BirdLife Conserv. Ser. no. 1. Cambridge, U.K.: BirdLife International.

Gochfeld, M., J. Burger, and I. C. T. Nisbet. 1998. Roseate Tern (*Sterna dougallii*). In Poole, A., and F. Gill, eds., *The birds of North America*, no. 370. Philadelphia: Birds of North America.

Gochfeld, M., J. Burger, J. E. Saliva, and D. Gochfeld. 1988. Herald Petrel new to the West Indies. *Am. Birds* 42: 1254–1258.

Gochfeld, M., D. O. Hill, and G. Tudor. 1973. A second population of the recently described Elfin Woods Warbler and other bird records from the West Indies. *Carib. J. Sci.* 13: 231–235.

Godman, F. du C. 1907–1910. *A monograph of the petrels (order Tubinares).* London: Witherby and Company.

Golding, P. 1985. Birding around Jamaica in 1984. *Gosse Bird Club Broads.* 44: 11.

———. 1987. At Mona Reservoir on March 20, 6.00–8.30 a.m. with A. Downer and Catherine Levy. *Gosse Bird Club Broads.* 49: 9–10.

———. 1995. Mona Reservoir, St. Andrew. *Gosse Bird Club Broads.* 64: 17.

———. 1996. Brown Pelican. *Gosse Bird Club Broads.* 66: 31.

González, A., J. Alvarez, and A. Kirkconnell. 1992. Aves observadas en Cayo Cruz, Archipiélago Sabana-Camagüey, Cuba. *Comunicaciones Breves de Zoología* (Instituto de Ecología y Sistemática, Academia de Ciencias de Cuba): 25–26.

Gosse, P. H. [Assisted by Richard Hill. Esq., of Spanish Town]. 1847. *The birds of Jamaica.* London: John Van Voorst.

Government of Jamaica. 1995. *Green paper: Toward a national system of protected areas for Jamaica (draft)*. Kingston, Jamaica: Natural Resources Conservation Authority.

Graham, D. J. 1984. A sighting of a Black-legged Kittiwake in Saint Lucia. *Am. Birds* 38: 256.

Graham, R. 1971. White-tailed Tropic Birds. *Gosse Bird Club Broads.* 16: 17–18.

———. 1973. White-tailed Tropicbird. *Gosse Bird Club Broads.* 21: 17–18.

Granger, S. 1976. White-tailed Tropicbird. *Gosse Bird Club Broads.* 26: 16.

Grayce, R. L. 1957. Range extensions in Puerto Rico. *Auk* 74: 106.

Gremone, C., and J. Gómez. 1983. *Isla de Aves como área de desove de la tortuga verde (Cheloni mydas). Biología reproductiva y morfometría. Observaciones adicionales sobre el ecosistema y las aves.* Caracas, Venezuela: Fundacion para la Defensa de la Naturaleza (FUNDENA).

Grieve, S. 1906. *Notes upon the island of Dominica.* London: Adam and Charles Black.

———. 1925. Notes on some Dominican birds. *Proc. Royal Physical Soc.* 21: 19–28.

Griscom, L. 1937. Herring Gull at Barbados. *Auk* 54: 539.

Grisdale, T. 1882. On the birds of Montserrat. *Ibis* 6: 485–493.

Groome, J. R. 1970. *A natural history of the island of Grenada, West Indies.* Arima, Trinidad: Caribbean Printers.

Gross, A. O. 1912. Observations on the Yellow-billed Tropicbird (*Phaethon americanus* Grant) at the Bermuda Islands. *Auk* 29: 49.

———. 1940. The migration of Kent Island Herring Gulls. *Bird-Banding* 11: 129–155.

Ground, D., and M. Pienkowski (eds.). 2004. *Guidelines for the development of a strategy for action to implement an environment charter.* Peterborough, U.K.: U.K. Overseas Territories Conservation Forum. www.ukotcf.org (Env. Charter/Strat. Development).

Ground, R. 2001. *The birds of the Turks and Caicos.* Providenciales: Turks and Caicos National Trust.

Gundlach, J. 1857. Beiträge zur ornithologie Cuba's. Nach mittheilungen des reisenden an Hr. Bez.—Dir. Sezekorn in Cassel; von Letzterem zusammengestellt. Mit zusatzen und anmerkungen geordnet vom herausgeber. *J. Ornithol.* 5(28): 225–242.

———. 1859. Ornithologisches aus briefen von Cuba. *J. Ornithol.* 7(40): 294–299.

———. 1859. Ornithologisches aus briefen von Cuba. *J. Ornithol.* 7(41): 347–351.

———. 1861. Tabellarische uebersicht aller bisher auf Cuba beobachteten vögel. *J. Ornithol.* 9(53): 321–349.

———. 1862. Zusätze und berichtigungen zu den "Beiträgen zur ornithologie Cuba's." *J. Ornithol.* 10(56): 81–96.

———. 1862. Zusätze und berichtigungen zu den "Beiträgen zur ornithologie Cuba's." *J. Ornithol.* 10(57): 177–191.

———. 1865–1866. Revista y catálogo de las aves Cubanas. Pp. 165–180 in Poey, F., ed., *Repertorio Fisico Natural de la Isla de Cuba*, vol. 1. La Habana, Cuba: Imprenta del Gobierno y Capitanía General.

———. 1865–1866. Revista y catálogo de las Aves Cubanas. Pp. 386–403 in Poey, F., ed., *Repertorio Fisico-Natural Capitanía General*, Vol. 1. La Habana, Cuba: Imprenta del Gobierno y Capitanía General.

———. 1871. Neue beiträge zur ornithologie Cubas, nach eigenen 30 jährigen beobachtungen zusammengestellt. *J. Ornithol.* 19(112): 265–295.

————. 1873. Catálogo de las aves cubanas. *An. Soc. Española Hist. Nat., Madrid* 2: 81–191.

————. 1873–1876. *Contribución á la ornitología cubana.* La Habana, Cuba: Imprenta "La Antilla" de N. Cacho-Negrette.

————. 1874. Beiträg zur ornithologie der insel Portorico. *J. Ornithol.* 22(127): 304–315.

————. 1875. Neue beiträge zur ornithologie Cubas: Nach eigenen 30 jährigen beobachtungen zusammengestellt. *J. Ornithol.* 23(132): 353–407.

————. 1878. Apuntes para la fauna Puerto-Riquena. Segunda parte (Aves). *An. Soc. Española Hist. Nat., Madrid* 7: 343–422.

————. 1878. Neue beiträge zur ornithologie der insel Portorico. *J. Ornithol.* 26(142): 157–194.

————. 1878. Briefliches über eine neue *Dysporus*-art auf Cuba. *J. Ornithol.* 26(143): 298.

————. 1881. Nachträge zur ornithologie Cuba's. *J. Ornithol.* 29(156): 400–401.

————. 1891. Notes on some species of birds of the island of Cuba. *Auk* 8: 187–191.

————. 1893. *Ornithología cubana ó catálogo descriptivo de todas las especies de aves tanto indígenas como de paso anual o accidental observadas en 53 años.* Archivos de la policlínica ed. La Habana, Cuba: Imprenta "La Moderna."

[Gurney, J. J.] 1841. Mr. J. J. Gurney on Santa Cruz, St. Thomas, and Dominica. *Ann. Mag. Nat. Hist.* 6: 527–529.

Guzmán, H., and R. W. Schreiber. 1987. Distribution and status of Brown Pelicans in Venezuela in 1983. *Wilson Bull.* 99: 275–279.

Halewijn, R. van. 1985. *Report on 1984 survey of marine birds of Aruba, Netherlands Antilles.* Unpublished report. The Netherlands: Stinapa-Aruba and Foundation for Scientific Research in Suriname and the Netherlands Antilles.

————. 1986. *Marine birds of Aruba: Report on 1985 survey and conservation campaign.* Unpublished report. The Netherlands: Stinapa-Aruba and Foundation for Scientific Research in Suriname and the Netherlands Antilles.

————. 1988. History of the seabird population of San Nicolas Bay keys, Aruba. Pp. 33–59 *in* van der Steen, L. J., ed., *Studies in honour of Dr. Pieter Wagenaar Hummelinck*, no. 123. Amsterdam, Netherlands: Foundation for Scientific Research in Suriname and the Netherlands Antilles.

Halewijn, R. van., and R. L. Norton. 1984. The status and conservation of seabirds in the Caribbean. Pp. 169–222 *in* Croxall, J. P., P. G. H. Evans, and R. W. Schreiber, eds., *Status and conservation of the world's seabirds.* ICBP Tech. Publ. no. 2. Cambridge, U.K.: International Council for Bird Preservation.

Halewyn, R. van. See Halewijn, R. van.

Hamilton, J. 1981. Recoveries of wintering Roseate Terns. *J. Field Ornithol.* 52: 36–42.

Haney, J. C. 1986. Seabird patchiness in tropical oceanic waters: The influence of *Sargassum* "reefs." *Auk* 103: 141–151.

————. 1987. Aspects of the pelagic ecology and behavior of the Black-capped Petrel (*Pterodroma hasitata*). *Wilson Bull.* 99: 153–168.

Hanlon, R. 1955. Notes on some birds of Long and Great Inagua Islands, Bahamas. *Flicker* 27: 98–104.

Hansen, J., M. Sato, R. Ruedy, A. Lacis, and V. Oinas. 2005. Global warming in the twenty-first century: An alternative scenario. *Geophysics* 97: 9875–9880.

Harkness, A. 1994. Birds at (A) Hermitage Dam and (B) Stony Hill. *Gosse Bird Club Broads.* 62: 17.

Harrington, B. A. 1974. Colony visitation behavior and breeding ages of Sooty Terns (*Sterna fuscata*). *Bird-Banding* 45: 115–144.

Harrington, M. W. 1899. Fauna and flora of Puerto Rico. *Science*, n. s., 10: 286–288.

Harris, A. 1988. Identification of adult Sooty and Bridled terns. *Br. Birds* 81: 525–530.

Hart, P. 1965. Was this the last of the line? *Gosse Bird Club Broads.* 5: 6–7.

Hartert, E. 1893 On the birds of the islands of Aruba, Curaçao and Bonaire. *Ibis*, 6th ser., 5: 289–338.

Hartlaub, G. 1847. Den heutigen zustand unserer kenntnisse von Westindiens ornithologie. *Isis* (Oken) 1847: 604–615.

Harvey, J. 1966. Of pelicans and frigate birds. *Gosse Bird Club Broads.* 7: 15.

Hatch, J. J. 1974. Homing experiment with Audubon's Shearwaters. *Auk* 91: 830–832.

Hawkes, A. D. 1971. Sea birds at Savanna-La-Mar. *Gosse Bird Club Broads.* 16: 15–16.

————. 1971. Frigatebirds. *Gosse Bird Club Broads.* 16: 22.

————. 1971. Birds at Paradise, Westmoreland. *Gosse Bird Club Broads.* 17: 18–19.

————. 1973. Birds at Naggo Head Beach. *Gosse Bird Club Broads.* 20: 12–13.

————. 1975. Magnificent Frigatebird. *Gosse Bird Club Broads.* 25: 20.

Hay, D. B. 2006. *Biological survey of the Pedro Cays.* Report prepared for the Nature Conservancy, Kingston, Jamaica.

Hays, H., P. Lima, L. Monteiro, J. Dicostanzo, G. Cormons, I. C. T. Nisbet, J. E. Saliva, J. A. Spendelow, J. Burger, J. Pierce, and M. Gochfeld. 1999. A nonbreeding concentration of Roseate and Common Terns in Bahia, Brazil. *Journal of Field Ornithology* 70: 455–464.

Hayes, F. E. 1996. Noteworthy bird records for Trinidad & Tobago, 1993–1994. *Living World, J. Trinidad and Tobago Field Naturalists' Club* 1995–96: 20–21.

————. 1998. Noteworthy bird records for Trinidad and Tobago, 1995–1996. *Pitirre* 11: 5–6.

————. 2001. Identification of Least Tern *Sterna antillarum* and Yellow-billed Tern *S. superciliaris*, with a sight record of Yellow-billed Tern from Tobago, West Indies. *Cotinga* 15: 10–13.

————. 2002. Seabird densities at sea in Saint Vincent and the Grenadines, with comments on their historic and current potential breeding status. *Pitirre* 15: 49–54.

————. 2004. Variability and interbreeding of Sandwich Terns

and Cayenne Terns in the Virgin Islands, with comments on their systematic relationships. *N. Am. Birds* 57: 566–572.

Hayes, F. E., C. L. Ramjohn, and F. B. Lucas. 1998. *Checklist of the birds of proposed Matura National Park and adjacent areas in northeastern Trinidad.* St. Augustine, Trinidad and Tobago: Department of Life Sciences, University of the West Indies.

Hayes, F. E., and I. Samad. 2002. Avifauna of the "dragon's teeth": the Bocas Islands, northern Gulf of Paria, between Venezuela and Trinidad. *Department of Life Sciences, University of the West Indies, St. Augustine, Occasional Paper* 11: 62–85.

Hayes, F. E., and G. White. 2000. First report of the Trinidad and Tobago Rare Bird Committee. *Living World, J. Trinidad and Tobago Field Naturalists' Club* 1999–2000: 39–45.

Hayes, F. E., G. L. White, M. D. Frost, B. Sanasie, H. Kilpatrick, and E. B. Massiah. 2002. First records of Kelp Gull *Larus dominicanus* for Trinidad and Barbados. *Cotinga* 18: 85–88.

Hayes, F. E., G. L. White, M. Kenefick, and H. Kilpatrick. 2002. Status of the Lesser Black-backed Gull *Larus fuscus* in Trinidad and Tobago. *Atlantic Seabirds* 4: 91–100.

Hayes, F. E., G. L. White, M. Kenefick, H. Kilpatrick, and N. Lallsingh. 2004. Seasonal variation in gull populations along Trinidad's west coast, Trinidad and Tobago. *Living World, J. Trinidad and Tobago Field Naturalists' Club* 2004: 3–5.

Hayes, W. K. 2003. Can San Salvador's iguanas and seabirds be saved? *Bahamas J. Sci.* 11: 2–8.

Haymes, G. T., and H. Blokpoel. 1978. Seasonal distribution and site tenacity of the Great Lakes Common Tern. *Bird-Banding* 49: 142–151.

Haynes, A. 1983. Conservation and ecology of *Sterna fuscata* and *Anous stolidus* in Jamaica. Pp. 92–100 in Pérez-Rivera, R. A., L. O. Nieves-Rivera, and E. Ortiz-Corp's, eds., *Memorias del cuarto simposio sobre la fauna de Puerto Rico y el Caribe.* Humacao: Universidad de Puerto Rico.

Haynes, A. M. 1986a. *Report on a visit to Pedro Cays, October 1986.* Unpublished report. Kingston, Jamaica: Natural Resources Conservation Department.

———. 1986b. Masked Boobies nesting at Pedro Cays. *Gosse Bird Club Broads.* 47: 2–3.

———. 1986. *Preliminary report on status & conservation of 'booby' terns at Morant Cays, Jamaica 1982–1985,* vol. 2. Unpublished report. Kingston, Jamaica: Natural Resources Conservation Division.

———. 1987. Human exploitation of seabirds in Jamaica. *Biol. Conserv.* 41: 99–124.

Haynes, A. M., and R. L. Sutton. 1988. Bird banding recoveries. *Gosse Bird Club Broads.* 50: 11–12.

Haynes, A. M., R. L. Sutton, and K. D. Harvey. 1989. Conservation trends, and the threats to endemic birds in Jamaica. Pp. 827–838 in Woods, C. A., ed., *Biogeography in the West Indies: Past, present, and future.* Gainesville, Fla.: Sandhill Crane Press.

Haynes-Sutton, A. M. 1987. The value of seabirds as a socio-economic resource in Jamaica. Pp. 77–81 in Diamond, A. W., and F. Filion, eds., *The value of birds.* ICBP Tech. Publ. no. 6. Cambridge, U.K.: International Council for Bird Preservation.

———. 1989. Banding and recaptures of Sooty Terns and Brown Noddies at Morant Cays, Jamaica. *Pitirre* 2(2): 7.

———. 1995. *On the nesting ecology of seabirds at the Morant Cays (Jamaica) with special reference to nest site selection, conservation and management.* Ph.D. dissertation. Mona, Jamaica: University of the West Indies.

———. 1996. *Sooty Tern and Brown Noddy management plan.* 2 vols. Unpublished report. Kingston, Jamaica: Natural Resources Conservation Agency.

Haynes-Sutton, A. M., and K. Aiken. 1992. *Off-shore cays—site report: Plan for a system of protected natural areas for Jamaica.* Unpublished report. Kingston: Jamaica Conservation and Development Trust.

Hays, H., J. DiCostanzo, G. Cormons, P. T. Z. Antas, J. L. X. do Nascimento, I. L. S. do Nascimento, and R. E. Bremer. 1997. Recoveries of Roseate and Common terns in South America. *J. Field Ornithol.* 68: 79–90.

Hays, H., P. Lima, L. Monteiro, J. DiCostanzo, G. Cormons, I. C. T. Nisbet, J. E. Saliva, J. A. Spendelow, J. Burger, J. Pierce, and M. Gochfeld. 1999. A non-breeding concentration of Roseate and Common terns in Bahia, Brazil. *J. Field Ornithol.* 70: 455–464.

Hayward, S. J., V. H. Gomez and W. Sterrer (eds.). 1981. *Bermuda's delicate balance: People and the environment.* Hamilton: Bermuda National Trust.

Hellmayr, C. E. 1906. On the birds of the island of Trinidad. *Novit. Zool.* 13: 1–60.

Henrard, L. 1995. Mona Reservoir, St. Andrew. *Gosse Bird Club Broads.* 64: 17.

Herklots, G. A. C. 1961. *The birds of Trinidad and Tobago.* London: Collins.

Hilder, P. 1989. *The birds of Nevis.* Charlestown, Nevis: Nevis Historical and Conservation Society.

Hill, M. 1970. White-tailed tropic birds. *Gosse Bird Club Broads.* 15: 17.

Hobley, C. W. 1932. Rediscovery of Dominica diablotin. *J. Soc. Preserv. Fauna Empire,* n.s., 17: 17–20.

Hodges, M. 1993. Visit to the Morant Cays, May 1993. *Gosse Bird Club Broads.* 61: 12.

Hodgson, M. 1974. Black Tern. *Gosse Bird Club Broads.* 23: 23.

Hofman, C. L., and M. L. P. Hoogland. 2003. Plum Piece: Evidence for archaic seasonal occupation on Saba, Northern Lesser Antilles around 3300 BP. *J. Carib. Archaeol.* 4: 12–27.

Holland, C. S., and J. M. Williams. 1978. Observations on the birds of Antigua. *Am. Birds* 32: 1095–1105.

Holliday, S. H. 2003. *Birds of Anguilla 2000–2003.* Report to Anguilla National Trust, Anguilla, B.W.I. and Royal Society for the Protection of Birds, Sandy, Bedfordshire, U.K.

Holliday, S. H., and K. V. D. Hodge. 2003. *A revised list of the birds of Anguilla.* Unpublished report: Royal Society for the Protection of Birds and Anguilla National Trust, Sandy, Bedfordshire, U.K.

Holman, J. P. 1952. West Indian Black-capped Petrel, *Pterodro-*

ma hasitata, picked up on Fairfield Beach, Connecticut. *Auk* 69: 459–460.

Hoogerwerf, A. 1977. Notes on the birds of St. Martin, Saba and St. Eustatius. *Studies on the Fauna of Curaçao and Other Caribbean Isl*ands 54(176): 60–123.

Horwith, B., and K. Lindsay. 1997. *A biodiversity profile: Antigua, Barbuda and Redonda.* Eastern Caribbean Biodiversity Programme, Biodiversity Publ. no.3. Washington, D.C: Island Resources Foundation.

Houston, W. H. 1963. Laughing Gull and Caspian Tern. *Gosse Bird Club Broads.* 1: 7.

———. 1968. Some notes on the birds of the U.S. Virgin Islands. *Gosse Bird Club Broads.* 11: 9–11.

Houston, W. H., and T. Davis. 1967. Forster's Tern. *Gosse Bird Club Broads.* 8: 16.

———. 1967. Black Tern. *Gosse Bird Club Broads.* 8: 16.

———. 1967. Sandwich Tern. *Gosse Bird Club Broads.* 8: 16.

Houston, W. H., and E. R. G. Kidd. 1964. Laughing Gull. *Gosse Bird Club Broads.* 2: 19.

Howard, M., E. Connolly, E. Taylor, and J. Mow. 2003. Community-based development of multiple-use marine protected areas: Promoting stewardship and sharing responsibility for conservation in the San Andres Archipelago, Colombia. *Gulf and Caribbean Research* 14: 155–162.

Howe, W. H., D. M. Taylor, and D. A. Jett. 1989. Additional records of birds from Cat Island, Bahamas. *Wilson Bull.* 101: 115–117.

Howell, C. 1991. *Antigua and Barbuda: Country environmental profile.* St. Michael, Barbados: Caribbean Conservation Association.

Howes, P. G. 1917. Bird collecting in eastern Colombia. *Oölogist* 34: 95–98.

Hudson, R. 1968. The Great Skua in the Caribbean. *Bird Study* 15: 33–34.

Hughes, G. 1750. *The natural history of Barbados: In ten books.* London: printed for the author (reprint, New York: Arno Press, 1972).

Huggins, A. E., S. Keel, P. Kramer, F. Nunez, S. Schill, R. Jeo, A. Chatwin, K. Thurlow, M. McPherson, M. Libby, R. Tingey, M. Palmer, and R. Seybert. 2007. *Biodiversity conservation assessment of the insular Caribbean using the Caribbean Decision Support System. Technical Report,* Nature Conservancy, Arlington, Va.

Hughes, J. 2000. *Birds and potential IBAs in Anguilla.* Sabbatical report: January February 2000. Sandy, Bedfordshire, U.K.: Royal Society for the Protection of Birds.

Hughes, J., K. Hodge, I. Christian, J. Stevenson, S. Holliday, I. Fisher, and M. Bryer. 2001. *Towards a bird conservation strategy in Anguilla.* Presentation to Soc. Carib. Ornithol., Cuba, July 2001, and report with the Anguilla National Trust, The Valley, Anguilla.

Hummelinck, P. W. 1953. Islote Aves, een vogeleiland in de Caraibische Zee. *J. West-Indische Gids* 33: 23–34.

Hundley, M. H., and C. R. Mason. 1963. *Field check list of the birds of the Bahama Islands.* Maitland: Florida Audubon Society.

Hurst, L. 1980. Magnificent Frigatebird. *Gosse Bird Club Broads.* 35: 13.

ICBP. 1988. *Report of the 1978 University of East Anglia-ICBP St Lucia expedition.* Cambridge, U.K.: International Council for Bird Preservation.

ICF Consulting. 1998. *Biological surveys on Sombrero Island.* Unpublished report to Beal Aerospace. Fairfax, Virginia: ICF Consulting.

———. 1999. *Supplemental biological surveys on Sombrero Island and other Anguillan islands.* Unpublished report to Beal Aerospace. Fairfax, Virginia: ICF Consulting.

Imber, M. J. 1991. The Jamaican Petrel—dead or alive? *Gosse Bird Club Broads.* 57: 4–9.

———. 1991. The Jamaican Petrel—dead or alive? P. 481 *in* Bell, B. D., ed., *Acta XX Congressus Internationalis Ornithologici, Christchurch, New Zealand, 2–9 December 1990.* Wellington: New Zealand Ornithological Congress Trust Board.

Intergovernmental Panel on Climate Change (IPCC). 2007. *Climate Change 2007: The physical science basis.* Contribution of Working Group I to the Fourth Assessment Report of the IPCC, Paris. Cambridge, U.K.: Cambridge University Press.

Island Resources Foundation. 1996. *Parham Harbour Facilitation Project Antigua and Barbuda, Northeast Coast Management Area and Bird Island Marine Reserve and Wildlife Sanctuary: Pollution stresses and impacts.* Unpublished report to Organization of American States. Island Resources Foundation. St. Thomas, U.S. Virgin Islands.

IUCN 2006. *2006 IUCN Red List of threatened species.* <http://www.iucnredlist.org>.

Jackson, J. A. 2000. Distribution, population changes and threats to Least Terns in the Caribbean and adjacent waters of the Atlantic and Gulf of Mexico. Pp. 109–117 *in* Schreiber, E. A., and D. S. Lee, eds., *Status and conservation of West Indian seabirds.* Special Publication no. 1. Ruston, La.: Society of Caribbean Ornithology.

Jacobs, S. S., C. F. Giulivi, and P. A. Mele. 2002. Freshening of the Ross Sea during the late 20th Century. *Science* 297: 386–389.

Jeffrey-Smith, M. T. 1947. [White Ibis and Sandwich Tern]. *Nat. Hist. Notes Nat. Hist. Soc. Jamaica* 3: 116.

———. 1956. *Bird-watching in Jamaica.* Kingston, Jamaica: Pioneer Press.

———. 1966. Magnificent Frigate Bird. *Gosse Bird Club Broads.* 7: 16.

Jennings, A. H. 1888. List of birds observed at New Providence, Bahama Islands, March-June, 1887. *Johns Hopkins Univ. Circulars* 7: 39.

Jérémie, S. 2003. *Réserve naturelle des îlets de Sainte-Anne, suiví ornithologique 2002.* Unpublished report. Fort-de-France, Martinique: Association Ornithologique de la Martinique (AOMA), Parc Naturel Régional de la Martinique.

———. 2005. *Réserve naturelle des îlets de Sainte-Anne, suiví ornithologique et contrôle de l'éradication de la population de*

Rattus rattus *sur la, année 2003.* Unpublished report. Fort-de-France, Martinique: Association de Carouge, Parc Naturel Régional de la Martinique.

Jérémie, S., and R. Brithmer. 2005. *Réserve naturelle des îlets de Sainte-Anne, suivi ornithologique et contrôle de l'éradication de la population de Rattus rattus, année 2003.* Unpublished report. Fort-de-France, Martinique: Association Ornithologique de la Martinique (AOMA), Parc Naturel Régional de la Martinique.

Jiménez, A., A. Rodríguez, S. Aguilar, and J. Morales. 2004. Some aspects of the breeding biology of Brown Pelican (*Pelecanus occidentalis*) and Double-crested Cormorant (*Phalacrocorax auritus*) in Río Maximo Fauna Refuge, Cuba. 31st Annual Meeting, Pacific Seabird Group, La Paz, Mexico.

Johnson, T. H. 1988. *Biodiversity and conservation in the Caribbean: Profiles of selected islands.* ICBP Monograph no. 1. Cambridge, U.K.: International Council for Bird Preservation.

Johnson, T. H., and A. J. Stattersfield. 1990. A global review of island endemic birds. *Ibis* 132: 167–180.

Johnston, D. W. 1965. Grand Cayman Island in early May. *Gosse Bird Club Broads.* 5: 4–5.

———. 1975. Ecological analysis of the Cayman Island avifauna. *Bull. Fla. State Mus., Biol. Sci.* 19: 235–300.

Johnston, D. W., C. H. Blake, and D. W. Buden. 1971. Avifauna of the Cayman Islands. *Q. J. Fla. Acad. Sci.* 34: 141–156.

Jones, J. H. 1979. *The guide to Bermuda's public parks and beaches.* Hamilton, Bermuda: Department of Agriculture and Fisheries.

Jones, M. A. J. 1991. Beach tar pollution: A threat to nesting sites? *Gosse Bird Club Broads.* 56: 9–11.

Jones, M., and P. R. Bacon. 1990. Beach tar contamination in Jamaica. *Marine Pollution Bull.* 21: 331–34.

Jouanin, C. 1962. Inventaire des oiseaux éteints ou en voie d'extinction conservés au Museum de Paris. *Terre Vie* 109: 257–301.

Junge, G. C. A., and G. F. Mees. 1958. The avifauna of Trinidad and Tobago. *Zool. Verhand.* 37: 1–172.

Junge, G. C. A., and K. H. Voous. 1955. The distribution and relationship of *Sterna eurygnatha. Ardea* 43: 226–47.

Keegan, W. F. 1997. *Bahamian archaeology: Life in the Bahamas and Turks and Caicos before Columbus.* Nassau: Media Publishing.

Keith, A. R. 1997. *The birds of St. Lucia.* BOU Check-list no. 15. Tring, U.K.: British Ornithologists' Union.

Keith, A. R., J. W. Wiley, S. C. Latta, and J. A. Ottenwalder. 2003. *The birds of Hispaniola: Haiti and the Dominican Republic. BOU* Checklist no. 21. Tring, U.K.: British Ornithologists' Union.

Kelly, J. B., and E. Roy. 1989. The status of Antigua's and Barbuda's wildlife, a mixed bag in habitat. Pp. 14–18 *in* Lugo, A. E., and L. B. Ford, eds., *Wildlife management in the Caribbean islands: Proceedings of the Fourth Meeting of Caribbean Foresters.* Río Piedras, Puerto Rico: Institute of Tropical Forestry and Caribbean National Forest.

Kenny, J. S., and P. R. Bacon. 1981. Aquatic resources. Pp. 112–144 *in* Kenny, J. S., and P. R. Bacon, eds., *The natural resources of Trinidad and Tobago.* London: Edward Arnold.

Kepler, C. B. 1971. *Bird survey of St. Thomas (offshore islands) and St. John, Virgin Islands.* Unpublished report. Laurel, Md.: Patuxent Wildlife Research Center.

———. 1978. The breeding ecology of sea birds on Monito Island, Puerto Rico. *Condor* 80: 72–87.

Kepler, C. B., and A. K. Kepler. 1978. The sea-birds of Culebra and its adjacent islands, Puerto Rico. *Living Bird* 16: 21–50.

Kerr-Jarrett, I. 1972. Breeding of the Least Tern in Jamaica. *Gosse Bird Club Broads.* 18: 18–19.

Kidd, E. R. G. 1963. Black Tern. *Gosse Bird Club Broads.* 1: 7.

———. 1965. Brown Noddy. *Gosse Bird Club Broads.* 4: 18.

———. 1965. Sooty Tern. *Gosse Bird Club Broads.* 4: 18.

King, W. B., G. V. Byrd, J. J. Hickey, C. B. Kepler, W. Post, H. A. Raffaele, P. F. Springer, H. F. Snyder, C. M. White, and J. W. Wiley. 1976. Report of the American Ornithologists' Union Committee on Conservation 1975–76. *Auk* 93(4, Suppl.): 1DD–19DD.

King, W. B., and A. T. Fenn. 1967. A short Jamaican bird-watching tour. *Gosse Bird Club Broads.* 9: 9–10.

Kirk, J. 1884. List of birds of Tobago. Pp. xviii–xxxiii *in* Hay, L. G., ed., *A handbook of the island of Tobago: A brief historical, geographic, and general account of the island.* Scarborough, Tobago: Government Printer.

Kirkconnell, A., and R. M. Posada Rodríguez. 1988. Adiciones a la fauna de Cayo Romano, Cuba. *Misc. Zool., Inst. Zool. Acad. Cienc. Cuba* 37: 4.

Kirkconnell, A., O. H. Garrido, R. M. Posada Rodríguez, and S. O. Cubillas. 1992. Los grupos tróficos en la avifauna cubana. *Poeyana* 415: 1–21.

Kirkconnell, A., R. M. Posada Rodríguez, V. Berovides Alvarez, and J. A. Morales. 1993. Aves de Cayo Guillermo, Archipiélago Sabana-Camagüey, Cuba. *Poeyana* 430: 1–7.

Knapp, C. 1995. A flora and fauna survey of Guana Cay, with an emphasis on its rock iguana. *Bahamas J. Sci.* 2: 2–7.

Knox, J. P. 1852. *A historical account of St. Thomas, West Indies, with . . . incidental notices of St. Croix and St. Johns, etc.* New York: C. Scribner.

Knutson, T. R., and R. E. Tuleya. 2004. Impact of global warming on hurricane intensity. *J. Climate* 17: 3477–3495.

Kohler, B. F. 1964. Brown Pelican. *Gosse Bird Club Broads.* 2: 16.

———. 1967. Behavior of some Jamaican birds. *Gosse Bird Club Broads.* 8: 12.

Kress, S. 1998. Applying research for effective management: Case studies in seabird restoration. Pp. 141–154 *in* Marzluff, J. M., and R. Sallabanks, eds., *Avian conservation.* Washington, D.C.: Island Press.

Kushlan, J. A., M. J. Steinkamp, K. C. Parsons, J. Capp, M. A. Cruz, M. Coulter, I. Davidson, L. Dickson, N. Edelson, R. Elliot, R. M. Erwin, S. Hatch, S. Kress, R. Milko, S. Miller, K. Mills, R. Paul, R. Phillips, J. E. Saliva, B. Sydeman, J. Happ, J. Wheeler, and K. Wohl. 2002. *Waterbird conservation for* the Americas: *The North American Waterbird Conservation Plan, Version 1.* Washington, D.C.: Waterbird Conservation for the Americas.

Kwok, R., and J. C. Comiso. 2002. Southern ocean climate and sea ice anomalies associated with the Southern Oscillation. *J. Climate* 15: 487–501.

Labastille, A., and M. Richmond. 1973. Birds and mammals of Anegada Island, British Virgin Islands. *Carib. J. Sci.* 13: 91–109.

Labat, J. B. 1722. *Nouveau voyage aux îsles de l'Amérique. Contenant l'histoire naturelle de ces pays, l'origine, les moeurs, la réligion & le gouvernement des habitants anciens & modernes: Les guerres & les évènements singuliers qui y sont arrivez pendant le long séjour que l'auteur y a fait. Le commerce et les manufactures quey sont établies, & les moyens de les augmenter. Ouvrage enrichi d'un grand nombre de cartes, plans & figures en taille-douce.* Paris: Guillaume Cavelier.

Lack, P. C., C. D. Taylor, and E. K. Dunn. 1973. *The Oxford expedition to Montserrat, 1973.* Unpublished report, Oxford University Exploration Club. Oxford, U.K.: Oxford University.

Lafresnaye, F. de. 1844. Description de quelques oiseaux de la Guadeloupe. *Rev. Zool.* 7: 167–169.

Laist, D. W. 1997. Impacts of marine debris: Entanglement of marine life in marine debris including a comprehensive list of species with entanglement and ingestions records. Pp 99–139 *in* Coe, J. M., and D. B. Rogers, eds., *Marine debris: Sources, impacts, and solutions.* New York: Springer-Verlag.

Lamb, G. R. 1957. *On the endangered species of birds of the U.S. Virgin Islands.* Research Report no. 2. New York: Pan-American Section, International Committee for Bird Preservation.

———. 1958. On the endangered species of birds in the U.S. Virgin Islands. *Bull. Intl. Council Bird Preserv.* 7: 144–148.

Larsen, N. J., M. Heegaard, and B. J. Baptiste. 2005. Recent bird observations from Dominica, West Indies. *J. Carib. Ornithol.* 18: 52–53.

Lawrence, G. N. 1862. Description of a new species of bird of the genus *Phaeton*, also of a new species of humming bird of the genus *Heliopaedica*. *Ann. Lyceum Nat. Hist. N.Y.* 7: 142–145.

———. 1862. Notes on some Cuban birds, with descriptions of new species. *Ann. Lyceum Nat. Hist. N.Y.* 7: 247–275.

———. 1864. VIII Catalogue of birds collected at the island of Sombrero, W.I., with observations by A. A. Julien. *Ann. Lyceum Nat. Hist. N.Y.* 8: 92–106.

———. 1867. Catalogue of birds collected at the island of Sombrero, W.I., with observations by A. A. Julien. *Ann. Lyceum Nat. Hist. N.Y.* 8: 92–106.

———. 1877. A provisional list of the birds procured and noticed by Mr. Fred. A. Ober in the island of Dominica. *For. Stream, New York* 9: 345.

———. 1879. Catalogue of the birds of Dominica from collections made for the Smithsonian Institution by Frederick A. Ober, together with his notes and observations. *Proc. U.S. Natl. Mus.* (1878) 1: 48–69.

———. 1879. Catalogue of the birds of St. Vincent, from collections made by Mr. Fred. A. Ober, under the directions of the Smithsonian Institution, with his notes thereon. *Proc. U.S. Natl. Mus.* (1878) 1: 185–198.

———. 1879. Catalogue of the birds of Antigua and Barbuda, from collections made for the Smithsonian Institution, by Mr. Fred. A. Ober, with his observations. *Proc. U.S. Natl. Mus.* (1878) 1: 232–242.

———. 1879. Catalogue of the birds of Grenada, from a collection made by Mr. Fred. A. Ober for the Smithsonian Institution, including others seen by him, but not obtained. *Proc. U.S. Natl. Mus.* (1878) 1: 265–278.

———. 1879. Catalogue of the birds collected in Martinique by Mr. Fred. A. Ober for the Smithsonian Institution. *Proc. U.S. Natl. Mus.* (1878) 1: 349–360.

———. 1879. Catalogue of a collection of birds obtained in Guadeloupe for the Smithsonian Institution, by Mr. Fred. A. Ober. *Proc. U.S. Natl. Mus.* (1878) 1: 449–462.

———. 1879. A general catalogue of the birds noted from the islands of the Lesser Antilles visited by Mr. Fred. A. Ober; with a table showing their distribution, and those found in the United States. *Proc. U.S. Natl. Mus.* (1878) 1: 486–488.

———. 1886. List of a few species of birds new to the fauna of Guadeloupe, West Indies, with a description of a new species of *Ceryle. Proc. U.S. Natl. Mus.* (1885) 8: 621–625.

———. 1891. Description of a new subspecies of Cypselidae of the genus *Chaetura*, with a note on the diablotin. *Auk* 8: 59–62.

Lazell, J. D., Jr. 1964. The reptiles of Sombrero, West Indies. *Copeia* 1964: 716–718.

———. 1967. The ternery on Aves Island in March. *Condor* 69: 87–88.

———. 1981. Tropic birds. *Virgin Islands* 6: 23.

———. 1986. *A Guana guide: Wildlife and natural history.* Jamestown, R.I.: Conservation Agency and Guana Island Wildlife Sanctuary.

———. 1989. *Guana: A natural history guide.* Jamestown, R.I.: Conservation Agency.

Leblond, G. 2003a. *Les oiseaux marins de Guadeloupe, de Saint Martin and de Saint Barthélemy.* Première partie. Guadeloupe: Bios/DIREN.

———. 2003b. *Les oiseaux marins de Guadeloupe, de Saint Martin and de Saint Barthélemy.* Deuxième partie. Guadeloupe: Bios/DIREN.

———. 2005. *Etude de faisabilité de la réserve naturelle terrestre et marine de Marie-Galante: La patrimoine faunistique terrestre.* Unpublished report. Guadeloupe: BIOS/Caraïbe Environnement.

Leck, C. F. 1972. U.S. Virgin Islands, St. Croix. *Birding* 4: 281.

———. 1974. Avifauna of St. Croix. Pp. 245–255 *in* Multer, H. G., and L. C. Gerhard, eds., *Guidebook to the geology and ecology of some marine and terrestrial environments, St. Croix, U.S. Virgin Islands.* Special Publication no. 5. Madison, N.J.: West Indies Laboratory, Fairleigh Dickinson University.

———. 1975. Notes on unusual and rare birds of St. Croix. *Condor* 77: 107.

Leck, C. F., and R. L. Norton. 1991. *An annotated checklist of the birds of the U.S. Virgin Islands.* Christiansted, St. Croix: Antilles Press.

LeCroy, M. 1976. Bird observations in Los Roques, Venezuela. *Amer. Mus. Novitates* 2599: 1–30.

Lee, D. S. 1995. The pelagic ecology of Manx Shearwaters *Puffinus puffinus* off the southeastern United States of America. *Marine Ornithology* 23: 107–119.

———. 2000a. Status and conservation priorities for Black-capped Petrels in the West Indies. Pp 11–18 *in* Schreiber, E. A., and D. S. Lee, eds., *Status and conservation of West Indian seabirds.* Special Publication no. 1. Ruston, La.: Society of Caribbean Ornithology.

———. 2000b. Status and conservation priorities for Audubon's Shearwaters in the West Indies. Pp. 25–30 *in* Schreiber, E. A., and D. S. Lee, eds., *Status and conservation of West Indian seabirds.* Special Publication no. 1. Ruston, La.: Society of Caribbean Ornithology.

Lee, D. S., and M. K. Clark. 1994. Seabirds of the Exuma Land and Sea Park. *Bahamas J. Sci.* 2: 2–9.

———. 1995. Seabirds of the Bahamas Land and Sea Park, Part 2. *Bahamas J. Sci.* 2: 15–21.

Lee, D. S., M. K. Clark, and W. Mackin. 2004. Demise of a White-tailed Tropicbird colony in the Exumas Land and Sea Park. *Bahamas J. Sci.* 11(2): 2–12.

Lee, D. S., and N. Viña. 1993. A re-evaluation of the status of the endangered Black-capped Petrel, *Pterodroma hasitata*, in Cuba. *Ornitol. Neotrop.* 4: 99–101.

Lee, D. S., and M. Walsh-McGehee. 1998. White-tailed Tropicbird (*Phaethon lepturus*). *In* Poole, A., and F. Gill, eds., *The birds of North America*, no. 353. Philadelphia: Birds of North America.

———. 2000. Population estimates, conservation concerns, and management of tropicbirds in the Western Atlantic. *Carib. J. Sci.* 36: 267–279.

Lee, D. S., O. H. Garrido, R. W. Dickerman, and J. C. Haney. 1993. Reassessment of Black-capped Petrel in Cuba. *Pitirre* 6(1): 4.

Lee, G. C. 1990. Puerto Rico's Least Tern status survey. *Pitirre* 3(3): 8.

Leeuwen, W. C. J. van. 1947. *Tempels in Woestijnen.* Willemstad, Curaçao: Imprenta Bolivar.

Le Faucheux, O. 1953. Quelques observations ornithologiques dans l'océan Atlantique. *Oiseau Rev. Fr. Ornithol.* 23: 303–304.

Lefroy, J. H. (ed.). 1877–1879. *Memorials of the discovery and early settlement of the Bermudas or Somers islands, 1515–1685.* Compiled from colonial records and other original sources. 2 vols. London: Longmans, Green and Company.

———. 1981. *Memorials of the discovery and early settlement of the Bermudas or Somers islands, 1515–1685.* 2 vols. Hamilton: Bermuda Historical Society and Bermuda National Trust.

Lembeye, J. 1850. *Aves de la isla de Cuba.* La Habana, Cuba: Imprenta del Tiempo.

Lentino, M. 2004. Ornitofauna de Capure y Pedernales, Delta del Orinoco, Venezuela. Pp. 125–136 *in* Lasso, C. A., L. E. Alonso, A. L. Flores, and G. Love, eds., *Rapid assessment of the biodiversity and social aspects of the aquatic ecosystems of the Orinoco Delta and Gulf of Paria, Venezuela.* RAP Bull. Biological Assessment 37. Washington, D.C.: Conservation International.

Lentino, M., A. Luy, and A. R. Bruni. 1994. *Lista de aves del Parque Nacional Archipiélago de los Roques y otras islas de las Dependencias Federales.* Caracas, Venezuela: Sociedad Conservacionista Audubon de Venezuela.

Lentino, M., and C. Rodner. 2003. Aves de Los Roques, una muestra de la riqueza de nuestra avifauna insular. Pp. 143–165 *in* Zamarro, J., ed., *Los Roques.* Caracas, Venezuela: Agencia Española de Cooperación Internacional–Ecograph.

Leopold, N. F., Jr. 1963. A checklist of the birds of Puerto Rico and the Virgin Islands. *Agricultural Experiment Station of the University of Puerto Rico Bulletin* 168: 1–119.

Leotaud, A. 1866. *Oiseaux de l'ile de la Trinidad.* Port of Spain, Trinidad: Chronicle Press.

Lesson, R. P. 1828. *Manuel d'ornithologie ou description des genres et des principales espèces d'oiseaux.* Paris: Roret.

———. 1847. *Oeuvres complètes de Buffon aves la nomenclatum linnéenne et la classification de Cuvier. Revues sur l'édition in 4o de l'Imprimerie royale annotées par M. Flourens.* Vol. 20. Paris: Garnier Frères.

Lever, C. 1984. Conservation success for two Bermudan bird species. *Oryx* 18: 138–143.

Lévesque, A. 2004. *L'avifaune du rocher du Diamant, Martinique—statut et proposition de gestion.* Unpublished report. Fort-de-France, Martinique: Association Amazona, Parc Naturel Régional de la Martinique.

Levy, C. 1987. 1987 diary of nests and juveniles. *Gosse Bird Club Broads.* 49: 2–6.

———. 1988. Observations on the effects of Hurricane Gilbert on bird-life in Jamaica: St. Andrew (Seymour Lands). *Gosse Bird Club Broads.* 51: 3–5.

———. 1988. Birds at Treasure Beach, Mar. 26–29, 1988. *Gosse Bird Club Broads.* 51: 10–11.

———. 1990. Report on recent activities made to the Inaugural Meeting November 15, 1989. *Gosse Bird Club Broads.* 54: 2–5.

———. 1990. Laughing Gulls. *Gosse Bird Club Broads.* 54: 20.

———. 1991. Christmas bird count 1990. *Gosse Bird Club Broads.* 56: 5–8.

———. 1991. Goat Island. *Gosse Bird Club Broads.* 56: 20.

———. 1992. Christmas count 1991. *Gosse Bird Club Broads.* 58: 4–6.

———. 1993. Christmas Bird Count 1992. *Gosse Bird Club Broads.* 60: 18–19.

———. (ed.). 1993. [Recoveries and recaptures in Jamaica]. *Gosse Bird Club Broads.* 60: 24.

[———]. 1994. Christmas Bird Count 1993. *Gosse Bird Club Broads.* 62: 13.

Levy, C., and L. Douglas. 1996. Christmas Bird Count 1995. *Gosse Bird Club Broads.* 66: 18–19.

Lewis, C. B. 1940. *Report on the decline in the yield of booby eggs on Pedro and Morant cays, with recommendations for conservation.* Internal report. Kingston: Institute of Jamaica.

———. 1942. Booby eggs. *Nat. Hist. Notes Nat. Hist. Soc. Jamaica* 1: 4–5.

———. 1947. A trip to the Morant and Pedro cays. *Nat. Hist. Notes Nat. Hist. Soc. Jamaica* 3: 105–108.

———. 1948. [Terns]. *Nat. Hist. Notes Nat. Hist. Soc. Jamaica* 3: 203.

———. 1948. The history of the Pedro and Morant Cays. *Jamaica Hist. Review* 1: 302–309.

———. 1949. Booby eggs. Pp. 34–36 in Lewis, C. B., and C. Swabey, eds., *Glimpses of Jamaican natural history*, vol. 1. Kingston: Institute of Jamaica.

[———]. 1951. The Cahow. *Nat. Hist. Notes Nat. Hist. Soc. Jamaica* 5: 6,8.

———. 1954. Bird notes. *Nat. Hist. Notes Nat. Hist. Soc. Jamaica* 6: 155.

———. 1961. Caspian Terns in Jamaica. *Auk* 78: 264–265.

———. 1970. Brown Pelican. *Gosse Bird Club Broads.* 14: 22–23

Ligon, R. 1673. *A true & exact history of the island of Barbadoes . . . [with] principal trees and plants.* London: P. Parker and T. Guy.

Lincoln, F. C. 1936. Returns of banded birds: Third paper (Some recoveries of water birds from Latin America). *Bird-Banding* 7: 139–148.

———. 1940. Caspian Tern in Haiti. *Auk* 57: 569.

Lindblad, J. 1969. *Journey to red birds.* New York: Hill and Wang.

Lindsay, K., and B. Horwith. 1997a. *A vegetation classification of Antigua, Barbuda and Redonda.* Eastern Caribbean Biodiversity Programme, Biodiversity Publ. no. 2. Washington D.C. Island Resources Foundation.

Lindsay, K., and B. Horwith. 1997b. *Seabird conservation status report: Antigua-Barbuda-Redonda.* Eastern Caribbean Biodiversity Programme, Biodiversity Publ. no. 4. St. Thomas, U.S. Virgin Islands: Island Resources Foundation.

Lindsay, K., B. Horwith, and E. A. Schreiber. 2000. Status of the Magnificent Frigatebird in the West Indies. Pp. 58–64 in Schreiber, E. A., and D. S. Lee, eds., *Status and conservation of West Indian seabirds.* Special Publication no. 1. Ruston, La.: Society of Caribbean Ornithology.

Llanes Sosa, A., A. Kirkconnell, R. M. Posada Rodríguez, and S. Cubillas. 1987. Aves de Cayo Saetía, archipiélago de Camagüey, Cuba. *Misc. Zool., Inst. Zool. Acad. Cienc. Cuba* 35: 3–4.

Lönnberg, E. 1929. Några ord om en samling fåglar från Haiti. *Fauna Flora* (Stockholm) 3: 97–112.

Lovgren, S. 2004a. Greenland melt may swamp LA, other cities, study says. *Natl. Geograph. News,* April 8, 2004: http://news. nationalgeographic.com/news/2004/04/0408_040408_ greeenlandicemelt.html.

———. 2004b. Warming to cause catastrophic rise in sea level? *Natl. Geograph. News,* updated April 26, 2004: http://news. nationalgeographic.com/news/2004/04/0420_040420_ earthday.html.

Lowe, P. R. 1909. Notes on some birds collected during a cruise in the Caribbean Sea. *Ibis* 3: 304–347.

———. 1911a. *A naturalist on desert islands.* London: Witherby and Company.

———. 1911. On the birds of the Cayman Islands, West Indies. *Ibis* 9 5: 137–161.

Lowery, G. H., Jr., and R. J. Newman. 1954. The birds of the Gulf of Mexico. Pp. 519–540 in Galtshoff, P. S., ed., *Gulf of Mexico, its origin, waters and marine life.* Fishery Bull. 89. Fish and Wildlife Service vol. 55.

Ludwig, F. E. 1942. Migration of Caspian Terns banded in the Great Lakes area. *Bird-Banding* 13: 1–9.

Ludwig, J. P. 1965. Biology and structure of the Caspian Tern (*Hydroprogne caspia*) population of the Great Lakes from 1896–1964. *Bird-Banding* 36: 217–233.

Luy, A. 1997. Caracterización de la avifauna del Parque Nacional Archipiélago Los Roques. Pp. 265–269 in Novo, I., M. L. González, C. T. Rodríguez, G. Martínez, and I. De Hertelendy, eds., *Ciencia y conservación en el sistema de Parques Nacionales de Venezuela.* Caracas, Venezuela: Econatura.

Machado, J. G. 1972. Magnificent Frigatebird. *Gosse Bird Club Broads.* 19: 22.

Mackin, W. A. 2000. A geographic information system for seabird breeding sites in the West Indies. Pp. 174–181 in Schreiber, E. A., and D. S. Lee, eds., *Status and conservation of West Indian seabirds.* Special Publication no. 1. Ruston, La.: Society of Caribbean Ornithology.

———. 2004. *Communication and breeding behavior of Audubon's Shearwater.* Ph.D. dissertation. Chapel Hill: University of North Carolina.

———. 2005. Neighbor-stranger discrimination in Audubon's Shearwater (*Puffinus l. lherminieri*) explained by a "real enemy" effect. *Behavioral Ecology and Sociobiology* 59: 326–332.

Maddison, P. R. 1977. White-tailed Tropicbirds at Hector's River. *Gosse Bird Club Broads.* 28: 17–18.

Maddison, P. R., and A. Maddison. 1977a. Bird Notes: White-tailed Tropicbird. *Gosse Bird Club Broads.* 28: 23.

———. 1977b. Bird Notes: White-tailed Tropicbird. *Gosse Bird Club Broads* 29: 13.

———. 1977. Bridled Tern. *Gosse Bird Club Broads.* 28: 25.

———. 1977. Common Tern. *Gosse Bird Club Broads.* 28: 25.

———. 1977. Laughing Gull. *Gosse Bird Club Broads.* 28: 25.

———. 1977. Sandwich Tern. *Gosse Bird Club Broads.* 28: 25.

———. 1977. Sooty Tern. *Gosse Bird Club Broads.* 28: 25.

———. 1977. Least Tern. *Gosse Bird Club Broads.* 29: 14.

Madeiros, J. L. 2002. Bermuda's remarkable Cahow. *World Birdwatch* 24: 16–18.

———. 2004. Translocation of the Cahow. Pp. 21–23 *in The Bermuda Audubon Society: 50th anniversary 1954–2004.* Hamilton, Bermuda: Bermuda Audubon Society.

Manning, C. J. 1896. Ueber den vogelzug auf Barbados im jahre 1886. *Ornis Int. z. gesam. Ornithol.* 8: 365–372.

Manolis, T. 1981. First sight record of South Polar Skua *Catharacta maccormicki*, for Trinidad, West Indies. *Am. Birds* 35: 982.

Manon Arredondo, M. de J. 1968. Gaviotas y ratas. *Listin Diario*, supl. del 12 Mayo 1968.

Manser, P. 1990. White-tailed Tropicbird. *Gosse Bird Club Broads.* 56: 21.

March, E. W. 1948. [Magnificent Frigatebird]. *Nat. Hist. Notes Nat. Hist. Soc. Jamaica* 3: 172.

Marsden, H. W. 1887. Nidification of the Noddy and Sooty terns in the West Indies. *Zoologist* 3 11: 429–430.

Mason, C. R. 1945. Pelican travels. *Bird-Banding* 16: 134–143.

———. 1964. Grand Bahama Island. *Fla. Nat.* 37: 116.

Mathews, G. M. 1915. *Phaëthon catesbyi* Brandt. *Auk* 32: 195–197.

Maynard, C. J. 1889a. Description of a supposed new species of gannet. *Ornitholog. Oölogist* 14: 40–41.

———. 1889. Notes on certain West Indian birds. *Bull. Newton Nat. Hist. Soc.* 1: 35–46.

———. 1889. Description of a supposed new species of gannet (*Sula coryi*) from Little Cayman. *Contr. Sci.* 1: 40–48.

———. 1889. Description of a supposed new species of gannet (*Sula coryi*) from Little Cayman. *Contr. Sci.* 1: 51–57.

———. 1889. On the probable evolution of the totipalmate birds, pelicans, gannets, etc. *Contr. Sci.* 1: 82–88.

———. 1889. Breeding habits of the Bridled Tern. *Oölogist* 6: 7–8.

———. 1889. Observations on Cory's Gannet. Ornitholog. *Oölogist* 14: 59.

———. 1890. Notes on West Indian birds. *Contr. Sci.* 1: 171–181.

———. 1896. *The birds of eastern North America; with original descriptions of all the species which occur east of the Mississippi River, between the Arctic Circle and the Gulf of Mexico, with full notes upon their habits, etc.*, rev. ed., Newtonville, Mass.: C. J. Maynard and Company.

———. 1898. *A catalogue of the birds of the West Indies which do not occur elsewhere in North America north of Mexico.* Newtonville, Mass.: published by the author.

———. 1899. The man-of-war bird and Cory's gannet. *Nat. Study Schools* 1: 229–243.

———. 1918. Notes on some remarkable birds. *Records of Walks and Talks with Nature* 10: 20–25, 34–38, 40–46, 48–51. Newtonville, Mass.: published by the author.

———. 1919. Some remarkable birds. *Records of Walks and Talks with Nature* 11: 4–7, 10–16, 19–20, 49–53, 55–57, 153–156. Newtonville, Mass.: published by the author.

———. 1920. Bahama gulls and terns. *Records of Walks and Talks with Nature* 12: 155–157. Newtonville, Mass.: published by the author.

Mayr, E. 1953. Additional notes on the birds of Bimini, Bahamas. *Auk* 70: 499–501.

McAtee, W. L. 1945. Catesby's Tropic-bird. *Auk* 62: 137–139.

McCandless, J. B. 1961. Bird life in southwestern Puerto Rico. I: Fall migration. *Carib. J. Sci.* 1: 3–12.

———. 1962. Birdlife in southwestern Puerto Rico. II: The winter season. *Carib. J. Sci.* 2: 27–39.

McCormick, C. 1999. *Anexo 3—Informe de investigaciones de campo durante 1999: Avifauna residente y migratoria de los cayos Bolívar, Albuquerque, Roncador, Serrana y Serranilla.* Field report. San Andrés: CORALINA.

McGowan, A., A. C. Broderick, S. Gore, G. Hilton, N. K. Woodfield, and B. J. Godley. 2006a. Breeding seabirds in the British Virgin Islands. *Endang. Species Res.* 2: 15–20.

McGowan, A., A. C. Broderick, C. Clubbe, S. Gore, B. J. Godley, M. Hamilton, B. Lettsome, J. Smith-Abbott, and N. K. Woodfield. 2006b. Darwin Initiative Action Plan for the coastal biodiversity of Anegada, British Virgin Islands. Darwin Initiative Secretariat, London. http://www.seaturtle.org/mtrg/projects/anegada/.

McKenzie, P. M., W. C. Barrow, Jr., J. Collazo, and C. A. Staicer. 1990. First summer record of the Common Black-headed Gull for Puerto Rico. *Am. Birds* 44: 1092–1093.

McNair, D. B., F. E. Hayes, and G. L. White. 2002. First occurrences of Franklin's Gull (*Larus pipixan*) for Trinidad. *Dept. Life Sci., Univ. West Indies, St. Augustine, Occ. Pap.* 11: 201–203.

Meier, A. J., R. E. Noble, and H. A. Raffaele. 1989. The birds of Desecheo Island, Puerto Rico, including a new record for Puerto Rican territory. *Carib. J. Sci.* 25: 24–29.

Melzer, J. P. 1935. Another Common Tern recovery in Puerto Rico. *Bird-Banding* 6: 69.

Menzies, G. 2002. *1421: The year China discovered the world.* London: Bantam Books.

Meyer de Schauensee, R., and W. H. Phelps, Jr. 1978. *A guide to the birds of Venezuela.* Princeton, N.J.: Princeton University Press.

Miller, J. R. 1978. Notes on birds of San Salvador Island (Watlings), the Bahamas. *Auk* 95: 281–287.

Milliman, J. 1969. Four southwestern Caribbean atolls: Courtown Cays, Albuquerque Cays, Roncador Bank and Serrana Bank. *Atoll Res. Bull.* 129(1–4): 1–22.

Mills, H. N. 1989. Wildlife management in St. Kitts. Pp. 53–62 *in* Lugo, A. E., and L. B. Ford, eds., *Wildlife management in the Caribbean islands: Proceedings of the Fourth Meeting of Caribbean Foresters.* Río Piedras, Puerto Rico: Institute of Tropical Forestry and Caribbean National Forest.

Mirecki, D. N. 1976. *Report of the Cambridge ornithological expedition to the British Virgin Islands.* Cambridge, U.K.: Churchill College.

Mirecki, D. N., J. M. Hutton, C. M. Pannell, T. J. Stowe, and R. W. Unite. 1977. *Report of the Cambridge Ornithological Expedition to the British Virgin Islands 1976.* Cambridge, U.K.: Churchill College.

Mitchell, P. I., S. F. Newton, N. Ratcliffe, and T. E. Dunn. 2004.

Seabird populations in Britain and Ireland. London, U.K.: Joint Nature Conservancy Committee–T & A. D. Poyser.

Mlodinow, S. 2004 Aruba, Dutch Caribbean, 26th March–3rd April 2004. http://www.surfbirds.com/mb/trips/aruba-dc-0404.html.

Moffatt, E. M. 1972. Magnificent Frigatebird. *Gosse Bird Club Broads*. 19: 22.

Mohan, D. 1982. Birdwatching at Yallahs Pond. *Gosse Bird Club Broads*. 39: 9.

Moltoni, E. 1929. Primo Elenco degli Uccelli dell'Isola di Haiti. *Atti Soc. Ital. Sci. Nat. Mus. Civ. Stor. Nat. Milano* 68: 306–326.

Montañez Huguez, L., V. Berovides Alvarez, A. Sampedro Marin, and L. Mugica Valdés. 1985. Vertebrados del embalse "Leonero," Provincia Granma. *Misc. Zool., Inst. Zool. Acad. Cienc. Cuba* 25: 1–2.

Moody, C. 1991. Least Tern. *Gosse Bird Club Broads*. 57: 21.

Moore, A. G. 1985. Winter status of birds on Grand Cayman Island. *Bull. Br. Ornithol. Club* 105: 8–17.

Moore, N. B. 1878. List of birds, chiefly visitors from N. America, seen and killed in the Bahamas in July, Aug., Oct., Nov., and Dec., 1876. *Proc. Boston Soc. Nat. Hist.* 19: 241–243.

Moors, P. J., and I. A. E. Atkinson. 1984. Predation on seabirds by introduced animals, and factors affecting its severity. Pp. 667–690 *in* Croxall, J. P., P. G. H. Evans, and R. W. Schreiber, eds., Status and conservation of the world's seabirds. ICBP Tech. Publ. no. 2. Cambridge, U.K.: International Council for Bird Preservation.

Morales Leal, J., and O. H. Garrido. 1988. Nuevo estercorario (Aves: Stercorariinae) para Cuba. *Misc. Zool., Inst. Zool. Acad. Cienc. Cuba* 39: 3–4.

Morales Leal, J., and O. H. Garrido. 1996. Aves y reptiles de Cayo Sabinal, Archipiélago de Sabana-Camagüey, Cuba. *Pitirre* 9(3): 9–11.

Morales Leal, J. de la C., E. Suares Falcon, A. Cardona Fuentes, and V. Berovides Alvarez. 1991. Conducta reproductiva y nidificacion del Rabihorcado (*Fregata magnificens*). *Rev. Biol.* 5: 3–8.

Moreau De Saint-Méry, M. L. E. 1796. *Description topographique et politique de la partie Espagnole de l'île de Saint-Domingue*. Philadelphia: printed and sold by the author.

———. 1797–1798. *Description topographique, physique, civile, politique et historique de la partie Française de l'île Saint-Dominigue*. Paris: Chez DuPont–Société Française d'Histoire d'Outre-mer.

Moreno, J. A. 1980. *Wildlife management considerations for La Cordillera with recommendations for other areas in northeast Puerto Rico*. San Juan, Puerto Rico: Department of Natural Resources.

Moreno, J. A., N. I. Perez, and A. Garcia-Moll. 1980. *Management plan for the seabirds and shorebirds of Puerto Rico*. San Juan: Division of Coastal Resources and Wildlife Planning, Puerto Rico Department of Natural Resources.

Moreno, M. I., M. I. García, and T. McNish. 2003. *Formulario de nominación y formulario para la base de datos para Áreas Importantes para la Conservación de las Aves AICAS de Colombia Reserva de Biosfera Seaflower: Archipiélago de San Andrés, Providencia y Santa Catalina. August 29, 2003*. Bogotá, Colombia: Fundación ProAves–Conservation Internacional–CORALINA, Instituto de Investigación de Recursos Biológicos Alexander Von Humboldt, and BirdLife International.

Moreno Bonilla, A. 1946. Notas ornitologicas. *Mem. Soc. Cubana Hist. Nat. "Felipe Poey"* 18: 185–188.

Morgan, A. 1993a. Black Tern. *Gosse Bird Club Broads*. 61: 18.

———. 1993. Effects of habitat manipulation on the waterbird populations of Hellshire. *Gosse Bird Club Broads*. 60: 16–17.

Morgan, G. S. 1977. *Late Pleistocene fossil vertebrates from the Cayman Islands, British West Indies*. M.S. thesis. Gainesville: University of Florida.

———. 1985. Taxonomic status and relationships of the Swan Island hutia, *Geocapromys thoracatus* (Mammalia: Rodentia: Capromyidae), and the zoogeography of the Swan Island vertebrate fauna. *Proc. Biol. Soc. Wash.* 98: 29–46.

———. 1994. Late Quaternary fossil vertebrates from the Cayman Islands. Pp. 465–509 *in* Brunt, M. A., and J. Davis, eds., *The Cayman Islands: Natural history and biogeography*. Netherlands: Kluwer Academic Publishers.

Moritz, C. 1836. Notizen zur fauna der insel Puertorico. *Wiegmann's Arch. für Naturg.* 2: 373–392.

Morris, M. M. J., and R. E. Lemon. 1982. *The effects of development on the avifauna of St. Kitts, W.I.* Unpublished report prepared for the Sub-committee on Wildlife and Natural History of the St. Kitts–Nevis National Heritage Trust. Montreal, Quebec: McGill University.

Morris, R. D. 1977a. Seabirds of Little Tobago. *Living World, J. Trinidad and Tobago Field Naturalists' Club* 1977: 2–6.

———. 1977. Methods for collection of sea-[bird] breeding data. *Living World, J. Trinidad and Tobago Field Naturalists' Club* 1977: 7–8.

———. 1984. Breeding chronology and reproductive success of seabirds on Little Tobago, Trinidad, 1975–1976. *Colon. Waterbirds* 7: 1–9.

Morris, R. D., and J. W. Chardine. 1989. Some preliminary observations on age of first breeding, survival rates, and mate/site fidelity in a tropical seabird: The Brown Noddy. *Colon. Waterbird Soc. Newsl.* 13: 25.

———. 1990. Costs of parental neglect in the Brown Noddy (*Anous stolidus*). *Can. J. Zool.* 68: 2025–2027.

———. 1990. Brown Noddies in Culebra: Trends in breeding biology 1985–1990. *Colon. Waterbird Soc. Newsl.* 14: 22.

———. 1991. Recent trends in breeding and survival of Brown Noddies nesting near Culebra, PR. *Colon. Waterbird Soc. Newsl.* 15: 32.

———. 1992. The breeding biology and aspects of the feeding ecology of Brown Noddies *Anous stolidus* nesting near Culebra, Puerto Rico, 1985–1989. *J. Zoology* (London) 226: 65–79.

———. 1995. Brown Noddies on Cayo Noroeste, Culebra, Puerto Rico: What happened in 1990? *Auk* 112: 326–334.

Morris, R. D., H. Blokpoel, and B. Ramdial. 1982. Common Terns. *Trinidad Nat.* 4(5): 37, 83–88.

Morris, S. 1967. The birds of South Cay. *Gosse Bird Club Broads.* 9: 5–6.

Mortensen, T. N. 1909. Dyrelivet Dansk Vestindien: Atlanten Medlemsblan fur Foreningen. *Dan. Atlanterhavsuer* 5: 639–651.

———. 1910. Fuglelivet paa de Dansk-Vestindiske Oer. *Dan. Ornithol. Foren. Tidsskr.* 3: 151–161.

Mortimer, C. 1732. A continuation of an account of an Essay towards a natural history of Carolina and the Bahama Islands, by Mark Catesby, F.R.S. with some extracts out of the fifth set. *Philos. Trans.* (Royal Soc. Lond.) 37: 447–450.

Mörzer Bruyns, W. F. J. 1967. Black-capped Petrels (*Pterodroma hasitata*) in the Caribbean. *Ardea* 55: 144–145.

Moser, M. L., and D. S. Lee. 1992. A fourteen-year survey of plastic ingestion by Western North Atlantic seabirds. *Colon. Waterbirds* 15: 83–94.

Mott, S. 1977. St. John, Virgin Islands. *Birding* 9: 264.

Mudd, S. H., and M. H. Mudd. 1973. White-tailed Tropic Bird colony near Ocho Rios. *Gosse Bird Club Broads.* 21: 6–8.

———. 1974. White-tailed Tropicbird colony revisited. *Gosse Bird Club Broads.* 23: 12–13.

Mugica Valdés, L., and M. Acosta Cruz. 1992. Breve caracterización de la comunidad de aves de Cayo Largo y Cayo Hicacos (grupo insular de los Canarreos). *Cienc. Biol. Acad. Cienc. Cuba* 25: 20–29.

Murphy, R. C. 1915. The Atlantic range of Leach's Petrel (*Oceanodroma leucorhoa* (Vieillot)). *Auk* 32: 170–173.

Murphy, R. C., and L. S. Mowbray. 1951. New light on the Cahow, *Pterodroma cahow. Auk* 68: 266–280.

Murphy, R. C., and W. Vogt. 1933. The Dovekie influx of 1932. *Auk* 50: 325–349.

Murphy, W. L. 1986. *A birder's guide to Trinidad and Tobago.* College Park, Md.: Peregrine Enterprises.

———. 1995. *A birder's guide to Trinidad and Tobago,* 2nd ed. College Park, Md.: Peregrine Enterprises.

———. 2004. *A birdwatcher's guide to Trinidad and Tobago.* Cley, U.K.: Prion.

Murray, T. 1999. *Birds of Anguilla, Lesser Antilles: 7–24 November 1999.* Report to Royal Society for the Protection of Birds and Anguilla National Trust.

Myers, N., R. A. Mittermeier, C. G. Mittermeier, G. A. B. Da Fonseca, and J. Kent. 2000. Biodiversity hotspots for conservation priorities. *Nature* 403: 853–858.

Naranjo, L. G. 1979. *Las aves marinas del Caribe colombiano: Taxonomía, zoogeografía y anotaciones ecológicas.* Thesis. Bogotá, Colombia: Universidad de Bogotá Jorge Tadeo Lozano.

NASA. 2004. First documented hurricane in the South Atlantic Ocean since geostationary satellite records began in 1966. http://www.ncdc.noaa.gov/img/climate/research/2004/mar/catarina-large.gif.

Natural History Society of Jamaica. 1945. *Glimpses of Jamaican natural history.* Kingston: Institute of Jamaica.

———. 1949. *Glimpses of Jamaican natural history,* 2nd ed., vol. I. Kingston: Institute of Jamaica.

Negron Gonzalez, L., R. A. Pérez-Rivera, and F. Cuevas Vergara. 1984. Evaluacion ecologica del sistema estuarino-lagunar de Humacao como habitaculo de vida silvestre. Pp. 63–89 in Ortiz Corp's, E., R. A. Pérez-Rivera, M. E. Rivera Rosa, and A. M. del Llano, eds., *Memorias del quinto simposio de la fauna de Puerto Rico y el Caribe.* Humacao: Universidad de Puerto Rico.

Nellis, D. W. 1984. Status of the breeding pelicaniformes in the U.S. Virgin Islands. *Colon. Waterbirds Group Newsl.* 8: 28.

[———]. 1985. *Breeding age and recruitment of Sooty Terns (Sterna fuscata fuscata) on the Eastern Puerto Rico Bank.* Unpublished report. St. Thomas, U.S. Virgin Islands: Division of Fish and Wildlife.

Nellis, D. W., and R. H. Boulon. 1986. *Nest habitat manipulation of the Blue-faced Booby.* Unpublished report, Study FW-3–IIG 1981–1985. St. Thomas, U.S. Virgin Islands: Virgin Islands Division of Fish and Wildlife.

Nellis, D. W., and J. J. Pierce. 1990. *Aspects of the breeding biology of the Brown Booby on Frenchcap Cay, U.S. Virgin Islands.* Final Report. Pittman-Robertson W-5, Study II. St. Thomas, U.S. Virgin Islands: Division of Fish and Wildlife, St. Thomas, U.S. Virgin Islands, 9 pp.

———. 1991. *Masked Booby colony establishment by egg translocation.* Final Report. Pittman-Robertson Wildlife Restoration Aid Grant W-5, Study 6. St. Thomas, U.S. Virgin Islands: Division of Fish and Wildlife, St. Thomas, 12 pp.

Nellis, D. W., J. Pierce, and C. Amrani. 1989. Brown Booby (*Sula leucogaster*) nesting habitat preference and reproductive success at Frenchcap Cay, U.S. Virgin Islands. *Colon. Waterbird Soc. Newsl.* 13: 25.

Nelson, J. B. 1978. *The Sulidae: Gannets and boobies.* Oxford, U.K.: Oxford University Press.

———. 1983. Contrasts in breeding strategies between some tropical and temperate marine Pelecaniformes. *Studies in Avian Biology* 8: 95–114.

Newton, A., and E. Newton. 1859. Observations on the birds of St. Croix, West Indies, made between February 20th and August 6th, 1857 by Alfred Newton, and between March 4th and September 28th, 1858 by Edward Newton. *Ibis* 1: 365–379.

Newton, I., and L. C. Dale. 1996. Bird migration at different latitudes in eastern North America. *Auk* 113: 626–635.

Newton, R. 1953. Terns (various). *Nat. Hist. Notes Nat. Hist. Soc. Jamaica* 6: 36.

Nichols, J. T. 1913. Notes on offshore birds. *Auk* 30: 505–511.

———. 1916. Limicolae at Porto Rico in July. *Auk* 33: 320–321.

Nichols, J. T., and L. L. Mowbray. 1916. Two new forms of petrels from the Bermudas. *Auk* 33: 194–195.

Nichols, R. A. 1943. The breeding birds of St. Thomas and St. John, Virgin Islands. *Mem. Soc. Cubana Hist. Nat. "Felipe Poey"* 17: 23–37.

Nicoll, M. J. 1904. On a collection of birds made during the cruise of the "Valhalla," R.Y.S., in the West Indies (1903–4). *Ibis* 4: 555–591.

Nisbet, I. C. T. 1980. *Status and trends of the Roseate Tern (Sterna dougallii) in North America and the Caribbean*, vol. 3. Unpublished Contract Report 50181–084–9 to U.S. Fish and Wildlife Service, Office of Endangered Species. Lincoln: Massachusetts Audubon Society.

———. 1981. *Biological characteristics of the Roseate Tern Sterna dougallii*. Unpublished report to U.S. Fish and Wildlife Service. Lincoln: Massachusetts Audubon Society.

———. 1984. Migration and winter quarters of North American Roseate Terns as shown by banding recoveries. *J. Field Ornithol.* 55: 1–17.

Noble, G. K. 1916. The resident birds of Guadeloupe. *Bull. Mus. Comp. Zool.* 60: 359–396.

Nogales, M., A. Martín, B. R. Tershy, C. J. Donlan, D. Veitch, N. Puerta, B. Wood, and J. Alonso. 2004. A review of feral cat eradication on islands. *Cons. Biol.* 18: 310–319.

Northrop, J. I. 1891. The birds of Andros Island, Bahamas. *Auk* 8: 64–80.

———. 1910. *A naturalist in the Bahamas, October 12, 1861–June 25, 1891: A memorial volume edited with a biographical introduction by Henry Fairfield Osborn*. New York: Columbia University Press.

Norton, R. L. 1979. New records of birds for the Virgin Islands. *Am. Birds* 33: 145–146.

———. 1984. Distribution and population status of Sterninae in the American Virgin Islands. *Colon. Waterbirds Group Newsl.* 8: 39.

———. 1984. Cayenne × Sandwich terns nesting in Virgin Islands, Greater Antilles. *J. Field Ornithol.* 55: 243–246.

———. 1985. *Effects of habitat manipulation on Sooty Terns (Sterna fuscata) in the Virgin Islands*. Unpublished report. St. Thomas, U.S. Virgin Islands: Division of Fish and Wildlife.

———. 1986a. Recoveries of Sooty Terns (*Sterna fuscata*) on Saba Cay, St. Thomas, U.S. Virgin Islands. *J. Field Ornithol.* 57: 226–228.

———. 1986b. Case of botulism in Laughing Gulls at a landfill in the Virgin Islands, Greater Antilles. *Fla. Field Nat.* 14: 97–98.

———. 1986. United States Virgin Islands. Pp. 585–586 in Scott, D. A., and M. Carbonell, eds., *A directory of neotropical wetlands*. Cambridge, U.K.: Conservation Monitoring Service, International Union for Conservation of Nature and Natural Resources, and International Wildfowl Research Bureau (Slimbridge).

———. 1986. Climatic influences on seabird populations of the tropical Western Atlantic. *Pacific Seabird Group Bull.* 13: 44.

———. 1987. Climate influences on breeding seabirds of the eastern Puerto Rico Bank. *In* Pérez-Rivera, R., and J. Moreno, eds., *Proc. Segundo Simposio Añual de la Sociedad Ornitología de Puerto Rico*. Unpaginated. San Juan: Sociedad Ornitología de Puerto Rico and Conservation Trust.

———. 1988a. The density and relative abundance of Pelecaniformes on the eastern Puerto Rico Bank in December 1982. *Carib. J. Sci.* 24: 28–31.

———. 1988. Extra-egg clutches and interspecific egg-dumping of the Roseate Tern (*Sterna dougallii*) in the West Indies. *Fla. Field Nat.* 16: 67–70.

———. 1989. First West Indian record of the Black Noddy and nesting of Masked Booby at Sombrero Island, Lesser Antilles. *Colon. Waterbirds* 12: 120–122.

———. 1993. Avifauna of Little San Salvador, Bahamas. *Fla. Field Nat.* 21: 16–17.

———. 1997a. Spring migration: West Indies region. *Field Notes* 51: 932–933.

———. 1997b. The nesting season: West Indies region. *Field Notes* 51: 1058–1059.

———. 1998. The nesting season: West Indies region. *Field Notes* 52: 507–508.

———. 2000. Status and conservation of Sandwich and Cayenne terns in the West Indies. Pp. 80–86 in Schreiber, E. A., and D. S. Lee, eds., *Status and conservation of West Indian seabirds*. Special Publication no. 1. Ruston, La.: Society of Caribbean Ornithology.

———. 2002. The nesting season: West Indies region. *N. Am. Birds* 56: 496–497.

———. 2003. Spring migration: West Indies region. *N. Am. Birds* 57: 417–419.

———. 2004. The nesting season: West Indies and Bermuda region. *N. Am. Birds* 57: 555–557.

Norton, R. L., and N. V. Clarke. 1989. Additions to the birds of the Turks and Caicos Islands. *Fla. Field Nat.* 17: 32–39.

Norton, R. L., and R. Teytaud. 1992. Bird study on St. John, U.S. Virgin Islands. *Ornitol. Caribeña* 3: 4–9.

Norton, R. L., and A. White. 2001. The nesting season: West Indies region. *N. Am. Birds* 55: 493–494.

Norton, R. L., A. White, and A. Dobson. 2002a. The spring migration: West Indies region. *N. Am. Birds* 56: 372–374.

———. 2002b. The nesting season: West Indies region. *N. Am. Birds* 56: 496–497.

———. 2003. Spring migration: West Indies region. *N. Am. Birds* 57: 417–419.

———. 2004. The nesting season: West Indies and Bermuda region. *N. Am. Birds* 57: 555–557.

Norton, R. L., R. M. Chipley, and J. D. Lazell, Jr. 1989. A contribution to the ornithology of the British Virgin Islands. *Carib. J. Sci.* 25: 115–118.

Nosel, J. 1994. Parc Naturel Regional de la Martinique. *Pitirre* 7(3): 11.

Nuttall, P. A. 1984. Tick-borne viruses in seabird colonies. *Seabird* 7: 31–41.

Nutting, C. C. 1895. Narrative and preliminary report of Bahama Expedition. *Bull. Lab. Nat. Hist. State Univ. Iowa* 3: 1–251.

Ober, F. A. 1880. *Camps in the Caribbees*. Boston, Mass.: Lee and Shepard, Publishers.

———. 1899. *Camps in the Caribbees: The adventures of a natu-*

ralist in the Lesser Antilles, 2nd ed. Boston, Mass.: Lee and Shepard, Publishers.

Oexmelin, A.-O. 1775. Histoire des aventuriers filibustiers qui se sont signalés dans les Indes . . . [avec] la vie, les moeurs & les coutumes des boucanie & des habitans de St. Domingue & de la Tortue. Nouvelle ed. Paris: Trévoux, La Compagnie.

Ogden, N. B., W. B. Gladfelter, J. C. Ogden, and E. H. Gladfelter. 1985. Marine and terrestrial flora and fauna notes on Sombrero Island in the Caribbean. Atoll Res. Bull. 292: 61–74.

Ogilvie-Grant, W. R. 1898. [Remarks on tropicbirds]. Bull. Br. Ornithol. Club 7: 23–24.

Olson, S. L. 1978. A paleontological perspective of West Indian birds and mammals. Pp. 99–117 in Gill, F. B., ed., Zoogeography in the Caribbean. Special Publ. no. 13. Philadelphia: Academy of Natural Science.

———. 1982. Biological archeology in the West Indies. Fla. Anthropol. 35: 162–168.

Olson, S. L., and P. J. Hearty. 2003. Probable extirpation of a breeding colony of Short-tailed Albatross (Phoebastria albatrus) on Bermuda by Pleistocene sea-level rise. Proc. Natl. Acad. Sci. 100(22): 12825–12829.

Olson, S. L., and W. B. Hilgartner. 1982. Fossil and subfossil birds from the Bahamas. Pp. 22–56 in Olson, S. L., ed., Fossil vertebrates from the Bahamas. Smithson. Contrib. Paleobiol. 48. Washington, D.C.: Smithsonian Institution Press.

Olson, S. L., H. F. James, and C. A. Meister. 1981. Winter field notes and specimen weights of Cayman Island birds. Bull. Br. Ornithol. Club 101: 339–346.

Olson, S. L., G. K. Pregill, and W. B. Hilgartner. 1990. Studies on fossil and extant vertebrates from San Salvador (Watling's) Island, Bahamas. Smithsonian Contrib. Zool. no. 508. Washington, D.C.: Smithsonian Inst. Press.

Olson, S. L., D. B. Wingate, P. J. Hearty, and F. V. Grady. 2005. Prodromus of vertebrate paleontology and geochronology of Bermuda. Pp. 1–14 in Alcover, J. A., and P. Bover, eds., Proceedings of the International Symposium "Insular Vertebrate Evolution: the Palaeontological Approach." Monografies de la Societat d'Historia Natural de les Balears, 12.

Orbigny, A. D. d.' 1839. [Mamiferos y] Aves [de la Isla de Cuba]. In Sagra, R. de la, ed., Historia fisica politica y natural de la isla de Cuba. Segunda parte: Historia natural, vol. 3. Paris: Arthus Bertrand.

———. 1839. Ornithologie [de l'île de Cuba]. In Sagra, R. de la, ed., Histoire physique, politique et naturelle de l'Ile de Cuba. 1839–56 [i.e., 1857], vol. 3. Paris: Arthus Bertrand.

Ortega Ricaurte, D. 1941. Los cayos colombianos del Caribe. Boletín de la Sociedad Geográfica de Colombia 7(3): 279–291.

Orton-Palmer, A. 1990. Nest site selection and reproductive success in the Brown Noddy (Anous stolidus) on Frenchcap Cay, U.S. Virgin Islands. M.S. thesis. Dekalb: Northern Illinois University.

Osborne, D. R. 1993. Nest site selection in Least Terns (Sterna antillarum). Pp. 97–102 in Eshbaugh, W. H., ed., Proceedings of the fourth symposium on the natural history of the

Bahamas. San Salvador, Bahama Islands: Bahamian Field Station.

Ottenwalder, J. A. 1979. Aves de la Isla Alto Velo. NP-15/79, pp. 161–162 in Cicero J., ed., Naturalista Postal 1976–1979. Carta Ocasional del Herbario. Santo Domingo, República Dominicana: Universidad Autonoma de Santo Domingo.

———. 1979. Una visita a la Isla Alto Velo. Zoodom 3: 20–31.

———. 1982. Primer registro del Rabijunco de Pico Rojo, Phaeton aethereus, (Phaethontidae: Pelecaniformes) en la Republica Dominicana. NP-30/82, pp. 1–2 in Cicero, J., ed., Naturalista Postal, 1982. Carta Ocasional del Herbario. Santo Domingo, República Dominicana: Universidad Autonoma de Santo Domingo.

———. 1992. Recovery plan for the Black-capped Petrel (Pterodroma hasitata) in southern Haiti. Prepared for the Macaya National Park Project–University of Florida, MacArthur Foundation, and USAID–Haiti. Gainesville: University of Florida.

Ottenwalder, J. A., and T. A. Vargas Mora. 1981. Nueva localidad para el Diabotin en la República Dominicana. NP-36/79, pp. 185–186 in Marcano F., E. de J., and J. Cicero, eds., Naturalista Postal 1976–1979. Carta Ocasional del Herbario. Santo Domingo, República Dominicana: Universidad Autonoma de Santo Domingo.

Overpeck, J., M. Sturm, J. Francis, D. Perovich, M. Serreze, R. Benner, E. Carmack, E. Chapin, S. Gerlach, L. Hamilton, L. H. and M. Holland, H. Huntington, J. Key, A. Lloyd, G. MacDonald, J. McFadden, D. Noone, T. Prowse, P. Schlosser, and C. Vörösmarty. 2005. Arctic system on trajectory to new, seasonally ice-free state. Eos, Transactions, American Geophysical Union 86(309): 312–13.

Oviedo y Valdés, G. F. de. 1526. De la natural hystoria de las Indias. Toledo, Spain: Remón de Petras.

———. 1851–55. In Historia general y natural de las Indias, islas y tierra firme del Mar Océano. Madrid, Spain: Imprenta de la Real Academia de la Historia.

Palmer, R. S. (ed.). 1962. Handbook of North American birds. New Haven, Conn.: Yale University Press.

Parkes, K. C. 1952. Taxonomic notes on the Laughing Gull. Proc. Biol. Soc. Wash. 65: 193–195.

Parnell, J. F., D. G. Ainley, H. Blokpoel, B. Cain, T. W. Custer, J. L. Dust, S. Kress, J. A. Kushlan, W. E. Southern, L. E. Stenzel, and B. C. Thompson. 1988. Colonial waterbird management in North America. Colonial Waterbirds 11: 129–169.

Paterson, A. 1968. New species records for the Bahamas. Bull. Br. Ornithol. Club 88: 109–110.

———. 1968. The birds of Fresh Creek. Fla. Nat. 41: 117–118, 120.

Paulson, D. R. 1966. New records of birds from the Bahama Islands. Notulae Naturae, Acad. Nat. Sci. Philadelphia 394: 1–15.

Paulson, D. R., G. H. Orians, and C. F. Leck. 1969. Notes on birds of Isla San Andrés. Auk 86: 755–758.

Paynter, R. A., Jr. 1947. The fate of banded Kent Island Herring Gulls. Bird-Banding 18: 156–170.

———. 1956. Birds of the Swan Islands. *Wilson Bull.* 68: 103–110.

Peña Franjul, M. 1978. Investigacion de seis (6) habitats de la fauna autoctoma Dominicana. III: Laguna Salada. *Zoodom* 1: 51–98.

Pennycuick, C. J., F. C. Schaffner, M. R. Fuller, H. H. Obrecht, III, and L. Sternberg. 1990. Foraging flights of the White-tailed Tropicbird (*Phaethon lepturus*): Radiotracking and doubly-labelled water. *Colon. Waterbirds* 13: 96–102.

Pérez Mena, E., P. Rodríguez Casariego, D. Rodríguez Batista, A. Parada Isada, O. Barrios, and E. Ruiz Rojas. 2005. Primer registro de *Sterna sandvicensis eurygnatha* para Cuba. *J. Carib. Ornithol.* 18: 29–30.

Pérez-Rivera, R. A. 1979. *Lista revisada de los animales vulnerables, amenazados o en peligro de extincion en Puerto Rico.* Cuadernos de La Revista Cayey no. 3. Cayey: Universidad de Puerto Rico.

———. 1981. Algunos de los problemas que podrían causar los exóticos que han alcanzado el estado silvestre en Puerto Rico. Pp. 35–46 *in* Nieves Rivera, L. O., R. A. Pérez-Rivera, G. Malavé Gutiérrez, C. Goenaga Portela, and M. E. Rivera Rosa, eds., *Memorias del Segundo Coloquio sobre la Fauna de Puerto Rico.* Humacao, Puerto Rico: Colegio Universitario de Humacao.

———. 1983. Nuevos informes y comentarios sobre las aves de la Isla de Mona. *Science-Ciencia* 10: 97–101.

———. 1984. Aspects of the reproductive ecology of the White-tailed Tropicbird on Mona Island. *Colon. Waterbirds Group Newsl.* 8: 38.

———. 1987. Additional records and notes on migratory water birds in Puerto Rico, West Indies. *Carib. J. Sci.* 23: 368–372.

Pérez-Rivera, R. A., and G. Bonilla. 1982. Los huracanes: Algunos de sus efectos sobre aves en Puerto Rico, incluyendo sus patrones de comportamiento. Pp. 123–135 *in* Nievas Rivera, L. O., and R. A. Pérez-Rivera, eds., *Memorias del Tercer Simposio sobre la Fauna de Puerto Rico.* Humacao: Universidad de Puerto Rico.

Pérez-Rivera, R. A., and L. Miranda. 1994. Corroboración de algunos registros de aves para Puerto Rico. *Pitirre* 7(1): 2–3.

Peters, J. L. 1917. Birds of the northern coast of the Dominican Republic. *Bull. Mus. Comp. Zool.* 61: 391–426.

———. 1927. Birds of the island of Anguilla, West Indies. *Auk* 44: 532–538.

Phelps, W. H., Jr. 1945 (1944). Las aves de las Islas Los Testigos, Los Frailes y la Tortuga. *Bol. Soc. Venez. Cienc. Nat.* 9(60): 257–283.

———. 1948. Las aves de la Isla La Blanquilla y de Los Morros El Fondeadero y La Horquilla del Archipiélago de Los Hermanos. *Bol. Soc. Venez. Cienc. Nat.* 11(71): 85–118.

Phelps, W. H., Sr., and W. H. Phelps, Jr. 1950. Las aves de las Islas los Roques y las Aves y descripción de un nuevo canario de mangle. *Bol. Soc. Venez. Cienc. Nat.* 13(76): 7–30.

———. 1957. Las aves de Isla de Aves, Venezuela. *Bol. Soc. Venez. Cienc. Nat.* 18(88): 63–72.

———. 1959a. Las aves de la Isla La Orchila. *Bol. Soc. Venez. Cienc. Nat.* 20(93): 252–266.

———. 1959b. La nidificación de las aves marinas en el Archipiélago de Los Roques. *Bol. Soc. Venez. Cienc. Nat.* 20(94): 325–336.

Philibosian, R. 1975. *Census of nesting birds in the Virgin Islands.* Unpublished report. Fredericksted, St. Croix, U.S. Virgin Islands: Information Services.

Philipon, A. 1931. Note sur une Fregate marine. *Oiseau Rev. Fr. Ornithol.* 1: 724.

Philipson, W. R. 1940. Notes on birds seen on a voyage to the West Indies and back. *Br. Birds* 33: 245–247.

Pienkowski, M. (ed.). 2002a. *Plan for biodiversity management and sustainable development around Turks & Caicos Ramsar Site.* U.K. Overseas Territories Conservation Forum, Peterborough, U.K. www.ukotcf.org (Publications).

———. 2002. *Plan for biodiversity management and sustainable development around Turks and Caicos Ramsar Site.* Output from the Darwin Initiative project "Developing biodiversity management capacity around the Ramsar site in Turks and Caicos Islands." Provenciales, Turks and Caicos Islands: Turks & Caicos National Trust.

——— (ed.). 2005. *Review of existing and potential Ramsar sites in UK Overseas Territories and Crown Dependencies.* Final Report on Contract CR0294 to the U.K. Department of Environment, Food and Rural Affairs. U.K. Overseas Territories Conservation Forum. Pp. 946. www.ukotcf.org

——— (ed.). 2006. Important Bird Areas in the Turks & Caicos Islands. Pp.247–272 *in* Sanders S. M., ed., *Important Bird Areas in the UK Overseas Territories: Priority sites for conservation.* Sandy, Bedfordshire, U.K.: Royal Society for the Protection of Birds.

Pienkowski, M., A. E. Pienkowski, and B. N. Manco. 2005. Birds on the outer cays of the Turks and Caicos Islands. *J. Carib. Ornithol.* 18: 31–43.

Pierce, J. J. 1990. Effects of Hurricane Hugo on cay-nesting avifauna in the U.S. Virgin Islands. *Colon. Waterbird Soc. Newsl.* 14: 23.

———. 1991. Red-billed Tropicbird breeding in the United States Virgin Islands. *Colon. Waterbird Soc. Newsl.* 15: 33.

———. 1992. *Red-billed Tropicbird (Phaethon aethereus) breeding in the U.S. Virgin Islands.* Final Report. Pittman Robertson Wildlife Restoration Aid Grant W-5-7, Study 1. St. Thomas, U.S. Virgin Islands: Division of Fish and Wildlife.

———. 1996a. *Survey of cay nesting avifauna in the U.S. Virgin Islands.* Pittman-Robertson Wildlife Restoration Aid Grant W5-11, Study 2. St. Thomas, U.S. Virgin Islands: Division of Fish and Wildlife.

———. 1996b. *Comparative habitat use and reproductive success of Sooty Terns (Sterna fuscata) on Saba Island, U.S. Virgin Islands.* Final Report. Pittman-Robertson Wildlife Restoration Aid Grant W5-10, Study 6. St. Thomas, U.S. Virgin Islands: Division of Fish and Wildlife.

———. 1997. *Nesting habitat and nesting success of Sooty Terns* on Saba Island, U.S. Virgin Islands. M.S. thesis. Tampa: University of South Florida.

———. 2001. *Survey of Roseate Tern (Sterna dougallii) breeding colonies in the U.S. Virgin Islands.* Final Report. U.S. Fish and Wildlife Service, Pittman-Robertson Wildlife Restoration Aid Grant W-5. St. Thomas, U.S. Virgin Islands: Division of Fish and Wildlife.

Pierce, K. E., R. Harris, L. S. Larned and M. A. Pokras. 2004. Obstruction and starvation associated with plastic ingestion in a Northern Gannet *Morus bassanus* and a Greater Shearwater *Puffinus gravis. Marine Ornithology* 32: 187–189.

Pinchon, P. R. 1953. Aperçu sur l'avifaune de la Désirade (Dépendence de la Guadeloupe). *Oiseau Rev. Fr. Ornithol.* 23: 161–170.

———. 1961. Deuxième note complémentaire sur l'avifaune des Antilles Françaises. *Oiseau Rev. Fr. Ornithol.* 31: 85–99.

———. 1963. *Faune des Antilles Françaises: Les oiseaux.* Fort-de-France, Martinique: Muséum National d'Histoire Naturelle.

———. 1976. *Faune des Antilles Françaises: Les oiseaux.* 2ème ed. Fort-de-France, Martinique: Muséum National d'Histoire Naturelle.

Pinchon, P. R., and M. Bon Saint-Côme. 1951. Notes et observations sur les oiseaux des Antilles Françaises. *Oiseau Rev. Fr. Ornithol.* 21: 229–277.

———. 1952. Note complémentaire sur l'avifaune des Antilles Française. *Oiseau Rev. Fr. Ornithol.* 22: 113–119.

Platenburg, R., F. E. Hayes, D. B. McNair, and J. J. Pierce. 2005. *A comprehensive wildlife conservation strategy for the U.S. Virgin Islands.* St. Thomas, U.S. Virgin Islands: Division of Fish and Wildlife.

Podolsky, R. H., and S. W. Kress. 1989. Plastic debris incorporated into Double-crested Cormorant nest in the Gulf of Maine. *J. Field Ornithol.* 60: 248–250.

Poey, F. 1851–1858. *Memorias sobre la historia natural de la Isla de Cuba, acompañadas de sumarios latinos y extractos en francés.* La Habana, Cuba: Imprenta de Barcina.

———. 1851–1855. Apuntes sobre la fauna de la Isla de Piños. Pp. 424–431 in *Memorias sobre la Historia Natural de la Isla de Cuba, acompañadas de sumarios Latinos y extractos en Frances,* vol. I. La Habana, Cuba: Imprenta de Barcina.

Poey y Aguirre, A. 1848. Catalogo Metodico de las Aves de la Isla de Cuba. *Mem. Real Soc. Econ., La Habana,* ser. 2, 6: 97–108.

Porter, S. 1930. Notes on the birds of Dominica. *Avicult. Mag.* 8: 114–126.

———. 1930. Notes on the birds of Dominica. *Avicult. Mag.* 8: 146–158.

———. 1936. A West Indian diary. *Avicult. Mag.* 1: 96–112.

Posada Rodríguez, R. M., A. Kirkconnell, F. de Arazoza, and A. Llanes Sosa. 1989. Ornitocenosis de los cayos Campos, Avalos y Cantiles, Archipiélago de los Canarreos, Cuba. *Poeyana* 365: 1–9.

Pregill, G. K., D. W. Steadman, S. L. Olson, and F. V. Grady. 1988. Late Holocene fossil vertebrates from Burma Quarry,

Antigua, Lesser Antilles. *Smithsonian Contrib. Zool.* no. 463. Washington, D.C.: Smithsonian Inst. Press.

Pregill, G. K., D. W. Steadman, and D. R. Watters. 1994. Late Quaternary vertebrate faunas of the Lesser Antilles: Historical components of Caribbean biogeography. *Bull. Carnegie Mus. Nat. Hist.* 30: 1–51.

Rabié, M. René-G. de. [1773–1784]. [*Histoire naturelle de St. Domingo*]. Paris: [Fabrique toutes sortes de Registres & Portfeu].

Raffaele, H. A. 1973. Assessment of Mona Island avifauna. Apéndice: K. Pp. K1–K32 in *Mona and Monito islands: An assessment of their natural and historical resources,* vol. 2. San Juan: Estado Libre Asociado de Puerto Rico Oficina del Gobernador, Junta de Calidad Ambiental.

———. 1973. *The fauna of Vieques Island.* Unpublished report. San Juan: Puerto Rico Department of Natural Resources.

———. 1975. *Important natural wildlife areas.* Unpublished report. San Juan: Puerto Rico Department of Natural Resources.

———. 1977. La fauna de vertebrados de Puerto Rico. Pp. 261–303 in Baez, V., ed., *El Gran Enciclopedia de Puerto Rico,* vol. 9. San Juan, Puerto Rico: Tome lo Editorial Obre.

———. 1981. New records of bird species for Puerto Rico and one for the West Indies. *Am. Birds* 35: 142–143.

Raffaele, H. A., J. M. Duffield, and J. A. Moreno. 1979. *Critical wildlife areas of Puerto Rico.* Federal Aid Project PW-1-7. San Juan: Department of Natural Resources, Commonwealth of Puerto Rico, Area of Planning and Resource Analysis.

Raffaele, H. A., J. Wiley, O. Garrido, A. Keith, and J. Raffaele. 1998a. *A guide to the birds of the West Indies.* Princeton, N.J.: Princeton University Press.

———. 1998b. *Birds of the West Indies.* Helm identification Guides. London: Christopher Helm Publisher, A & C Black.

Rams Beceña, A. 1987. Segundo reporte para Cuba de *Phaeton aethereus mesonauta* Peters, Rabijunco de Pico Rojo. *Garciana* 2: 3–4.

Rams Beceña, A., A. Coy Otero, and J. Espinosa. 1987. Contribucion al conocimiento de la fauna de Cayo Fragoso, costa norte de Cuba, Parte III: Vertebrados. *Garciana* 5: 2–3.

Ramsden, C. T. 1911. Nesting of man-o'-war-bird (*Fregata aquila*) in Cuba. *Auk* 28: 254.

———. 1912. *Phœtusa magnirostris* Licht. in Cuba. *Auk* 29: 100.

Rappole, J. H., E. S. Morton, T. E. Lovejoy, III, and J. L. Ruos. 1983. *Nearctic avian migrants in the Neotropics: With an appendix on Latin American laws by Byron Swift.* Washington, D.C.: U.S. Department of the Interior, Fish and Wildlife Service.

———. 1993. *Aves migratorias nearticas en los neotropicos.* Front Royal, Va.: Conservation and Research Center, National Zoological Park, Smithsonian Institution.

Read, A. C. 1912. Birds observed on the Isle of Pines, Cuba, 1912. *Oölogist* 30: 130–131.

———. 1913. Birds seen on a long journey. *Oölogist* 30: 264–268.

Reid, K., and J. P. Croxall. 2001. Environmental response of upper tropic-level predators reveals a system change in an Antarctic marine ecosystem. *Proc. Royal Soc. London B* 268: 377–384.

Reis, K. R., and D. W. Steadman. 1999. Archaeology of Trants, Montserrat. Part 5: Prehistoric avifauna. *Annals of Carnegie Museum* 68(4): 275–287.

[Richardson, J.]. 1993a. Tern, Roseate. *Gosse Bird Club Broads.* 61: 18.

[———]. 1993b. Bridled Tern. *Gosse Bird Club Broads.* 61: 18.

Richmond, C. W. 1899. *Pelecanus occidentalis* vs. *P. fuscus. Auk* 16: 178.

Ridgway, R. 1888. Catalogue of a collection of birds made by Mr. Chas. H. Townsend, on islands in the Caribbean Sea and in Honduras. *Proc. U.S. Natl. Mus.* (1887) 10: 572–597.

———. 1891. List of birds collected on the Bahama Islands by the naturalists of the Fish Commission steamer *Albatross. Auk* 8: 333–339.

Riley, J. H. 1904. Catalogue of a collection of birds from Barbuda and Antigua, British West Indies. *Smithson. Misc. Coll.* 47: 277–291.

———. 1905. Birds of the Bahama Islands. Pp. 347–368 *in* Shattuck, G. B., ed., *The Bahama Islands*. New York: Macmillan–Geographic Society of Baltimore.

———. 1905. List of birds collected or observed during the Bahama Expedition of the Geographic Society of Baltimore. *Auk* 22: 349–360.

Ripley, S. D., and G. E. Watson, III. 1956. Cuban bird notes. *Postilla* 26: 1–6.

Ritter, K. 1836. *Naturhistorische Reise nach der Westindieschen Insel Hayti, Auf Kosten Sr. Majestät des Kaisers von Oesterreich.* Stuttgart: Hallberger.

———. 1920. *Voyage d'histoire naturelle et d'études botaniques dans les Indes Occidentales, île d'Haiti.* Port-au-Prince, Haiti: Collection bibliothèque Edmond Mangones deposited at Bibliothèque de Saint Louis de Gonzague.

Robertson, W. B., Jr. 1960. *Observations on the birds of St. John, Virgin Islands.* Project completion report to the National Park Service. Washington, D.C.: U.S. Department of the Interior.

———. 1962. Observations on the birds of St. John, Virgin Islands. *Auk* 79: 44–76.

———. 1964. The terns of the Dry Tortugas. *Bull. Fla. State Mus., Biol. Sci.* 8: 1–95.

———. 1969. Transatlantic migration of juvenile Sooty Terns. *Nature* 222: 632–634.

Robinson, K. L. 1986. Culebra National Wildlife Refuge, Puerto Rico. *Am. Birds* 40: 217–223.

[Rochefort, C. C. de]. 1658. *Histoire naturelle et morale des îles Antilles de l'Amérique.* Rotterdam: Arnout Leers.

[———]. 1666. *The history of the Caribby-Islands, viz. Barbados, St. Christophers, St. Vincents, Martinico, Dominico, Barbouthos, Montserrat, Mevis, Antego, &c. In two books.* Trans. John Davies. London: Thomas Dring and John Starkey.

[———]. 1681. *Histoire Naturelle et Morale des îles Antilles de l'Amérique, Enrichie d'un grand nombre de belles figures en taille douce, qui représentent au naturel les places, & les Raretéz les plus considérables qui y sont décrites. Avec un Vocabulaire Caraïbe.* Rotterdam: Dernière ed. Reinier Leers.

Rodríguez, P., A. Parada, E. Pérez, D. Rodríguez, O. Barrios, E. Ruiz, and P. Blanco. In press. Primer registro de nidificación del Pampero de Audubon *Puffinus lherminieri* (Aves: Procelariidae) en Cuba. *J. Carib. Ornithol.*

Rodríguez Batista, D., and M. E. Garcia Romero. 1987. Ornitocenosis de una vegetación litoral al norte de La Habana. *Poeyana* 347: 1–7.

Rodríguez Ferrer, M. 1876. *Naturaleza y civilización de la grandiosa Isla de Cuba, ó estudios variados y científicos, al alcance de todos, y otros históricos, estadísticos y políticos. Parte primera: Naturaleza.* Madrid: Imprenta de J. Noguera á Cargo de M. Martinez.

Rojer, A. 1997a. *Biological inventory of Saba.* Unpublished report. Curaçao, Netherlands Antilles: Carmabi Foundation.

———. 1997b. *Biological inventory of Saint Eustatius.* Unpublished report. Curaçao, Netherlands Antilles: Carmabi Foundation.

Rolle, F. J. 1961. The avifauna of Mona Island, Puerto Rico. *Fla. Nat.* 34: 195–202.

———. 1961. Notes and records of little-known species of birds from Puerto Rico. *J. Agric. Univ. P.R.* 45: 333–341.

———. 1966. Notes on birds from some West Indian islands. *Stahlia* 7: 1–4.

Rolle, F. J., H. Heatwole, R. Levins, and F. Torres. 1964. Fauna notes on Monito Island, Puerto Rico. *Carib. J. Sci.* 4: 321–322.

Rooks, D. 1988. Bird observations in Tobago December 1985 to November 1987. *Living World, J. Trinidad and Tobago Field Naturalists' Club* 1987–1988: 41–42.

Root, T. L., J. T. Price, K. R. Hall, S. H. Schneider, C. Rosenzweig, and J. A. Pounds. 2003. Fingerprints of global warming on wild animals and plants. *Nature* 421: 37–42.

Rose, P. M., and D. A. Scott. 1997. Waterfowl population estimates. Wetlands International Special Publication 44. Wageningen, Netherlands: Wetlands International.

Rothschild, L. W. 1907. *Extinct Birds: An attempt to unite in one volume a short account of those birds which have become extinct in historical times—that is, within the last six or seven hundred years. To which are added a few which still exist, but are on the verge of extinction. With 45 colored plates, embracing 63 subjects and other illustrations.* London: Hutchinson and Company.

———. 1907. On extinct and vanishing birds. Pp. 191–217 *in* Hartert. E. J. O., and J. L. Bonhote, eds., *Proceedings of the Fourth International Ornithological Congress (1905).* London: Dulan and Company.

———. 1907. On the genus *Fregata. Novit. Zool.* 22: 145–146.

Rothstein, S. I. 1973. Plastic particle pollution of the surface of the Atlantic Ocean: Evidence from a seabird. *Condor* 75: 344–345.

Rowlands, B. W. 2001a. St. Helena and the dependencies of

Ascension Island and Tristan da Cunha, including Gough Island. Pp. 711–725 in Fishpool, L. D. C., and M. I. Evans, eds., *Important Bird Areas in Africa and associated islands: Priorities for conservation*. BirdLife Conservation Series no. 11. Newbury, U.K.: Pisces Publications.

———. 2001. St. Helena and the dependencies of Ascension Island and Tristan da Cunha, including Gough Islands, June 2002. *J. Carib. Ornithol.* 18: 31–43.

Rowlands, B. W., T. Trueman, S. L. Olson, M. N. McCulloch, and R. K. Brooke. 1998. *The birds of St Helena*. BOU Checklist no. 16. Tring, U.K.: British Ornithologists' Union.

Russell, S. M., J. C. Barlow, and D. W. Lamm. 1979. Status of some birds on Isla San Andres and Isla Providencia, Colombia. *Condor* 81: 98–100.

Rutten, M. 1934. Observations on Cuban birds. *Ardea* 23: 109–126.

Sagra, R. de la. 1842. *Album de aves cubanas reunidas durante el viage de D. Ramon de la Sagra*. Paris: Imprenta y Litografia de Maulde y Renou.

———. 1842. *Album d'oiseaux de Cuba réunis pendant le voyage de M. Ramonde la Sagra dédié à S. M. la Reine Isabelle II*. Paris: Imprimerie et lithographie de Maulde et Renou.

Saliva, J. E. 1989. Possible effects of Hurricane Hugo on the seabird populations of Culebra Island. *Colon. Waterbird Soc. Newsl.* 13: 33.

———. 1989. Behavioral thermoregulation of breeding Sooty Terns. *Colon. Waterbird Soc. Newsl.* 13: 26.

———. 1990. El rol de la vegetación en los habitos de anidamiento de la gaviota oscura, *Sterna fuscata*. Pp. 130–134 *in XVI Simposio de los Recursos Naturales*. San Juan: Departamento de Recursos Naturales de Puerto Rico.

———. 1990. Laughing Gull foraging technique at a Sooty Tern colony. *Colon. Waterbird Soc. Newsl.* 14: 24.

———. 1993. *Caribbean Roseate Tern Recovery Plan*. Atlanta, Ga.: U.S. Fish and Wildlife Service.

———. 1994. *Vieques y su fauna. Vieques wildlife manual*. Boquerón, Puerto Rico: U.S. Department of the Interior, U.S. Fish and Wildlife Service.

———. 1995. *The importance of vegetation in the ecology and behavior of Sooty Terns in a Caribbean colony*. Ph.D. dissertation. Piscataway, N.J.: Rutgers University.

———. 2000a. Conservation priorities for Sooty Terns in the West Indies. Pp. 103–108 *in* Schreiber, E. A., and D. S. Lee, eds., *Status and conservation of West Indian seabirds*. Special Publication no. 1. Ruston, La.: Society of Caribbean Ornithology.

———. 2000b. Conservation priorities for Roseate Terns in the West Indies. Pp. 87–95 *in* Schreiber, E. A., and D. S. Lee, eds., *Status and conservation of West Indian seabirds*. Special Publication no. 1. Ruston, La.: Society of Caribbean Ornithology.

Saliva, J. E., and J. Burger. 1988. Dense vegetation as a nesting habitat of Sooty Terns (*Sterna fuscata*). *Bull. Ecol. Soc. Am.* 69: 284.

———. 1989. Effect of experimental manipulation of vegeta-tion density on nest-site selection in Sooty Terns. *Condor* 91: 689–698.

———. 1995. Thermal stress and behavior of Sooty Terns nesting under variable vegetation density. *Colon. Waterbird Soc. Bull.* 19: 62.

Saliva, J. E., and J. Pierce. 1993. Distribution of Roseate Tern colonies in the Puerto Rico Bank. *Colon. Waterbird Soc. Bull.* 17: 53.

———. 1996. *Survey of Roseate Tern breeding colonies in the British Virgin Islands*. USFWS Annual Report. Boquerón, Puerto Rico: U.S. Fish and Wildlife Service, Caribbean Field Office.

Saliva, J. E., and D. A. Shealer. 1991. Factors influencing reproductive success and colony site fidelity of Roseate Terns in the Caribbean. *Colon. Waterbird Soc. Newsl.* 15: 34.

———. 1991. Aspects of the breeding biology of Roseate Terns in Puerto Rico. *Pitirre* 4(3): 8.

Sallé, M. A. 1857. Liste des oiseaux rapportés et observés dans la République Dominicaine (Ancienne Partie Espagnole de l'île St. Domingue ou d'Haiti), pendant son voyage de 1849 à 1851. *Proc. Zool. Soc. London* 25: 230–237.

Salmon, L. 1965. Caspian Tern. *Gosse Bird Club Broads.* 5: 22.

———. 1967. Black Tern. *Gosse Bird Club Broads.* 8: 16.

———. 1970. White-tailed tropic birds. *Gosse Bird Club Broads.* 15: 18.

Sanchez, B., V. Berovides Alvarez, and A. Gonzalez. 1992. Aspectos ecológicos de la avifauna de la Reserva Natural Cayo Caguanes provincia de Sancti Spíritus, Cuba. *Rep. Invest. Inst. Ecol. Sistem.* Diciembre: 1–16.

Sanchez, B., M. E. Garcia Romero, and D. Rodríguez Batista. 1991. Aves de Cayo Levisa, Archipiélago de los Colorados, Pinar del Río, Cuba. *Invest. Mar. CICIMAR* 6: 247–249.

Sanchez Falcon, C. 1940. Nuevo hallazgo del "Dovekie" (*Alle alle*) en Cuba. *Mem. Soc. Cubana Hist. Nat. "Felipe Poey"* 14: 98.

Sanders, S. M. (ed.). 2006. *Important Bird Areas in the UK Overseas Territories: Priority sites for conservation*. Sandy, Bedfordshire, U.K.: Royal Society for the Protection of Birds.

Sanderson, D. J. 1982. Birds of the Turks and Caicos Islands. *Turks and Caicos Current* 1982: 35–42.

Saunders, J. B. 1957. Bird life on Soldado Rock. *Trinidad Regent News* 7(3): 4–7.

Scambos, T., J. Bohlander, C. Shuman, and P. Skvarca. 2004. Glacier acceleration and thinning after ice shelf collapse in the Larsen B embayment, Antarctica. *Geophysical Res. News* 31, L18402 doi: 10.1029/2004GL02670.

Schaffner, F. C. 1984. White-tailed Tropicbird breeding at Culebra, Puerto Rico in 1984. *Colon. Waterbirds Group Newsl.* 8: 30.

———. 1985. *White-tailed Tropicbird (Phaethon lepturus) breeding at Culebra, Puerto Rico: Report for 1984–1985 and outline of continued study*. Unpublished report to U.S. Fish and Wildlife Service. Coral Gables, Fla.: University of Miami.

———. 1986. White-tailed Tropicbird breeding at Cayo Luis Peña, Puerto Rico. *Colon. Waterbird Soc. Newsl.* 10: 36.

———. 1987. *White-tailed Tropicbird (Phaethon lepturus) breeding at Cayo Luis Peña, Culebra National Wildlife Refuge, Puerto Rico: Report for 1984–1986.* Unpublished report. Cabo Rojo, Puerto Rico: U.S. Fish and Wildlife Service.

———. 1988. *The breeding biology and energetics of the White-tailed Tropicbird (Phaethon lepturus) at Culebra, Puerto Rico.* Ph.D. dissertation, Coral Gables, Fla.: University of Miami.

———. 1989. Regulation of food provisioning patterns of White-tailed Tropicbirds. *Colon. Waterbird Soc. Newsl.* 13: 26.

———. 1990. Feed size and feeding periodicity in pelagic birds: Notes on methodology. *Colon. Waterbirds* 13: 7–15.

———. 1990. Food provisioning by White-tailed Tropicbirds: Effects on the developmental pattern of chicks. *Ecology* 71: 375–390.

———. 1991. Nest-site selection and nesting success of White-tailed Tropicbirds (*Phaethon lepturus*) at Cayo Luís Peña, Puerto Rico. *Auk* 108: 911–922.

Schaffner, F. C., M. R. Fuller, C. J. Pennycuick, and H. H. Obrecht, III. 1989. Radio tracking of White-tailed Tropicbirds over the Caribbean Sea. *Pacific Seabird Group Bull.* 16: 41.

Schaffner, F. C., R. L. Norton, and J. Taylor. 1986. Range extension of Cayenne Terns on the Puerto Rico Bank. *Wilson Bull.* 98: 317–318.

Schaffner, F. C., and P. K. Swart. 1991. Influence of diet and environmental water on the carbon and oxygen isotopic signatures of seabird eggshell carbonate. *Bull. Mar. Sci.* 48: 23–38.

Schmidt, K. P. 1926. The amphibians and reptiles of Mona Island, West Indies. *Field Mus. Nat. Hist. Zoology Ser.* 12: 147–163.

Schreiber, B. A. 1996. *Barbuda frigatebird colony status report. Preserving the birds as an economic resource.* Report to the Organisation of Eastern Caribbean States, Natural Resources Management Unit. Castries, St. Lucia.

Schreiber, E. A. 1997. *Barbuda Magnificent Frigatebird colony management and monitoring plan.* Report to the Organisation of Eastern Caribbean States. Castries, St. Lucia: OECS.

———. 1997. *Barbuda Magnificent Frigatebird colony: Status report and management recommendations.* Report to Environmental and Coastal Resources (Encore). Castries, St. Lucia: Encore.

———. 2000a. Action plan for conservation of West Indian seabirds. Pp. 182–191 *in* Schreiber, E. A., and D. S. Lee, eds., *Status and conservation of West Indian seabirds.* Special Publication no. 1. Ruston, La.: Society of Caribbean Ornithology.

———. 2000b. Status of Red-footed, Brown and Masked boobies in the West Indies. Pp 46–57 *in* Schreiber, E. A., and D. S. Lee, eds., *Status and conservation of West Indian seabirds.* Special Publication no. 1. Ruston, La.: Society of Caribbean Ornithology.

———. 2000c. The vital role of research and museum collections in the conservation of seabirds. Pp. 126–133 *in* Schreiber, E. A., and D. S. Lee, eds., *Status and conservation of West In-

dian seabirds.* Special Publication no. 1. Ruston, La.: Society of Caribbean Ornithology.

———, and J. Burger. 2002. *Biology of marine birds.* Boca Ratón, Fla.: CRC Press.

Schreiber, E. A., and D. S. Lee (eds.). 2000a. *Status and conservation of West Indian seabirds.* Special Publication no. 1. Ruston, La.: Society of Caribbean Ornithology.

Schreiber, E. A., and D. S. Lee. 2000b. West Indian seabirds: A disappearing natural resource. Pp. 1–10 *in* Schreiber, E. A., and D. S. Lee, eds., *Status and conservation of West Indian seabirds.* Special Publication no. 1. Ruston, La.: Society of Caribbean Ornithology.

Schreiber, E. A., R. W. Schreiber, and G. A. Schenk. 1996. Red-footed Booby (*Sula sula*). In Poole, A., and F. Gill, eds., *The birds of North America*, no. 241. Philadelphia: Birds of North America.

Schreiber, R. W. 1979. Reproductive performance of the eastern Brown Pelican *Pelecanus occidentalis*. Contributions to Science no. 317. Natural History Museum of Los Angeles County.

Schreiber, R. W., D. W. Belitsky, and B. A. Sorrie. 1981. Notes on Brown Pelicans in Puerto Rico. *Wilson Bull.* 93: 397–400.

Schreiber, R. W., and P. J. Mock. 1988. Eastern Brown Pelicans: What does 60 years of banding tell us? *J. Field Ornithol.* 59: 171–182.

Schreiber, R. W., and E. A. Schreiber. 1983. Reproductive failure of marine birds on Christmas Island, fall 1982. *Trop. Ocean-Atmos. Newsl.* 16: 10–12.

Schwartz, A. 1969. Land birds of Isla Saona, República Dominicana. *Q. J. Florida Acad. Sci.* 32: 291–306.

Schwartz, A., and R. F. Klinikowski. 1963. Observations on West Indian birds. *Proc. Acad. Nat. Sci. Philadelphia* 115: 53–77.

———. 1965. Additional observations on West Indian birds. *Notulae Naturae, Acad. Nat. Sci. Philadelphia* 376: 1–16.

Sclater, P. L. 1910. Revised list of the birds of Jamaica. Pp. 596–619 *in* Ford, J. C., and F. Cundall, eds., *The handbook of Jamaica for 1910: Comprising historical, statistical and general information concerning the island, compiled from official and other reliable records.* Kingston: Institute of Jamaica.

Scott, W. E. D. 1891a. Observations on the birds of Jamaica, West Indies. I: Notes on the habits of the Yellow-billed Tropic Bird (*Phaëthon flavirostris*). *Auk* 8: 249–256.

———. 1891b. Observations on the birds of Jamaica, West Indies. II: A list of the birds recorded from the island, with annotations. *Auk* 8: 353–365.

SEA/DVS. 1992. *Reconocimiento y evaluación de los recursos naturales de la zona costera del este.* Santo Domingo, República Dominicana: Secretaria de Estado de Agricultura, Secretaría de vida Silvestre.

Sealey, N. E. 1994. *Bahamian landscapes: An introduction to the geography of the Bahamas*, 2nd ed. Nassau: Media Publishing.

Seaman, G. A. 1951. Wildlife resources survey of the Virgin Islands. *Pittman-Robertson Quart.* 11: 110–111.

———. 1961. *Wildlife resources survey of the Virgin Islands No.

4-R: Quarterly Rept., June. Unpublished report. St. Croix., U.S. Virgin Islands: Division of Fish and Wildlife.

Seaman, G. A., and J. E. Randall. 1962. The mongoose as a predator in the Virgin Islands. *J. Mammal.* 43: 544–546.

Shealer, D. A. 1995. *Comparative feeding ecology of Roseate and Sandwich terns in Puerto Rico and its relation to breeding performance.* Ph.D. dissertation. New Brunswick, N.J.: Rutgers University.

———. 1996. Foraging habitat use and profitability in tropical Roseate Terns and Sandwich Terns. *Auk* 113: 209–217.

———. 1999. Sandwich Tern (*Sterna sandvicensis*). *In* Poole, A., and F. Gill, eds., *The birds of North America,* no. 405. Philadelphia: Birds of North America.

Shealer, D. A., and J. Burger. 1991. Comparative foraging success between adult and immature Roseate and Sandwich terns. *Colon. Waterbird Soc. Newsl.* 15: 35.

———. 1992. A "good" versus a "bad" year for Roseate Terns breeding in Puerto Rico. *Colon. Waterbird Soc. Bull.* 16: 56–57.

———. 1992. Differential responses of tropical Roseate Terns to aerial intruders throughout the nesting cycle. *Condor* 94: 712–719.

———. 1993. Effects of interference competition on the foraging activity of tropical Roseate Terns. *Condor* 95: 322–329.

———. 1993. Prey selection by tropical Roseate and Sandwich terns during years of food abundance and food stress. *Colon. Waterbird Soc. Bull.* 17: 43.

———. 1995. Comparative foraging success between adult and one-year-old Roseate and Sandwich terns. *Colon. Waterbirds* 18: 93–99.

Shealer, D. A., and J. E. Saliva. 1992. Northeastern Roseate Terns seen at Puerto Rican colony during breeding season. *Colon. Waterbirds* 15: 152–154.

Shealer, D. A., and J. G. Zurovchak. 1995. Three extremely large clutches of Roseate Tern eggs in the Caribbean. *Colon. Waterbirds* 18: 105–107.

Shealer, D. A., J. E. Saliva, and J. Pierce. 2005. Annual survival and movement patterns of Roseate Terns breeding in Puerto Rico and the U.S. Virgin Islands. *Waterbirds* 28: 79–86.

Siegel, A. 1983. *Birds of Montserrat.* Plymouth, Montserrat: Montserrat National Trust.

Siegenthaler, U., T. F. Stocker, E. Monnin, D. Lüthi, J. Schwander, B. Stauffer, D. Raynaud, J.-M. Barnola, H. Fischer, V. Masson-Delmotte, and J. Jouzel. 2004. Stable carbon cycle–climate relationship during the Late Pleistocene. *Science* 310(5752): 1313–1317.

Simons, T. R., J. Collanzo, D. Lee, and J. Gerwin. 2002. *Conservation status of the Black-capped Petrel (Pterdroma hasitata): Colony surveys at Sierra de Baoruco, Dominican Republic, January 2002.* Unpublished report. Raleigh: North Carolina State University.

Siphron, J. 1973. Reef birds. *Gosse Bird Club Broads.* 21: 14.

———. 1976. Tropicbirds. *Gosse Bird Club Broads.* 27: 13–14.

Siri Nuñez, D. 1986. Reportes de aves anilladas: *Plegadis fal-* *cinellus* (Linnaeus) y *Sterna maximus* (Boddaert). *Hispaniolana, Publ. Ocas.* 1: 13–14.

Sladen, F. W. 1988. *Checklist of birds of St. Croix, U.S. Virgin Islands.* Revised 1988 ed. Christiansted, St. Croix, U.S. Virgin Islands: published by author.

———. 1988. Some new records and observations of birds in the Virgin Islands. *Am. Birds* 42: 1227–1231.

———. 1992. Abundance and distribution of waterbirds in two types of wetlands on St. Croix, U.S. Virgin Islands. *Ornitol. Caribeña* 3: 35–42.

Sladen, F. W., and J. Pierce. 1988. *Least Tern nesting in St. Croix, USVI.* Final Report. Pittman-Robertson Wildlife Restoration Aid Grant W-5. St. Croix, U.S. Virgin Islands: Division of Fish and Wildlife.

———. 1989. *Survey of Least Tern nesting in St. Croix.* Final Report. Pittman-Robertson Wildlife Restoration Program Grant W-5, Study 3. St. Thomas, U.S. Virgin Islands: Division of Fish and Wildlife.

Sladen, F. W., and R. H. Wauer. 1992. Third record of White-winged Tern for the West Indies. *Ornitol. Caribeña* 3: 49–50.

Sloane, H. 1707. *A voyage to the islands Madera, Barbados, Nieves, S. Christophers and Jamaica, with the natural history of the herbs and trees, four-footed beasts, fishes, birds, insects, reptiles &c.* London: printed by B. M. for the author.

Smith, D. 1994. Brown Pelican. *Gosse Bird Club Broads.* 62: 19.

———. 1994. Herring Gull. *Gosse Bird Club Broads.* 62: 21.

Smith, D., and C. Keller. 1995. Birds at mouth of the Black River, St. Elizabeth. *Gosse Bird Club Broads.* 65: 16.

———. 1995. Common Tern. *Gosse Bird Club Broads.* 65: 20.

Smith, P. W., and S. A. Smith. 1993. Tern, Sandwich. *Gosse Bird Club Broads.* 61: 17.

Smith, R. W. 1964. Bird banding in Jamaica. *Gosse Bird Club Broads.* 2: 4–5.

———. 1964. Bird banding: January to June 1964. *Gosse Bird Club Broads.* 3: 5–6.

———. 1964. Black Tern. *Gosse Bird Club Broads.* 3: 16.

———. 1965. Bird banding, 1964. *Gosse Bird Club Broads.* 4: 5–7.

———. 1965. Bird banding. *Gosse Bird Club Broads.* 5: 7–9.

———. 1966. A trip to Morant Cays. *Gosse Bird Club Broads.* 6: 5–6.

———. 1966. Bird banding. *Gosse Bird Club Broads.* 6: 7–10.

———. 1966. Colour-marked Sooty Terns. *Gosse Bird Club Broads.* 6: 10.

———. 1967. Bird banding. *Gosse Bird Club Broads.* 8: 4–6.

———. 1967. Bird banding. *Gosse Bird Club Broads.* 9: 15.

———. 1969. Informal conversations on Jamaican birds. *Gosse Bird Club Broads.* 12: 22–23.

———. 1969. Further searches for the Blue Mountain Duck. *Gosse Bird Club Broads.* 12: 11–15.

———. 1970a. Tropic birds in Jamaica. *Gosse Bird Club Broads.* 14: 3–7.

———. 1970b. White-tailed tropic birds. *Gosse Bird Club Broads.* 15: 18.

———. 1970. White-tailed Tropic Bird. *Gosse Bird Club Broads.* 14: 23.

———. 1970. Birds of Port Henderson—1894. *Gosse Bird Club Broads.* 15: 22–23.

———. 1971. Recovery of a banded noddy. *Gosse Bird Club Broads.* 16: 13.

———. 1971. White-tailed Tropic Bird. *Gosse Bird Club Broads.* 17: 26.

———. 1972a. White-tailed Tropic Bird. *Gosse Bird Club Broads.* 18: 19.

———. 1972. Conservation areas—birds—April 1969. *Gosse Bird Club Broads.* 19: 2–4.

———. 1973. Conservation areas—birds (Contd.) April 1969. *Gosse Bird Club Broads.* 20: 2–4.

Smith, R. W., and N. Agar. 1967. Common Tern. *Gosse Bird Club Broads.* 8: 16.

Smith, R. W., N. Agar, and P. M. Smith (eds.). 1967. Distribution of Jamaican species. *Gosse Bird Club Broads.* 8: 9.

Smith, R. W., and M. Gochfeld. 1965. Black-capped Petrel (*Pteradroma hasitata*). *Gosse Bird Club Broads.* 4: 14.

Smith, R. W., and W. H. Houston. 1964. Parasitic Jaeger. *Gosse Bird Club Broads.* 3: 15.

Smyth, J. A. 1937. Audubon's Shearwater nesting on Mona Island, Puerto Rico. *Wilson Bull.* 50: 203–204.

Sorenson, L. G., and P. Bradley. 2000. Update on the West Indian Whistling-Duck (WIWD) and Wetland Conservation Project. Report from the WIWD Working Group. *Pitirre* 13: 57–63.

Sorenson, L. G., P. E. Bradley, and A. Haynes Sutton. 2004. The West Indian Whistling-Duck and wetland conservation project: A model for species and wetlands conservation and education. *J. Carib. Ornithol.* 17: 72–80.

Sorenson, L. G., P. E. Bradley, L. Mugica, and K. Wallace. 2005. West Indian Whistling-Duck and Wetlands Conservation Project: Symposium report and project news. *J. Carib. Ornithol.* 18: 102–105.

Sorrie, B. A. 1975. Observations on the birds of Vieques Island, Puerto Rico. *Carib. J. Sci.* 15: 89–103.

Southern, W. E. 1974. Florida distribution of Ring-billed Gulls from the Great Lakes regions. *Bird-Banding* 45: 341–352.

Soy, J. P., and S. O. Cubillas. 1991. Conducta de asociación de varias especies de aves como factor de supervivencia. P. 67 *in Preservar la Biodiversidad, Premisa del Verdadero Desarrollo: II Simposio de Zoologia, 18–23 de junio 1991.* La Habana, Cuba: Universidad de La Habana.

Soy, J. P., and S. O. Cubillas. 1991. Conducta de asociacion de varias especies de aves como factor de supervivencia. *Pitirre* 4(2): 7.

Spaans, A. L. 1973. Some observations on the sea-birds of St. Giles. *J. Trin. Field Nat. Club* 1973: 83–84.

Spence, S. 1973. Magnificent Frigatebird. *Gosse Bird Club Broads.* 20: 20.

———. 1974. Sooty Shearwater. *Gosse Bird Club Broads.* 23: 20.

Spencer, W. 1981. *A guide to the birds of Antigua.* Antigua: privately published.

Sprunt, A., IV. 1984a. The status and conservation of seabirds of the Bahama Islands. Pp. 157–168 *in* Croxall, J. P., P. G. H. Evans, and R. W. Schreiber, eds., *Status and conservation of the world's seabirds.* ICBP Tech. Publ. no. 2. Cambridge, U.K.: International Council for Bird Preservation.

———. 1984. Some aspects of breeding seabirds in the Bahamas. *Colon. Waterbirds Group Newsl.* 8: 37.

Stahl, A. 1882. *Fauna de Puerto-Rico: Clasificacion sistemática de los animales que corresponden á esta fauna y catálogo del gabinete zoológico del Dr. A. Stahl en Bayamon.* Bayamón, Puerto Rico: Imprenta del "Boletin Mercantil."

———. 1887. Beitrag zur Vogelfauna von Portorico. *Ornis* 3: 448–453.

Starrett, W. C., and K. L. Dixon. 1947. Notes on the Pomarine Jaeger in the Atlantic and Caribbean. *Auk* 64: 320.

Steadman, D. W., R. L. Norton, M. R. Browning, and W. J. Arendt. 1997. The birds of St. Kitts, Lesser Antilles. *Carib. J. Sci.* 33: 1–20.

Sterrer, W. 1986. *Marine flora and fauna of Bermuda.* New York: John Wiley and Sons.

Stoddart, D. R., and F. R. Fosberg. 1991. Plants of the Jamaican cays. *Atoll Res. Bull.* 352: 1–24.

Stoddart, D. R., and M. E. C. Giglioli. 1980. Geography and ecology of Little Cayman. *Atoll Res. Bull.* 241: 181.

Stoffers, A. L. 1956. *Studies on the flora of Curaçao and other Caribbean islands. Vol. 1: The vegetation of the Netherlands Antilles.* Publ. Found. Sci Res. Surinam. Neth. Ant. 15. Utrecht, Netherlands: Kemink and Zn.

Stokes, A. V., and W. F. Keegan. 1993. *A settlement survey from prehistoric archeological sites on Grand Cayman.* Misc. Project Report no. 52. Gainesville: Florida Museum of Natural History.

Strong, A. 1996. Brown Booby. *Gosse Bird Club Broads.* 66: 31.

———. 1996. Black Tern. *Gosse Bird Club Broads.* 66: 33.

Struthers, P. H. 1923. Observations on the bird life of Porto Rico. *Auk* 40: 469–478.

———. 1927. Notes on the bird-life of Mona and Desecheo Islands. *Auk* 44: 539–544.

Sturm, M. G. de L. 1991. The living resources of the Caribbean Sea and adjacent regions. *Carib. Mar. Stud.* 2(1–2): 18–44.

Sundevall, C. J. 1869. Foglarne på ön St Barthelemy, efter de af Dr. A. von Goës hemsända samlingarna bestämde. *Öfvers. af K. Vetensk. Ak. Förhandl.* (Stockholm) 25: 579–591.

———. 1869. Foglarne på ön Porto Rico, efter Hr Hjalmarsons insamlingar framställda. *Öfvers. af K. Vetensk. Ak. Förhandl.* (Stockholm) 25: 593–603.

Sutton, A. M., and R. L. Sutton. 1988. Bird banding recoveries. *Gosse Bird Club Broads.* 50: 11–12.

Sutton, R. L. 1976. Morant Cays. *Gosse Bird Club Broads.* 27: 15.

———. 1979. Bird recoveries. *Gosse Bird Club Broads.* 32: 11–12.

———. 1979. Visit to south coast areas. *Gosse Bird Club Broads.* 32: 11.

———. 1991. Banded birds recaptured or recovered in Jamaica: Returns from US Fish & Wildlife Service for 3rd quarter 1990/91. *Gosse Bird Club Broads.* 57: 3.

Sutton, R. L., and J. Siphron. 1976. White-tailed Tropicbird. *Gosse Bird Club Broads.* 27: 20.

Sutton, R. L., and A. Sutton. 1989. Recent recoveries in Jamaica of birds banded elsewhere. *Gosse Bird Club Broads.* 53: 22.

Swank, W. G., and C. R. Julien. 1975. *Wildlife management and protection. Dominica: Distribution and status of wildlife in Dominica.* Project Working Document no. 1. Rome, Italy: Food and Agriculture Organization of the United Nations.

Taylor, E. C. 1864. Five months in the West Indies. Part II: Martinique, Dominica, and Porto Rico. *Ibis* 6: 157–173.

Taylor, J. P. 1984. Nesting habitat improvement for Sandwich Terns. *Colon. Waterbirds Group Newsl.* 8: 39.

———. 1985. [Status and management of seabirds in the Culebra National Wildlife Refuge]. *Colon. Waterbirds Group Newsl.* 9: 23–24.

Taylor, R. G. T. 1970. White-tailed Tropic Birds. *Gosse Bird Club Broads.* 15: 18.

Terborgh, J., and J. Faaborg. 1973. Turnover and ecological release in the avifauna of Mona Island, Puerto Rico. *Auk* 90: 759–779.

Terrill, S. B. 1990. *Field notes from San Salvador, Bahamas.* Unpublished list. Loudonville, N.Y.: Siena College.

Thaly, D. 1934. The re-discovery of the Diablotin. *Country Life* 76: 286.

Thayer, G. H. N.d. (assumed to be 1925). *Preliminary list of St. Vincent birds (April 1924–April 1925).* Unpublished report. New York: American Museum of Natural History.

Thienemann, F. A. L. 1857. Ueber die von Dr. Gundlach eingesendeten Eier und Nester cubanischer Vögel. *J. Ornithol.* 5(27): 145–159.

Thomas, C. D., A. Cameron, R. E. Green, M. Bakkenes, L. J. Beaumont, Y. C. Collingham, B. F. N. Erasmus, M. Ferreira de Siqueira, A. Grainger, L. Hannah, L. Hughes, B. Huntley, A. S. Van Jaarsveld, G. F. Midgley, L. Miles, M. A. Ortega-Huerta, A. T. Peterson, O. L. Phillips, and S. E. Williams. 2004. Extinction risk from climate change. *Nature* 427: 145–148.

Thomas, R. 1997. *Birds of Anguilla.* Report to Anguilla National Trust (unpublished). The Valley, Anguilla.

Thompson, B. C., J. A. Jackson, J. Burger, L. A. Hill, E. M. Kirsch, and J. Atwood. 1997. Least Tern (*Sterna antillarum*). *In* Poole, A., and F. Gill, eds., *The birds of North America,* no. 290. Philadelphia: Birds of North America.

Thompson, R., and K. C. Hamer. 2000. Stress in seabirds: Causes, consequences and diagnostic value. *J. Aquatic Ecosystem Stress and Recovery* 7(1): 91–109.

Threlfall, W. 1978. Dispersal of Herring Gulls from the Witless Bay Sea Bird Sanctuary, Newfoundland. *Bird-Banding* 49: 116–124.

Thwaites, P. 1991. Brown Pelican. *Gosse Bird Club Broads.* 57: 21.

Timmers, W. W. 1979. Wetgeving natuurbeheer op de Nederlandse Antillen in 1978. STINAPA Doc. Ser. no. 6. Willemstad, Curaçao: STINAPA.

Tippenhauer, L. G. 1892 (1893). *Die Insel Haiti.* Leipzig, Germany: F. A. Brockhaus.

Todd, W. E. C. 1916. The birds of the Isle of Pines: Incorporating the substance of field-notes by Gustav A. Link. *Ann. Carnegie Mus.* 10: 146–296.

Todd, W. E. C., and W. W. Worthington. 1911. A contribution to the ornithology of the Bahama Islands. *Ann. Carnegie Mus.* 7: 388–464.

Toro, L., D. Hernández, R. Newball, M. Robinson, and M. Peralta. 1999. *Plan de manejo de aguas subterráneas para la Isla de San Andrés 2000–2009.* San Andres, Colombia: CORALINA.

Torres, A. 1994. Listado de las aves observadas dentro del corredor migratorio de Gibara, Provincia Holguín, Cuba. *Garciana* 22: 1–4.

Torres Leyva, A., C. Peña, and A. Rams Beceña. 1989. Aves observadas en las cienagas de Birama, Cauto Norte y Carena, Provincia Granma, Cuba. *Garciana* 20: 1–2.

Towle, E. L., A. Archer, P. J. Butler, K. E. Coulianos, M. H. Goodwin, S. T. Goodwin, I. Jackson, D. Nicholson, W. E. Rainey, J. A. Towle, W. Wernicke, and N. J. O. Liverpool (eds.). 1986. *Environmental assessment report on the proposed southeast peninsula access road, St. Kitts, West Indies.* Report to U.S. Agency for International Development/USDA Forest Service. St. Thomas, U.S. Virgin Islands: Islands Research Foundation.

Towle, J. A., and E. A. Towle (eds.). 1991. *St. Lucia country environmental profile.* Bridgetown, Barbados: USAID.

Trimm, N. A., Jr. 2004. Behavioral ecology of Audubon's Shearwaters at San Salvador, Bahamas. Unpublished Ph.D. dissertation. Loma Linda, Calif.: Loma Linda University.

Tye, A., and H. Tye. 1991. Bird species on St. Andrew and Old Providence Islands, West Caribbean. *Wilson Bull.* 103: 493–497.

U.S. Department of the Interior. 1981. *Final environmental impact statement: Proposed disposition and administration of lands declared excess by the U.S. Navy on the islands of Culebra and Culebrita in Puerto Rico.* Atlanta, Ga.: U.S. Department of the Interior.

U.S. Fish and Wildlife Service. 1986. *Brown Pelican in Puerto Rico and the U.S. Virgin Islands recovery plan.* Atlanta, Ga.: U.S. Fish and Wildlife Service.

———. 1987. Endangered and threatened wildlife and plants: Determination of endangered and threatened status for two populations of the Roseate Tern. *Fed. Reg.* 52: 42064–42071.

———. 1993. *Caribbean Roseate Tern recovery plan.* Atlanta, Ga.: U.S. Fish and Wildlife Service.

Valdés Miro, V. 1984. Datos de nidificación sobre las aves que crían en Cuba. *Poeyana* 282: 1–27.

Vargas Mora, T. A. 1984. *Informe sobre las aves acuaticas y ribereñas del Lago Enriquillo.* Santo Domingo, República Dominicana: Seccion de Ornitologia, Departamento de Vida Silvestre, Secretaria de Estado de Agricultura.

———. 1984. Contribucion al conocimiento del estado actual de las aves acuaticas en el Lago Enriquillo. Pp. 168–169 *in Memoria de la Segunda Jornada Cientifica: Medio Ambiente y Recursos Naturales en homenaje al Profesor Ricardo Ramírez*

Núñez, 5 al 7 de septiembre, 1984. Santo Domingo, República Dominicana: CENAPEC.

Vargas Mora, T. A., and M. Gonzalez Castillo. 1984. Informe sobre la avifauna de la Peninsula de Barahona e Isla Beata. Pp. 225–253 *in Estudios en las areas silvestres de la Peninsula de Barahona e Isla Beata: Propuesta para la creacion de una zona protegida (parque nacional).* Santo Domingo, República Dominicana: Departamento de Vida Silvestre, Secretaria de Estado de Agricultura.

Varnham, K. 2001 *Restoration of Green Island, Antigua, West Indies: Rat eradication project.* Cambridge, U.K.: Antiguan Racer Conservation Project, Flora and Fauna International.

Varona, L. S., and O. H. Garrido. 1970. Vertebrados de los Cayos de San Felipe, Cuba, incluyendo una nueva especie de jutia. *Poeyana* A 75: 1–26.

Vaurie, C. 1953. Observations and new records of birds from the Biminis, northwestern Bahamas. *Auk* 70: 38–48.

———. 1961. List of and notes on the birds of the Iles des Saintes, French West Indies. *Auk* 78: 57–62.

Vermeij, G. J. 1993. Biogeography of recently extinct marine species: Implications for conservation. *Cons. Biol.* 7: 391–397.

Verrill, A. H. ca. 1905. *Additions to the avifauna of Dominica: Notes on species hitherto unrecorded with descriptions of three new species and a list of all birds known to occur on the island.* Barbados: privately printed.

Verrill, G. E. 1892. Notes on the fauna of the island of Dominica, British West Indies, with lists of the species obtained and observed by G. E. and A. H. Verrill. *Trans. Conn. Acad. Arts Sci.* 8: 315–355.

Verrill, G. E., and A. H. Verrill. 1909. Notes on the birds of San Domingo, with a list of the species, including a new hawk. *Proc. Acad. Nat. Sci. Philadelphia* 61: 352–366.

Vieillot, L. J. P., and M. P. Oudart. 1825. *La galérie des oiseaux, dédiée à son Altesse Royale Madame, Duchesse de Berri.* Paris: Constant-Chantpie.

Vieillot, L. J. P., and M. P. Oudart. 1834. *La galérie des oiseaux.* Tome Primier. Paris: Carpentier-Mericourt.

Vincente, V. P. 1979. The occurrence of a nesting colony of the Royal Tern, *Sterna (Thalasseus) maxima* on the south coast of Puerto Rico. *Am. Birds* 33: 147.

Vivaldi, J. L. 1986. La conservacion de la ornitofauna y el desarollo de Puerto Rico. *Ornitol. Caribeña* 2: 3–8.

Voous, K. H. 1955a. The birds of St. Martin, Saba, and St. Eustatius. *Stud. Fauna Curaçao and Other Carib. Isl.* 6(25): 1–82.

———. 1955a. *The birds of the Netherlands Antilles.* Curaçao: Uitg. Natuurwetenschappelijke Werkgroep Nederlandse Antillen.

———. 1957. *The birds of Aruba, Curaçao, and Bonaire.* Studies of the fauna of Curaçao and other Caribbean islands, no. 29. The Hague: Martinus Nijoff.

———. 1963. Tern colonies in Aruba, Curaçao and Bonaire, South Caribbean Sea. Pp. 1214–1216 *in* Sibley, C. G., ed., *Proceedings XIII International Ornithological Congress,* Ithaca 17–24 June 1962. Baton Rouge, La.: American Ornithologists' Union.

———. 1965. Nesting and nest sites of Common Terns and Dougall's terns in the Netherlands Antilles. *Ibis* 107: 430–431.

———. 1983. *Birds of the Netherlands Antilles,* 2nd ed. Zutphen–Utrecht, Netherlands: De Walburg Press.

Voous, K. H., and H. J. Koelers. 1967. Check-list of the birds of St. Martin, Saba, and St. Eustatius. *Ardea* 55: 115–137.

Wallace, G. E., and D. R. Fillman. 1994. Sighting of a Northern Gannet in Cuba. *Fla. Field Nat.* 22: 114–117.

Walsh-McGehee, M. 2000. Status and conservation priorities for White-tailed and Red-billed tropicbirds in the West Indies. Pp. 31–38 *in* Schreiber, E. A., and D. S. Lee, eds., *Status and conservation of West Indian seabirds.* Special Publication no. 1. Ruston, La.: Society of Caribbean Ornithology.

Walsh-McGehee, M., D. S. Lee, and J. M. Wunderle. 1998. A report of aquatic birds encountered in December from the Caicos Islands. *Bahamas J. Sci.* 6: 28–33.

Walsh-McGehee, M., D. S. Lee, and D. Claridge. 1999. Distribution and population status of White-tailed Tropicbirds nesting in the Bahamas. *Bahamas J. Sci.* 6(2): 44–48.

Warham, J. 1990. *The petrels: Their ecology and breeding systems.* London: Academic Press.

Watson, G. E. 1966. *Seabirds of the tropical Atlantic Ocean.* Washington, D.C.: Smithsonian Press.

Wauer, R. H., and J. M. Wunderle, Jr. 1992. The effect of Hurricane Hugo on bird populations on St. Croix, U.S. Virgin Islands. *Wilson Bull.* 104: 656–673.

Weaver, J. D., H. Heatwole, J. R. Goreham, and F. J. Rolle. 1961. Institute of Caribbean Studies field excursion to Isla Mona. Ornithology (5th.–7th. November 1960). *Carib. J. Sci.* 1: 30–35.

Webster, P. J., G. J. Holland, J. A. Curry, and H.-R. Chang. 2005. Changes in tropic cyclone number, duration, and intensity in a warming environment. *Science* 309(5742): 1844–1846.

Wege, D. C. 2002. *Important Bird Areas in the Caribbean: Resource book.* Unpublished Report. Cambridge, U.K.: BirdLife International. Sandy, Bedfordshire. UK.

Wells, A., and J. Wells. 2000. Lesser Antilles—cruise: St. Lucia, St. Vincent, and the Grenadines. Unpublished report. <http://maybank.tripod.com/Caribbean/Cruise-12-2000.htm>.

Wells, J. G. 1887. A catalogue of the birds of Grenada, West Indies, with observations thereon. *Proc. U.S. Natl. Mus.* (1886) 9: 609–633.

———. 1902. Birds of the island of Carriacou. Part I: Water birds. *Auk* 19: 237–246.

Wells, S. 1988. *Coral reefs of the world. Vol. 1: Atlantic and eastern Pacific.* Cambridge, U.K.: UNEP–IUCN.

Werf, P. A., J. S. van Zaneveld, and K. H. Voous. 1958. Field observations on the birds of the Islas Las Aves, in the southern Caribbean Sea. *Ardea* 46: 37–58.

Westermann, J. H. 1953. Nature preservation in the Caribbean: A review of literature on the destruction and preservation of flora and fauna in the Caribbean area. *Stud. Fauna Curaçao and Other Carib. Isl.* 9: 1–106.

Wetmore, A. 1916. Birds of Porto Rico. *U.S. Dept. Agric. Bull.* 326: 1–140.

———. 1916. The birds of Vieques Island, Porto Rico. *Auk* 33: 403–419.

———. 1917. The birds of Culebra Island, Porto Rico. *Auk* 34: 51–62.

———. 1918a. Bones of birds collected by Theodore de Booy from kitchen midden deposits in the islands of St. Thomas and St. Croix. *Proc. U.S. Natl. Mus.* 54: 513–523.

———. 1918. The birds of Desecheo Island, Porto Rico. *Auk* 35: 333–340.

———. 1927. *Birds of Porto Rico and the Virgin Islands: New York Academy of Science Scientific Survey of Porto Rico and the Virgin Islands.* Vol. 9, parts 3 & 4, pp. 245–406. New York: New York Academy of Science.

———. 1930. The Rabie paintings of Haitian birds. *Auk* 47: 481–486.

———. 1932a. Birds collected in Cuba and Haiti by the Parrish-Smithsonian Expedition of 1930. *Proc. U.S. Natl. Mus.* 81: 1–40.

———. 1932. Notes from Dr. R. Ciferri on the birds of Hispaniola. *Auk* 49: 107–108.

———. 1932. The breeding of the Brown Booby in Porto Rican territory. *Auk* 49: 341.

———. 1932. The diablotin in Dominica. *Auk* 49: 456–457.

———. 1937. Ancient records of birds from the island of St. Croix with observations on extinct and living birds of Puerto Rico. *J. Agric. Univ. P.R.* 21: 5–16.

———. 1938. A skua in the Caribbean Sea. *Auk* 55: 277.

———. 1938. Bird remains from the West Indies. *Auk* 55: 51–55.

———. 1939. A record of the Black-capped Petrel from Haiti. *Auk* 56: 73.

———. 1940. A specimen of the Black-capped Petrel. *Auk* 57: 105.

———. 1944. The subspecific characters and distribution of the New World skimmers (*Rynchops nigra*). *Caldasia* 3: 111–118.

———. 1945. A review of the forms of the Brown Pelican. *Auk* 62: 577–586.

———. 1952. A record for the Black-capped Petrel, *Pterodroma hasitata* in Martinique. *Auk* 69: 460.

———. 1962. Bones of birds from Cockroach Island, Bermuda. Pp. 15–17 *in* Wetmore, A., Notes on fossil and subfossil birds. *Smithson. Misc. Coll.* 142(2).

———. 1965. *The birds of the Republic of Panama: Part I (Tinamidae—Rhynocriptidae).* Smithson. Misc. Coll. 150 (1).

Wetmore, A., and F. C. Lincoln. 1933. Additional notes on the birds of Haiti and the Dominican Republic. *Proc. U.S. Natl. Mus.* 82: 1–68.

Wetmore, A., and W. M. Perrygo. 1931. The cruise of the *Esperanza* to Haiti. Pp. 59–66 *in Exploration and field work of the Smithsonian Institute in 1930*, Smithson. Publ. no. 3111. Washington, D.C.: Smithsonian Institution.

Wetmore, A., and B. H. Swales. 1931. The birds of Haiti and the Dominican Republic. *U.S. Natl. Mus. Bull.* 155.

White, A. W. 1998. *A birder's guide to the Bahama Islands (including Turks and Caicos).* Colorado Springs, Colo.: American Birding Association.

———. 2002. Checklist of Bimini Birds. *Bahamas J. Sci.* 9(2): 63–66.

———. 2004. Seabirds in the Bahamian archipelago and adjacent waters: Transient, wintering and rare nesting species. *N. Am. Birds* 57: 436–451.

White, A. W., and D. S. Lee. 2000. Bahamian seabirds: An international resource. Pp 59–66 *in* Carey, E., S. D. Buckner, A. C. Alberts, R. D. Hudson, and D. S. Lee, eds., *Protected areas management strategy for Bahamian terrestrial vertebrates: Iguanas and seabirds.* Apple Valley, Minn.: IUCN–SSC Conservation Breeding Specialist Group.

White, A. W., B. Hallett, and A. M. Bainton. 1996. Red-footed Boobies nest on White Cay, San Salvador. *Bahamas J. Sci.* 3: 33–34.

White, A. W., E. Carey, and P. Dean. 1999. Report of a visit to Cay Santo Domingo, Cay Verde and Cay Lobos. *Bahamas J. Sci.* 7: 40–44.

White, B. 1991. *Common birds of San Salvador Island, Bahamas.* San Salvador, Bahamas: Bahamian Field Station.

White, G., and F. E. Hayes. 2002. Second report of the Trinidad and Tobago Rare Bird Committee. *Living World, J. Trinidad and Tobago Field Naturalists' Club* 2002: 51–56.

Wiese, F. K., and I. L. Jones. 2001. Experimental support for a new drift block design to assess seabird mortality from oil pollution. *Auk* 118: 1062–1068.

Wiley, J. W. 1985. Bird conservation in the United States Caribbean. Pp. 107–159 *in* Temple, S. A., ed., *Bird Conservation 2.* Madison: University of Wisconsin Press for International Council for Bird Preservation.

———. 1996. Ornithology in Puerto Rico and the Virgin Islands. Pp. 149–179 *in* Figueroa Colón, J. C., ed., *The Scientific Survey of Puerto Rico and the Virgin Islands: An eighty-year reassessment of the islands' natural history.* Annals of the New York Academy of Sciences vol. 776. New York: New York Academy of Sciences.

———, and J. A. Ottenwalder. 1990. Birds of Islas Beata and Alto Velo, Dominican Republic. *Stud. Neotrop. Fauna Environ.* 25: 65–88.

Wiley, J. W., and J. M. Wunderle, Jr. 1993. The effects of hurricanes on birds, with special reference to Caribbean islands. *Bird Conserv. Intl.* 3: 319–349.

Williams, E. H., Jr., and L. Bunkley-Williams. 1992. Two unusual sea bird records from Puerto Rico. *Carib. J. Sci.* 28: 105.

Williams, E. H., Jr., L. Bunkley-Williams, and I. Lopez-Irizarry. 1992. Die-off of Brown Pelicans in Puerto Rico and the United States Virgin Islands. *Am. Birds* 46: 1106–1108.

Williams, R. S. R., G. M. Kirwan, and C. G. Bradshaw. 1996. The status of the Black-capped Petrel *Pterodroma hasitata* in the Dominican Republic. *Cotinga* 6: 29–30.

Williams, W. T. 1980. *Las maravillosas islas Venezolanas.* Caracas, Venezuela: Publicaciones Seleven, C.A.

Willmann, P. A. 1970. Black Skimmer, *Rynchops nigra*, on Puerto Rico. *Fla. Nat.* 43: 180.

———. 1971. Birding in southwest Puerto Rico. *Birding* 3: Unpaginated insert between pages 22–23.

Wing, E. S. 1969. Vertebrate remains excavated from San Salvador Island, Bahamas. *Carib. J. Sci.* 9: 25–29.

Wing, E. S., C. A. Hoffman, Jr., and C. E. Ray. 1968. Vertebrate remains from Indian sites on Antigua, West Indies. *Carib. J. Sci.* 8: 123–139.

Wingate, D. B. (ed.) 1959. A check list of the birds, mammals, reptiles and amphibians of Bermuda. Hamilton, Bermuda: Bermuda Audubon Society.

———. 1964a. Discovery of breeding Black-capped Petrels on Hispaniola. *Auk* 81: 147–159.

———. 1964. Does the Blue Mountain Duck of Jamaica survive? *Gosse Bird Club Broads.* 2: 1–2.

———. 1965. John Tavenier Bartram (1811–1889). *Bermuda Historical Quarterly* (Hamilton) 21 (4) 1964, 22 (2, 3, 4)

———. 1973. *A checklist and guide to the birds of Bermuda.* Hamilton, Bermuda: Published by the author.

———. 1975. White-tailed Tropicbirds. *Gosse Bird Club Broads.* 24: 6–7.

———. 1977. Excluding competitors from Bermuda Petrel nesting burrows. Pp. 93–103 *in* Temple, S. A., ed., *Proceedings of the Symposium on Management Techniques for Preserving Endangered Birds.* Madison: University of Wisconsin Press and Croom Helm.

———. 1978. Attracting longtails to artificial nesting holes with decoys. *Month. Bull. Bermuda Dept. Agric. Fish. Parks* 48: 80–83.

———. 1985. The restoration of Nonsuch Island as a living museum of Bermuda's pre-colonial terrestrial biome. Pp. 225–238 *in* Moors, P. J., ed., *Conservation of island birds.* ICBP Tech. Publ. no. 3. Cambridge, U.K.: International Council for Bird Preservation.

———. 1988. Making safe artificial nesting sites for longtails. *Heritage* 1988: 129–131.

———. 1995. The 1994/1995 Cahow season summary: A year of crisis overcome, Hurricane "Felix" devastates Cahow nesting islets, and the saga of Cahow chick. IPOB4. *Month. Bull. Bermuda Dept. Agric. Fish. Parks* 66: 102–105.

Wingate, D. B., I. K. Barber, and N. W. King. 1980. Poxvirus infection of the White-tailed Tropicbird (*Phaethon lepturus*) in Bermuda. *Journal of Wildlife Disease* 16: 619–622.

Wingate, D. B., T. Hass, E. S. Brinkley, and J. B. Patteson. 1998. Identification of Bermuda Petrel. *Birding* 30: 18–36.

Witt, H.-H. 1978. Black Tern. *Gosse Bird Club Broads.* 30: 13.

———. 1978. Least Tern. *Gosse Bird Club Broads.* 30: 13.

Witt, H., A. Maddison, P. Maddison, and R. Sutton. 1977. Bird Notes: Cattle Egrets. *Gosse Bird Club Broads.* 29: 11.

Wood, C. A. 1923. The fossil eggs of Bermudan birds. *Ibis*, ser. 11, 5: 193–207.

Wood, P., S. Babbs, S. Ling, and P. Robertson. 1987. *Report of the 1986 University of East Anglia Martinique Oriole Expedition.* ICBP Study Report no. 23. Cambridge, U.K.: International Council for Bird Preservation.

Woodbury, R. C., L. F. Martorell, and J. C. Garcia Tuduri. 1971. The flora of Desecheo Island, Puerto Rico. *J. Agric. Univ. P.R.* 55: 478–505.

Woodfield, N. K. 1999. The conservation status of birds in British Virgin Islands National Parks. *Pitirre* 12(2): 68–69.

Woods, C. A. 1987. The threatened and endangered birds of Haiti: Lost horizons and new hopes. Pp. 385–429 *in* Risser, A. C., ed., *Proceedings of the Jean Delacour Symposium on Breeding Birds in Captivity.* Los Angeles, Calif.: International Foundation for the Conservation of Birds.

Woods, C. A., and J. A. Ottenwalder. 1983. The montane avifauna of Haiti. Pp. 607–622, 576–590 *in* Risser, A. C., Jr., and F. S. Todd, eds., *Proceedings of the Jean Delacour–IFCB Symposium on Breeding Birds in Captivity.* Los Angeles, Calif.: International Foundation for the Conservation of Birds.

Woods, C. A., and J. A. Ottenwalder. 1992. *The natural history of southern Haiti.* Gainesville: Florida Museum of Natural History, University of Florida.

World Gazetteer. 2002. Colombia. Website, accessed September 10, 2003. http://www.world-gazetteer.com/fr/fr_co.htm.

Worth, C. B. 1967. *A naturalist in Trinidad.* Philadelphia: J. B. Lippincott.

Worth, C. B., and W. G. Downs. 1962. Recoveries in the West Indian region of birds banded in North America, 1951–1960, and their possible relationship to the transport of arthropod-borne viruses. *Journal of Wildlife Disease* 24: 17.

Wurster, C. F., and D. B. Wingate. 1968. DDT residues and declining reproduction in the Bermuda Petrel. *Science* 159: 979–981.

Yarrell, W. 1871–1885. *A history of British birds,* 4th ed., vol. 3. London: John Van Voorst.

Yates, G. S. 1955. Notes on the Diablotin and Saffron Finch. *Nat. Hist. Notes Nat. Hist. Soc. Jamaica* 6: 16.

———. 1977. Notes on the Diablotin and Saffron Finch. *Nat. Hist. Notes Nat. Hist. Soc. Jamaica,* n.s., 1: 1–22.

Yépez Tamayo, G. 1963a. Ornitología de las Islas Margarita, Coche y Cubagua (Venezuela), Primera Parte. *Mem. Soc. Cienc. Nat. La Salle* 23(65): 75–112.

———. 1963b. Ornitología de las Islas Margarita, Coche y Cubagua (Venezuela), Segunda Parte. *Mem. Soc. Cienc. Nat. La Salle* 23(66): 167–249.

———. 1964a. Ornitología de las Islas Margarita, Coche y Cubagua (Venezuela), Tercera Parte. *Mem. Soc. Cienc. Nat. La Salle* 24(67): 5–39.

———. 1964b. Ornitología de las Islas Margarita, Coche y Cubagua (Venezuela), Cuarta Parte. *Mem. Soc. Cienc. Nat. La Salle* 24(68): 103–162.

Zans, V. A. 1958. The Pedro Cays and the Pedro Bank: Report on the survey of the cays 1955–57. *Bulletin of the Geological Survey Department* (Kingston, Jamaica) 3: 1–47.

Zimmerman, D. R. 1975. *To save a bird in peril.* New York: Coward, McCann, and Geohagan.

Zuloaga, G. 1955. The Isla de Aves story. *Geogr. Rev.* 45: 172–180.

Appendix A. Seabird Species and Corresponding Codes

Table A.1. English and Latin names of seabirds and codes

English name	Latin name	Letter Code	Number Code for GIS
Bermuda Petrel	*Pterodroma cahow*	BEPE	1
Black-capped Petrel	*Pterodroma hasitata*	BCPE	2
Jamaican Petrel	*Pterodroma caribbaea*	JAPE	3
Audubon's Shearwater	*Puffinus lherminieri*	AUSH	4
White-tailed Tropicbird	*Phaethon lepturus*	WTTR	5
Red-billed Tropicbird	*Phaethon aethereus*	RBTR	6
Masked Booby	*Sula dactylatra*	MABO	7
Brown Booby	*Sula leucogaster*	BRBO	8
Red-footed Booby	*Sula sula*	RFBO	9
Brown Pelican	*Pelecanus occidentalis*	BRPE	10
Magnificent Frigatebird	*Fregata magnificens*	MAFR	11
Laughing Gull	*Larus atricilla*	LAGU	12
Brown Noddy	*Anous stolidus*	BRNO	13
Black Noddy	*Anous minutus*	BLNO	14
Sooty Tern	*Onychoprion fuscatus*	SOTE	15
Bridled Tern	*Onychoprion anaethetus*	BRTE	16
Least Tern	*Sternula antillarum*	LETE	17
Gull-billed Tern	*Gelochelidon nilotica*	GBTE	18
Roseate Tern	*Sterna dougallii*	ROTE	19
Common Tern	*Sterna hirundo*	COTE	20
Royal Tern	*Thalasseus maximus*	RYTE	21
Sandwich Tern	*Thalasseus sandvicensis*	SATE	22
Cayenne Tern	*T. s. eurygnatha*	CYTE	23

Appendix B. Breeding Seabirds in the British Virgin Islands, 2004 and 2005

ANDREW MCGOWAN, ANNETTE C. BRODERICK, SHANNON GORE, GEOFF HILTON,
NANCY K. WOODFIELD, AND BRENDAN J. GODLEY

Our original intention was to survey all 43 islands and cays in the BVI archipelago during each of the two years of this study (2004 and 2005), but this was not possible due to logistical constraints and inclement weather. We thus surveyed a total of 42 different islands and cays; 25 in 2004 and 40 in 2005, 23 of which were surveyed in both years (tables B.1 and B.2).

Surveys were typically carried out during May. Exceptions were Great Tobago (surveyed in February 2004 and May 2005) and Anegada (surveyed in May and July in both years). The decision to carry out the bulk of surveying in May was based on the phenological information available (Schreiber and Lee 2000a). This enabled maximum detection of tropicbird, gull, and tern nesting (breeding May to August) in addition to other seabird species (breeding October to May). Surveys were carried out between 08:00 and 18:00 hours. Excluding Anegada, a total of three and five days were spent conducting surveys across the entire archipelago in 2004 and 2005, respectively. An additional six days were spent surveying Anegada for seabird colonies in each survey year (total 12 days).

For all islands, we estimated the number of breeding pairs of each seabird species present, and species were confirmed as breeding if one of the following was observed: (i) mating behavior, (ii) nest building, (iii) active nests, or (iv) recently fledged chicks. Potential breeding sites on all islands, with the exception of Anegada, were observed from a boat due to inaccessibility. Each island was slowly circumnavigated, and a direct count of the number of apparently occupied nests (AONs) for each species of seabird present was recorded. Wherever possible, islands were ground-truthed on foot, and direct counts of all AONs were made. In most cases where ground-truthing took place, a combination of direct counts and boat observations was used to estimate breeding numbers. As birds were not marked, we divided the archipelago up into discrete geographical units and surveyed islands that were in close proximity to one another on the same day, in order to reduce the potential problem of double counting.

Table B.1. Breeding seabird counts, British Virgin Islands, 2004

Species	Anegada	Carrot Rock	Carval Rock	Cockroach Island	Cooper Island	Deadmans Chest	East Seal Dog	Fallen Jeru-salem	Ginger Island
Audubon's Shearwater									
White-tailed Tropicbird									
Red-billed Tropicbird		4	4						
Brown Booby			10						10
Brown Pelican									
Magnificent Frigatebird									
Laughing Gull	245					15	10	150	
Brown Noddy					3				75
Bridled Tern		4	25				15	10	20
Least Tern	60								
Gull-billed Tern									
Roseate Tern				550					
Common Tern	2								
Royal Tern									
Sandwich Tern	20								

Note: The following islands were surveyed with no seabird nesting being recorded: Beef, Great Camanoe, Great Thatch, Green Cay, Little Thatch, Peter, Prickly Pear, Salt, Sandy Cay, Sandy Spit and Tortola.

Table B.2. Breeding seabird counts, British Virgin Islands, 2005

	Anegada	Broken Jerusalem	Carrot Rock	Carval Rock	Cistern Rock	Cockroach Island	Deadmans Chest	East Seal Dog	Fallen Jerusalem	George Dog	Ginger Island
Audubon's Shearwater											
White-tailed Tropicbird											
Red-billed Tropicbird								5			
Brown Booby											
Brown Pelican											
Magnificent Frigatebird											
Laughing Gull	175		15		5	11	22	20	150		
Brown Noddy				10							38
Bridled Tern		20	15	25		5		10	4	8	5
Least Tern	55										
Gull-billed Tern	4										
Roseate Tern					20						
Common Tern											
Royal Tern											
Sandwich Tern	25										

Note: The following islands were surveyed with no seabird nesting being recorded: Beef, Cooper, Eustatia, Great Dog, Great Thatch, Green Cay, Little Camanoe, Marina Cay, Mosquito, Pete, Prickly Pear, Salt, Sandy Spit, Scrub and Tortola.

Great Tobago	Guana Island	Norman Island	The Indians	West Dog	West Seal Dog	Total
						0
						0
2						10
125						145
		100				100
800						800
	30			50	5	505
						78
			4	8	2	88
						60
						0
						550
						2
						0
						20

Great Camanoe	Great Tobago	Guana Island	Little Tobago	Necker Island	Norman Island	Pelican Island	Round Rock	Sandy Cay	The Indians	Virgin Gorda	Watsons Rock	West Dog	West Seal Dog	Total
														0
				3						2				5
2	3													10
	32		55											87
		35			30									65
	500													500
20		25		40								40		523
							15				40			103
				15		2	5	5	3	1	5	8	4	140
														55
														4
				10						5				35
														0
														0
														25

Contributors

Allcorn, Richard I. Ornithologist with the Royal Society for the Protection of Birds (RSPB) while on Montserrat, 2002–2005. Royal Society for the Protection of Birds, The Lodge, Sandy, Bedfordshire SG19 2DL, United Kingdom. richard.allcorn@gmail.com

Anthony, Donald. Senior Wildlife Officer. Forestry Department, Ministry of Agriculture, Forestry and Fisheries, Castries, St. Lucia. kioko59@yahoo.com

Blanco, Pedro R. Researcher, specializing in the Order Charadriiformes, Vertebrate Department, Ecology and Systematic Institute, Havana, Cuba.

Bodnar, Stefan. An ecologist working on seabirds, particularly storm petrels, on the outer Scottish isles. Studied passerines and seabirds on Little Tobago and St. Giles Island, 1999–2000. 995 Chester Road, Birmingham B24 0HG, United Kingdom. stefan_bodnar@birmingham.gov.uk

Boogerd, Coen. Graduate in nature management sciences at the Hogeschool Delft in the Netherlands; field studies on Curaçao and Bonaire were required for his degree. Carmabi Foundation, Piscaderabaai z/n, P.O. Box 2090, Curaçao, Netherlands Antilles.

Bosque, Carlos. Professor; ornithological studies involve seabird surveys on Los Roques, use of plant material by birds, and physiological and ecological consequences of processing such foods. Departamento de Biología de Organismos, Universidad Simón Bolívar, Caracas 1080, Venezuela. carlos@usb.ve

Bradley, Patricia E. Conservation biologist in the Cayman Islands and in 2007 was honored with the Lifetime Achievement Award of the Society for the Conservation and Study of Caribbean Birds. She is the author of *Birds of the Cayman Islands* (1985, 1995), the BOU Checklist of Cayman Islands Birds and is lead author on the Cayman Islands section of *Important Bird Areas in the UK Overseas Territories*, among other publications. P.O. Box 2394, Grand Cayman, Cayman Islands, KY1-1105. pebrad@candw.ky

Broeck, Dieter van den. Graduate in nature management sciences at the Hogeschool Delft in the Netherlands; field studies on Curaçao and Bonaire were required for his degree. Carmabi Foundation, Piscaderabaai z/n, P.O. Box 2090, Curaçao, Netherlands Antilles.

Brown, Adam. Science director and co-founder of the nonprofit organization Environmental Protection in the Caribbean (EPIC), based in St. Martin and the United States, focusing on the ecology and conservation of Caribbean birds. Environmental Protection in the Caribbean, 200 Dr. Martin Luther King Jr. Blvd, Rivera Beach, FL 33404. info@epicislands.org

Collier, Natalia. President and co-founder of the nonprofit organization Environmental Protection in the Caribbean (EPIC), based in St. Martin and the United States, focusing on surveying seabird colonies and on conservation issues in the Lesser Antilles. Environmental Protection in the Caribbean, 200 Dr. Martin Luther King Jr. Blvd, Rivera Beach, FL 33404. info@epicislands.org

Daley, J. "Scriber." Forestry Officer, Forestry Department, Ministry of Agriculture, Housing, Land and the Environment, Brades, Montserrat.

Debrot, Adolphe O. Director of Carmabi Foundation, Curaçao, and author of more than 70 publications in reports and scientific journals on biological and environmental conservation. Carmabi Foundation, Piscaderabaai z/n, P.O. Box 2090, Curaçao, Netherlands Antilles. adebrot@cura.net

Dornelly, Alwin. Wildlife officer with Forestry Department, Ministry of Agriculture, Forestry and Fisheries, Castries, St Lucia. biom@candw.lc

Dubief, Lionel. Consultant for seabird monitoring in Martinique for the French government in the Department of the Environment (DIREN); member of conservation NGO Société pour l'Etude, la Protection et l'Aménagement de la Nature en Martinique (SEPANMAR). 36 Chemin Bois Thibault, Appartement no. 5, 97200 Fort de France, Martinique, French West Indies. dubief.lionel@wanadoo.fr

Esclasans, Diana. Biologist with Colección Ornitológica Phelps, Venezuela, since 2004. Identification of IBAs; co-author for Venezuela, *Neotropical Migrants in the Tropical Andes;* GIS database for seabirds; censusing and monitoring seabirds on Los Roques since 2001. Instituto de Tecnología y Ciencias Marinas (INTECMAR), Edif. Básico I, Piso 2, Oficina 208, Universidad Simón Bolívar, Caracas 89000, Venezuela. diana@intecmar.usb.ve

Frost, Martin D. Resident ornithologist in Barbados and co-author of *Birds of Barbados*. Featherbed Lane, St. John, Barbados. mfrost@hornabbot.bb

García, Martha Inés. Director of the Corporation for the Sustainable Development of the Archipelago of San Andres, Old Providence, and Santa Catalina (CORALINA), San Luis Road, Bight, San Andres Island, Colombia.

Genesseaux, Valérie. Member of Société pour l'Etude, la Protection et l'Aménagement de la Nature en Martinique (SEPANMAR) and volunteer on the seabird monitoring program. 36 Chemin Bois Thibault, Appartement no. 5, 97200 Fort de France, Martinique, French West Indies.

Halewijn (also Halewyn), Ruud van. Studied at-sea distribution of marine birds in the southeast sector of the Caribbean Sea and adjacent Atlantic Ocean, 1970–72. Contributor to *The Birds of the Netherlands Antilles* (Voous 1983); co-author of the first inventory of Caribbean seabirds (1984) with Norton; published on Cayenne Tern and worked on larid monitoring and conservation on cays off San Nicolas, Aruba, 1984–90. vanhale@wanadoo.nl

Hallett, Bruce. Naturalist, birder, and noted photographer in the Caribbean, with over 25 years of observations on Bahamian birds; author of *Birds of the Bahamas*. 697 Darlington Road NE, Atlanta, GA 30305.

Hay, Brandon. Scientific officer for the Caribbean Coastal Area Management Foundation (C-CAM) in Jamaica. Co-chair, Society for the Conservation and Study of Caribbean Birds White-crowned Pigeon Working Group, and involved in seabird surveys throughout the Caribbean since 1999. Marshall's Pen, P.O. Box 58, Mandeville, Jamaica, West Indies. brandonhay@cwjamaica.com

Hayes, Floyd. E. Professor of biology at Pacific Union College, California. Lecturer in Trinidad and Tobago at the University of Southern Caribbean (University of the West Indies), 1994–2002. Co-editor, *Journal of Caribbean Ornithology*, since 2005. Department of Biology, Pacific Union College, 1 Angwin Avenue, Angwin, CA 94508. floyd_hayes@hotmail.com

Haynes Sutton, Ann M. Resident conservation ecologist in Jamaica, working for the Jamaican government, University of the West Indies, and currently for local and international NGOs. Founder member Society for the Conservation and Study of Caribbean Birds (as secretary to the board, and co-chair of the Seabirds and Monitoring groups). Her ornithological interests include seabirds, a long-term banding study, and environmental education. Marshall's Pen, P.O. Box 58, Mandeville, Jamaica, West Indies. asutton@cwjamaica.com

Hodge, Karim V. D. Director of environment with the government of Anguilla. He has many years' experience in environmental management and natural resource conservation. He worked for the Anguilla National Trust from its inception in 19995, becoming its associate executive director in 2000 and its president from 2003–2005. He is a co-author of and contributor to books on Anguilla's birds and reptiles, and contributed to the Anguilla sections of the Important Bird Area publications for the Caribbean and U.K. Overseas Territories.

Holliday, Steve H. Director of the Midlands Regional Office for the Royal Society for the Protection of Birds (RSPB) and leads seabird monitoring and training with the Anguilla National Trust. Co-author, *Birds of Anguilla*. RSPB Central England, 46 The Green, South Bar, Banbury, Oxfordshire OX 16 9AB, United Kingdom. steve.holliday@rspb.org.uk

Howard, Marion. Director, Sustainable International Development Programs, Heller School for Social Policy; management and policy director until 2005, Corporation for the Sustainable Development of the Archipelago of San Andres, Old Providence, and Santa Catalina (COR-ALINA), San Andres Island, Colombia. Heller School for Social Policy and Management, Brandeis University, Mailstop 035, Waltham, MA 02454. mwhoward@brandeis.edu

Jiménez, Ariam. Instructor, professor, and researcher at Faculty of Biology, working in avian ecology and conservation and focusing on shorebirds and seabirds; author and co-author of 19 scientific publications. Faculty of Biology, University of Havana, Cuba. ariam@fbio.uh.cu

Joseph, Victor. Biologist and volunteer in Antigua and Barbuda with the local NGO Environmental Awareness Group (EAG) and a member of the seabird monitoring and conservation programs. P.O. Box 2103, Long Street, St. John's, Antigua and Barbuda. eag@candw.ag

Keith, Allan. Author of Birds of St Lucia and co-author of The Birds of Hispaniola; former president of the American Birding Association. Box 247, Chilmark, MA 02535. keiths@vineyard.net

Leblond, Gilles. Consultant biologist and director of the environmental research company BIOS, monitoring avifauna since 1995; work for the French government's Department of the Environment (DIREN) included a report on the northern French Antilles in 2003; current studies on Martinique. Rue Brindeau, Marie-Gaillard, 97190 Gosier, Guadeloupe. leblond@wanadoo.fr

Lemoine, Vincent. Director of the NGO Société pour l'Etude, la Protection et l'Aménagement de la Nature en Martinique (SEPANMAR), specializing in seabird monitoring. SEPANMAR, 140 cité Saint-Georges, 97233 Schoelcher, Martinique, French West Indies. lemoine_v@yahoo.fr

Lentino, Miguel. Curator since 1993 of the bird collection, Museo de Historia Natural La Salle, and curator of Colección Ornitológica Phelps, Caracas, Venezuela. Research associate with Sociedad Conservacionista Audubon de Venezuela (SCAV), working on the ecology of flamingos and wetlands. Over 100 published papers include the Important Bird Areas of Venezuela; co-author of Birds of Northern South America. Edif. Gran Sabana, Piso 3, Boulevard de Sabana Grande, Caracas 1050, Venezuela. mlentino@reacciun.ve

Luy, Alejandro. General manager and biologist with the NGO Fundación Tierra Viva, Caracas, since 2001, promoting sustainable development programs in four states of Venezuela. Work includes technical management, advocacy and production of outreach materials for conservation. Fundación Tierra Viva, Apartado Postal 69046, Caracas 1062, Venezuela. alejandro@tierraviva.org

Mackin, William A. Ecological consultant with Jadora International LLC. Until 2008, adjunct professor of biology at Elon University, North Carolina. Manages a database of seabird breeding sites in the Caribbean; doctoral and postdoctoral studies on Audubon's Shearwater and White-tailed Tropicbirds in the Bahamas. www.wicbirds.net

Madeiros, Jeremy L. Resident chief wildlife and conservation officer on Bermuda and director of the endangered Bermuda Petrel program since 2000; author of many papers on indigenous wildlife and conservation issues. Department of Conservation Services, Bermuda, Ministry of the Environment, P.O. Box Fl 117, Flatts FLBX, Smiths Parish, Bermuda. cahowman@yahoo.com

McGowan, Andrew. Biologist, worked in the British Virgin Islands on seabirds, 2004–2005. Centre for Ecology and Conservation, University of Exeter, Cornwall Campus, Tremough, Penryn TR10 9EZ, Cornwall, United Kingdom. a.mcgowan@exeter.ac.uk

Moreno, Maria Isabel. Director of Fundación ProAves, with responsibility for the San Andreas Archipelago. Fundación ProAves, Carrera 20, #36–61, Bogotá, Colombia. mmoreno@proaves.org

Norton, Robert L. Environmental planner and biologist, studied seabirds in the U.S. Virgin Islands and British Virgin Islands since 1983. Originator and co-editor of the West Indies regional report in American Birds, Field Notes, and North American Birds since 1980. Co-author with E. A. Schreiber, Brown Booby account in Birds of North America; comprehensive chapter with R. van Halewijn on seabirds of the Caribbean in Status and Conservation of the World's Seabirds (1984). 8960 NE Waldo Road, Gainesville, FL 32609. corvus0486@aol.com

Pienkowski, Michael W. Surveys (including seabirds) since 1997 in the Turks and Caicos Islands; chair since 1995, U.K. Overseas Territories Conservation Forum. Director, Joint Nature Conservation Committee (the U.K. government's statutory advisor), 1991–95; editor, *Journal of Applied Ecology* (1994–99); assistant chief scientist, Nature Conservancy Council, 1990–91; headed International Legislation and Funding Department, Royal Society for the Protection of Birds, 1995–97. U.K. Overseas Territories Conservation Forum, 102 Broadway, Peterborough PE1 4DG, United Kingdom. pienkowski@cix.co.uk

Pierce, Judy. Chief of wildlife of the U.S. Virgin Islands Division, U.S. Fish and Wildlife Service; worked for over 20 years managing seabird nesting sites, with special interest in Red-billed Tropicbird, Masked Booby, and Roseate Tern. Author of many publications on Caribbean seabirds. Division of Fish and Wildlife, 6291 Estate Nazareth, St. Thomas, VI 00802. sula@vitelcom.net

Prosper, Junior. Biologist and volunteer in Antigua and Barbuda with local NGO Environmental Awareness Group (EAG) and co-coordinator of the seabird monitoring and conservation programs; director, Society for the Conservation and Study of Caribbean Birds, 2006–2008. P.O. Box 2103, Long Street, St. John's, Antigua and Barbuda. eag@candw.ag

Prosper, Shanee. Volunteer in Antigua and Barbuda with local NGO Environmental Awareness Group (EAG) and part of the seabird monitoring team. P.O. Box 2103, Long Street, St. John's, Antigua and Barbuda.

Rodríguez, Patricia. Researcher specializing in the study of ecology and conservation of colonial seabirds, especially gulls and terns; co-author of the Important Bird Areas program for Cuba (BirdLife International). Ecology and Systematic Institute, Havana, Cuba. sterna@ecologia.cu

Salaman, Paul. Research officer with American Bird Conservancy; consultant, 2000–2002, to Fundacion ProAves, Carrera 20, #36–61, Bogotá, Colombia.

Saliva, Jorge E. Senior wildlife officer with the Caribbean Office in Puerto Rico of U.S. Fish and Wildlife Service, responsible for seabird monitoring and training in the Puerto Rican archipelago. Author on many publications on Caribbean seabirds. U.S. Fish and Wildlife Service, Caribbean Field Office, P.O. Box 491, Boquerón, Puerto Rico. jorge_saliva@fws.gov

Schreiber, E. A. Research associate in the Bird Department at the Smithsonian Museum's National Museum of Natural History, Washington, D.C. Published over 60 scientific papers, edited *Biology of Marine Birds*, and has maintained an active pantropical research program on seabirds over 35 years. Specialist on all aspects of Pelicaniformes ecology, population dynamics, and systematics; designer and consultant on pantropical monitoring and training programs. Pelican Springs Lodge, 122 Jump Cove Road, Weaverville, NC 28787. SchreiberE@aol.com

Sylvester, Ingrid. Director in Antigua and Barbuda of the NGO Environmental Awareness Group (EAG), 1996–2004, and initiated monitoring and conservation programs for seabirds. Organization of Eastern Caribbean States (OECS), Environment and Sustainable Development Unit, P.O. Box 1383, Morne Fortuné, Castries, St. Lucia. isylvester2001@yahoo.com

Wiley, James W. Renowned ornithologist with U.S. Geological Survey and other government conservation agencies for 35 years. Co-author of *Birds of the West Indies* (1998), author of *A Bibliography of Ornithology of West Indian Birds* and many other publications, chiefly on endangered amazons in the West Indies. First editor of *El Pitirre* (now *Journal of Caribbean Ornithology*). Western Foundation of Vertebrate Zoology, 5757 Charles Cannon Road, Marion Station, MD 21838. jwwiley@mail.umes.edu

Index

Page numbers in *italics* refer to illustrations.